Northern Hospitality

Northern Hospitality

Cooking by the Book in New England

Keith Stavely and Kathleen Fitzgerald

University of Massachusetts Press

Amherst and Boston

LC 2010054340
ISBN 978-1-55849-861-7 (paper); 860-0 (library cloth)

Designed by Sally Nichols
Set in Goudy Old Style, Gill Sans, and Simmissa
Printed and bound by Thomson-Shore, Inc.

Library of Congress Cataloging-in-Publication Data

Stavely, Keith W. F., 1942–
Northern hospitality : cooking by the book in New England / Keith Stavely
and Kathleen Fitzgerald.
p. cm.
Includes bibliographical references and index.
ISBN 978-1-55849-861-7 (pbk. : alk. paper) — ISBN 978-1-55849-860-0 (library
cloth : alk. paper)
1. Cooking, American—New England style. 2. Cooking—New England.
3. Cookbooks. I. Fitzgerald, Kathleen, 1952– II. Title.
TX715.2.N48S7435 2011
641.5974—dc22
2010054340

British Library Cataloguing in Publication data are available.

Frontispiece: Illustration published in "Mother" by Kathleen Norris, *Ladies Home Journal*,
August 1912). Courtesy Cabinet of American Illustration (Library of Congress)

To Tony and Jary
K. S.

To Maryanne and Mark
K. F.

Contents

Illustrations

Preface

Where does a reader or cook turn to get a good taste of traditional New England cuisine? Up till now, those exploring the region's culinary past have found mostly adaptations of historic recipes. Usually highlighted within this narrow repertoire are dishes that were developed during the colonial revival of the late nineteenth and early twentieth centuries. While based on long-established everyday foods, these exemplars of the tradition are frequently sweetened beyond recognition or otherwise re-worked to appeal to modern palates. For those who remained convinced that more was involved than baked beans and clam chowder, the only alternative was a confusing array of single cookbook reprints.

Both the adaptive and reprint approaches leave out much of the three-hundred-year history of the changing gastronomic customs and styles of New England. The good news is that numerous cookbooks reflecting and helping to build that tradition were imported into or created in the region. They offer a reservoir of significant historical information.

In an earlier book, *America's Founding Food,* we told a large part of the complex, colorful, sometimes controversial story of New England cooking. The present book represents our attempt to tell the rest of the story, through a generous selection of unaltered historic recipes, combined with analysis of the writers and cookbooks that most influenced the food habits of New Englanders from the seventeenth to the early twentieth centuries. The gastronomy found in their pages tells a rich and evolving tale. Adding to the fun is the fact that the recipes, while rarely written with the precision to which we have become accustomed, are neverthe-less accessible to any mildly adventurous cook.

Over the past several years, we have discussed with many audiences and individual readers the social context of cooking and eating in New England, along the way describing particular recipes, methods of prepa-ration, and ingredients. Frequently people have asked where they could go to learn more. They have told us that they would like to begin or to deepen their own encounters with historic cooking. Others, avid students of history and recipe readers, have said they were hungry for primary source material on New England food history. This critical anthology is our attempt to further those encounters and feed those reading habits. We hope readers will find as much relish in the reading as we have in the compiling and writing.

Acknowledgments

In our study of New England food history we have relied on the work of many scholars, curators, and librarians. First among those to whom we are indebted is the staff of the Schlesinger Library, Radcliffe Institute, Harvard University, which has again guided us unerringly through the Library's invaluable trove of collections and services. We have also drawn on the resources of the University of Rhode Island Library and its HELIN consortium, the Newport Public Library and its OSL consortium, the Fall River Public Library and its SAILS consortium (this also means you, VirtCat), and the Boston Public Library. *Feeding America,* an on-line collection of eighteenth- to twentieth-century cookbooks produced and maintained by the Michigan State University Libraries, and Google Books, which now includes hundreds of cookbooks in its ever-increasing repository of historical materials, have transformed the lives of culinary researchers. The American Antiquarian Society kindly granted permission to quote a passage from the unpublished manuscript portions of the diary of Ebenezer Parkman.

Foremost among the individuals who have supported this work is Bruce Wilcox, director of the University of Massachusetts Press. From the very first, we have been the lucky recipients of his unfailing advocacy and great acuity. We also wish to express our gratitude to the entire staff of the Press, especially managing editor Carol Betsch, and to copy editor David Coen. The greatest compliment to any writer is a careful reader. We have had the good fortune to have two such readers in Robert S. Cox and Joseph A. Conforti. Their energetic engagement with our work amounted to encouragement of the most helpful sort.

At the Oxford Symposium on Food and Cookery, several of our friends and fellow laborers in the vineyards of culinary history gave us the benefit of their responses to a paper we presented there that was subsequently published in one of the Symposium's *Proceedings* volumes (*Food and*

Morality, Prospect Books, 2008) and that appears here in part, somewhat altered, in chapter 1. For ongoing support both of the present project and of our overall endeavors as food historians, we wish to thank Barbara Ketcham Wheaton, Joseph M. Carlin, and Andrew F. Smith.

Finally, our loving families have once again provided an emotional atmosphere that could not be more congenial to the pursuit of our passions. In particular our son Jonathan has fed our spirits with great conversation and warm laughter. Who could ask for more?

Northern Hospitality

Introduction

Cookbooks are big business. Titles in the *America's Test Kitchen* series regularly show up on the best-seller lists, and *The Joy of Cooking*, a fixture in American middle-class households for two generations, could still become a best seller in its 2006, seventy-fifth-anniversary incarnation. Anyone who has ever worked in a public library, as we both have, knows that cookbooks rank near the top when such libraries' collections are evaluated in terms of the types of materials that are most frequently checked out. The reading public's love affair with cookbooks is aptly summarized in a recent article in *The Economist*, where it is observed that "even a medium-sized bookshop contains many more recipes than one person could hope to cook in a lifetime."[1]

The popularity of cookbooks is nothing new. Amelia Simmons's *American Cookery*, now generally considered the first American cookbook, was reprinted (not to mention plagiarized) for almost thirty years after its initial publication in 1796. Simmons's successor as a widely read New England cookbook author was Lydia Maria Child, whose *American Frugal Housewife* (originally *The Frugal Housewife*) went through thirty-one editions between 1829 and 1845. In 1843, Child was lauded by a

New Hampshire farming periodical as having "won unfading laurels" for her cookbook, in that it contained the type of material "which is calculated to benefit the greatest number."[2]

Similar success stories can be told about eighteenth-century British cookbooks. Of the three best-selling works of that era, E. Smith's *The Compleat Housewife* remained in print for nearly half a century, while Hannah Glasse's *The Art of Cookery Made Plain and Easy* and Elizabeth Raffald's *The Experienced English House-keeper* were both, like *The Joy of Cooking*, extant in current editions almost seventy-five years after their initial publications. All three were published in North American editions.

Cookbooks of past times such as these, which are known to have been in great demand, constitute valuable historical evidence. However, it is evidence that must be used with caution. As some culinary historians have emphasized, cookbooks do not directly hold the mirror up to dietary reality. Until quite recently, their content reflected almost exclusively "the fare of the . . . well-fed." Most of the people of nineteenth-century America, for example, "had no time or wealth to exercise the kinds of prescribed refinements or self-conscious style promoted by the Beechers or Sarah J. Hale"—that is, Harriet Beecher Stowe, her sister Catharine Beecher, and the editor of *Godey's Lady's Book*.[3]

But that doesn't mean that such people wouldn't have liked to have had the time and wealth to engage in the elegant cookery offered in the works of these and other authors of the era. Since ancient times, bread made with the highest grade of wheat was consumed on a regular basis only by the upper classes. For just as long—in other words, well before the invention of the printing press began the process of making cookbooks widely available—people of the lower classes also wanted to eat bread of this type. And there was more to this than just the fact that bread made with "clean wheat" tasted better. To eat the bread of the upper classes was to partake to some small degree of the upper-class way of life. The invention of printing and with it the ever-broadening dissemination of cookbooks further stimulated this symbolic role of food and cooking as an expression of social aspiration. This is what primarily accounts for the popularity of cookbooks throughout the modern era.[4]

So the cookbooks of past times tell us what a few well-off people actually ate, and in so doing these books give us clues about what a great many more people wanted to eat, or were being encouraged to want to eat. We can see the latter dynamic at work in our own society. Consider the difference between the McDonald's menu of today, on which salads and "gourmet" coffee are offered alongside the burgers and fries, with the fare offered by this same fast-food behemoth just a few years ago, when little beyond the burgers, fries, and ordinary coffee were to be had. Or take a walk down the aisles of any supermarket and measure the amount of shelf space devoted to "international" or purportedly super-nutritious or organically grown items, in comparison to the many fewer linear feet set aside for these types of foods in a comparable supermarket in, say, the 1980s. By the early twenty-first century, more Americans were eating more food defined as healthy or fancy or cosmopolitan. There are no doubt many reasons for this change, but one of the most important is surely the publication in the 1960s and 1970s of such books as *Mastering the Art of French Cooking* and *Diet for a Small Planet*.

Of course, the interaction between dietary realities and cookbooks moves in the opposite direction as well. As we shall see, when Amelia Simmons included distinctively American dishes in her 1796 *American Cookery*, she was bringing more fully into the open the tendency in elite New England circles during the several previous decades to confer greater prestige on such heretofore everyday fare as Indian pudding, chowder, and johnnycake. In England toward the end of the seventeenth century, the manuscript "receipt books" kept by gentry women recorded instances of the new French culinary fashions well before they appeared in any English cookbooks.[5]

But once such material appeared in cookbooks, from whatever source, it was thereby both identified as part of the repertoire of the culinarily legitimate and disseminated among participants in and aspirants to a way of life founded on such norms. This is not to say that cookbook users do not make their own creative alterations and adaptations of the recipes presented to them. They do. British food writer Nigel Slater's likening of a recipe to a straitjacket is not really well founded. Much of the history of cookbooks, like much of the history of all literature, is a history of alterations and adaptations of material from earlier sources. To take a look at cookbook material over time is therefore to be introduced to the evolving definition of what has been considered desirable to cook and eat.[6]

The chicken-and-egg question about origins—whether an established dish was primarily the result of reaching a kind of critical mass of kitchen practice or was rather derived mostly from printed sources—cannot ultimately be answered, and perhaps it need not be answered. A more important issue for historians of food is one of assessment. What place did the dish or food hold in the overall cuisine? How does one make a case for the importance of this dish over that, this food over that?

Part of the answer to these questions emerges from looking, as we do in the present work, at the print record of a cuisine. Recipe reproductions are a major indication of a dish's popularity and influence. Some recipes enjoyed widespread dissemination not only through the multiple editions of the best-selling cookbooks in which they originally appeared but also through the plagiarism that went unchecked throughout the period under study. Because uncredited as well as credited copyings are found throughout the manuscript recipe books and printed cookbooks of the day, we make a concerted effort to consider both a dish's first known appearance in print and its subsequent reprints, copyings, and adaptations.

In Part One of this book, we place the cookbooks and authors that played the most important parts in the culinary history of New England in social and cultural context. Then, in Part Two, we provide representative selections of Anglo-American recipes of the seventeenth, eighteenth, nineteenth, and early twentieth centuries, transcribed from the cookbooks in which they were first published with their original wording, spelling, and punctuation left intact. Most of the recipes are accompanied by commentaries to aid historical understanding. Our aim is to give readers the opportunity to inhabit, so far as possible, the culinary environments of these earlier times. To put it another way, Part One amounts to our map of the forest, while Part Two offers both description of the trees and guidance to species we anticipate will be unfamiliar to many. Our hope is that by the time readers turn the last page, they will feel that they've had full, revealing views of a remarkable culinary landscape.

PART
1
Cooks and Cookbooks

CHAPTER ONE

~≋≋≋≫~

Culinarily Colonized
Cookbooks in Colonial New England

*D*uring the colonial era, New England cooks in a position to make use of printed recipe sources had to rely on English cookbooks, since, as noted in the Introduction, the first American cookbook was not published until 1796. In the seventeenth century, the most popular of these was Gervase Markham's *The English Hus-wife*, first published in 1615 and frequently reprinted until late in the century. Copies of this work were shipped to Virginia in 1620, and it seems likely that before long other copies made their way to New England. Miles Standish of Plymouth Colony, who died in 1656, may have owned it. By the 1680s, if not earlier, it appeared on lists of titles imported from London by Boston booksellers.[1]

Two other cookbooks appeared on these 1680s Boston booksellers' import lists: *The Queens Closet Opened,* by "W. M.," and *The Queen-like Closet,* by Hannah Woolley. The former, purporting to enshrine the domestic "secrets" of Henrietta Maria, the wife of Charles I, had first been published in 1655 and was destined to be reprinted until 1713. The Hannah Woolley book, entitled with an eye to the success of *The Queens*

Closet Opened, first appeared in 1670, with several reprints and supplements in the 1670s and 1680s.[2]

In the eighteenth century, cookery titles continued to be imported for sale to those colonists participating in the expanding colonial book market. In the second quarter of the century, E. Smith's *The Compleat Housewife* (1727), which has been called "the best seller of the early eighteenth century" in Britain, was widely advertised in newspapers "throughout the colonies," including New England. Its successful sale prompted an edition on this side of the Atlantic, in Williamsburg, Virginia, in 1742, the first cookbook publication in British North America.[3]

Hannah Glasse's *The Art of Cookery Made Plain and Easy* (1747), by far the most popular cookbook in eighteenth-century Britain, achieved a similar status in the colonies. Along with Glasse's later and somewhat less popular *The Compleat Confectioner* (1760), *The Art of Cookery* was listed in the 1765 catalog of the circulating library of John Mein, a Boston bookseller. In the manuscript cookbook begun in 1763 by Anne Gibbons Gardiner of Boston, more than ninety of the recipes "can easily be traced" to *The Art of Cookery*. The popularity of Hannah Glasse in New England persisted after the achievement of American independence, if at the turn of the nineteenth century the region was anything like New York was at that time, as described by a memoirist writing in the 1840s: "Persons of a certain age were very much under the domination of that absurd style which was emphatically called 'GOOD OLD ENGLISH COOKERY.' We had emancipated ourselves from the sceptre of King George, but that of Hannah Glasse was extended without challenge over our fire-sides and dinner-tables, with a sway far more imperative and absolute."[4]

John Mein's 1765 catalog also listed *The House-Keeper's Pocket-Book* (1733), by Sarah Harrison, and *Madam Johnson's Present; or, The Best Instructions for Young Women in Useful and Universal Knowledge* (1754). Another Boston bookselling firm, that of Edward Cox and Edward Berry, listed *The British Housewife* (1756), by Martha Bradley, in its 1772 sale catalog.[5]

The Cox and Berry catalog featured a full-page advertisement for the first cookbook published in New England, the 1772 Boston printing (with copper plates by Paul Revere) of Susannah Carter's *The Frugal Housewife*, originally published in London in 1765. By this time, the most important and popular British cookbook of the closing decades of the eighteenth century, Elizabeth Raffald's *The Experienced English House-keeper* (1769), had made its way to New England, as indicated by the fact that the Gardiner manuscript cookbook contains approximately fifty recipes copied or adapted from Raffald.[6]

COOKBOOK WRITERS AND READERS IN ENGLAND

Of the three cookbooks definitely known to have been imported into seventeenth-century New England, two of them represent the two major types produced in England in the sixteenth and seventeenth centuries. Markham's *English Hus-wife* is an instance of the country household management manual, combining instruction in cookery with that in "Physicke [medicine] . . . Wooll, Hemp, Flax, Dayries, Brewing, . . . and all other things belonging to an Houshould." In *The Queens Closet Opened* and other works with similar titles, esoteric knowledge—associated either with the seats of power, as here, or with such mysterious figures as alchemists—is alleged to be divulged for the first time to a wider public. As with the household management manual, the type of instruction imparted in "secrets" books was not confined to cooking alone but also included "confectionery" and "remedies." Indeed, cooking was considered the least prestigious among these three types of domestic activity.[7]

In many ways, these two types of books were similar. They both presented cooking as one domestic endeavor among many. Both were addressed primarily to women. Since by 1640 the rate of full literacy among English women was probably no more than 10 percent, both are likely to have reached an audience extending no lower in English society than "the gentry, the clergy, and the professions."[8]

Most of the recipes in *The English Hus-wife* are included with this upper level of society in mind—those with a sophisticated cosmopolitan aura, for example ("To make a Quelquechose"; "To make an excellent *Olepotrige*, which is the onely principall dish of boild meate which is esteemed in all *Spaine*"). But Markham states that he is aiming at a broader audience than this. His *Hus-wife* is "intended to be generall," and it therefore includes such recipes as the one for pottage, which he characterizes as "those ordinary wholsome boild-meats, which are of vse in euery good mans [average farmer's] house."[9]

Although it is unlikely that the typical seventeenth-century English "goodman" purchased a copy of *The English Hus-wife*, the presence of his food in the book points to an important difference between it and *The Queens Closet Opened* and other such titles. Markham projects an image of a securely stratified, relatively stable society. The goodman is in his place, contented with his pottage, and the squire, vicar, or lord is in his, dining on his continental Quelquechose and *Olepotrige*.

Some scholars have argued that *The English Hus-wife* is replete with indications of the conspicuous consumption and social climbing that were already by the early seventeenth century turning such claims of ageless social hierarchy into exercises in nostalgia. The strongest evidence for such arguments is the section devoted to "Banquetting stuffe and conceited dishes." The banquet course at the end of a dinner gathering in the upper reaches of society was an innovation of the Elizabethan era. It consisted of sweetmeats of all sorts, presented in such a way as to produce "a glamorous show." There was "lavish provision of sugar in every conceivable form"—even the plates and cups might be made of molded sugar, and there were also apt to be sculpted sugar or marchpane birds, snails, "playing-cards, slices of bacon and suchlike." Hostesses vied with each other to bring off the most dazzling "display of wealth." To the traditional role of the feast or entertainment as a display of power and preeminence with respect to the lower orders was now added an element of bidding for admission into the charmed circle of the elite or competitively striving for a superior position within it.[10]

Nevertheless, the fact that *The English Hus-wife* makes room for the cookery of humbler people, thereby embodying traditional hierarchical ideals, distinguishes Markham's book from those of the *Queens Closet Opened* type. There, the only pottages on offer, for example, are elaborate concoctions made with beef tongues or capons, "Champignions," veal sweetbreads, and orange or lemon juice. But the fact that the cuisine being described is more exclusively upper class than that found in Markham is precisely what makes the book more forward looking than his. "The Queens Closet Opened": the work's very raison d'être is to cater to social climbing, otherwise known as upward mobility. Only high-status dishes are paraded before readers because the act of throwing open the queen's closet presumes that readers are more inclined to emulate those above them than they are to abide in tranquility in their assigned stations.[11]

This brings us to the third of the English cookbooks known to have made its way to New England in the course of the seventeenth century. Hannah Woolley's *The Queen-like Closet* illustrates two major trends in the development of English cookbooks. The first of these amounts to a subsequent phase in the emergence of upward mobility. Retaining *The Queens Closet Opened*'s traditional separation of "preserving" and "candying" from cooking, Woolley "adapts the complex receipts of aristocratic cookery to make them more accessible." Thus, instead of the foods of the great world retaining their full exaltation and glamour, beckoning temptingly but perhaps all but unattainably, as they did in *The Queens Closet Opened*, they now in Woolley's pages stoop to conquer, becoming "simplified versions of court dishes," suited to the limitations of the more modest kitchens and households inhabited by Woolley's readership, which consisted of members of "an aspiring middle class striving for gentility."[12]

This was one of the two directions that English cookbook writing was primarily to take in the course of the eighteenth century: ever increasing adaptation of courtly and aristocratic cookery to the circumstances and needs of the ever increasing middle class. Woolley also anticipates the other major eighteenth-century development, the increasing dominance of women, as opposed to male professional chefs, in the ranks of cookbook authors. And most of Woolley's eighteenth-century successors were to resemble her in being either former housekeepers/cooks for the nobility or greater gentry or women of middle-class or gentle birth whose circumstances required them to write cookbooks for money, or both.[13]

The Compleat Housewife (1727), as noted already well established as "the best seller of the early eighteenth century" by the time of its publication in a British North American edition in 1742, was written by someone who had served the great and noble. E. Smith explains in the preface that the book is "the Product of my own Experience," having been for more than thirty years "constantly employed in fashionable and noble Families, in which the Provisions ordered according to the following Directions, have had the general Approbation of such as have been at many noble Entertainments." Like Woolley, Smith offers the traditional aristocratic subdivisions (along with cookery and confectionery, Smith restores the medicinal section omitted by Woolley), with the cookery section filled with "adapted versions of grand court dishes." Thus were

Smith's middling readers reassured that they were getting as reasonable a facsimile as possible of the genuine high culinary style.[14]

With Hannah Glasse's *The Art of Cookery* (1747), as popular in the colonies as in the mother country, a new dimension was added to the role of the cookbook as an aid to upward mobility. By this time, more than half the women in London were fully literate, and "literacy was the rule rather than the exception" among London servants. Meanwhile, in a development to be explored more fully later on, within the lower gentry and upwardly aspiring middle class, an idea was gaining increasing acceptance that the mistress of the household should be a lady of leisure, not only not herself engaged in cookery and other housework but also not involved, or at worst only minimally involved, in instructing her servants.[15]

Glasse addressed this situation by designing her cookbook in such a way "that every Servant who can but read will be capable of making a tollerable good Cook, and those who have the least Notion of Cookery can't miss of being very good ones." The result would be to "save the Ladies a great deal of Trouble." The servants would learn how to cook, some of them to cook well, and thereby possibly themselves begin climbing the social ladder, while the mistress would be freed of the "Trouble" of involvement of any sort in housework, knowing all the while that from her kitchen would emerge "fashionable dishes without excessive expense."[16]

Ironically, Glasse herself, the illegitimate daughter of a lesser gentry family, married imprudently, spent time as a servant in an aristocratic household, and was forced to write *The Art of Cookery* in an effort "to rescue the family fortunes." In other words, downwardly mobile, she entered vicariously, by composing a cookbook, into exactly the household labor from which it was the aim of her book to liberate those women who were traveling in the opposite direction on the social ladder.[17]

In Elizabeth Raffald's *The Experienced English House-keeper* (1769), Hannah Glasse's redefinition of the readership of cookbooks as consisting primarily of servants can be seen to have been successful. "In as plain a Style as possible, so as to be understood by the weakest Capacity," Raffald writes for "young Persons who are willing to improve themselves." The instruction of servants, which Glasse had trumpeted as "a Branch of Cookery which Nobody has yet thought worth their while to write upon," and which would empower them for upward mobility, could now be quietly identified as a cookbook's principal purpose.[18]

ELIZABETH RAFFALD.

Frontispiece to Elizabeth Raffald, *The Experienced English Housekeeper*, 10th ed., 1786. Raffald offers her cookbook to her readers. (Courtesy the Schlesinger Library, Radcliffe Institute, Harvard University)

As far as cookbook authorship is concerned, Raffald had been a "young Person" in service who had most distinctly demonstrated a capacity and a willingness to improve herself. She became a housekeeper in a gentry household, married the gardener, and with her husband established her own business in Manchester, a combination "fine food and confectionery" emporium and employment clearinghouse for servants. She began giving cooking classes as part of this enterprise, and before long she was writing *The Experienced English House-keeper*. According to its modern editor, this cookbook was unusual at the time in not copying, or even much adapting, material from other cookbooks. It contained, its title page proclaimed, "800 Original Receipts," all of which the author had personally prepared.[19]

The success of *The Experienced English House-keeper* led to other lucrative publishing ventures, and the book doubtless also served to advertise the Manchester business in the manner that Raffald anticipated: "The Receipts for the Confectionary are such as I daily sell in my own Shop, which any Lady may examine at pleasure, as I still continue my best Endeavours to give Satisfaction to all who are pleased to favour me with their Custom." Raffald's career provided those endeavoring to propagate the ethos of entrepreneurship and the career open to talents, and more specifically "the myth of social betterment through service," with a case study almost exactly suited to their requirements.[20]

English Cookery

In the seventeenth century, the cookbooks sent over from England to the colonies presented a cuisine that was very much in process of definition. One writer has drawn a distinction between a courtly and aristocratic style, descended from medieval elite cookery, and a style that "can be termed yeoman." In the former, diverse ingredients were thoroughly mixed and "flavored with wine and spices." In the latter, "ingredients . . . retain[ed] their individuality with a minimum of blending and seasoning." The writer asserts that Markham's *English Hus-wife* is a prime manifestation of this latter, yeoman tradition.[21]

The culinary landscape of seventeenth-century England was not so neatly bifurcated as this, however. We have already mentioned the broad range of sources and influences to be found in Markham. Some recipes are yeoman and/or native; others are aristocratic and/or international. Even at the highest level of society, at court, such eclecticism prevailed. The cookery section of *The Queens Closet Opened* amounted to the manuscript cookbook for the court of Charles I. While as noted earlier the recipes in this collection are more predominantly upper-class than those in Markham, a sprinkling of contributions from various "Mrs." and one "Master" coexist with those from "Earl" and "Lady" and "Lord" and "Countess" So-and-so.[22]

There are no recipes in *The Queens Closet Opened* explicitly identified as appropriate for a "goodman," but many of them are simple and straightforward, more or less in the "yeoman" manner. For example, there is little to distinguish the recipe for fresh fish that found favor with Queen Henrietta Maria from the fresh fish recipe in *The English Hus-wife* that the writer quoted above considers the epitome of yeoman cooking. In both, the fish is essentially boiled in wine and flavored with herbs. Another writer's characterization of the aristocratic cooking of this period as consisting in great part of food that would be "abundant on a country estate" was equally true of court cooking at this time.[23]

The more clearly aristocratic and cosmopolitan recipes in *The Queens Closet Opened* share the same breadth of national styles as already noted in Markham. Dishes labeled as French in origin are the most numerous of those with any national designation at all, but recipes in the Italian, Spanish, Portuguese, and even Persian styles are also to be found. However, French cooking had already been launched toward ascendancy in English elite circles with the publication in 1653 of *The French Cook*, the first English translation of *Cuisinier françois* (1651), by François Pierre de la Varenne. This is the work that is generally considered to have inaugurated what has come to be thought of as French cuisine. In part reflecting a paradigm shift in the medical profession from the Galenic or humoral to a Paracelsian, or "fermentation," theory of food, digestion, and health, la Varenne and his successors (who tended to denounce him as retaining too much medieval baggage) stressed the separation of savory flavors from sweet. Within the domain of the savory thus created, they combined "rich, intensely-flavoured sauces" with meat, fowl, or fish and vegetables to produce "made dishes."[24]

After 1660, with Charles II and his retinue having become great admirers of all things Gallic while exiled in France during the Cromwellian interlude of the 1650s, French influences, including culinary influences, were dominant at the English court. From there, French cooking spread outward and downward in English society, as seen to a considerable degree as early as 1670 in Hannah Woolley's *Queen-like Closet*. Manuscript cookbooks compiled in subsequent decades by members of the country gentry and those in the upper reaches of the professions betray an even more marked French influence. In these books and manuscripts of the closing years of the seventeenth century, the proportion of made dishes that included the residually medieval sugar or dried fruit among their ingredients was steadily on the decline, while the proportion of such dishes featuring the wine and/or anchovies that la Varenne and his followers had made fashionable was steadily on the increase.[25]

This trend continued in the first half of the eighteenth century. Separate stewing stoves ("a sort of furnace . . . made of Brick Work, furnish'd with chaffing dishes above and an ash-pan underneath") were imported from France and installed in the kitchens of many aristocratic households, where they were used to "dress pottages, and . . . prepare ragoes [ragouts]"—in other words, specifically to cook French-derived made dishes. By midcentury, stewing stoves were evidently to be found in less exalted households as well, for Hannah Glasse, who aimed her cookbook at gentry and middle-class readers, provides special instructions in her "Eel Soop" recipe for any reader who might "have a Stew-hole."[26]

Glasse's *Art of Cookery* supplies far more evidence than this for the popularity of French cooking in eighteenth-century England. By Glasse's day, French cooking "was synonymous with dishes in sauce, enriched with such extras as truffles, morels, cockscombs, and artichoke bottoms (to mention only those which recur most frequently)." Such dishes in sauce, along with exactly such enrichments, are found throughout *The Art of Cookery*. For example, in "Pigeons *in compote with white sauce*," the birds are stewed with "Veal Sweetbreads, Cocks Combs, Mushrooms, Truffles, [and] Morels," as though Glasse (or her source, *The Whole Duty of a Woman*) were taking directions from the 1702 English translation of François Massialot's *Le Cuisinier roïal et bourgeois:* "In order to make a proper Ragoo for [pigeons, in a recipe for "Bisk of Pigeons"], 'tis requisite to take some Veal-Sweet-breads cut into two parts, Mushrooms cut into small pieces, Truffles in Slices, Artichoke-bottoms cut into four quarters, and one whole, to be put into the middle of the Potage." Glasse's second-longest chapter is the one for made dishes (that is, dishes in sauce), and more dishes of this sort are to be found scattered through several other chapters.[27]

Nor was Glasse the first to manifest such thoroughgoing French influence. E. Smith, her predecessor as a best-selling female English cookbook author, offers, along with five other ragouts, "A Ragoo for made Dishes," containing "Lamb-stones [lamb's testicles], Cock's-Combs, . . . Oysters, Mushrooms, Truffles, and Murrells." Smith's "Bisk of Pigeons" features lambstones, sweetbreads, and palates. Her repertoire also includes recipes proclaiming their French ancestry in their names: "A Goose, Turkey, or Leg of Mutton, A-la-daube"; "A Leg of Mutton A-la-royal." Elizabeth Raffald, Hannah Glasse's successor in cookbook popularity and significance, likewise remained in part in the French mode. As with Glasse, the made-dish chapter is one of her longest, and she explains at its outset that "you may use pickled Mushrooms, Artichoke Bottoms, Morels, Truffles, and Forcemeat Balls in almost every Made Dish."[28]

French cuisine did not succeed in permeating English cuisine to this degree without provoking a reaction. In 1709, Joseph Addison complained in *The Tatler* about his visit to the house of a friend who was "a great admirer of the *French* cookery." The table was "covered with a great Variety of unknown Dishes. . . . That which stood before me I took to be a roasted Porcupine, however did not Care for asking Questions; and have since been informed that it was only a larded Turkey. I afterwards passed my Eye over several Hashes which I do not know the Names of to this Day, and hearing they were Delicacies, did not think fit to meddle with them." This was not the end of Addison's difficulties: "Among other Dainties I saw something like a Pheasant, and therefore desired to be helped to a Wing of it; but to my great Surprize my Friend told me it was a Rabbit, which is a sort of Meat I never cared for."

Solace finally came when Addison detected "the agreeable Savour of Roast Beef" emanating from "a noble Sirloin upon the Side of the Table smoking in the most delicious Manner." He "had Recourse to it more than once." But his pleasure was mixed with "some Indignation" at seeing "that substantial *English* Dish banished in so ignominious a Manner to make way for *French* Kickshaws."[29]

The anti-French conventions found in virtually all eighteenth-century English cookbooks are seen here in fully developed form. Just as in the supposed contrast between the aristocratic and yeoman cookery of the sixteenth and seventeenth centuries, overly sophisticated and refined, vaguely effeminate ("Delicacies, . . . Dainties"), not to mention deceptive (fowl disguised as flesh, flesh as fowl) French methods of preparing food are pitted against solid, honest English fare.[30]

The reader will perhaps have grasped that if such anti-French rhetoric was found in virtually all eighteenth-century English cookbooks, then it was found in the very same cookbooks in which recipes based on French-inspired procedures were also to be found throughout. This was indeed exactly the case. E. Smith felt obliged to apologize for the French dimension of *The Compleat Housewife,* attributing it to book-marketing necessities and insisting that she had minimized it as much as possible: "I have so far temporized, as, since we have to our disgrace, so fondly admired the *French* Tongue, *French* Modes, and also *French* Messes, to present you now and then with such Receipts of *French* Cookery, as I think may not be disagreeable to *English* Palates."[31]

Most notoriously, Hannah Glasse, in the front matter of a book replete with food of French origin, inveighed against "*French* cooks" and the "*French* tricks" they invariably played, such as making an unsuspecting "*English* Lord" pay as much for "dressing one Dish" as should suffice for "a fine Dinner of twenty Dishes," or such as wasting "six Pounds of Butter to fry twelve Eggs; when every Body knows, that understands Cooking, that Half a Pound is full enough, or more than need be used." Alas, "so much is the blind Folly of this Age, that [Gentlemen] would rather be impos'd on by a *French* Booby, than give Encouragement to a good *English* Cook!"[32]

What makes English cooking superior to French, then, is that, in the words of one of Glasse's contemporaries, it can turn out dishes "in the most elegant manner," just as French cooking can do, but it can do so "at a small Expence," which French cooking cannot do. English cooking is more economical. E. Smith's remarks suggest a gastronomic difference as well. She has included only "such Receipts of the *French* cookery" as she thinks "may not be disagreeable to *English* Palates." Around this same time, a French observer offered a clue as to what was not disagreeable to English palates when he stated that English cookery was "simple and unadorned," a characterization in agreement with Addison's earlier description of roast beef as a "substantial" dish.[33]

By 1769, this emerging positive valence to native English culinary preferences had become more explicit. Elizabeth Raffald assures her readers that such of her recipes as have "French names" will not only be found to be inexpensive but also to be uncomplicated, "as plain as the nature of the dish will admit of." The suggestion here that a less elaborated cuisine is a better cuisine is further seen in Raffald's particular phrasing of the now standard formula quoted above about combining elegance with "small Expence": she explains that in her career as a housekeeper and cook she was "always endeavouring to join Oeconomy with Neatness and Elegance." The addition of "Neatness" to the catalog of kitchen desiderata increases the sense that it is a positive aesthetic of restraint, of containment within carefully considered boundaries, that determines Raffald's entire presentation. The same note is struck in the assessment of the length of *The Experienced English House-keeper:* "The Number of Receipts in this Book are not so numerous as in some others, but they are what will be found useful and sufficient for any Gentleman's Family." The point is not that the book is small but rather that it is properly proportioned, like the cookery that it makes available and the genteel way of life that it enables.[34]

The principle that less is more is brought to bear in recipe after recipe in *The Experienced English House-keeper*—for example, in "A savory Chicken Pye":

> Let your Chickens be small, season them with Mace, Pepper and Salt, put a Lump of Butter into every one of them, lay them in the Dish with the Breasts up, and lay a thin Slice of Bacon over them, it will give them a pleasant Flavour, then put in a Pint of strong Gravy, and make a good puff Paste, lid it and bake it in a moderate Oven; French cooks generally put Morels and Yolks of Eggs chopped small.

Chickens specified as small, seasonings as few, bacon as thin, puff paste as good, an oven as moderate, and a flavor as pleasant. The minimalism of this ensemble, if anything accentuated by the strength of the gravy, prepares the way for the concluding, devastatingly laconic acknowledgment of what French cooks do. Frenchification is retained but reduced to a mere option, "chopped small." Thus did a cuisine of economy joined with neatness and elegance move beyond negation and begin expressing and affirming itself.[35]

COOKBOOK READERS IN COLONIAL NEW ENGLAND

Who (besides Mrs. Gardiner of Boston) might have made use of the English cookbooks imported into or reprinted in colonial New England? Evidence bearing on this question is unfortunately scarce. The first factor to be considered is the number of people in the region—or rather, since cookbook readers and users were overwhelmingly likely to have been female, the number of women and girls in the region—who could, as Hannah Glasse put it, "but read." The most recent estimates are that the percentage of females able to read and write rose from at most 40 percent at the end of the seventeenth century, to 60 percent in the 1760s, to 80 percent in the 1790s.[36]

It is generally agreed that more women and girls were able to "but read" than to read and write as well, although, as was the case for England during this period, there are no available quantitative measures of reading literacy only. What is known is that within the first few decades of settlement, all the New England colonies except Rhode Island passed legislation requiring all households to teach reading to their children, girls as well as boys; that most of this reading instruction in the home was conducted by women; and that the first instruction in reading outside the home for children of both sexes most often took place in "dame schools" run by women. One of the most thoughtful scholars of reading in colonial New England came to the conclusion that relatively soon after settlement, "when defined as the skill of reading English [as opposed to Latin], literacy was almost universal."[37]

So not only could New England women of the late eighteenth century read Elizabeth Raffald's *Experienced English House-keeper*, and not only could their mothers read Hannah Glasse's *Art of Cookery*, but the vast majority of their great- and great-great-grandmothers could have read Hannah Woolley's *Queen-like Closet* and Gervase Markham's *English Hus-wife*. Whether very many of them actually did read books of this sort is another question, however. A recent study of the standard of living in southern New England during the seventeenth and eighteenth centuries indicates that during the seventeenth century, while "religious books" were owned by more than half of even the least wealthy of those surveyed, ownership of "secular books," a category presumably including cookbooks, was found only among the wealthiest group.[38]

So, not surprisingly, the audience for cookbooks in seventeenth-century New England at best corresponded to that in seventeenth-century England: larger rural landowners and farmers (such as Miles Standish of Plymouth Colony, who as noted owned a work by Markham that may have been *The English Hus-wife*), the clergy, and those participating in the embryonic professional and mercantile communities, concentrated as yet almost entirely in Boston. The rest of the population, mostly freehold farmers (Markham's "goodmen"), did not yet have the resources to prepare the type of diversified diet that the use of a cookbook presupposes. Studies of the material culture of this group show them to have been for the most part "ill-furnished farmer-settlers" who had achieved by the end of the century no more than "a modicum of comfort and convenience." Analysis of the structures and interiors of seventeenth- and early-eighteenth-century houses shows that even the more prosperous life of the merchants and larger farmers was signaled not by "the character or quality of the furnishings" but rather by sheer numbers—"a greater number of rooms and greater quantities of goods."[39]

The dietary aspirations of seventeenth-century freeholders were likewise focused on quantity, not quality or variety, the latter of which was provided only by such fresh meat, fish, vegetables, and fruits as became seasonally available. The scholar who has made the most thorough study of the colonial New England diet concludes that apart from such seasonal variation, the majority of seventeenth-century New Englanders ate "'one continued round' of [salt] meat and legume or [root] vegetable stews morning, noon, and night." Obviously people subsisting in such circumstances had little occasion to consult *The English Hus-wife*, not to mention *The Queens Closet Opened* or Woolley's *Queen-like Closet*.[40]

Evidence has been accumulating recently that during the eighteenth century this situation of material and cultural minimalism changed significantly. We have already referred to developments relating to the availability and use of books. While female literacy was doubling, book imports and local imprints were increasing by factors of ten and five respectively. Beginning in the middle decades of the century, social and circulating libraries further augmented the readership of the already growing stock of available titles. The catalogs of these libraries, as well as those of booksellers, indicate that "secular books," including, as stated earlier, cookbooks, were now in demand below the elite level. A Williamsburg, Virginia, printer who issued a book called *Every Man His Own Doctor* in 1734 was the same one who brought out E. Smith's *Compleat Housewife* eight years later. The conjunction suggests an emerging colonial market for works that would help non-elite readers educate themselves.[41]

More reading of books, especially nonreligious books, was an aspect of what historians have come to agree was a "consumer revolution" that occurred in the eighteenth century in both Great Britain and its North American colonies. In all the spheres in which it manifested itself, the eighteenth-century consumer revolution was, like the evolution of cookbooks that was a part of it, a top-down affair. Those at the apex of colonial society were the first to go in search of a more refined mode of existence and the material goods that would enable it. Turn-of-the-eighteenth-century Boston merchants may have been the first members of the colonial elite to "distance themselves more obviously from their less wealthy neighbors" by stocking their residences with imported textiles and with silverware and furniture upon which, whether imported or locally made, a noticeably greater degree of craftsmanship had been bestowed. It was in these same Boston and Salem mercantile circles that new French styles of domestic interiors were first adopted: "the division of houses into state rooms and domestic apartments, their arrangement into suites of rooms in ascending order of importance and intimacy as one approached the owner's inner sanctum, the creation of specialized entertaining rooms for use by his family, friends, and closest associates, and the unified decoration of rooms into which this invited public was admitted."[42]

One such new type of design- and color-coordinated space for the exhibition of refinement and gentility was the "dyning room," in which one was to partake of meals with one's social equals. Here were to be found oval or round tables, matched sets of chairs, flatware, drinking vessels, and silverware, and glass cases in which to display much of this paraphernalia. It is worth taking a second to ponder one item from this inventory of the apparatus of refined food consumption. As opposed to previous drinking vessels that had to be grasped with both hands, new-style wineglasses could be "elegantly held by pinching either the stem or the foot between the thumb and forefingers" of one hand, leaving the other hand free "to engage in the practiced gestures that accompanied genteel conversations."

Such conversations were "the real substance of the dinner table performance," and it was likewise in order to facilitate them that the tables were made oval or round and that the chairs, plate, and silver came in matched sets.[43]

This stage for the "performance" of gentility was not complete without an elaborated cuisine, comprising a variety of dishes composed from a variety of ingredients, a ritualized placement of these gastronomic offerings on the table, and a ritualized sequence in which to consume them, the succession of courses. And the role of the cookbooks read by the same top-tier groups that lived in houses equipped in this fashion was to provide instruction, "very necessary for all Ladies and Gentlewomen," in all these elements of the fully genteel repast.[44]

How far down the social ladder were such rituals observed? In fully developed form, not very far. On the other hand, as the eighteenth century wore on, people below the elite level were increasingly capable of participating in them. The most notable example of this trend is tea drinking, which "required new containers and utensils and new skills to use them successfully and gracefully." According to an English observer visiting New England in 1740, all the tradesmen's wives in the region were spending an hour every morning and another hour every afternoon sipping tea. From the evidence of probate inventories, it appears that around this same time farming families in Worcester County, Massachusetts, and other rural districts counted not only porcelain teacups and other tea service items but also knives, forks, and "many kinds of imported tableware" among their possessions. When Stephen Brewer, a blacksmith and barber in Roxbury, Massachusetts, died in 1770, his house was found to contain a dining room furnished with an oval dining table, a separate tea table, and accompanying plates, glasses, cups, and teapot.[45]

A Connecticut author of a 1749 agricultural manual, listing the ways in which "the Country may be considered as Improving & Advancing very much," mentioned "better Food" among his pieces of evidence. His claim has been confirmed by modern scholarship. The same historian quoted earlier regarding the dietary monotony experienced by the typical seventeenth-century New England farm family has documented the ways in which this situation was transformed by the end of the eighteenth century. By increased agricultural production and more efficient use of traditional methods of storage and preservation, grains, salt meats, cider, dairy

Porcelain teapot, ca. 1740–1760. Tea drinking was the most widely adopted custom associated with the emergence at this time of consumerism. (Courtesy Newport Historical Society; photograph by Michael Osean)

products, root vegetables, and fruits came to be available for consumption year-round instead of the supplies of these staples approaching exhaustion by the end of the cold season. The result was more choices at mealtime, especially in warm weather, when the family could draw upon both the remaining stocks of preserved foodstuffs and the fresh game, fowl, fish, fruits, and green vegetables it was also usually in a position to obtain.[46]

The social distance may seem vast between an average central Massachusetts farming family and the Gardiners of Boston. The former would be sitting down one day to boiled dinner supplemented with garden "sass," the next to trout from the local stream accompanied by cheese and newly picked huckleberries, all of it washed down with cider. The latter would, on a Monday, be savoring the mistress's own variation on a giblet pie theme drawn from Raffald's *Experienced English House-keeper* and would be following this up on Tuesday with Mrs. Gardiner's more closely imitated version of Hannah Glasse's Scotch barley broth.[47]

We have very little direct evidence regarding who in eighteenth-century New England actually owned and used cookbooks. However, it is not at all improbable that there might have been a copy of Hannah Glasse in the household of Stephen Brewer of Roxbury, the barber and blacksmith with the fully equipped dining room. Books were to be had in the village, or perhaps Brewer got ahold of Glasse from the circulating library in Boston, not far away. His wife might have made a scotch barley broth quite similar to the one prepared by Mistress Gardiner. Similarly, if our well-provisioned central Massachusetts farm household was one of those that had adopted the genteel custom of drinking tea, the housewife may have felt a hankering for the latest English fashions in food preparation as well and may have found a way to get access to the best source of information, a wildly popular book on "the art of cookery . . . by a lady." We don't know how many of these sub-elite New England families made use of cookbooks in this way, but there is every reason to believe that at least some of them did. After all, the wives of thriving artisans and farmers were squarely among the sorts of people for whom Glasse and Raffald were writing.[48]

COLONIAL NEW ENGLAND COOKERY

The idea that English Puritanism caused English cookery to become simple and plain, instead of complex and sophisticated like French cookery, has been effectively discredited. By the time English culinary preferences began to become more fully conscious of themselves as English, in the eighteenth century, Puritanism had long been on the wane as a decisive presence in English society and culture. It may be, however, that a stronger case for Puritan culinary influence can be made for New England, where, after all, this more intense form of English Protestantism enjoyed a much longer and much less contested interval of hegemony. One prominent American historian has argued as much: "The Puritans of Massachusetts created one of the more austere food ways in the Western world. For three centuries, New England families gave thanks to their Calvinist God for cold baked beans and stale brown bread, while lobsters abounded in the waters of Massachusetts Bay and succulent gamebirds orbited slowly overhead. Rarely does history supply so strong a proof of the power of faith."[49]

The writer bases these uncompromising assertions on passages from John Winthrop's account of his spiritual life, written in the 1630s. In a portion of the account the historian does not quote, the first governor of Massachusetts sketches the framework within which dietary choices should be made:

> The fleshe is eagerly inclined to pride, and wantonnesse, by which it playes the tirant over the poore soule, makinge it a verye slave; the workes of our callings beinge diligently followed, are a speciall meanes to tame it, and so is temperance in diet, for idlenesse (under which are all suche workes as are doone to full-fill the will of the fleshe rather then of the spirit,) and gluttonie are the 2 maine pillars of the fleshe hir kingdome.

Temperance in diet is the partner of energetic devotion to one's work in the world ("the workes of our callings beinge diligently followed") in living a life in which the "soule" rather than the "fleshe" is dominant.[50]

By flesh, Winthrop does not mean primarily the body but rather worldliness—the pursuit of pleasure, wealth, or power as an end in itself. The opposite of temperance in diet, what Winthrop calls "gluttonie," would thus be, as stated by John Cotton, the leading minister of early Massachusetts, to "chear our bodies" with food in such a way that we "terminate . . . in eating and drinking." To approach eating and drinking as ends in themselves, for mere pleasure, is to turn the taking of nourishment into "a lust of the flesh" rather than a reenergizing of the soul.[51]

There is reason to believe that this view of food and eating was widely accepted in seventeenth-century New England. Suppression of "the fleshe" in order that "the soule" might hold sway in one's life constituted the core message of the manuals of popular piety by English Puritan clerics that were, along with the Bible, the "steady sellers" among books circulating in the region. Roger Williams, the prime dissenter from the political and ecclesiastical order erected by the likes of Winthrop and Cotton, was nevertheless in entire agreement with them about the perils of eating in the fleshly rather than the soulful mode. "What are all the Contentions and Wars of this World about (generally) but for greater Dishes and Bowles of Porridge, of wch (if We believe Gods Spirit in Scripture) Esau and Jacob were types? Esau will part with the heavenly Birthright for his Supping (after his hunting) for God Belly."[52]

As Williams goes on to say, the logic of the biblical episode of Jacob and Esau points to abstention from food altogether as the means to secure the soul in its properly superior position: "and Jacob will part with his porridge for an Eternal Inheritance." Certainly fast days in atonement for communal sins were an important New England custom. Nevertheless, it should be stressed that the principle of "temperance in diet" did not necessarily entail food austerity, either quantitatively or qualitatively. John Cotton described what Winthrop called "the workes of our callings beinge diligently followed" in a manner exactly parallel to the way he described temperance in diet. Someone diligently pursuing his calling, he wrote, was apt to "rise early and goe to bed late." Such a person would "avoid idleness, cannot indure to spend any idle time, takes all opportunities to be doing something, early and late . . . go anyway and bestir himselfe for profit, this will he doe most diligently in his calling: And yet bee a man deadhearted to the world." Nonstop pursuit of profit was perfectly acceptable, indeed worthy of the highest praise, so long as the soul rather than the flesh continued to govern one's frame of mind and one thereby remained "deadhearted to the world." Correspondingly, temperance in diet might allow one to devote oneself to "chearing" one's body with food and drink of the highest quality, as long as one managed to remain as deadhearted to the world gastronomically as Cotton's pious businessman allegedly remained economically.[53]

So, with Puritan doctrines of food consumption as elastic in principle as was the famous Protestant ethic that smiled on "the spirit of capitalism" and granted absolution to many a striving entrepreneur, the thin upper stratum of New England gentry, professionals, and merchants who might have consulted Gervase Markham or *The Queens Closet Opened* were free to cook and eat just about anything they found in those volumes. Regarding what the early New England upper classes actually ate on a regular basis we know very little. One chronicler of early New England, Edward Johnson, boasted in the 1650s that beef, pork, mutton, and poultry were "frequent in many houses," that there was "great plenty of wine and sugar," allowing for the making of diverse fruit tarts, and that "in their feasts" the colonists had not "forgotten the English fashion of stirring up their appetites with variety of cooking their food." That description, quite possibly accurate for the upper classes, is perfectly consistent with an unfettered recourse to the recipes in Markham's *English Hus-wife* and does not in the least suggest "one of the more austere food ways in the Western world."[54]

It is probable, nevertheless, that the seventeenth-century New England elite abstained from anything that was noticeably elaborate, certainly from anything that was the least bit gaudy, in Markham or the other cookbooks available to it. Puritan teaching did produce temperaments exhibiting moderation and restraint, and what this might mean culinarily is suggested by some lines from a sonnet by the greatest English Puritan poet John Milton. Sometime in the 1650s, Milton invited his young friend Edward Lawrence, "of virtuous father virtuous son," to dine with him, making his offer in the form of a rhetorical question: "What neat repast shall feast us, light and choice, / Of Attic taste, with Wine, whence we may rise / To hear the lute well toucht, or artful voice / Warble immortal notes and Tuscan Air?"[55]

Unlike Ben Jonson, who similarly, several decades before, had proposed in verse to an acquaintance that they partake together of a sequence of culinary pleasures, Milton does not entice his friend with a specific menu. Jonson had promised "an olive, capers, or some better sallade," mutton, egg-stuffed "hen" with lemon and wine sauce, "a coney," a variety of "succulent gamebirds," pastry (perhaps with the game birds inside), "digestive cheese, and fruit," and "a pure cup of rich *Canary*-wine," all to be partaken of freely, "but moderately."[56]

Ben Jonson was no Puritan. Indeed, he dramatized his hostility to Puritanism in *Bartholomew Fair* and other plays. Nevertheless, with the number of courses perhaps a bit reduced, this was a menu that might well have qualified as "a neat repast . . . light and choice" in the eyes of Milton and his young guest. Similarly, one can readily imagine Milton's New England cousins sitting down to Jonson's menu during this same decade, as one of "their feasts" in which they had not forgotten "the English fashion of stirring up their appetites with variety of cooking their food."[57]

As discussed earlier, a more widespread use of cookbooks was an aspect of the eighteenth-century consumer revolution, and by these cookbooks New Englanders were introduced to the sophistications of postmedieval French cooking, as adapted by such authors as E. Smith and Hannah Glasse. The first cookbook printed in New England, Susannah Carter's *The Frugal Housewife*, likewise exhibits what had become the conventional degree of frenchification. There is a chapter "Of Ragouts" filled with recipes, many of them copied from Glasse and/or Smith, calling for truffles, morels, sweetbreads, lambstones, and cockscombs. Many of

Carter's stews are also French made dishes by way of Glasse and Smith, and Carter reproduces Glasse's "Essence of Ham," a variation on the *coulis*, or cullis, that was the fundamental saucing component of seventeenth- and eighteenth-century French cuisine.[58]

One historian has recently argued that once conflict arose in the 1760s between Britain and her North American colonies, opposition to the consumer revolution became one of the most important means of organizing the colonial population into the political force that made the American Revolution. Consumption of foreign commodities was equated with extravagance and luxury, while making do with simpler, domestically produced goods showed one's heart was morally and politically in the right place. In 1767, a writer in a Connecticut newspaper rhetorically asked if a man could be "a true lover of his country" if he would prefer to be seen "strutting about the streets, clad in foreign [i.e., British] fripperies," rather than to remain "nobly independent in . . . russet grey." As regards consumption of food and drink, sentiments of this sort took such forms as the resolution adopted around this same time by the village of Windham, Connecticut, to "discourage and discountenance . . . the excessive use of all foreign teas, china ware, spices, and black pepper, all British and foreign superfluities and manufactures."[59]

If foreign tea, spices, and black pepper were off-limits, then certainly foreign culinary sophistications would have been as well. One might therefore expect to find that Revolutionary-era New England witnessed an adaptation of the stereotyped confrontation presented in eighteenth-century British cookbooks between the honest simplicity of English cooks and the devious sophistications of French boobies. Now New Englanders and Americans would be cast as the exemplars of honest simplicity, and the English would be forced to play the French part, turned into purveyors of depraved culinary practices. The publication in 1772, in the midst of the prime decade of xenophobic anticonsumerism, of a cookbook titled *The Frugal Housewife*, complete with woodcuts by Paul Revere, an energetic participant in the consumer boycott movement, might seem to be consistent with such an understanding of what transpired.

That, however, is not the way things went. Such a scenario is contradicted by the fact that the cookbook in question was itself a British import, and also by the fact that, as we've just seen, the contents of this cookbook were by no means as frugal and plain as its title promised. Indeed, the approach in the contemporary manuscript cookbook by Mrs. Anne Gibbons Gardiner, whose family became Tories when the revolutionary crisis came to a head and who was therefore highly unlikely to have sympathized with the movement to boycott British goods, is closer to the plain style than what is found in Carter. Gardiner calls for the "French" enhancements only occasionally and limits herself to truffles and morels the few times that she does. For Glasse's and Carter's frenchified essence of ham Gardiner substitutes a "Gravy for Sauce" that she bluntly characterizes as "rich and cheap." This mistress of the domestic establishment of a wealthy Boston physician and merchant was more truly a frugal housewife than would have been an uncritical Boston user of the recipes of Susannah Carter of the London district of Clerkenwell.[60]

The evidence suggests that the development of New England cuisine during the eighteenth century was more subtle and interesting than a simple replay of the recent and continuing psychodrama of the English vis-à-vis the French. Along with notions of "temperance in diet," a sense of the unique value of New England institutions and the New England way of life had been drummed into the populace pretty much continuously since the first settlement. As time passed, New England's cherishing of itself began to take historical form, and by the eighteenth century, enough time had passed for this to take the particular historical form of ritual commemoration. In 1720, the centennial of the landing of the Mayflower was observed in Plymouth with, among other things, a meal in two parts: "first a Wooden Dish of Indian Corn and Clams to represent how our Fathers fed in 1620, then an elegant Dinner to shew 1720." So, as of 1720, the foods that the first settlers borrowed from the Indians—Indian corn and North American forms of shellfish—were apparently still regarded as they mostly were in the seventeenth century, as the foods of survival, not the foods of civilization. To progress culinarily was to move from plainness and economy, which were merely a temporary necessity, to elegance.[61]

By 1769, however, commemoration of the founding of Plymouth had become institutionalized in the Old Colony Club, which that year held the first Forefathers' Day celebration. The menu for the day included "a large baked Indian whortleberry pudding, a dish of sauquetash [succotash], a dish of clams, a dish of oysters and a dish of codfish, . . . a course of cranberry tarts, and cheese made in the Old Colony," along with other items. In club records, the banquet was described as "dressed in the plain-est manner (all appearances of luxury and extravagance being avoided, in imitation of our worthy ancestors whose memory we shall ever respect)." A newspaper account of the 1772 Forefathers' Day feast characterized the food that year as "plain and elegant." So now the plainness of a cook-ery composed of ingredients and preparations native to the region was being not contrasted with elegance but rather conjoined with it. The same formula for a positive aesthetic of culinary restraint surfaced at just about the same time in New as in old England.[62]

A historian of residential architecture has argued that around the middle of the eighteenth century portions of the colonial elite, including "some of the very wealthiest" people, reacting against forms of consump-tion that were in their eyes, as practiced by the lower orders, already becoming conspicuous, "came to argue for an aesthetic of simplicity and restraint." Such views found favor in New England, with its "religiously imbued traditions of moderation." A preference for "neoclassical simplic-ity" in architecture did not constitute a renunciation of consumerism, however, but rather an alternative form of it. "For those who could read the new stylistic code, the austerity, restraint, and seeming simplicity of [neoclassic houses] also communicated wealth, luxury, and cosmopoli-tan taste." By the end of the century, the "country seats and neoclassi-cal town houses" designed by Charles Bulfinch that were to be found in Boston and vicinity "were among the most austere and most expensive in America."[63]

The Forefathers' Day banquet, in which austerity was made to harmonize with elegance, represents a parallel set of developments in the history of New England cooking. Nor did the tendency remain confined to ritual oc-casions like Forefathers' Day. In May 1760, the Reverend Ebenezer Parkman of Westborough, Massachusetts, in town for the Harvard Commencement, as well as for the annual elections and ministerial convention, enjoyed a cruise around Boston Harbor with "a number of Gentlemen & Ladies." The party sailed to the lighthouse and had tea there, then "re-embark'd— Eat our Chowder 'o board [aboard] in good order—returnd & landed just after nine at Eve." Chowder, a simple "vernacular" dish, merges easily with tea, the very epitome of genteel consumerism, to constitute the fare for an outing of gentlemen and ladies.[64]

We can also see this pattern at work in the life and writings of a much more famous eighteenth-century American and, at least originally, New Englander. Benjamin Franklin recounts in his autobiography the moment when the consumer revolution most distinctly announced its entrance into his household:

> My breakfast was a long time bread and milk (no tea), and I ate it out of a twopenny earthen porringer, with a pewter spoon. But mark how luxury will enter families, and make a progress, in spite of principle: being called one morning to breakfast, I found it in a china bowl, with a spoon of silver! They had been bought for me without my knowledge by my wife, and had cost her the enormous sum of three-and-twenty shillings, for which she had no other excuse or apology to make, but that she thought *her* husband deserved a silver spoon and china bowl as well as any of his neighbors. This was the first appearance of plate and china in our house, which afterward, in a course of years, as our wealth increased, augmented gradually to several hundred pounds in value.

Just as in the Plymouth centennial, Franklin's breakfast equipage makes the progressive journey from the austerity of "a twopenny earthen porringer" and a pewter spoon to the luxury and elegance of a china bowl and silver spoon.[65]

But also as in the Plymouth anniversary observances, the world of earthenware and pewter was not to be left behind as one moved into the world of china and silver but was rather to be reconceived as a participant in the brave new realm of prosperity and refinement. In 1765, Franklin was in London representing the colonies in an official capacity. An anonymous Englishman wrote a letter to a newspaper belittling the movement to protest against the Stamp Act by boycotting tea, stating that the Americans would be unable to do without tea, "their Indian corn not affording an agreeable or easily digestible breakfast."

Franklin wrote back to "inform the gentleman, who seems ignorant of the matter, that Indian corn, take it for all in all, is one of the most agreeable and wholesome grains in the world; that its green [ears] roasted are a delicacy beyond expression; that samp, hominy, succatash, and nokehock, made of it, are so many pleasing varieties; and that johny or hoecake, hot from the fire, is better than a Yorkshire muffin." American corn-based dishes, in all their native rudeness, are defended not in terms of moral or political virtue but rather in the language of genteel gastronomy, as delicacies, as constituting a pleasing diversity and a superior alternative. Clearly by the 1760s, with such distinct savoring at diverse points of the New England compass of Indian pudding, chowder, and johnnycake, Puritan temperance in diet, crossed with Yankee insistence on the value of local traditions, was modulating into a set of aesthetic and consumerist preferences that amounted to a New England variation on the English theme of economy, neatness, and elegance blending harmoniously together.[66]

CHAPTER TWO

———※———

The Young Republic

Amelia Simmons, Lydia Maria Child, Mrs. Lee

*A*mong the slimmest volumes on the bookshelf of early British and American cookbooks is *American Cookery*, published in Hartford in 1796, as noted the first cookbook written by an American author and the first with a distinct focus on American cooking.[1] *American Cookery* was an immediate commercial success, with a second edition appearing in Albany later the same year. It was printed, as stated on the title page, "For the Author," making the first American cookbook self-published. Nothing is known about Simmons except the few details she herself tells us, the most tantalizing of which is her assertion that she is "An American Orphan."[2]

Simmons's straightforward main title leads us to expect a straightforward book. Yet from its first days in print the work has been surrounded by contention, beginning with a clash between the author and the anonymous person who helped prepare the manuscript for the printer. In an early indication of difficulty, the original edition—a cheap, paperbound forty-seven pages—exists in two versions, one of which Simmons found full of errors. She placed an "Advertisement" in later printings to correct omissions of "several articles very essential in some of the receipts" as well as unauthorized interpolations "which were highly injurious to them." She complains bitterly that these and other changes were made without her consent, "with a design to . . . injure the sale of the book" and were "unknown to her, till after publication."[3]

It was easy enough for Simmons to correct in the second edition the quantity of butter in her rice pudding recipe (half a pound rather than a pound) and the amount of time needed to boil Indian pudding—six hours. Yet she continued to grumble about the flaws in the first edition as she wrote the preface to the second. Even the evident consumer interest that led to that edition seems not to have been enough to assuage her pique. She still takes as a personal matter the "egregious blunders" entered into the text "which were occasioned either by the ignorance, or evil intention of the transcriber for the press." These remain grave charges, and we will consider them at some length below. But first let us review the more recent debate about *American Cookery*, which amounts to a discussion of what exactly makes the book important to subsequent generations.[4]

The historian who first sparked interest in *American Cookery* (and, it should be noted, the book did not receive much attention until 1957) believed that its importance derived, as we might expect, from its being "the first cookbook of American authorship to be published in the United States." However, the next historian to consider the matter (thirty-nine years later) took a different tack. For her, it was neither American authorship nor American ingredients and terms that made *American Cookery* consequential to the story of American cuisine. Rather, it was the combination of American products and British practices that gave the work its lasting significance. To this writer, *American Cookery*'s Anglo-Americanism assured its place in American history.

One could say that these variant approaches to the book's importance—one, that it was the first cookbook by an American author, and two, that it melded British and American elements—are really not at odds. Simmons *was* unique in being the first person to publish a book emphasizing a distinctly American style of cooking. (One wonders why it took two decades of independence for someone to think of it.) But she was equally clever at adapting British recipes—many of them, by the way, lifted from the pages of Susannah Carter's *The Frugal Housewife*—to the ingredients available to American cooks. Certainly both assessments have merit. But *American Cookery* is important for other reasons as well.[5]

As those who have written about such matters in recent decades have emphasized, the success of the American Revolution brought not only a new political dispensation but also a changed cultural atmosphere, one that found a particularly positive reception among American women because of the new emphasis on homes and families as "crucial to the success of the nation." The idea of the family as the crib of the Republic rested in turn on the ideal of motherhood. The exertions of the woman who ran the household were perceived as public duties, the importance of which are conveyed in the term historians use to describe the woman herself—the "Republican Mother." It was only a matter of time before someone thought to search for expressions of this new national consciousness in the kitchen. By highlighting indigenous American ingredients and preparations, and by introducing into print American slang terms for common foods, Simmons capitalized on this shift in the public mood.[6]

Her effort to produce "recipes in a vernacular idiom for food preparation in the New World" were, to be sure, nothing if not timely. One writer even wonders if Simmons herself might not be "a trope for the new society and culture? . . . Orphaned much like the new republican country, she was without parents, lineage, genealogy . . . She had broken from her parents, as did colonial America." This may be stretching the case, but certainly we can agree with Mary Tolford Wilson that *American Cookery* is, "in its minor sphere, another declaration of American independence." Simmons's unabashed assertion that "An American Orphan" was the author gives the book at least a mild sense of bravado, in keeping with the pluckiness that was beginning to be attributed to the American character. *American Cookery* can therefore be read as a landmark, small but visible, along the road not only to gastronomic but also to overall national personality.[7]

But we must take Simmons at her word and presume that her self-identification as an orphan was not merely a literary device. This leads us to wonder how her life was affected by her familial status. The short answer is that orphans in eighteenth-century America did not have it easy. Most were made indentured servants or apprenticed for years in agricultural or domestic work. They were required to participate in the building of the new country but were rarely the beneficiaries of political changes. The rhetoric of freedom and egalitarianism seems not to have applied to them, as indicated by the fact that well into the nineteenth century orphans remained more likely than not to become indentured servants.[8]

Domestic service as a solution to the problem of orphaned girls went back to the seventeenth century, when poor orphans—grouped for legal and all practical purposes with illegitimate, neglected, and abandoned children—were placed in families until they reached the age of eighteen or twenty-one, or even, in some instances, the advanced age of twenty-four. Under the government, as it was called, of a respectable family unit, the orphan was expected to receive a good dose of "decent and Christian education," along with some training in a craft or trade. But as a bound servant, even when well treated, the orphan occupied a distinctly inferior position within the host family. One fortunate enough to be left with an estate might secure an apprenticeship or live under the care of a guardian who was compensated for his efforts. Even in these cases the orphan's social status was apt to be reduced from what it would have been had he or she retained true family ties.[9]

The woes of orphanhood envelop *American Cookery*, from Simmons's complaint in her first preface about the social limitations her status imposed on her, to her errata-page apology for the mess her recipes were in. While asserting that the book is "calculated for the improvement" of all American young women, Simmons singles out "those females in this country, who by the loss of their parents, or other unfortunate circumstances, are reduced to the necessity of going into families in the line of domestics."[10]

So although she aims her book mainly at an audience of literate servants of much the same type as the intended audiences of Glasse and Raffald, who wrote "improving" works for those coming up in the world, Simmons sees the American domestic servant as someone who is as likely to be in a reduced condition as to be on the rise. She encourages all women to better themselves, but among her reasons for this advice is the unhappy possibility that they might be forced, at some point, to find "an opinion and determination of . . . [their] own." For her, developing a culinary repertoire is a way to preserve "the *female character*" even in straitened circumstances.[11]

We might think that an American work of this type would be more optimistic at a time when the national mood supported the loosening of social (including gender) boundaries. But even as Simmons strives for a tone of republican optimism in her preface, she cannot help but remind readers of those women who are left on the sidelines of social mobility simply by virtue of their gender, combined with such accidents of fate as orphanhood or widowhood. The continued precariousness of women's social and economic position highlights the incompleteness of the revolution. So the author of America's first cookbook may promote republicanism through her cookery, but she cannot disguise a subtext of disappointment in the fixed realities that her own autobiography represents.

By comparison, Glasse and Raffald, writing within a more stratified society, nevertheless seem more hopeful. Opportunities for advancement were beginning to appear for clever and diligent British servants to move up to or within the expanding middle class. Having no republican standards against which women's progress must be compared, these writers were able to embrace more enthusiastically the social mobility that was possible.[12]

Around the time of the American Revolution, social attitudes, especially in the wealthy mercantile homes of the North, began to shift toward the use of paid help, what one writer has called "the earliest forerunners of the domestic." From an opposite social direction, this trend among Northern elites was also influenced by the long-standing practice among European aristocrats of keeping cadres of domestic servants. Thus for an array of reasons the market for well-trained help was expanding among the American gentry. In this way, too, Simmons's cookbook was suited to the times.[13]

Within Simmons's overall concern for women in need of respectable employment were those "taking refuge with their friends or relations." These spinster aunts, sisters, daughters, cousins, and friends ended up as housekeepers for those sheltering them. For women without husbands, the assumption of the role of housekeeper in exchange for room, board, and the conviviality of family life—an arrangement often arrived at informally yet lasting indefinitely—had long antecedents in both Britain and the colonies. But in the eighteenth century, this type of service in Britain had begun to be seen as "ignoble," mainly because "the gulf between polite society above stairs and the servants in the basement became ever more marked." This shift in attitudes had not yet occurred in America; wage relations and the associated removal of servants from proximity to the family unit were in an early stage. If these changes had been completely effected, Simmons, a keen reader, literate or not, of the American social code, would not have promoted the domestic role as a suitable livelihood for her genteel female readers.[14]

Finally for Simmons, knowledge of cookery serves not only as a bulwark for orphans and genteel single ladies but also as a way to "improve the minds" of her sex in general. By this time we might think that Simmons has cast her net rather widely for a forty-seven-page paperbound book. But happily, the early success of her work—for which "the call has been so great, and the sale so rapid"—allowed her to focus these somewhat scattershot promotional efforts. By the second edition, her pitch is distinctly more confident: she finds herself, she says, "not only encouraged, but under a necessity of publishing a second edition, to accommodate a large and extensive circle of reputable characters, who wish to countenance the exertions of an orphan, in that which is designed for general utility to all ranks of people in this Republic." Even in victory, Simmons remains motivated by her two main passions: respectability and republicanism.[15]

Now to return to the intriguing question of who if anyone but Simmons herself introduced errors into the first edition of *American Cookery*. In the errata page to the first edition Simmons addresses such matters as whether fourteen or eight eggs should be put into a rice pudding, and whether an Indian pudding should boil for twelve hours or only six. These are significant errors in a text designed for a working cook, yet the seventeen pages of "Directions for Catering, or the procuring the best Viands, Fish, &c.," which Simmons claims were interpolated without her consent, amount to a far more significant alteration of her work. Of these marketing and horticultural tips, which precede the recipes, she says in the second edition preface, "This is a matter, with which, the Authoress does not pretend to be acquainted, much less to give directions to others; nor does she consider any way connected, with that branch which she has undertaken." The addition of such material to her cookbook, or to any cookbook, she considers an assault on "good sense." "Long experience" should have taught both city and country dwellers "how to distinguish good and bad" in the marketplace.[16]

Yet in the material in question, there is nothing but perfectly good advice, if not on cookery then on the closely related topics of purchasing and growing food. Why then is Simmons so adamant that this section does not belong in her book? She claims to know nothing of the subject, at the same time asserting that experience teaches everyone how to make judgments in such matters. Apparently, some readers took a different view and found the marketing information valuable: editions of *American Cookery* that include the "Directions for Catering" appeared in Hartford in 1798 and in Troy, New York, in 1808.[17]

The vehemence of Simmons's objections remains something of a puzzle. Marketing advice had been incorporated into English cookbooks at least since Glasse, in the middle of the eighteenth century (although it is not found in Carter, Simmons's most immediate English source), and since the latter part of the seventeenth century the purchase of food had been a standard part of the duties of housekeepers in English gentry households. There is some evidence that in the United States, around the time Simmons was writing and for a few decades thereafter, it was men who did much of the shopping for food. But the majority of American cookbook imprints (other than Simmons) tell a different story. Marketing advice is dispensed in almost all of them, from the 1807 Boston edition of Maria Rundell's *New System of Domestic Cookery*, through Child's *American Frugal Housewife* and the contemporaneous *Cook's Own Book*, to Beecher's *Domestic Receipt-Book* and beyond.[18]

If marketing advice had been included in most English cookbooks of the second half of the eighteenth century, and particularly in one, that of Glasse, which remained highly popular on this side of the Atlantic, then the most likely explanation for the insertion of such advice into *American Cookery* is that the printer or transcriber had determined that this would boost sales. This theory is all but confirmed by the fact that portions of the advice are clearly derived from Glasse.[19]

As for Simmons's subsequent discountenancing and deletion of this material, the most likely explanation for this is her sensitivity regarding the limited education that she, as an orphan, had received("This is a matter, with which, the Authoress does not pretend to be acquainted, much less to give directions to others"). Having struggled mightily to achieve the exalted status of "Authoress," she was not about to put this hard-won position in jeopardy by seeming to claim to know anything beyond what she actually did know. Her further comments to the effect that everybody already knows how to shop for food anyway represent an awkward attempt to direct attention away from the ignorance on her own part that she has just acknowledged.

But what exactly was Simmons's level of literacy? Was she "all but illiterate," as one commentator infers from the errors the author failed to correct in the first edition? As we have noted, by the late eighteenth century the vast majority of American women—80 percent—could both read and write. Even within the minority, moreover, many women were able to read but not to write. Simmons's substantial borrowing from Carter's *Frugal Housewife* indicates that she could read. Perhaps, as an orphan put out to service early in life, her education ended after she had learned to read but before she mastered writing. This was one of "those disadvantages, which usually attend, an Orphan," and it may have been the reason that she was unable to prepare her manuscript for publication on her own.[20] As the reader will doubtless realize, this supposition, plausible in many respects, leaves us with one loose end: Simmons would have been capable of reviewing her work before its initial publication. Yet it appears that she didn't. The solution to this further mystery may be provided by Simmons herself, who after all contends that the person who prepared her manuscript for the press set out to trick her. Certainly this is possible. But it is also possible that her amanuensis or publisher simply believed that he knew better than the author on several points and, without telling her, revised accordingly. Finally, we must consider the possibility that, despite Simmons's accusation, the recipe errors at least were no more nor less than simple mistakes.[21]

Simmons tells us that the infringement of her authorial role turned her against her former associate. Her expression of anger against an anonymous enemy for a difficult-to-explain grievance, forever a part of her unique and original cookbook, may now seem a misjudgment. But this was the only means at Simmons's disposal to assert her intellectual property rights. Ironically, while she complained that her opus had been tampered with, she herself stole from the work of Susannah Carter (just as the offending transcriber or printer stole from Glasse for the marketing section). Carter, in turn, had lifted many a recipe from her predecessors, Glasse, Smith, and others.[22]

If the front matter of *American Cookery* offers a case study of the interplay between the new American ideals and the social mores constraining women, orphans, and others on the margins of late-eighteenth-century society, the main text of the cookbook offers something quite different—succinct and useful directions for cooks both novice and experienced. Here we find the kind of workaday instructions with which modern cookbook readers are familiar. The techniques, ingredients, and recipes in *American Cookery*, some old, some new, some an amalgamation of both, amount to Simmons's prescription for an American cooking style.

One writer has described Simmons's gastronomy as embodying "Old and New World flavors, language, and ideas, simultaneously merging and distinguishing the two cultures, American and English." This statement could serve almost as a roadmap to the debate about the cookbook among historians that we mentioned at the outset of this chapter: some emphasize its use of "native . . . products," others stress its conformance with "English culinary traditions." On the title page the bold proclamations of "American Cookery" by "An American Orphan" bracket a list of traditional English foods—puddings, pies, cakes, custards, and preserves. Simmons even gives a nod to the old English practice of including simplified recipes for court luxuries by including the "Imperial Plumb" cake. Despite the titular emphasis on American cooking, the lengthy subtitle fails to mention even one uniquely American product or process. Simmons has packed substantial American kitchen know-how into her small book, but you would never know it from her title page.[23]

Nevertheless, the enumeration made by Mary Tolford Wilson, the first scholar to study *American Cookery*, of Simmons's use of American products, recipes, and slang terms shows the uniqueness of Simmons's work: cornmeal (called in Simmons's day "Indian" and used to make Indian Pudding, "Johny" Cake, and Indian "Slapjacks"), pumpkin pie (the American custard style rather than the British deep-dish style), crookneck squash, whortleberries, Jerusalem artichokes, spruce beer (thought to prevent scurvy), corn cobs used to smoke bacon, "cramberry-sauce," watermelon rinds to make "American citron," pearl ash (chemical leavener made from wood ashes), soft gingerbread (crisp was the rule in Europe), molasses (Simmons steers clear of the British term "treacle"), colloquialisms such as "emptins" for "emptyings" (the lees of beer, cider, or wine, used as yeast), "Hannah Hill" for sea bass, "shortning" for "shortening," and two Dutch terms just coming into common use in America—

"cookey," instead of the British "little cake," and "slaw" from *sla,* for salad. In the second edition, Simmons continues to wave the American flag with the addition of "Independence Cake," "Election Cake," and "Federal Pan Cake."[24]

Karen Hess disputes the distinctively American nature of many of the items on this list. Such foodstuffs as corn, although originating in the Americas, appeared in British and continental cookbooks before Simmons. But a scattering of references to American products and recipes across the vast European culinary repertoire—for instance, to maize in *Le Parfait Boulanger* (1778) or to pumpkin pie in Hannah Woolley's 1673 *The Gentlewoman's Companion*—does not tarnish Simmons's reputation as the author of the first "uniquely American" cookbook. Her accomplishment was to highlight and codify the legitimization of American ingredients and preparations that, as we have seen, was taking place in a variety of ways toward the end of the colonial period. She gathers together in one small, convenient book some of the best American—and British—recipes of the day, illustrating how these dishes could be cooked using American products and described using American terms, making them truly *American* food.[25]

Simmons presented an emerging cuisine within an emerging postcolonial society. Given the republican consciousness that permeates it, her cookbook is indeed "strikingly original." But can we really claim that with *American Cookery* a distinctly American cuisine came before the reading public? If one mostly tastes the "English precedents" of Simmons's American dishes (not to mention the many recipes that are lifted directly from English sources), questions arise not only about her originality but also about the integrity of the notion of the uniquely "American" quality of her cookbook. To resolve the matter, let us look at two issues: the "Englishness" of the English food in *American Cookery,* and the changes that occur when nontraditional ingredients and practices (in this case, American) are substituted in the making of standard dishes.[26]

The "Puff-Pastes, Pies, Tarts, Puddings, Custards and Preserves, and All Kinds of Cakes" of Simmons's title page catalog "the more traditional areas of English cookery" of the earlier eighteenth century, as one British food historian has put it. Pies, for example, were considered chiefly English fare: "By the middle of the seventeenth century [pies were] . . . a peculiarly English speciality; even the French were prepared to concede supe-

Pompkin.

No. 1. One quart ftewed and ftrained, 3 pints cream, 9 beaten eggs, fugar, mace, nutmeg and ginger, laid into pafte No. 7 or 3, and with a dough fpur, crofs and chequer it, and baked in difhes three quarters of an hour.

No. 2. One quart of milk, 1 pint pompkin, 4 eggs, molaffes, allfpice and ginger in a cruft, bake 1 hour.

Orange Pudding.

Put fixteen yolks with half a pound butter melted, grate in the rinds of two Seville oranges, beat in half pound of fine Sugar, add two fpoons orange water, two of rofe-water, one gill of wine, half pint cream, two naples bifcuit or the crumbs of a fine loaf, or roll foaked in cream, mix all together, put it into rich puff-pafte, which let be double round the edges of the difh; bake like a cuftard.

Amelia Simmons, *American Cookery*, Hartford edition, 1796. These two recipes, an Americanized pumpkin pie and a verbatim copy of an English recipe for orange pudding, exemplify the dual nature of Simmons's work. (Courtesy American Antiquarian Society)

riority." In keeping with English practice, Simmons's pies run the gamut from fowl and flesh pies made with pigeon, chicken, beef, veal, and mutton to apple, currant, and custard pies. Creams were also "peculiar to English cookery" of the period, and here again Simmons displays her lingering cultural allegiance with her syllabubs, trifles, and fruit creams. As we have discussed, Glasse and many others had expressed ambivalence about high-style French cooking. Carter's *Frugal Housewife*, from which Simmons borrowed so much, followed this emerging preference for a simpler, middle-class style of cooking.[27]

But as with any cooking tradition, these distinctions—high style for the upper class and plainer pies and pastries for the middle—do not hold up in any strict sense. For instance, we find antecedents to the English meat pie in the venison pasties served "at the wedding feast of the Duke of Mantua in 1581." Styles were mixed up and reinterpreted by such middle-class practitioners of the culinary arts as Glasse and Carter, themselves the inheritors of the seventeenth-century adaptations of court cooking to gentry and middle-class requirements. But the original "point of diffusion" downward—what one writer calls "the embourgeoisement of haute cuisine"—was not England but France. Thus while Simmons's work relies on "English precedents," the classic dishes of that repertoire are themselves the product of older influences emanating from the continent.[28]

As to whether the introduction of a new main ingredient constitutes a newly created dish if a traditional method of preparation is still employed, this may be a question not only of a culinary tipping point but also of a cultural one. The issue arises in relation to Simmons's recipes for such foods as Indian (cornmeal) pudding, turkey with cranberry sauce, "Pompkin" pudding or pie, "Johny Cake," and "Indian Slapjack." These dishes, it is claimed, are not particularly original because they are prepared in the same manner as such standard English dishes as flour and oatmeal hearth cakes, roast game garnished with barberries, and parsnip puddings. But the differences between these Old and New World foods far outweigh the similarities in their preparation. No one would confuse pumpkin pie with parsnip pudding.[29]

There may well be an underlying continuity in method of preparation between many English and American dishes, but in the application of those methods to new ingredients Simmons was the first to record the emergence of a distinctly American cuisine. Just as "the more traditional areas of English cookery" arose as a result of many kinds of adaptations, some major, some minor, from traditional areas of continental cookery, so American culinary traditions arose from a similar process of adaptation, primarily from English practices. To these many creative kitchen adaptations, Simmons was a central contributor.

American Cookery was a runaway success. Many editions and reprints followed the first, as did plagiarized texts passed off as original works along with blatant, if acknowledged, copies produced in New York in 1805; Montpelier, Vermont, in 1808; and Boston in 1819. As Simmons had intended, it is likely that among the first users, if not the first buyers, of the first American cookbook were young female orphans in domestic service. But Simmons was also a hit with the spinsters and widows who worked as housekeepers, with young farm girls who "lived out" for a few years before marriage, with genteel ladies, and with the wives of the upwardly mobile professional and mercantile classes who populated America's growing cities and towns—in other words, with a wide range of American women whose almost universal literacy might lead them to participate in the "consumer revolution" and take their part in the young republican enterprise by owning and using *American Cookery*.[30]

Despite its broad appeal, Simmons's little book was primarily intended for servants. The frequent appearance in the recipes of such phrases as "may be served," "send them hot to the table," and "you may send it up" indicates that she designed or, when borrowing from Carter, chose recipes with the cook rather than the woman of the house in mind. This assumption that servants would be preparing her recipes is perhaps contradicted in one instance, the recipe for Foot Pie (see below, Chapter 10, #34), where she advises: "put carefully together and serve up, by this means you can have hot pies through the winter, and enrich'd singly to your company." Even here the final phrase is ambiguous. And taken together with an absence of the typical references to a housewife's concerns—leftovers, frugality, family members' preferences—the preponderance of evidence suggests that Simmons's aim for her recipes is mainly to provide instruction for women in domestic service, as she states in her first preface.[31]

By the early nineteenth century, most American editions of British cookbooks, such as Glasse's *Art of Cookery*, Carter's *Frugal Housewife*, and Maria Rundell's *A New System of Domestic Cookery*, had been revised to include foods either considered uniquely American, such as doughnuts and cornmeal dishes, or made according to the "American Mode of Cooking," such as soft gingerbread. The surprise success of Amelia Simmons's little cookbook had made these editions necessary.[32]

On the other hand, the very fact that it was deemed profitable to issue American editions of English cookbooks indicates that Simmons bequeathed a dual heritage to the nineteenth century. As seen with our next author, cookbooks would continue to emphasize Americanness, calling for ingredients and methods "adapted to the wants of this country," while other works such as that of our author-after-next, "Mrs. N. K. M. Lee," would reveal that dependence on British sources and techniques continued to be a major factor in New England's culinary evolution.

Lydia Maria Child

As much is known about Lydia Maria Child as is obscure about Amelia Simmons. Born February 11, 1802, she was the youngest of the five surviving offspring of Susannah and Convers Francis, middle-class householders in Medford, Massachusetts, a shipbuilding town six miles up the Mystic River from Boston. Her father, a baker, had achieved prosperity and a certain level of fame with the invention of the popular sea biscuit known as the "Medford cracker." Although Francis was a strict Calvinist and "great believer in manual labor" who frowned on intellectual pur-

Engraving from a portrait of Lydia Maria Francis (Child) by Francis Alexander, 1826. Original held by Medford Historical Society. (Courtesy Library of Congress)

suits, two of his children became influential members of Boston's cultural elite. Child's favorite brother, also named Convers, served as pastor of the Unitarian First Parish in Watertown, Massachusetts. But it was Child herself who had the greater career, as a writer, editor, and reformer.[33]

Her berth in the literary world was gained at the tender age of twenty-two with the publication of a romantic novel, *Hobomok, A Tale of Early Times*. Involving the love relationship of an Indian and a Puritan woman, the story appealed to a New England audience whose newfound concern for Indian rights coincided with the dwindling numbers of actual Indians in the region. Despite the avant-garde love match, the tale ultimately left unbreached the racial boundaries of the day. Nevertheless, its depiction of an interracial, if short-lived, marriage brought *Hobomok* and its creator some notoriety. Reacting as she would throughout her long career, the young writer did not shrink from the controversy surrounding her work; indeed, she seemed to relish her place at the center of the storm. With *Hobomok* came a brief period of favor for Child among Boston's literary and cultural elite as a writer of great promise. However, she soon fell from grace for taking a stance in favor of the abolition of slavery well before that position became orthodoxy among wealthy Bostonians.[34]

In a strange way, the misfortunes of her girlhood years probably helped the adult to weather the vicissitudes of fame. During much of her youth, her mother was invalided with tuberculosis, dying when the girl was twelve. Three years later her father sold his business, moved in with his eldest son, and sent fifteen-year-old Lydia to live with her newly married older sister in rural Norridgewock, Maine. Lydia remained with her sister's family for five years. She then took a job teaching school in Gardiner, Maine, a town forty miles south of Norridgewock. After a year, she relocated again, this time into the household of her minister brother, Convers, in the prosperous Boston suburb of Watertown. Thus by her early twenties, Child had experienced life as a foster teen, a teacher in rural Maine, a young adult dependent on a brother and sister-in-law, and, finally, as a successful author. For the young Lydia Francis, writing was as much a means to achieve independence as it was a source of pleasure and self-expression. For the mature Lydia Child, this would also be the case.

Four years after her stellar literary debut, Lydia married David Child, a promising young lawyer and editor of the *Massachusetts Journal,* who, it turned out, had a greater knack for becoming involved in protracted and expensive legal wrangles than for the practice of law or the wielding of an editor's pen. David Child found it impossible to hold a job for very long. It thus fell to his wife to shoulder most of the family's financial burdens during their married life, a task she accomplished, as she had done in her early adulthood, mainly through writing.[35]

It was not only the ups and downs of her childhood and married life that shaped Lydia Maria Child's career as a writer. As a nineteenth-century girl with a prosperous but determinedly anti-intellectual father, Child found her creative opportunities circumscribed from the start. She felt isolated, for instance, when her brother Convers left home for Harvard in 1811 after having, with great difficulty, convinced their father to allow him to pursue a college education. But the dual educational deficits Convers's youngest sister faced—coming from a home in which academic pursuits were little prized and growing up at a time when all women were kept out of the first-class coach when it came to education—seem ultimately to have motivated as much as constrained her.[36]

However, the effort Child expended to overcome her class and gender circumstances took a toll, as the following anecdote illustrates. In early adulthood, she surprised her friends by requesting that they cease calling her Lydia, a name she claimed was "unpleasant" to her because of "some associations of childhood." Henceforth, they were to call her Maria, the name she had recently taken for herself at an adult baptism. The melodic similarity between the two names is apparent, as is the pain that must have occasioned Child's unusual request. As we know, her own preference never became primary and has survived only as a pretty placeholder.[37]

Child experienced tensions between loyalty to her family and aspirations to live on a level better suited to her literary talents. Her most intimate allegiances—to her hapless husband and ailing father—forced her to take on household tasks more suited to a mechanic's wife than to the distinguished woman of letters she had become. Her husband's lifelong financial difficulties caused Child to fall back on the pinching virtues of her childhood. "Industry, frugality, and perseverance" were traits that, while admirable, were more dutifully espoused the farther down the social scale one went. They were the special bulwark of the striving artisan class from which she had struggled, by becoming a writer, to distance herself. In better circumstances, Child might have been free to emphasize other qualities in her work and life. Despite her talent, energy, and accomplishments, she remained for all practical purposes at the social level she had occupied when she was a prosperous baker's daughter.[38]

But we get ahead of ourselves. In 1829, Child published *The Frugal Housewife*, the domestic advice manual and cookbook that is her contribution to kitchen literature. A compact little book, packed somewhat randomly with advice and recipes, it became an immediate success. With the eighth edition, published in 1832, Child changed the title to *The American Frugal Housewife*, including the modifier because, as she explained, "there is an *English* work of the same name, not adapted to the wants of this country." That work was Carter's *Frugal Housewife*, which had escaped Child's attention until she began to prepare an English edition of her own work.[39]

Like Simmons, Child set out to provide recipes suited to the resources available to her American audience. But an examination of the front matter of both works reveals their differences. Simmons's proclamation of *American Cookery* fits a young, assertive nation, while Child's *American Frugal Housewife* suggests limitation—financial, domestic, and, in later editions, geographic. Her choice of the phrase "the wants of this country," meant in the sense of requirements, may also be read as deficiencies. We highlight below some of the merits of her prudence. Nevertheless, her emphasis is indisputably on thrift. The tone of the book is all the more striking when we recall that it first appeared not in the midst of the terrible financial crisis of the late 1830s but during the relatively prosperous 1820s and early 1830s. Child's extreme antipathy to waste, whether in good times or bad, and her creativity in the face of limits are exactly the traits that we have come to see as the hallmarks of the New England character. While not all New Englanders embodied such characteristics, in writing her book Child certainly did.

The differences between the works of Child and Simmons are also apparent in their contents. Whereas Simmons wishes to expunge everything but cooking instructions, and her recipes generally assume a household with servants, Child offers a scrapbook of moral advice, household tutelage, and health remedies for the servantless classes. Her recipes are inexpensive, practical, and easily prepared by the mistress of a moderate home. In other words, Simmons, for all her emphasis on orphanhood, produces a cookbook that suits wealthy households, whereas Child provides parsimonious recipes and gives advice economical enough for a house full of orphans.

But perhaps a comparison between Simmons and Child is somewhat beside the point. After all, the publication dates of the two works are separated by thirty-three years. And although influential, Simmons's little book never reached the broad market attained by the most popular English cookbooks. Several American works were beginning to achieve comparable fame at the time Child wrote, primary among them Mary Randolph's *The Virginia Housewife* and Philadelphian Eliza Leslie's *Seventy-five Receipts for Pastry, Cakes and Sweetmeats.* It was against these American cookbooks, and several British titles, that Child's work competed.[40]

Randolph's book, first published in 1824, appeared in at least nineteen antebellum editions. Some critics claim that *The Virginia Housewife* was the most "influential American cookbook of the nineteenth century." Although reflecting the diet of the upper classes of bountiful Virginia, the work "had some circulation even in New England." But Randolph's impact on New England regional cooking was minimal. New Englanders were no doubt curious about the fashions, diet, and living styles of their historic rivals, the Virginians. But the legendary New England quest for knowledge did not in this instance lead to a change in practice.[41]

A story inscribed inside the front cover of one New Hampshire copy of *The Virginia Housewife* illustrates the point: "This was my mother's first cook-book. She sent to town by my father. He bought one of the only kind they had. Mother was so disappointed, she cried. My mother became a very nice cook, although she did not use the Virginia Housewife. Ma's next cook book was by Mrs. Child." The story reveals something of one New England family's economic status as well as its food preferences: the inscriber's mother may have had sufficient disposable resources (presumably when she was a new housewife) to purchase a cookbook, but when that book failed to provide a satisfactory return on her investment she was just poor or thrifty enough to feel the disappointment acutely. While it is only implied in the brief tale that it was Mrs. Randolph's expensive mode of cooking that was the source of the New Hampshire mother's long-ago tears, the mention of Child is surely meant to point a contrast. Here was exactly the young, striving, literate American female audience Child primarily aimed to assist.[42]

Carolyn L. Karcher believes that "at the height of *The Frugal Housewife*'s popularity in the 1830s, the readers Child addressed probably constituted a majority of the nation's adult female population." Her audience consisted mostly of the "poor and 'middling' sort"; they lived on farms, and in small towns and rural villages, but more and more they were moving to the nation's growing cities; they had little in the way of household technology to help them in their daily tasks (for instance, Child still assumed that her readers cooked over open hearth fires) and few could afford "help" with their domestic responsibilities.[43]

Despite the strained economic circumstances of most housewives, cookbook writers continued to do as Mrs. Randolph had profitably done and direct their gaze up the social ladder to the smaller but more affluent (and therefore more apt to be book-buying) group of female readers. Eliza Leslie's *Seventy-five Receipts* is a case in point, with costly recipes, such as those for ice cream and French almond cake.[44]

Child was well aware that Randolph's and Leslie's works, along with many British cookbooks and domestic advice manuals then flooding the market, were aimed at wealthy readers and those wishing to imitate them. Shrewdly, she set her sights on the as yet untapped downscale market, dedicating her domestic guide "to Those Who Are Not Ashamed of Economy." In other words, she addressed those who *were* ashamed of economy but whose feelings of inferiority she was resolved to erase through a mixture of inspirational rhetoric and recipes. With this strategy, she carved for herself a new and sizable audience, in a sense creating a market for her work ex nihilo.[45]

Child's advice about running a modest home did help poor and middle-class women to economize. While she could not change their social status, she could help them modulate their feelings about the social opprobrium commonly associated with the necessity of living on a limited budget. Child understood that women in such circumstances were keenly sensitive to the social condescension of those with greater financial resources. Her goal was restoration of the traditional New England insistence on the dignity of any and every domestic task, and transformation of attitudes about penny-pinching from resignation to bleak necessity to social acceptance, indeed beyond, to social esteem. She wanted frugality to be the mode of life preferred by enlightened American women. It was Dickens's *Christmas Carol* in reverse, with frivolous spending the benighted enemy of enlightened Scroogism. Of course the need to argue as vehemently as Child did for frugality suggests that the dominant view of the matter was more and more residing, as it still resides, elsewhere.

We might well ask why careful consideration of household finances and a willingness to perform housework signified low social status in a young nation ostensibly dedicated to the democratic virtues of egalitarianism and self-reliance. What made exertions of this sort in the domestic sphere undignified, when agricultural and industrial labor were being upheld as virtuous? The literature on the rise of the ethos of refinement answers these questions in detail. For our purposes, it is enough to note that housewives had descended, philosophically speaking, from assuming the crucial civic role of nurturing future citizens—the ideology of

Study for Lilly Martin Spencer, *The Young Wife: First Stew*, 1856. The work portrays the emotional toll taken by the loss of culinary skill among nineteenth-century young women, a loss Child's *American Frugal Housewife* addresses. (Courtesy Ohio Historical Society)

the Republican Mother—to participating in the genteel consumerism that, evolving from the eighteenth-century "empire of goods," was accompanying the emergence of a market-based social order. In short, the Victorian era was at hand.[46]

Living a pampered domestic life may have been the ideal to which American women were beginning to aspire, but for most in the broad middle class such a costly choice was simply out of reach. Little was being done to assuage the feelings of inadequacy brought on by the distance between the real-world domestic arrangements of the majority of women and this unattainable goal. Furthermore, as Child's contemporary the vegetarian activist William Alcott stated, echoing Child herself, for many young women domestic "education has been so defective, as to leave [them] ignorant on the subject of house-keeping." As young families followed the movement of jobs to the newly settled western territories (today's Midwest) or into the ever-growing cities, freshly minted housewives were forced to set up housekeeping without the advice and support of their older and more experienced sisters, aunts, mothers, and grandmothers. These often lonely and inexperienced young women enthusiastically invited Mrs. Child into their homes, making her book an immediate hit that sold, as she herself proudly pointed out, "more than six thousand copies in one year."[47]

Child's story of the three "mechanics," or artisans, who supported their families on twelve, eight, and six hundred dollars a year respectively will serve to illustrate how she goes about improving frugality's reputation among American housewives. Ironically, she offers little by way of specific advice on the subject of economizing, only mentioning that the six-hundred-a-year man's "wife and children were in the habit of picking up paper and twine." This admirable practice may have helped to conserve some of the family's resources, but it could hardly have saved half a breadwinner's annual wages. The real point of the story is to offer not tips on economizing but rather a rationale for economy, and permission to boast about it, as this exchange reveals: "'I keep house, and comfortably too with a wife and children, for six hundred a year; but I suppose they would have thought me mean, if I had told them so.' I did not think him mean . . . the man who is economical, is laying up for himself the permanent power of being useful and generous."[48]

In the revised moral universe Child creates, being *mean* has become being *economical,* and the person who is economical has gained the permanent power to exercise his (or her) higher nobility. Child's readers are encouraged to move beyond genteel ostentation in order to be able to practice two virtues: one—generosity—usually associated with aristocracy; the other—usefulness—the quintessence of practical New England. Child's adoption of a moral vocabulary to rehabilitate the social status of frugality within the emerging world of capitalist middle-class gentility would have immense appeal to many Americans but especially to Calvinist New Englanders and their financially struggling offspring. Representing the Northern Protestant cultural tradition, Child was not merely speaking their language; she was writing them back into the cultural mainstream, which, through an emphasis on material consumption as the definition of middle-class refinement, had threatened to leave them behind.[49]

At the end of the book, in the section "Travelling and Public Amusements," Child relates the story of a farmer and his wife who spend foolishly on a leisure trip to Quebec. Her choice of a Catholic and Francophone region as the couple's destination would have set off immediate alarms for her Protestant, English-descended readers. For them, French Canada was as much the moral and social antipode of their way of life as was the plantation South. From the couple's accounts of seasickness, the theft of a watch, the disarray in which they found farm and family on their return, and the expense of returning the hospitality of the relatives and friends with whom they had stayed on their journey, the first-level meaning of the story is clear: there are vast hidden costs to the leisure travel that had recently come into vogue among the middle classes.[50]

But as in the previous example, the deeper meaning of the story is somewhat more complicated. Again Child aims to make "republican simplicity, industry, and virtue" not only acceptable but fashionable. She concludes her story with this exhortation: "I would not have . . . people who have little to spend . . . sacrifice permanent respectability and comfort to present gentility and love of excitement." But in the story as she tells it "present gentility" is hardly the point. Love of excitement is. Child describes the consequences of giving in to that passion. Her readers understood her message perfectly: good breeding does not mean pursuing such passing fancies as the new vogue for exotic leisure travel. Costly displays such as these are marks not of refinement but rather of vulgarity. From the lower rungs of the social ladder rather than from the upper, Child was preaching an aesthetic of restraint similar to the one that found favor in eighteenth-century elite circles in response to aspects of the consumer revolution of that era.[51]

In addition to western migration and the growth of cities, Child's readers of the 1820s faced enormous changes to the structure of their social lives, as America was on the cusp of the Industrial Revolution and its impact on domestic life was just beginning to be felt, if at first mostly by the wealthy. The path by which many technological improvements found their way into the average American home is exemplified by an ingenious cooking appliance known as the Rumford stove, the plans for which were first published in the United States in 1796. This wall-mounted combination stew hole and cylindrical metal oven box was outrageously expensive, tricky to operate, and difficult to install. Yet once in place and mastered, it offered the cook a revolutionary new cooking experience—regulated heat. To those who had long labored over hearth fires it also provided the ability to stand rather than stoop while cooking. These combined advantages proved irresistible, and while few families could afford a Rumford stove, its existence stimulated interest in stove technology. Within a short time, the cast iron cookstove, a mass-produced, reasonably priced alternative to the Rumford stove, would enter countless American households, forever changing domestic cooking.[52]

Despite these early signs of the changes to come, at the time Child published *The Frugal Housewife* the manner of food preparation remained for most women what it had been for their mothers, grandmothers, and great-grandmothers. Work still revolved around open hearths. As they had been for centuries, heavy iron cooking pots were suspended on lug poles and cranes over hearth fires. Housewives stooped to tend bake kettles and rotate the spits of tin kitchens, and they reached into brick ovens to sweep out ashes and insert loaves of bread, pots of beans, and dishes of pudding or custard. With wet clay from their yards, women sealed their oven doors to keep in the hard-won heat. The "modest investment in cooking equipment" that had been the norm since settlement was still the rule for most American families into the early nineteenth century.[53]

Perhaps the most significant development in domestic circumstances in the 1820s and '30s was not any actual change in mode of living but rather a new sense that permanent change such as had already taken place with the Industrial Revolution in Britain was on the horizon. New appliances were beginning to come within reach of the middle class. These inventions held the potential to transform daily life. For example, despite the still-high costs and mechanical quirks of the new stoves, they were immediately popular because they offered something to both men and women. When we consider that "to feed a family in those [pre-stove] days was fully one man's work" in chopping wood, we can better understand the great appeal of an appliance that significantly reduced, or even eliminated, the need for firewood. And for women, hearth cooking required "constant maneuvering, adjusting, and vigilance." Here was an appliance that allowed women not only to stand while cooking but also to tend their fires less often, and even to walk away from their pots and pans for extended periods of time. We can hardly comprehend the pleasure householders felt at these improvements to their daily lives.[54]

Nevertheless, adoption of such new domestic technologies required both substantial changes in attitude and considerable investment of a family's limited capital. On the question of attitudes, let us look again at the transition from open hearth to stove. New Englanders in particular were reluctant to adopt the new technology wholeheartedly, in no small part because the hearth symbolized the independent, agrarian way of life which they viewed as their cultural inheritance. Thus the Griggs family of Dover, Massachusetts, decided in the 1830s not to brick up their "ancient" fireplace after purchasing a cookstove. They wished occasionally to sit by an open fire, exercising their patrimony, as it were. It also had long been noted that New Englanders, being the most English of all the North American colonists, followed the predilection of their forbears in liking "open fires." This was true despite the known fuel inefficiency of eighteenth- and nineteenth-century fireplaces as compared to stoves (which had been widely used in continental Europe since the sixteenth century). According to one estimate, "fireplaces lost 80 percent of their heat up the chimney."[55]

Given the New England fondness for fireplaces, Child's assumption in her recipes that her readers would be cooking over open hearths fits with an opposite social current in the early years of the Industrial Revolution—the desire to slow down the rapid, at times overwhelming, rate of change. Resistance to technology was then, as it is now, as integral a part of technological innovation as the inventions themselves.[56]

In spite of such efforts, the changes wrought by mechanized industry were not easy to keep at bay. At the same time that cast iron stoves were entering homes in significant numbers, anthracite coal was being promoted for domestic use in both heating and cooking. Canal transportation had greatly reduced the price of coal to eastern markets, making it an appealing alternative to scarce and expensive firewood. But the new fuel, like the new stoves, had drawbacks. For one thing, it was much more difficult to light coal than wood. The story of coal versus wood—new fuel versus old—highlights the hidden costs involved in a transition to a physically easier yet culturally more dissociated life, the classic two-edged sword of modern life.[57]

But even the promised ease was sometimes elusive. Consider one domestic advice writer's painfully exact directions for lighting a coal fire, given in 1827. "This is a great mystery," he begins. After the grate has been "perfectly cleared," one is to add a layer of kindling, followed by a layer of live coals, which are to be obtained, in this infinitely regressive universe, from an already existing coal fire. This fire cake is to be topped by pieces of coal cut to "about the size of a half-pint tumbler." Finally— here the author seems to sigh—"if the process . . . fails, begin all over again." Despite such daunting instructions, it appears that even the mere promise of ease was powerful enough for many consumers to outweigh the troublesome aspects of the early versions of these "improvements."[58]

So change was coming, one way or another, and economics was the key. In 1817, for example, before the opening of the Erie Canal, carriage costs between Buffalo and New York City averaged 19.12 cents per ton mile; in 1840, fifteen years after the canal opened, the price had fallen to 1.68 cents. There were countless additional consequences of lowered transportation costs. For example, the canal system led quite rapidly to higher rates of settlement and to a vast increase in wheat, corn, and rye production in the Midwest. As a result, New England farmers no longer found it profitable to grow these crops for their own tables or local markets. Grains, heretofore locally grown and milled whole were quickly replaced by the new "superfine" western flours that had been bleached of germ and bran to prevent deterioration during the extended periods of storage that long-distance transport required. Previously, highly processed grains had been used only for export or in commercial bakeries making rot-resistant (and, of course, nutritionally inferior) foods such as sea biscuits and army hardtack. As one historian notes, the transition for the average farm family from growing and milling their own grain, or perhaps bartering locally, to purchasing "fine and superfine wheat flours . . . [from] large automated flour mills" amounted to "the first stages of the industrialization of their household."[59]

Into this world of rapid and profound change came Child's *Frugal Housewife,* with its economizing recipes and old-fashioned advice and instructions. However, many of the housewives Child aimed to reach did not need any advice about living in an old-fashioned manner. They already were, and it was no picnic. Of her existence in the 1820s in Illinois, for instance, one diarist reflected: "You may feel I have attached undue notice to the meals given and the calls on our hospitality, but could you know the labor of bringing from raw materials anything at all presentable for family use, you would understand why the impression was so lasting." This woman writes from the far side of a great experiential divide; she is aware that her readers will never know the backbreaking household labor of which she speaks. Yet it is just such an old-fashioned, labor-intensive home that Child implicitly held up as her ideal in her cookbook.[60]

Another such home was labored into existence by what Caroline Clapp Briggs, born in 1822 in Northampton, Massachusetts, called "sturdy, self-reliant independent Yankee women." Ironically, Briggs was describing not the wives of freeholders but rather "help," women whose economic circumstances led them to work in the homes of others, in this case in the author's childhood household. These unique characters "would have scorned to be called servants," reports Briggs. Invoking the New England mystique, Briggs describes their temperament and character this way: their "faithfulness made up for all grace of manner . . . [they were] often saucy and impertinent, but in sickness they were ready to work all day and nurse all night."[61]

For our purposes, the most interesting aspect of Briggs's statement is her conflation of the old republican values of self-reliance, sturdiness, and industry with the vaunted independence of the "Yankee." She published her memoir in 1897, at a time when all "Yankee" rhetoric was cli-chéd at best and nativist at worst. Although the equation of Yankee ethnicity with republican virtues may have become threadbare by the late nineteenth century, the formula was fresh in the 1820s; and it was in part forged by Lydia Maria Child in her *Frugal Housewife*. As Joseph Conforti argues, Child's emphasis on the putatively traditional New England values of "industry, economy, frugality, simplicity, and self-discipline" was designed to supplant an alternative view of the Yankee, rooted in the alleged practices of peddlers, as an acquisitive trickster. Paradoxically, it was the recent mechanization and consolidation of the publishing industry that allowed Child to broadcast to the nation this backward-looking perspective.[62]

At least one other contemporaneous domestic advice writer shared Child's emphasis on self-reliance, although for very different reasons. William Alcott, whose concerns regarding failures in domestic education we have noted, "argued that keeping servants was unnecessary, costly, destructive of family privacy, bad for the children, and highly unrepubli-can." But Alcott's domestic ideal, the foundation of which was a radical (for its time) whole grain diet, was so extreme that he attracted a good deal of attention but few endorsements or followers.[63]

Child also complains of the deleterious effects of domestic servants: "Now, how few, even of the sons of plain farmers and industrious me-chanics, have moral courage enough to do without a servant." Yet where Alcott's disapproval was part of his philosophical objection to almost all aspects of middle-class life, including hot food, Child opposed the use of servants primarily because they made it easier for people to entangle themselves in spoiling leisure. In view of her subsequent involvement in the antislavery movement, it is tempting to see a connection between this perspective on keeping servants and the opinion long entertained in the North that the effect of slaveholding on the slaveholders of the South was likewise the encouragement of laziness and extravagance. In her first and most significant abolitionist work, published four years after the ini-tial appearance of *The Frugal Housewife*, Child indeed entertained the possibility of such a connection: "Whether the undue importance at-tached to merely external gentility, and the increasing tendency to indo-lence and extravagance throughout this country, ought to be attributed, in any degree, to [slavery], I am unable to say; if *any* influence comes to us from the example . . . of the slaveholding states, it certainly must be of this nature."[64]

But Child also emphasizes Northern complicity in the slave system in her abolitionist writings, striving to promote self-criticism among her Northern readers: "They tell us that Northern ships and Northern capital have been engaged in this wicked business, and the reproach is true. Several fortunes in [Boston] have been made by the sale of negro blood." Self-criticism and reform was likewise her purpose in *The Frugal Housewife*. What concerned her was the way in which extravagance and luxury were eroding the New England veneration and practice of industry and frugal-ity, considered traditional. Alluding to a standardized contrast with the South in which Northerners remained possessed of these virtues would have run counter to her rhetorical design.[65]

Child does refer at one point in *The Frugal Housewife* to a more basic abolitionist theme: "A luxurious and idle *republic*! Look at the phrase!—The words were never made to be married together." Luxury and idleness, imbibed from whatever source, are as oxymoronic in a republic, as threatening to its survival, as is slavery. Child invokes antislavery motifs only when they might, she hopes, encourage not self-satisfaction but rather self-examination.[66]

Thus, insofar as keeping servants was a consequence of the pursuit of idleness and luxury, Child agreed with Alcott that it was "highly unrepublican." Her self-consciously republican vision of the "useful" helpmeet who, in a servantless household, aids her husband in escaping debt—and even in building wealth—by practicing "economy" (in effect, an alternate form of old-fashioned domestic production) is fundamentally a preindustrial domestic model. In essence, she reasserts for women a crucial role within the family economy, and by extension within the national economy, at a time when the removal of economic production from the home had diminished women's social and familial importance.

In other words, Child saw a place, even within increasingly industrialized, market-based social arrangements, for the array of agrarian-derived domestic skills and habits that had facilitated self-sufficiency for generations, especially in New England. Puritan and Yankee farmers famously surmounted enormous obstacles to their prosperity—a poor soil, a harsh climate, and an often hostile Native population; Child implies that the new forces arrayed against their descendants—an unpredictable economy, mechanization, and an impersonal workplace—can be tamed with old tricks. She holds out the hope in uncertain times that her readers can gain control over their destinies by practicing the tried and true virtues of Puritanism—vigilance in all worldly and spiritual matters, restraint, steady habits, fierce frugality, and a renewed dedication to "manual employment," the legendary honest labor of yore.[67]

In some of our commentaries on Child's recipes, we call attention to her relatively relaxed, almost conversational style, highly unusual in a cookbook, both then and now (see Chapter 12, #s 3 and 26). According to one literary critic, this manner is typical of Child's writing as a whole. She invariably utilizes an unassertive rhetoric, bespeaking a posture of "common sense and moderation," and because of this demeanor, this critic further argues, Child always managed to attract readers of all classes, even after her embrace of Garrisonian abolitionism.[68]

This invitation to friendly dialogue determines not only the tone of individual recipes but also the overall organization of *The Frugal Housewife*.

Many have found the book to be haphazard, at best, especially as compared with those of later domestic advice writers such as Catharine Beecher, who emphasize system in all aspects of housework. Child begins with "Odd Scraps for the Economical," in which, for instance, methods for extending the life of tortoiseshell and horn combs abut instructions for preventing the fermentation of cornmeal and rye flour. But her "Odd Scraps" section is not the only place in her work where she seems more intent on creating a repository of skill and knowledge than on developing a comprehensive system of housework. Her jumble of tips, tales, and recipes has been attributed to the speed with which her own financial predicament forced her to work. More fundamentally, though, the lack of overt structure reflects Child's refusal of the standard cookbook instructional mode, her commitment instead to the ebbs and flows of engagement and interchange.[69]

Two decades after Child produced a manual rich with life lessons and organic knowledge of the domestic arts, the tension between skill and organization lurking just beneath the surface of her work was made explicit by none other than Catharine Beecher's sister, Harriet Beecher Stowe, in *Uncle Tom's Cabin* (1852). Stowe uses the character of Dinah, an immensely talented African slave cook, to illustrate her point. According to Stowe, Dinah is "inflexibly attached to time-honored inconveniences." For instance, she refuses to trade her "great old-fashioned fireplace" for a "modern cook-stove," a resistance that we now understand was essentially a refusal to make a major paradigm shift. Stowe describes Dinah's disorganization this way: she washes dishes "with a dinner-napkin one day, and with a fragment of old petticoat the next . . . [yet] she gets up glorious dinners . . . and you must judge her . . . by her success." The first level of implication is that skill and experience produce tastier results than do organization and modern improvements. But Stowe also suggests that the magical qualities of Dinah's cooking may actually thrive amid chaos. Like some rare and delicate species, her marvels cannot be created in a highly rationalized environment.[70] In this respect, Child differs not only from her successors but also from her contemporaries. Mary Randolph takes as her motto for *The Virginia Housewife*, "Method Is the Soul of Management." Child, we suspect, would have countered with the notion that soul, mixed with plenty of good old elbow grease, is all the method she needs.[71]

A word about Child and posterity. She had a reputation among her contemporaries as a courageous reformer and versatile writer of novels, children's literature, domestic advice manuals, and political tracts. She is now mostly remembered, if at all, as the author of the Thanksgiving poem that today we know as "Over the river, and through the wood."

"Mrs. N. K. M. Lee"

Although the Library of Congress attributes authorship of *The Cook's Own Book* (1832) to someone with this name, no biographical information regarding such an individual has ever been found. On the title page of the first as well as subsequent editions, the author is identified only as "A Boston Housekeeper." The "housekeeper" component of this moniker associates the work with the eighteenth-century British tradition of cookbooks authored by such housekeepers to the well-born as Smith, Glasse, and Raffald, while the "Boston" component evokes the city's growing cultural and intellectual prestige.[72]

That the "housekeeper" part of the author's identity constitutes a reference to British culinary tradition is confirmed by the fact that the book consists almost entirely of recipes lifted from British sources. The title page boasts of "comprehending all valuable receipts . . . that have been published or invented during the last twenty years," specifically mentioning "the very best" of the recipes in William Kitchiner's *The Cook's Oracle* and William Dolby's *The Cook's Dictionary*. Of the forty-five recipes from Lee (as we shall sometimes for the sake of convenience refer to the volume) that we have considered for inclusion in the present book, all but three are from these two British sources and from one other not directly acknowledged on the title page, *The Practice of Cookery*, by "Mrs. Dalgairns."

Two of the three exceptions are copied from Eliza Leslie's *Seventy-five Receipts* (for which see Chapter 3). This leaves one recipe, "Squash Pie" (Chapter 12, #4), for which we could not identify a source. Thus, if our sample is at all representative, the "numerous original receipts" claimed on the title page amount to about 2 percent of the book's total contents. Our sample also suggests that in the view of whoever compiled *The Cook's Own Book*, 93 percent of the "valuable receipts" published in the early decades of the nineteenth century were British.[73]

The "Boston" part of the authorial persona is also fully appropriate to such an overwhelmingly British collection. During these years, "European travelers often described Boston as the most 'English' of American cities and its higher circles as the most Anglophile of American elites." Among the most avid of the Boston Anglophiles were the leading citizens responsible for the founding or transformation of such institutions as the Boston Athenaeum and Harvard College, designed after English precedents and models. Our "Boston Housekeeper" putting together a 93 percent English "Complete Culinary Encyclopedia" fits squarely into this pattern. Since the book was hugely popular—it was frequently reprinted through the end of the Civil War—and since a number of the recipes turned up in other cookbooks popular in New England, such as those by Hale and Webster, the project must be judged to have been successful in perpetuating the English cooking tradition, unadulterated, in nineteenth-century New England and America.[74]

CHAPTER THREE

Cuisine and Culture at Midcentury

Sarah Josepha Hale and Catharine Beecher

*O*ur next writer was what her century might have called a "true New Englander." What they would have meant was that Sarah Josepha Hale was white, Protestant, middle class, and from a rural (in her case New Hampshire) farming family. It would only add to her pedigree that the patriarch of her family had fought in the American War for Independence.

Hale was born and raised in Newport, New Hampshire, growing up on a farm but moving as a young adult to town when the family exchanged the hardships of farm life for tavern keeping. Her father, Gordon Buell, had served as an officer of the Continental Army under General Horatio Gates. Her brother Horatio, presumably named for her father's commanding officer, was a Dartmouth graduate. After teaching school for several years, Sarah Josepha Buell married the young and dashing David Hale, an up-and-coming lawyer who had recently taken up residence in her hometown.[1]

Like the other American women in our story, Hale was moved by personal financial hardship to become a writer and eventually a writer

65

of cookbooks. In her case, money problems followed the sudden death of her relatively young husband, who left her with five small children to support. Hale, like her contemporary Lydia Maria Child, took readily to writing and, also like Child, to writing across genres as different as novels, poetry, and domestic guides. Her literary career, once started, never ceased. She even found time to compile a thousand-page biographical dictionary of women.

Her first book, *The Genius of Oblivion*, published in 1823 with the help of her deceased husband's Masonic friends, was an unremarkable (and largely unsold) collection of poems. Success came four years later with the publication of her novel *Northwood; A Tale of New England,* whose themes of slavery and sectional differences struck a chord with the reading public. Set largely in "a New England country village" in her beloved "Old Granite State," the book helped establish the nineteenth-century stereotype of the thrifty, morally upright New Englander whose values and manner of living derived from small-scale farming. As we have just seen, this was the same ideological project on which Child would soon be embarking in her *Frugal Housewife*. Hale wrote in a foreword to the novel's twenty-fifth-anniversary edition that she had received many favorable notices for "the portraitures of American character . . . particularly that phase generally known as *the Yankee.* The habits and tone of feeling characterizing the real yeomanry of this class are nowhere so clearly marked as in New Hampshire. There, the Farmers are really lords of the soil." She brought these lords of the soil to life.[2]

Although a successful novelist and prolific writer in many forms, Hale, once again like Child, did not hew strictly to the writer's path. In her case, it was not advocacy of social causes but rather work as an editor that drew her away from writing. Shortly after publishing *Northwood,* she took the helm of *The Ladies' Magazine,* published in Boston, one of the earliest successful journals for women. Less than a decade later, as part of a merger between this periodical and *Godey's Lady's Book,* she became the latter's editor in chief. Her tenure at *Godey's* lasted for a remarkable forty years, from 1837 to 1877, a record even by the nineteenth century's unhurried standards.[3]

Under Hale's editorial leadership (the magazine's owner, publisher, and namesake, Louis A. Godey, wisely confined himself to the management of business affairs), *Godey's* became the gold standard for American wom-

Engraving from a portrait of Sarah Josepha Hale by W. B.
Chambers, *Godey's Lady's Book*, December 1850. (Courtesy
the Schlesinger Library, Radcliffe Institute, Harvard University)

en's magazines, a vehicle for good literature and an organ of social influence. Through *Godey's* Hale not only helped to mold American fashions
in clothing, house design, furnishings, manners, child-rearing, and food,
she also played a role in forming the contours of the American literary
landscape, publishing the stories and poems of Hawthorne, Longfellow,
Emerson, Stowe, Whittier, and Poe, among others.[4]

In yet another parallel with Child, Hale is now best known as the author of a classic children's verse, "Mary Had a Little Lamb." But controversy surrounds the authorship of the poem. Questions raised initially in the 1870s about who composed the first twelve lines—in other words, who first thought of Mary and her lamb—have never been settled convincingly in Hale's favor.[5]

Although both Child and Hale were propelled into writing, at least in part, by financial need, Hale was born into a higher social class, if to a less prosperous family, than was Child. Her lifelong attitudes and affiliations reflected these origins. In one case at least, she directly expressed the differences between her perspective and Child's. Reviewing *The Frugal Housewife*, she wrote: "Now we do not think that either in earning or saving money consists the chief importance of life . . . Our men are sufficiently money-making. Let us keep our women and children from the contagion as long as possible." Carolyn L. Karcher contends that "Hale tellingly misconstrued the purpose of *The Frugal Housewife*, confusing a strategy for survival with a program for getting rich—an error symptomatic of her class blinders." Hale seems to have been little influenced by her brief stint as a penurious young widow.[6]

Before proceeding further with Hale, we turn briefly to one of her contemporaries, on whom she frequently drew for recipes. Like Child and Hale, Eliza Leslie was at least partly led to write her first cookbook by the need to earn money. Since her father's death in 1803, she and her mother had taken in boarders to make ends meet. She had attended the first American cooking school, Mrs. Goodfellow's in Philadelphia, to improve the fare offered at the boardinghouse and in the process collected a number of the school's recipes. The eventual result was *Seventy-five Receipts for Pastry, Cakes, and Sweetmeats*, first issued by the Boston firm of Munroe and Francis in 1828.[7]

We argue elsewhere that in the first half of the nineteenth century New England writers cast their cooking manuals in national rather than regional terms. Although Leslie, a Philadelphian, was not strictly speaking a New England author, her culinary style was shaped by the same Northern, white, Protestant, middle-class characteristics and values implicit to greater and lesser degrees in Child, Beecher, and Hale, and her work was read avidly by New England women. The style of cooking found in the work of these writers varied in minor ways, but their differences are less notable than their similarities. The existence of Mary Randolph's regionally styled and titled *Virginia Housewife*, published in 1824, just before the appearances in print of these Northern authors, served to call attention to the similarities among them by calling attention to their mutual differences from her.[8]

Leslie's contribution to the Northern style influenced many New England housewives and cookbook writers. She was one of the century's best-selling domestic authors; her *Directions for Cookery, in Its Various Branches* was reprinted more than sixty times between 1837 and 1892.[9]

All of the writers under discussion lived in a time of rapid social and technological change, as we have begun to see. To consider further the transformations that took place during the first half of the nineteenth century, we will look first to Britain, the source of so many of the developments that eventually affected American life. A simple tale of biscuit-making serves to illustrate some of the relevant issues.

Felipe Fernandez-Armesto tells us that "the most commercially successful biscuits of the nineteenth century came in tins which depicted an idyll. Along a neatly paved street with a quaint, bow-fronted shop, elegant officers in Number One dress escorted daintily crinolined ladies." Similar scenes adorn the tins of cheap cookies we find on our supermarket shelves today. Fernandez-Armesto also notes that "in reality, London Road, Reading, where Joseph Huntley started his biscuit business in 1822, was a mud track where the coach from London stopped on its way west. The coach brought custom virtually to the shop door and diffused patronage along the coaching routes of the realm."

Huntley's biscuit business ran on a relatively small scale for years. The biscuits were made, as hardtack had long been, "by human assembly lines in eighteenth-century dockyards." But then a change occurred: "In the late 1830s . . . Jonathan Dickson Carr of Carlisle . . . invented the mechanical biscuit stamp, which enabled numerous biscuits to be cut from a strip of dough. . . . He [also] made the process of rolling it reversible, which halved the time taken, as the rollers sped back and forth." By 1859, the company, now Carr's, was making 6 million pounds of biscuits per year, and by the 1870s, 37 million pounds per year. The scenes of rural gentility reproduced on millions of biscuit tins remained unchanged because they were the most saleable images in which to wrap a food that, in actuality, had been produced in a large, urban factory and distributed along a muddy coach route.[10]

While Carr was aiding the British economy by inventing his mechanical biscuit stamp, on U.S. shores economic retrenchment was causing depression and even panic in the newly capitalized markets of the 1830s. Women were particularly vulnerable to economic vagaries because, as Ruth E. Finley points out, "no woman controlled a penny in 1830 save in exceptions so rare as to prove the rule." This had not been a matter of concern to most women when the economy had been structured in a way they understood—around the bartering of goods and services. In those days, "family-centered units of economic production" dominated both the actual and the financial landscape. But as family farms and backyard enterprises were displaced by "remunerative employment in expanding capitalist arenas," women found themselves powerless either to secure berths within these new workplaces or to control much of the financial benefits resulting from their husbands' involvement in the new world of work.[11]

As we have seen, Child's rehabilitation of frugality and industry was a reasonable response to the stresses everyone was experiencing during the transition to a capitalist economy. Taking a far different approach, Hale unequivocally embraced technological change, as is evident from her 1838 pronouncement in *Godey's* that "steam . . . will annihilate space and time. . . . Cross the Atlantic in *twelve* days! and how much time is *redeemed!*" It is unlikely that an experienced editor and writer inadvertently used a term as fraught with religious connotation as "redeemed." Hale chose her words carefully to communicate her belief in the social value of machines and the machine age. For her, industrialization's benefits greatly outweighed its destabilizing effects.[12]

Leslie, on assignment for *Godey's*, echoed her editor's enthusiasm for industrialization in her report on a railroad and steamboat trip that she took from her home in Philadelphia to the new travel destination, Niagara Falls, New York. Undaunted by crude fellow passengers, Leslie wrapped the account of her journey in the purplest nineteenth-century prose: "Our anticipation cannot keep pace with the realities that are continually overtaking them. . . . But we have only to be true to ourselves . . . and the power exists not . . . that can stop us on our onward course. A bright light is forever gleaming through the mist that veils the futurity of America." Leslie's image of a bright light was meant to stir a sense of hopefulness. But for us it also brings to mind the Buchanans' green dock light in *The Great Gatsby,* that symbol of the open American future turning into a will-o'-the-wisp.[13]

Recalling Child's view of such excursions as at best frivolous and at worst ruinous, we are struck by the stark contrast with Leslie and her backers, Hale and *Godey's:* "And the whole expense to each person [for a trip from Philadelphia or New York City to Niagara Falls] need not exceed fifty dollars including everything." That final phrase, "including everything," is the telltale sign of the sales pitch. Leslie's mercenary purpose was successful beyond all expectations, as "Niagara Falls became the most fashionable wedding journey in the entire history of the world." The irony of two unmarried professional women, a single writer and a widowed editor, fashioning one of America's most enduring honeymoon destinations seems to have been lost on *Godey's* readers. But a larger irony also went unremarked: the women who were now writing the most influential American cookbooks and domestic manuals were no more apt to be real cooks and housekeepers than Leslie and Hale were likely to be honeymooning at Niagara Falls.[14]

We may be skeptical about the benefits of the Industrial Revolution as applied to discretionary travel and other light entertainments, but we must nevertheless acknowledge the advantages of the industrialism that Hale, Leslie, and indeed most of the elite welcomed. Take, for instance, the differences between the pre- and post-1840s diets of most Americans, as Susan Strasser describes them: "Close-to-subsistence farmers ate monotonous diets, heavily dependent on a few staples . . . fresh meat . . . was 'unwholesome,' . . . something to be left to 'those who have a mind to swallow or be swallowed by flies.' . . . milk spoiled in the summer hot weather. . . . Leafy vegetables also spoiled, and many farmers did not plant them because of the need for constant care . . . a steady fare of bread, butter, coffee, and bacon, appears accurate for farmers everywhere before the middle of the nineteenth century who depended almost entirely on their own efforts for their living."[15]

Many urban dwellers also dined on generally poor fare before industrialization brought railroads and refrigeration. Their diets, Strasser recalls, "lacked milk, fresh fruits and vegetables; produce was scarce in winter and perishable in summer. . . . The growing urban wage-earning class subsisted . . . on bread, potatoes, salt pork, and . . . sausage." Despite the gradual introduction of dietary variety during the eighteenth century, a fully modernized gastronomic world began to emerge only after about 1840, with "the opening of railroads [that] stimulated consumption of fresh dairy products and produce. Even before the introduction of refrigerator cars, the railroads of the 1840s were shipping such items regionally, and the existence of railroads stimulated the development of truck farming in districts adjacent to cities."

Priscilla Brewer points out that "processed meat, milk, fruits, and vegetables also began to appear on store shelves." Of course, food on store shelves does not necessarily translate into food on home shelves—cash increasingly being the nexus of nutritional well-being—but possibilities for a better diet were expanding.[16]

Nutritional improvements during these steam-driven decades were accompanied, as we've begun to note, by domestic technologies. Along with cookstoves and coal, the 1830s and '40s brought a torrent of inventions into the average home, from such simple devices as the rotary eggbeater and "double skillet for boiling milk" to sewing and washing machines. Hale was as big a promoter of these domestic improvements as she was of Niagara excursions. For example, in the pages of *Godey's* she implored the "inventors of the country to put their heads together and come up with a machine for washing clothes."[17]

As we have seen, the advent of the cast iron cookstove spawned a fireplace cult in reaction. It is surprising to find the usually pro-technology Hale among fireplace enthusiasts, expressing particular admiration for the brick oven. In 1857 she stated that the brick oven was "far superior . . . for baking . . . being much more easy to regulate, as well as more economical, than an iron one." The final part of the comment is particularly striking, since as Brewer explains, "If there was one thing on which [Hale's] contemporaries agreed, it was the fact that stoves were 'economical.'" Brewer concludes that Hale's attachment to the brick oven was rooted in the old yearning for stability: "It was difficult for proponents of the 'cult of domesticity' to come to terms with the new technology of domestic heating and cooking." But that is only a statement of the contradiction in Hale, not an explanation of it.[18]

The key to this conundrum lies in the date of Hale's brick-oven pronouncement. In the 1830s and '40s, she was a wholehearted advocate of the young American Industrial Revolution. But by the late 1850s her sentiments had modulated. On the most obvious level, her change of heart can be explained by the fact that she herself had long since left behind the role of housewife. This displaced New Englander employed a cook, and it would have been her job, not Hale's, to maintain hearth and brick oven. But the causes of Hale's attitudinal shift lay deeper still.

In an earlier period of patriotic zeal, she and other New England writers had embarked on a campaign to describe the uniqueness of American life and character. Nicole Tonkovich explains the dynamic in relation to Hale's educational writing: "Through her ability, indeed duty, to represent American women, . . . [writers like Hale] can specify the customs and behaviors that will be identifiable as American. . . . Books such as [Hale's *The Countries of Europe and the Manners and Customs of Its Various Nations*] . . . were a part of the process of constituting American identity." By the 1850s, in response to a number of unexpected and unwanted changes brought on by the industrialization they had once championed, Hale and her fellow writers began to turn again to those earlier features of American life, this time in order to promote selective aspects of the past, a kind of smorgasbord antiquarianism. The old brick oven, with its antique New England associations, was revived as part of this new canon of American "customs and behaviors."[19]

A decade after her encomium to brick ovens, Hale asserted that "there are, in the texture of American life, certain threads, that, like telegraphic wires, reach across all obstacles and awaken the sympathies of the world." As industrialism congested the American landscape with its telegraph wires, steam, and steel—not to mention its waves of immigrants—one of its staunchest proponents was deftly working to smooth out the wrinkles that women especially perceived in the fabric of this new myth of progress. Hale was weaving together her vision of the virtuous American character of the past with her hope that America's industrial power would attain global reach, and she was selling this dream to American women, in effect asking them to ignore the spiritual and material ugliness the Industrial Revolution had wrought.[20]

But would it be easy to convince Americans that the changes in their lives were for the good? American kitchens were now equipped with "many technical devices and improvements better understood by the thermodynamics engineer than the cook." Householders might be able to afford such "improvements," along with a flood of other consumer goods, but they could no longer build the equivalent of their old kitchen hearths and brick ovens themselves, nor could they call on local artisans for help. Amateurs often found that it was no easy matter to repair the new cookstoves. Autonomy and self-sufficiency had been sacrificed to progress.[21]

Leonore Davidoff and Catherine Hall describe the trend toward the gargantuan levels of domestic consumption and display that typified the Victorian era. Again, this trend found its first expression in Britain: "By the 1830s . . . taste which favoured lightness and space was giving way to the heavy upholstered cluttered effect of the mid and late Victorians." They offer a colorful contemporaneous account of increased consumption from one who more honored it in the breach than in the observance: "Arthur Biddell, the bluff Suffolk farmer who prided himself on his simplicity despite a substantial income, maintained: 'Gay Plates require Silver Spoons, Glasses instead of Black and White Mugs—a clean cloth and nice knives and forks and all this necessitates food and wine to match the plates.'" Biddell grasped the compounding dynamic of accumulation and the near impossibility of stepping out of the consumer stream once the first fancy plate has been snagged. But neither Biddell's nor Davidoff's and Hall's descriptions explain why the increase in the demand for goods occurred in the first place.[22]

It seems like simple logic to posit a causal connection between better methods of production and transportation and a growing public taste for gewgaws, gadgets, elaborate table settings, and elaborated cuisines. But as Cary Carson has demonstrated regarding the quantum leap in consumption during the eighteenth century, increases in demand were not primarily the result of increases in supply. Other factors, particularly geographic mobility, were more important. Carson connects the "widespread possession and use of fashion-bearing, status-giving artifacts" with the relocation and emigration of the middle classes in Britain, a process that began in the seventeenth century and developed inexorably thereafter.[23]

Geographic mobility continued to dominate middle-class experience on this side of the Atlantic, and specifically in New England: "The initial settlements were followed by innumerable dislocations and out-migrations as new towns hived off old ones, land-poor grandsons went searching for greener pastures, and individual wageworkers followed whatever opportunities beckoned." This was "a setting-out process that never ceased in the generations that followed. . . . Persistence rates, which measure the stability of stay-at-home populations, began to decline in New England towns in the 1730s from which they never recovered."[24]

New England, a compact, islandlike region, replicated the mother country's pattern of sending many of its offspring away from home. It also followed the English strategy for attaining "instant respectability" through the display of consumer goods. As we have seen, these patterns were established relatively early. For instance, in the seventeenth century the "merchant princes of Boston were the first Americans to remodel their sleeping apartments." Following London and Amsterdam, Boston quickly became a locus of fashion.[25]

The city also led in matters of etiquette. In light of constant geographic mobility, the "new system of manners that spurred the consumption of fashionable goods solved major problems of social communications . . . [and] offered a universal code of behavior to smooth reception in faraway places." Of course, not everyone relocated. But even for those who stayed put, consumer goods offered "an all-embracing ecumenical gentility."[26]

The point is not that fashion traveled but rather that travel necessitated fashion—it was the only way to establish the newcomer's social status. And whether newly arrived or about to depart, no one traveled more than New Englanders; it follows that no one understood the social uses of consumer fashion better than New Englanders.

As Carson also indicates, the purchase of prestige was not confined to upper-class Bostonians but was practiced by all New Englanders. For example, "inventory studies of the upland counties . . . settled in central Massachusetts and Connecticut indicate . . . heavy investments in material goods once the hardships of homesteading were past."[27]

Keeping in mind Carson's analysis of a goods- and manners-defined gentility as "a regulator of social interaction," we can now take another look at Hale's mid-nineteenth-century position on stoves versus brick ovens. Since much of Hale's writing was intended to present her readers with news of the products whose acquisition would give them social status, by promoting brick ovens just as most consumers were gaining access to cast iron cookstoves she was creating a new vogue for antiquarianism in order to assert that the group boundaries had again shifted. The audience who followed her advice in *Godey's* and fired up their hearths would thus be differentiated from—superior to—the generality who didn't. But it is not only, or even particularly, the old brick oven that Hale was selling. She was peddling the *knowledge* of the superiority of the brick oven to the cast iron cookstove.

As one of the most influential prescribers of genteel behavior, Hale had astutely determined by midcentury that portable status markers, because they were so quickly susceptible to democratization in the industrial age, were bound to be less important than the kind of boundary-setting knowledge she was in a perfect position to dispense. Just at the time that the proliferation of the paraphernalia of refinement threatened to erase the differences between the rude and the refined, Hale found an easy way to reestablish rank—by portraying certain arbitrary tastes and fashions as systems of "education" and "domestic order."[28]

As consumer goods were devalued by mass production they could not adequately serve as compensation for the loss of mastery over one's environment caused by industrialization. By moving status-marking out of the realm of goods altogether and into the ether of education and domestic management, Hale could transcend the continual need to adjust her opinions about individual consumer goods as the new and rare became, with astonishing speed, the cheap and common.

But a complete denigration of the consumer goods market wouldn't work either. After all, *Godey's* had to sell the latest fashions, furnishings, home designs, and the like. What was needed from Hale was a combination of approaches that lured readers to the magazine's illustrations and patterns of an endlessly changing parade of goods but also compelled them, through a fear of being left behind the intellectual fashion, to search for the subtle changes in perspective on the latest goods and styles embedded in Hale's commentary. In a democratic republic of goods, only such knowledgeable patrons of the marketplace as *Godey's* readers would know in each new season both what to consume and what to disavow. By continually inducing both the desire for goods *and* the need to keep current on changing attitudes toward goods, Hale earned her status as a premier American magazine editor.

Hale often decried the increase in "luxury" and promoted "economy," making her sound like Child. But her critique of luxury was always half-hearted at best. For instance, she maintains that "excessive luxury and rational liberty were never yet found compatible," making "excessive" luxury rather than luxury itself the enemy of the stern old republican virtues. In introducing the section on "Cheap Dishes" in *The Good Housekeeper*, she stresses that economy is a requisite virtue for all those who "mean to be rich" or "who love comfort and independence." This contrasts sharply with Child, for whom independence and comfort are invariably antago-nists, not bedfellows.[29]

More broadly, while Hale advocated dress reform on the *Godey's* edito-rial page, she was not really attempting to distance herself from the incul-cation of fashion itself, which was the prime purpose of the magazine she edited, as is clear from this rationale for the fashions-in-dress department that she offered in 1853: "Our fashions are selected with particular care, and the plates prepared at great expense, in order to benefit that large por-tion of our friends who, residing in the country, naturally wish to know the style of city-made clothing. . . . Our plates are their patterns." Thus, we would amend Tonkovich's argument that the dissemination of "the lan-guage of fashion" in *Godey's* "contributed significantly to the ideology of American democratic classlessness, particularly among women." It was the combination of Hale's now disseminating this language, now discounte-nancing it, that was crucial. This was the cue to her readers that what was important above all else was the adoption of a fashionable attitude.[30]

With her first enterprise, *The Ladies' Magazine*, Hale had fit neatly within the phenomenon of "the golden age of local publishing in America," as David Hall characterizes the publishing industry between 1800 and 1840. In her subsequent association with *Godey's*, she followed the industry's consolidation phase, which began in the 1830s. Hall dis-cusses the success of the Philadelphia firm of Carey, Lea, noting "all of the advantages accruing to publishers who seized a metropolitan loca-tion." He could as well have been speaking of Hale's decision to follow *Godey's* to that city.[31]

But before Hale left Boston for the larger metropolitan area of Philadelphia (she remained in Boston while her youngest son attended Harvard), she published her first cookbook, *The Good Housekeeper; or, The Way to Live Well and to Be Well While We Live* (1839). With her customary moderate approach, she proclaims that her goal is to combine the elegance of William Kitchiner's *The Cook's Oracle* with the frugality of Child's *Frugal Housewife*, all the while "keeping in view the important object of preserving health." A moderate in health matters as in every-thing else, Hale was far less stringent in her dietary recommendations than were reformers Sylvester Graham or William Alcott in theirs. Her temperate approach had wide appeal. *The Good Housekeeper's* first edi-tion of two thousand copies sold out in less than two months.[32]

Actually, Hale's recommendations for preserving health are, when taken as a whole, remarkably consistent with modern theories of healthy eating. She advocates a "mixed" diet of bread, meat, vegetables, and fruit as "the only right regimen for the healthy." But she also emphasizes that the *quantity* of food one consumes should be proportionate to one's level of activity and age. Families, she thinks, should have regular mealtimes and eat a variety of foods, and everyone should eat only limited amounts of rich pastries, gravies, and meat. On meat, in particular, she cautions: "The tendency in our country has been to excess in animal food."[33]

Among Hale's recommendations are some that would still save money if followed today. For instance, she suggests that every housekeeper make her own wheat bread once a week. She gives easy-to-follow instructions for a basic wheat bread (which she calls "fine bread" and which we now call white bread) and for another with the bran left in (which she calls "brown or dyspepsia bread" and we now call whole wheat bread). She mentions that this "dyspepsia" (meaning *anti*-dyspepsia) bread was best known as "Graham" bread, after the staunchest whole wheat advocate. As well, Hale offers a simple formula for the traditional New England loaf made of rye and cornmeal, along with directions for a bread made with cooked rice and wheat flour. With only slight modifications—Hale's quantities for a week's worth of bread for the average family would produce too much for the average-sized family today—all of these recipes could be followed by modern cooks.[34]

Citing the popular contemporary writer Catharine Sedgwick, Hale asserts that "Italian and music are worthless accomplishments compared with the knowledge of bread-making." It is "a thousand times more important that the bread necessary to the health and comfort of those we love . . . should be made in the best manner, . . . than the cake made for 'the dear five hundred friends,' who attend a fashionable party." As with dress reform, Hale disguises an endorsement of an alternate fashion—for what we would now call "artisanal" baking—as a moral statement in opposition to fashion.[35]

Hale's endorsement of bread-making is part of her overall presentation of what it means to be a "good housekeeper." Like Child and, as we shall see, Beecher, she stresses that "it is only the frivolous . . . who despise and neglect the ordinary duties of life as beneath their notice." Unlike Child and Beecher, however, she does not perceive "the frivolous" as posing much of a threat. Due to "the rational institutions" of "our republican land, . . . our richest and most fashionable women are often models of good housekeeping."[36]

Hale's affirmation of American republicanism is also the basis of her view of the servant question, which is more relaxed than that of Beecher (as we shall shortly see) and many others. Unlike the situation in other countries, in America people work in domestic service only temporarily, according to Hale, "to obtain a living and a little cash, so that they may begin business or house-keeping for themselves. . . . I would wish every young female domestic to *hope* that she may some time be mistress of her *own house*." In this sunny world in which everyone at the bottom is on the rise and no one at the top puts on airs, rational self-interest provides the servant with the strongest possible motivation to "improve every opportunity she has of learning the best and most prudent manner of doing all kinds of work. Then she will be fitted to make her husband happy, and bring up her children to be respectable members of society."[37]

In addition to those from *The Good Housekeeper*, we have also selected in Part 2 recipes from Hale's cookbook of 1852, *The Ladies' New Book of Cookery*, of which it has been said that "the bounty of a prosperous America can be found here." This unashamed celebration of genteel consumerism is reflected, for instance, in the recommendation to use only silver teapots, and in the directions for roasting a haunch of venison, indeed in the entire chapter on venison, which includes a disconcerting illustration of a live buck. As in *The Good Housekeeper*, Hale also includes recipes for less expensive dishes, such as a mutton recipe designed "to make it taste like venison." The secret is to rub the well-hung (that is, aged) meat with olive oil, whole pepper, garlic, sweet herbs, and vinegar.[38]

In a gesture of accommodation to the dietary requirements of Catholic immigrants, *The Ladies' New Book of Cookery* includes "a greater variety of receipts for preparing *Fish, Vegetables, and Soups*." And reflecting the Victorian interest in children, the book has a section on cooking for them.[39]

Hale was also an adherent of the new science of domestic economy, championed by Beecher (one biographer claims Hale coined the phrase "domestic science"). She wanted cookbooks to take their place among the honored texts in American "Seminaries for Female Education."

Such institutions had sprouted up everywhere and were one of the great spurs to progress for women. As we have noted, through the course of her life Hale shifted her allegiance from republican views of women to the Victorian idea of separate spheres. Nevertheless, her contributions to women's education were substantial.[40]

Like Ben Franklin and many New Englanders before and after her (so many, in fact, that it could be called a minor New England tradition), Hale abandoned her home region when social advancement beckoned, all the while asserting its superiority in everything from fireplaces to moral outlook. Such contradictions in her life, as in her domestic philosophy, went unnoticed by an audience eager to embrace every new thing, even when the newest thing was the "old times." Hale rode a new wave of popular publishing and national expansion, all the while invoking the ethos of old New England.

CATHARINE BEECHER

Born in East Hampton, Long Island, in 1800, Catharine Beecher was the eldest child of Lyman Beecher and Roxana Foote Beecher. Her father was a young clergyman who, having studied at Yale under the grandson of Jonathan Edwards (one of the most prominent leaders of the mid-eighteenth-century First Great Awakening), became during Catharine's childhood one of the most prominent leaders of the early-nineteenth-century Second Great Awakening. Her mother was from an illustrious Connecticut family that belonged to the wing of the New England elite that had defected from the Puritan establishment to Anglicanism during the eighteenth century. She died when Catharine was sixteen, leaving her to manage the household of her father and seven younger brothers and sisters. A year later, Lyman Beecher took Harriet Porter as his second wife.[41]

Meanwhile, in 1810 Lyman Beecher had moved the family from East Hampton to the larger and more prestigious parish and community of Litchfield, Connecticut. In 1822, in the midst of her father's efforts to assist her in (or, as we might be more apt to say now, to pressure her into) having a Calvinist experience of spiritual rebirth, Catharine's fiancé, a clergyman-in-training who himself could not yet testify to such a con-

Daguerreotype portrait of Catharine Beecher, 1848. (Courtesy the Schlesinger Library, Radcliffe Institute, Harvard University)

version experience, died at sea. She responded to this emotional and spiritual crisis by moving to Hartford and founding the Hartford Female Seminary, enrolling her young sister Harriet in the school (Harriet would later herself be a teacher there). This was the first of a lifelong series of initiatives in the education of women.[42]

Beecher published her first book in 1829, and she remained a prolific author throughout her life, with titles on a wide range of topics appearing under her name until within a few years of her death in 1878: religion, slavery and abolitionism, the condition of women in general and women's suffrage in particular, health, and various aspects of domestic life. It was in the 1840s that Beecher devoted herself particularly to domesticity, with *A Treatise on Domestic Economy* (1841), *Letters to Persons Who Are Engaged in Domestic Service* (1842), and *Miss Beecher's Domestic Receipt-Book* (1846).

The *Receipt-Book*, the only cookbook Beecher ever wrote, was reissued almost annually into the 1870s. Its subtitle indicates its position within the corpus of Beecher's writings on matters domestic: "Designed as a Supplement to Her Treatise on Domestic Economy." Instruction in the specifics and details of cookery was offered as part of an analysis of the woman's realm of the household, which Beecher aspired to have taken as seriously as systematic elucidations of such traditional male preserves as religion (e.g., Jonathan Edwards's *A Treatise concerning Religious Affections*) and politics (e.g., John Locke's *Two Treatises of Government*) had always been taken. In pursuit of this aim, she considered at length in the *Treatise* such major issues impinging on domestic life as the overall direction and pace of social change; the education and role of women; the relations between Puritan traditions of hard work and restraint and an emerging culture of abundance, refinement, and leisure; and the position of servants in a democracy. To ensure that these larger concerns would not be forgotten in a book dealing mostly with the nitty-gritty of the kitchen, she included summary discussions of them within the *Receipt-Book* itself.

On the issue of servants, we have argued that Child sought to encourage people like herself who had never been able to afford servants not to be ashamed of themselves, reminding them of the traditional New England insistence on the dignity of labor. On the other hand, Beecher, herself of upper-class origin, assumed that her readers did keep servants, to whom her books would be passed along. She had endeavored in the *Receipt-Book* "to give all directions so minutely as that the book can be kept in the kitchen, and be used by any domestic who can read, as a guide in *every one* of her employments in the kitchen." This hearkens back to Hannah Glasse's assertion that "every servant who can but read" and who does read her *Art of Cookery* "will be capable of making a tollerable good Cook."[43]

But Glasse's further definition of her purpose as being to "save the Ladies a great deal of Trouble" points to the way in which Beecher differed from Glasse and resembled Child. As we have observed, at the time Glasse was writing, eighteenth-century England was increasingly becoming a society in which the less a woman had to trouble herself with domestic concerns and labors, the more she could devote herself to matters of high refinement and culture and the more her status as a lady was confirmed. Beecher, on the other hand, wrote her systematic *Treatise on Domestic Economy* "for the use of young ladies at home and at school." All girls, she insisted, and especially young ladies, girls from families that have the "means of securing hired service," should be educated in such a way that, rather than coming to view "domestic employments" as "degrading and unbecoming," they would gain "a thorough practical knowledge" of them. Like Child, in other words, Beecher wrote in opposition to the English norm of the lady of leisure to which Glasse had subscribed and which both Child and Beecher saw making alarming headway in the antebellum American North.[44]

In emphasizing that women able to employ servants ought nevertheless to be possessed of housewifely knowledge and skills, Beecher was reaffirming a distinctively New England set of values. The English ideal of the lady of leisure was articulated by English writer Eliza Haywood, around the same time that Glasse published her cookbook: "a lady of condition should learn just as much of cookery and of work, as to know when she is imposed upon by those she employs, . . . but no more:—to pass too much of her time" in such pursuits would impair her reputation as "a woman of *fine taste*," one capable of "polite conversation, or of entertaining herself agreeably when alone."[45]

In New England, however, the dignity of labor—John Winthrop's "the workes of our callings beinge diligently followed"—had been upheld too insistently for too long to be much eroded as a prime social value by the consumer revolution of the eighteenth century. Two upper-class women, one from each end of the Revolutionary-era political spectrum, will serve as our cases in point. As we have seen, Anne Gibbons Gardiner, the wife of a wealthy Boston physician, merchant, and Tory, kept a manuscript cookbook filled with recipes from Glasse and Raffald. Her comments and emendations indicate her interest and skill as a cook. She thus implicitly disavows the aim of her sources of saving "the Ladies a great deal of Trouble." Her seasoned, hands-on use of material from these English cookbooks means that for her such cookbooks are made to subserve the ideal of the lady not of leisure but rather of labor.[46]

Our representative upper-class Revolutionary-era woman from the Patriot camp is Abigail Adams, the second First Lady of the United States. Throughout her life, Adams manifested an engagement in domestic tasks, indeed an enthusiasm for them, that makes Salem, Massachusetts, diarist William Bentley's remark upon her death—"the first time I ever saw Madam was at her own house shelling her beans for a family dinner"—an appropriate obituary tribute. In 1809, Adams formulated the issue of the place of housewifery in the education of young women almost exactly as would Child and Beecher a few decades later: "It behoves us . . . to give our daughters and granddaughters . . . such an education as shall qualify them for the useful and domestic duties of life. . . . The finer accomplishments, such as music, dancing, and painting, serve to set off and embellish the picture; but the groundwork must be formed of more durable colors."[47]

It is not surprising that Catharine Beecher should have striven to propagate in nineteenth-century America the colonial New England values of the Protestant work ethic in general and of the upper-class "notable housewife" in particular. Her father was a leading Protestant clergyman, and her mother had been, according to both her own and Lyman Beecher's recollections, just such a housewife, who had taught her "to perform properly many kinds of domestic labors." Nor is it surprising that she should have seen no conflict between this tradition and that of keeping servants. Just as Abigail Adams, throughout her housekeeping career, both engaged directly in domestic tasks and supervised her servants' performance of them, so Roxana Foote Beecher both "did her own work" (to quote the title of an essay on the subject by her daughter Harriet) and oversaw the work of at least three servants. Beecher's echo of Hannah Glasse, in publishing a cookbook that would be instructive to servants, and her dissent from Glasse's definition of domestic activities as inherently unrefined, were equally rooted in her own formative experiences.[48]

But Beecher's similarity to Glasse in respect of addressing herself to servants quickly turns into a difference. After the Preface, servants go unmentioned in the remainder of Glasse's *Art of Cookery*. In Beecher's domestic works, on the other hand, they are a constant nagging presence, meriting a chapter in the *Treatise*, two chapters in the *Receipt-Book*, and yet another entirely rewritten chapter a quarter of a century later in *American Woman's Home* (which Beecher coauthored with her sister

Harriet Beecher Stowe). And this catalog doesn't even include the separate title devoted exclusively to the topic—*Letters to Persons Who Are Engaged in Domestic Service*. Why all the fuss?

A full exploration of this question, which has engaged the attention of a number of historians, cannot be attempted here. What can be stated with confidence is that whatever problems there were in the mistress-servant relationship in eighteenth-century England (Abigail Adams thought that "3 Americans would do the whole work of the Eight" servants she employed in London in the 1780s "and think they had no hard task"), they were in many ways different problems from those besetting this relationship in the nineteenth-century American North. Among other factors, the definition of the independent United States as a democratic republic and the transition to an economy characterized increasingly by wage labor introduced myriad uncertainties and tensions into relations that had hitherto constituted part of a relatively stable constellation of social hierarchies. Along with many others, Beecher came forward with her recommendations for unsnarling "the servant question."[49]

Her prescriptions look back, on the one hand, to her Puritan and colonial/hierarchical heritage and look forward, on the other hand, to the workplace world of written contracts, minutely defined goals and objectives, and staff manuals with which we have become familiar. As far as the former is concerned, Beecher advises mistresses, for example, to act like true mistresses, neither exhibiting "a severe and imperious mode of giving orders and finding fault," nor relinquishing "proper authority and control" for fear that a discontented servant will, in a world of wage relations and mobility, depart for a new place. Rather, the mistress should adopt "a course of real kindness in manner and treatment, attended with the manifestation of a calm determination, that the plans and will of the *housekeeper,* and not of the domestic, shall control the family arrangements." More broadly, in a summary injunction to bring back the colonial world in which servants were defined as part of the family, Beecher urges the mistress and master "so far as may be, to supply the place of parents."[50]

Although mistresses are warned not to long for "the cringing, submissive, well-trained, servants of aristocratic lands," servants themselves, when directly addressed, are for the most part counseled to exhibit the virtues traditionally associated with stable, long-term subordination—

faithfulness, loyalty, patience, forbearance. However unhappy a servant may be with her lot in a particular household, she should "remember that you never can find a place in this world where everything will be just as you want it, and that it is a bad thing for you, as well as for your employers, to keep roving about from one place to another."[51]

But the very need to place such emphasis upon "the plans and will of the *housekeeper*" and the very acknowledgment that servants would "keep roving about from one place to another"—both suggest the high degree of wishful thinking in this reliance on the mores and practices of the vanishing past. Elsewhere, Beecher took the realities of the present more fully into account, as when she told mistresses to stop complaining that servants "exact exorbitant wages." This was only to be expected in a society under the governance of "the universal law of labor and of trade, that an article is to be valued, according to its scarcity and the demand." Only two pages after urging mistresses to treat their servants as though they were members of the family, Beecher excludes servants from the family circle. She justifies what had become the standard prohibition against servants taking their meals with their employers (a departure from what had to some degree prevailed in colonial New England) with the argument that the family would be unable "to talk freely of their private affairs, when they meet at meals . . . if restrained by the constant presence of a stranger."[52]

Beecher's more workable remedies for the circumstances of the emerging modern world—strangers thrown together under the same roof, assertive, mobile employees, and frustrated, dissatisfied employers—are versions of the sorts of explicit, written contractual arrangements that have become characteristic of the modern workplace: "Much trouble . . . is saved by hiring persons *on trial*, in order to ascertain whether they are willing and able to do the work of the family in the manner which the housekeeper wishes." And both the trial period and, if this is negotiated successfully, the ongoing employment will be made less tense and more durable if "the mistress of the family arranges the work for each domestic, and writes it on a large card, which is suspended in the kitchen for guidance and reference. On hiring a new [servant], these details are read to her, and the agreement made, with a full understanding, on both sides, of what is expected."[53]

In a sense, Beecher's *Receipt-Book* as a whole—designed, as we've

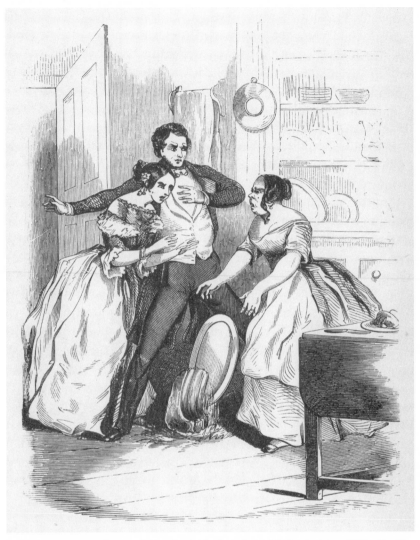

Engraving for Kate Sutherland, "Cooks," *Godey's Lady's Book*, May 1852. Conflict between householders and servants was a constant theme in nineteenth-century domestic manuals and cookbooks. As here, servants were often depicted as coarse and disobedient. (Courtesy the Schlesinger Library, Radcliffe Institute, Harvard University)

noted, "to give all directions so minutely as that [it] can be kept in the kitchen, and be used by any domestic who can read, as a guide in *every one* of her employments in the kitchen"—is one of these large cards, a combination employment contract, set of weekly objectives, and staff manual. This forward-looking dimension of Beecher's contribution to the servant question is also a case of creative, as opposed to nostalgically futile, looking backward. Puritan New England was nothing if not a culture of the Word—of constant writing and reading. Beecher here applies these inclinations and capabilities to the vexed household of the nineteenth-century American North.[54]

Another resemblance between Beecher and Glasse relates more directly to the nature of the cuisine that each offers. Just as Glasse denounces French cooking in her preface and then proceeds to fill her book with French-derived recipes, so Beecher disapproves of "rich and elegant dishes" and then proceeds to include chapters on "Rich Puddings and Pies," "Rich Cakes," and "Articles for Desserts and Evening Parties."[55]

The category "rich" that Beecher in principle rejects extends well beyond sweet preparations. She sets the tone for her book with an opening chapter ("On Selecting Food and Drinks with Reference to Health") in the course of which both seasonings and fats—in other words, the major resources for cooking so as to succeed in "gratifying the palate"—are roundly condemned: "A housekeeper that will . . . avoid oily dishes, oily cooking, and condiments, will double the chances of good health for her family." And since "fat is an unhealthful aliment, and when heated becomes still more so," it follows that "*fried* food of all kinds is injurious." Nevertheless, there is a chapter in the *Receipt-Book* on "Fried and Broiled Meats," not to mention numerous recipes in other chapters in which fats and seasonings are utilized no less liberally than in other contemporary cookbooks.[56]

Beecher acknowledges the contradiction much more explicitly than Glasse. "No book of this kind will sell without receipts for the rich articles which custom requires," she writes in her preface, immediately drawing upon her Puritan heritage for a curious supplementary rationale: "In furnishing [such receipts], the writer has aimed to follow the example of Providence, which scatters profusely both good and ill, and combines therewith the caution alike of experience, revelation, and conscience, 'choose ye that which is good, that ye and your seed may live.'" Later, as an excuse for giving recipes for pie crust—"an article which, if the laws of health were obeyed, would be banished from every table, for it unites the three evils of animal fat, *cooked animal fat,* and heavy bread"—she states that "this work does not profess to leave out unhealthy dishes, but only to set forth an abundance of healthful ones, and the reasons for preferring them."[57]

So Catharine Beecher inserted fatty, highly seasoned foods throughout *Miss Beecher's Domestic Receipt-Book* for the same reason that God placed the Tree of the Knowledge of Good and Evil in the Garden of Eden, as an educational tool and moral challenge, a continuous reminder of the need to resist temptation and make wise dietary choices. An argument that makes fats, oils, and condiments participate in the age-old conundrums surrounding the presence of evil in a God-given universe strains credibility, to say the least. There are more plausible explanations for Beecher's blatant culinary inconsistencies.

One of these arises from the way that *Miss Beecher's Domestic Receipt-Book* was written. Following a tradition that went back to the era of manuscript cookbooks, Beecher obtained much of the material for the book by consulting among "friends, relatives, even servants" and leaving evidence of this form of research in the names of many of the recipes. So, just as in seventeenth-century England *The Queens Closet Opened* contains such items as "The Countesse of Rutlands Receipt of making the rare Banbury Cake which was so much praised at her Daughters (the right Honourable the Lady Chawerths) wedding," so in nineteenth-century America Beecher's *Receipt-Book* contains such similarly (if less floridly) named items as "Mrs. H.'s Raised Wedding Cake (very fine)," "Bridget's Bread Cake (excellent)," and "Macaroni Soup (Mrs. F.'s Receipt)."[58]

Beecher appears to have quarried for material most systematically in one particular sector of her circle of acquaintance. According to a Hartford Female Seminary alumnae reunion account, as the deadline for submission of the *Receipt-Book* manuscript approached, Beecher gathered together "ten or twelve old pupils," to each of whom she assigned "a certain number of pages of receipts upon fish, flesh, fowl, cakes and dainties." Since the student body of the Hartford Female Seminary had been deliberately recruited from the Hartford upper class, it is highly probable that many of the dishes contributed to the *Receipt-Book* by its alumnae were of the "rich and elegant" variety that its author both discountenanced and was nevertheless unwilling entirely to prohibit.[59]

But the presence of the rich and elegant dishes in the *Receipt-Book* had much deeper roots than this. Beecher sought for students among the Hartford upper class in part because she herself had attended a school, the Litchfield Female Academy, the students of which had been drawn from this level of society. Her entrée into this world had been, along with her father's position as the minister of the established church in town, the genteel culture that her mother, with her elite Anglican background, had already imparted to her. Foods prepared with unapologetic reliance upon the oils and seasonings that made them rich constituted as basic a part of Catharine Beecher's personal heritage—the part bestowed by her mother—as did the part bestowed by her father—a puritanical wariness of appetite and pleasure that Beecher secularized as the promotion of good health.[60]

Kathryn Kish Sklar characterizes Beecher's career as a lifelong effort to unite these polar opposites that she inherited from her parents, to synthesize "refined culture with evangelical morality." That is also not a bad way to characterize one of the major efforts made by American culture as a whole during the nineteenth century, as the evangelical ardor of the Second Great Awakening evolved into tightly wound mid-Victorian parlor rectitude, while the amenities enjoyed by the colonial elite since the eighteenth-century consumer revolution came to be, in a time of industrial revolution and constantly increasing wealth, much more widely enjoyed, coalescing as mid-Victorian parlor gentility.[61]

On the evidence of *Miss Beecher's Domestic Receipt-Book*, this was a synthesis that remained unconsummated. Although Beecher was strongly influenced by both her parents, all accounts agree that the dominant presence in her childhood was her evangelical father, not her refined, Anglican mother. Similarly, in the *Receipt-Book*, the framing, overriding concern is the good health that is central to Beecher's evangelical promulgation of domesticity, not the gastronomic pleasure that is always a core component of a refined way of living. Pages and pages of the opening chapter are devoted to the unappetizing details of the digestive process: "Minuteness of division is a great aid to easy digestion. For this reason food should be well chewed before swallowing, not only to divide it minutely, but to mix it with the saliva, which aids in digestion." That cooking and eating might contribute to making life more agreeable is mentioned only to be minimized, in a quotation from Beecher's dietary guru, Dr. J. Pereira: "The relish for flavoring, or seasoning ingredients, manifested by almost every person, would lead us to suppose that these substances serve some useful purpose beyond that of merely gratifying the palate. At present, however, we have no evidence that they do." Gratifying the palate is therefore "merely" tolerated in *Miss Beecher's Domestic Receipt-Book*, surviving covertly here and there as the pepper and powdered sage in the recipe "to roast a spare rib," or the "spices, and wine, or brandy" in the recipe for "portable soup," but nowhere openly avowed, let alone celebrated.[62]

Beecher's focus on health and digestion both derives from Puritan asceticism (eating and drinking must never be ends in themselves) and looks forward to the end-of-the-century domestic science movement, which would give birth to the tasteless school cafeteria repasts quite a few of us grew up with. Likewise Janus-faced is Beecher's emphasis on "*a habit of system and order*," her insistence that "nothing secures ease and success in housekeeping so much as *system* in arranging work." Rooted most broadly in the Puritan determination to take control of a sinful, chaotic world, rooted more particularly in Beecher's youthful experience of the minutely regulated environment of the Litchfield Female Academy, constituting a manifestation of what has been called "the Second Great Awakening as an organizing process," Beecher's domestic "system and order" takes the form of comprehensive inventories of kitchen equipment and functional analyses of domestic spaces and bodily interiors. It anticipates the myriad bureaucratized arrangements of the twentieth and twenty-first centuries. More specifically, just as her sister Harriet helped prepare the way for the late-nineteenth-century colonial revival movement, with her four novels set in the New England of bygone days, so Beecher's systematic approach to the household anticipated, as did her emphasis on health, the domestic science movement.[63]

In relation to Beecher's endeavor to forge a synthesis of "refined culture with evangelical morality," systematized domesticity produces singularly unfortunate results. The *Receipt-Book* chapters "Directions for Dinner and Evening Parties" and "Setting Tables and Preparing Various Articles of Food for the Table" are "designed for a young and inexperienced housekeeper, in moderate circumstances, who receives visitors at her table from the most wealthy circles." Each step to be taken, each item to be placed and arranged, is specified with insane exactitude:

> After soup and fish, and the plates are removed by the waiters . . . and clean plates put around, wine or conversation will fill up the time, while the meats are brought on, which are to be placed on the table, covered, and in the order marked in the drawing, Fig. 7.
>
> When all are prepared, the host gives a sign to the waiters, and the covers are all to be removed, and so adroitly that no steam be spilt on the table-cloth or guests. To do this, the covers must be first inverted, *holding them directly over the dishes they cover,* and this the hostess must teach the waiter to do before-hand, if need be.

Here and throughout these two chapters Beecher's attempted synthesis of refinement and moralism becomes the nightmare of every young family confronted with the task of getting along and getting ahead in modern America. Externally dictated rituals of gentility generate tedium ("wine or conversation will fill up the time") and clenched-fist contemplation of the ever-present specter of a disastrous misstep (as in Beecher's emphatic injunction to avoid spilling steam).[64]

In her writings on domesticity as a whole, Catharine Beecher strives mightily to bestow dignity upon women's traditional tasks and activities, and she imparts an abundance of practical advice that was doubtless helpful to her many readers. In *Miss Beecher's Domestic Receipt-Book* in particular, she provides "a great variety of simple and well-cooked dishes, designed for every-day comfort and enjoyment." Unfortunately, all this is presented in a framework and laid out in a manner that discourages pleasure and engagement and instead demands obedience to a code. Catharine Beecher was the nineteenth century's Martha Stewart, not its Julia Child.[65]

CHAPTER FOUR

~~~~

The Civil War and After

Community Cookbooks, Colonial Revival, Domestic Science

By now we can see that industrialization and consolidation of resources, on the one hand, and nostalgia for a past that was imagined as disciplined, pastoral, and more humanly cohesive, on the other, were the warp and weft of the fabric of New England life in the nineteenth century and as such formed the social circumstances out of which the idea of a particular and noteworthy New England style of cooking emerged. We know further that beginning among wealthy Americans in the 1820s, and spreading like concentric circles outward to ever larger segments of society, domestic change was felt throughout the century in everything from eggbeaters to ovens, from the availability of fresh milk and meat to the disappearance of the homely fireside.

In time, these changes—with the Civil War giving particular impetus to the process—would lead to the world of mass-produced and globally moved goods and services with which we are familiar. The disadvantages of the new social order, such as anonymity, homogenization, and economic insecurity, are now generally more commented upon by middle-class Americans than are the advantages. But from the inception of the

Industrial Revolution until well into the twentieth century, Americans, and especially New England writers and intellectuals, domestic writers and cookbook creators among them, struggled quite explicitly to come to terms with all aspects of their new world, sometimes emphasizing its vast improvements and seemingly endless possibilities but at other times mourning the loss of a way of life in which everything from food to social relations was, or seemed, both richer and simpler.

Sometimes, ironically, the developments that might seem to lead furthest from the imagined agrarian utopia of the past, as in the creation and expansion of the railroads, had the opposite effect of bringing agricultural bounty within the reach of average families living in the region's small towns and expanding cities. In 1841, wealthy Bostonians endorsed building a railroad between Boston and Pittsfield, Massachusetts, as the best way to feed their urban workers at minimum expense. The new line, and others like it, had a stimulating effect on the markets for wheat, fruit, vegetables, dairy products, and meat. For example, the season during which strawberries, grapes, tomatoes, string beans, and peaches were on sale in Northern cities increased on average by three to four months between 1835 and 1865. Thus, the nostalgic and seemingly rarefied zeal for a vegetable and whole grain regimen espoused by such dietary reformers as Sylvester Graham and William Alcott was turned into a practical possibility by railroads, a pivotal feature of the otherwise past-obliterating Industrial Revolution.[1]

This is not to say that social reformers were wrong in suspecting that industrialization contributed to ill health of body and soul. Poor living and working conditions and many of the products of the industrialized food processes themselves were both the legitimate targets of temperance and health advocates who worried about the well-being of a population subsisting on denatured wheat, white sugar, fatty foods, and intoxicating beverages.

Yet the expanding market in fresh foods was experienced as a veritable cornucopia by the majority in both town and country who had long gotten by on a diet of little more than starch, fat, and salt meat. To appreciate the change in circumstances, we might recall how the average New England breakfast table, a farmer's table at that, appeared to a European visitor at the beginning of the nineteenth century. Constantin Volney wrote that farmers at breakfast "deluge their stomach with a quart of hot water, impregnated with tea, or so slightly with coffee that it is mere colored water; and they swallow, almost without chewing, hot bread, half baked, toast soaked in butter, cheese of the fattest kind, slices of salt or hung beef, ham, etc., all of which is nearly insoluble." Dinner was no better, consisting of "boiled pastes under the name of puddings," more melted butter, potatoes in hog's lard, yet more butter or fat, and pumpkin pie in a pastry that was "nothing but a greasy paste, never sufficiently baked."[2]

So increased mechanization as the century progressed resulted in a surplus that both delighted and perplexed. The sometimes salutary, sometimes damaging abundance produced by industrial processes was the overriding change in circumstances with which the nineteenth century had to cope. Abundance, long pursued and finally achieved, turned out to be a two-edged sword.

Those more impressed by the damaging than the salutary consequences of the industrial cornucopia undertook various initiatives to reconstruct a sense of small-scale traditional community as an alternative to the nationalized scope of the new order. For example, Louisa May Alcott's father (and William Alcott's cousin) Bronson Alcott started a vegetarian commune in a pastoral setting in protest against the incursions of industry. In 1844, on a newly acquired farm in Harvard, Massachusetts, Alcott, his family, and followers undertook to live on whole grain breads, garden produce, and fruit. Unfortunately, their "Fruitlands" experiment was a failure, lasting a mere seven months and bringing its most ardent members close to starvation. Was it better ultimately to build a railroad to bring fresh foods, but also cheap, adulterated bread, to an expanding urban population, or was it better to take a personal stand against mechanization by eating an alternative diet and growing one's own food? In many ways, these are still the options between which those concerned with food, health, and the environment must choose.[3]

What may seem to us an alternative or oppositional dimension in these communal ventures is sometimes more apparent than real, however. We are perhaps inclined, for instance, to think of the community cookbooks that emerged after the Civil War and have endured into our own day as offering views of a more authentically local cuisine. Ann Romines tells us that throughout her life such cookbooks "put local cooking into words and into print so that I could carry them with me, wherever I moved, and serve up the tastes of Houston [Missouri] on my own table."[4]

While Romines's extended testimony regarding the power of community cookbooks to evoke the face-to-face world of her childhood is eloquent and compelling, we nevertheless find it necessary to stress that, both in origin and content, the genre as a whole was not an antidote to but rather a product of the processes of culinary industrialization and consolidation that we have been describing. As far as origins are concerned, the community cookbook was an offshoot of the charitable cookbook, and the first charitable cookbook (fancifully titled A *Poetical Cook Book*) was issued in 1864 in conjunction with the Philadelphia Sanitary Fair. Both the fair and its accompanying cookbook were part of not local but rather coordinated national efforts by women's relief organizations to raise funds for Civil War soldiers and their families.[5]

After the war, women's relief organizations continued to use fairs to raise money for wounded veterans and war widows. In time these efforts were extended into other areas of need, and a national women's charitable movement to establish and support hospitals, schools, settlement houses, and more was under way. As in the worlds of commerce and industry, the development of systems was often seen as integral to charitable success. Few women civic leaders of the nineteenth century would have understood the current bromide about "random acts of kindness." For them, as often as not, success depended upon massive assemblages of people and resources.[6]

Not only did charity fairs and expositions often involve cooperation with commercial interests, they also mimicked their sponsors' structures and procedures. As Barbara Kirshenblatt-Giblett explains, "To achieve greater coherence, fair organizers arranged merchandise by category and created a temporary department store." The community cookbooks invariably printed in conjunction with the fairs provided a souvenir of the new marriage of merchandizing and social organization that fairgoers could take home.[7]

As for the culinary content of community cookbooks, it was for the most part indistinguishable from that of national cookbooks, as can be seen by comparison of the community cookbook recipes we have included in Part 2 with our selection of contemporaneous recipes from more widely distributed works. Indeed, some community cookbooks included recipes copied from national cookbooks. In New England, community cookbooks offered mostly regional standbys and newer recipes reflecting influential recent trends.[8]

xx

Back matter page, *Meriden Cook Book*, 1898[?]. Product promotion was regularly featured in community cookbooks. (Courtesy the Schlesinger Library, Radcliffe Institute, Harvard University)

The content of community cookbooks also reflected the companionable relationship with commerce that we have seen in the origin and early history of the form. Recipes for products using Jell-O or Borden's Eagle Brand condensed milk were found alongside more traditional dishes and grandmotherly heirloom recipes. So pervasive could this brand-name presence become, in both recipes and advertisements, that sometimes community cookbooks resembled the promotional pamphlets, featuring appliances and food products, that manufacturers began disseminating around the same time that community cookbooks were being developed. The end result of the intersection of mass food production, women's broadly organized charitable endeavors, and community cookbooks is nicely illustrated by the advertising copy in one of Ann Romines's Methodist charity cookbooks: "What a Delicious Cake! How Good Your Bread Is! That is what one Houston housewife said to another. Here is the secret: they were made from GILT EDGE FLOUR."[9]

THE COLONIAL REVIVAL

The North's victory in the Civil War led to the nationalizing trends we have been discussing. Yet another effect of that triumph was the power of the North to shape the national story and to advance the idea that New England's colonial past was normative for the entire country. For novelists, artists, and historians in particular, New England became "the heart and soul," as one historian has put it, of the reunified nation. From a taste for colonial architecture to a tendency to tell the story of American origins from a Puritan perspective, New England dominated—some would say monopolized—both the artistic and popular imagination. To "see New Englandly" was Emily Dickinson's apt phrase for the phenomenon that was to become known as the colonial revival.[10]

But the special regard for colonial New England life arose as much from a revulsion at the present as from a celebration of recent victories. Amid the material prosperity and practical conveniences wrought by industrialization, not only the small number influenced by social reform movements but also many other Americans in the latter half of the nineteenth and the early twentieth century worried that they had unwittingly created, in the words of Edith Wharton, "a world without traditions, without reverence, without stability." Among those who offered an alternative, if only an imaginative one, to the perceived shortcomings of progress was the hugely popular novelist Harriet Beecher Stowe. For Stowe, select aspects of the New England way of life—in particular the New England family farm and small town—served as a moral and cultural lodestar. The region represented to her and to many others the first and best that American democracy, built on Puritan principles, had to offer.[11]

Stowe propounded these views in a series of novels written between 1859 and 1878 but set in the early republican period. In them she probed such facets of the New England story as the emotional constraints of strict Calvinism as personified by an evangelical minister in Newport, Rhode Island (*The Minister's Wooing*, 1859); a cohesive if materially poor fishing community on the craggy Maine coast (*The Pearl of Orr's Island*, 1862); the conflicts in mores between country town and city as viewed from a fictional version of Natick, Massachusetts, where Stowe's husband Calvin had grown up (*Oldtown Folks*, 1869); and the panoply of local characters and patriotic customs to be found in Poganuc, a fictionalization of Litchfield, Connecticut, Stowe's hometown (*Poganuc People*, 1878). In Stowe's day as in our own, these books were overshadowed by *Uncle Tom's Cabin*. Yet from the vantage point of the early twenty-first century, they offer a warm, humorous, and complex, if idealized, treatment of a decisive time and place in American history.[12]

It is somewhat surprising, therefore, to find that contemporary criticism of Stowe's New England fiction could be almost virulently negative, as in this review by Bret Harte in the October 1869 issue of *Overland Monthly*: "Mrs. Stowe's treatment of 'Oldtown Folks' is even more provincial than her subject." Harte went on to complain that Stowe treated her "much-used stock of New England provincials . . . with the provincial satisfaction of a village gossip recalling other village worthies."[13]

Harte was not alone in his negative assessment of Stowe and her beloved region. Writers in the *Nation* magazine reported with satisfaction on New England's decline in national standing. Of *Oldtown Folks* its reviewer dryly noted that "it is some years since our New Englanders have even been a little tedious." He complained of Stowe's "Puritan parson, and the Puritan deacon, and the Puritan tithing-man; and the Puritan Thanksgiving, and 'Lection cake, and May Training; and the Puritan 'revivals,' and 'doctrines,' and donation parties." These of course were the very things that Stowe held up as foundational to the way of life she was extolling.[14]

But even ardent New England boosters such as Stowe had to admit that the old ways needed some updating. She did not uniformly praise her Puritan characters. For instance, she was critical of Dr. Hopkins's rigid moralism in *The Minister's Wooing*. In her own life, she tempered the spiritual inflexibility of her father's Calvinism. But she also believed that the excesses of Victorian conspicuous consumption needed to be restrained. She criticized those who "have the best of everything and are perfectly miserable," while at the same time encouraging those who were apt to be content with mediocrity to raise their standards and strive to do better. In other words, as her biographer Joan D. Hedrick puts it, "she helped the middle class find the middle ground."[15]

To find any ground at all was no mean accomplishment amid a sea of damask, mahogany, oriental carpets, ornate silver table settings, and all the curious extravagances that, as one commentator notes, "were to make Tiffany's famous." This was the overendowed material world of Victorianism that was forming around Stowe's readers and into which she introduced her homely rural characters with their antique turns of phrase. This was also a world in which there were no social safety nets—wealth one day might become penury the next, despite the preponderance of newspaper stories and popular novels peddling the reverse trope of rags to riches. For many readers, Stowe's stable, commonsensical, close-knit fictional world served both as antidote to their extravagance and as emotional balm in their precarious lives.[16]

Joseph Conforti argues that Stowe represents colonial and early national New England as an implicit critique of the excesses of the Gilded Age, adding that she places "women, domesticity, moral character, and daily life at the center of New England's historic distinctiveness." And she paints this female side of "Old New England" with the wealth of plausibly rendered domestic detail and good humor that were her hallmarks as a novelist.[17]

According to Conforti, as the colonial revival turned into a more distinct movement, author Alice Morse Earle emerged as the heir to Stowe's perspective. In a series of highly readable histories of popular customs and "the artifacts of colonial domesticity," Earle invidiously contrasted the way of life of her own day—"the 'disorder' of ethnic tenement life and the material excesses of Victorian consumers"—with that of the colonial era—"the true dignity which comes from simplicity of living, simplicity in dress, in home-furnishing, in all social and domestic relations."[18]

Earle intended her recreations of "home life in colonial days" to be not "nostalgic representations of an unrecoverable past" but rather encouragements to "native-born Victorians to reaffirm tradition." However, like more recent movements for the adoption of "alternative" or "traditional" ways of living, and indeed like its predecessor, the late-eighteenth-century vogue for neoclassical simplicity in domestic architecture, the colonial revival was in essence an aesthetic movement that required leisure and resources to pursue. It made a considerable cultural impact but could be ardently pursued only by the privileged few.[19]

Domestic Science Meets Colonial Revival

At roughly the time of the colonial revival, another movement that also got its start in New England and was inspired in part by Stowe's sister Catharine Beecher seemed to confront more realistically what was amiss in contemporary domestic life. Laura Shapiro summarizes this movement's forward-looking approach: "Domesticity expanded into an objective body of knowledge that had to be actively pursued; it was no longer to be treated as a God-given expertise insensibly commanded by all women. The most popular way to refer to this approach was to call it 'scientific.'"[20] Here was a different form of inoculation against the extremes to which the Victorian love of extravagance and display might lead. The Puritan-inspired moral restraint and material simplicity that Stowe and Earle espoused was appealing, even comforting, but it always had about it a rather hopeless air of antiquity. The reader might well imagine those better-balanced bygone days, but how could she re-create them? Following "scientific" methods of domestic management, on the other hand, would integrate women into the world of progress and moderate the tendency to lavish display, all the while continuing to assert the need for a separate sphere of women's activity.[21]

With the newly professionalized home came the new profession of teaching home science. And at the heart of the new teaching was the discipline of cooking. Since the days of the Puritan divines, Boston had been home to movements for moral and spiritual renewal. By the nineteenth century, the city had a substantial educated female population, making it a suitable testing ground for new charitable and social ideas. Boston would become the premier location of the domestic science movement and the Boston Cooking School would become its incubator.

Founded in 1879, the school was the brainchild of the Woman's Education Association (WEA), one of the city's most powerful philanthropic groups. Although it was not the first cooking school for women in the nation—New York claimed that honor—the renown attaching to Boston educational institutions and the efforts of the WEA to promote their new enterprise quickly earned a national standing for the school.[22]

The school's first mission was to educate the "daughters of mechanics," that is, students from a low social stratum for whom economical ways in the kitchen and a marketable skill could mean both great savings and a route to gainful employment. This was, at least in terms of economy in the kitchen, an updating of Lydia Maria Child's approach. The school argued that teaching these girls how to cook would be a boon for the entire family; with a new devotion to "science," the philanthropic ladies of Boston had determined that knowledge of cookery was best gained through methodical instruction by trained teachers.[23]

In furtherance of this mission, the WEA initially hired two teachers: an experienced but relatively unknown young woman of Irish descent, Joanna Sweeney, and the celebrated author of the popular *Appledore Cook Book*, Maria Parloa. The dishes in which Sweeney was to give instruction were those of working-class Boston—"tomato soup, Irish stew with mutton and potatoes, and steamed apple pudding." Parloa, on the other hand, was encouraged to offer tutelage in a much more lavish style of cooking. Parloa's sessions proved so popular, however, that soon they took precedence over the school's program for its working-class students. Rationalizing the quick retreat from their original mission, the school's leaders wrote in their annual report: "That a woman is rich seems no sufficient reason for excluding her from the advantages offered her of becoming practi-

Engraving, "Young Ladies' Cooking School of Boston," *Frank Leslie's Illustrated Newspaper*, 3 April 1880. (Courtesy Harvard College Library, Widener Library, XPS 527PF, vol. 48)

cally conversant with some of the most important duties of woman's home life." Apparently, those duties included knowing how to make Parloa's "larded grouse with bread sauce, lobster croquettes, potato soufflé, cream meringues, and orange sherbet."[24]

Yet for several years under Sweeney, the Boston Cooking School continued to offer lessons to students of modest means at its North End branch. The evening and weekend classes were attended by hundreds of women. Nevertheless, the future of the school lay not in educating poor and working women in the ethnic North End but rather in enlightening a "class of housekeepers who could afford to pay for their lessons" in the school's tonier quarters on Tremont Street. Within a few years of its founding, the Boston Cooking School had separated completely from the charitable Woman's Education Association and incorporated as an independent enterprise.[25]

Along with a desire to learn to cook, many of the wealthy women who attended the Boston Cooking School did so in order that they might better instruct and supervise their servants. In Boston, as elsewhere, management of domestic staff was famously, or infamously, known as "the servant problem." This was a problem upon which, as we have seen, Child, Beecher, and many others had weighed in. If Alice Morse Earle's colonial revivalism was meant to reaffirm tradition, or her version of tradition, among "native-born Victorians," then domestic science as practiced at the Boston Cooking School was developed with similar goals in mind: to provide "native-born" mistresses with the knowledge they needed to run their households. Put more simply, the Boston Cooking School, and many others like it, taught white Anglo-Saxon Protestant upper-class women what they needed to know about cooking and household management in order to indoctrinate their cooks and servants in the proper—in this case the proper Bostonian—cooking styles and manners.[26]

Who were the servants, sometimes called "faithless strangers," so in need of guidance? As Faye E. Dudden puts it, they were mostly "the Irish domestic, stereotypically referred to as 'Biddy,' who dominated the labor market at mid-century and therefore drew the blame for servant problems." These immigrant women were "most faithless, because so greatly in need of money, and most strange, not just personally but culturally." Although Dudden is discussing the middle of the century, clearly the perceived "servant problem" had not abated later in the century. Of course most households had no such problem, being "staffed" by the mothers and daughters of the families themselves. But the wealthiest and most influential members of the community, as well as those a few notches below that status, did employ servants, whether occasionally or permanently, and their concerns dominated social discourse.[27]

So the reasons for a new interest in domestic science in the latter half of the nineteenth century, as exemplified by the history of the Boston Cooking School, were various and sometimes overlapping:

a desire to help the poor; an interest in professionalizing women's work; a wish to achieve social elevation through culinary display; and a hope to improve the work of domestic servants, who were often cultural—and culinary—aliens. The next character in our story embodies aspects of all these trends. Through the cuisine she chose to highlight she brought the domestic science movement close to intersection with the colonial revival.

Like many cookbook writers and skilled cooks before her, Mary J. Lincoln came to her life's work partly because of a personal financial crisis caused by her husband's business "reversals" and "his consequent ill health." She had only minimal cooking experience when she was hired to replace Joanna Sweeney as head of the Boston Cooking School. Perhaps for ethnic or class reasons, Sweeney was considered unsuitable for a permanent leadership position by the school's directors, even though Lincoln's culinary education amounted to nothing but a few lessons "in fancy dishes" from Sweeney herself.

In her first months as principal of the Boston Cooking School, Lincoln was deemed an unsatisfactory teacher by many students. Nevertheless, she was encouraged to enroll in a class to prepare cooking teachers then being offered at the school by Parloa. Luckily, Lincoln was a quick study. Within months, Parloa was off the payroll, Sweeney was back teaching working-class students at the school's remote North Bennett Street location, and Mary Lincoln, the student whom both of them had helped to train, was launched on what was to be a long, successful career.[28]

Despite the education in fancy cooking she had received at the school she now headed, Lincoln, like so many New Englanders ambivalent about luxury, included, indeed emphasized, the plainer New England fare with which she had grown up. From her position of authority, she taught generations of wealthy women, as well as some servants and daughters of mechanics, how to cook "baked beans, brown bread, fish balls, doughnuts, and Indian pudding." Of course she interspersed these lessons with others in the "dainty" dishes her upper-class students found appealing, among them such Victorian favorites as the lightly spiced "Turkish pilaf," the still-popular, dough-encrusted sausage hors d'oeuvre called "pigs in blankets," and the meringue concoction "floating island."

To amalgamate plain New England cooking with the Victorian taste for luxury, Lincoln relied on the strategy adopted by most colonial revival cooks—sweetening of both individual dishes and overall meals. In her curriculum, "a sweet concluded every lesson in every course, with the occasional exception of breakfast." In the "Richer" and "Fancy" courses she taught, each lesson included between two and five desserts. And the baked beans, steamed brown bread, and Indian pudding recipes she imparted were sweetened beyond anything her ancestors would have recognized as their everyday food. The outlines of a colonial revival cuisine, based on the quotidian foods of the white Protestants of New England but greatly enriched to suit Victorian tastes, were reflected in Lincoln's repertoire.[29]

Aiding in the dissemination of the types of foods favored by Mrs. Lincoln was the fact that by the 1890s two of the Boston Cooking School's three cooking classes involved dietary planning for public schools—"Cookery Applied to Public School Work" and "Observation and Assistance at Public Schools." Preparing many of its students for employment in school cafeterias amounted to designing a menu for the masses of American children who passed every day through the public school. Whether by introducing immigrant children to butter-drenched sweet corn and molasses-soaked pork and beans, or by reinforcing (and making more appetizing) the home cuisine of native-born youth, Boston-trained cooks working in the nation's expanding public school system helped to bring New England cooking—or at least their fattened and sweetened version of it—to the fore as standard American food.[30]

But the national dissemination of this type of gussied-up New England cookery could not have been accomplished solely through the education of cooks, cooking teachers, and institutional dietitians. Several other organs of diffusion were needed to accomplish the goal. The popularity of cooking classes at the height of the domestic science movement also led to a rise in the number of cooking-related columns to appear in magazines and newspapers.[31]

Even more important were the domestic science–inspired cookbooks. As a graduate of the Boston Cooking School reported from Asheville, North Carolina: "What do you think I found on one of the very first trips I made into this delightful town? A cooking class in full session poring over 'The Boston Cook Book.'" The full title of that book was *Mrs. Lincoln's Boston Cook Book*. Lincoln's work was the basic text of the school for over ten years, and it served to disseminate both domestic science theory and New England cooking to a national audience.[32]

Popular as she may have been in her time, few of us nowadays have heard of Mrs. Lincoln or her Boston cookbook. Many more of us know a book that borrowed extensively from Lincoln—Fannie Farmer's *Boston Cooking-School Cook Book*, first published in 1896. Despite the debt to Lincoln, evident in the book's original title, the work came to be so closely identified with the author that its title is now given as *The Fannie Farmer Cookbook*.

This title is appropriate in that it acknowledges not only Farmer's success and fame but also her substantial alteration of the work. Essentially, she imbued it more fully with the spirit of the domestic science movement. Where Lincoln was chatty, Farmer was concise, intending her version to be consulted rather than read. Her spare prose style paralleled her advocacy of level measurements. As Joseph Carlin has shown, a movement toward utilizing standardized weights and measures in cooking had been gathering momentum throughout the nineteenth century and had achieved a "major breakthrough" in *Mrs. Lincoln's Boston Cook Book*. Farmer, "one of the first cookbook writers to be trained from the very beginning on standardized measuring cups and spoons," proceeded to dispense with the residues of vagueness still to be found in Lincoln, and, with her immense popularity, made strictly level measurement and "scientific" recipe presentation once and for all the norm.[33]

Farmer's devotion to precise measurements, together with her easily consulted cooking text, won her an enormous and loyal audience in her day. Her book was reprinted every year from 1897 until her death in 1915, at which time more than 360,000 copies had been sold. A revised edition prepared by Marion Cunningham is still, a century later, a perennial best seller. In addition, a facsimile of the original 1896 edition has been in print since the 1970s.

Fannie Farmer eventually opened her own cooking school and wrote a number of other cookbooks: *Chafing Dish Possibilities* (1898), *Food and Cookery for the Sick and Convalescent* (1904), *What to Have for Dinner* (1905), *Catering for Special Occasions* (1911), and *A New Book*

Cover, *Harper's Weekly*, 21 January 1911. The dialogue between cookbook writer and cook, depicted earlier in the frontispiece to Elizabeth Raffald's *Experienced English Housekeeper*, continues into the twentieth century. (Courtesy Harvard College Library, Widener Library, P207.6F, vol. 55)

of Cookery (1912). Despite her enthusiasm for boiled-down prose and scientific analysis, she tended to promote not only the New England "plain" style but also a rich cuisine based in large part on the menus of the fancy restaurants she frequented after becoming wealthy. At the time of her death at age fifty-seven—probably from arteriosclerosis—many of the sumptuous dishes from her *New Book of Cookery* were being incorporated into the latest edition of *The Boston Cooking-School Cook Book*. Yet Farmer's personal and professional origins in Boston, the no-nonsense tone of her work, and the continued inclusion in her primary work of New England culinary "classics" in sweetened form means that not only domestic science but also the colonial revival continue to be associated with her name.[34]

Despite its ostensible plainness, colonial revival cooking was motivated by ulterior social motives. What might seem like a backward-looking cuisine, New England cooking, was transformed by practitioners like Lincoln and Farmer into a sophisticated modern strategy. When so-called traditional dishes were prepared using the most up-to-date scientific methods, enhanced with molasses, butter, and eggs, and evangelically promoted to eager middle-class audiences as well as to captive audiences of schoolchildren across the nation, they could hardly be seen as anything but a means to a social end. That end was the promotion of "Old New England."[35]

For some, enthusiasm for New England domestic culture extended beyond the composition of their meals and the contents of their cookbooks. These devotees created a realm made up of equal parts fantasy and reality—the "Olde Tyme" or "New England Kitchen Exhibit," popular from the 1860s to the 1890s. As one historian points out, in a highly conflicted response to industrialization, "These allegedly rural, preindustrial spaces [were] set up in the most thoroughly urbanized area of the industrial North." Fair committees were busy from the Philadelphia International Centennial, to the Chicago Columbian Exposition, to smaller affairs in New York, Indianapolis, St. Louis, and towns across the country. The scale of the endeavors might differ, but the goal was the same: "The idea is to present a faithful picture of New-England farm-house life of the last century. The grand old fire-place shall glow again—the spinning wheel shall whirl as of old—the walls shall be garnished with the products of the forest and the field—the quilting, the donation, and the wedding party shall assemble once more, while the apple-paring shall not be forgotten—and the dinner table, always set, shall be loaded with substantial New England cheer."[36]

The menu on that always-set dinner table was, naturally, colonial, or more accurately, colonial revival: "bountiful supplies of toothsome viands—pork and beans, cider apple-sauce, Boston brown bread, pitchers of cider, pumpkin, mince, and apple pies, doughnuts, and all the savory and delicate wealth of the New England larder." The exhibit fireplace may have been continually glowing, but the cooking required to serve to the masses of exhibition-goers an approximation of what they saw in the exhibit was more often carried out in modern kitchens outfitted with cast iron ranges. Fantasy nevertheless prevailed with such claims as the one made in Indianapolis, where the "Yankee Kitchen" was proclaimed to be "under the management of live yankees." A list of the cast of characters staffing the Yankee exhibit at the fair in St. Louis sums up the ethnocentric ideal: "Grandma Brown, Jonathan Jones (he sold genuine nutmegs), Mr. Deacon Twitchell from Iowa, Miss Polly Bluestocking, sundry country cousins, Aunties Nabby, Sally and Polly from Cape Cod, Miss Prissy the village dressmaker, Miss Rogers the Yankee schoolmarm." And so on.[37]

As complex responses to modernism, domestic science and the colonial revival took opposite tacks, one emphasizing women's place within the science-inspired world of progress, the other emphasizing old-fashioned domesticity as a haven in a tumultuous world. Yet, as we can see, progress and tradition often overlapped and might be represented by one and the same figure, such as Fannie Farmer, or one and the same genre, such as the community cookbook. The complexity of late-nineteenth- and early-twentieth-century life permitted, perhaps required, that the same phenomena be assigned multiple meanings.

As to the multiple meanings attaching themselves to the idea of New England in the colonial revival period, there is good, bad, and indifferent to report. Sometimes the promotion of the region and its Protestant "stock"—a favorite term of the time—took the fairly innocuous form of a bit of chauvinism expressed by a group living with the stresses of geographic dispersion and cultural dissipation. But at other times, the assertion of a blood connection to New England amounted to a declaration of social superiority over newer immigrants. Celebrating the heritage of New England sometimes also implied disparagement of other regions, such as the defeated South and the newly settled Midwest and West. Eras of change can produce both brilliant exemplars like Harriet Beecher Stowe, Alice Morse Earle, and Fannie Farmer and stunning inanities, such as the New England Kitchen exhibits managed by "live yankees."

PART

2

Recipes and Commentaries

CHAPTER FIVE

Pottages, Chowders, Soups, and Stews

THE CHOWDER PARTY.

*I*t could be said that New England history began when English met Indian, so we think it is fitting to begin this collection of recipes with a dish that, in its New England form, is a mixture of Indian and English influences. Most commonly known as pottage, it is the progenitor of the baked beans and chowders for which New England is still famous. At the outset, pottage was no more than a pot of boiled meat, fowl, or fish, grain, seasoning, and whatever vegetables were on hand.

Long before the colonization of New England, similar mixed dishes were the basis of many of the world's cuisines. The English were known to have been particularly devoted to pottage. In the sixteenth century it was said to be "not so much used in all Christendom" as it was in England. When they settled New England a century later, the English brought iron pots with them so that they could prepare their pottage. But when they arrived they found that the Indians also lived on a kind of pottage, which they cooked in European pots or kettles acquired in trade.

While the Indian kettles full of broth and grain "made thicke with Fishes, Fowles, and Beasts" may have looked similar to English pottage, the taste and texture were less so. For one thing, the Indians were apt to toss into their cooking pots the bones as well as the meat of animals and fish. (The English marveled at the Indians' ability quickly to remove dangerous small bones with their teeth as they ate.) However, the primary difference between Indian and English pottage was the grain. The Indians used maize, or as the English called it, Indian corn, which had been grown in southern Europe since 1493 but which, insofar as it was known at all, was met with skepticism by the English. In his *Herball* (1597), John Gerard opined that Indian corn "doth nourish far lesse than either wheat, rie, barly, or otes," and it was these traditional European grains that the English settlers would have preferred in their pottages.

Unfortunately, the English soon found that the grains they liked best did not grow well in New England. It took them a while to get used to pottages, puddings, and breads made with Indian corn. But get used to it they did. From this combination of European pottage and Indian corn many of the classic foods of New England are descended.

English Grain Pottages

In the Middle Ages, thicker English pottages were known as "stondyng," thinner as "ronnyng." The "standing" dishes made with cereals, shreds of meat or fish, spices, and other emoluments such as eggs and bread crumbs were sometimes known by other names, depending on variations in their spicing, meat, and cereal components—brewets, egerdouces, mortrews, mawmenees, blancmanges, and blanc dessores. These substantial pottages continued to proliferate in the sixteenth century—after all, they were both filling and a successful vehicle for almost any medley of ingredients. Their less heavy counterparts, the "running" pottages, early forms of soup, were less prominent in early English cuisine.

1. OF BOILD MEATS ORDINARY

It resteth now that we speak of boild meats and broths, which forasmuch as our House wife is intended to be generall, one that can as well feed the poore as the rich, we will first beginne with those ordinary wholsome boild meats, which are of vse in euery goodman's house: therefore to make the best ordinary pottage: you shall take a racke of mutton cut into peeces, or a legge of mutton cut into peeces: for this meat and these ioints, are the best, Although any other ioint, or any fresh beefe will likewise make good pottage: And having washt your meat well, put it into a cleane pot with faire water, and set it on the fire: then take violet leaues, endiue, succory, strawberie leaues, spinage, langdebeefe, marygold flowers, Scallions, and a little persly, and chop them very small together, then take halfe so much oatmeale well beaten as there is herbes, and mix it with the herbes, and chop it all very wel together: then when the pot is ready to boile, skumme it very wel, and then put in your herbes: And so let it boile with a quicke fire, stirring the meat oft in the pot, till the meat be boild enough, and that the hearbes and water are mixt together without any seperation, which will be after the consumption of more then a third part: Then season them with salt, and serue them vp with the meate either with sippets or without.

—Markham, *English Hus-wife* (1615), pp. 47–48

This classic "ordinary" pottage recipe (more sophisticated dishes were also referred to as pottage or "potage"; see below, #38 commentary), published just before the English settlement of New England, follows the pattern outlined in Andrew Boorde's *Dyetary of Helth* (1542): "Pottage is made of the liquor in the which flesh is sodden in, with putting-to chopped herbs, and oatmeal and salt." Such items as "marigold flowers" and "violet leaves" in herb mixtures were quite common in medieval cookery and persisted into the eighteenth century (as in #2, below). In Markham's day, chicory was called succory. Langdebeef, more commonly known as borage, is a cucumber-flavored herb. Sippets, from the diminutive form of sop (see "Soups" introduction later in the chapter), were small pieces of fried or toasted bread. Large numbers of ingredients and a final garnish of sippets (often with barberries and lemon) were culinary innovations of this period. The sippet was used less frequently by the eighteenth century, but it nevertheless endured as "a distant echo of the trenchers of the Middle Ages."

2. TO MAKE SCOTCH BARLEY BROTH

Take a Leg of Beef, chop it all to Pieces, boil it in three Gallons of Water, with a Piece of Carrot and a Crust of Bread, till it is half boiled away; then strain it off, and put it into the Pot again, with half a Pound of Barley, four or five Heads of Salary washed clean and cut small, a large Onion, a Bundle of Sweet Herbs, and a little Parsley chopped small, and a few Marigolds. Let this boil an Hour; take a Cock or large Fowl, clean picked and washed, and put into the Pot; boil it till the Broth is quite good, then season with Salt, and send it to the Table, with the Fowl in the Middle. This Broth is very good without the Fowl; take out the Onion and Sweet Herbs, before you send it to the Table.

—Glasse, *Art of Cookery* (1747), p. 65

With minor alterations and "without the Fowl," this recipe made its way to New England, as indicated by its presence in *Mrs. Gardiner's Family Receipts* (ca. 1770).

We find sweet herbs mentioned frequently in early English cookbooks. Karen Hess says that sweet herbs are similar to the French *fine herbes*, including parsley, chervil, thyme, but rarely tarragon. According to C. Anne Wilson, the terms "fine" and "sweet" herbs are synonymous. They both entered seventeenth-century French cookbooks, which in turn influenced the English. After the Restoration, the "faggot of sweet herbs" (the French *bouquet garni*) became common in English cooking. The modern editors of an eighteenth-century manuscript cookbook list basil, marjoram, rosemary, parsley, bay leaves, coriander, and thyme as sweet herbs "seldom absent from any savoury dish" of the period. Sometimes even lettuce and spinach were classified as sweet herbs.

What herbs were not sweet? Markham mentions radishes, chives, coleworts (kale), chervil, cresses, lettuces, basil, leeks, scallions, fennel, and coriander. Others include onions, shallots, turnips, carrots, and celery among pot herbs, that is, herbs to be added to stock. Herb was a catchall term for the plant material "used primarily as flavorings, and in relatively small amounts." Many of the herbs that remain in use today were first introduced into northern Europe by the Romans. The range of acceptable herbs narrowed in the eighteenth century: green beets, mallows, orache, mercury, bugloss, smallage, nettles, and turnip tops, all used in the Middle Ages, fell from favor.

Indian Succotash

As made by the Indians from whom the English settlers of the New England area learned about it, succotash was a far cry from the insipid mixture of canned corn and lima beans that many of us were served in the school cafeteria at lunchtime.

3. PONDOMENAST

The Indians have another sort of Provision out of this Corne, which they call Pondomenast—the English call it sweete Corne, which they prepare in this manner: When the Corne in the Eare is full, whiles it is yet greene it hath then a very sweete tast, this they gather and boyle a convenient time, and then they drie it, and put it up into Baggs or Basketts, for their store, and so use it as they have occasion boyleing of it againe either by it selfe, or amongst their Fish or Venison or Beavers Flesh, or such as they have, and this they account a principall Dish, either at their ordinary Meales or Feastivall times, they boyle it whole, or beaten Gross.

—Mood, quoting John Winthrop Jr., "Indian Corne" (1662), p. 131

4. THE INDIANS' POTTAGE

Their food is generally boiled maize or Indian corn, mixed with kidney beans, or sometimes without. Also they frequently boil in this pottage fish and flesh of all sorts, either new taken or dried, as shads, eels, alewives, or a kind of herring, or any other sort of fish. But they dry mostly those sorts before mentioned. These they cut in pieces, bones and all, and boil them in the aforesaid pottage. I have wondered many times that they were not in danger of being choked with fish bones; but they are so dextrous to separate the bones from the fish in their eating thereof that they are in no hazard. Also they boil in this furmenty all sorts of flesh they take in hunting: as venison, beaver, bear's flesh, moose, otters, raccoons, or any kind that they take in hunting, cutting this flesh in small pieces and boiling it as aforesaid. Also they mix with the said pottage several sorts of roots: as Jerusalem artichokes, and ground nuts and other roots, and pumpions and squashes, and also several sorts of nuts or masts, as oak acorns, chestnuts, walnuts; these husked and dried and powdered, they thicken their pottage therewith.

—Karr, quoting Daniel Gookin, "Historical Collections" (1674), pp. 80–81

Gookin's description of the Indians' pottage bears a resemblance to a culinary historian's description of the typical peasant diet of the Emilia region of Italy: "Peasants ate more or less the same meals in the early twentieth century as when Gregory the Great ruled Rome. A typical Lombard-period family meal in winter comprised a loaf of bread, a pot of minestra and a thick foccaccia made of beans and millet, spread with animal fats or oil. . . . A modern menu in the same season would be little changed: the minestra would have pasta as well as beans, cooked in water with lard or onions for flavor and herring or bacon and ground chestnuts spread on polenta."

While Gookin only wonders at the Indians' dexterity in eating pottage with bones in it, a modern Italian historian, adopting an attitude unfortunately common among European explorers and later "scientific" observers, disparages the local diet: "It bears a strong peasant stamp—simple, crude, rooted in barbarian traditions."

"Furmenty" or frumenty was a type of wheat or barley pottage.

New England Succotash

According to one historian of early New Hampshire, the "most common dish" of that colony's first settlers was a type of "bean porridge" that was clearly an adaptation of succotash: "It was made by boiling the beans very soft, thickening the liquor with a little meal and adding a piece of pork to season it. A handful of corn was often put in."

In his poem "The Hasty Pudding," published near the end of the eighteenth century, Joel Barlow assumed that meat, in the form of "a long slice of bacon," remained a standard ingredient in succotash, just as it always had been in the succotash of the New England Indians and the first English settlers. But in the succotashes of New England's nineteenth century, meat was sometimes included, sometimes not. This was probably because succotash was changing from being a pottage, a traditional mixed dish constituting virtually the entire meal, to being a vegetable side dish in what the archaeologist James Deetz calls "the ideal American meal of meat, potato, and vegetable."

5. SUCCOTASH

If you wish to make succotash, boil the beans from half to three quarters of an hour, in water a little salt, meantime cutting off the corn and throwing the cobs to boil with the beans. Take care not to cut too close to the cob, as it imparts a bad taste. When the beans have boiled the time above mentioned, take out the cobs, and add the corn, and let the whole boil from fifteen to twenty minutes, for young corn, and longer for older corn. Make the proportions two-thirds corn and one-third beans. Where you have a mess amounting to two quarts of corn and one quart of beans, take two tablespoonfuls of flour, wet it into a thin paste, and stir it into the succotash, and let it boil up for five minutes. Then lay some butter in a dish, take it up into it, and add more salt if need be.

—Beecher, *Domestic Receipt-Book* (1846), p. 77

6. SUCCOTASH

Take one dozen ears of sweet corn, cut off the kernels, and boil the cobs in three pints of water; wash one quart of Lima, or other fresh-shelled beans, and put them into the water with the cobs; scald one pound of salt pork, and add it to the beans and cobs; let the whole boil together three quarters of an hour, then take out the cobs, add the kernels of corn previously cut from them, and let the kernels, the beans, and the pork boil together fifteen minutes; when done, there should remain water only sufficient to keep them from burning, in the pot; serve the pork on a flat, and the succotash in a deep dish.

Succotash is a favorite dish in New England; some prefer it without the salt pork, in that case, butter and salt must be added when the succotash is dished.

—Bliss, *Practical Cook Book* (1850), p. 97

Hasty Pudding

Like many other traditional foods, among them gingerbread (not a bread, as we understand the term) and johnnycake (not a cake, as we know it), Hasty Pudding is, depending on the recipe, an instance of greater or lesser dissociation between name and thing. In some cases, it is made in haste. In others, haste will ruin it. Sometimes it is, with certain amendments, indisputably a pudding, enriched with eggs, milk, or cream. More basically, however, hasty pudding is a simple pottage—grain (in England, wheat or oats) stirred into boiling liquid until thoroughly cooked and of a creamy consistency.

In America, hasty pudding was always made in this simple way, with cornmeal serving as the grain. A culinary assertion of democracy and self-sufficiency, it inspired Joel Barlow's "The Hasty Pudding," which in turn may have influenced Harvard students to choose "Hasty Pudding" as the name for the secret society they formed in 1795 to cultivate "friendship and patriotism." Democracy and patriotism aside, cornmeal hasty pudding is identical to that Italian classic polenta.

7. HASTY PUDDING

Boil water, a quart, three pints, or two quarts, according to the size of your family; sift your meal, stir five or six spoonfuls of it thoroughly into a bowl of water; when the water in the kettle boils, pour into it the contents of the bowl; stir it well, and let it boil up thick; put in salt to suit your own taste, then stand over the kettle, and sprinkle in meal, handful after handful, stirring it very thoroughly all the time, and letting it boil between whiles. When it is so thick that you stir it with great difficulty, it is about right. It takes about half an hour's cooking. Eat it with milk or molasses. Either Indian meal or rye meal may be used. If the system is in a restricted state, nothing can be better than *rye* hasty pudding and *West India* molasses. This diet would save many a one the horrors of dyspepsia.

—Child, *American Frugal Housewife* (1833), p. 65

Child gives a straightforward rendition, although her suggestion of rye is out of the ordinary for American writers. In *The Good Housekeeper* (1839), Hale copied this recipe.

8. MUSH, OR HASTY PUDDING

Wet up the Indian meal in cold water, till there are no lumps, stir it gradually into boiling water which has been salted, till so thick that the stick will stand in it. Boil slowly, and so as not to burn, stirring often. Two or three hours' boiling is needed. Pour it into a broad, deep dish, let it grow cold, cut it into slices half an inch thick, flour them, and fry them on a griddle with a little lard, or bake them in a stove oven.

—Beecher, *Domestic Receipt-Book* (1846), p. 108

Beecher's instructions are complex and time-consuming (after lengthy boiling, the mixture must be cooled and subsequently fried or baked). Nevertheless, in keeping with New England practice, she retains the name "Hasty Pudding," though making that a secondary choice after the more common "Mush."

Hominy

Learned from the Indians, hominy was also called samp. It can be eaten alone, added to soups or stews, or fried. In the mid-seventeenth century, Roger Williams described hominy as "a kind of meale pottage," adding that the difference between the Indian and English versions was that while the Indians ate their hulled corn mixed with "plaine water," the English had theirs with milk or butter, which were "mercies beyond" the Indian prepa-ration. Maple syrup, molasses, sugar, or honey were also sometimes added.

The dish is made by removing the hulls of the dried corn kernels through winnowing or boiling in an alkaline solution of lye or lime. Early Americans did not need to go far to obtain lye. Fireplaces were built with ash pits; later, cookstoves were equipped with ash hoppers. When water passes over ashes, brown lye (caustic potash or potassium hydroxide), also known as quicklime, is leached out. Jars were placed beneath the drain holes of outdoor ash pits to catch the lye leached after rain.

Corn was soaked in lye to loosen the outer skin, or pericarp. Repeated washings were then required to remove the lye, after which the loos-ened outer skin was removed by rubbing. Any remaining skin was washed away in a final rinse.

9. SAMPE

They first Water the Corne, if with Colde Water a little longer, if with Water a little warmed a shorter time about halfe an hower more or less, as they find it needfull, according to the driness of the Corne, then they either beate it in a Mortar . . . to be about the Biggness of Rice, though some will be a little smaller, and some a little greater, or Grind it gross as neere as they can about the big-ness of Rice in handmills or other Mills, out of which they sift the Flower or Meale very cleane (for whether they beate it or Grinde it there wilbe some little Quantity of Meale amongst it) then they winnow it in the wind, and so seperate the hulls from the rest this is to be boyled or Stued with a gentle Fire, till it be tender, of a fitt consistence, as of Rice so boyled, into which if Milke, or butter be put either with Sugar or without, it is a food very pleasant and wholesome, being easy of Digestion, and is of a nature Divertical and Clensing.

—Mood, quoting John Winthrop Jr., "Indian Corne" (1662), p. 130

Winthrop also declared that hominy was "the best sort of Food" the early English settlers made from corn and their "most common diet" during the very first years of settlement. He added that hominy was good for what ails you, whether fever, "the Stone," scurvy, or "other acute Diseases."

10. BOILING HOMMONY

Boiling Hommony.—To two quarts of hommony pour four quarts of water, stir it up well that the hulls may rise; then pour off the water through a sieve in order to separate the hulls. Turn the same water again into the hommony, stir it well, and pour it off again in the same several times. Pour back the water, add a little salt, and, if necessary, a little more water, and hang it over a slow fire to boil. It will need stirring often, if not constantly, during the first hour. Let it boil from three to six hours.

—Alcott, *Young House-Keeper* (1838), p. 408

11. BEATING HOMMONY

Beating Hommony.—Soak the hommony corn ten minutes in boiling water; then take the corn up and put it into the hommony mortar, and beat it until the hulls are all separated from the corn. Once or twice, while beating, take it out of the mortar and fan it; that is, throw it up on a tray or bowl so as to allow the hulls to fly off. When sufficiently beaten, fan it until all the hulls are out.

—Alcott, *Young House-Keeper* (1838), p. 409

In what amounts to a reversion to Indian practice, Alcott's two recipes for making "hommony" neither prohibit emoluments nor recommend them. However, if you have achieved a good hominy by following either of Alcott's methods, which you certainly may, go ahead and dress the results as you like.

12. FRIED HOMINY

When cold hominy is left of the previous day, it is very good wet up with an egg and a little flour, and fried.

—Beecher, *Domestic Receipt-Book* (1846), p. 97

Baked Beans

This dish, eventually to be esteemed a New England classic, got its start in the pottage kettle or stewpot, as peas or beans and bacon, which one historian says was among the oldest of English dishes. In medieval times, the legumes were softened in water, drained, and stewed gently in bacon broth. A piece of bacon would be put in the pot when the peas were almost done.

By the time of the settlement of New England, there had developed in the Midlands county of Staffordshire a baked version of beans and bacon, called "blanks & prises." The beans were soaked overnight, then baked, along with onions, leeks, and honey-and-mustard-cured ham. "Staffordshire was also famous for its brown earthenware pottery, and in all probability its recipe for baked beans diffused with the special narrow necked pot employed in their preparation," writes Jay Allan Anderson. Sound familiar? The Staffordshire pot certainly sounds like the famous Boston Bean Pot.

13. TO DRESS BEANS AND BACON

When you dress Beans and Bacon, boil the Bacon by itself and the Beans by themselves, for the Bacon will spoil the Colour of the Beans. Always throw some Salt into the Water, and some Parsley nicely pick'd. When the Beans are enough (which you will know by their being tender) throw them into a Cullender to drain: Take up the Bacon and skin it; throw some Raspings of Bread over the Top, and if you have an Iron make it red-hot and hold over it, to brown the Top of the Bacon: If you have not one, set it before the Fire to brown. Lay the Beans in the Dish, and the Bacon in the Middle on the Top, and send them to Table, with Butter in a Bason.

—Glasse, *Art of Cookery* (1747), p. 12

The way this stewed dish was served up turned it into something not all that different from what we know as baked beans. Whereas one medieval recipe recommends taking steps to prevent the legumes spoiling the appearance of the bacon, Glasse's beans-and-bacon aesthetics are reversed—the bacon must not be allowed to disfigure the beans.

14. BEANS AND PEAS

Baked beans are a very simple dish, yet few cook them well. They should be put in cold water, and hung over the fire, the night before they are baked. In the morning, they should be put in a colander, and rinsed two or three times; then again placed in a kettle, with the pork you intend to bake, covered with water, and kept scalding hot, an hour or more. A pound of pork is quite enough for a quart of beans, and that is a large dinner for a common family. The rind of the pork should be slashed. Pieces of pork alternately fat and lean, are the most suitable; the cheeks are the best. A little pepper sprinkled among the beans, when they are placed in the bean-pot, will render them less unhealthy. They should be just covered with water, when put into the oven; and the pork should be sunk a little below the surface of the beans. Bake three or four hours.

Stewed beans are prepared the same way. The only difference is, they are not taken out of the scalding water, but are allowed to stew in more water, with a piece of pork and a little pepper, three hours or more.

—Child, *American Frugal Housewife* (1833), p. 51

For quite a long time, colonial New Englanders ate what one historian has called "daily pottage fare" as their basic diet, probably more often

than not the sort of hybrid of succotash and beans and bacon that we described, under the name "bean porridge," in the section on New England
succotash earlier in the chapter. It was in the eighteenth century, as
bake ovens came to be installed in many households (and taverns), that
stewed beans and bacon evolved into baked beans. But as Child's recipe
indicates, stewed beans and bacon didn't disappear altogether.

15. BAKED BEANS

The species of beans used for baking is called the white field bean. There are
two varieties,—the large and the small, or pea-bean,—the last is considered
the best.

Soak one quart in cold, soft water, over night; the next morning remove the
water in which the beans have soaked, and wash the beans in fresh water; then
put them into a pot with two quarts of cold water, set the pot over a slow fire,
and let simmer two hours, then score one and a half pounds of fat salt pork,
and put it into the pot, concealing it, except the rind, in the middle of the beans;
pour in a tea-spoonful of salt, and water enough to cover the pork and beans,
set the pot in a hot oven and bake six hours; if the water wastes so that the
beans become too dry, add a little more.

Baked beans, after having stood a day or two, are very good warmed over.
In some parts of New England they are considered indispensable at a Sunday
breakfast.

Lima and kidney beans, and other varieties, are sometimes dried and baked
as above; they cook in a shorter time than the white field bean.

—Bliss, *Practical Cook Book* (1850), p. 90

This recipe illustrates the standard mid-nineteenth-century practice—
both in using the white field bean and in minimal seasoning, in this case
with salt only. Beecher felt that "all the garden beans are better for baking" than "the common field bean." Her opinion gained few adherents
however. One writer recommended adding saleratus, an early form of
baking soda, to the dish just before it was baked.

16. BAKED BEANS, (WITHOUT PORK.)

Take one quart of clean, plump white beans, put them in a pan with sufficient
water to keep them covered while soaking over night, (10 or 12 hours); pour off
the water and put them in an iron kettle, to boil a half an hour, or until they can
be crushed by a squeeze of the thumb and finger, and they are then ready to be
poured into the baking pan, when a little brown sugar and salt may be added;
pour sufficient water in the pan to keep them from burning at the bottom, and

if the pan is covered it will prevent the beans at the top from being scorched. Bake from 3 to 4 hours.

—Hunt, *Good Bread* (1858), p. 17

The most important development in the subsequent history of New England baked beans was the addition of a sweetener to the beans (in this instance baked in a pan rather than a pot). It is ironic that one of the earliest occurrences of this innovation appears in this cookbook, which is otherwise notable for its austerity and proclaimed adherence to tradition.

17. NEW ENGLAND BAKED BEANS

Pick over and wash one quart of white beans and soak them over night in cold water; turn off the water, renew it with fresh, and boil steadily, keeping them covered with water until they begin to crack; drain and put them in the baking pot with not over half a pound of salt pork; cut the pork rind through across several times and have it a little above the beans; add two teaspoons of salt and one tablespoon of molasses; cover with water and bake slowly, all night is better; if cooked in a quick oven the water will dry away faster; keep sufficient water on them until done.

—*Aunt Mary's New England Cook Book* (1881), p. 20

Since the middle of the nineteenth century, molasses has been the sweetener of choice, as in this recipe.

Chowder

Now the dish identified more than any other with New England, chowder developed as a seagoing version of pottage, using ingredients adapted to long storage, such as hardtack (or pilot crackers, thinner than hardtack and baked until they made a crackling sound), salt pork, salt fish, and root vegetables. For the dish to become an everyday affair required a change in culinary norms. In the Anglo-American world, the end of meatless Lenten and fast days made meat and fish mixtures permissible, whether in individual dishes or bills of fare.

18. TO MAKE CHOUDER, A SEA-DISH

Take a Belly-piece of pickled Pork, slice off the fatter Parts, and lay them at the Bottom of the Kettle, strew over it Onions, and such sweet Herbs as you can procure. Take a middling large Cod, bone and slice it as for Crimping, pepper, salt, all-spice, and flour it a little, make a Layer with Part of the Slices; upon that a slight Layer of Pork again, and on that a Layer of Bisket, and so on, pursuing the like Rule, until the Kettle is filled to about four Inches; cover it with nice Paste, pour in about a Pint of Water, lute down the Cover of the Kettle, and let the Top be supplied with live Wood-embers. Keep it over a slow Fire about four Hours.

When you take it up, lay it in the Dish, pour in a Glass of hot *Madeira* Wine, and a very little *India* Pepper: If you have Oysters or Truffles, and Morels, it is still better; thicken it with Butter. Observe, before you put this Sauce in, to skim the Stew, and then lay on the Crust, and send it to Table reverse as in the Kettle; cover it close with the Paste, which should be brown.

—Glasse, *Art of Cookery* (1758), p. 368

This is one of the earliest known Anglo-American chowder recipes, appearing for the first time in the greatly expanded appendix found in this edition of Glasse. Crimping, a practice common in Glasse's day, involved cutting gashes in a living or very recently killed fish, causing the flesh to contract. Lute means to seal with "tenacious clay or cement." Clay was also used to seal chimney-side bake ovens in colonial New England.

François Pierre de la Varenne describes morels as "a kind of excellent smal red Mushrums." Mushrooms in general were rediscovered as food during the Renaissance and invariably connoted luxury.

Sealing a pint of water in the dish while at the same time covering the kettle with hot embers results in a preparation that is simultaneously steamed and baked, an interesting but now rarely used technique for the simple reason that few of us cook on open fires. The principle is retained, however, in our pot pies, preparations (explored in Chapters 10 and 11) full of stewed gravies in which solids simmer, all cooked under a steam-retaining baked crust.

India pepper is cayenne pepper (*Capsicum annuum longum*).

19. CHOUDER

Take a bass weighing four pounds, boil half an hour; take six slices raw salt pork, fry them till the lard is nearly extracted, one dozen crackers soaked in cold water five minutes; put the bass into the lard, also the pieces of pork and crackers, cover close, and fry for 20 minutes; serve with potatoes, pickles, apple-sauce or mangoes; garnish with green parsley.

—Simmons, *American Cookery* (Albany, 1796), pp. 22–23

As Richard J. Hooker points out, Simmons's bass chowder, in which the fish is first boiled, then fried in lard, and to which pieces of salt pork and a dozen sodden crackers are added, is "very dry," even "strange."

Serving a dish such as chowder with pickles, applesauce, or mangoes might also seem strange to us, but as late as 1971 Imogene Wolcott recommends serving her milk-based "Gloucester Fish Chowder" with pickles as well as common crackers. Simmons serves her roasted turkey not only with boiled onions and cranberry sauce but also with "mangoes, pickles or celery," and in the 1830s Lee (copying Dolby) concludes a stewed chicken recipe with the suggestion to "add some gherkins cut in thin slices."

20. CHOWDER

Four pounds of fish are enough to make a chowder for four or five people; half a dozen slices of salt pork in the bottom of the pot; hang it high, so that the pork may not burn; take it out when done very brown; put in a layer of fish, cut in lengthwise slices, then a layer formed of crackers, small or sliced onions, and potatoes sliced as thin as a four-pence, mixed with pieces of pork you have fried; then a layer of fish again, and so on. Six crackers are enough. Strew a little salt and pepper over each layer; over the whole pour a bowl-full of flour and water, enough to come up even with the surface of what you have in the pot. A sliced lemon adds to the flavor. A cup of tomato catsup is very excellent. Some people put in a cup of beer. A few clams are a pleasant addition. It should be covered so as not to let a particle of steam escape, if possible. Do not open it, except when nearly done, to taste if it be well seasoned.

—Child, *American Frugal Housewife* (1833), p. 59

While the kettle containing it is not stoppered with clay or covered with hot embers, Child's chowder broadly resembles Glasse's in being sealed tightly and steamed. But in other respects, it reflects the emerging nineteenth-century norm for the dish: a simple meal of layered white fish, crackers, onions, and salt pork, covered with a water-flour mixture, seasoned with salt and pepper, and boiled. With Child's "potatoes sliced as thin as a four-pence" and her "few clams" that are "a pleasant addition," we see for the first time in our selections two ingredients that were to become increasingly important in the history of chowder. The story of the beginnings of clams and potatoes in chowder recipes is a bit complex, however, and is best told in the commentary on the next recipe. A "catsup" made with tomatoes was something relatively new in Child's day. For more on ketchups, see the commentary on #36, below.

21. CHOWDER

Lay some slices cut from the fat part of a belly-piece of pork, in a deep stew-pan, mix sliced onions with a variety of sweet herbs, and lay them on the pork. Bone and cut a fresh cod into thin slices, and place them on the pork; then put a layer of pork, on that a layer of biscuit, then alternately the other materials until the pan is nearly full, season with pepper and salt, put in about a pint and a half of water, lay a paste over the whole, cover the stewpan very close, and let it stand, with fire above as well as below, for four hours; then skim it well, and put it in a dish, pour a glass of Madeira made hot over it, also some Jamaica pepper, stewed mushrooms, truffles, and oysters; brown the paste slightly, and lay it over the whole.

—Lee, *Cook's Own Book* (1832), p. 51

While this recipe is in most respects an adaptation of Glasse's pioneering "Chouder" (above, #18), it arrives in New England via Dolby's *Cook's Dictionary* (1830). A small but telling difference between Glasse and Dolby/Lee indicates that the later chowder practitioners misread or misunderstood their source: Glasse seasons her sliced but as yet uncooked cod with salt, pepper, and "all-spice," whereas Dolby/Lee add allspice (called by them by its alternate name of Jamaica pepper) at the end of the dish. Compounding the error, Dolby/Lee, who seem to mistake Jamaica pepper (allspice) for Glasse's India (capsicum or red) pepper, leave out the latter seasoning altogether. Common black pepper (*Piper nigrum*) is used to season the fresh, uncooked cod in both Glasse and Dolby/Lee. Glasse's sweet herbs, browned top paste, hot Madeira, truffles, and oysters are retained, but the archaic terms "crimping" and "luting" are removed.

There are two additional chowder recipes in Lee, taken from Kitchiner's *Cook's Oracle* (1822). In the first, also a fish chowder, sliced potatoes are introduced. In the second, clams are substituted for fish and the recipe, made in the same way as a conventional fish chowder, is now called "Clam Chowder." Kitchiner/Lee go on to remark that "many prefer" clam to fish chowder—thus we can virtually pinpoint the beginnings of the clam chowder tradition. Kitchiner was writing several years before Child, the first American to include the iconic clams and potatoes in a New England chowder. So not only was the first published recipe for any type of chowder, that of Glasse, an English one, but also the first recipes to include potatoes and clams were English ones. However, the cultural ties extended in the other direction as well. Kitchiner, taking a characteristically British pride in America's forebears, records the common report that "the pilgrims to Plymouth . . . could cook [clams] and lobsters in nearly 50 different ways, and even as puddings, pancakes, &c." With this aside, we have an Englishman adding his mite to the mythologizing of the Plymouth settlement, the bicentennial of which had just been observed. His contribution is then sent back to America and New England by way of Lee, the supposed "Boston Housekeeper." Kitchiner and Lee thus engage in the cultural reimportation trade long before rhythm and blues music was made more wildly popular than ever in America by British rockers such as the Beatles and the Rolling Stones.

22. TO MAKE A CHOWDER

Lay some slices of good fat pork in the bottom of your pot, cut a fresh cod into thin slices and lay them top of the pork, then a layer of biscuit, and alternately the other materials till you have used them all, then put in about a quart of water. Let it simmer till the fish is done; previously to its being thoroughly done add pepper, salt, and such seasoning as you like, and a thickening flour, with a coffee cup of good cream, or rich milk.

—*Roger Cookery* (1838), p. 18

Potatoes, clams, and now milk or cream. We are not, however, making steady progress toward clam chowder as we know it today, for even as the milk or cream is being added, the potatoes are being subtracted. The author does include a recipe for clam chowder, like Kitchiner/Lee merely substituting the clams for the cod: "*Clam Chowder*, is made in the same way, only the heads and hard leathery parts must be cut off."

23. FISH CHOWDER

1. Fry a large bit of well-salted pork in the kettle over the fire. Fry it thoroughly. 2. Pour in a sufficient quantity of water, and then put in the head and shoulders of a codfish, and a fine, well-dressed haddock, both recently caught. 3. Put in three or four good Irish potatoes, for which none better can be found than at Marshfield, and then boil them well together. An old fisherman generally puts in two or three onions. 4. When they are about done, throw in a few of the largest Boston crackers, and then apply the pepper and salt to suit the fancy. Such

a dish, smoking hot, placed before you, after a long morning spent in the most exhilarating sport, will make you no longer envy the gods.

—Daniel Webster (1842), quoted in Hooker, *Book of Chowder*, p. 38

This recipe was originally part of a letter from Webster to his biographer, S. P. Lyman, written at a time when the senator was sojourning at his coastal home in Marshfield, Massachusetts. Aside from the fact that it was written by the most celebrated New England politician of the day, the recipe is of interest for its rough-and-ready sportsman's aura. The potatoes are not sliced and other ingredients are casually tossed in. When, in contrast, Harriet Beecher Stowe describes chowder-making in the rough, as part of a picnic, in *The Pearl of Orr's Island* (1862), the potatoes are thinly sliced, and all ingredients are as carefully "arranged" in "alternate layers" as they would have been had the dish been prepared indoors.

24. CHOWDER

Cut some slices of pork very thin, and fry it out dry in the dinner-pot; then put in a layer of fish cut in slices, on the pork and fat, then a layer of onions, and then potatoes, all cut in thin slices; then fish, onions, and potatoes again, till your materials are all in, putting some salt and pepper on each layer of onions; split some crackers, and dip them in water, and put them around the sides and over the top; put in water enough to come up in sight; boil about half an hour, till the potatoes are done; add half a pint of milk, or a tea-cup of sweet cream, five minutes before you take it up.

—Howland, *New England Economical Housekeeper* (1845), p. 62

Mrs. Howland's 1845 chowder conforms to the standard dish as it had become codified (so to speak). Increasingly, the basic pattern included milk or cream and potatoes.

25. CLAM CHOWDER

Boil the clams until the shells open, pick them from the shell and slip the sheath from the head. All the water must be strained through a thick piece of cloth, and saved. Wash them in two or three waters. Fry out six slices of pork for one bucket of clams, also a good-sized onion. First put a layer of the pork which has been fried, then clams, then onions, salt, pepper, and crackers split; shake in considerable flour, more clams, onions, salt, pepper, and crackers. When all are in the pot, put in what water the clams were boiled in. Always be sure to save enough for this. When you boil your clams, it is best to put half a pint of water in the pot, that you may have enough to wash them with.

—Chadwick, *Home Cookery* (1853), pp. 84–85

Here is a fully rendered recipe for clam chowder. However, it remains the solid casserole we have seen repeatedly. It lacks both the potatoes and the milk or cream that were being introduced into fish chowders, although potatoes are to be found in both Chadwick's fish chowder and her second clam chowder.

26. NEW ENGLAND CHOWDER

Take a good haddock, cod, or any other solid fish, cut it in pieces three inches square; put a pound of fat, salt pork, cut into strips, into the pot; set it on hot coals and fry out the grease; take out the pork, but leave the grease in the bottom of the pot, and put in a layer of fish, over that a layer of sliced onions, over that a layer of fish, with slips of the fried pork, then another layer of onions and a few sliced raw potatoes, and so on alternately until your fish is all in; mix some flour with as much water as will fill the pot; season to suit your taste, and boil for half an hour; have ready some pilot bread, soaked in water, and throw them into your chowder five minutes before taking off; serve in a tureen.

—Turner, *New England Cook Book* (1905), p. 52

In this early-twentieth-century example, the honor of being designated the representative regional chowder is conferred, with less nostalgia and more genuine sense of history than we might have expected, on a truly traditional chowder, with salt pork, layered fish and potatoes, and "pilot bread." One of the chowders in this same book to which milk is added is not a "New England" chowder but a plain old "Fish Chowder."

27. NEW ENGLAND CLAM CHOWDER

Chop 24 large, hard-shelled clams and let stand on ice, in their own liquor. Fry ¼ pound of fine cut larding pork until crisp, add 2 quarts of boiling water, 1 cup each of diced carrot, and finely chopped onion and white stalks of celery; boil until the carrots are tender; add 4 cups of peeled potatoes cut in small pieces, ½ tablespoonful of salt, ½ teaspoonful pepper, let boil ten minutes, add 1 pint of canned tomatoes, 1 teaspoonful of thyme, cook 20 minutes, then add the clams with their liquor, thicken with 1 tablespoonful of flour rubbed into 1 tablespoonful of butter, cook 10 minutes, and serve.

—Wright, *New England Cook Book* (1912), p. 21

There could be no better illustration than this recipe that the chowder categories that most of us grew up with came into existence quite recently. It is 1912, a recipe is offered under the name "New England Clam Chowder," and not only does it leave out the milk, it puts in some tomatoes. We solemnly assure you that the author is no Manhattanite subversive. Her book is suffused with nostalgia for "the New England tradition." Larding pork is salt pork.

28. CLAM CHOWDER

Fry 4 slices of mixed salt pork until brown; add 2 onions sliced and fry.

Remove pork and onion from pork fat and add to it 4 cups water, 4 cups diced potato. Cook until potatoes are nearly done then add 4 cups of chopped clams from which all black parts have been removed. Salt and pepper to taste.

Scald 3 cups rich milk, add to first mixture. Let it all boil up once and pour into toureen in which 4 crackers have been broken, together with 1/8 pound of butter.

—Inman, *Rhode Island Rule Book* (1939), p. 11

At long last, the end of the road—a clam chowder as we in New England have "always" known it.

Soups

In the Middle Ages, all pottages were served over pieces of bread, called sops. In the case of the thinner or "running" pottages, the name of the pieces of bread eventually got transferred to the strained liquid that was poured over them. Hence, "soup," which became a fashionable dish in England toward the end of the seventeenth century. The distinction between soup and pottage was by no means hard and fast, however. The terms were treated as though synonymous in the title of a recipe ("A Soop or Pottage") in E. Smith's early-eighteenth-century best seller, *The Compleat Housewife*.

29. A POTTAGE OF BEEF PALLATS

Take Beefe Pallats after they be boyled tender in the Beefe Kettle, or Pot among some other meat, blanch and serve them cleane, then cut each Pallat in two, and set them a stewing between two Dishes with a piece of leer Bacon, an handful of Champignions, five or six sweetbreads of Veale, a Ladle-full or two of strong broth, and as much gravy of Mutton, an Onion or two, five or six Cloves, and a blade or two of Mace, and a piece of Orange Pils; as your Pallats stew, make ready your Dish with the bottoms and tops of two or three Cheat Loaves dryed and moystned with some Gravy of Mutton, and the broth your Palats stew in, you must have the Marrow of two or three beef-bones stewed in a little broth between two Dishes in great pieces; when your Pallats and Marrow iss stewed, and you['re] ready to Dish it, take out all the Spices, Onyon and Bacon, and lay it in your Plates, sweetbread, and Champigneons, pour in the Broath they were stewed in & lay on your peices of Marrow, wring the juyce of two or three Oranges; and so serve it to the Table very hot.

—*Compleat Cook* (1658, 2nd ed.), p. 34

This elaborate dish, served over pieces of dried cheat bread, a less refined wheat loaf or a mixed loaf of wheat and rye or wheat and barley (there is a recipe in Markham), is an example of the type of pottage that evolved into soup. Intensely flavored broths and gravies made of onion, mutton, and pig's cheeks ("leer Bacon"), mixed garnishes of mushrooms, sweetbreads, and marrow—all this influenced by the new-style cuisine just coming into vogue from France—are combined with more backwardlooking high spicing with cloves, mace, and orange peel, such as typified medieval court dishes.

30. ANOTHER GRAVY SOOP

Take a Leg of Beef, and a piece of the Neck, and boil it till you have all the goodness out of it; then strain it from the Meat; take half a pound of fresh Butter, and put it in a Stew-pan and brown it; then put in an Onion stuck with Cloves, some Endive, Sellary and Spinage, and your strong Broth, and Season it to your Palate with Salt, Pepper, and Spices; and let it boil together; and put in chips of *French* bread dried by the Fire, and serve it up with a *French* roll toasted in the middle.

—Smith, *Compleat Housewife* (1728), p. 2

With minor alterations, this recipe reappeared in Carter's *Frugal Housewife*. This gravy soup adopts techniques of the French *coulis*, also called cullis. Though the classic coulis was based on ham or veal, the techniques of boiling, straining, and thickening with crusts of bread can all be found a generation earlier in François Massialot's influential *Le cuisinier roïal et bourgeois* (1691), and, in Smith's time, in Vincent La Chapelle's *The Modern Cook* (1733), which ushered in the simplified *nouvelle cuisine* of the day.

31. AN EEL SOOP

Take Eels, according to the Quantity of Soop you would make, a Pound of Eels will make a Pint of good Soop; so to every Pound of Eels put a Quart of Water, a Crust of Bread, two or three Blades of Mace, a little whole Pepper, an Onion, and a Bundle of Sweet Herbs. Cover them close, and let them boil till half the Liquor is wasted; then strain it, and toast some Bread, and cut it small, lay the Bread into the Dish, and pour in your Soop. If you have a Stew-hole, set the Dish over it for a Minute, and send it to Table. If you find your Soop not rich enough, you must let it boil till it is as strong as you would have it. You may make this Soop as rich and good as if it was Meat: You may add a Piece of Carrot to brown it.

—Glasse, *Art of Cookery* (1747), p. 77 —

This and oyster soup were two of the most popular soups in the eighteenth century. As with the previous recipe, Carter copied this one. The stew-hole, a progenitor of the cast iron range (as discussed in Chapters 1 and 2), interested Thomas Jefferson, who installed one at Monticello.

32. VEAL SOUP

Take a shoulder of veal, boil in five quarts water three hours, with two spoons rice, four onions, six potatoes, and a few carrots, sweet marjorum, parsley and summersavory, salt and pepper sufficiently; half a pound butter worked into four spoons flour, to be stirred in while hot.

—Simmons, *American Cookery* (Albany, 1796), pp. 19–20

By and large, in eighteenth-century English soups, the solid matter from which the broth was obtained was not served with the soup. Rather, the broth was served over bread, as in the two preceding examples. In more elaborate soups, such as #29 above or Smith's "Soop or Pottage," other solids would be added before serving. But the meat or fish that was the basis of the broth hardly ever made it to the table.

It comes as somewhat of a surprise, therefore, that this veal soup, along with the other two soups added to the second edition of Simmons's *American Cookery,* was not strained. Although the recipe is ambiguous, it appears that fragments of boiled meat, along with broth-simmered grain and vegetables, are part of the final product. The resulting dish resembles English pottage and New England succotash more than English soup.

33. CLAM SOUP

Wash a peck of clams and boil them in a pint of water, till those on the top open and they come out easily. Strain the liquor, and add a quart of milk. When it just boils thicken with two and a half spoonfuls of flour, worked into three of butter, with pepper, mace, and other spices to your taste. It is better without spice.

—Beecher, *Domestic Receipt-Book* (1846), p. 60

A peck is equal to eight quarts. Beaten egg yolks are called for in several eighteenth-century English soups, but only a handful include milk or cream. By contrast, a respectable number of the soups in Gardiner's eighteenth-century New England manuscript collection include milk or cream. Highlighting the difference are two recipes for "Soup Meagre": Gardiner's is served with half a pint of cream; the Englishwoman, Glasse, presents hers with two beaten egg yolks as a final enrichment. The soups of nineteenth-century New England are in keeping with the pattern found in the Gardiner collection. Milk is to be added to Beecher's "Oyster Soup" just before serving, something that is never recommended in the innumerable oyster soup recipes in eighteenth-century English cookbooks. Beecher's "Clam Soup," with milk and thickened clam liquor, more closely resembles our modern New England clam chowders than do the chowders of the day, including Beecher's own. Beecher includes other recipes, such as her macaroni and giblet soups, that are more in the English tradition of strained meat or fish broth.

34. PIGEON SOUP

Of eight pigeons, cut up two and put them into four quarts of cold water, with the necks, livers and pinions of the rest; when they have simmered and boiled till the substance is extracted, strain out the soup, then restore it to the kettle with a handful of parsley, a handful of spinach, chopped and mixed with a pint of cream, in which a handful of bread crumbs have been boiled. Truss and season the pigeons with salt and a little mace, and boil them in the soup till they are tender.

—Mann, *Christianity in the Kitchen* (1857), p. 137

This recipe, offered by the wife of the Massachusetts educational reformer Horace Mann, further exemplifies the prominence of cream in the world of New England soups. Recipes for pigeon were ubiquitous in the nineteenth century, until nonstop hunting of the passenger pigeon resulted in its extinction.

Stews

In the seventeenth century and for most of the eighteenth, the term "stew" was used primarily as a verb. The earliest use as a noun in our sources is Glasse's calling her 1756 chowder (#18) "the stew." A decade later, Raffald explained how to adapt her recipe for Ox Cheek Soup so that it would "eat like stew." In our selections from nineteenth-century New England sources, only one of the recipes conforms (albeit rather imperfectly) to our modern idea of stew as a preparation of meat or fish and vegetables simmered and served in broth. To compound the confusion, that recipe (#37) is not given the name "stew." At least one nineteenth-century recipe denominated "stew" more resembles the thick, layered chowders of the day than modern stews. Most of the following recipes that are titled with verbal forms of "stew" amount to sauced meat or fish—a modern equivalent would be beef stroganoff. Clearly, our modern category stew remained elusive until quite recently.

35. TO MAKE ORDINARY STEWED BROTH

To make ordinary stewed broth, you shall take a necke of veale, or a leg or marybones [marrow bones] of beefe, or a pullet, or mutton, and, after the meat is washt put it into a pot with faire water, and being ready to boile skumme it well; then you shall take a couple of manchets and paring away the crust cut it into thicke slices and lay them in a dish, and couer them with hot broth out of the pot, when they are steept put them and some of the broth into a strainer, and straine it, and then put it into the pot; then take halfe a pound of Prunes, half a pound of Raisins, and a quarter of a pound Currants clean pickt & washt with a little whole Mace of [*sic*] and two or three brused Cloues, and put them into the pot and stirre all well together, and so let them boile till the meate be enough; then if you will alter the colour of the broth put in a little Turnsole, or red Saunders, and so serue it vp upon Sippets, and the fruit vppermost.

—Markham, *English Hus-wife* (1615), pp. 48–49

Somewhat surprisingly, this, the most antique offering in our selection, bears a greater likeness (in texture if not in taste) to stew as we now know it than do most of the following recipes, with the dried fruits, surviving from medieval cookery, playing the part of the root vegetables in modern stew. Markham's technique of soaking manchets (the best wheat bread, baked in small loaves) in broth, straining, and recombining with the stew approximates the modern use of roux to thicken soups and stews.

The term currant can confuse, being the name of both the fresh berry (white currant, black currant, red currant) of the northern temperate climes and the dried grape or tiny raisin. In the second sense, it is a corruption of "raisins of Corinth," Corinthia being the region of southern Greece where the grapes are grown and from whence they were first exported to Western Europe. Turnsole or heliotrope, a plant so named because its flowers follow the sun, produces a red or purple hue; the red sanders (sandalwood) of India was also used in both meats and sweetmeats to give a "pleasing red colour."

36. FISH TO STEW, ANOTHER WAY

Scrape your Fish very clean, then gut them, and wash them in a pint of good stale Beer, to preserve the Blood. Then boil your Fish in a little Salt and Water. In the meantime strain the Beer, and put it into a Sauce-pan, with a pint of red Wine, two or three blades of Mace, some whole Pepper, an Onion stuck with Cloves, half a Nutmeg bruised, a bundle of sweet Herbs or peice of Lemon Peel as big as an Eighth of a Dollar, an Anchovy and a little piece of Horse-radish. Stew these together softly for half an Hour, covering your Sauce pan close; then strain it, and add to it two or three Spoonsfull of Catchup, a quarter of a pound of fresh Butter, and a Spoonfull of Mushroom Pickle or Lemon Pickle or both. Set it on the Fire, and let it boil, observing to keep it stirring untill the Sauce is thick enough, adding Salt if it wants it. When your Fish are sufficiently boiled take them up and drain them in the usual Way, before the Fire; then lay them in your Dish, and pour your Sauce over them.

—Gardiner, *Family Receipts* (ca. 1770), p. 31

Martha Washington's Booke of Cookery includes a recipe for boiling a carp in its blood, in which the blood is mixed with wine. Here the blood is mixed with beer as well as wine and stewed separately from the fish itself.

Gardiner's use of citrus, wine, and anchovy, the trinity of flavors that came to dominate high-style English cuisine for a few decades after the Restoration, indicates her devotion to genteel, if somewhat dated, fare.

Ketchups (or catchups or catsups) of the period were prepared using different ingredients, not including tomatoes. Only in the nineteenth century did tomatoes gain general acceptance as a food item. When left unspecified, as in this recipe, "catchup" usually meant a thick sauce made from mushrooms, anchovies, dried oysters, or walnuts. Lemon pickle was a brew of dried lemon quarters, steeped for months in vinegar seasoned with a spice mixture.

The use of ketchup and lemon or mushroom pickle represents the eighteenth-century English gentry interpretation of noble French cuisine, made popular by Glasse and especially Raffald, in which the complicated and expensive broth or coulis that was the basis of the best French dishes is replaced with cheap, off-the-shelf flavoring poured in at the last minute.

37. CHICKEN BROTH

Cut a chicken in quarters; put it into three or four quarts of water; put in a cup of rice while the water is cold; season it with pepper and salt; some use nutmeg. Let it stew gently, until the chicken falls apart. A little parsley, shred fine, is an improvement. Some slice up a small onion and stew with it. A few pieces of cracker may be thrown in if you like.

—Child, *American Frugal Housewife* (1833), p. 55

Obviously, terminology remained fluid (so to speak), but Child's broth, with its chicken pieces, rice, and onion, is in effect a stew, reminiscent in title and overall result of Markham's "ordinary stewed broth" (#35).

38. BEEF STEWED

Take ten pounds of a brisket of beef, cut the short ribs, and put it into a saucepan, with two large onions, stuck with three or four cloves, two or three carrots cut into quarters, a bunch of sweet herbs, a small lemon sliced, and five quarts of water; skim it well; let it stew seven hours. Strain and clarify the gravy—thicken it with butter and flour. Chop the carrots with some capers, mushroom catsup, or Cayenne. Any other pickle that is liked may be added.

—Hale, *Good Housekeeper* (1841), p. 39

Hale's recipe is a lightly seasoned sauced-meat dish rather than the more liquid dish we call a stew. Essentially it is an aristocratic potage in the tradition of the French *olios* (which themselves were based on the fashionable Spanish spiced meat dish of the seventeenth century—olla podrida), bisques, and terrines (at that time, these terms connoted types of potage).

These substantial and showy dishes of mixed meats and broth were introduced to privileged English diners by Massialot; they quickly became fashionable.

Surprisingly little changed between 1698 and 1839 in terms of the basic flavors of the potage, although the French technique—and one could therefore say the overall depth and complexity of the broth—was greatly pared down by Hale's time. The continuities, however, are worth noting: in Massialot's "Bisk of Pigeons" we see an "Onion stuck with Cloves, and two Slices of Lemmon," and in Hale, "two large onions, stuck with three or four cloves" and "a small lemon sliced"; in Massialot's "Oil for Flesh-days" we find an olio of meats and seasoned broth much like Hale's ten-pound beef stew. Admittedly, Hale has streamlined the garnish, or ragout, until it is nothing but chopped carrots, capers, mushroom ketchup (see #39), or "any other pickle." Her broth is strained like the court dishes, and while at first French chefs thickened with crusts of bread, since La Chapelle cooks almost invariably used a flour roux, as Hale does.

So, despite its simplifications, Hale's stew is at least a remnant of the high style that found its way into English gentry cooking in the late seventeenth century and was carried forward by Glasse, Raffald, and other less ambivalently Francophile eighteenth-century cooks. The particular marks of this style are preferences for mixtures or made dishes over simpler roasts, the use of a large number of ingredients and a great—indeed sometimes amazing—quantity of various meats.

Finally, Hale's seasonings and garnish reflect the distinct legacy of two French chefs: la Varenne used capers and citrus juice, while Massialot relied on meat juices and lemon.

39. MUSHROOM CATSUP

4 quarts of mushrooms,	1 oz. of mace, in powder,
2 spoonfuls of salt,	1 Cayenne pepper,
4 oz. of shallots,	1 oz. of cloves, all in powder.
1 oz. of ginger,	

Wipe and clean the mushrooms, see there are none worm-eaten, sprinkle the salt in as you put the mushrooms in, and set them over a slow fire. They will produce a great deal of liquor, which you must strain, and then put in the above seasoning. Boil and skim very well. When cold, bottle and cork close. In two months boil it up again with a little fresh spice and sticks of horseradish, and it will then keep the year, which it seldom does, if not boiled the second time.

—Allen, *Housekeeper's Assistant* (1845), p. 76

Here is an example of the mushroom ketchup called for in the preceding recipe. One of the earliest recipes for the blend is found in a late-seventeenth-century English manuscript cookbook kept by the daughter of a country gentleman.

CHAPTER SIX

Fish and Shellfish

In China, fish have always been highly esteemed, not only nutritionally and gastronomically but also culturally, thought to symbolize such desirable conditions as wealth, freedom, and marital harmony and such virtues as perseverance and courage. Mostly because of guilt by association—in Europe with Lenten deprivation, in North America with the scarcities of the earliest years of English settlement, as well as with Indian "savagery"—Anglo-American attitudes toward fish have been more wary, as indicated by the fact that the English word "fishy" means worthy of suspicion.

In the mid-nineteenth century, orthodox English medical opinion held that fish "affords upon the whole, but little nourishment, and is, for the most part, of difficult digestion." Around the same time on this side of the Atlantic, Sarah Josepha Hale offered a variation on this view, asserting that there was no type of fish that had it all. Those that were easier to digest, "the white kinds" such as cod and haddock, were "the least nutritious," while those that were somewhat more nutritious, "the oily kinds" such as salmon and eels, were "more difficult to digest." Nowadays, fish are viewed more favorably, but a lingering ambivalence is perhaps suggested by the fact that while per capita poultry consumption in the United States increased by 80 percent during the quarter century beginning in 1980, per capita fish consumption during the same period increased by only 30 percent.

A regional breakdown of these figures might well produce a rather larger increase in fish consumption for New England. Certainly fish and shellfish—live boiled lobster, fried clams—have defined New England cooking for twentieth- and twenty-first-century visitors to the region. While fish did not occupy such a central culinary position much before this, there is nevertheless ample earlier testimony to a willingness to relish the region's piscatory abundance. In England—"an island surrounded by fish"—a sixteenth-century writer boasted that "of all nacyons and countres, England is best served of Fysshe, not onely of al maner of see-fysshe, but also of fresshe-water fysshe, and of al maner of sortes of salte-fysshe." Similarly in earliest New England, Edward Winslow delightedly reported from Plymouth that "Skote, Cod, Turbot, and Herring wee have tasted of; abundance of Musles the greatest & best that ever we saw; Crabs and Lobsters, in their time infinite."

Such appreciation is echoed in the multitude of fish recipes found in English and New England cookbooks during the next three centuries. So when a 1916 diner in Beverly, Massachusetts, exulted in the "magnificent tureenful of steamed clams" on which she and her sister had lunched, she was both extending an existing tradition and helping to hoist fish and shellfish to the top of the culinary pedestal, where, in New England, they are still to be found.

Eels

Most Americans today are scarcely aware of eels as an edible variety of fish, although they continue to be consumed at significant levels elsewhere, especially Japan. In medieval Europe, they were popular among all classes. Being relatively cheap, they "were probably the only fresh variety, other than shellfish, bought by poor people." On the other hand, in Italy the highest-ranking, most comfortable clergy regularly dined on eels, and in anticlerical satires "the rubicund faces of monks and canons" were made to look like fat eels. In England in the early sixteenth century, just before the Protestant Reformation, eels were a particular favorite among the monks of Westminster Abbey, with conger (saltwater) eel often making an appearance on feast days, "eaten with a sauce of bread, herbs, spices, garlic and vinegar."

Eels remained popular a century later, when Europeans began living in North America, and the English colonizers were pleased to find that they were in abundant supply in their new surroundings. Edward Winslow was as appreciative of the eels in the Plymouth area as of other species, noting that "in September we can take a Hogshead [up to 150 gallons] of Eeles in a night, with small labour, & can dig them out of their beds, all the Winter." Winslow and his compatriots undoubtedly knew what to do with all these slithery creatures once they got them into their kitchens. But for any who may have been unsure about the best procedures to follow to turn slippery fish into edible dish, published eel recipes, like eels themselves, abounded. For instance, a year after Winslow's words appeared in print, a new edition of Markham's *English Hus-wife* offered a recipe for baked eel pie. For the next two centuries and more, until the mid-nineteenth century, every cookbook used in New England or produced there offered ample instruction in eel cookery. Perhaps the selection that follows will pique your curiosity about the taste for these snake-like fish that prevailed among many generations of New Englanders.

1. TO STEW EELS

Take them without their heads, flay them and cut them in pieces, then fill a Posnet with them, and set them all on end one by one close to one another, and put in so much White Wine and Water as will cover them, then put in good store of Currans to them, whole Spice, sweet herbs, and a little Salt, cover them and let them stew, and when they are very tender, put in some Butter, and so shake them well, and serve them upon Sippets; Garnish your Dish with Orange or Limon and raw Parsley.

—Woolley, *Queen-like Closet* (1670), p. 105

A few years after the publication of Woolley's cookbook, English traveler John Josselyn reported that the best eels in the world were to be found in

New England and that as far as he was concerned the best way of cooking them was in a manner similar to the procedures outlined here. A posnet was a small pot for boiling or simmering, with a handle and three feet. Woolley frequently calls for whole spice, as in a recipe similar to this one "To boil Pigeons." Whole spice would most likely have been cloves, cinnamon, nutmeg, or combinations thereof and may or may not have been tied up in a muslin bag. In Woolley's recipe for the honey-based drink metheglin, the whole spice is tied up in a bag, whereas in the recipe for venison or hare sauce in Henry Howard's *England's Newest Way* (1710), the whole spice consists of slices of cinnamon and nutmeg and is not tied up in a bag. Unlike Howard, Woolley leaves it as understood that the whole spice is to be removed after its essence has been infused into the broth. Eels are skinned by loosening a flap of the skin at the head end (nowadays a pair of pliers is recommended for this part of the operation) and then pulling the skin apart with both hands along the middle and tail in such a way that it comes off in one tube-shaped piece.

Woolley ignores the real difficulty with eels, which is that they are "a tricky fish to kill." Kate Colquhoun says that medieval cooks skinned them alive. She also reports on a nineteenth-century approach to the business, involving "fixing it while still thrashing to a thick board with a sharp knife through the base of the skull, pulling off the skin the moment it died."

2. TO PITCHCOCK EELS

You must split a large Eel down the Back, and joint the Bones, cut it into two or three Pieces, melt a little Butter, put in a little Vinegar and Salt, let your Eel lay in two or three Minutes, then take the Pieces up, one by one, turn them round with a little fine Skewer, roll them in Crumbs of Bread, and broil them of a fine Brown. Let your Sauce be plain Butter, with the Juice of Lemon.

—Glasse, *Art of Cookery* (1747), p. 92

Except for the fact that Americans no longer eat eels, these chunks of fish—marinated, skewered, breaded, broiled "of a fine Brown," and served with lemon juice and butter—would be right at home at a contemporary backyard barbecue. "Pitchcock" is Glasse's alteration of "spitchcock," a term for the method of cooking eels described here that, according to the *OED*, was in use by 1601. In *The Whole Duty of a Woman*, from which Glasse copied this recipe, "spitchcock" is the term used. A similar-sounding word for broiling fowl, "spatchcock," in use in eighteenth-century Anglo-

Ireland, was short for "dispatch cock," meaning that the bird was cooked in a hurry, under emergency conditions. Carter copied Glasse's recipe but corrected the name back to "spitchcock," whereas Raffald offered a different recipe but replicated Glasse's variation on the name. The term survived into nineteenth-century New England, once as Lee's "spitch-cocked" and once in a yet more creative variation, Allen's "Spilchrock."

3. EELS STEWED (1)

Cut the eels into pieces about four inches long; take two onions, two shallots, a bunch of parsley, thyme, two bay leaves, a little mace, black and Jamaica pepper, a pint of good gravy, the same of Port wine, and the same of vinegar, six anchovies bruised; let all boil together for ten minutes; take out the eels; boil the sauce till reduced to a quart; strain and thicken it with a table-spoonful of flour, mixed smooth in a little cold water. Put in the eels, and boil them till they are tender. Eels may also be roasted with a common stuffing.

—Lee, *Cook's Own Book* (1832), p. 69

In a recipe copied from Dalgairns's *Practice of Cookery* (1830), Lee eliminates Woolley's currants and whole spice, relics of medieval cookery, and relies instead on the types of ingredients, seasonings, and procedures—wine, anchovies, fewer herbs and spices, broth reduced and thickened into a sauce—that indicate the French influence on English cuisine that made an early appearance in other recipes in Woolley's book and that became widespread during the eighteenth century. A recipe for roasted, stuffed eels, copied by Carter, is found in Smith.

4. TO BAKE EELS

Joint and lay them in a deep dish, with bits of salt pork, peppered and salted; cover with pounded rusked bread, and bake thirty minutes.

—Webster, *Improved Housewife* (1844), p. 72

In this austere New England form of spitchcocking, salt pork replaces butter, and the bread crumbs are spread over the top of the fish in a baking dish, rather than coating skewered chunks. Rusked bread is bread that has been hardened by additional toasting. The modern equivalents are melba toast or zweiback. Chapter 14, #20 is a recipe for an enriched type of rusk.

They should be rolled in yolk of eggs and bread-crumbs, or a thick coating of sweet herbs, and fried a pale brown. They may be served with any savory or acid sauce that may be preferred.

—Hale, *Ladies' New Book of Cookery* (1852), p. 54

Hale gives the gist of any number of nineteenth-century recipes for fried eels, all of which amount to spitchcocking in the fried rather than the broiled version. At the end of the century, under the influence of the colonial revival's elevation of humdrum colonial subsistence into nostalgic Victorian symbol, Fanny Farmer would require that the eels be coated with cornmeal and fried in pork fat.

Other Fish in the Sea (Not to Mention Rivers and Lakes)

Seventeenth-century observers such as early Salem, Massachusetts, clergyman Francis Higginson, William Wood (author of *New Englands Prospect* [1634]), and traveler John Josselyn were amazed at the abundance, variety, and dimensions of the fish in New England waters, both fresh and salt. They specifically mentioned several of the species—salmon, sturgeon, bass, halibut, cusk—included in the following selection of recipes. Salmon and sturgeon (the former a pygmy of three feet compared to the eighteen-foot, two-hundred-pound potential of the latter) had long enjoyed particularly high status in Britain, and the colonists readily partook of their hearty, pinkish-to-reddish flesh. Halibut and cusk—the one a huge flatfish capable of growing to six feet in length and six hundred pounds in weight, with flesh that could be either white or gray; the other a relative of the cod—were also known quantities but did not become particularly popular in New England until the nineteenth century. The bass seen by these observers and featured in one of our recipes was the striped bass, a native of the North American East Coast. William Wood wrote that "though men are soone wearied with other fish, yet they are never with Basse."

Of the remaining species comprising our selection, mackerel is a relatively small (one to two foot) fish whose "flashy" appearance led to its name becoming a slang term for a dandy. Its oily flesh makes it vulnerable to spoilage, so that it was as often marketed in salted as in fresh form. The name trout is used for a variety of both saltwater and freshwater species, of which the freshwater have long been especially popular in both Englands. Amelia Simmons (or whoever was responsible for the marketing advice in the first edition of her book) felt that "Salmon Trout . . . when caught under a fall or cataract . . . and hurried into dress . . . take rank in point of superiority of flavor, of most other fish."

Shad, like salmon, bass, and eel a fish that lives in both fresh and salt waters, was particularly plentiful in New England, especially Connecticut, and was therefore used for fertilizer and hog feed as well as for human consumption. Shad runs up the Connecticut River resulted in huge harvests, which is why from 1785 to 1852 the official seal of the city of Hartford depicted a catch of shad and salmon.

"Waiter, bring me shad roe," Cole Porter famously wrote, and indeed there was a time when its roe so eclipsed the shad itself that fish vendors could sell only their female shads and were forced to give away the males. But before Porter's day, in nineteenth-century New England, shad, as distinguished from its eggs, was "much-esteemed and cheap" (although its extreme boniness limited its popularity somewhat). Even in Porter's day, in the 1930s, the virtues of shad were extolled in a passage in a Soviet cookbook (there being species of shad native to the Black Sea) that Joseph Stalin himself may have authored.

These distinctive traits of particular species of fish notwithstanding, different species were often considered interchangeable in the kettle or skillet, to the point that most cookbooks included recipes for which it was claimed that any type at all would work as well as any other type. This feature of the fish cookery of colonial and nineteenth-century New England is amply represented in our selection.

6. TO ROST FRESH STURGEON

If you will roast a peece of fresh Sturgeon which is a dainty dishe, you shall first stop it all ouer with cloues, then spit it and let it roast at greate leasure, plying it continually with basting, which will take away the hardnes: then when it is enough, you shall draw it and serue it vppon Venison sauce with salt onely throwne ouer it.

—Markham, *English Hus-wife* (1615), p. 59

The recipe is similar to Markham's recipe for roasting venison, which immediately precedes it and concludes with the sauce called for here (see Chapter 8, #1). A "peece of fresh sturgeon" may have been a piece as large as five pounds, what Sandra L. Oliver calls "a sort of roast of fish."

7. TO CAVEACH FISH, AS PRACTISED IN THE WEST INDIES

Boil as much Vinegar, lowering it with Water to your Taste as you think will be sufficient for your Purpose, putting in black Pepper, mace, and Salt, and boiling all together gently. Slice as many Onions as you chuse, and fry well in the best of Olive Oyl (commonly called sweet Oyl, and Sallad Oyl). Let your Fish, which must be of the large kind cheifly, and also of those sorts which have firm, hard Flesh (In the West Indies they chiefly caveach Groupers, King Fish, Barrecooters and Hynds) be cut into Junks and fried in Oyl. When all is done put your Fish and fried Onions [in] a Jar or Stone Pot, laying first a Layer of Onions, then of fried Fish, then fried Onions, then Fish again, & so on untill all is put in. Lastly pour in your prepared Vinegar, and as much cold Oyl as you chuse. Tie Down the Pot close. . . .

In this Country, Bass and white, or silver, Perch, seem to be as proper as any Sort of Fish to caveach. The Caveached Fish will keep good six months, even in the West Indies, as I have often experienced, keeping it in a dry, cool place. It is an excellent Dish for Supper, and is allways ready to sit upon Table.

—Gardiner, *Family Receipts* (ca. 1770), p. 21

Caveach is the anglicized form of the Spanish *escabeche*, the name, in Alan Davidson's words, for "a preparation of fried fish which has been allowed to cool and is then soused with a hot marinade of vinegar and other ingredients." It is not to be confused with ceviche, which, as Davidson also explains, is "raw fish (usually fillets) marinated in lime or lemon juice with olive oil and spices." Martha Washington's manuscript cookbook includes a recipe for pickled mackerel, soles, or sprats that Karen Hess calls "a classic *escabeche* recipe." Recipes for pickled mackerel in which the terms "caveack" or "caveach" make an appearance are found in Smith and Glasse, with Glasse's recipe being essentially an amplification of Smith's. Like Gardiner, Martha Washington calls for the seasonings to be added to the marinating liquid as it boils, whereas both Smith and Glasse say to rub the seasonings into the fish. None of the other recipes includes fried onions.

Groupers are tropical fish that, in the variety found in the Caribbean, have been known to grow to a length of eight feet. As for kingfish,

Gardiner seems to have been misinformed regarding their dimensions, as they achieve a maximum length of only fifteen inches. Barracudas ("Barrecooters") can approach six feet in length. Hind fish are of the same genus as groupers, but like kingfish, they are not particularly large. The maximum length of the rock hind is two feet, that of the speckled hind 19 inches. Striped bass range in size from one to three feet. The white perch, or sea perch, is also a type of grouper. By "junks," Gardiner means chunks.

8. TO DRESS A BASS

Season high with salt, pepper and cayenne, one slice salt pork, one of bread, one egg, sweet marjoram, summersavory and parsley, minced fine and well mixed, one gill wine, four ounces butter; stuff the bass—bake in the oven one hour; thin slices of pork laid on the fish as it goes into the oven; when done pour over dissolved butter: serve up with stewed oysters, cramberries, boiled onions or potatoes.

The same method may be observed with fresh *Shad, Codfish, Blackfish* and *Salmon*.

—Simmons, *American Cookery* (Albany, 1796), pp. 21–22

Here is our first instance of what was to become a standard nineteenth-century baked stuffed fish entrée, and a delicious one it is. The salt pork is placed atop the fish during baking to prevent drying out. The amount of butter—in the stuffing and poured over at serving—is perhaps comparable to that included in or with a restaurant fish entrée today. A gill is equal to a quarter of a standard pint, or four ounces.

9. TO DRESS STURGEON

Clean your sturgeon well, parboil it in a large quantity of water till it is quite tender, then change the water and boil it till sufficiently done, then hash it as you would beef, adding the usual articles for seasoning. Some prefer it done in the form of veal cutlet, which is, by taking slices of sturgeon, dipping them in the yolks of eggs well beat, then rolled in flour and fried in butter.

—Simmons, *American Cookery* (Albany, 1796), p. 22

Just as Markham aligns his roast sturgeon recipe with his roast venison recipe (see #6), so Simmons parallels her hashed sturgeon recipe with hashed beef, for which she herself does not provide any recipes. Carter, upon whom Simmons often relies, makes her beef hash with thin slices of roast (not boiled) beef, which she adds to a sauce made with gravy, water, onion, salt, pepper, butter, capers, mushrooms, and walnut pickle or ketchup. Davidson notes that "sturgeon meat has often been compared to that of veal" and that it has therefore often been fried like veal cutlets.

10. TO BROIL SHAD

Take a fresh shad, salt and pepper it well, broil half an hour; make a smoke with small chips while broiling, when done add butter, and wine if agreeable.

Salmon or any kind of fresh fish may be prepared in the same manner.

—Simmons, *American Cookery* (Albany, 1796), p. 22

In hearth cooking, broiling involved "rubbing the gridiron with a bit of fat and heating it before the open fire" before placing the fish or meat on the heated iron and the iron over the fire. A gridiron was "a framework of parallel metal bars" that was either handheld or rested on three legs.

The recommendation of smoking during broiling we have not found replicated elsewhere. Davidson reports that in Ghana "a kind of shad called bonga is smoked and cooked (indeed, often burnt black) in simple kilns made from oil drums."

11. TO ROAST A SHAD

Fill the inside with good force meat; sew it up; tie it on a suitable board, (not pine;) cover it with bread crumbs, a little salt, and pepper, and place it before the fire; when done one side, turn it; and when sufficiently done, pull out the thread; dish it; and serve it out with drawn butter and parsley.

—Webster, *Improved Housewife* (1844), p. 68

Webster's own recipe for fish stuffing—bread, butter, salt, pepper, eggs, spices—is less interesting than the one given by Simmons, above #8. According to Oliver, writing in the 1990s, Webster's recommended method of cooking the shad "before a fire supported by a piece of wood"— in other words, planked shad—was not widely practiced in New England until "recent decades." Hardwoods are recommended for plank cookery, so pine, decidedly a softwood, would not qualify. The fact that Webster feels the need to explain such an elementary point of plank cookery perhaps supports Oliver's view. However, another exception to the argument that planked shad is a quite recent development is Fannie Farmer's recipe for an oven version of "Planked Shad or Whitefish."

12. MACKEREL

Mackerel is fine well broiled, having been split open and salted, peppered, and strewed with summer savory, and parsley, or fennel. Or boiled with salt and served with drawn butter and fennel. Or, baked with a stuffing of crumbs and fennel, chopped fine. If they are barrelled, they should be laid in water to freshen, until they will answer to broil; then let them hang and dry a little, broil and spread with butter.

—Allen, *Housekeeper's Assistant* (1845), p. 129

Allen applies the standard broiling, boiling, and baking instructions to mackerel, although she innovates slightly with her use of fennel. Note the concluding acknowledgment of the prevalence of salted mackerel.

13. FRESH SALMON, BOILED

From the middle of a salmon weighing sixteen or eighteen pounds, take four pounds, wash it carefully, rub the inside with salt, tie it up in a cloth, and boil it slowly forty minutes; when half cooked turn it over in the pot,—serve with egg sauce, or drawn butter and parsley.

If any remains from dinner, pour one tea-cup of vinegar into two table-spoonfuls of the liquor in which the fish was boiled, heat it scalding hot and pour it over the salmon. This makes a fine relish for breakfast. Or you may mince the fish with potato, as minced cod.

—Bliss, *Practical Cook Book* (1850), p. 36

As we have already to an extent seen, melted or drawn butter and parsley was poured over every type of fish after every type of cooking. As we shall see, egg sauce was more likely to accompany cod than anything else, and for Bliss cod is indeed the default fish. This is indicated here by the concluding recommendation of salmon-potato cakes on the model of codfish cakes or balls.

14. TO FRY FISH

Fry some slices of salt pork, say a slice for each pound, and when brown take them up, and add lard enough to cover the fish. Skim it well, and have it hot, then dip the fish in flour, without salting it, and fry a light brown. Then take the fish up, and add to the gravy a little flour paste, pepper, salt; also wine, catsup, and spices, if you like. Put the fish and pork on a dish, and, after one boil, pour this gravy over the whole.

Fish are good dipped first in egg and then in Indian meal, or cracker crumbs and egg, previous to frying.

—Beecher, *Domestic Receipt-Book* (1846), p. 63

Beecher provides two alternative coatings for fried fish. Either way, whether the fish is coated in flour or in meal/crumbs and egg, it is to be fried in a considerable amount of hot fat, although not so much and so hot as to be deep fat.

15. CUSK, À LA CRÈME

A cusk, cod or haddock, weighing five or six pounds; one quart of milk, two ta-ble-spoonfuls of flour, one of butter, one small slice of onion, two sprigs of parsley, salt, pepper. Put the fish on in boiling water enough to cover, and which contains one table-spoonful of salt. Cook gently twenty minutes; then lift out of the water, but let it remain on the tray. Now carefully remove all the skin and the head; then turn the fish over into the dish in which it is to be served (it should be stone china), and scrape off the skin from the other side. Pick out all the small bones. You will find them the whole length of the back, and a few in the lower part of the fish, near the tail. They are in rows like pins in a paper, and if you start all right it will take but a few minutes to remove them. Then take out the back-bone, starting at the head and working gently down toward the tail. Great care must be taken, that the fish may keep its shape. Cover with the cream, and bake about ten minutes, just to brown it a little. Garnish with parsley or little puff-paste cakes; or, you can cover it with the whites of three eggs, beaten to a stiff froth, and then slightly brown.

To prepare the cream: Put the milk, parsley and onion on to boil, reserving half a cupful of milk to mix with the flour. When it boils, stir in the flour, which has been mixed smoothly with the cold milk. Cook eight minutes. Season highly with salt and pepper, add the butter, strain on the fish, and proceed as directed.

— Parloa, *Miss Parloa's New Cook Book* (1882), pp. 112–13

In this gastronomic nullity, genteel appearance is all, from deboning the fish in such a way that it "may keep its shape," to piling the whiteness of frothed egg whites on top of the whiteness of a cream sauce that has been browned "just a little," on top of the whiteness of the skinned cusk, cod, or haddock itself. The age-old (in the West) preference for paleness in food—seen among other places in the realms of bread and sweeteners, and which Oliver informs us also governed the attitudes of nineteenth-century New Englanders toward fish—here achieves what must surely be its ultimate expression.

16. BAKED HALIBUT WITH TOMATOES

Take two pounds of halibut cut out as a steak; lay in a baking dish. Cover with layer of stewed tomatoes; then a layer of bread crumbs, butter, pepper, and salt; last of all, layer of tomatoes. Bake in hot oven twenty minutes.

—*Durham Cook Book* (1898), pp. 18–19

Well into the nineteenth century, tomatoes were included among the fresh fruits and vegetables that languished in city markets because of a suspicion that the consumption of summer produce was somehow associated with the higher incidence in summertime of dreaded communicable diseases such as cholera. Gradually, especially when cooked, tomatoes gained in popular acceptance, although the absolute passion for them among Americans did not become full blown until the twentieth century. For additional discussion, see Chapter 12, #13.

17. STEWED TROUT

Clean and wash the fish with care, and wipe it perfectly dry; put into a stewpan two tablespoonfuls of butter, dredge in as it melts a little flour, grate half a nutmeg, a few blades of mace, a little cayenne, and a teaspoonful of salt; mix it all together; then lay in the fish, let it brown slightly; pour over some veal gravy, a lemon thinly sliced; stew very slowly for forty minutes; take out the fish, and add two glasses of wine to the gravy. Lay the fish on a hot dish, and pour over it some of the gravy. Serve the rest in a sauce-tureen.

—Turner, *New England Cook Book* (1905), pp. 50–51

In ingredients and seasonings, this resembles much earlier recipes for stewed fish (see #1); it differs in utilizing the standard modern stewing sequence in which the main ingredient is browned in fat and seasonings before being simmered in liquid.

The Oyster: That Charming Bivalve

Of the four shellfish—lobsters, clams, oysters, scallops—that are central to the modern New England self-image (as well as to its tourist industry), oysters are the only one whose popularity is not a relatively recent development. "He was a bold Man that first eat an Oyster," Jonathan Swift has one of the characters in his *Polite Conversation in Three Dialogues* remark. But once that first bold move was made, there ensued "a vast and widespread consumption of this food by prehistoric man." Abundant in the Mediterranean, oysters were already a favorite of the Romans at the time of the conquest of Britain. "The palm and pleasure of the table," the naturalist Pliny the Elder called them, and Britain was soon added to the roster of locales called upon to satisfy the oyster lust of Rome itself.

Throughout the Middle Ages, oysters, along with other shellfish, remained relatively cheap and so were regularly eaten by the poorer people of London. Yet being cheap and common was not held against oysters as it was against other foods. Both royal and aristocratic households supplied themselves liberally with them.

The English love of oysters had not abated at the time of the colonization of North America. In a 1630s fish day feast menu, the first two courses are monopolized by stewed oysters, pickled oysters, fried oysters, and oyster pie. The species of oyster inhabiting the eastern coast of North America (*Crassostrea virginica*) was larger than the type with which the colonists were familiar (*Ostrea edulis*) but was nevertheless reported to be "fully as good," and oysters quickly became part of the colonial diet.

The nineteenth century was the great age of oyster consumption in the United States. In New York City in 1859, more was spent on oysters than on butchers' meat. Indeed, the demand for this item was such that in many urban areas it generated "the first freestanding restaurants in the nation"—oyster houses or saloons, some catering to a wealthy clientele, others of a more rough-and-ready character that were essentially lunchtime fast-food joints. Oysters could also be purchased at virtually any time from street vendors, and such peddlers also brought oysters, "packed in small wooden kegs, or in tin containers surrounded with ice," to people in rural and inland districts who were just as eager for them as were their city and coastal cousins.

The nineteenth-century demand for oysters ultimately could not be satisfied, with overfishing leading, despite efforts to replant depleted beds with oysters from elsewhere, and despite the development of methods of oyster cultivation, to a greatly reduced supply. The U.S. oyster harvest at the end of the twentieth century was less than a third of what it had been a century earlier. For those who agree with Karen Hess and Eleanor Clark (and disagree with the early European oyster eaters quoted above) that *Crassostrea virginica* is distinctly inferior to *Ostrea edulis* (the latter has to the former "the relation of love to tedium" is the way Clark puts it), this is perhaps just as well. On the other hand, M. F. K. Fisher makes no invidious comparisons along these lines, and more recently

Rowan Jacobsen has offered a gastronomic survey of American oysters, demonstrating that they run the full gamut from delectable to ho-hum. Moonstone oysters from Point Judith Pond, in Rhode Island, for example, not far from where we live, have, he says, "that full body; the taste fills your mouth with minerals and brothy . . . richness."

Jacobsen means to evoke here only the experience of eating such an oyster raw, on the half shell, of course, but he also states that it is possible to cook oysters properly, in such a way that "their essence survives." Fisher's view is that the farther south one travels in the continental United States, the "less interesting" become the oysters "served in the shell." They "almost cry out for such decadences as horseradish or even cooking, which would be sacrilege in Boston or Bordeaux." Certainly neither Fisher nor Jacobsen would endorse Hess's claim that the American oyster in general is "fatter and blander" than the European. So maybe all those nineteenth-century New Englanders happily frequenting oyster saloons, or making oysters at home in the myriad ways that cookbooks and tradition explained they could be made, weren't heading down the wrong culinary path after all. We invite you to try some of the following recipes and find out for yourself.

18. TO STEW OYSTERS, AND ALL SORTS OF SHELL FISH

When you have opened your Oysters, put their Liquor into a Tossing Pan, with a little beaten Mace, thicken it with Flour and Butter, boil it three or four Minutes, toast a Slice of white Bread, and cut it into three-cornered Pieces, lay them round your Dish, put in a Spoonful of good Cream, put in your Oysters, and shake them round in your Pan, you must not let them boil, for if they do it will make them hard and look small, serve them up in a little Soup Dish or Plate.

N. B. You may stew Cockles, Muscles or any Shell Fish the same Way.

—Raffald, *Experienced English House-keeper* (1769), p. 31

The sequence of events here isn't particularly clear, since it seems as though the carefully shaped and positioned pieces of toast are then to be rudely jostled around in the same tossing pan (sauté pan) in which the seasoned and thickened oyster liquor has already been simmering. Probably Raffald elides the steps explained more clearly in a similar recipe that Lee copied from Kitchiner: the cream is stirred into the simmering oyster liquor until the mixture is smooth, the oysters are added but (as here) not allowed to boil, the pieces of toast are placed in the serving dish, and the oysters and sauce are poured over them. Note the concern with appearance—the three-cornered pieces of toast, the overcooked oysters that will not only be impaired for eating but will also "look small."

19. ESCALOPED OYSTERS

Put crumbled bread around the sides and bottom of a buttered dish. Put oysters in a skillet, and let the heat just strike them through; then take them out of the shells, and rinse them thoroughly in the water they have stewed in. Put half of them on the layer of crumbled bread, and season with mace and pepper; cover them with crumbs of bread and bits of butter; put in the rest of the oysters, season and cover them in the same way. Strain their liquor, and pour over. If you fear they will be too salt, put fresh water instead. Bake fifteen or twenty minutes.

—Child, *American Frugal Housewife* (1833), p. 120

This recipe, part of the appendix to Child's book that did not appear in the earliest editions, was the mother of all the scalloped (or escalloped or scolloped) oyster recipes that would be found in virtually every cookbook produced in nineteenth-century New England. (Toward the end of the century, recipes for scalloped clams also began to appear.) The term derives from the French *escalope* or *eschalop*, which meant both (and this would be a source of confusion) a shell and a slice of meat. In the latter signification, it emerged into English cookery early on as collops and eggs (a form of bacon and eggs) and Scotch collops (thin slices of meat in sauce). Escaloped or scalloped denoting something, usually oysters, cooked with buttered bread crumbs in shells or shell-shaped dishes was a usage that arose in the eighteenth century. The *OED* cites an occurrence of scalloped or scolloped as a verb in this cookery sense from 1737. However, Smith refers to "scollop'd Oysters" earlier than this, in the preliminary menu section of her 1728 (2nd) edition, although there is no such recipe within the book itself (in the menu section of a later edition, Smith lists "Scolloped Lobsters" as well, again with no actual recipe provided later). Glasse introduces further confusion by giving the name "Collups of Oysters" to her recipe for broiled oysters and buttered bread crumbs in "Scollop-shells." (Gardiner copied this recipe, altering the name to "Scolloped Oysters.") Raffald's recipe, "To scollop Oysters," in which the oysters, bread crumbs, and butter are layered in "scolloped shells" and then baked in a Dutch oven, may have been Child's source.

Child's explanation for stewing and rinsing the oysters may seem confusing. Raffald also is not particularly clear about this step: "wash them out of their own Liquor." However, John Thorne explains the same process with respect to clams: "Remove clams from their shells, holding them over a bowl so all liquid is saved . . . rinse the clams in their own juices, reserving them in a separate dish. Then let those juices settle until the grit falls to the bottom."

For her economically stretched readers, Child omits the requirement of the shell-shaped baking and serving vessels. Perhaps she felt that a sufficient aura of elegance was produced by the antiquated form "escaloped" in the name of the dish.

20. TO FRY OYSTERS

Select the fattest of large size, dip them in beaten eggs, then in flour, or fine bread crumbs; fry them in lard till of a light brown. They are a fine garnish for calves' head, fish, or most modern dishes.

—Webster, *Improved Housewife* (1844), p. 74

The basic fish frying methodology applied to oysters. Beecher offers a variation in which the oysters are dipped in a batter consisting of their own liquor, flour, and eggs. What Webster means by "modern dishes" is anyone's guess, and it's unfortunate that those calves together have only one head.

21. OYSTERS, ROASTED

Select single oysters in the shell, and put them, with the rounded side down, upon a gridiron and over a sharp fire. They will roast in a very short time. Send them to the table in the shell, with coffee, cold-slaw, and fresh bread and butter.

—Bliss, *Practical Cook Book* (1850), p. 39

Another item that could easily be added to today's backyard or "in the rough" restaurant repertoire. Beecher offers similar advice. Roasting shellfish in their shells dates from prehistoric times; in Britain, larger-sized oysters have been cooked by roasting since at least the sixteenth century. Like most oyster aficionados, Rowan Jacobsen basically disapproves of cooking them. His book nevertheless includes a section of recipes, one of which is for an "Oyster Roast," to be executed either outdoors on a grill or indoors in an oven.

Clams

Among shellfish, clams are often paired with mussels, but the latter have been a much more significant presence in world cuisine. Think of the mussels being shown off in their half-opened shells in paella. Clams on the other hand, though they inhabit the European as well as the North American side of the Atlantic, have rarely been consumed in Britain (when at all, by the poor) and only a bit more frequently elsewhere in Europe. Though mussels were in ill repute along with clams in early New England, both, as noted, being associated with the scarcities of initial settlement, as well as with the diet of the "savage" natives, it was only clams that bore the additional stigma of being, as William Wood reported, "a great commoditie for the feeding of Swine."

Recipes for mussels appear in English medieval cookbooks, as well as in the cookbooks in use in colonial New England. Clams, on the other hand, did not make their print debut until the early nineteenth century, in American imprints of English cookbooks. The first American author to deal with clams was Child, whose advice is given below.

Clams gained somewhat in prestige in the course of the nineteenth century, mostly in coastal New England and in great part due to the emergence of the festival known as the clambake. "O the sweetness of winter clams—they taste as if boiled in sugar," exclaimed one Connecticut clammer of the 1870s.

Of the varieties of clam, the hard-shell or round, also called quahogs, are often eaten raw (cherrystones) or used (the largest ones) in clam chowder, while soft-shell or long clams are almost always steamed or fried. Bowls of clam chowder and heaping plates of steamers and fried clams are key among the images used to promote New England tourism. That such efforts have met with considerable success is implied by the assertion that "most soft-shell clams are consumed 'within five miles of the coast from Boston to Bar Harbor, Maine.'" Clam chowder, steamed clams, and fried clams are inventions of the twentieth century, but their prehistory can be discerned in the following recipes from an earlier day.

22. CLAMS

Clams should boil about fifteen minutes in their own water; no other need be added, except a spoonful to keep the bottom shells from burning. It is easy to tell when they are done, by the shells starting wide open. After they are done, they should be taken from the shells, washed thoroughly in their own water, and put in a stewing pan. The water should then be strained through a cloth, so as to get out all the grit; the clams should be simmered in it ten or fifteen minutes; a little thickening of flour and water added; half a dozen slices of toasted bread or cracker; and pepper, vinegar and butter to your taste. Salt is not needed.

—Child, *American Frugal Housewife* (1833), pp. 58–59

The procedure for rinsing the clams is explained above in the commentary on a recipe for oysters (#19). Recipes varying from this one only in some details are found in Webster, Beecher, Bliss, and Chadwick. Bliss states that long clams and small round clams—in other words, soft-shelled clams and cherrystones—are best for this procedure, which, at least as far as the specification of soft-shelled clams is concerned, puts us on the road to steamed clams. Steamers as we know them today are made simply by boiling the clams as Child directs at the outset of her recipe (although with the pot or kettle tightly covered), straining the resulting broth, and serving the clams in their shells, accompanied by the broth and melted butter in separate little cups. The clams are removed from their shells by the diner, not the cook, rinsed one by one in the broth, and dipped in the butter before being "ingurgitated," as one modern writer puts it. In this writer's recipe, as in Child's, there is the option of mixing vinegar with the melted butter.

23. TO ROAST CLAMS.—SUPERIOR MODE OF COOKING THEM

Select according to taste as to size, (those with thin edges are the tenderest, never buy those of a *thick* edge,) wash them clean, place them flatwise in an old tin or iron pan, so as to save the liquor, and set the pan over a furnace of ignited coal. As they become sufficiently roasted, take them out singly, empty the liquor of each into your dish, then take out and add the clam, either cut in pieces or whole; add butter, salt, and pepper; other seasoning to taste.

—Webster, *Improved Housewife* (1844), p. 73

Beecher and Bliss offer almost identical recipes, Beecher admonishing to keep the salt to a minimum, Bliss (like Child with simmered clams) omitting it altogether. Bliss states that large quahogs, the kind now used primarily for chowder, are the ones that are the most suitable for roasting, and she recommends eating the roasted clams from their shells.

24. TO FRY HARD-SHELL CLAMS

Take the large sand clams; wash them in their own liquor; beat well the yolks of 4 eggs with a little pepper and a table-spoonful of fine flour. Dip in the clams and fry them in butter a light brown.

—Hale, *Ladies' New Book of Cookery* (1852), p. 63

This is one of the few recipes for fried clams before the twentieth century. As compared with such later recipes (see below, #s 26–27 and commentary), one difference is that Hale makes quahogs rather than soft-shelled clams the default choice for frying. Hale later says to fry soft-shelled clams the same way as stipulated here. The other, more significant way that Hale's recipe differs from the later ones is that she proposes a much lighter batter. The clams are to be lightly coated in flour and egg yolk and fried in butter, in a manner similar to what we have seen, in some cases from Hale herself, in other recipes for frying fish or shellfish; see #s 5 and 20. With the later fried clams, the batter contains much more flour as well as a good deal of milk, and they are deep-fat fried, producing the crustier, crispier result with which we are today familiar.

Among Hale's contemporaries, Beecher comments that "clams are good put into a batter and fried," but she does not elaborate. In Leslie's 1847 recipe for clam fritters, the clams are minced "as fine as possible," then mixed into the batter, so the dish is not really recognizable as fried clams. It amounts, rather, to clam-studded fried dough, which today is a Rhode Island specialty, the stuffie. Like Hale, Leslie makes her clam fritters with what she calls sand clams.

25. STEAMED CLAMS

Select clams in the shell, wash and scrub thoroughly, and change the water until clean. Put them in a kettle with a pint of water for half a peck of clams. Cover tightly and cook them until the shells open. Take out the clams, pour off the liquor carefully into a pitcher, and let it stand until clear, then pour off again from the sediment. Serve the clams in the shell with cups of the broth and small dishes of melted butter.

—Lincoln and Barrows, *Home Science Cook Book* (1911), p. 122

Here are steamed clams made according to the best-known formula, exactly as relished by countless New Englanders and tourists in the century since this recipe appeared. In subsequent instructions regarding the steaming broth, the authors state that the broth may be served "with a garnish of whipped cream." But a later writer comments that "to the true *cognoscente* this is superfluity."

26. FRIED CLAMS

Remove steamed clams from the shells, taking off the thin membrane on the edge and the black heads. Rinse thoroughly, dry on a cloth, dip in batter . . . and fry.

—Lincoln and Barrows, *Home Science Cook Book* (1911), p. 122

27. FRITTER BATTER

Two eggs, one-half cup of milk, one cup of flour, one saltspoon of salt, one teaspoon of sugar, one tablespoon of oil or melted butter. . . . separate the yolks and whites of the eggs[, mix the yolks with the other ingredients, beat the . . . mixture together until smooth,] and fold in the whites last. One teaspoon of baking powder may be added and one egg left out.

The yolks of the eggs are sometimes omitted. . . . One tablespoon of lemon juice or vinegar often is added to the batter for meat or fish.

—Lincoln and Barrows, *Home Science Cook Book* (1911), pp. 90–91

Other recipes for twentieth-century crusty, crisp fried clams and clam fritters utilize essentially this batter; in some, both contemporaneous with Lincoln and Barrows and later, the liquor from the clams is mixed in. Salt spoons vary in size, but they tend to be small. Probably one-quarter teaspoon of salt, at most, is being called for.

Lobsters

Part of the British diet at least since Roman times, lobsters have enjoyed a status that, while never as exalted as that of oysters, has never been less than respectable. As we've already heard from Edward Winslow, early observers included lobsters on their exclamatory rosters of the New England region's fish plenitude. Francis Higginson also remarked on their (to him) unusually large size, an attribute he associated with their capacity to satisfy his appetite: "I was soone cloyed with them, they were so great, and fat, and luscious."

Some have dissented from this positive assessment. William Bradford spoke apologetically about how during the early years in Plymouth, the "best dish" that could be offered by way of hospitality was "a lobster or a piece of fish without bread or anything else but a cup of fair spring water." Two and a half centuries later, a Connecticut lobsterman opined that "lobsters are very good as an article of commerce, and pretty enough to look at, after they're b'iled; but as to eating them, I prefer castoff rubber shoes."

In both these cases, distaste is readily explained away as arising from the contempt that familiarity breeds, accentuated in early Plymouth by the lack of alternatives. Most people enjoyed lobsters as fully as had Francis Higginson, and a steady demand for them soon developed. Live lobsters were being shipped to New York by the 1740s, and colonial readers of English cookbooks were instructed in a variety of forms of lobster cookery. Glasse offers a recipe she calls "a Fine Dish of Lobsters" that involves an elaborate presentation producing "if nicely done . . . a pretty Dish." Gardiner has five lobster recipes, one (for potted lobster, a dish in vogue in England since the seventeenth century) copied from Raffald, another (for lobster pie) copied from Glasse.

In the middle of the nineteenth century, Webster ranked lobster alongside salmon as the two most popular forms of aquatic sustenance in the United States, and her impression is substantiated, as far as lobster is concerned, by a modern analysis that concludes there are as many recipes for lobster in nineteenth-century cookbooks as there are for cod, salt cod, and generic fish. Such a level of demand is further indicated by the continued supply of such cities as New York and Boston with lobsters both live and preboiled.

The sale of preboiled lobsters in Boston is attested by 1832, and as Oliver points out, "cooking lobsters for market paved the way for canning." From the 1840s until the end of the nineteenth century, a lobster canning industry flourished along the Maine coast and in the Canadian Maritime Provinces. Canned lobster was also produced in nineteenth-century Britain. During the Sepoy Mutiny in India in the 1850s, a box of "regimental stores" of the British Army came into the possession of the mutineers, "who thinking that a great capture of some kind of deadly and destructive ammunition had been made, rammed the painted tin cases, with goodly charges of powder behind them, into their immense guns, laid them steadily on the . . . British troops, and then with a flash and a thundering roar, preserved lobster, from Fortnum and Mason's, was scattered far and wide over the battlefield."

This incident did not (at least not all by itself) put the lobster canning industry on the skids, but on the skids the industry did indeed eventually find itself. Canned lobster was not manufactured in New England after 1895. It was eventually replaced, as we all know, by a renewed emphasis on live lobster, which was now defined as vastly superior when it was boiled in the kitchen of the home or restaurant where it was to be consumed. The idea that this supreme item must be obtained only from the coast of Maine is, as Davidson says, owing to "the hard work put in by Maine publicists." In fact, "the Canadian catch is more than twice the size of the United States one, and the southern part of the Gulf of St. Lawrence is the richest lobster-breeding ground in the world."

As we shall see, boiling had long been one of the primary ways not only of preparing lobster for sale but also of cooking it for eating. But no particular fuss had ever been made about this. It took the marketing genius of the twentieth century—more hard work by those Maine publicists—to accomplish the makeover whereby the "bright scarlet" of the preboiled lobsters filling the stalls of nineteenth-century Boston fish markets became the "cardinal's hat" hue of the dainty-dish crustaceans set before the king-for-a-meal diners of contemporary New England. This metamorphosis was not really accomplished until after the period from which we are drawing our selections. But as with clams, the diverse elements that contributed to it had long been part of the Anglo-American culinary repertoire, as this next set of recipes will show.

28. TO ROAST LOBSTERS

Tie your Lobsters to the Spit alive, baste them with Water and Salt till they look very red, and are enough; then baste them with Butter and Salt, take them up, and set little Dishes round with the Sauce, some plain melted Butter, some Oyster Sauce.

—Smith, *Compleat Housewife* (1732), p. 25

In a similar recipe by Woolley, the oyster sauce consists of stewed oysters, anchovies, and melted butter. When eaten with the plain melted butter instead of with the oyster sauce, Smith's roasted lobsters (and Woolley's

as well), cooked alive "till they look very red," have most of the properties of modern live boiled lobster. Indeed, Glasse's recipe for roast lobsters
recommends boiling them, then placing them "before the Fire," then
serving them with plain melted butter: "This is as good a Way to the
full as roasting them, and not half the Trouble." Raffald concurs. This
adoption of a method of boiling prior to roasting may have been due not
only to convenience but also to having had the experience of the meat
turning mushy when the fire didn't cook the lobster fast enough. Harold
McGee explains that because of this danger—caused by the particular
nature of crustacean muscle fiber—"boiling and steaming," being "the
most rapid heating methods," are now "the usual treatments for shrimp,
lobster, and crab."

29. LOBSTER SALAD

The meat of one lobster is extracted from the shell, and cut up fine. Have fresh
hard lettuce cut up very fine; mix it with the lobster. Make a dressing, in a deep
plate, of the yolks of four eggs cut up, a gill of sweet oil, a gill of vinegar, half a gill
of mustard, half a teaspoonful of cayenne, half a teaspoonful of salt; all mixed
well together. To be prepared just before eaten. Chicken salad is prepared in the
same way, only chicken is used instead of lobster, and celery instead of lettuce.

—Child, *American Frugal Housewife* (1833), p. 120

Like Child's escaloped oysters, this recipe is not found in the earliest
editions of her book. The dressing is mayonnaise in all but name, and
the dish could easily be served up on a toasted hot dog roll at a modern
tumbledown roadside seafood eatery.

30. LOBSTER FRICASSEE

Break the shells, and take out the meat carefully, cut it and the red part, or coral,
into pieces, adding the spawn; thicken with flour and butter some white stock,
with which the shells have been boiled; season it with white pepper, mace, and
salt, put in the lobster and heat it up; just before serving, add a little lemon-juice,
or lemon pickle. The stock may be made with the shells, only boiled in a pint
of water, with some white pepper, salt, and a little mace, thickened with cream,
flour, and butter.

—Lee, *Cook's Own Book* (1832), p. 111

This recipe, taken from Dalgairns, is similar to Raffald's for stewing
"Oysters, and All Sorts of Shell Fish" (#18), with the stock made from

the shells the equivalent of the oyster liquor used by Raffald. Harold McGee notes that "the shells of lobsters, crayfish, and some crabs are often cooked to extract both flavor and color for sauces . . . soups, and aspics." The coral is the ovary of the female lobster (again quoting McGee), "a mass containing thousands of 1–2 mm eggs, which turns red-pink when cooked; hence its name 'coral.'" Along with its eggs (here called "the spawn"), the coral also contributes color and flavor to a lobster dish. Subsequent recipes for stewed lobster in Bliss, Chadwick, and Mendall offer minor variations on the theme. Instead of the coral, Mendall says to put in "the green meat of the lobster," by which she means the liver or tomalley. The elements of Lobster Newburg can be found scattered among these recipes: take the butter from them all, the creamy sauce from Raffald and Dalgairns/Lee, the coral from the latter, the tomalley from Mendall, the sherry or port also from Mendall, and the serving over toast from Raffald.

31. LOBSTERS AND CRABS

Have your water boil, put in and boil them from thirty to forty-five minutes. Boil six spoonfuls of salt to every four pounds of fish. When cold, break the shell, take out the meat, be cautious to extract the blue veins, and what is called the lady in the lobster; these are very unhealthy.

Eat cold with a dressing of vinegar, mustard, sweet oil, salt and cayenne; or warm them up with a little water, vinegar, salt, pepper; and add a rich gravy and grated nutmeg, if liked. . . .

—Webster, *Improved Housewife* (1844), p. 72

In a tradition perhaps based on experience of the behavior of lobster meat during cooking (see #28 commentary), boiling, in plain water or brine, and eating cold, dressed with vinegar, had long been the most prevalent form of lobster cookery and consumption in Britain. Raffald's recipe for boiled lobster says to salt the water (and also to "put a skewer in the vent of the tail to prevent the water getting into the body of the lobster"), but gives no directions regarding subsequent dressing and eating. Beecher likewise says nothing about what is to happen after boiling is completed. Perhaps they both take it for granted that boiled lobster is to be eaten cold. The "lady in the lobster" is, according to Betty Fussell, "the stomach sac near the head."

32. BOILED LOBSTER

To properly boil lobsters, throw them living into a kettle of fast-boiling salt and water, that life may be destroyed in an instant. Let them boil for about half an hour. When done, take them out of the kettle, wipe them clean, and rub the shell with a little salad-oil, which will give a clear red appearance. Crack the large claws without mashing them, and with a sharp knife split the body and tail from end to end. The head, which is never eaten, should also be separated from the body, but laid so near it that the division is almost imperceptible. Dress in any way preferred.

—Turner, *New England Cook Book* (1905), p. 57

The concluding open-mindedness regarding dressing indicates that the twentieth-century orthodoxy of melted butter has not yet taken hold. Raffald similarly counsels rubbing after boiling with "a Lump of Butter in a Cloth," which will "strike the Colour and make it look bright." A concern with appearance, also evident here in the insistence that decapitation be disguised, seems to have been a major theme in Anglo-American lobster cookery. We have heard it expressed by Glasse and Raffald, as well as in this recipe. Much earlier, however, the lobster's appearance could be cause for concern of another sort. One seventeenth-century English satirist has his canting Puritan preacher intone that "Lobsters seeme to be in red coats like Cardinals."

Cod

Inhabiting the North Atlantic from the vicinity of the Arctic down the western coast of Europe to the Bay of Biscay and down the eastern coast of North America to Cape Hatteras, the cod is a bottom-dwelling fish that can grow to a length of more than six feet and a weight of more than one hundred pounds. It feeds primarily on other fish and crustaceans but is famed for its propensity to ingest just about anything. English fishermen of our day have reported finding Styrofoam cups in the bellies of cod they have caught. A nineteenth-century sea captain retrieved his keys from a codfish's stomach a few days after and "very many miles distant from where . . . he had dropped them overboard from a North Sea trawler." A "book in three treatises" was removed from a cod captured "on Midsummer-eve, 1626." The volume was eventually presented to the vice chancellor of Cambridge University.

There is no other fish that even begins to approach the importance of cod in the economic history of Europe and North America. In the Middle Ages, Roman Catholic dietary rules meant that large supplies of cheap preserved fish were needed to feed the people of Europe. Cod, available in abundance and adapting readily to both drying and salting preservation methods, was the most obvious candidate to meet this need.

Fishing for cod on a major scale took place in Norwegian waters as early as the tenth century. Scandinavian fishermen began venturing ever farther into the Atlantic in search of additional sources of supply, which they found first off Iceland and then off the North American coast near Newfoundland, an area that came to be known as the Grand Banks. The Grand Banks had "a greater density of cod than anything ever seen in Europe," and Mark Kurlansky believes that fishermen from the Basque country (the area of the European Atlantic coast adjoining both sides of what is now the border between Spain and France) had, like the fabled Northmen, found their way to it well before Columbus and had proceeded to fish it much more extensively and continuously than the Northmen ever had.

English fishermen began harvesting Icelandic cod in the fifteenth century. Toward the end of the century, voyagers financed by merchants from Bristol, on the western coast of England, may also have made their way, prior to Columbus, to the Grand Banks. John Cabot's 1497 expedition, underwritten jointly by Bristol merchants and the English monarch, confirmed that this area was indeed "teeming with cod," and fishermen from the English west country—as well as from France, Spain, and Portugal— thereafter joined those from the Basque country in a determined effort "to exploit this resource seriously."

In the first decade of the seventeenth century, Bristol merchants received reports from more than one exploratory voyage that the waters of what would become New England offered "excellent fishing for cod which are better than those of Newfound-land." So impressed was Bartholomew Gosnold, the first of these explorers, that he gave the name Cape Cod to a promontory shaped like an arm bent upward at the elbow off whose shores the species was particularly plentiful. The prospect of exploiting this resource seriously was one of the prime motivations in the establishment of both the Plymouth and the Massachusetts Bay colonies, and indeed the cod fishery became crucial to the economy of colonial New England.

The factors of periodic abstinence from meat and plentiful supplies meant that cod, for the most part in preserved form, was a dietary staple in medieval England. Records from both monasteries and gentry households, from the thirteenth century into the sixteenth, show that half or more of the fish consumed even on these upper social levels was cod or closely related species. The Protestant Reformation did not bring the observation of "fysshe days" in Britain to an end. As late as the middle of the eighteenth century, the longest chapter in a best-selling cookbook, that of Glasse, is the one "for Lent," in which are to be found nine recipes for fresh cod and two for salt cod. On this side of the Atlantic, Puritan New England had by this time developed a Sabbatarian form of quasi-Lenten weekly observance in which salt cod constituted the fare for Saturday dinner.

In the nineteenth century, "eating fish meant eating cod, particularly salt cod" for most New Englanders. Samuel Adams Drake, writing in 1875, stated that the custom of a weekly fish dinner was still being observed "by every family in New England"; he went so far as to claim that "the cod-fish is to New England what roast beef is to old Albion." By this time, the proportion of fresh cod in New England cod consumption had considerably increased.

Although the reported eighteenth-century weekly codfish dining took place in the upper-class venues of New England and featured elegant dressings and sauces, cod was viewed for the most part as everyday food for everyday people. It was eaten but not particularly relished. To the extent that it was revered, as in the white pine carving of the "Sacred Cod" that has overseen the deliberations of the Massachusetts legislature since 1784, this was for its value not as a comestible but rather as a commodity. The twentieth-century development of New England tourism that elevated clam chowder, steamed and fried clams, and live boiled lobster to iconic status pretty much bypassed the cod, except perhaps for scrod ("young cod or haddock"), which, as seen below, emerged into print in the middle of the nineteenth century and plays the leading cod part on restaurant menus today.

33. TO STEW COD

Cut your Cod in thin slices, and lay them one by one in the bottom of a Dish; put in a pint of White-wine, half a pound of Butter, some Oysters, and their

Liquor, two or three blades of Mace, a few crumbs of Bread, some Pepper and Salt, and let it stew till 'tis enough. Garnish the dish with Lemon.

—Smith, *Compleat Housewife* (1728), p. 35

A recipe that is in essence the same as the various stewed fish and shellfish recipes we have previously encountered, from the white wine mixed with other liquid (here oyster liquor), to the butter and grain (here bread crumb) thickening agents, to the seasoning. We see oysters playing here the same part vis-à-vis cod that we shall repeatedly see it playing in fowl cookery.

34. TO DRESS SALT FISH

Old Ling, which is the best Sort of Salt Fish, lay it in Water twelve Hours, then lay twelve Hours on a Board, then twelve more in Water. When you boil it, put it into the Water cold; if it is good, it will take about fifteen Minutes boiling softly. Boil Parsnips very tender, scrape them, and put them into a Sauce-pan, put to them some Milk, stir them till thick, then stir in a good Piece of Butter, and a little Salt; when they are enough, lay them in a Plate, the Fish by itself dry, and Butter and Hard Eggs chopped in a Bason.

As to Water-Cod, that need only be boiled and well skimmed.

Scotch-Haddocks you must lay in Water all Night. You may boil or broil them; if you broil, you must split them in two.—You may garnish your Dishes with hard Eggs and Parsnips.

—Glasse, *Art of Cookery* (1747), p. 91

Ling (*Molva molva*) is a member of the cod family found primarily not on the Grand Banks but rather in the waters between Iceland and Britain. It is not to be confused with lingcod (*Ophiodon elongatus*), "a family of fish unique to the west coast of North America," which is not in fact a species of cod at all. In Glasse's day, the term "ling" was being used to denote salt cod in general, but in praising it as "the best Sort of Salt Fish," Glasse probably had *Molva molva* in mind, since it "is considered to be close to fresh cod in merit; and in dried or salted and dried form it is almost as highly esteemed as the corresponding cod products." A member of Boston's emergent "codfish aristocracy" probably used cod caught closer to home, rather than ling, for the Saturday dinner of "salt cod fish" with which he entertained a visitor from Maryland in 1744. But the dish was in at least one respect prepared in accordance with what would be Glasse's instructions three years later, "being elegantly dressed with a sauce of butter and eggs." The fact that even "the best Sort of Salt Fish" required thirty-six hours of desalinating and remoisturizing perhaps helps to explain why historically cod did not attain to a level of prestige much superior to mediocre.

Davidson guesses that the term "water-cod . . . may refer to the practice of keeping cod alive in salt water until the time came to sell them; or it may just mean fresh as opposed to salt cod." By "Scotch-Haddocks," Glasse doubtless means the smoked haddock for which Scotland had become famous (preservation with salt being less efficacious with haddock than with cod), and that now goes under the name Finnan Haddie. "Haddie" is a Scottish colloquialism for haddock; "Finnan" has been identified as a corruption of the names of either of two fishing villages: Findon near Aberdeen, or Findhorn, about eighty miles northwest of Aberdeen. Toward the end of the nineteenth century, Finnan Haddie was being exported from New England to the Canadian Maritime Provinces, with their large numbers of people of Scottish descent.

35. SALT FISH

Salt fish should be put in a deep plate, with just water enough to cover it, the night before you intend to cook it. It should not be boiled an instant; boiling renders it hard. It should lie in scalding hot water two or three hours. The less water is used, and the more [the] fish is cooked at once, the better. Water thickened with flour and water while boiling, with sweet butter put in to melt, is the common sauce. It is more economical to cut salt pork into small bits, and try it till the pork is brown and crispy. It should not be done too fast, lest the sweetness be scorched out. . . .

Salt fish mashed with potatoes, with good butter or pork scraps to moisten it, is nicer the second day than it was the first. The fish should be minced very fine, while it is warm. After it has got cold and dry, it is difficult to do it nicely. Salt fish needs plenty of vegetables, such as onions, beets, carrots, &c.

There is no way of preparing salt fish for breakfast, so nice as to roll it up in little balls, after it is mixed with mashed potatoes; dip it into an egg, and fry it brown.

Child, *American Frugal Housewife* (1833), pp. 59–60

In these paragraphs, Child summarizes the essence of New England salt cod cookery for the next century and more. During her 1820s childhood in a wealthy Salem, Massachusetts, family, Caroline King had a version of this repast for dinner on Saturdays, although naturally on a level of society that was more exalted than the one inhabited by Child's intended readers, various refining touches were applied to the fish and vegetables, so that the diner's plate ended up looking "like a painter's pallet."

This "dainty mixture," as King calls it, would eventually go by the name of Cape Cod Turkey. But this terminology had evidently not taken hold by 1850 when Bliss offered recipes for "Salt Cod, or Dun Fish" and "Cod Fish Balls." For some reason, Bliss makes the vegetables available only in combination with one type of sauce: "Serve with egg sauce . . . and boiled beets; or, if you prefer, with drawn butter and pork scraps." After the dish had been fully standardized, mid-twentieth-century readers would be warned that the boiled potatoes in Cape Cod Turkey must be "of uniform size" and that the beets must be "small buttered."

Child's "salt fish mashed with potatoes" that is "nicer the second day" recurs repeatedly—for example, as Beecher's "To Cook Cold Codfish" or much later, in 1939, as Nellie I. Brown's "Old Hundred Codfish Cakes."

36. COD BAKED (2)

Choose a fine large cod, clean it well, and open the under part to the bone, and put in a stuffing made with beef suet, parsley, sweet herbs shred fine, an egg, and seasoned with salt, pepper, nutmeg, mace and grated lemon-peel; put this inside the cod, sew it up, wrap it in a buttered paper, and bake it; baste it well with melted butter.

—Lee, *Cook's Own Book* (1832), p. 52

An alternative stuffing and method of basting to the one Simmons provides in #8 for bass. Just as that recipe works for cod and other fish, so this one, taken from Dolby, would doubtless work for bass and other fish.

37. COD SOUNDS, BROILED

Let them lie in boiling water till it is nearly cold, rub them with salt, and pull off the black and dirty skin, boil them in hot water, drain, and dust them with flour, rub them over with butter, season with white pepper and salt, and broil them. Put a table-spoonful of catchup, half a one of soy, and a little Cayenne, into melted butter, heat and pour it over them.

—Lee, *Cook's Own Book* (1832), p. 53

Mark Kurlansky explains that the cod sound is an "air bladder, . . . a long tube against the backbone that can fill [with] or release gas to adjust swimming depth." Glasse has two recipes for broiled cod sounds (one of them copied by Carter) that may have been the basis for this one (by Dalgairns and copied by Lee). In the early twentieth century, the wife of the captain of a New England fishing boat compared cod sounds to "deep sea scallops," and indeed the saucing instructions here would constitute a pleasant variation with broiled scallops.

38. COD'S HEAD AND SHOULDERS, TO BOIL

Wash it clean; tie it up, and dry it with a cloth. Allow in the proportion of every three measures of water, one of salt; when it boils, take off the scum; put in the fish and keep it boiling very fast for twenty-five or thirty minutes. Serve with the roe and milt parboiled, cut into slices, and fried, and garnish with curled parsley and horse-radish. Sauces;—oyster, melted butter, or anchovy butter.

—Lee, *Cook's Own Book* (1832), p. 53

A recipe taken from Dalgairns. Davidson remarks that "the head of a cod, in places where people are knowledgeable about such things, is greatly prized." Early modern England and colonial New England must have been such places, for recipes for cod's head and shoulders—boiled, roasted, or baked—are found in just about all of the seventeenth- and eighteenth-century cookbooks sent across the Atlantic or reprinted there. Raffald also calls for an accompaniment of sliced roe, although she does not mention the milt, "the roe or spawn of the male fish." In one way or another, horse-radish is utilized in all these recipes. A standard anchovy sauce of the time was made with three teaspoons of anchovy extract (several pounds of the fish boiled and strained through a hair sieve) mixed into half a pint of melted butter. This may have been the "anchovy butter" called for here.

Hale and Webster copied this recipe, while Bliss offered a simplified version.

39. TO BROIL SALT COD FISH

Put your fish in soak over night; in the morning, let it drain and dry on the gridiron, front of the fire, a few minutes; grease your gridiron well, then broil your fish thoroughly brown on both sides; then put it on a board, and beat it with a pestle, or hammer, till it becomes entirely soft; then pour on boiling water, and after a minute drain it off. If the fish is very salt, repeat the boiling water two or three times, then pour over sweet cream, or a little butter. If the fish is not very salt, you may omit the soaking over night.

—Howland, *New England Economical Housekeeper* (1845), pp. 61–62

This daunting recipe, which requires overnight soaking before broiling and beating with a hammer and additional soaking after broiling, returns us to the Middle Ages, when it was recommended that stockfish, dried cod, be beaten with a hammer "for a full hour." However, if one follows Bliss and uses "a large and tender dunfish"—in other words, cod that is "not very salt"—the total soaking time is reduced to only six minutes.

40. PICKED-UP CODFISH

Pick off one-pound of salt cod or dunfish in small bits, wash them in a little water; pour on half a pint of clear water, and set over a slow fire, let it scald three minutes, turn off the water; pour over the fish two tea-cupsful of milk, a table-spoonful of butter, and break one egg into it, dredge with a little flour; stir one minute and serve hot.

This is a good breakfast dish.

—Bliss, *Practical Cook Book* (1850), p. 34

This dish—essentially creamed, chipped salt cod—became a New England standard. The "Old Hundred" version a century later is virtually identical.

41. SCRODE OR YOUNG COD, ROASTED

Procure a fat scrode, and require the fishmonger to open and dress it; sprinkle a little salt and pepper upon it; spread it out flat and fasten it to a board, stand the board up before a brisk fire, that the fish may roast; when browned on one side, unfasten it from the board, and by means of a tin sheet, turn it on to a gridiron, that the other side may be browned. Be careful not to break the fish in transferring it from the board to the gridiron. Dish it, pour a spoonful of melted butter over it, and serve hot.

Haddock may be cooked in the same way, and is considered more delicate than cod.

—Bliss, *Practical Cook Book* (1850), p. 34

42. SCRODE, FRIED

Score a small scrode, dredge it with pepper and salt, roll it in Indian meal, fry it in hot pork fat. If you put the fish into fat that is not very hot, it will fall in pieces before it crisps. Dish and serve hot, but never cover it before sending to the table.

Haddock may be cooked in the same manner.

—Bliss, *Practical Cook Book* (1850), pp. 34–35

The term "scrod" (variant spellings include "scrode," "schrod," and "schrode") first emerged in New England not long before the publication of Bliss's cookbook. It occurs the year before, in 1849, in another cookbook, as "Broiled Scrod." In 1844, it is used in a collection of children's stories published in Boston. The first use of the term that the mid-twentieth-century *Dictionary of Americanisms* was able to find was in 1841, in the New York weekly paper *The Spirit of the Times*. In the 1877 edition of John Russell Bartlett's *Dictionary of Americanisms*, scrod is defined as "pieces of fish, or small fish, for broiling; small codfish split open and salted." The 1849 broiled scrod recipe mentioned above may have contributed to this definition, as it begins by saying to "take a small cod, or the tail of a large one, sprinkle a little salt over it, and let it remain over night." The emphasis upon the tail turned up again a century later, when the *Chicago Tribune* stated that "as served in famous Boston restaurants, scrod is simply a tail piece of filleted haddock or cod dipped in oil, then bread crumbs and broiled in a moderate oven."

The cumbersome combination of planking and broiling in Bliss's first recipe is due to the difficulty of getting a "fat scrode" turned over without its falling apart. Hale agrees with Bliss that "hot pork fat" is best for frying cod, and that a coating of cornmeal helps, as Hale puts it, "to prevent breaking." We've already seen cornmeal being used to fry eels (#5 commentary) and generic fish (#14).

As scrod has approached canonical status, the most common methods of cooking it have been broiling (though not always in accordance with the *Chicago Tribune* account) or baking (with or without a wine-based sauce). In either guise, it has become customary to attach the tritely honorific "Boston" prefix.

CHAPTER SEVEN

Fowl, Wild and Tame

Dame Trot came home one wintry night,
A shivring, starving soul,
But Pufs had made a blazing fire
And nicely trufs'd a Fowl.

owl is fair in our time. While Americans still eat more beef than chicken, for reasons of both health and convenience the little bird is pecking out a larger market share each year—chicken consumption increased by 70 percent in the last quarter of the twentieth century, at the same time that annual beef consumption fell by twenty-five pounds per capita. Yet the Anglo-American taste for fowl is much older than the current craze. Whereas now chicken and turkey dominate the fowl category to the virtual exclusion of other species (in current American usage, "fowl" means any domestic bird; in Britain, the word refers to the domestic cock or hen), in earlier centuries these were just two among many winged creatures, wild and tame, that ended up on the spit or in the pot. Nature's entire aviary was fair game, from birds we may still see on fancy restaurant menus, like pheasant and quail, to those we would find ethically if not gustatorily unpalatable, such as songbirds.

Of sixteenth-century bird cookery Colin Spencer writes: "The crane, the bittern, the wild and tame swan, the brant, the lark and two kinds of plover, teal, widgeon, mallard, shelldrake and shoveller, the peewit, scamen knot, olicet, dun bird, partridge and pheasant, were all hunted or snared, eaten and enjoyed." He also mentions Sir Hugh Plat's recipe for sparrows, gives the price per dozen for larks (from 1d to 10d), and says that pigeons were frowned upon "by reason of their multitude."

Since the Middle Ages, the nobility, for whom pageantry was as important as flavor in the design of their menus, had found the large number of edible bird species appealing. The success of noble feasts depended on this kind of diversity. It would be painting a distorted picture to deny that roasted flesh meat, including some fancy cuts of pork but most especially beef and mutton, dominated the noble diet. Yet fowl—and game—provided the greatest pleasure and variety.

Fowl could be taken fresh at almost any time of year. Before refrigeration, this was especially important in winter and spring, when all wearied of salt meat. To make them more palatable, wildfowl might be spiced and larded, or garnished with forcemeat, lemons, Seville oranges, and sweetbreads, or cooked in broth or cream sauce, or basted with butter and bread crumbs, then baked or roasted. Then as now, the larger birds were considered best for the rack. For display, their feathers and skin were saved and reassembled on the cooked carcass to imitate—or improve upon—the bird in life.

In time, tame chickens, geese, ducks, peahens, and—after the Columbian exchange had left its indelible mark on the European diet—turkeys took the place of rarer wildfowl, first on the gentry's boards and eventually on just about everybody's table, high and low. But whether wild or domestic, potted or poached, spitted or sauced, fricasseed or fried, fowl have long been considered among the most delectable of foods. "Oh, my dear Sir, what a glorious bit!" exclaimed a guest dining on a wild turkey roasted by the famous French gourmet Anthelme Brillat-Savarin after a hunt near Hartford, Connecticut, in 1794. Cook some of the following neglected classics in ways that approximate the authors' methods and you might well hear similar expressions of gratitude from your amazed guests.

Wildfowl, Ducks, Geese

Despite their sometimes strong flavor, stringy flesh, and the difficulties of hunting, wildfowl, ducks, and geese long constituted a prestigious if relatively minor part of the Anglo-American diet. As with any nondomesticated animals, birds were "in good grease" (that is, in season) at different times of the year depending upon the species, although many were best taken in autumn and winter, as stated in a mid-sixteenth-century cookbook: "Cygnets be best between All Halloween day and Lent. A mallard is good after a frost, till Candlemas, so is a teal and other wild fowl that swimmeth. A woodcock is best from October to Lent; and so be all other birds as ousels and throstles, robins and such other. Herons, curlews, crane, bittern, bustard, be at all times good; but best in winter. Pheasants, partridge and rail be ever good, but best when they be taken with a hawk. Quail and larks be ever in season . . . and so be pigeons if they be young."

We include in this section ducks and geese, which might come to the kitchen from the barnyard or the wild. (Turkeys may also be had wild or tame, but they merit a section of their own for their greater culinary and symbolic importance in the American story.) The Renaissance Italian cook and author, Bartolomeo Scappi, who flourished from 1540 to 1570, says that all species of wild duck are in season from October to the end of February but are best when taken during the coldest months. Geese were in eating order both in early summer, when young, and in early autumn, when fattened. From the seventeenth to the nineteenth centuries, on both sides of the Atlantic, large flocks of tame geese were herded great distances to market in late summer and early autumn, their death march sometimes taking months.

1. TO BOYLE DUCKS AFTER THE FRENCH FASHION

Take and lard them and put them upon a spit, and halfe roast them, then draw them & put them into a Pipkin, and put a quart of Clarit Wine into it, and Chesnuts, & a pint of great Oysters taking the beards from them, and three Onyons minced very small, some Mace and a little beaten Ginger, a little Tyme stript, a Crust of a French Rowle grated put into it to thicken it, and so dish it upon sops. This may be diversified, if there be strong broth there need not be so much Wine put in, and if there be no oysters or Chesnuts you may put in Hartichoak bottoms, Turnips, Colliflowers, Bacon in thin slices, Sweet bread's, &c.

—*Compleat Cook* (1658, 2nd ed.), pp. 36–37

The ingredients used to flavor these ducks—chestnuts, oysters, and onions or artichoke bottoms, turnips, cauliflower, etc.—were not destined to become the flavors of the next century. The most forward-looking recipe of the day for duck in "the French fashion," by Robert May, was a plainer one, reflecting the moderation and subtle seasoning introduced by la Varenne. It called for duck with green peas and sweet herbs, and was taken up in the eighteenth century by Hannah Glasse (see #3). Though elite modern tastes might again run more to the spiced, multifarious garnishes of this recipe, the simpler duck with peas and sweet herbs reflects the fashion that came to dominate aristocratic English dining in the eighteenth century and to influence elite New England tastes as well. Despite its recommendation in this recipe for a varied garnish, *The Compleat Cook* mostly reflected progressive trends, such as reduced sugar in savory recipes and liberal use of anchovies. Sweetbreads are the thymus gland and pancreas of a calf, a lamb, or, less frequently, a pig.

Although the recipe does not specify the number of ducks, the quantities of other ingredients—a quart of claret, a pint of oysters, three onions, the crust of one French roll—suggest a brace.

2. TO ROAST A GOOSE

Take a little sage, and a small onion chopt small, some pepper and salt, and a bit of butter; mix these together, and put it into the belly of the goose. Then spit it, singe it with a bit of white paper, drudge it with a little flour, and baste it with butter. When it is done, which may be known by the leg being tender, take it up, and pour thro' it two glasses of red wine, and serve it up in the same dish, and apple sauce in a bason.

—Smith, *Compleat Housewife* (1750), p. 22

This recipe first appeared in the fourteenth edition of *The Compleat Housewife*, eighteen years after the author's death. In an amusing reversal of the fact that Glasse, in her first edition of 1747, draws a good deal of her material from the earlier editions of Smith, all sections added to post-1747 editions of Smith appear to be heavily indebted to Glasse. Most of the elements of this particular recipe are found in Glasse's three different sets of directions for roasting a goose.

Smith's modest stuffing and final wine soaking, with good English applesauce as an accompaniment, mark a style of cooking that strove to unite a measure of elegance—and a hint of French fashion—with a concern for economy and ease of preparation, allowing the English gentry, and even urban tradesmen and others a few notches below the gentry, to eat well and stylishly while avoiding undue trouble and expense. Roasting had long been the favorite method of preparing fowl. On the question of when your goose is cooked, Glasse (Smith's source) states that "three Quarters of an Hour will do it at a quick Fire." Under modern conditions, Sandra L. Oliver recommends a roasting time of thirty minutes per pound in moderate heat.

3. TO DRESS A DUCK WITH GREEN PEAS

Put a deep Stew-pan over the Fire, with a Piece of fresh Butter, singe your Duck and flour it, turn it in the Pan two or three Minutes, then pour out all the Fat, but let the Duck remain in the Pan; put to it Half a Pint of good Gravy, a Pint of Pease, two Lettuces cut small, a small Bundle of Sweet Herbs, a little Pepper and Salt, cover them close, and let them stew for Half an Hour, now and then give the Pan a shake; when they are just done grate in a little Nutmeg, and put in a very little beaten Mace, and thicken it either with a Piece of Butter rolled in Flour, or the Yolk of an Egg beat up with two or three Spoonfuls of Cream; shake it all together for three or four Minutes, take out the Sweet Herbs, lay the Duck in the Dish and pour the Sauce over it: You may garnish with boiled Mint chopped, or let it alone.

—Glasse, *Art of Cookery* (1747), p. 41

As mentioned above (#1), this became the most popular English stewed duck dish of the period, both for obvious reasons—it takes little time to cook—and less obvious ones—its delicate sauce imitated, in a scaled-down version, the new French style popular with the aristocracy. It is characteristic of Glasse's interpretation of culinary fashion—cost is reduced and preparation is simplified.

Lehmann cites several later English recipes by Raffald, Mary Smith (*Complete House-keeper*, 1772), and others to demonstrate the English technique of half-roasting the duck on a spit, then cooking it in sauce with peas. But this is exactly the method that we've just seen *The Compleat Cook* call French. Whether French or English, this is not the procedure followed by Glasse. Then again, neither does Glasse follow what Lehmann describes as the French method, as when Clermont braises the duck and peas separately, then combines and enriches the sauce with a *coulis*. Despite the confusion, Glasse's recipe illustrates Lehmann's point that once a dish has been thoroughly anglicized, as here, it can be played with rather more freely, producing "variations on the theme in the same way as the French diversified their own repertoire."

4. WILD DUCKS, WIDGEONS, OR TEAL

Wild fowl are in general liked rather under done; and if your fire is very good and brisk, a duck or widgeon will be done in a quarter of an hour; for as soon as they are well hot through, they begin to loose their gravy, and if not drawn off, will eat hard. A teal is done in little more than ten minutes.

—Carter, *Frugal Housewife* (1772), p. 11

Carter expands on Glasse's instructions regarding roasting times for these birds. This recipe illustrates that game birds, with their aristocratic associations, still held a special appeal for many. Carter also offers preparations for pigeons, woodcocks, snipes, quails, pheasants, partridges, plovers, larks, ortolans, ruffs (sandpipers) and reifs (birds of prey). Her citrus garnishes include orange and lemon for woodcocks, snipes, and partridges; Seville orange and lemon, with anchovy and shallots, for quails; lemon for pheasants; squeezed lemon and orange, with a forcemeat of artichoke bottoms, for plovers; and orange for larks. She recommends that ortolans be roasted with a vine leaf between each, then garnished with fried bread crumbs, lemon, and gravy; only ruffs and reifs, served on buttered toast with gravy, receive no citrus garnish. All of the birds are served with bread in some form, whether on sippets, covered with bread sauce, or basted with bread crumbs and butter.

In her emphasis on citrus, Carter follows French fashion, which, in English translations since the early eighteenth century, had recommended garnishes of lemon or orange slices or squeezes of juice as final flavorings to sauces for boiled meats. English cooks such as William Verral (*Complete System of Cookery*, 1759) continued the trend, bringing French technique to English aristocratic kitchens. It is doubtful that Carter knew Massialot, Clouet, Verral, and the like. Yet strands of influence can be traced from continental to British kitchens, from the aristocracy to the gentry and middle class, and finally, with an American edition of Carter, to the colonies.

5. TO STUFF AND ROAST A GOSLIN

Boil the inwards tender, chop them fine, put double quantity of grated bread, 4 ounces butter, pepper, salt, (and sweet herbs if you like) 2 eggs moulded into the stuffing, parboil 4 onions and chop them into the stuffing, add wine, and roast the bird.

The above is a good stuffing for every kind of Water Fowl, which requires onion sauce.

—Simmons, *American Cookery* (Hartford, 1796), p. 19

Simmons's recommendation to use her goslin stuffing with waterfowl reminds us that geese could come to the table either from the barnyard or the wild. The technique for taming wild ducks and geese was brought to Britain in the late Iron Age by the Celts, who probably learned it from the Gauls. As we mention in the introduction to this section, goose was popular not least because it was in season twice a year, the goslin in early summer and the fattened goose at Michaelmas (September 29).

6. DUCK, DRESSED IN DIFFERENT WAYS

Take either a large duck, or two ducklings, which truss like a fowl for boiling; put it into a pot (just about large enough to hold the duck) with thin slices of bacon, a little stock, a glass of wine, pepper, salt, onions, carrots, a head of celery sliced, a bunch of sweet herbs, two cloves and a bay-leaf; when done, take out the duck, wipe the fat off very clean, and serve with what sauce or ragout you choose, such as sweetbreads, green-peas, turnips, chestnuts, olives, cucumbers, or any sort of stewed greens, according to the season.

—Lee, *Cook's Own Book* (1832), p. 66

This recipe (which might alternately be titled, "Ways to Make Ducklings") is copied from Dolby. It's therefore not surprising that it alludes to the French preparation—ragout—popularized in English cooking in the eighteenth century. There the similarity to French style ends. In the French mode, complex sauces combined with the new idea of standardizing preparation produced a multitude of dishes. The English interpretation of the French method followed the pattern Lee presents here: meat is boiled or roasted, and sauces accompany but are not really integral to the cooked meat. For the French, sauces were given as much attention as the meat itself. The sauce was no afterthought but part of the process of cooking the meat. New Englander Helen Wright, who copied many of Lee's wildfowl recipes, brought the English practice forward to the twentieth century by copying this one.

7. TO STEW PARTRIDGES

Truss two partridges as fowls are done for boiling; pound the livers with double the quantity of fat bacon and bread crumbs boiled in milk, add some chopped parsley, and mushrooms; season with pepper, salt, grated lemon-peel, and mace. Stuff the inside of the birds, tie them at both ends, and put them into a stewpan lined with slices of bacon; add a quart of good gravy, if you have it, otherwise water, two onions, a bunch of sweet herbs, and a few blades of mace; let them stew gently till tender; take them out, strain and thicken the sauce with flour and butter, make it hot and pour it over the partridges.

—Hale, *Good Housekeeper* (1841), p. 54

Partridges were hunted with hawks, as we mention in the introduction. The larger hawks were owned by the nobility and hunted the larger fowl; smaller hawks, such as the kestrel, which ordinary people might own, were flown at smaller birds such as young partridges. One might say that the big wigs had the big wings.

Hale concludes the previous recipe for stewing pigeons with the comment that "partridges may be roasted like pigeons; but they are better stewed, because such dry meat." This opinion was shared by Elizabethan cooks. However, as we see in the next recipe, some cooks thought pigeon meat dry.

8. PIGEONS

Pigeons are either roasted, broiled, potted, or stewed. *Potting* is the best way, and the least trouble. After they are picked and cleaned, put a small slice of salt pork and a little ball of stuffing into the body of each bird. The stuffing may be made of one egg to one cracker, and an equal quantity of suet or butter, seasoned with sweet marjoram or sage. Baste them well, lay them close together in the bottom of the pot, merely cover them with water, put in a bit of butter, and let them stew an hour and a quarter, if young; an hour and three quarters, if old. *Stewed* pigeons are cooked nearly as above, omitting the stuffing. Being dry meat, they require a good deal of butter. To *Roast* pigeons, put them on a small spit, and tie both ends close. Baste with butter. They will be done in fifteen or twenty minutes. To make a *Pigeon Pie,* put inside of every bird a piece of butter and the yolk of an egg boiled hard.

—Prescott, *Valuable Receipts* (1845), p. 6

As in sixteenth-century England, pigeons were abundant in nineteenth-century New England. But the response to this situation was exactly the opposite—cooking and eating them constantly rather than rarely. They are the only wildfowl species regularly to be encountered in the cookbooks of the day.

Preserving fowl and meat in pies, often with the addition of clarified butter or lard, was practiced before potting took hold as a favored method for short-term preservation (three weeks to a month). By the time of Elizabeth I, small birds, pieces of flesh meat, and some fishes, especially lamprey eels, were often potted. Prescott has gotten his methods confused. While he says that potting is the best way to prepare pigeons, the preparation he describes calls for a covering of water and a bit of butter, which amounts to stewing; potted flesh might be parboiled, but it was then sealed in butter. Prescott's distinction between potted pigeon (with stuffing) and stewed pigeon (without stuffing) is also idiosyncratic.

9. WOODCOCK

Skin the head and neck of the bird, pluck the feathers, and truss it by bringing the beak of the bird under the wing, and fastening the pinion to the thigh; twist the legs at the knuckles and press the feet upon the thigh, bind the bird with strings to the spit, put a piece of bread under each bird to catch the drippings, baste with butter, dredge with flour, and roast fifteen or twenty minutes before a sharp fire. When done, cut the bread in diamond shape, each piece large enough to stand one bird upon, place them aslant on your dish, and serve with gravy enough to moisten the bread, serve some in the dish and some in the tureen; garnish with slices of lemon.

—Bliss, *Practical Cook Book* (1850), p. 86

The woodcock ranges in Eurasia from Britain and northern Spain to Siberia and Japan. The American woodcock is smaller but equally valued as a game bird. Presumably referring to the European species *Scolopax rusticola*, Davidson says that one woodcock feeds one person. He also notes that "it is usually roasted, without first being cleaned, since the entrail is accounted essential to full enjoyment of the bird's fine flavour." Thus Bliss's directions to bind the bird to the spit, rather than pierce the body. The pieces of diamond-shaped bread aslant in the dish are latter-day sippets. The lemon garnish for woodcock follows Carter.

10. ROAST SNIPE

Clean and truss, but do not stuff. Lay in rows in the dripping-pan, sprinkle with salt, and baste well with butter, then with butter and water. When they begin to brown, cut as many slices of bread as there are birds. Toast quickly, butter, and lay in the dripping-pan, a bird upon each. When the birds are done, serve upon the toast, with the gravy poured over it. The toast should lie under them while cooking at least five minutes, during which time the birds should be basted with melted butter seasoned with pepper. The largest snipe will not require above twenty minutes to roast. Or, dip an oyster in melted butter, then in bread-crumbs, seasoned with pepper and salt, and put in each bird before roasting. Small birds are especially delicious cooked in this way.

—Turner, *New England Cook Book* (1905), pp. 66–67

A northern hemisphere shore and marsh bird with a long bill, the snipe weighs on average only four ounces, thus Turner's recommendation to roast a number of them. She doesn't mention the old-fashioned citrus accompaniment, although she does serve the birds on sippet-like toast. Hunting snipe is difficult and rarely done anymore—indeed, the phrase snipe hunt is synonymous with wild goose chase (an instance of birds of a futile feather flocking rhetorically together).

According to Barbara Wheaton, the use of shellfish to stuff birds dates to the time of la Varenne (1651).

Chicken

Harold McGee says that chickens were domesticated in the vicinity of Thailand before 7500 BCE and arrived in the Mediterranean around 500 BCE. It is likely that the Celts brought them to Britain in the first century BCE.

Most medieval English farm families kept chickens, which they themselves ate, but only after eggs were no longer forthcoming. By the sixteenth century, chicken was becoming a luxury food. With the development of cities and markets, the price more than doubled, and yeoman farmers therefore tended to sell their flocks to the wealthy rather than consume them at home.

By the end of the first decade of settlement at Plymouth, chickens, along with swine, were considered too numerous to inventory. In choosing breeds, the colonists were guided by tradition as well as by such works as Markham's *Cheape and Good Husbandry* (1614). They probably favored the red dunghill fowl, as did their counterparts in England.

Abundant in early Plymouth, hens and roosters were used both as gifts to and in exchange with the native population. In 1623, Edward Winslow gave chickens to the ailing Wampanoag sachem Massasoit, instructing him on how to make that well-known curative, chicken broth. Instead, Massasoit kept the birds for breeding. Indians referred to chickens primarily by the term "netasuaog," meaning "ones that are house fed."

As in England, New England farm families, along with servants, widows, and others of limited means, began to sell both chickens and eggs to supplement their incomes. Chickens reserved for home use were not—again as in England—killed and eaten until their egg production had declined. Some New England recipes address the problem of cooking tough, old hens, and we give one as our final offering in this section.

The usefulness of this easily kept, easily bred species is clear. But chicken has a downside. Like an invasive plant, it has all but obliterated other domesticated fowl, not only in the United States but throughout the world. Moreover, there has been an emphasis on some breeds of chicken to the detriment of others. As Davidson remarks, "chicken dishes are possibly the most nearly ubiquitous menu items of a non-vegetarian kind." The chicken meat most of us eat is insipid, made tasty only by seasoning or sauce. American factory farms can produce a four-pound chicken on eight pounds of feed in six weeks. As Harold McGee points out, "because such a bird grows very fast and lives very little, its meat is fairly bland."

In the past, chickens were a more diverse lot. The Romans favored a breed that produced a heavy, docile hen; some speculate that a similar old English type, the Dorking, may trace its ancestry to Roman Britain. Queen Victoria loved the Cochin, from China. The French *poulet de Bresse*, long considered especially delicious, is sold with a leg ring in place to assure authenticity. In North America, the Indian Game Fowl developed into the delectable Cornish Game Hen, and the Mediterranean Leghorn (bred for its eggs) was crossed with Asian breeds to become the famed Rhode Island Red. There were other composite breeds as well—the Plymouth Rock was bred from Cochin, Dorking, and Malay; the Wyandotte evolved from Cochin, Hamburgh, and Sebright bantam (meaning miniature) genes.

Some of these new breeds, especially the Plymouth Rock, overwhelmed the others, becoming the basis of an industry so intensive and efficient in its meat production that it left little either to the imagination (the pecking farmyard chicken now exists only in children's picture books) or the taste buds. The modern poultry industry standard is for flesh that is disproportionately white, mostly from the breast. For obvious commercial reasons, modern birds must mature early. In other words, McGee's eight pounds of feed + six weeks of maturation = four pounds of "chicken."

How do today's practices compare with the marketing and breeding procedures of the past? The extensive shopping advice found in many early cookbooks indicates that deceptions to make birds look younger and fresher were common. Certainly product uniformity was impossible to achieve before the advent of the factory farm. Writers from Markham to the twentieth-century women of South County, Rhode Island, understood that their readers would be faced with a variety of chickens—young and old, tender and tough, fat and scrawny. Quality and age were challenges, as was the need to use all parts of the bird. Is the hen old? Boil, stew, or fricassee it. Is it young and succulent? Then it is ready for the spit. Are there remnants left over from a curry or a chicken pie? They can be pulverized into forcemeat.

Many superb chicken recipes appear in the cookbooks we consulted. We have tried to select a few of the best, and to emphasize dishes that had the longest legacy in the New England tradition. Your efforts at preparing them are most likely to be successful if you use fresh, unadulterated chickens.

11. TO ROST A CAPON WITH OYSTERS AND CHESNUTS

Take some boiled Chesnuts, and take off their shells, and take as many parboil'd Oysters, then spit your Capon, and put these into the belly of it, with some sweet Butter, rost it and bast it with sweet Butter, save the Gravie, and some of the Chesnuts, and some of the Oysters, then add to them half a Pint of Claret Wine, and a pice of sweet Butter and a little Pepper, and a little Salt, stew these altogether till the Capon be ready, then serve them in with it; Garnish your Dish as you please.

—Woolley, *Queen-like Closet* (1670), p. 128

This recipe demonstrates why Woolley's book dominated the later seventeenth century. As mentioned in Chapter 1, her primary audience was the aspiring gentry, whose budgets might permit some chestnuts, wine, and butter to enhance an expensive capon. Oysters (along with morels and artichoke bottoms) in fowl dishes became fashionable in the seventeenth century. Woolley permits the cook latitude in garnishing the dish, as does *The Compleat Cook* (for both points, see above #1). Just after Woolley's time, a distinction would be drawn between sweet and savory dishes, with chestnuts accompanying the sweeter chicken dishes and oysters the savory ones.

12. TO FORCE CHICKENS

Roast your Chickens better than half, take off the Skin, then the Meat, and chop it small with shread Parsley and Crumbs of Bread, Pepper and Salt, and a little good Cream, then put in the Meat and close the Skin, brown it with a Salamander, and serve it up with White Sauce.

—Raffald, *Experienced English House-keeper* (1769), p. 111

Bread crumbs could also be applied to the skin, as in Markham's "To roast a Pigge," (Chapter 8, #21). Here, the bread crumbs are combined with the chicken meat and seasoning and forced back between the skin and carcass before undergoing a final browning. This technique produces a kind of chicken sausage wrapped in its own crispy skin. Raffald's use of the chicken meat itself as the basis of the dish's forcemeat is a variation on a French method introduced by la Varenne and described by Wheaton: "Well-seasoned mixtures of meat, poultry, and fish, either used as farces or formed into meatballs, were very widely used. The custom, still artfully practiced in France, of slipping a well-seasoned forcemeat between the skin and breast of a bird dates from this time." The salamander for browning Raffald's forced chicken "consists of an iron disc mounted on the end of an iron rod, which is furnished with a wooden handle. The disc is heated red-hot, then passed to and fro over and close to the dish" to be browned. The name of this device comes from that of a "mythical lizard-like animal" that was reputed to be able to survive being thrown in the fire, indeed to prefer such an environment. Only the wealthiest of Raffald's colonial readers would have possessed this specialized and expensive implement.

13. TO SMOTHER A FOWL IN OYSTERS

Fill the bird with dry Oysters, and sew up and boil in water just sufficient to cover the bird, salt and season to your taste—when done tender, put into a deep dish and pour over it a pint of stewed oysters, well buttered and peppered, garnish a turkey with sprigs of parsley or leaves of cellery: a fowl is best with a parsley sauce.

—Simmons, *American Cookery* (Hartford, 1796), p. 19

In the United States, the term "fowl" could be applied to the domestic duck or turkey, but in Simmons's day the prevailing meaning was the domestic cock or hen of the genus *Gallus*. Elsewhere, Simmons (or whoever wrote the marketing section of her cookbook) opines regarding fowl that "the female in almost every instance, is preferable to the male . . . [but] *chickens*, of either kind are good, and the yellow leg'd the best, and their taste the sweetest."

As we have seen in *The Compleat Cook* (above, #1) and Woolley (above, #11), oysters were often used in English cookery to enhance the taste of both roasted and boiled fowl. New Englanders followed suit, as we saw in Turner's stuffing for roast snipe (above, #10). Here, Simmons uses them for both stuffing and sauce.

Simmons also gives a description of a method for making fresh parsley available all winter. It involves boring holes in an old cask, filling the cask half-full of rich garden mold, planting parsley through the holes with roots inside, branches out, repeating the boring and planting up the sides of the cask, running an iron bar through the cask, filling it with water, letting it stand on the south or east side of your house until the first frost, then lugging it by the iron bar into the basement where, as the author concludes, "during the winter, I clip with my scissars the fresh parsley . . . and in the spring transplant the roots in the bed in the garden."

Simmons provides no recipe for parsley sauce, but does warn: "In dressing all sorts of kitchen garden herbs, take care they are clean washed; that there be no small snails, or caterpillars between the leaves."

Parsley is the most common aromatic herb; its use in English cooking dates to about 1000 CE. Parsley or green sauce has been a standard of English cooking since the Middle Ages. One medieval recipe calls for ground spices—ginger, cinnamon, pepper, nutmeg, and cloves—to be mixed with salt, bread crumbs, parsley, sage, and two or three cloves of garlic, all moistened with vinegar or verjuice. Markham's green sauce recipe is simpler—butter, verjuice, and parsley.

Verjuice (also verges or verjus, from the Old French, meaning green juice) is made by pressing unripe (one could say sour) grapes and sometimes other fruit such as plums and crab apples. Harold McGee describes it as "a tart alternative to vinegar or lemon juice." But that is backward as far as northern European cooking is concerned, because there the use of verjuice predates that of lemons, a Mediterranean import.

14. FRICASSEED CHICKEN, BROWN

Singe the chickens; cut them in pieces; pepper, salt, and flour them; fry them in fresh butter, till they are very brown: take the chickens out, and make a good gravy, into which put sweet herbs (marjoram or sage) according to your taste; if necessary, add pepper and salt; butter and flour must be used in making the gravy, in such quantities as to suit yourself for thickness and richness. After this is all prepared, the chicken must be stewed in it, for half an hour, closely covered. A pint of gravy is about enough for two chickens; I should think a piece of butter about as big as a walnut, and a table-spoonful of flour, would be enough for the gravy. The herbs should, of course, be pounded and sifted. Some, who love onions, slice two or three, and brown them with the chicken. Some slice a half lemon, and stew with the chicken. Some add tomatoes catsup.

—Child, *American Frugal Housewife* (1833), p. 54

15. FRICASSEED CHICKEN, WHITE

The chickens are cut to pieces, and covered with warm water, to draw out the blood. Then put into a stew-pan, with three quarters of a pint of water, or veal broth, salt, pepper, flour, butter, mace, sweet herbs pounded and sifted; boil it half an hour. If it is too fat, skim it a little. Just before it is done, mix the yolk of two eggs with a gill of cream, grate in a little nutmeg, stir it up till it is thick and smooth, squeeze in half a lemon. If you like onions, stew some slices with the other ingredients.

—Child, *American Frugal Housewife* (1833), p. 54

With these two fricassees Child harks back—no doubt unconsciously—to the very beginnings of the English imitation of French cooking, from the "fricases" of the sixteenth and early seventeenth centuries, to the court cooking of la Varenne in the mid-seventeenth century, to Massialot's blockbuster of French style at the beginning of the eighteenth. By Child's day, the lineage of these dishes was so attenuated that her fricassees were appropriate even for frugal family mealtimes.

Fricassees usually involved frying and then simmering, although sometimes the sequence was reversed. Child's first recipe follows the classic pattern, but there is no frying at all in the second. Most fricassees had an element of tartness, supplied in the earliest versions by verjuice or vinegar, later on, after la Varenne inaugurated modern French cuisine and the English began to imitate it, by lemon juice. The earliest fricassees often called for egg yolks, but by the eighteenth century, under the influence of current French style, egg yolks had become one of a number of options, along with cream sauce, flour-thickened broth, and various combinations of these and other ingredients. Many of these features are found, in one form or another, in Child's two offerings.

Lemon in the form of a final garnish, part of the genteel English tradition since the sixteenth century, became almost indiscriminate. But the French too favored a squeeze of lemon at the very end. Raffald, and many English cooks who followed her, substituted "Lemon Pickle" (defined in Chapter 5, #36) or "Browning" ("caramel dissolved in red wine," with spices, mushroom ketchup, salt, and lemon rind) for the more subtle and expensive French coulis. In Child this becomes a final dollop of humble "tomatoes catsup." (However, ketchup made with tomatoes was an exciting new condiment just at this time.)

16. CHICKEN, COLD FRIED

Cut the chicken in quarters, and take off the skin, rub it with an egg beaten up, and cover it with grated bread seasoned with pepper, salt, grated lemon-peel, and chopped parsley, fry it in butter, thicken a little brown gravy with flour and butter, add a little Cayenne, lemon pickle, and mushroom catchup.

—Lee, *Cook's Own Book* (1832), p. 49

The emphasis on gravy, even with cold chicken, and the addition of lemon pickle and mushroom ketchup, are permutations on the eighteenth-century high style we have been discussing in the preceding recipes. Without these additions, this is fried chicken as we would expect to find it in a modern picnic basket. The recipe is taken from Dalgairns.

17. ROAST CHICKENS

Wash them clean outside and inside, stuff them as directed for turkeys, baste them with butter, lard, or drippings, and roast them about an hour. Chickens should be cooked thoroughly. Stew the inwards till tender, and till there is but little water, chop them and mix in gravy from the dripping-pan, thicken with brown flour, and season with salt, pepper, and butter. Cranberry, or new-made apple sauce, is good with them.

—Beecher, *Domestic Receipt-Book* (1846), p. 47

18. ROAST TURKEY [OR CHICKEN] STUFFING

Take bread crumbs, grated or chopped, about enough to fill the turkey, chop a bit of salt pork, the size of a good egg, and mix it in, with butter, the size of an egg, pepper, salt, and sweet herbs to your taste. Then beat up an egg and work in.
—Beecher, *Domestic Receipt-Book* (1846), p. 46

The use of brown (probably whole wheat) flour to thicken gravy is unusual, but otherwise Beecher's directions are modern. She also recommends this bread stuffing for boiled pigeons.

19. CURRIED DISHES

Chickens and veal are most suitable for curries. Boil the meat till tender, and separate the joints. Put a little butter in a stew-pan with the chickens, pour on a part of the liquor in which the meat was boiled, enough nearly to cover it, and let it stew twenty minutes more.

Prepare the curry thus: for four pounds of meat, take a tablespoonful of curry powder, a tea-cup of *boiled* rice, a tablespoonful of flour, and another of melted butter, a tea-cup of the liquor, and half a teaspoonful of salt, mix them, and pour them over the meat and let it stew ten minutes more.

Rice should be boiled for an accompaniment.

—Beecher, *Domestic Receipt-Book* (1846), pp. 39–40

20. TO PREPARE CURRY POWDER

One ounce of ginger, one ounce of mustard, one of pepper, three of coriander seed, three of tumeric, half an ounce of cardamums, quarter of an ounce of Cayenne pepper, quarter of an ounce of cinnamon, and quarter of an ounce of cummin seed. Pound them fine, sift them, and cork them tight in a bottle.

—Beecher, *Domestic Receipt-Book* (1846), p. 40

"Currey," a spiced dish of fowls or rabbits, first appeared in print in Glasse in 1747. Her version of what was to become curry powder consisted of pepper and coriander only, but later mixtures might include cayenne, turmeric, and ginger. Curry recipes utilizing ready-made powder became common toward the end of the century. Rice was always included. This was a case of a London fashion, derived from a colonial import, evolving into a thoroughly English made dish, then spreading to provincial areas. Prepared curry powder was also "proof of the growing commercialization of food products."

21. CHICKENS TO BROIL

After dressing and washing the chickens as previously directed, split them open through the back-bone; frog them by cutting the cords under the wings and laying the wings out flat; cut the sinews under the second joint of the leg and turn the leg down; press down the breast bone, without breaking it.

Season the chicken with salt and pepper, lay it upon the gridiron with the inside first to the fire: put the gridiron over a slow fire, and place a tin sheet and weight upon the chicken, to keep it flat; let it broil ten minutes, then turn and proceed in the same manner with the other side.

The chicken should be perfectly cooked, but not scorched. A broiled chicken brought to the table with its wings and legs burnt, and its breast half cooked, is very disagreeable. To avoid this, the chicken must be closely watched while broiling, and the fire must be arranged so that the heat shall be equally dispensed. When the fire is too hot under any one part of the chicken, put a little ashes on the fire under that part, that the heat may be reduced.

Dish a broiled chicken on a hot plate, putting a large lump of butter and a tablespoonful of hot water upon the plate, and turning the chicken two or three times that it may absorb as much of the butter as possible. Serve with poached eggs on a separate dish. It takes from thirty to forty minutes to broil a chicken well.

—Bliss, *Practical Cook Book* (1850), pp. 82–83

Bliss's instructions for dressing and washing chickens and turkeys are part of #33, below. As in her "To Bone a Fowl" (Chapter 10, #9), Bliss offers expert advice on fowl cookery. By 1850, unless driven by a romantic desire to return to the old way of doing things, cooks were using coal cookstoves rather than woodburning open hearths. Yet Bliss's discussion of arranging the fire, measuring the heat, and adjusting the ashes implies an open fire. Perhaps she reverted to the open hearth only when broiling, which, as this recipe illustrates, produces superb flavor.

22. GUMBO, (A FAVORITE SOUTHERN DISH)

Cut up a pair of good sized chickens, as for a fricassee, flour them well, and put into a pan with a good sized piece of butter, and fry a nice brown, then lay them in a soup pot, pour on three quarts of hot water, and let them simmer slowly for two hours. Braid a little flour and butter together for a thickening, and stir in a little pepper and salt. Strain a quart or three pints of oysters, and add the juice to the soup. Next add four or five slices of cold boiled ham, and let all boil slowly together for ten minutes. Just before you take up the soup, stir in two large spoonfuls of finely powdered sassafras leaves, and let it simmer five minutes, then add your oysters. If you have no ham, it is very nice without it. Serve in a deep dish, and garnish the dish with rice.

—Knight, *Tit-Bits* (1864), p. 28

In the midst of the Civil War, a Northern cook offers a "favorite Southern Dish," which was "New Orleans's most famous Creole creation." In Knight's New England hands, the dish turns out to be a wetter version of fricassee, with the addition of powdered sassafras to thicken the broth. Also called filé, dried and powdered sassafras is "among the Choctaw's lasting contributions to Creole cuisine." Although a roux—flour and fat cooked to a dark color—is generally considered essential to gumbo, Knight forgoes it, adding only uncooked flour and butter for thickening. Essentially, she smothers the fowl in oysters, a long-established practice, as we have seen (#s 1, 13). North and South agree about this, as gumbos often mix seafood and poultry.

The garnish of rice is aligned with a different convention, as rice was often served with curried dishes (#19), which are in many ways similar to gumbo. For centuries rice had been the main crop of the lowland South, especially South Carolina and Georgia, and as such was found in countless regional dishes, including jambalayas, pilaus, and gumbos. In the North rice was eaten less frequently, usually as a component of puddings or soups.

23. FRICASSEE CHICKEN

Clean and then boil the chickens until tender. If old (and they can be purchased cheaper and are as good), boil three to four hours; if young, one hour will do. Keep them covered with water while cooking, skimming when needed. Cut them up; put two slices of pork into the spider, and fry brown; take out the pork, and fry the chicken brown in the fat; remove as fast as brown, and lay in a deep dish. Thicken the liquor left from boiling the poultry with flour mixed smooth in cold water; boil it well; salt it; add a little butter, if not rich enough, and turn on to the chicken. Toast relishes well dipped or spread with this gravy.

—*Aunt Mary's New England Cook Book* (1881), p. 10

Here is a fricassee in which simmering (in this instance all-out boiling) precedes frying (see #15 commentary). This sequence was especially useful in giving tenderness and flavor to many "a tough, old bird," although here and in the following recipe it was also employed with younger birds. Fricasseed chicken remained in the New England repertoire well into the twentieth century.

Black frying pans were known as spiders because initially they were made with three legs to stand before the hearth fire.

24. BROWN FRICASSEE OF CHICKEN

Cut 2 chickens, or fowl, in pieces, and parboil them in just water enough to cover, and when tender take them up and drain dry. Dredge with salt, pepper and flour and fry a dark brown in pork fat. When all is fried stir into the remaining fat a cup of dry flour. Stir until a dark brown, then pour on it one quart of boiling liquor, in which the chicken had been cooked. Season with salt and pepper. Lay chicken in this gravy, simmer 20 minutes and serve.

—Whatsoever Circle, *King's Daughters Cook Book* (1903), p. 35

There is no difference between this recipe in a community cookbook and the previous fricassee, from a Boston publisher, except for the assumption here that only young, tender birds, which need only be parboiled, will be used.

25. SOUTH COUNTY CHICKEN

(Rabbit may also be used in place of chicken and is equally good)

Cut rabbit or fowl in pieces and soak overnight with one medium onion. Then drain, cover with water and boil until tender. Drain, discard onion, dredge heavily with flour and brown in a frying pan. Place pieces in a roaster, fill with water not quite covering, season with salt and pepper and a pinch of sugar (add stalk of dried celery for chicken). Cover and bake 1 hour for rabbit, 2 hours for fowl. This recipe is excellent for tough fowl.

—*Echoes from South County Kitchens* (194?), p. 25

This recipe illustrates the lengths to which cooks were prepared to go, even as late as the mid-twentieth century, to make tough fowl palatable.

The inclusion of sugar in meat, fish, and other savory dishes is, as we discuss elsewhere, a tradition that extends back to the Middle Ages. This recipe appears to be one of the last unself-conscious "echoes" of that hoary practice. Honey had first sweetened the pot in Europe. As trade with the Arab world increased, sugar arrived along with other valuable spices. In one medieval recipe for "chicken in sauge," the sauce of broth, wine, pounded egg yolk, parsley, and sage is spiced with an ounce of cinnamon, a bit of saffron, and an ounce of sugar. The rural Rhode Island home cook who provides the last of our chicken recipes unwittingly follows this ancient practice with her bit of sweetening.

Engraving, "The Day before Thanksgiving, *Harper's Weekly,* 22 November 1890. (Courtesy Harvard College Library, Widener Library, P207.6F, vol. 34)

Turkey

It is the centerpiece of the Thanksgiving table, a symbol of bounty and peace, reminding Americans of their blessings and of the early cooperation between Pilgrims and Indians. Norman Rockwell's 1943 painting *Freedom from Want,* corny as it may be, still sums up the sentimental attachment many Americans feel to the Turkey Day turkey. The bizarre-looking bird with its plume of tail feathers, protuberant snood, and wobbling throat wattle is one of the first figures U.S. schoolchildren learn to draw and color, giving the bird a permanent place of endearment in our national psyche. Turkeys are so tightly woven into the fabric of modern American celebration that few stop to ask how they achieved their celebrity status. So let us ask now: why turkeys? Or, to put it another way, why not roast beef? After all, beef is equally all-American and arguably more prestigious. Why isn't the noble sirloin rather than the comical gobbler the gustatory Polaris of our winter holidays?

To answer the question of why poultry, and turkey in particular, became the main attraction when U.S. holiday menus were codified in the nineteenth century we must first look into the British culinary past.

Despite declarations of political independence, the United States has long found itself—at times placed itself—under British cultural influence. This affinity has ebbed and flowed, to be sure. But the period in the mid to late nineteenth century when communal celebrations and their attendant culinary displays were used most assiduously to advance a uniquely American identity was, ironically, also a time when the continuity of the nation's English heritage and the persistence of its English habits were most enthusiastically asserted and protected.

To begin our backward glance, let us consider a 1517 royal proclamation discussed by Colin Spencer. The primary purpose of the decree was to regulate food consumption—and display—on the basis of social status. Turkeys had been introduced into Europe only about six years earlier, so they were yet to figure in sumptuary laws, although we can easily see how they would, in time, fit very nicely into this (ahem) pecking order:

> A cardinal may have nine dishes served at one meal; a duke, archbishop, marquis, earl or bishop could have seven; lords "under the degree of earl", mayors of the city of London, knights of the garter and abbots could have six; and so on down until those with an income of between £40 and £100 a year could have three dishes. As a dish meant one swan, bustard, peacock or "fowls of like greatness", or four plovers, partridge, woodcock or similar birds (except in the case of the cardinal, who was allowed six), eight quail, dotterels and twelve very small birds such as larks, they were hardly limited in their choice.

As high-status fare, poultry of all sorts was among the first foods in London to be the subject of price controls, preceding veal, beef, and mutton. (In time, the king's council brought these valuable commodities under its purview as well.) As the population of Britain increased, and London in particular grew to gargantuan size, provisions were sought from (literally) farther afield. The pressure was on to make once infertile areas productive: "Buckwheat liked sandy soil and was used for fattening poultry and pigs. . . . It helped to promote the poultry business in Norfolk and Suffolk where the largest acreages of buckwheat were grown on the sands and brecks where hundreds of turkeys, geese, chickens and ducks were fattened for the table."

Poultry in general, but especially turkeys, not only supplied the expanding consumer markets of urban areas, they also provided fresh meat and valuable supplemental income to the rural lower classes: "They earned something from the sale of feathers and grease as well as the meat." Introduced from Mexico after 1510, turkeys became central to the agriculture of East Anglia by the end of the sixteenth century. In time, the number of turkeys driven to the great London market each autumn from these incubating counties was astounding. Daniel Defoe, writing in 1720, says that three hundred droves of turkeys and geese were counted during one season as they passed over the River Stour on their way to London. Each drove held three hundred to a thousand birds. As they walked along, the animals fed on the stubble left behind in harvested fields. One wonders how these rural counties found room for any human inhabitants. Along with buckwheat, carrots, turnips, sodden barley, and oats were used as turkey feed.

Turkeys quickly took the place of the larger game birds eaten whenever the aristocracy and its imitators wished to put on a show. Turkeys, unlike other New World foods such as tomatoes and potatoes, "appear . . . to have diffused swiftly and been consumed enthusiastically" in Europe. Samuel Pepys, whose diary records the intimate details of life among the London gentry and nobility in the 1660s, mentions five gifts of turkey, four of them at Christmastime. But then, by Pepys's day, turkey had long been a holiday dish—Thomas Tusser lists the bird as Christmas fare as early as 1557. Roasting was the favored method of preparation, followed by baking into pies, tarts, and pasties. Pepys apparently learned from the Duke of York (later James II) to make a parsley sauce to accompany the bird. The future king had gotten the recipe from the Spanish ambassador: it consisted of parsley ground up with toast, vinegar, salt, and pepper.

That the Spanish ambassador had opinions about how to sauce turkey is perhaps explained by the fact that the birds had made their way to Spain from Mexico, whence they spread to the rest of Europe. According to Wheaton, "In the sixteenth century, the only New World food immediately accepted in France was the turkey." The French called it *coq d'inde* (Indian rooster), the Germans, *Indianischer Henn,* examples of nomenclatural confusion that reflect the widespread European idea of "a supposed eastern origin." The French term was corrupted to *dinde* or *dindon.*

Wheaton explains the ease with which the new species was accepted:

"Its use spread quickly through Europe, replacing peacock as an important roast for banquets, though as far as I know it was never served sewn back into its skin. It resembled the peacock closely enough to give cooks and diners a model in using it." Turkey remained a "luxury meat." Sixty-six turkeys were served at a banquet held in Paris in 1549 in honor of Catherine de Medici. Yet some resisted the replacement of the earlier banquet birds. One turkey grower opined in 1564: "It is very true that his flesh is fine and delicate, but without taste and of hard digestion."

This remained a minority view. The turkey's popularity in the Old World replicated the esteem in which it had been held throughout the New World, especially in Mexico and Central America. The Mexican turkey, probably domesticated in the late second millennium BCE, was especially favored. A. W. Schorger provides this remarkable story from the first decades of European contact with Mexico: "Every person in Misquiahuala had to contribute to Montezuma one turkey every twenty days. The population of the town in 1519 was estimated at 7,500 persons. . . . Assuming that only adults were intended to contribute [say, 3,000 persons] . . . the number of turkeys would be 54,000 [annually]." During the same era, turkeys "were the most conspicuous and cheapest source of meat in Mexico."

The seventeenth-century cookbooks in our sample include only a few recipes for turkey but all involve cooking the bird in familiar ways, especially roasting and baking in a pie. Markham recommends serving roast turkey with onion sauce. Discussing pastry and baked meats, he lists turkey among foods suitable for encasing in good (though not the best) wheaten pie crusts (see Chapter 9, #1). Woolley also gives a turkey pie. In this, neither Markham nor Woolley were original: turkey quickly became a favorite Elizabethan bakemeat and was featured in Christmas pies.

But between Woolley in 1670 and the first edition of Smith in 1727, the idea that roasting was far and away the best method by which to prepare the large fowl had taken firm hold in the cooking manuals. The roast turkey was soon at home in aristocratic settings, on gentry tables, and, for holidays at least, in all manner of humbler households. Successfully fending off the old favorites—among wildfowl, herons, swans, and bustards; among tame varieties, peacocks, geese, ducks, and chickens—turkey has never lost its culinary preeminence since it first sailed eastward across the Atlantic under the Spanish flag.

We have selected the following recipes in order to showcase the classic formulas for the cooking methods most widely used in New England—roasting and, to a lesser extent, boiling. (Turkey used as bakemeat did not survive the eighteenth century.) Our major emphasis in this section is on the gastronomic pleasure provided by roast turkey, a deceptively simple dish that, according to Thomas Robinson Hazard, the nineteenth-century Rhode Island raconteur, must first be "well-killed, well-picked, well-dry-dressed." Along with proper butchering methods, skill in roasting is also required to produce the perfect turkey dinner. And the English and New England cooks who roasted their turkeys in the days when open-hearth fires were the norm were indeed highly skilled. The superiority of English and American roasting techniques was widely acknowledged, even by the French.

26. TO ROAST A TURKEY

Take a quarter of a pound of lean veal, a little thyme, parsley, sweet marjoram, a sprig of winter savory, a bit of lemon peel, one onion, a nutmeg grated, a dram of mace, a little salt, and half a pound of butter; cut your herbs very small, pound your meat as small as possible, and mix all together with three eggs, and as much flour, or bread, as will make it of a proper consistence. Then fill the crop of your turkey with it, paper the breast and lay it down at a good distance from the fire. An hour and a quarter will roast it if not very large.

—Smith, *Compleat Housewife* (1750), p. 22

Another posthumous offering from Smith, in this instance not lifted from Glasse. Smith fills the crop of the bird rather than the body cavity with the stuffing. The crop (or craw) is a baglike organ in the breast of the turkey above the gizzard. It is part of the turkey's digestive tract and in the live turkey can hold more than a pound of feed. In recipes #27 and #31 below, Raffald and Lee also stuff the crop, while Beecher (#32) fills both crop and body. Bliss (#33) gives a thorough description of how to clean the crop and prepare the breast for forcemeat.

Papering the breast and setting the fowl to roast at a distance from the fire is what was once known as white roasting, a method by which the flesh is kept pale and the bird thoroughly cooked but not scorched. The alternative method, brown roasting—the only one now in use—involved longer cooking before a slower fire, and was once used only for large birds with dark flesh, such as swans, cranes, and bustards. Papering derives from the French *surtout* (overcoat), a dish of roasted game bird that has first been larded and wrapped in paper. Patrick Lamb includes *surtouts* among the "choicest recipes" in his *Royal Cookery* of 1710.

27. TO STEW A TURKEY WITH CELERY SAUCE

Take a large Turkey, and make a good white Force-meat of Veal, and stuff the Craw of the Turkey, skewer it as for boiling, then boil it in soft Water 'till it is almost enough, and then take up your Turkey, and put it in a Pot with some of the Water it was boiled in, to keep it hot, put seven or eight Heads of Celery that is washed and cleaned very well into the Water that the Turkey was boiled in, 'till they are tender, then take them up, and put in your Turkey with the Breast down, and stew it a quarter of an Hour, then take it up, and thicken your Sauce with half a Pound of Butter and Flour to make it pretty thick, and a quarter of a Pint of rich Cream, then put in your Celery; pour the Sauce and Celery hot upon the Turkey's Breast, and serve it up.

It is a proper Top Dish for Dinner or Supper.

—Raffald, *Experienced English House-keeper* (1769), p. 108

In eighteenth-century Britain and colonial New England, turkey was more likely to be stewed (simmered in or along with sauce) than boiled— that is, when it was not roasted. Both Smith and Glasse have recipes for stewed turkey but none for boiled. Coming a bit later and perhaps anticipating the nineteenth-century trend, Raffald does include a recipe for boiled turkey along with this and one other for stewing the bird. A top dish, referring to placement on a formal dining table, was essentially a main course.

28. GRAVY SAUCE FOR A BOILED TURKEY

Take a little water, or mutton Gravy, a blade of Mace, an Onion, a little Thyme, a little Bit of Lemon Peel, and an Anchovy. Stew all together very gently. When done enough, strain through an hair Sieve. Melt some Butter and add to this Gravy.

—Gardiner, *Family Receipts* (ca. 1770), p. 11

Gardiner does not offer recipes for preparing fowl per se but includes in her manuscript cookbook a number of preparations for saucing birds, all except two, this one and one other, taken from Glasse or Raffald. A hair sieve, sometimes called a hair bag, was made of horse hair. Glasse utilizes one in a fowl sauce recipe not copied by Gardiner.

29. TO STUFF AND ROAST A TURKEY, OR FOWL

One pound soft wheat bread, 3 ounces beef suet, 3 eggs, a little sweet thyme, sweet marjoram, pepper and salt, and some add a gill of wine; fill the bird therewith and sew up, hang down to a steady solid fire, basting frequently with salt and water, and roast until a steam emits from the breast, put one third of a pound of butter into the gravy, dust flour over the bird and baste with the gravy; serve up with boiled onions and cramberry-sauce, mangoes, pickles or celery.

2. Others omit the sweet herbs, and add parsley done with potatoes.

3. Boil and mash 3 pints potatoes, wet them with butter, add sweet herbs, pepper, salt, fill and roast as above.

—Simmons, *American Cookery* (Hartford, 1796), p. 18

Seasoning poultry stuffing with the herbs Simmons uses here for her bread stuffing—thyme and marjoram—along with those she recommends in another bread stuffing—summer savory and sage—remains customary. Bell's Seasoning, created in 1867 and still the most popular poultry blend, adds rosemary, oregano, and ginger to Simmons's selections, but the predominant aromatics are the same. Of course we do not follow Simmons in stuffing the bird with potatoes, mashed or otherwise.

30. TO CARVE A TURKEY

Fix the fork firmly on one side of the thin bone that rises in the centre of the breast; the fork should be placed *parallel* with the bone, and as close to it as possible. Cut the meat from the breast lengthwise, in slices of about half an inch in thickness. Then turn the turkey upon the side nearest you, and cut off the leg and the wing; when the knife is passed between the limbs and the body, and pressed outward, the joint will be easily perceived. Then turn the turkey on the other side, and cut off the other leg and wing. Separate the drum-sticks from the leg-bones, and the pinions from the wings; it is hardly possible to mistake the joint. Cut the stuffing in thin slices, lengthwise. Take off the neck-bones, which are two triangular bones on each side of the breast; this is done by passing the knife from the back under the blade-part of each neck-bone, until it reaches the end; by raising the knife, the other branch will easily crack off. Separate the carcass from the back by passing the knife lengthwise from the neck downward. Turn the back upwards, and lay the edge of the knife across the back-bone, about midway between the legs and wings; at the same moment, place the fork within the lower part of the turkey, and lift it up; this will make the back-bone crack at the knife. The croup, or lower part of the back, being cut off, put it on the plate, with the rump from you, and split off the side-bones by forcing the knife through from the rump to the other end.

The choicest parts of a turkey are the side-bones, the breast, and the thigh-bones. The breast and wings are called light meat; the thigh-bones and side-bones dark meat. When a person declines expressing a preference, it is polite to help to both kinds.

—Child, *American Frugal Housewife* (1833), pp. 122–23

The thoroughness and precision of these instructions, together with serving tips aimed at those aspiring to gentility, help explain why Child's cookbook was an immediate and long-lasting success.

31. TURKEY, TURKEY POULTS, AND OTHER POULTRY

A fowl and a turkey require the same management at the fire, only the latter will take longer time.

Many a Christmas dinner has been spoiled by the turkey having been hung up in a cold larder, and becoming thoroughly frozen; *Jack Frost* has ruined the reputation of many a turkey roaster.

Let them be carefully picked, &c. and break the breast bone (to make them look plump), twist up a sheet of clean writing paper, light it, and thoroughly singe the turkey all over, turning it about over the flame.

Turkeys, fowls, and capons have a much better appearance, if, instead of trussing them with the legs close together, and the feet cut off, the legs are extended on each side of the bird, and the toes only cut off, with a skewer through each foot, to keep them at a proper distance.

Be careful, when you draw it, to preserve the liver, and not to break the gall-bag, as no washing will take off the bitter taste it gives, where it once touches.

Prepare a nice, clear, brisk fire for it.

Make stuffing; stuff it under the breast, where the craw was taken out and make some into balls, and boil or fry them, and lay them round the dish; they are handy to help, and you can then reserve some of the inside stuffing to eat with the cold turkey, or to enrich a hash.

—Lee, *Cook's Own Book* (1832), p. 227

To hear Lee speak of "a fowl and a turkey" as distinct species may strike us as odd, but as we mention in the introduction to this chapter, in Britain the term "fowl" refers only to the domestic cock or hen, not to domestic poultry in general as it does in the United States. Lee follows British usage—hardly surprising, since the instructions are lifted verbatim from Kitchiner.

The warning about frozen turkey in the larder reminds us that, as Brian Fagan notes, the nineteenth-century Atlantic world was a colder place than it is now. Before refrigeration, many cooks hung meat to improve taste and texture. Harold McGee explains how hanging and aging ward off the toughness that results when fresh meat is cooked in a state of rigor mortis: "Carcasses are hung up in such a way that most of their muscles are stretched by gravity, so that the protein filaments can't contract and overlap very much; otherwise the filaments bunch up and bond very tightly and the meat becomes exceptionally tough. Eventually, protein-digesting enzymes within the muscle fibers begin to eat away the framework that holds the actin and myosin filaments in place . . . and the meat texture softens."

Drawing a turkey, that is, removing the gizzard, liver, and heart, is described in detail by Bliss (below, #33). As mentioned in the commentary to #26, the craw is the crop.

32. TO BOIL A TURKEY

Make a stuffing for the craw, of chopped bread and butter, cream, oysters, and the yolks of eggs. Sew it in, and dredge flour over the turkey, and put it to boil in cold water, with a spoonful of salt in it, and enough water to cover it well. Let it simmer for two hours and a half, or if small, less time. Skim it while boiling. It looks nicer if wrapped in a cloth dredged with flour.

Serve it with drawn butter, in which are put some oysters.

—Beecher, *Domestic Receipt-Book* (1846), p. 42

Beecher's suggestion to wrap the turkey in a floured pudding cloth (see Chapter 13) before boiling in order to minimize discoloration was a technique more often presented as mandatory than optional in nineteenth-century New England recipes for boiled turkey.

Drawn butter is simply melted butter. In New England, it is nowadays usually served with steamed clams or boiled lobster. The word "drawn" has long been used to mean strained, as in drawn gruel or gravy. Glasse mentions "a little good drawn Gravy." In 1812, William Windham provided what was to become a typical nineteenth-century indictment of this aspect of his national cuisine: "It was the sort of poverty of conception, reproached by some foreigner to English cookery, that we had but one sauce, and that that sauce was melted butter."

33. TURKEY TO ROAST

A turkey weighing twelve pounds has usually the best flavor, being neither too young nor too old; a turkey of this size requires three hours to roast; prepare as follows:—

Cut the neck very close to the body, and take off the legs at the joint of "the drum stick;" singe the turkey with white paper or newspaper,—brown paper and straw paper will smut it; take out the crop by carefully cutting a slit on the back of the neck, just above the breast,—this will leave the breast whole for the forcemeat; draw the turkey by putting the fingers of the right hand up the vent, quite to the throat, and, with the middle finger close to the sides of the back-bone, loosen the lights and draw them out with the liver, gizzard, and heart; be careful to take them *all* firmly in your hand, in order not to break the gall, which you will do if you pull them out separately; then wash the turkey clean, rub the inside well with salt, and, if you desire to stuff the body, take out the sole,—which is the dark-colored meat adhering to the little ribs near the middle of the back; the sole will discolor the stuffing; but if you intend to stuff the breast only, the sole may be left in, as it will keep the meat from becoming dry in roasting.

When the turkey is thus prepared, fill the place from which the crop was taken with a forcemeat of bread crumbs, salt pork, sweet marjoram, pepper, and salt, well mixed; fasten up the place by drawing the skin of the neck over it and putting a small bird skewer through to keep it tight,—this way is much more convenient and expeditious than fastening by a needle and thread; then put a long skewer through the body, under the second joint of the leg, so that the lower end of the drum stick will only reach to the vent; put a short skewer through the flap at the side of the vent; bring both the drum sticks down, put the same skewer through them, bringing it out through the other side of the flap and binding it fast with a tape; then fasten the wings to the side of the turkey with another long skewer, spit the turkey, but never put a skewer through the breast to fasten it to the spit; dredge it with flour; if the turkey is not very fat, put small bits of butter on the breast, if it is fat, no butter will be requisite; place it before a slow fire and turn it frequently until all the flour begins to brown; baste it continually with salt and water from the dripping-pan, and when half done, dredge it again with flour. If the breast is browning too fast, put a piece of paper over it. Fifteen minutes before you wish to serve it, drip a little melted butter all over it, from the basting-spoon; dredge it with flour, let it brown,—and the turkey is roasted.

Gravy.—Make a gravy by boiling the neck, heart, liver, and gizzard in a stew-pan with a pint of water; when these have become quite tender take them out of the water, chop the heart and gizzard, mash the liver, throw away the neck; return the heart, gizzard, and liver to the liquor in which they were stewed; add to this the liquor in the dripping-pan of the roaster, skim off the fat from the surface of the stew-pan; set the stew-pan over the fire, boil three minutes, and thicken with flour,—if you have basted the turkey as directed, you will need no burnt flour to color the gravy.

Serve turkey with cranberry sauce, and boiled ham or tongue. Some people serve it with sausages.

—Bliss, *Practical Cook Book* (1850), pp. 79–80

Bliss's description of how to prepare and roast turkey before an open fire cannot be topped: she gives ideal weight and roasting time, precise instructions for drawing, stuffing, skewering, basting, and flouring, and directions for classic giblet gravy. She even recommends appropriate side dishes, which, for the meat-crazy nineteenth century, were as apt to be other meats as cranberry sauce.

The ideal turkey, weighing about twelve pounds and "being neither too young nor too old," was a fairly recent commodity in the mid-nineteenth-century marketplace. In the late eighteenth century, one English visitor to the eastern United States, speaking of the wild turkey of the Western Hemisphere, wondered: "Why do not the Americans domesticate this noble bird? They are much better adapted to bear this climate than the puny breed their ancestors imported from England." The larger dimensions of the wild turkey had long been noted, and both accidental and intentional interbreeding between wild and domesticated birds had occurred, but it was not as easy as it might seem to crossbreed wild and tame birds. Schorger points out that "the development of a heavy domestic turkey was slow in coming."

Despite the glories of the carefully bred and well-roasted domesticated turkey, the large wild breed should not be overlooked in telling the American story. Wild turkeys served the pioneers as a kind of "emergency ration." In West Virginia in 1773, for instance, Joseph and Samuel Martin lived on nothing but boiled turkey—without even salt—for two or three months until they could harvest their first crop of corn. And in 1779, after being wounded in a battle with Indians in the same area, a Captain R. Benham and his companions survived until they were well enough to travel by shooting and eating the wild turkeys that came near their camp. Daniel Boone escaped captivity on June 16, 1778, when the Indians who held him near Chillicothe, Ohio, left him in camp to pursue a flock of wild turkeys.

CHAPTER EIGHT

Game and Meat

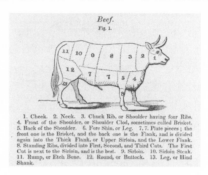

Beef.
Fig. 1.

1. Cheek. 2. Neck. 3. Chuck Rib, or Shoulder having four Ribs.
4. Front of the Shoulder, or Shoulder Clod, sometimes called Brisket.
5. Back of the Shoulder. 6. Fore Shin, or Leg. 7, 7. Plate pieces; the
front one is the Brisket, and the back one is the Flank, and is divided
again into the Thick Flank, or Upper Sirloin, and the Lower Flank.
8. Standing Ribs, divided into First, Second, and Third Cuts. The First
Cut is next to the Sirloin, and is the beef. 9. Sirloin. 10. Sirloin Steak.
11. Rump, or Etch Bone. 12. Round, or Buttock. 13. Leg, or Hind
Shank.

Touring England in the 1690s, Henri Misson was only one of many continental travelers who had "always heard that [the English] were great flesh-eaters" and who found that this was indeed true. While the people he observed would only "nibble a few crumbs" of bread, meat they would "chew . . . by whole mouthfuls. . . . Among the middling sort of people they have ten or twelve sorts of common meats which infallibly take their turns at their tables." Around this same time it was calculated that English annual per capita meat consumption was 140 pounds. A bit earlier, in 1639, English flesh-eating was associated with a charge of heresy against one Puritan radical. John Everarde was alleged to have denied the doctrine of the resurrection of the body because he "did not beleeve that our bodyes nourished of and by beefe mutton and Capon and the like could rise againe and goe to heaven."

The settlers of New England were primarily drawn from the meat-eating, "middling sort of people," but in the seventeenth century most of them were not yet prosperous enough to place flesh meat at the core of their diet. As we noted in Chapter 5, pottage was the staple dish of early New England, with the legume and grain component dominating the meat component and increasingly so as time passed since autumn slaughtering.

By the middle of the eighteenth century, things had begun to change. Food preservation techniques in general, and meat preservation techniques in particular, had steadily improved, so that in a great many households salted meat supplies lasted the entire year. Frequently apt to be found in the "ample depths" of "the huge dinner pot," steaming on "the genial open kitchen-fire" (to quote a nostalgic evocation by Harriet Beecher Stowe), were "beets, carrots, potatoes, and turnips [boiling] in jolly sociability with the pork or corned beef which they were destined to flank at the coming meal." Boiled dinner, and the meat that was central to it, was supplanting pottage as the daily fare of New England.

By the first half of the nineteenth century, the former English colonies had equaled or surpassed their onetime mother country in reputed flesh-eating avidity. A native observer, Timothy Dwight, found that in New England meat was consumed two or three times a day by even the poorer sort. An English visitor, forgetting his own nation's achievements in this regard, stated that "as a flesh-consuming people, the Americans have no equal in the world." This writer had seen a typical gentleman "choose as many as seven or eight different kinds of animal food from the bill of fare, and after having all arranged before him in a row, . . . commence at one end and eat his way through in half a dozen minutes."

Sarah Josepha Hale made flesh consumption the key to a dietary theory of human development and the configurations of power among the nations of the world. Since "a portion of animal food" was required "to develop and sustain the human constitution, in its most perfect state of physical, intellectual, and moral strength and beauty," it was only to be expected that "it is that portion of the human family, who have the means of obtaining [such animal food] at least once a day, who now hold dominion over the earth." More specifically, "Forty thousand of the beef-fed British govern and control ninety millions of the rice-eating natives of India," while "in our own country, . . . the severe and unremitting labors of every kind, which were requisite to subdue and obtain dominion of a wilderness world" were enabled by "a generous diet" based on meat.

The importance of meat to the English and the English-Americans is on display elsewhere in this volume in other meat-based preparations, such as pies. Here we offer a representative selection of the ways in which flesh meat was more directly transformed into good eating.

Game

Game, especially venison, enjoyed great prestige in England as the food of the aristocracy, and there were certainly plenty of deer and other forest animals in North America for the early settlers to hunt or trap, cook, and eat. Nevertheless, game did not become particularly prominent in New England cookery. This was so in spite of the further fact that game—especially deer—were hunted to virtual extinction in New England during the seventeenth and eighteenth centuries and so must have been consumed there on a regular basis. New Englanders' relative silence about game cookery may have been due to the fact that it—especially venison—was a staple of the native peoples, so that embarrassment about eating what the Indians ate outweighed this food's traditional association with the aristocracy. However, there were some recipes for venison and other game meats in English and New England cookbooks, of which we offer a few tasty examples.

1. TO ROAST VENISON

If you will roast any Venison after you haue washt it, and clensed all blood from it, you shal sticke it with cloues all ouer on the out side, and if it be leane you shall larde it either with Mutton lard, or porke larde, but mutton is the best: then spit it and roast it by a good soking fire, then take vinegar, bread crummes, and some of the grauie which comes from the Venison, and boile them well in a dish; then season it with sugar, cinamon, ginger, and salt, And so serue the Venison foorth vpon the sauce when it is roasted enough.

—Markham, *English Hus-wife* (1615), p. 59

In 1617, Englishman Fynes Moryson, in a multivolume account of his travels across Europe, commented that "the English Cookes, in comparison with other Nations, are most commended for roasted meates." As if in confirmation of this reputation, Markham prefaces his recipes for roasting specific meats with more than two pages of detailed instructions on all aspects of roasting procedures. In the section on how "to know when meate is rosted enough . . . neither too moist nor too drie," the signs of doneness for "large ioints of meate" are "when the stemme [steam] or smoake of the meat ascendeth, either vpright, or els goeth from the fire [i.e., toward the room rather than farther back in the hearth], when it beginneth a little to shrinke [i.e., separate] from the spit, or when the grauy which droppeth from it is cleere without bloodinesse."

Larding could mean either drawing strips of fat through the meat with a larding needle or spreading it all over the outside (sometimes called barding); the former is the more common meaning and is probably what Markham intends. Venison is usually larded since "it is generally very lean and inclined to be dry." A soaking ("soking") fire is one that has been maintained at a steady temperature for an extended period. Markham calls for a seasoning mixture for the sauce, with sugar and cinnamon, that could have been used at a medieval banquet.

2. TO JUG A HARE

Having cased the hare, turn the blood out of the body into the jug. Then cut the hare to pieces, but do not wash it. Then cut three quarters of a pound of fat bacon into thin slices. Pour upon the blood about a pint of strong old pale beer: put into the jug a middling sized onion, stuck with three or four cloves, and a bunch of sweet herbs: and having seasoned the hare with pepper, salt, nutmeg, and lemon-peel grated, put in the meat, a layer of hare, and a layer of bacon. Then stop the jug close, so that the steam be kept in entirely; put the jug into a kettle of water over the fire, and let it stew three hours, then strain off the liquor, and having thickened it with burnt butter, serve it up hot, garnished with lemon sliced.

—Carter, *Frugal Housewife* (1772), pp. 67–68

Although the sixteenth-century writer Andrew Boorde, along with others, feared that in eating hare one ran the risk of falling into melancholy, it was a risk he was willing to run, as hare flesh was, he felt, "best of all wylde beestes." There were many recipes for hare, explicitly distinguished from domesticated rabbits or conies, in seventeenth- and eighteenth-century cookbooks, and jugged hare was a standard item. Carter's recipe appears to be adapted from one in Smith, with the primary difference between the two being that Smith does not steam the hare in its own blood. To case an animal carcass is to remove the skin. The instruction to "put in the meat, a layer of hare, and a layer of bacon" is initially confusing, since no meat other than hare is mentioned in the recipe. Presumably the words, "a layer of hare, and a layer of bacon," are intended to specify the types of meat being put in.

3. FRICASSEED RABBITS

The best way of cooking rabbits is to fricassee them. Take a couple of fine ones, and cut them up, or disjoint them. Put them into a stew-pan; season them with cayenne pepper and salt, some chopped parsley, and some powdered mace. Pour in a pint of warm water (or of veal broth, if you have it) and stew it over a slow fire till the rabbits are quite tender; adding (when they are about half done) some bits of butter rolled in flour. Just before you take it from the fire, enrich the gravy with a jill or more of thick cream with some nutmeg grated into it. Stir the gravy well, but take care not to let it boil after the cream is in, lest it curdle.

Put the pieces of rabbit on a hot dish, and pour the gravy over them.

—Leslie, *Directions for Cookery* (1840), p. 138

While rabbits formed part of the livestock resources of the typical English yeoman of the seventeenth century, they were not domesticated with such regularity in North American husbandry. We have included this dish in the game section because wild rabbits were used for food in North America. When Lee (or rather, Kitchiner) states that "a fine, well-grown (but young) warren rabbit, kept sometime after it has been killed, and roasted with a stuffing in its belly, eats very like a hare, to the nature of which it approaches," it is likely, given the claim of resemblance to a hare, that what is meant is a rabbit from a warren in the sense of "a piece of uncultivated ground in which rabbits breed wild in burrows." Certainly two rabbits of this type could easily be the "couple of fine ones" that Leslie calls for. The dish is similar to the recipes for white fricasseed chicken we've seen in Chapter 7.

4. TO ROAST VENISON

Spit a haunch of venison, and butter well four sheets of paper, two of which put on the haunch. Then make a paste with flour, butter, and water; roll it out half as big as the haunch, and put it over the fat part; then put the other two sheets of paper on, and tie them with pack-thread; lay it to a brisk fire, and baste it well all the time of roasting. If a large haunch of twenty-four pounds, it will take three hours and a half, unless there is a very large fire; then three hours will do: smaller in proportion.

—Howland, *New England Economical Housekeeper* (1845), p. 52

Howland's recipe reflects changes in standard roasting techniques since the time of Markham. The use of buttered paper to prevent the meat from scorching was recommended in any number of eighteenth-century English recipes. Markham protects against excessive dryness by larding, whereas Howland, again following standard eighteenth-century English practice, calls for basting, presumably with drippings captured in a dripping pan. Dryness was also averted by dredging with flour, oatmeal, or bread crumbs; Howland employs a simple pie crust covering "the fat part" to accomplish the same purpose. It is an indication of the emerging New England plain style that Howland eliminates not only Markham's sugared-and-spiced gravy but also the more modern seasonings, enhancements, and garnishes found in most eighteenth-century recipes.

Veal

Until well into the nineteenth century, veal was for most people an opportunity to partake of fresh meat during the late spring and early summer, when most calves were slaughtered. The carcasses were small enough that there was no difficulty about warm-weather preservation of unconsumed portions. In one western Massachusetts town in the eighteenth century, veal constituted 8 percent of the meat diet. Yet it constituted a rather higher proportion than this of the meat recipes in both English and American cookbooks—no doubt mainly because cookbooks were mostly used by urban people who could afford fresh meat and who traded with butchers who could meet their demand year-round.

5. VEALE TOSTS

To make the best veale tosts, take the kidney fat and all of a loine of veale rosted, and shred it as small as possible; Then take a couple of egges and beat them very well, which done take spinage, succory, violet leaues, and marigold leaues, and beat them, and straine out the iuice, and mix it with the egges: Then put it to your veale and stirre it exceedingly well in a dish; then put to good store of currance cleane washt and pickt, cloues, mace, sinamon, nutmeg, sugar, and salt, and mix them all perfectly well together: then take a manchet and cut it into tosts, and tost them well before the fire; then with a spoone lay vpon the toste in a good thickenesse the veale, prepared as before said; which done put into your frying pan good store of sweet butter, and when it is well melted and very hot, put your tosts into the same with the bread side vpward, and the flesh side downeward: And assoone as you see they are fried browne, lay vpon the vpper side of the toasts which are bare more of the flesh meate; and then turne them, and frie that side browne also: Then take them out of the pan and dish them vp, and strow suger vpon them, and so serue them forth. There be some Cookes which will do this but vpon one side of the tostes, but to do it on both is much better: If you adde creame it is not amisse.

—Markham, *English Hus-wife* (1615), pp. 45–46

This type of meat topping (and in this case bottoming) for toast became popular in the sixteenth century and was usually, as in most medieval cookery, semisweet. Markham mixes the hashed veal and kidney fat with sugar and currants, as well as with eggs, additional spices, and the juice of various herbs. Most of the fruits, spices, and herbs he also utilizes elsewhere (see Chapter 5, #1; Chapter 10, #13).

6. TO STUFF A LEG OF VEAL

Take one pound of veal, half pound pork (salted,) one pound grated bread, chop all very fine, with a handful of green parsley, pepper it, add 3 ounces butter and 3 eggs, (and sweet herbs if you like them,) cut the leg round like a ham and stab it full of holes, and fill in all the stuffing; then salt and pepper the leg and dust on some flour; if baked in an oven, put into a sauce pan with a little water, if potted, lay some scewers at the bottom of the pot, put in a little water and lay the leg on the scewers, with a gentle fire render it tender, (frequently adding water,) when done take out the leg, put butter in the pot and brown the leg, the gravy in a separate vessel must be thickened and buttered and a spoonful of ketchup added.

—Simmons, *American Cookery* (Hartford, 1796), p. 19

The stuffing is a standard eighteenth-century forcemeat. Cutting the leg "round like a ham" would make it narrow at the top and bottom with a round bulge in the middle. Simmons allows for the dish either to be baked in a brick oven or simmered in a pot or kettle. Until well into the nineteenth century, baking cuts of meat in an oven was considered more akin to stewing than to roasting. Mushroom ketchup, in the same amount Simmons recommends here, is added to Raffald's recipe for stewing a leg of veal. Chapter 5, #39 is a nineteenth-century recipe for such a ketchup.

7. THE KNUCKLE IS BEST STEWED,

as the whimsical receipt of Gay, the poet, testifies:—

"Take a knuckle of veal,

(You may buy it or steal,)

In a few pieces cut it,

In a stewing pan put it."

Where it must remain (seasoned with a great variety of sweet herbs) about three hours, when it is fit for any dignitary.

—Hale, *Good Housekeeper* (1841), p. 48

The knuckle is the lower part of either the hind or front leg. The lines Hale quotes were actually written by Alexander Pope, as part of a humorous letter to Jonathan Swift on which Pope and a group of his and Swift's mutual friends, including John Gay, collaborated. The sweet herbs and other seasonings Pope mentions in the portion of his versified recipe that Hale does not quote are mace, celery, sorrel, parsley, spinach, endive, lettuce, beet leaves, salt, and pepper. Pope also says to "put no water at all" in the stewing pan but rather to place the entire pan in a "hot boiling kettle." Since Hale says nothing about water, you may well wish to follow Pope's directions, essentially making jugged knuckle of veal (see #2). Or you may wish to be guided by the first of Glasse's two recipes for stewed knuckle of veal, which calls for simmering a knuckle left whole in two quarts of water. Smith, Pope's contemporary, puts heavy cream and egg yolk into the sauce for her stewed knuckle of veal.

8. VEAL CHEESE

Prepare equal quantities of sliced boiled veal and smoked tongue, boiled, skinned, and sliced.

Pound each separately in a mortar, moistening with butter as you proceed.

Then take a stone jar, or tin can, and mix them in it, so that it will, when cut, look mottled and variegated. Press it hard and pour on melted butter. Keep it covered in a dry place. To be used at tea in slices.

—Beecher, *Domestic Receipt-Book* (1846), p. 56

This is a veal (and smoked tongue) variation on a pâté-like preparation found in many nineteenth-century cookbooks: pig's-head cheese, an example of which is given below (#29). The term "cheese" could be applied to any food product made by pressing a foodstuff into a dense, solid mass, as in Beecher's own "Fruit Cheese." The circumstances that called this recipe into existence are evoked by the concluding sentence: "To be used at tea in slices." The reputation of pork declined during the nineteenth century. By midcentury, when Beecher was writing, pig's-head cheese would have been a dubious choice for such an occasion as a tea party, whereas veal cheese would have been perfectly acceptable.

9. POT-ROASTED [VEAL] FILLET

Remove the bone and fill the cavity with a force-meat made of bread-crumbs, a very little salt, pork chopped fine, sage, pepper, salt, and ground cloves. Lay in the pot a layer of slices of salt pork; put in the fillet, fastened with skewers, cover with additional pork, pour over it a pint of good stock, cover down close, and let it cook slowly two or three hours; then take off the cover and let it brown. Serve hot.

—Turner, *New England Cook Book* (1905), p. 77

The emergence around this time of pot roast as a name for a simmered cut of beef is discussed in #49. This recipe uses a stuffing, as in beef pot roast's predecessor, beef à la mode. It calls for browning the meat after simmering rather than before, as is usual in modern pot roast.

Lamb

Like veal, lamb was available primarily during spring and summer slaughtering time and had to be consumed while fresh, although Hale states that "it requires to be kept a few days, when the weather will permit." In the same eighteenth-century western Massachusetts town where veal constituted 8 percent of the meat diet, lamb and mutton together represented 12 percent of meat consumption. This calls into question the assertion made by one food historian that "lamb and mutton met considerable prejudice, even in New England where they were most used." So do the recipes appearing in the region's cookbooks.

10. TO MAKE A RAGOO OF LAMB

Take a Fore-Quarter of Lamb, cut the Knuckle Bone off, lard it with little thin Bits of Bacon, flour it, fry it of a fine Brown, and then put it into an Earthen Pot or Stew-pan; put to it a Quart of Broth or good Gravy, a Bundle of Herbs, a little Mace, two or three Cloves, and a little Whole Pepper; cover it close, and let it stew pretty fast for Half an Hour, pour the Liquor all out, strain it, keep the Lamb hot in the Pot till the Sauce is ready, take Half a Pint of Oysters, flour them, fry them Brown, drain out all the Fat clean that you fry'd them in, skim all the Fat off the Gravy, then pour it into the Oysters, put in an Anchovy, and two Spoonfuls of either Red or White Wine; boil all together until there is just enough for Sauce, add some fresh Mushrooms (if you can get them) and some pickled Ones, with a Spoonful of the Pickle, or the Juice of Half a Lemon; lay your Lamb in the Dish, and pour the Sauce over it. Garnish with Lemon.

—Glasse, *Art of Cookery* (1747), p. 27

In eighteenth-century England, the term "Ragoo," an anglicization of the French *ragoût*, could mean either, as here, an entire dish, usually of meat simmered in garnished sauce or simply the garnish alone. With its bundle of herbs, anchovy, wine, and mushrooms, Glasse's dish is in keeping with the ragouts found in influential French authorities. The knuckle, or shank, of a lamb is cut from the front leg.

11. ROAST LAMB

Lay down to a clear good fire that will not want stirring or altering, baste with butter, dust on flour, baste with the dripping, and before you take it up, add more butter and sprinkle on a little salt and parsley shred fine; send to table with a nice sallad, green peas, fresh beans, or a colliflower, or asparagus.

—Simmons, *American Cookery* (Hartford, 1796), p. 18

Like the venison dish in #4, this recipe utilizes standard eighteenth-century English roasting practices—in this instance, dredging (or dusting) and basting. In the seventeenth century, for example in Markham, the term "sallad" or "sallet" could refer to vegetable mixtures composed primarily of cooked or pickled ingredients as well as to mixtures comprising mainly raw ingredients. By Simmons's time, a definition propounded in 1699 that is more in accordance with our modern understanding had taken hold: "We are by *Sallet* to understand a particular Composition of certain *Crude* and fresh Herbs, such as usually are, or may safely be eaten with some *Acetous* Juice, *Oyl*, *Salt*, &c. to give them a grateful Gust and Vehicle."

12. TO COOK A SHOULDER OF LAMB

Check the shoulder with cuts an inch deep, rub on first butter, then salt, pepper, and sweet herbs, over these put the yolk of an egg and bread crumbs, and then bake or roast it a light brown. Make a gravy of the drippings, seasoning with pepper, salt, and tomato catsup, and also the grated rind and juice of a lemon; thicken with a very little flour.

—Beecher, *Domestic Receipt-Book* (1846), p. 49

Beecher keeps her baked or roasted meat moist not with water or basting but with a coating of butter, egg yolk, and bread crumbs. Beecher's own recipe for tomato ketchup is decidedly more interesting than what we get today out of a bottle.

13. TOMATO CATSUP

Pour boiling water on the tomatoes, let them stand until you can rub off the skin, then cover them with salt, and let them stand twenty-four hours. Then strain them, and to two quarts put three ounces of cloves, two ounces of pepper, two nutmegs. Boil half an hour, then add a pint of wine.

—Beecher, *Domestic Receipt-Book* (1846), p. 72

14. LAMB EN CASSEROLE

Brush lamb chops with melted butter, salt and pepper. Brown in spider. Parboil three-fourths cup carrot till nearly soft. Drain, fry in bacon fat, to which has been added three-fourths tablespoon chopped onion. Put chops in casserole, add the carrots, one cup potato balls, two cups thin brown sauce or water, three tablespoons sherry, salt, pepper. Cook till potatoes are done. Add twelve small onions (which have been cooked). Simmer one hour on back of range.

—Patten, *Our New England Family Recipes* (1910), pp. 12–13

There is little of the New England culinary tradition in this recipe from a cookbook bearing the imprimatur of the "National Society of New England Women," except for the perfunctory nostalgia of requiring the lamb chops to be browned in a spider—a black frying pan named, as noted in Chapter 7, for the three-legged version that stood before the hearth fire. Prior to the later nineteenth century, the term "lamb chop" appears in a New England cookbook only once, as an afterthought in a recipe for mutton chop. From its semi-French title, to its specification of delicately rounded pieces of potato, to its sherry, the recipe reflects its era's ethos—as given in its cookbook's prefatory quotation from the Victorian critic John Ruskin, that cooks "are to be perfectly and always ladies."

Mutton

At the time of the settlement of New England, mutton was an established part of the British diet. A sixteenth-century writer offered detailed analysis of the factors—county of origin, age at time of slaughter, method of cooking—that needed to be considered if one wished to be in a position to savor mutton to the fullest. So it is no surprise that Edward Johnson, seeking in 1654 to demonstrate the Englishness of New England, would list mutton alongside beef and pork among the flesh foods that had become "frequent in many houses."

In anecdotal sources, mutton is mentioned more frequently than lamb as having been purchased, cooked, or eaten by people on all levels of society. Like veal and lamb, mutton was mostly eaten fresh, after slaughtering, but there had been some salting of mutton in Britain. In the eighteenth century, Essex County, Massachusetts, fishing families, most of them eking out a precarious existence, bought salted mutton from storekeepers. Around this same time, better-off families in Boston and other urban centers could get fresh mutton from butchers almost year-round. As seen below (#17), in the 1820s Lydia Maria Child warned against fresh mutton because it was "apt to taste strong." Unless one had obtained some that was unusually "sweet," it was "best to corn it and boil it."

Since the newly married Child and her husband were none too prosperous, it was doubtless corned mutton that went into the mutton pie that, along with baked potatoes and Indian pudding, she served up to some dinner guests around this time. There would perhaps have been more gastronomic reward in the mutton, "unsurpassed even by the English South-down," raised by a prosperous merchant and farmer in Harriet Beecher Stowe's fictionalized antebellum Maine.

Just as boiled leg of mutton served as Christmas fare in eighteenth-century England, so "joints of . . . mutton" were occasionally part of Thanksgiving dinner in eighteenth- and nineteenth-century New England.

But mutton was most famously consumed, in the history of New England, in the opposite of festive circumstances—in the repasts of the Fall River, Massachusetts, Borden family that immediately preceded the infamous 1892 ax murders.

Few eat mutton nowadays. But just as the venue of the Borden murders has been reborn as a bed and breakfast hostelry, so perhaps the following recipes, mostly from mutton's pre–"Lizzie Borden took an ax" heyday, will help to reestablish this type of meat in the respectable culinary niche it once occupied.

15. TO ROAST A LEG OF MUTTON TO BE EATEN COLD

First take as much Lard as you thinke sufficient to Lard your Leg of Mutton with-all, cut your Lard in grosse long Lardors; season the Lard very deep with beaten Cloves, Pepper, Nutmeg, and Mace, and bay salt beaten fine and dryed, then take Parsley, Tyme, Marjoram, Onion, and the out-rine of an Orange, shred all these very small, and mix them with the Lard, then Lard your Legge of Mutton therewith, if any of the Herbs and Spice remaine, put them on the Legge of Mutton; then take a silver Dish, lay two stickes crosse the Dish to keepe the Mutton from sopping in the Gravy and fat that goes from it, lay the Legge of Mutton upon the stickes, and set it into an hot Oven, there let it roast, turne it once but baste it not at all, when it is enough and very tender, take it forth but serve it not till it be throughly cold; when you serve it, put in a saucer or two of Mustard, and Sugar, and two or three Lemons whole in the same dish.

—*Compleat Cook* (1658, 2nd ed.), pp. 40–41

As in #1, larding means drawing strips of fat through the meat. The lard provides sufficient fat without basting. Although before the nineteenth century oven cooking of a joint of meat was considered more akin to stewing than to roasting, it is called roasting in this seventeenth-century recipe. A few years later, Hannah Woolley presents a similar recipe, but the meat is to be roasted on a spit. Here, the leg is to be mounted on sticks just as the leg of veal in #6 is mounted on skewers. No water is used, though. Two centuries later, the "Steamed Leg of Mutton" in a New England community cookbook is also to be eaten cold, like deli meat.

16. MUTTON CUTLETS

Cut a Neck of Mutton bone by bone, and beat it flat with your cleaver; have ready seasoning, with grated bread, a little thyme rubb'd to powder, shred parsley, with grated nutmeg, and some lemon-peels minced; then beat up two eggs,

flour your Cutlets on both sides, and dip them in the egg beat up with a little
salt, and then roll them in the grated bread and seasoning, put some butter in
your frying-pan, and when it is hot, lay in your Cutlets, and fry them brown on
both sides; for sauce, take gravy or strong broth, an onion, some spice, a bit
of bacon and a bay-leaf, and boil them well together; then beat it up with an
anchovy, or some oysters, and a quarter of a pint of red wine; strow upon your
Cutlets pickled walnuts in quarters, barberries, samphire, or cucumbers, and a
little sliced lemon.

—Smith, *Compleat Housewife* (1739), pp. 42–43

Except for the garnishes, which cooks might consider reintroducing,
these mutton cutlets are prepared in basically the same way that veal
cutlets are prepared today. Of the two species of samphire, rock samphire,
(*Crithmum maritimum*) is doubtless meant. Into the eighteenth century,
samphire was "so popular and saleable in England that men risked their
necks to collect it from the cliffs" along the seacoast where it grew. Before
use in cooking, it was pickled.

17. MUTTON AND LAMB

Six or seven pounds of mutton will roast in an hour and a half. Lamb one hour.
Mutton is apt to taste strong; this may be helped by soaking the meat in a little
salt and water, for an hour before cooking. However, unless meat is very sweet,
it is best to corn it, and boil it.

Fresh meat should never be put in to cook till the water boils; and it should
be boiled in as little water as possible; otherwise the flavor is injured. Mutton
enough for a family of five or six should boil an hour and a half. A leg of lamb
should boil an hour, or little more than an hour, perhaps. Put a little thickening
into boiling water; strain it nicely; and put sweet butter in it for sauce. If your
family like broth, throw in some clear rice when you put in the meat. The rice
should be in proportion to the quantity of broth you mean to make. A large
table spoonful is enough for three pints of water. Seasoned with a very little
pepper and salt. Summer-savory, or sage, rubbed through a sieve, thrown in.

—Child, *American Frugal Housewife* (1833), p. 49

Although Child recommends using corned mutton more often than
not, she nevertheless shines a few rays of hope in the direction of her
struggling readers, frugal from necessity, suggesting how, in the best-case
scenario of "very sweet" fresh mutton, they can make the best of their
limited stock of provisions. Sweet butter, clear rice, and sieved, refined
herbs enhance an otherwise austere repast.

18. GRAVY FOR A MUTTON HASH, OR VENISON HASH

For a dish for six persons, take a tea-cup and a half of boiling water, and slice fine one small onion (say one an inch in diameter) into it, to give it a slight flavor of onion, and thus hide the strong mutton taste. Mix a thin paste made with a heaping teaspoonful of flour, wet with a great spoonful of water, stir it in, and let it boil three minutes, adding half a teaspoonful of black pepper, and rather more salt. Then set it where it will keep hot, but not boil, till wanted.

Cut the mutton into half-inch mouthfuls, leaving out most of the fat. Cut up the same number of mouthfuls of cold boiled potatoes, and half as much cold boiled turnips, and slice in two large peeled tomatoes, or cold boiled parsnips, or both. Mix them in a tin pan the size of a dining plate, stir two great spoonfuls of butter into the gravy, and, if you like, a great spoonful of tomato catsup, and pour it on to the hash. Cover it with a plate, and set it to heat ten minutes on the stove, or on a trivet over coals.

If you do not put in vegetables, take less water, salt, and pepper. If you do not put in onion, put in a wine-glass of currant, plum, or grape jelly, or squeeze in some lemon juice when you add the butter, and leave out the catsup, or not, as you like. Modify to suit your taste, and then write the proportions exactly, for all future cooks of your family.

—Beecher, *Domestic Receipt-Book* (1846), p. 68

In modern parlance, a hash is, as here, a way of "eking out minced left-over meat." But in the seventeenth and eighteenth centuries, hashes could also be more elegant preparations of thinly sliced meat. Examples are found in *Compleat Cook*, Woolley, and the Martha Washington manuscript cookbook. The tradition was kept alive in the eighteenth century by Smith and Raffald. (Glasse, on the other hand, requires in all her hashes that the meat be cut into "little Bits"; Woolley had anticipated Glasse and more modern hashes in one of her versions.)

Beecher's offering is a hash in the modern sense. It might be called "everything you wanted to know about how to disguise the strong taste of mutton but were afraid to ask." This can be accomplished by a countering strength (onion), by something sour (lemon juice), or by something sweet (the various fruit jellies). Beecher also oscillates strangely between a control freak's precision (measure the diameter of the onion!) and a bewildering variety of options. But in any case, no one subsequent to the ur-cook of the family will taste freedom in the kitchen.

19. TO BOIL A SHOULDER OF MUTTON WITH OYSTERS

Hang it some days, then salt it well for two days, bone it, and sprinkle it with pepper and a bit of mace pounded; lay some oysters over it, roll the meat up tight, and tie it. Stew it in a small quantity of water, with an onion and a few pepper-corns, till quite tender. Have ready a little good gravy, and some oysters stewed in it; thicken this with flour and butter, and pour over the mutton when the tape is taken off. The stew-pan should be kept close covered.

—Howland, *New England Economical Housekeeper* (1845), p. 57

A simple recipe, in which the disapprovals of the taste of fresh mutton found in Child and Beecher become outright banishment through an insistence on thoroughgoing preservation procedures. As we've seen (Chapter 7, #13), Simmons has a fowl recipe in which oysters are to be found, as here, in both stuffing and sauce.

20. IRISH STEW

Blanch three pounds of mutton chops by dipping them first in boiling water, for two or three minutes, and then into ice-cold water. Place them on the bottom of a clean stewpan, barely covering them with cold water. Bring them slowly to a boil; add one teaspoonful of salt; skim clean; add a little parsley, mace, and a few peppercorns. Simmer twenty minutes; add a dozen small onions whole, and two tablespoonfuls of flour mixed well with cold water. Let it simmer for an hour; add a dozen potatoes pared and cut to about the size of the onions. Boil till these are done; then dish, placing the chops around the edge of the plate, and pouring the onions and potatoes into the centre. Strain the gravy, add three tablespoonfuls of chopped parsley, and pour over the stew.

—Turner, *New England Cook Book* (1905), p. 84

Although Anglo-American recipes for Irish stew, such as this one and one that appears in Lee, call for mutton chops, rural Irish people had not been in a position to be so particular. Sheep were primarily valued there for the wool and dairy products they yielded, "and this insured that only old or economically nonviable animals ended up in the cooking pot, where they needed hours of slow boiling." The insistence here on blanching the meat and on a particular serving arrangement reflects the Gilded Age requirement that a middle-class person must maintain a genteel bearing. This respectable concoction is far removed in spirit from the Irish stew celebrated in an 1800 ballad: "then hurrah for an Irish Stew / That will stick to your belly like glue."

Pork

As far as flesh meat is concerned, pork and beef were the mainstays of the New England as they had been of the English diet. In England from the Middle Ages onward, the average farm family was more apt to be eating pork than beef, mainly because cattle were less likely to be slaughtered, being valued for dairy production. Pigs reproduced at a high rate, so they could be consumed frequently without exhausting the family's swine resources. In addition, pork was cheaper to preserve than beef, and the end product tasted better. For New England, scholars disagree about whether people ate pork more than beef, although everyone agrees that they ate at least as much pork as beef.

For whatever reason, there developed more of a mystique about beef in Anglo-American culture. But that is not to say that Anglo-American pork cookery was gastronomically impoverished. On the contrary, pork was so readily available that in households with sufficient resources cooks could not but begin exercising their imaginations in finding tasty ways to prepare it—from the whole roasted pigs and the brawns (increasingly made after the sixteenth century with pickled pork rather than wild boar meat) of festive occasions, to long-cured hams, to loins, legs, and ribs that could be brought to the table any number of ways.

Flavorings and seasonings of pork have followed an intriguing historical pattern in Anglo-American cuisine. Sweet and fruity flavors were frequently emphasized in medieval and early modern pork cookery and were still to be found in some recipes in the early nineteenth century. By that time, however, they were considered old-fashioned, since pork like other meats was now required to be seasoned in such a way, with sage and its ilk, that it could be placed on the savory side of the recently developed dividing line between sweet and savory. There are only a few remnants of the earlier mode to be found in our nineteenth-century selections. Late in the century, however, the old association of pork with sweetness was revived, at least in America. As Alan Davidson points out, "sweet ingredients" have become "characteristic of American pork cookery." Think, for example, of our standard way of preparing baked ham, with brown sugar and pineapple, as seen, as far as the brown sugar is concerned, in #32 below.

As notions of refinement took hold in many quarters, there developed some squeamishness about eating pork, in distinct contrast to the earlier days when even a child of a wealthy and well-bred Salem, Massachusetts, merchant family considered it a treat to have "'scraps' . . . little bits of pork, prepared in some mysterious way with sage and sweet marjoram." We hope the following recipes will help people appreciate the richness of New England pork cookery.

21. TO ROAST A PIGGE

To roast a Pigge curiously you shall not scald it, but draw it with the haire on, then hauing washt it, spit it and lay it to the fire so as it may not scorch; then being a quarter roasted and the skinne blistered from the flesh, with your hand pull away the haire and skinne, and leaue all the fat and flesh perfectly bare: then with your knife scorch all the flesh downe to the bones, then bast it exceedingly with sweet butter and creame, being no more but warme; then dredge it with fine bread crummes, currants, sugar and salt mixt together, and thus apply dredging vpon basting, and basting vpon dredging till you haue couered all the flesh a full inch deepe: Then the meat being fully roasted, draw it and serue it vp whole.

—Markham, *English Hus-wife* (1615), pp. 57–58

Curiously indeed. This is a muscular approach to pig-roasting, with the hair and skin pulled from the partially cooked carcass. Later authorities, such as Raffald and Ann Allen, would recommend scalding. Drawing, as used near the beginning of the recipe, means disembowelment. Perhaps to avoid confusion between the different senses of "scorch," beginning in the second edition (1623), the second appearance of "scorch" in the recipe is changed to another word for the same operation, "scotch." Currants and sugar survived into the eighteenth century in pig roasting procedures in recipes for accompanying sauces. Indeed, even in the nineteenth century, Lee (taking it from Kitchiner) notes that "currant sauce is still a favorite with some of the old school," while *The Roger Cookery* simply says that "currant sauce is very good with roasted pig." In his discussion of "when meat is enough," Markham explains that in the case of a pig, "when the eies are falne out . . . it is halfe rosted," and when "the body leaueth piping [steaming] . . . it is fully enough." As seen in #24 below, these same signs of doneness continued to be noted in nineteenth-century New England.

22. TO DRESS A PIG'S PETTITOES

Take up the Heart, Liver, and Lights when they have boiled ten Minutes, and shread them pretty small, but let the Feet boil till they are pretty tender, then take them out and split them; thicken your Gravy with Flour and Butter, put in your Mincemeat, a Slice of Lemon, a Spoonful of White Wine, a little Salt, and boil it a little, beat the Yolk of an Egg, add to it two Spoonfuls of good Cream, and a little grated Nutmeg, put it in your Pettitoes, shake it over the Fire, but don't let it boil: Lay Sippets round your Dish, pour in your Mincemeat, lay the Feet over them the Skin-side up, and send them to the Table.

—Raffald, *Experienced English House-keeper* (1769), p. 45

The pettitoes are the feet, the lights, the lungs. This recipe is yet another indication of how people of earlier times, on all social levels, had a broader conception than the majority does now of all the meat that's fit to eat. Organ meats and pig's feet gussied up with lemon, wine, butter, cream, and nutmeg, and served with first-quality bread, is something that is unlikely to emerge from most kitchens nowadays, although diners can find them on fancy restaurant menus.

23. TO BOIL HAM

This is an important article, and requires particular attention, in order to render it elegant and grateful. It should be boiled in a large quantity of water, and that for a long time, one quarter of an hour for each pound; the rind to be taken off when warm. It is most palatable when cold, and should be sent to the table with eggs, horse-radish or mustard.—This affords a sweet repast at any time of day.

—Simmons, *American Cookery* (Albany, 1796), pp. 20–21

Indeed, in our terms, with the eggs for breakfast or the mustard for lunch. No flavoring agents are called for during boiling, presumably because the ham has already been made sufficiently tasty during the pickling and smoking process. Simmons's own recipe for curing bacon or ham (the two terms were often used interchangeably), which is included in the first (Hartford) edition of her cookbook but that she removed from the second, Albany, edition, uses molasses during the pickling phase and specifies "cobs or malt fumes" during smoking.

24. ROAST PIG

Strew fine salt over it an hour before it is put down. It should not be cut entirely open; fill it up plump with thick slices of buttered bread, salt, sweet-marjoram and sage. Spit it with the head next the point of the spit; take off the joints of the leg, and boil them with the liver, with a little whole pepper, allspice, and salt, for gravy sauce. The upper part of the legs must be braced down with skewers. Shake on flour. Put a little water in the dripping-pan, and stir it often. When the eyes drop out, the pig is half done. When it is nearly done, baste it with butter. Cut off the head, split it open between the eyes. Take out the brains, and chop them fine with the liver and some sweet-marjoram and sage; put this into melted butter, and when it has boiled a few minutes, add it to the gravy in the dripping-pan. When your pig is cut open, lay it with the back to the edge of the dish; half a head to be placed at each end. A good sized pig needs to be roasted three hours.

—Child, *American Frugal Housewife* (1833), p. 50

Markham's bread-crumb coating applied in layers to the outside of the pig (#21) here becomes a simple bread stuffing. Stuffing is also called for in Smith, Carter, Raffald, and Simmons. Inclusion of the brains and entrails in the gravy was standard, although only Raffald provides precedent for adding the lower legs as well. Simmons puts the entrails into the stuffing rather than the gravy. Child does not mention baking rather than roasting the pig, although this option had been provided at least since Glasse. Lee (relying again on Kitchiner) stresses that a pig is "very troublesome . . . to roast," and that "most persons" therefore "have them baked" by a baker. Most persons reading Child's book, however, could not afford to send a pig to a baker, and many of them may not have lived in homes equipped with bake ovens.

25. PICKLED PORK

Pickled Pork takes more time than other meat. If you buy your pork ready salted, ask how many days it has been in salt; if many, it will require to be soaked in water before you dress it. When you cook it, wash and scrape it as clean as possible; when delicately dressed, it is a favorite dish with almost every body. Take care it does not boil fast; if it does, the knuckle will break to pieces, before the thick part of the meat is warm through; a leg of seven pounds takes three hours and a half very slow simmering. Skim your pot very carefully, and when you take the meat out of the boiler, scrape it clean.

The proper vegetables are parsnips, potatoes, turnips, or carrots. Some like cabbage; but it is a strong, rank vegetable, and does not agree with a delicate stomach. It should not be given to children.

—Hale, *Good Housekeeper* (1841), p. 44

Except for the second paragraph, this recipe is copied all but verbatim from Lee (who had herself copied it from Kitchiner). We include it in Hale's transcription because with the addition of the second paragraph it provides an example of boiled dinner made with pork rather than beef. Ironically, Hale's disapproval of cabbage is couched in terms similar to those that would be used later in the century, when boiled dinner was being sanctified as "New England Boiled Dinner," to disqualify pork from inclusion in the dish. Pickling and other methods of pork preservation are described in the commentary to #29.

26. LOIN AND NECK OF PORK

Simmer the best end of either of the joints till nearly fit for the table, strip off the skin, put it into a cradle-spit, wet it all over with yolks of eggs, and cover it thickly with crumbs of bread, sweet herbs and chives chopped fine for stuffing, and seasoned with pepper and salt. It will get a good brown in about half an hour.

Either of them may also be *rolled.*—Bone it: put a forcemeat of chopped sage, a very few crumbs of bread, salt, pepper, and two or three berries of allspice, over the inside; then roll the meat as tight as you can, and roast it slowly, and at a good distance at first from the fire.

To parboil it before the herbs are put on will be an improvement.

A hand of pork may likewise be boned, stuffed, rolled, and roasted, as above.

—Hale, *Ladies' New Book of Cookery* (1852), p. 140

The loin, from the midsection of the back, is the portion of the pig that is almost exclusively used for roast pork today. Hale still assumes that her readers will be roasting their pork over an open fire. A cradle spit was one with an open framework in the middle to hold the piece of meat. The garlicky flavor of chives is a mild imitation of the actual garlic (French) or onions (British) found in European pork cookery. Note that Hale warns against roasting the meat in too close proximity to direct heat, a precaution more necessary to pork, with its tendency to dryness, than to beef or lamb. For the same reason, simmering and parboiling are recommended. The hand of pork comes from the foreleg.

27. CHINE OF PORK

The chine is more usually salted, and served as an accompaniment to roast turkey. Salt the chine for three days, roast it, and serve it up with sauce made thus:
Fry in oil or butter two or three sliced onions until they take color; then pour off
the oil, and add some gravy-sauce, chopped mushrooms, and two tablespoonfuls of vinegar, with one teaspoonful of made mustard. Give the whole a boil,
and serve it up in the dish.

—Hale, *Ladies' New Book of Cookery* (1852), p. 141

Chine, from the French *échine* (spine), is the tender meat taken from
between the pig's shoulder blades, along with part of the backbone, some
fat, and, as Colin Spencer puts it, "a hefty bit of spinal marrow." Hale's
recommendation to serve the roasted chine as an accompaniment to another roast (in this instance, turkey) follows earlier British and American
practice, as evidenced by Carter's remark that pickled pork is "commonly
a sauce of itself to roasted fowls or veal," and by Lucy Emerson's copying
of this in her *New-England Cookery*.

Accompanying roast meat or fowl with vegetable-scented, wine-en-
riched ham sauce derives from the French coulis, which was, as Anne
Willan notes, "thick, concentrated, and very extravagant"—just the
impression given here. But according to Bliss, chine and spareribs were
also the preferred cuts for roasting and serving as stand-alone dishes. In
the meals served in the Inner Star Chamber to the Lords of the Privy
Council between 1567 and 1605, chine frequently appeared as a side to
beef or mutton. Despite this long and illustrious history, chine of pork is
little known today.

28. TO COOK A HAM (VERY FINE)

Boil a common-sized ham four or five hours, then skin the whole and fit it
for the table; then set it in an oven for half an hour, then cover it thickly with
pounded rusk or bread crumbs, and set it back for half an hour.

Boiled ham is always improved by setting it into an oven for near an hour,
till much of the fat fries out, and this also makes it more tender. Save the fat for
frying meat.

—Beecher, *Domestic Receipt-Book* (1846), pp. 36–37

Simmons (#23) suggests one-quarter hour of boiling for each pound of ham, so a common-sized ham of fifteen to twenty pounds could require four or five hours' boiling. Beecher's instruction to coat the ham with "pounded rusk or bread crumbs" is the latter-day equivalent of Markham's "dredge [roast pig] with fine bread crummes" (#21). Chapter 14, #20 is Beecher's recipe for rusk.

29. PRESSED HEAD

Boil the several parts of the entire head, and the feet, in the same way as for souse. All must be boiled so perfectly tender as to have the meat easily separate from the bones. After neatly separated, chop the meat fine, while warm, seasoning with salt, and pepper, and other spices to taste. Put it in a strong bag, and, placing a weight on it, let it remain till cold. Or put it in any convenient dish, placing a plate with a weight on it, to press the meat. Cut it in slices, roll in flour, and fry in lard.

—Webster, *Improved Housewife* (1844), p. 44

On the same page as this recipe, Webster explains how to make souse: "Clean pig's feet and ears thoroughly, and soak them a number of days in salt and water; boil them tender, and split them." But her alternative method introduces yet another term for this type of cured pork: "To souse them cold, pour boiling vinegar over them, spiced with mace and pepper-corns. Cloves give them a dark color, but they improve their taste. If a little salt be added, they will keep good, pickled, for a month or two." Pickling, sousing, salting, brining, and smoking were all ways to preserve pork, but nineteenth-century writers were often imprecise, and at times inconsistent, in applying terms to methods. Boiled or soaked cold, in brine or vinegar, spiced or unspiced, pickled, soused, or smoked? All of these techniques can be used to preserve pork, depending on the quantity of meat to be cured, the season, the time the meat is expected to last, and of course the curing agents available. Broadly speaking, making brine involves scalding salt in water and skimming, then adding salt until it will no longer melt in the water. In Webster's day, and earlier, brined pork that was to be kept only a few days was said to be "collared," while that kept for longer periods, often the whole winter, was "soused." Smoking the meat after brining, to create the famous flavor and keeping qualities of smoked ham, was optional.

As indicated earlier, head meat was not repugnant to Webster's audience. Pig's-head cheese such as this was a standard nineteenth-century dish, although as also indicated earlier (#8), versions without pork were gaining in popularity.

30. FRIED PORK STEAKS

Fry a few slices of salt pork, cut very thin; when done, take the slices out of the fat and put in your fresh pork; let them fry a light brown,—some people like onion and sage fried with the pork,—slices of apple fried are very nice with the pork.

—Bliss, *Practical Cook Book* (1850), p. 78

The fried or grilled pork chop was a creation of the nineteenth century, although here at midcentury it is still flying under the "steak" flag. While pork was beginning to suffer at this time under the perception that it was a low-class and often unhealthy food (given the average porker's diet of swill), fresh pork fared better than salt pork. Of Bliss's pork recipes, the majority call for various cuts of fresh meat. Sage and onion were British favorites to stuff roast pork and flavor its sauce. Applesauce as accompaniment also has British precedent, while the pork and apple combination is found in British pies (see Chapter 10, #21). For her frugal readers, Child suggests "fried salt pork and apples."

31. ROAST SPARERIB

Trim off the rough end of a 3 pound spare rib. Break the ribs across twice, sprinkle with salt and pepper, then spread on a dressing made of 1 cup bread crumbs, 1 small teaspoon sage, butter size of walnut, 1/3 teaspoon salt, little pepper. Roll up and tie securely. Roast 2 hours in a moderate oven. Add 1 gill of water and baste frequently. Turn over once.

—Whatsoever Circle, *King's Daughters Cook Book* (1903), p. 33

Spareribs are located behind the shoulder of the pig. This set of ribs, with its seasoned bread-crumb stuffing, would make for a pleasant alternative to barbecue.

32. BAKED BAM

Wash and scrape ham. Then place in a large iron pot and cover with cold water. Let it come to a boil and, if ham is very salty, pour water off and add fresh water. Boil until ham is done when testing fork will slip out easily. Let cool in liquor. Skin the ham and stick full of whole cloves and cover with as much brown sugar as possible and bake a few minutes until brown.

—Inman, *Rhode Island Rule Book* (1939), p. 12

As in Beecher's recipe (#28), this ham is boiled before baking. Inman glazes with brown sugar and cloves, as opposed to Beecher's coating of pounded rusk or bread crumbs. Although occasionally used earlier, it was not until the end of the nineteenth century that glazing became the standard treatment, as seen in recipes from Farmer, and Lincoln and Barrows. All kinds of savory foods, such as baked beans and brown bread, were at this time being sweetened more than previously.

Beef

As we have seen in Joseph Addison's tribute to the "noble Sirloin" presented in Chapter 1, the reputation of roast beef as the English national dish was established by the beginning of the eighteenth century, after escaping its medieval image as the food of the lower orders (the nobility preferred fowl and game). Henry Fielding helped the process along with a song published in his *Grub Street Opera* (1731): "When mighty roast beef was the Englishman's food, / It ennobled our hearts and enriched our blood, / Our soldiers were brave and our courtiers were good. / Oh the roast beef of England, / And Old England's roast beef!" William Hogarth depicted the hoariness of the roast beef tradition in his 1748 painting "O the Roast Beef of Old England" ("The Gate of Calais"), in which a belly-rubbing monk and two bayonet-toting grenadiers inspect a slab of beef so huge that it weighs down the cook who carries it. Various passersby look on with envy as the maw of Calais Gate looms in the background, its spikes seeming ready to take a bite out of the noble food that is the center of attention in the painting.

If roast beef's thoroughgoing Englishness still undergirds its appeal, that is no accident. In the eighteenth century, popular cookbook writers such as Raffald found that recipes for roast beef and plum pudding gave their up-and-coming urban readers just what they wanted—a patriotic means of display and an allusion to the prestige of the English countryside without the whiff of aristocratic decadence that clung to French-inspired dishes and the spoils of the hunt. Tory parsons entertained their parishioners with roast beef to suggest both ancient English hospitality and present-day camaraderie.

While always a favorite, roast beef never quite attained the status on New England tables that it held for the British. In a much-reprinted newspaper account of what New Englanders had for Thanksgiving dinner in the early nineteenth century, roast beef is mentioned along with joints of pork and (as noted earlier) mutton, but chickens, chicken pies, turkeys, and geese dominate the menu.

When later-nineteenth-century New England focused on roast beef, it was often to bemoan its loss, the result of the displacement of the open hearth fire by the cookstove. Many cooks and recipe writers considered roast beef prepared in the new way—that is, baked in a cast iron oven— not worth the effort. Some even refused to call it roast beef, sniffing that technically speaking it was *baked* beef.

It was not the women cooks and domestic writers, for whom the advantages of the cookstove were generally considered well worth the trade-off, but rather the men of the family who were most dismayed that their beef was no longer to be roasted at an open fire. As Adeline D. T. Whitney writes in an 1887 short story, "How the old gentlemen grumbled when the new inventions first came, and couldn't eat their roast beef that was no longer cooked by a wood-blaze." In *The American Woman's Home*, Catharine Beecher and her sister Harriet Beecher Stowe proposed an unusual remedy: remove the oven doors, set a tin roaster full of beef in front of the coal heat, and roast away.

As esteemed as roast beef was, for most people of the seventeenth through the nineteenth centuries, on both sides of the Atlantic, a nice piece of boiled beef was a perfectly fine thing in its own right. Fresh boiled beef on a farm family's table was not only an edible delight but also a sign that the family had moved beyond the subsistence level. Various cuts of fresh but tough beef might be softened by boiling in a kettle of water or broth or stewing in gravy. Leftover boiled beef could be shredded and mixed with butter and spices, or sliced and baked in a pie.

In New England, however, it was neither roasted nor boiled fresh beef that eventually achieved culinary fame. When New England Boiled Dinner was made with beef (it was also made with pork), it was the corned variety that ended up in the pot, in keeping with the region's stridently unassuming tastes. But New Englanders relished their beef whether fresh or salted, roasted, boiled, stewed, potted, or in a pie, as the following recipes reveal.

33. TO BAKE A BULLOKS CHEEK TO BE EATEN HOT

Take your Cheek and stuff it very well with Parsley and sweet herbs chopped, then put it into a Pot with some Claret wine and a little strong Beer, and some whole Spice, and so season it well with Salt to your taste, and cover your Pot and bake it, then take it out, and pull out the Bones, and serve it upon tosted bread with some of the Liquor.

—Woolley, Queen-like Closet (1670), p. 140

Anne Willan points out that the phenomenon of female cookbook authorship, which, as we've seen, began in England with Woolley and flourished thereafter, was "virtually unknown to the French until the twentieth century." The difference between French and English cooking instruction was one not only of gender but also of intent: English cookbooks by women promoted "domestic economy," while French works by male chefs aimed to purvey haute cuisine exclusively.

In Woolley, we find the balance that the English, and their New England cousins, strove to attain: simplicity of preparation combined with a bit of refinement. A very cheap piece of meat—the beef cheek muscle and lining of the mouth, with jaw bones in (the usual practice is to remove the bones, as well as the external lip and salivary glands)—is tenderized by braising in wine and beer and enhanced with herbs and spices. With a little sleuthing, you can find beef cheeks for sale today.

34. TO A-LA-MODE BEEF

Take the Bone out of a Rump of Beef, lard the Top with Bacon, then make a Force-meat of four Ounces of Marrow, two Heads of Garlick, the Crumbs of a Penny Loaf, a few sweet Herbs chopped small, Nutmeg, Pepper and Salt to your Taste, and the Yolks of four Eggs well beat, mix it up, and stuff your Beef w[h]ere the Bone came out, and in several Places in the lean part, skewer it round and bind it about with a Fillet, put it in a Pot with a Pint of Red Wine, and tie it down with strong Paper, bake it in the Oven for three Hours; when it comes out, if you want to eat it hot, skim the Fat off the Gravy, and add half an Ounce of Morels, a Spoonful of pickled Mushrooms, thicken it with Flour and Butter, dish up your Beef and pour on the Gravy, lay round it Force-meat Balls, and send it up.

—Raffald, Experienced English House-keeper (1769), p. 103

À *la mode:* "in the fashion" or style of a particular region or person, as in "*Potage à la [mode de] Rothschild.*" Davidson points out that in this sense the French phrase is problematic because the meaning changes "according to what it is that is being cooked or garnished." However, for the English, "à la mode Beef" came to mean a specific preparation (described below, #36).

That it became a specific preparation for the French as well is most memorably indicated near the end of Marcel Proust's vast masterpiece, *Remembrance of Things Past.* The narrator, contemplating the novel he intends to write (and also describing the novel that Proust has actually written), muses that "since in this book the individual entities, human or otherwise, would be constructed from numerous impressions which, derived from many young girls, many churches, many sonatas, would go to make up a single sonata, a single church, a single young girl, would I not be making my book the way Françoise [the family servant] made her *boeuf à la mode* . . . the jelly of which was enriched by so many carefully selected pieces of meat?"

Binding with a fillet in Raffald's sense does not mean, as we might think, adding a layer of thinly sliced meat to the rump roast but rather tying it with a strip of cloth.

35. TO ROAST BEEF

If it be a surloin or chump, butter a piece of writing-paper, and fasten it on to the back of your meat, with small skewers, and lay it down to a soaking fire, at a proper distance. As soon as your meat is warm, dust on some flour, and baste it with butter; then sprinkle some salt, and, at times, baste with what drips from it. About a quarter of an hour before you take it up, remove the paper, dust on a little flour, and baste with a piece of butter, that it may go to table with a good froth. Garnish your dish with scraped horseraddish; and serve it up with potatoes, broccoli, French beans, colliflower, horse raddish, or cellary.

—Carter, *Frugal Housewife* (1772), pp. 1–2

Here is a typical English recipe from roast beef's golden age. It takes pride of place in Susannah Carter's cookbook, following directly after her "General Rules to be observed in Roasting," the key element of which is "allowing a quarter of an hour for every pound of meat, at a steady fire." As we saw above, Carter's tips for a perfect roast—cover the beef with paper to prevent scorching and baste with butter and meat juices—were recommended by nineteenth-century writers as well and of course are still useful. Horseradish, potatoes, and hearty vegetables remain standard accompaniments.

36. TO ALAMODE A ROUND

Take fat pork cut in slices or mince, season it with pepper, salt, sweet marjoram and thyme, cloves, mace and nutmeg, make holes in the beef and stuff it the night before cooked; put some bones across the bottom of the pot to keep from burning, put in one quart Claret wine, one quart water and one onion; lay the round on the bones, cover close and stop it round the top with dough; hang on in the morning and stew gently two hours; turn it, and stop tight and stew two hours more; when done tender, grate a crust of bread on the top and brown it before the fire; scum the gravy and serve in a butter boat, serve it with the residue of the gravy in the dish.

—Simmons, *American Cookery* (Hartford, 1796), p. 20

In the nineteenth century, the anglicized term "alamode," already established as shorthand for an English preparation, came to be widely used in America as well. Simmons's readers would understand beef alamode as larding a tough cut such as a round (here with pork fat; in Raffald, above #34, with bacon, marrow, bread crumbs, and egg yolk comprising a lard-like stuffing), followed by stewing in wine, water, or seasoned broth, and serving with a rich gravy.

37. CALF'S HEAD

Calf's head should be cleansed with very great care; particularly the lights. The head, the heart, and the lights should boil full two hours; the liver should be boiled only one hour. It is better to leave the wind-pipe on, for if it hangs out of the pot while the head is cooking, all the froth will escape through it. The brains, after being thoroughly washed, should be put in a little bag; with one pounded cracker, or as much crumbled bread, seasoned with sifted sage, and tied up and boiled one hour. After the brains are boiled, they should be well broken up with a knife, and peppered, salted, and buttered. They should be put upon the table in a bowl by themselves. Boiling water, thickened with flour and water, with butter melted in it, is the proper sauce; some people love vinegar and pepper mixed with the melted butter; but all are not fond of it; and it is easy for each one to add it for themselves.

—Child, *American Frugal Housewife* (1833), pp. 47–48

As with #22, this recipe illustrates the distance between them and us—the unsqueamishness of earlier home cooks as compared to their successors today. Our attitudes were emerging in Child's day, however. In his review, Child's former boyfriend Nathaniel P. Willis ridiculed *The Frugal Housewife* for its commendation of ungenteel foods and its dwelling upon details "at which a palate of tolerable nicety would revolt." This recipe was one of Willis's examples, particularly the caution about not allowing the windpipe to hang out of the pot. Willis's point of view has come to prevail. John Thorne notwithstanding, most of us now eat finely seasoned calf's brains, heart, lights (lungs), and liver only if these delicacies appear on the menu of a multistar restaurant.

38. BEEF A-LA-MODE

Choose a piece of thick flank of a fine heifer or ox, cut into long slices; some fat bacon, but quite free from yellow; let each bit be near an inch thick; dip them into vinegar, and then into a seasoning ready prepared, of salt, black pepper, allspice, and a clove, all in a fine powder, with parsley, chives, thyme, savory, and knotted marjoram, shred as small as possible, and well mixed. With a sharp knife make holes deep enough to let in the larding, then rub the beef over with the seasoning, and bind it up tight with tape. Set it in a well-tinned pot over a fire, or rather stove; three or four onions must be fried brown and put to the beef, with two or three carrots, one turnip, a head or two of celery, and a small quantity of water; let it simmer gently ten or twelve hours, or till extremely tender, turning the meat twice; to be cut in slices, and eaten cold.

—Howland, *New England Economical Housekeeper* (1845), pp. 52–53

As Fannie Farmer remarks at the end of the century, beef alamode is the precursor of pot roast. The aspects of the preparation that survived the transition to the modern dish were boning and seasoning the joint, rolling and tying it, setting it in an inch or two of aromatic broth, and simmering it slowly and long. Left behind were the alamode's almost invariable larding and the sense that the cooking broth should be made as rich and complex as the seasoning, by inclusion of such enhancements as lemon rind, calf's foot, port, Jamaica pepper, nutmeg, bay leaf, thyme, and other sweet herbs. Lee, copying Dalgairns, had offered this kind of elaborate alamode, and Howland follows her closely, though with gestures toward plainness such as the elimination of lemon rind and port. In a minority of recipes, including one by Webster (plagiarized by Beecher), stuffing and covering the beef with a bread-egg-butter mixture amounted to an alternative form of larding similar to that found in Raffald (#34). Intersecting the trajectory of beef alamode into pot roast was the major technological change Howland mentions merely as an aside—"fire, or rather stove."

Knotted marjoram (so called because of the plant's appearance), also known as sweet marjoram, is an aromatic that has been used in cooking since ancient times and is closely related in botanical and taste terms to oregano. Marjoram is also dried for use in herbal mixtures such as Herbes de Provence.

The popularity of beef alamode into the nineteenth century (even in its less frequent cold form) is attested to by a visitor to the Bronson Alcott family of Concord, Massachusetts, in the winter of 1841, when daughter Louisa May was an infant. Miss Robie, a cousin of Mrs. Alcott, brought along for her visit tea, coffee, cayenne pepper, "and a small piece of cooked meat . . . which last article was a little piece of *a la mode* beef." It was Miss Robie's time of month to "expect a headache," as she writes, and she brought the beef "in case my wayward stomach should crave it." But in the presence of the Alcotts, who subsisted with neither "meat, nor butter, nor cheese, and only coarse brown sugar, bread, potatoes, apples, squash and simple puddings," Robie's plans collapsed. "I lived as they did, for I could not have the heart or the stomach to take out my beef."

39. BEEF TRIPE FRICASSEE

Let your tripe be very white, cut it into slips, put it into some boiled gravy, with a little cream and a bit of butter mixed with flour; stir it till the butter is melted; add a little white wine, lemon-peel grated, chopped parsley, pepper and salt, pickled mushrooms, or lemon-juice; shake all together; stew it a little.

—Lee, *Cook's Own Book* (1832), p. 18

"Let your tripe be very white" is Lee's (actually, Dolby's) way of telling the cook to be sure that the organ meat is fresh. Blanching, or covering with cold water, then simmering slowly, clears away any extraneous matter and bacteria from the surface of the meat (a common problem with the pockmarks and folds of organ meats), while also tenderizing it. A longer stewing time than Lee suggests is usually recommended for beef tripe, which is made from the first, second, or third stomach of the cow.

Lee also diverges from the norm in recommending wine, lemon, mushrooms, and parsley for seasoning—most recipes suggest a milk and onion broth. As discussed in Chapter 7, a fricassee was speedy pan-frying and light saucing of pieces of meat.

40. A GOOD BOILED DISH

Have ready a substantial fire, put your meat in the pot, covering it with cold water, and let it simmer some time without boiling; watch the scum as it rises and be sure and remove it, adding a little cold water after every skimming; see that the meat is covered during the process of boiling, but not beyond what is necessary. A good rule for the time of cooking the meat, is allowing twenty minutes for every pound, —this is when it boils very gently; always bear in mind, the slower it boils the more it will swell, and the more tender it will be. The above rule answers for beef and mutton; lamb, pork, and veal require to be more thoroughly done. Potatoes very nicely washed acquire an additional flavor by being boiled with the meat. Many cooks insert as many vegetables as the pot will allow, but in this, the cook must consult the taste of her employers.

—*Roger Cookery* (1838), p. 13

Fresh beef, mutton, lamb, pork, or veal, simmered together with potatoes and other vegetables, is little different from the boiled salt meat and vegetables that, as noted in the introduction to this chapter, became a staple of the New England diet in the eighteenth century. (At the end of the nineteenth century it would become enshrined as "New England Boiled Dinner.") Whether the meat is fresh, corned, or salted, the cook must be careful to keep it simmering gently for a prolonged period to ensure that it is tender and plump when it arrives on the dinner plate.

41. BEEF, OR VEAL STEWED WITH APPLES (VERY GOOD)

Rub a stew-pan with butter, cut the meat in thin slices, and put in, with pepper, salt, and apple sliced fine; some would add a little onion. Cover it tight, and stew till tender.

—Beecher, *Domestic Receipt-Book* (1846), p. 42

The best cooking apples retain their shape and texture yet release some of their juices, which here constitute the stewing liquid. Although some of the traditional varieties, for example the Newton Pippin, are now difficult to find, others such as the Granny Smith and the Golden Delicious have been bred both to be eaten raw and to be cooked. Although Beecher calls this a stewed dish, it is a hash in the old-fashioned sense described above (#18 commentary).

42. CORNED BEEF COOKED WITH DRY PEAS

Peas, also, are good to dry, and make a fine dish thus. Take six or eight pounds of corned beef, put it in a large pot and fill it with water, and put in two quarts of dried peas. Let them boil till soft, and then add the sweet herb seasoning, or take it up without any other seasoning than a little pepper and the salt of the meat.

Beef, cooked thus, is excellent when cold, and the pea soup, thus made, is highly relished. No dish is cheaper, or more easily prepared.

—Beecher, *Domestic Receipt-Book* (1846), pp. 226–27

More a discussion by a resourceful housekeeper on how to provide "a successive variety of food" than a recipe, this preparation follows Beecher's directions for drying sweet corn for winter use. We are again reminded that it was only by the heroic exertions of the nineteenth-century housewife in drying, salting, corning, smoking, and curing meats, vegetables, and fruits that an array of food was available to the average family through the winter. As for "the sweet herb seasoning," a few pages earlier Beecher recommends that "*Sweet Herbs* should be dried, and the stalks thrown away, and the rest be kept in corked large mouth bottles, or small tin boxes."

43. BEEF STEAKS

Those from the sirloin are best, those from the shoulder clod and round are not so good, but cheaper. Meat, if tough, is made more tender by pounding, if it is done very thoroughly, so as to break the fibres. Cut the steaks from half an inch to an inch thick. Broil on hot coals, and the quicker it is done the better. Ten or twelve minutes is enough time. Turn it four or five times, and when done put on butter, salt, and if you like pepper, and on both sides. Do not let your butter be turned to oil before putting it on. It is best to have beef tongs to turn beef, as pricking it lets out the juices. Often turning prevents the surface from hardening and cooks it more equally.

—Beecher, *Domestic Receipt-Book* (1846), pp. 54–55

The shoulder clod is the front of the shoulder; the round is the buttock, below the rump. Beecher's recommendation to cut sirloin steaks a half-inch or inch thick is telling. Most Americans today expect a two-inch steak, that is, one significantly oversized by nineteenth-century standards. Sirloin (from the Old French, *surlonge*, above the loin) comes from the upper part of the loin before the rump and remains the preferred cut for broiling, grilling, and pan-frying, in other words for cooking with dry rather than moist heat. The term "steak" is from the Old Norse meaning to roast on a stake or spit.

44. STEWED BRISKET

8 lbs. of beef,	4 turnips,
2 carrots,	Celery and pepper corns.
4 onions,	

Put the part that has the hard fat into a stew-pot, with a small quantity of water; let it boil up, and skim it thoroughly; then add the carrots, turnips, salt, onions, celery, all sliced up, and the pepper corns. Stew till extremely tender, then take out the flat bones and remove all the fat from the soup. Lay the meat on a dish; it will require more salt nicely strewed over; take some of the soup, rub some flour into butter, one spoonful of mushroom catsup, put in and boil up, and pour on the beef. Chop capers, walnuts, red cabbage, a pickled cucumber, chives, and parsley, together small, and put in separate heaps over it. Have boiled potatoes and other vegetables to use with it, after the soup.

—Allen, *Housekeeper's Assistant* (1845), p. 95

The ingredients list, standard in modern recipes, here makes one of its early appearances. However, Allen lists only the stew components, leaving out the ingredients necessary to the rest of the recipe. The separation of the meat from the soup and the side servings of potatoes and vegetables transforms a stewed, garnished brisket (in the tradition of the potage) into a version of boiled dinner. The brisket is a section of the breast behind the foreshank; moist heat softens it.

45. TO ROAST A FILLET OF BEEF

Raise the fillet from the inside of the sirloin, or from part of it, with a sharp knife; leave the fat on, trim off the skin, lard it through, or all over, or roast it quite plain; baste it with butter, and send it very hot to table, with tomato sauce, or sauce piquante, or eschalot sauce, in a tureen. It is sometimes served with brown gravy or currant jelly: it should then be garnished with forcemeat-balls. If not very large, an hour and a quarter will roast it well with a brisk fire.

Obs. The remainder of the joint may be boned, rolled, and roasted or braised; or made into meat cakes; or served as a miniature round of beef.

—Hale, *Ladies' New Book of Cookery* (1852), p. 80

Common Tomato Sauce. —Tomatoes are so juicy when ripe, that they require but little liquid to reduce them to a proper consistency for sauce; and they vary so exceedingly in size and quality that it is difficult to give precise directions for the exact quantity which is needed for them. Take off the stalks, halve the tomatoes, and gently squeeze out the seeds and watery pulp; then stew them softly with a few spoonsful of gravy or of strong broth until they are quite melted. Press the whole through a hair-sieve, and heat it afresh with a little additional gravy should it be too thick, and some Cayenne, and salt. Serve it very hot.

Fine ripe tomatoes, 6 or 8; gravy or strong broth, 4 table-spoonsful; half to three quarters of an hour, or longer if needed. Salt and Cayenne sufficient to season the sauce, and two or three spoonsful more of gravy if required.

—Hale, *Ladies' New Book of Cookery* (1852), p. 199

Shalot Sauce.—Put a few chopped shalots into a little gravy, boiled clear, and nearly half as much vinegar; season with pepper and salt; boil half an hour.

—Hale, *Ladies' New Book of Cookery* (1852), p. 200

Sauce Piquante.—Brown lightly, in an ounce and a half of butter, a table-spoonful of minced eschalots, or three of onions; add a tea-spoonful of flour when they are partially done; pour to them half a pint of gravy, or of good broth, and when it boils, add three chilies, a bay leaf, and a very small bunch of thyme. Let these simmer for 20 minutes; take out the thyme and bay leaf, add a high seasoning of black pepper, and half a wine-glassful of the best vinegar. A quarter of a tea-spoonful of Cayenne may be substituted for the chilies.

Eschalots, 1 table-spoonful, or 3 of onions; flour, 1 tea-spoonful; butter 1½ oz.: 10 to 15 minutes. Gravy or broth, half a pint; chilies, 3; bay leaf; thyme, small bunch: 20 minutes. Pepper, plenty; vinegar, half a wine-glassful.

—Hale, *Ladies' New Book of Cookery* (1852), pp. 202–3

The fillet of beef or tenderloin (from which the renowned filet mignon is taken) is an extremely tender cut. But because it is also relatively lean, Hale recommends enhancing its flavor by larding it or basting it with butter. It is served here with a sauce, as is customary with filet mignon.

46. BOILED DINNER
This is an old-fashioned but favorite dish.

For six or eight persons, put on six pounds of corned beef to boil about nine o'clock for dinner at noon; if the beets are old, put them on soon after the meat;

peel four white turnips and one rutabaga, which if large, cut in thick slices; wash the carrots; pare the parsnips thin; cut the cabbage, if large, into quarters, trimming it and cutting out the hard stump, leaving only enough to hold the leaves together; select large potatoes and a piece of squash; clean and pare them; lay all these vegetables in cold water until it is time to put them into the pot; if the carrots are old, boil them two hours; the turnips and cabbage, one and a half hours; and the potatoes, parsnips, and squash, from one half to three quarters of an hour. If a large kettle is used, boil all together, except beets; they will do no harm, unless in coloring. Some do not like to boil the cabbage with the meat; if so, boil it in some of the liquor taken from the pot, but fill up the meat pot again; do the same if desired with the other vegetables. Serve the meat and each kind of vegetables on separate dishes whole, excepting the squash and turnip, which should be mashed with a little butter.

—*Aunt Mary's New England Cook Book* (1881), p. 8

Adhering strictly to a set of instructions and a list of ingredients considered essential to a true New England boiled dinner—in other words, boiling the salt meat with this particular combination of vegetables, then separating the elements of the dish before serving—is, despite the author's claims, an invention of the late nineteenth century. This is a colonial revival period piece, given luster by adding unhistorical, labor-intensive presentation requirements (separate serving dishes) meant to emphasize both excess and refinement—the more food and crockery on a table, the higher the Victorian hostess's social status. New England Boiled Dinner's ultimate codification in newspapers, women's magazines, and cookbooks like *Aunt Mary's* indicates the prestige that regional affiliation and an allusion to one group's ethnic heritage had bestowed on the dish. So, in truth, boiled dinner was, as *Aunt Mary's* claimed, a "favorite dish" among those who called it theirs. But it was not, in the form in which she presents it, an "old-fashioned" one.

Aunt Mary's instructions seem aimed at the inexperienced cook, for who else would need to be told to leave some of the core to hold the cabbage together; to cut up over-large turnips and rutabaga before boiling them; or that old beets require extra-long cooking? After all, these were New England's most common root vegetables. Among those who might not know these things were the servants belowstairs in wealthy Yankee households (many of them recent Irish immigrants) and young housewives who were themselves immigrants of a sort on newly established farms and ranches in the Midwest and West and therefore beyond the reach of their mothers and other domestic mentors. Both of these groups would have stood in need of clear and explicit directions on how to make "proper" New England food.

47. BEEF STEW

Take a pound and a half of nice beef, and cut it into small pieces.

Place in the bottom of your saucepan a layer of sliced potatoes, a few slices of onion, a pinch of pepper, one of salt; then a layer of meat, another layer of potatoes, onions, salt, and pepper, with a layer of meat, and continue in this way till you have disposed of all of your meat; let the top layer be of potatoes, onions, and seasoning. Cover all with water, and let it stew for an hour and a half.

—Knight, *Tit-Bits* (1864), p. 9

Knight's "Beef Stew" is a meaty version of the more popular nineteenth-century layered dish considered in Chapter 5—chowder. All of Knight's eleven beef recipes but one (for roasted or baked beef heart) involve boiling the meat. Even her "Beef Steak" is fried, then stewed for two hours. Whether "Beef Tongue," "Bouilli" (ten pounds of tender beef), "Corned Beef," or "Stuffed Beefsteak"—"the slower it boils the better." It is reasonable to suppose that Knight recommends baths for her beef because she expects the meat to be tough, but her "Bouilli" is explicitly tender; so the only inference that is fully warranted is that as far as Knight is concerned wetter is better.

48. BRAISED BEEF

Take six or eight pounds of the round or the face of the rump, and lard with quarter of a pound of salt pork. Put six slices of pork in the bottom of the braising pan, and as soon as it begins to fry, add two onions, half a small carrot and half a small turnip, all cut fine. Cook these until they begin to brown; then draw them to one side of the pan and put in the beef, which has been well dredged with salt, pepper and flour. Brown on all sides, and then add one quart of boiling water and a bouquet of sweet herbs; cover, and cook *slowly* in the oven for four hours, basting every twenty minutes. Take up, and finish the gravy as for braised tongue. Or, add to the gravy half a can of tomatoes, and cook for ten minutes. Strain, pour around the beef, and serve.

—Parloa, *Miss Parloa's New Cook Book* (1882), p. 137

Although it has been claimed that the term "braising" was popularized by Fannie Farmer, we see here that Parloa (whose book appeared over a decade before Farmer's) not only uses the term in a recipe title but also refers offhandedly within the recipe to a braising pan and to another braised dish.

This recipe is the first in our sample to utilize the essentially modern technique of searing, giving the meat the caramelized appearance now considered indispensable in beef cookery. To prevent moisture from being squeezed from muscle fibers during boiling or steaming, slow cooking, as here, is recommended. Parloa's gravy for braised tongue is composed of cooking liquid and lemon juice, thickened with corn starch that has been mixed with cold water. The option of canned tomatoes indicates the emergence of new methods of food preservation, replacing such traditional techniques as salting and drying.

49. POT ROAST OR BRAISED BEEF

Four to six pounds from the middle or face of the rump, the vein, or the round. Wipe and sear all over in a frying-pan or under the gas flame. Add one cup of water, and place it where it will cook slowly. Use only water enough to keep the meat from burning, and have the cover fit closely to keep in the steam. Cook until very tender, but do not let it break. Serve hot or cold. The meat, cut in quarter-inch slices, may be reheated in hot butter.

—Lincoln and Barrows, *Home Science Cook Book* (1911), pp. 126–27

This braised beef—with the name pot roast now receiving top billing—is the plainest of plain. Unseasoned, steamy, gray roasts appeared around this time on many a polished silver platter on many a mahogany sideboard in the cavernous dining rooms of the Back Bay elite. Reheating the leftovers in hot butter offers a small reprieve.

CHAPTER NINE

Pie Crusts

ie crust's continental antecedents can be found in medieval courtly kitchens, but our story begins more recently and among lower, if aspiring, social groups—the English gentry and middle class—where forms of aristocratic display such as elaborate paste sculptures decorating the tops and sides of pies were simplified and reserved for special occasions. Nevertheless, English pies could be large, requiring many pounds of flour and butter or lard. By the early seventeenth century, a consensus had developed regarding the techniques and ingredients for making the various types of crust. But good pie crust, whether the sturdy raised variety used to contain unwieldy carcasses or the flaky puff paste put into little patty pans, could only be made by those who had attained a certain level of skill. Thus centuries of cookbook writers have thought it worth their while to offer detailed instructions.

By the middle of the eighteenth century, it was generally agreed that pies, confectionery, and puddings were the particular province of English cooks and bakers and that baked goods and roasted meats constituted most of what could be called traditional British fare. Pastry work had long been the forte of English ladies. One commentator in 1656 asserted that the English were "so well vers'd in the Pastry Art, as that they may out-vie the best Forreign Pastry Cooks." Pies remained vehicles of display to some degree, but superior taste and texture were more important. Pastes could contain the ancient sweet-savory mixtures, which in this form persisted beyond the Middle Ages. Or they could be filled, sweet or savory, with custards, fruits, vegetables, meats, fish, or poultry. The pie's shape or top decoration might indicate its filling.

Whatever was inside, pastes were taken seriously, and many cookery schools, themselves a phenomenon of the eighteenth century, specialized in teaching the art of baking. New England carried on this tradition with its own emphasis on pie-making. We give crusts a chapter of their own to emphasize the importance of the whole pie, not just the filling, to English and New England cooking.

Note: Well into the nineteenth century, sugar came to the kitchen in solid blocks or cones, to be cut and sifted, or searced, by the cook. When finely sifted, it was called powdered. The powdered sugar that appears as an ingredient in a number of recipes in this and following chapters is of this type and should not be confused with the modern product, also known as confectioners' sugar, which is pulverized to a true powder and mixed with an anti-clumping agent such as cornstarch.

1. OF THE PASTERY & BAKED MEATES

Next to these already rehearsed, our *English Hus-wife* must be skilfull in the pastrie, and know how and in what manner to bake all sorts of meate, and what paste is fit for euery meate, and how to handle and compound such pastes: as for example, red Deere venison, wilde Boare, gammons of Bacon, Swannes, Elkes, Porpas and such like standing dishes which must be kept long would bee bak't in a moist, thicke, tough, course and long lasting crust; and therefore of all other your Rie paste is best for that purpose: your Turkie, Capon, Pheasant,

Partridge, Veale, Peacocks, Lambe, and all sorts of water fowle which are to come to the table more then once (yet not many daies) would be bak't in a good white crust, somewhat thicke; therefore your wheat is fit for them: your Chickens, Calues feet, Oliues, Potatoes, Quinces, Fallow-deere and such like, which are most commonly eaten hot, would be in the finest, shortest & thinnest crust; therefore your fine wheat flower which is a little baked in the ouen before it be kneaded is the best for that purpose.

—Markham, *English Hus-wife* (1615), pp. 64–65

Markham's hierarchy of pastes resembles the English bread hierarchy, which (as will be discussed more fully in Chapter 14) ranged from a coarse product made with oats, barley, rye, unbolted wheat, seeds, and even weeds, to a refined white loaf. In the case of pie pastes, considerations other than the cost and availability of the grain dictated the level of refinement. The amount of food to be encased affected the length of time the pie was to be kept, which in turn dictated the strength and durability of the paste to be used. The "shortest crust" was a crust with the highest proportion of easily spoiled fats, making it suitable only for short-term preservation (a short crust indeed). Through the nineteenth century, cooks often had to dry (Markham's "baked") their wheat flour in the oven before use. By olives Markham means not the Mediterranean fruit but rather thin slices of meat (see Chapter 10, #13).

2. OF THE MIXTURE OF PASTS [*SIC*]

To speak then of the mixture and kneading of pastes, you shall vnderstand that your Rie paste would be kneaded only with hot water and a little butter, or sweet seame and Rie flour very finely sifted, and it would bee made tough and stiffe that it may stand well in the raising, for the coffin thereof must euer be verie deepe: your course wheat crust would bee kneaded with hot water, or Mutton broth and good store of butter, and the paste made stiffe and tough because that coffin must bee deepe also; your fine wheat crust must be kneaded with as much butter as water, and the paste made reasonable lythe and gentle, into which you must put three or fowre eggs or more according to the quantity you blend together, for they will giue it a sufficient stiffening.

—Markham, *English Hus-wife* (1615), p. 65

Markham's instructions for making different kinds of pastes to serve different purposes were standard into the nineteenth century. Raised crusts differ from short crusts and puff pastes in one crucial respect: they are strong enough to stand on their own as "coffins" for even the sturdiest fillings. This apt term was applied to the traditional pastry vault used to hold heavy fillings such as meat or oily Lenten fish and spice combinations; recipes frequently advised, "make fair coffins and let them hard in the oven" or "take harded coffins." They are made by mixing coarse wheat or rye flour, or a combination of the two, with a small amount of lard or butter until a crumbly texture is achieved, then adding more lard or butter that has been melted in boiling water, finally kneading all together to form a smooth dough. "Seam" is glossed in the modern edition of Markham as clarified animal fat; in the *OED*, it is simply hog's lard.

3. TO MAKE PUFF-PASTE FOR TARTS

Rub a quarter of a pound of Butter into a pound of fine Flour; then whip the whites of two Eggs to Snow, and with cold Water, and one yolk make it into a Paste: then roll it abroad, and put in by degrees a pound of Butter, flowering it over the Butter every time, and roll it up, and roll it out again, and put in more Butter: So do for six or seven times till it has taken up all the pound of Butter. This Paste is good for Tarts, or any small things.

—Smith, *Compleat Housewife* (1728), pp. 107–8

Puff paste made an early appearance in Hugh Plat's *Delightes for Ladies* (1602). A 1586 "butter paste" was probably the first instance of a puff paste recorded in English; the technique is believed to have originated in fifteenth-century Tuscany.

Tarts are here singled out for particular treatment. They were always made with a rich crust such as this one; usually the crust did not cover the top. Gilly Lehmann tells us that "the eighteenth century tended to use puff-pastry where we would use short-crust or sweet pastry." Lucky them.

4. PUFF PASTES FOR TARTS

NO. 1. Rub one pound of butter into one pound of flour, whip 2 whites and add with cold water and one yolk; make into paste, roll in[,] in six or seven times one pound of butter, flowring it each roll. This is good for any small thing.

NO. 2. Rub six pound of butter into fourteen pound of flour, eight eggs, add cold water, make a stiff paste.

NO. 3. To any quantity of flour, rub in three fourths of it's weight of butter, (twelve eggs to a peck) rub in one third or half, and roll in the rest.

NO. 4. Into two quarts flour (salted) and wet stiff with cold water roll in, in nine or ten times one and half pound of butter.

No. 5. One pound flour, three fourths of a pound of butter, beat well.

No. 6. To one pound of flour rub in one fourth of a pound of butter wet with three eggs and rolled in a half pound of butter.

—Simmons, American Cookery (Hartford, 1796), p. 29

Simmons's first recipe for puff paste in based on Smith (#3), but Simmons uses more butter (two pounds to Smith's one and a quarter pounds). Simmons reworked the ratio of butter to flour in her second edition (doubling the flour), in the process further removing the recipe from the Smith original. Simmons also modernized Smith's directions, dropping "roll it abroad" and "whip the whites of two eggs to snow." While certainly plagiaristic, this adaptive borrowing also illustrates an experienced cook's dialogue with a renowned predecessor. Simmons's fifth version of puff paste is copied from Glasse.

5. A PASTE FOR SWEET MEATS

No. 7. Rub one third of one pound of butter, and one pound of lard into two pound of flour, wet with four whites well beaten; water q:s: to make a paste, roll in the residue of shortning in ten or twelve rollings—bake quick.

No. 8. Rub in one and half pound of suet to six pounds of flour, and a spoon full of salt, wet with cream roll in, in six or eight times, two and half pounds of butter—good for chicken or meat pie.

—Simmons, American Cookery (Hartford, 1796), p. 29

The title must refer only to the first of the two recipes: "sweet meat" had signified sweet food since at least the fifteenth century, whereas the second recipe is "good for chicken or meat pie"—in other words, for what had become by Simmons's day distinctly "savory meat." Of Simmons's nine pastes, these are the only ones that call for lard or suet.

"Q.s.," which Simmons deploys in other recipes besides this one, is an abbreviation of the Latin phrase *quantum sufficit*, as much as suffices. This was not a standard notation in eighteenth-century English cookbooks and makes for an amusing parade of learning on the part of an author who makes no effort to conceal her illiteracy.

6. ROYAL PASTE

No. 9. Rub half a pound of butter into one pound of flour, four whites beat to a foam, add two yolks, two ounces of fine sugar; roll often, rubbing one third, and rolling two thirds of the butter is best; excellent for tarts and apple cakes.

—Simmons, *American Cookery* (Hartford, 1796), pp. 29–30

This recipe is based on Carter's "Paste Royal for Patty-pans." (Patty pans originally referred to miniature pastries, though the term came to be applied instead to the small pans themselves.) Simmons changed Carter by removing two of the egg yolks, beating the whites before adding them to the dough, and rubbing some of the fat into the dough before rolling in the rest. In her second edition, Simmons alters the recipe still further, removing all of the yolks as well as her own confusing reference to apple cakes. The Martha Washington manuscript cookbook also offers a "Royall" paste, with sugar rather than egg white as the defining ingredient. It is richer than either Carter's or Simmons's, calling for rosewater (see Chapter 12, #4) and sack (see Chapter 10, #2 commentary) along with sugar. This is the only paste to which Simmons adds sugar.

7. RAISED CRUST FOR MEAT-PIES, OR FOWLS, &C.

Boil water with a little fine lard, and an equal quantity of fresh dripping, or of butter, but not much of either. While hot, mix this with as much flour as you will want, making the paste as stiff as you can to be smooth, which you will make it by good kneading and beating it with the rolling-pin. When quite smooth, put in a lump into a cloth, or under a pan, to soak till near cold.

Those who have not a good hand at raising crust may do thus: Roll the paste of a proper thickness, and cut out the top and bottom of the pie, then a long piece for the sides. Cement the bottom to the sides with egg, bringing the former rather further out, and pinching both together; put egg between the edges of the paste, to make it adhere at the sides. Fill your pie, and put on the cover, and pinch it and the side crust together. The same mode of uniting the paste is to be observed if the sides are pressed into a tin form, in which the paste must be baked, after it shall be filled and covered; but in the latter case, the tin should be buttered, and carefully taken off when done enough; and as the form usually makes the sides of a lighter colour than is proper, the paste should be put into the oven again for a quarter of an hour. With a feather, put egg over at first.

—Rundell, *New System of Domestic Cookery* (1807), pp. 135–36

In this recipe, we see why this British writer was popular on both sides of the Atlantic. She combines classic techniques with tips that allow the home cook to approximate the achievements of the professional *pâtissier*. Rundell includes two alternatives to the basic technique for raising crust described above in the commentary on #2: forming the top, bottom, and sides separately and then pinching them together; or pressing all the dough into a tin pie mold. Rundell's instruction "to soak till near cold" apparently means to let the smooth lump of worked dough cool and rest before it is shaped.

8. POTATOE PASTE

Pound boiled potatoes very fine, and add, while warm, a sufficiency of butter to make the mash hold together, or you may mix with it an egg; then before it gets cold, flour the board pretty well to prevent it from sticking, and roll it to the thickness wanted.

If it is become quite cold before it be put on the dish, it will be apt to crack.

—Rundell, *New System of Domestic Cookery* (1807), p. 155

"Potatoe" (Dan Quayle vindicated!) pastes are also found in Leslie, Webster, and Beecher. Leslie maintains that it is "unfit for baking." Even when boiled, she says, it must be eaten "quite hot" or it will be "tough and heavy." In her "Veal and Chicken Potpie," Webster recommends potato crust as a worthy alternative to raised crust. For Beecher's view of the virtues of potato paste, see #12 and Chapter 10, #27.

9. PIE CRUST

To make pie crust for common use, a quarter of a pound of butter is enough for a half a pound of flour. Take out about a quarter part of the flour you intend to use, and lay it aside. Into the remainder of the flour rub butter thoroughly with your hands, until it is so short that a handful of it, clasped tight, will remain in a ball, without any tendency to fall in pieces. Then wet it with cold water, roll it out on a board, rub over the surface with flour, stick little lumps of butter all over it, sprinkle some flour over the butter, and roll the dough all up; flour the paste, and flour the rolling-pin; roll it lightly and quickly; flour it again; stick in bits of butter; do it up; flour the rolling-pin, and roll it quickly and lightly; and so on, till you have used up your butter. Always roll from you. Pie crust should be made as cold as possible, and set in a cool place; but be careful it does not freeze. Do not use more flour than you can help in sprinkling and rolling. The paste should not be rolled out more than three times; if rolled too much, it will not be flaky.

—Child, *American Frugal Housewife* (1833), p. 69

Child's small pie crust uses less fat than any of Simmons's recipes. The technique for adding more butter to the dough, then rolling, resembles the puff paste method, although Child's admonition to roll only three times, consistent with the reduced amount of fat in the dough, is new. The result is an adequate if unexciting crust, far less rich and flaky than its predecessors.

10. TART PASTE

Rub into eight ounces of flour, six of butter, and a spoonful of powdered sugar. Form it into a thick paste with hot water.

—Webster, *Improved Housewife* (1844), p. 92

11. SHORT PASTE FOR FRUIT PIES

Rub into twelve ounces of flour, four ounces of lard and a spoonful of powdered sugar. Form it into a paste with milk; roll it out, and add four ounces of butter. For a fruit tart, roll out half an inch thick.

—Webster, *Improved Housewife* (1844), p. 92

Webster's "Tart Paste," with three-fourths the amount of butter to flour, is richer than Child's (half the amount of butter to flour) but far less rich than equivalent offerings of the previous century—for instance, Smith's (#3, one and a quarter the amount of butter to flour) or Simmons's (#4.1, twice the butter to flour), both of which also include egg. With its spoonful of sugar and its hot water, Webster's recipe is a kind of hybrid short-royal-raised paste. Her "Short Paste for Fruit Pies" has a two-thirds proportion of fat (lard and butter) to flour, along with some milk, and is thus also richer than Child's "Pie Crust," though still utilitarian by eighteenth-century standards.

12. HEALTHFUL PIE CRUSTS

Good crusts for plain pies are made by wetting up the crust with rich milk turned sour, and sweetened with saleratus. Still better crusts are made of sour cream sweetened with saleratus.

Mealy potatoes boiled in salted water, and mixed with the same quantity of flour, and wet with sour milk sweetened with saleratus, make a good crust.

Good light bread rolled thin, makes a good crust for pandowdy, or pan pie, and also for the upper crust of fruit pies, to be made without bottom crusts.

—Beecher, *Domestic Receipt-Book* (1846), p. 128

13. PASTE MADE WITH BUTTER

Very plain paste is made by taking a quarter of a pound of butter for every pound of flour. Still richer allows three quarters of a pound of butter to a pound of flour. Very rich paste has a pound of butter to a pound of flour.

—Beecher, *Domestic Receipt-Book* (1846), p. 128

14. DIRECTIONS FOR MAKING PASTE

Take a quarter of the butter to be used, rub it thoroughly into the flour, and wet it with *cold* water to a stiff paste.

Next dredge the board thick with flour, and cut up the remainder of the butter into thin slices, and lay them upon the flour, and dredge flour over thick, and then roll out the butter into thin sheets and lay it aside.

Then roll out the paste thin, cover it with a sheet of this rolled butter, dredge on more flour, fold it up, and roll it out, and then repeat the process till all the butter is used up.

Paste should be made as quick and as cold as possible. Some use a marble table in order to keep it cold. Roll *from* you every time.

—Beecher, *Domestic Receipt-Book* (1846), p. 128

Beecher uses saleratus (sodium carbonate) to balance or "sweeten" the lactid acid in her first two "healthful" crusts, both made cheaply without butter or lard. Saleratus was produced from potash, a wood-ash-derived chemical also used as a fertilizer and in glass and soap manufacture. It comes as no surprise that the use of an industrial by-product in cooking initially caused some ripples of concern among health experts, especially when products baked with it were fed to children. Many American cooks were quickly won over, however, perhaps because pearl ash (potassium carbonate), a less effective chemical leaven from the same source, had been in use in American kitchens since the 1790s. Pearl ash had proved innocuous, if indelicious. Chemical leavens were readily adopted by New Englanders as quick and inexpensive alternatives to yeast and eggs in pie, cake, and bread doughs. Saleratus was in time replaced by baking soda (sodium bicarbonate) mixed with cream of tartar, which was eventually manufactured as baking powder. In *The Taste of America*, John and Karen Hess offer a stirring (so to speak) account of the American baking powder wars, including bribery charges that reached Congress.

The richest option in Beecher's "Paste made with Butter," with its one-to-one ratio of fat to flour, indicates that the nineteenth century's health concerns were nudging cooks away from the eighteenth century's extravagant two-to-one butter/flour puff pastes.

The last recipe presents a variation on the standard puff paste technique of dotting the dough with pieces of butter between rollings. Instead, Beecher creates thin sheets of butter coated with flour that are then rolled into the dough. This clever technique is used in her explicitly named "Puff Paste," the next recipe in her book.

15. PUFF PASTE

One quart of pastry flour, one pint of butter, one table-spoonful of salt, one of sugar, one and a quarter cupfuls of ice water. Wash the hands with soap and water, and dip them first in very hot, and then in cold, water. Rinse a large bowl or pan with boiling water and then with cold. Half fill it with cold water. Wash the butter in this, working it with the hands until it is light and waxy. This frees it of the salt and butter-milk, and lightens it, so that the pastry is more delicate. Shape the butter into two thin cakes, and put in a pan of ice water, to harden. Mix the salt and sugar with the flour. With the hands, rub one-third of the butter into the flour. Add the water, stirring with a knife. Stir quickly and vigorously until the paste is a smooth ball. Sprinkle the board *lightly* with flour. Turn the paste on this, and pound quickly and lightly with the rolling pin. Do not break the paste. Roll from you and to one side; or, if easier to roll from you all the while, turn the paste around. When it is about one-fourth of an inch thick, wipe the remaining butter, break it in bits, and spread these on the paste. Sprinkle lightly with flour. Fold the paste, one-third from each side, so that the edges meet. Now fold from the ends, but do not have these meet. Double the paste, pound lightly, and roll down to about one-third of an inch in thickness. Fold as before, and roll down again. Repeat this three times if for pies, and six times if for *vol-au-vents,* patties, tarts, etc. Place on the ice, to harden, when it has been rolled the last time. It should be in the ice chest at least an hour before being used. In hot weather if the paste sticks when being rolled down, put it on a tin sheet and place on ice. As soon as it is chilled it will roll easily. The less flour you use in rolling out the paste the tenderer it will be. No matter how carefully every part of the work may be done, the paste will not be good if much flour is used.

—Parloa, *Miss Parloa's New Cook Book* (1882), p. 255

Teacher to Mary Lincoln of Boston Cooking School fame, who in turn taught Fannie Farmer, Maria Parloa developed a procedure for making puff paste that was copied by both of those more illustrious cookbook authors. This author who in many ways epitomizes late-nineteenth-century excess and gentility actually recommends the same spare fat-flour ratio as does her militantly frugal predecessor Child (#9). The difference is that Parloa's excruciatingly precise instructions for folding the paste and rolling it to measured thicknesses are designed to produce a more layered, flakier, "puffier" paste. Parloa's thoroughness and specificity were anticipated in many respects by Leslie (as in her recipe for "Raised French Pie").

CHAPTER TEN

Pies — Mixed, Meat, Mince

HERE's great H, and I
With the Chriſtmas Pye ;
Who will eat the Plumbs out ?

avory foods baked in crusts, such as steak and kidney pie, pork pie, and Cornish pasties, have a long and continuous history as British favorites but are virtually unknown to the average American. We may occasionally pop a frozen, manufactured beef or chicken pot pie into the oven for dinner, but those soupy repasts crowned with industrial-strength pie dough hold little resemblance to the rich, substantial, hand-made pies of old England.

It may come as a surprise, then, to learn that both the custom of eating savory pies and the custom of disapproving of them have long if also long-forgotten roots in New England cooking. The decline of the meat, fowl, and fish pie on this side of the Atlantic resulted in part from the rise in the nineteenth century of health food fads, led most famously by

Sylvester Graham. Many domestic advice writers discouraged the eating of any type of pie, calling pie pastry "indigestible," a term of highest opprobrium for that century. As with many American dietary fashions, this anti-pie campaign, waged by the same trendsetters who advocated eating beefsteaks for breakfast, now serves merely to point up our paradoxical history as ill-informed consumers. But we cannot lay the entire blame at the feet of Graham and others of like mind. In truth, pies in this country were often so poorly made that disapproval of them on health grounds by the day's nutrition experts merely confirmed the public's suspicions based on direct experience.

The war was waged on pies in general, but surprisingly it was savory pies, not sugar-laden fruit pies, that were particularly targeted. Hale proclaimed bluntly that "meat pies . . . should never be made." It was also she who peevishly warned hostesses to "beware of the common practice of having too much." Competing with the abundance that improved technology and transportation brought to American tables around this time was the old Puritan ideal, now dressed in New England Brahmin guise, of gastronomic restraint. Food historian Felipe Fernandez-Armesto points out that while "individuals, for most of history, gained prestige in proportion to their food consumption," elites have also distinguished themselves by exalting "the nobility of austerity and simplicity." So, somewhat perversely, just as abundance came within common reach, traditional New England restraint was reasserted as the new standard of refinement.

In addition to its sometimes inexpertly cooked crust, the savory pie eventually became suspect for the very qualities that had once recommended it to both the frugal housewife and the feasting lord: it consolidated a mélange of foods within its solid envelope, and it remained edible for a surprisingly long time. As railroads delivered relatively inexpensive fresh meat to many American tables, and industrialists devised new chemical soups to preserve vast amounts of the abattoir's product, the advantages of the savory pie appeared to be outweighed by its challenges. Many cooks, then as now daunted by pie-making, simply abandoned the whole exercise. Fruit pies, on the other hand, got sweeter and more fashionable in an era unafraid of sugar. They will be treated in Chapter 12.

However, we have, in a sense, begun at the end of our story. For two and a half centuries New Englanders did indeed hew to the English tradition, taking much of their local bounty, combining it with imported luxuries when they could, and baking it all up into an array of meat, fowl, and fish pies. The recipes in this and the next chapter represent the English origins and the New England expressions of that forgotten, centuries-long pie extravaganza. Perhaps predictably, the end of New England savory pie-making coincided not only with the rise of health-food fads but also with an insistence upon Yankee-style plainness that resulted in the banishment of most of the enhancements and flavorings that had made the earlier pies so glorious.

Mixed Pies

While most traditional pies contained more than one ingredient—the term itself may derive from the habit of the magpie to collect all sorts of odd bits for its nest—in this category we include those that empha-sized combinations of primary ingredients, usually various sorts of game or meat coupled with various sorts of fowl. The fowl component tended to dominate, especially in the genre's more elaborate and festive incarna-tions. For the reasons just mentioned, mixed pies didn't survive in New England much past the colonial period—except as holiday specialties (#s 7–9), or as exercises in Anglophilia that failed to catch on (#6).

1. A CAUDLE FOR SWEET PYES

Take Sack and White-wine alike in quantity, a little Verjuice and Sugar, boil it, and brew it with two or three Eggs, as butter'd Ale; when the Pyes are baked, pour it in with a Funnel, and shake it together.

2. A LEAR FOR SAVOURY PYES

Take Claret, Gravy, Oyster Liquor, two or three Anchovies, a faggot of sweet Herbs and an Onion; boil it up and thicken it with brown Butter, then pour it into your savoury Pyes when called for.

—Smith, *Compleat Housewife* (1730), p. 4

The term "caudle" might refer to a gruel given to sick people, an ale-based, spiced beverage, or, as here, a rich sauce to be poured into pies just as they finished baking. The last two uses occur in the Martha Washington man-uscript cookbook. The first occurs in Glasse, as well as in Beecher and several other New England cookbooks. Lears were thickening sauces for pottages, as well as last-minute additions to pies. When a caudle or lear was added to a pie, the top crust was removed (or a funnel was inserted), the sauce poured in, the crust replaced, and the pie allowed to bake for an additional five or ten minutes, thereby warming and amalgamating the flavors of sauce and filling. Sack (from the French *vin sec*) was a popular Spanish wine.

3. A BATTALIA PYE

Take four small Chickens, four squab Pigeons, four sucking Rabbets; cut them in pieces, season them with savoury Spice; and lay 'em in the Pye, with four Sweet-breads sliced, and as many Sheep's-tongues, two shiver'd Palates, two pair of Lamb-stones, twenty or thirty Coxcombs, with savoury Balls and Oysters. Lay on Butter, and close the Pye. A Lear.

—Smith, *Compleat Housewife* (1730), pp. 8–9

Battalia is described in the *OED* as "Tit-bits, as cocks' combs, sweetbreads, etc. in a pie." In time, such compound pies were most often made with fowl, forcemeat balls, some type of pickled ingredient such as mushrooms or oysters, and perhaps offal (especially sweetbreads, brains, feet, lungs, testicles, liver, or kidneys). The name battalia probably derives from the medieval Latin term for samplers sewn by nuns—*beatillae*—meaning "small blessed articles."

It wasn't until Antonin Carême (1784–1833) simplified haute cuisine, insisting on "the principle of garnishing meat with meat, fish with fish, and dispens[ing] with such things as trimmings of cockscombs and sweetbreads" that dishes such as this fell completely out of favor. Such trends are not yet evident in Smith, whose aim was to introduce the older aristocratic style to women cooks. Spicing the meat, rather than seasoning with herbs, also suggests an older style. "Savoury spice" is salt, pepper, cloves, mace, and nutmeg. To shiver is "to break or split into small fragments or splinters." As for ox palates, "small pieces of the palate (roof of mouth) of an ox were used as garnish." Carter copied this recipe with slight modifications.

4. A YORKSHIRE GOOSE PYE

Take a large fat Goose, split it down the Back, and take all the Bones out, bone a Turkey and two Ducks the same Way, season them very well with Pepper and

Salt, with six Woodcocks, lay the Goose down on a clean Dish, with the Skin-side down, and lay the Turkey into the Goose, with the Skin down, have ready a large Hare cleaned well, cut in Pieces, and stewed in the Oven, with a Pound of Butter, a quarter of an Ounce of Mace beat fine, the same of White Pepper, and Salt to your Taste, 'till the Meat will leave the Bones, and scum the Butter off the Gravy, pick the Meat clean off, and beat it in a Marble Mortar very fine with the Butter you took off, and lay it in the Turkey, take twenty-four Pounds of the finest Flour, six Pounds of Butter, half a Pound of fresh rendered Suet, make the Paste pretty stiff, and raise the Pye oval, roll out a Lump of Paste, and cut it in Vine Leaves, or what form you please, rub the Pye with the Yolks of Eggs, and put on your Ornaments on the Walls, then turn the Hare, Turkey, and Goose Upside down, and lay them in your Pye, with the Ducks at each End, and the Woodcocks on the Sides, make your Lid pretty thick, and put it on; you may lay Flowers, or the Shape of the Fowls in Paste, on the Lid, and make a Hole in the Middle of your Lid; the Walls of the Pye is to be one Inch and a half higher than the Lid, then rub it all over with the Yolks of Eggs, and bind it round with three-fold Paper, and lay the same over the Top; it will take four Hours baking in a brown Bread Oven, when it comes out melt two Pounds of Butter in the Gravy that comes from the Hare, and pour it hot in the Pye through a Tun-dish, close it well up, and let it be eight or ten Days before you cut it; if you send it any Distance, make up the Hole in the Middle with cold Butter, to prevent the Air from getting in.

—Raffald, *Experienced English House-keeper* (1769), pp. 129–30

Glasse has a similar recipe that she calls "A Yorkshire Christmas-Pye." In it, she explains that "these pies are often sent to *London* in a Box as Presents; therefore the Walls must be well built." She also offers a simpler version, called "A Goose-Pye," made in the same Russian-nesting-doll fashion with goose, fowl, and pickled dried tongue. In the early nineteenth century, Rundell has two smaller pies along the same lines, a "Green-goose Pie," with one young goose stuffed inside the other, and a "Duck Pie," in which a duck is stuffed with a fowl that has in turn been stuffed with a pickled calf's tongue. She also explains the northern pie tradition: "The large pies in Staffordshire are made as above: but with a goose outwards, then a turkey, a duck next, then a fowl; and either tongue, small birds, or forcemeat, in the middle." In 1832 in Boston, Lee (Dalgairns) is still at it with a recipe for "Pie, Goose" involving goose, turkey, fowl, boiled ham, and tongue. Leslie and Bliss (#7) continue the tradition. A tun-dish is a type of funnel.

Preserving meat, fish, or fowl by sealing with butter was known as potting. It came into widespread use in the mid-seventeenth century but was known in Elizabethan days and perhaps earlier. An intermediate-range preservation technique, potting kept flesh "for three weeks or one whole month together," according to Sir Hugh Plat. Small birds such as pigeon and woodcock were especially well-suited to the process, although larger birds such as swans and geese were, as here, also potted.

Instructions for (de)boning a fowl are given below (#9).

5. A SEA PIE

Four pound of flour, one and half pound of butter rolled into paste, wet with coldwater, line the pot therewith, lay in split pigeons, turkey pies, veal, mutton or birds, with slices of pork, salt, pepper, and dust on flour, doing thus till the pot is full or your ingredients expended, add three pints water, cover tight with paste, and stew moderately two and half hours.

—Simmons, *American Cookery* (Hartford, 1796), p. 23

The sea pie, similar to the battalia in a watered-down sort of way, is sometimes identified as "double-" or "triple-decker" according to the number of layers. It originated in the ship's galley as a chowderlike stew of fresh and salt meat, paste, root vegetables, and water. This heavy concoction was soon found serviceable for hungry landlubbing families as well. In her second edition, Simmons specifies a dozen split pigeons and omits all the other flesh meats except the slices of pork, which, given the standard sea pie ingredients, we can assume to be salt pork. In this version, we take her "turkey pies" to be a misprint for turkey *pieces*. Lee offers a Sea Pie (stolen from Dalgairns, in turn stolen by Hale) which, she avers, "answers well for a family dinner." It is similar to Simmons's second version, but with salt beef replacing the slices of pork and with alternating layers of beef, paste, and fowl, stewed in water. About a century earlier, in a chapter titled "For Captains of Ships," Glasse offers a variation with salt pork and potatoes.

6. PIE, DEVIZES

Cut into very thin slices, after being dressed, cold calf's head, with some of the brains, pickled tongue, sweetbreads, lamb, veal, a few slices of bacon, and hard-boiled eggs; put them in layers into a pie-dish, with plenty of seasoning between each, of cayenne, white pepper, allspice, and salt; fill up the dish with rich gravy;

cover it with a flour and water paste; bake it in a slow oven, and when perfectly cold, take off the crust, and turn the pie out upon a dish; garnish it with parsley and pickled eggs cut into slices.

—Lee, *Cook's Own Book* (1832), p. 140

Lee's (Dalgairns's) simple flour and water crust, discarded after the pie is baked, serves as a protective covering for the filling as it slowly cooks. This use of paste harks back to the origins of pie: "In effect, the pastry became an oven, ensuring moderate heat thanks to its insulating properties."

7. A NEW YEAR'S PIE

Boil a neat's tongue, skin it, and put it into a boned chicken; put the boned chicken into a boned duck; put the boned duck into a boned turkey; put the boned turkey into a boned goose; season the whole with lemon and spice to your taste, and bake it in a hot oven. Make a jelly of beef's feet, as jelly is made of calf's feet, (chap. XXIII.;) when the fowls are baked, put them into a deep dish, or into a deep-plated dish cover, with the breast of the goose downwards; then pour upon them the jelly, covering the fowls with it; set the whole away, for the jelly to harden; when it has become hard and stiff, turn the whole out carefully upon your dish, and serve, cutting through all.

The dish may be garnished with small moulds of the jelly.

—Bliss, *Practical Cook Book* (1850), p. 244

The term for compressed meat encased in jelly—*pâté*—originally meant pastry, an association that Bliss recalls in naming this dish a "pie." Though crustless, it is nevertheless descended from the Yorkshire Christmas Pie. From the banquet tables of early modern England to the festive boards of New England, glistening, sculpted calf's foot jelly creations betokened elegance and refinement. The idea of stuffing multiple fowls one inside the next has made a recent comeback, although the dish now comes to the table with neither decorative paste nor shimmering jelly. In this bald state it is known as "turducken."

8. CALF'S FOOT JELLY

Cut up four calf's feet, and put them into a stew-pan and over the fire with six quarts of water; when it boils, remove it to a corner of the fire, and let it simmer slowly five hours, reducing it to two quarts; then strain it through a hair sieve into a bowl, and let it stand in a cool place until it becomes firm; then take off from the top as much of the oil as you can with a spoon, wash off the remainder quickly with a little hot water, wipe it dry, put it into a stew-pan with one pound of fine white sugar, the juice of six lemons, the grated rind of two lemons, the whites of six eggs with the shells, and one pint of Madeira wine; put the stew-pan over the fire, and whisk about its contents until they boil; strain it through a jelly-bag, pouring that which first runs through back again until it runs through clear, pour it into moulds, and keep it in a cool place until it is wanted.

This jelly may be flavored, while boiling, as you require.

—Bliss, *Practical Cook Book* (1850), p. 230

Many authors of the day warned against squeezing a jelly bag during straining, since this would, in Hale's words, allow "thicker particles" through and keep the jelly from becoming "brilliantly clear." Assisting in the production of a clear jelly was also the purpose of the egg shells, which were universally utilized in nineteenth-century New England to facilitate the settling of the grounds during coffee-making. Harold McGee explains how egg whites play a similar clarifying role in the making of consommé: "As the stock heats up, the abundant egg white proteins begin to coagulate into a fine cheesecloth-like network, and essentially strain the liquid from within."

9. TO BONE A FOWL

Clean the fowl as usual. With a sharp and pointed knife begin at the extremity of the wing, and pass the knife down close to the bone, cutting all the flesh from the bone, and preserving the skin whole; run the knife down each side of the breast-bone and up the legs, keeping close to the bone; then split the back half way up, and draw out the bones; fill the places whence the bones were taken with a stuffing, restoring the fowl to its natural form, and sew up all the incisions made in the skin.

—Bliss, *Practical Cook Book* (1850), p. 244

Meat Pies

The English love of meat pies is reflected in the vast number and astounding variety found in the classic cookbooks of the seventeenth and eighteenth centuries. But the New England offerings are almost as substantial—venison, veal, beef, and pork baked in raised crusts, puff pastes, plain pastes, even potato pastes. New Englanders rivaled the English in their devotion to meat pies, although the later New England examples show some wear.

10. TO SEASON AND BAKE A VENISON PASTY

Bone your Haunch or Side of Venison, and take out all the Sinews and Skin; then proportion it for your Pasty, by taking away from one part, and adding to another, till 'tis of an equal thickness; then season it with Pepper and Salt, about an ounce of Pepper; save a little of it whole, and beat the rest, and mix with twice as much Salt, and rub it all over your Venison, and let it lie till your Paste is ready. Make your Paste thus: A peck of fine Flour, six pounds of Butter, a dozen of Eggs; rub your Butter in your Flour; beat your Eggs, and with them and cold Water make up your Paste pretty stiff; then drive it forth for your Pasty; let it be the thickness of a Man's Thumb; put under it two or three Sheets of Cap-paper well floured: Then have two pounds of Beef-suet, shred exceeding fine; proportion it on the bottom to the breadth of your Venison, and leave a Verge round your Venison three Fingers broad; wash that Verge over with a bunch of Feathers or Brush dipped in an Egg beaten, and then lay a Border of your Paste on the place you washed, and lay your Venison on the Suet; put a little of your Seasoning on the top, and a few corns of whole Pepper, and two pounds of very good fresh Butter; then turn over your other Sheet of Paste, so close your Pasty. Garnish it on the top as you think fit; vent it in the middle, and set it in the Oven. It will ask five or six hours baking: Then break all the Bones, wash them and add to them more Bones, or Knuckles; season them with Pepper and Salt, and put them with a quart of Water, and half a pound of Butter, in a Pan or earthen Pot; cover it over with coarse Paste, and set it in with your Pasty; and when your Pasty is drawn and dished, fill it up with the Gravy that came from the Bones.

—Smith, *Compleat Housewife* (1728), pp. 108–9

Before the Imperial System became law in Britain in 1824, units of weight such as the peck varied slightly according to local custom. Nevertheless, we can assume that Smith's peck works out to about eight pounds of flour. This, along with six pounds of butter, makes for a huge pie.

Venison pasties were served on festive occasions, such as William Bradford's 1623 Plymouth wedding. Smith's version exemplifies the classic English procedure of encasing seasoned raw venison and suet in a crust, baking, and adding gravy upon serving. The seasoning here is simpler (salt and pepper only) than it probably was for the venison pasties at the Bradford festivities. The seventeenth-century recipe in the Martha Washington manuscript calls for lemon rind and lemon juice as well as salt and pepper. As Lehmann points out, a garnish including lemon was "part of English habits throughout the sixteenth and seventeenth centuries."

Sixty years before Smith, Woolley prescribes the proper order of service, depending on the rank of the diners, for venison in its various forms: the nobility, for whom venison was no rarity, might have both haunch and pasty during the less important first course, but the gentry served the pasty, sometimes made with that humbler meat, beef, for the first course and reserved the prestigious whole roasted haunch for the more important second course.

11. VENISON FOR PASTRY

Take out the bones, then beat the meat well, and season; lay it in a jar and set it in a kettle of water, with some nice gravy of any kind; if none, cover with water, season, boil three or four hours, take up the meat, and let the water get cold. Remove the fat the next day. The bones should be boiled with some fine old mutton, and cut the meat in nice pieces for a pie; season, rub flour into butter, and lay the fat between the pieces, that in cutting, it may be proportioned to each person. Cover with paste NO. 2, have plenty of good gravy to serve with the pie, and currant jelly always with venison.

If it is done out of the pie, add by pouring in some rice with a funnel in the middle. Shake the dish to settle it even.

—Allen, *Housekeeper's Assistant* (1845), p. 97

Allen has joined the traditional method of first beating the raw venison with what now seems a peculiar practice—placing meat and liquid in a jar to boil, as one would fruit preserves. Her recommendation for alternating layers of meat and fat is unusual, although it approximates the traditional bottom layer of suet. It appears that she uses only an upper crust. Allen's "paste No. 2" is a massive puff paste, made with six pounds of butter, a pound of lard, eight eggs, and fourteen pounds of flour. Although she gives no specific instructions about the quantity of meat in this pie, from the size of the crust we can assume that, like Smith, she intends a haunch or side.

12. VENISON PASTY

Cut a neck or breast into small steaks, rub them over with a seasoning of sweet herbs, grated nutmeg, pepper, and salt; fry them slightly in butter; line the sides and edges of a dish with puff paste, lay in the steaks, and add half a pint of rich gravy made with the trimmings of the venison; add a glass of port wine, and the juice of half a lemon, or a tea-spoonful of vinegar; cover the dish with puff paste, and bake it nearly 2 hours; some more gravy may be poured into the pie before serving it.

—Hale, *Ladies' New Book of Cookery* (1852), p. 272

Hale's recipe attempts to participate in the English venison pie tradition, even to the use of the antiquated term "pasty." However, she uses fried venison steaks instead of a boned haunch or flitch, omits the layer of suet, bakes the meat in gravy, and pours more gravy into the pie just before serving, whereas Smith prepares a more elaborate gravy from the bones and pours it into each diner's dish.

13. TO BAKE AN OLIUE PYE

To make an excellent Oliue pie; take sweet hearbes as Violet leaues, Strawberry leaues, Spinage, Succorie, Endiue, Time and Sorrell and chop them as small as may be, and if there be a Scallion or two amongst them it will giue the better taste; then take the yelks of hard egs with Currants, Cinamon, Cloues and Mace and chop them amongst the hearbes also; then hauing cut out long oliues of a legge of Veale, roule vp more then three parts of the hearbes so mixed within the Oliues, together with a good deale of sweet butter; then hauing raised your crust of the finest and best paste, strowe in the bottom the remainder of the hearbes, with a fewe great Raysins hauing the stones pickt out, then put in the Oliues and couer them with great Raysins and a fewe Prunes; then ouer all lay good store of butter and so bake them; then being sufficiently bak't, take Claret wine, Sugar, Cinamon, and two or three spoonefull of wine Vinegar and boile them together, and then drawing the pye, at a vent in the top of the lid put in the same, and then set into the Ouen againe a little space, and so serue it forth.

—Markham, *English Hus-wife* (1615), pp. 67–68

The olives of this recipe could refer either to thin slices of beef or veal or to the slices rolled up with herbs, hard-boiled egg yolks, onions, raisins, and other fillings. Wilson maintains that the term, applied to veal in the seventeenth century, is a "variant of the much older beef or mutton olives, called 'allowes' or 'aluander' of beef or mutton." Seasoned with suet, onion, egg, parsley, and spices, these earlier olives were also rolled and roasted or grilled. Both Smith and Rundell offer versions of this popular pie. In one of Smith's, she insists that "the Herbs must be Thyme, Parsley, and Spinage," a dictum she ignores in the other, where nutmeg, lemon peel, and gravy season the pie.

14. TO MAKE A LUMBER PYE

Take a pound and half of Veal, parboil it, and when 'tis cold chop it very small, with two pound of Beef-suet, and some candied Orange-peel; some Sweet-herbs, as Thyme, Sweet-marjoram, and a handful of Spinnage; mince the Herbs small before you put them to the other: So chop all together, and a Pippin or two; then add a handful or two of grated Bread, a pound and half of Currants, washed and dried; some Cloves, Mace, Nutmeg, a little Salt, Sugar and Sack, and put to all these as many yolks of raw Eggs, and whites of two as will make it a moist Forc'd-meat; work it with your hands into a Body, and make it into Balls as big as a Turkey's Egg; then having your Coffin made, put in your Balls. Take the Marrow out of three or four Bones as whole as you can: Let your Marrow lie a little in Water, to take out the Blood and Splinters; then dry it, and dip it in yolks of Eggs; season it with a little Salt, Nutmeg grated, and grated Bread; lay it on and between your Forc'd-meat Balls, and over that sliced Citron, candied Orange and Lemon, Eringoe-roots preserved, Barberries; then lay on sliced Lemon, and thin slices of Butter over all; then lid your Pye, and bake it; and when 'tis drawn, have in readiness a Cawdle made of White-wine and Sugar, and thickened with Butter and Eggs, and pour it hot into your Pye.

—Smith, *Compleat Housewife* (1728), pp. 103–4

While Smith's Lumber Pie is made with meatballs of parboiled veal, pies of the same name might also feature fish. The name makes more sense when we realize that it was sometimes spelled "lumbar" and, as the *OED* suggests, derives from Lombard or Lombardy. Eringo is sea holly, pickled or candied. The barberries in this recipe may or may not be preserved; Simmons includes a recipe for barberries preserved in white wine vinegar and water in which only "the worst of your barberries" are used.

Regarding the breaded marrow with which Smith surrounds her veal forcemeat in this pie, Felipe Fernandez-Armesto provides context. "Viscous textures" were all the rage among the educated diners of ancient Rome (glands, jowls, feet, udders, wombs, and testicles, along with marrow and other delicacies, satisfied their craving). According to Wilson, the Roman love of marrow specifically was transmitted to "the Middle Ages and beyond" by way of Pliny.

15. VEAL PIE

Cut your veal up in small pieces, boil it an hour, season it with salt, and pepper, and a small piece of butter; mix your flour with sour milk, saleratus, and a small piece of lard, and mould it for the crust; line the sides of a tin dish or basin with the crust, put the meat in, and fill up the basin with the gravy as full as you can handle it; shake some flour in it, and cover it over with the crust, leaving a hole in the centre, for a vent. Bake from one and a half to two hours. If preferred, cream tartar crust may be used. See *Cream Tartar Bread*.

—Howland, *New England Economical Housekeeper* (1845), p. 41

Howland's gravy-soaked, flour-thickened, hashed veal pie, with only salt and pepper for seasoning, is given a lard-sour milk crust, leavened with saleratus. Lest we think things can't get any worse, the Economical Housekeeper, promoting a gastronomic austerity that would come to define New England cooking, offers an even plainer crust as an alternative (see the next recipe).

16. CREAM TARTAR BREAD

One quart of flour, two tea-spoonfuls of cream tartar, one of saleratus, two and a half cups of milk; bake twenty minutes.

—Howland, *New England Economical Housekeeper* (1845), p. 16

As we've noted, the American fondness for chemicals in cooking was reflected in the popularity of saleratus. Howland, like her more famous contemporary Catharine Beecher, was devoted to it. As for cream of tartar (tartaric acid), it is one of the more rapidly acting of the leavening agents that can be mixed with baking soda to form baking powder.

17. TO MAKE A GOOD PIE OF BEEF

Take the Buttock of a fat Oxe, slice it thin, mince it small and beat it in a Mortar to a Paste, then lard it very well with Lard, and season it with beaten Spice, then make your Pie, and put it in with some Butter and Claret Wine, and so bake it well, and serve it in cold with Mustard and Sugar, and garnish it with Bay-leaves.

—Woolley, *Queen-like Closet* (1670), p. 116

This type of pie—venison pasty made with beef—is found in virtually every seventeenth-century English cookbook. Woolley's spices, claret, and butter are found in all these recipes, as well as in recipes for venison pasty made with venison (including Woolley's own version of the latter). Instructions similar to Woolley's to beat the thin-sliced beef "in a Mortar to a Paste" are also found in some of these recipes. This advice does not appear in the "Red Dear of Beefe" recipe in the Martha Washington manuscript cookbook that specifies "a piece of young buttock beefe." But in another such recipe in the same cookbook, which does not stipulate young tender meat, the reader is told to "beat it extremely." In other words, the likely reason that Woolley's oxen buttock must be beaten to a paste is that, as Wilson explains, in the sixteenth and seventeenth centuries "oxen . . . had a long working life before they were butchered." As a result, "their meat must often have been dry and of poor quality." These realities also underlie Woolley's (and others') requirement of larding venison-imitating beef. Larding was called for in most venison pasty recipes made with venison because, as we've noted (Chapter 8, #1) venison is generally lean and dry.

Since the Middle Ages, when the carvers of great households served roasted meats with appropriate sauces, mustard sauce had been considered the proper accompaniment for beef (as it was for brawn, pork, and salted mutton).

18. BEEF-STEAK PIE

Butter a deep dish, and spread a sheet of paste all over the bottom, sides, and edge.

Cut away from your beef-steak all the bone, fat, gristle, and skin. Cut the lean in small thin pieces, about as large, generally, as the palm of your hand. Beat the meat well with the rolling-pin, to make it juicy and tender. If you put in the fat, it will make the gravy too greasy and strong, as it cannot be skimmed.

Put a layer of meat over the bottom-crust of your dish, and season it to your taste, with pepper, salt, and, if you choose, a little nutmeg. A small quantity of mushroom ketchup is an improvement; so, also, is a little minced onion.

Have ready some cold boiled potatoes sliced thin. Spread over the meat, a layer of potatoes, and a small piece of butter; then another layer of meat, seasoned, and then a layer of potatoes, and so on till the dish is full and heaped up in the middle, having a layer of meat on the top. Pour in a little water.

Cover the pie with a sheet of paste, and trim the edges. Notch it handsomely with a knife; and, if you choose, make a tulip of paste, and stick it in the middle of the lid, and lay leaves of paste round it.

Fresh oysters will greatly improve a beef-steak pie. So also will mushrooms. Any meat pie may be made in a similar manner.

—Leslie, *Seventy-five Receipts* (1830), pp. 26–27

Leslie's beefsteak pie recipe is a descendant of the British versions in

Glasse and Raffald. Simmons includes a steak pie in her second edition. All these earlier versions, and Leslie's as well, proceed from what Dalgairns (addressing New England readers via Lee) calls the "common but mistaken opinion, that it is necessary to put stock or water into meat pies." Only Simmons and Leslie, however, pour the water over a bottom crust (many meat pies sported only top and verge crusts). The layering of the steak and potatoes makes Leslie's pie into a distant cousin of chowder. Like Leslie, Dalgairns and Lee suggest oysters as an enhancement.

19. BEEF STEAK PIE

Choose steak that has been long hung, cut it into moderately-sized pieces, and trim off all skin or sinews; season them with pepper, salt, and minced shalot or onion, and lay them in the dish; put crust on the ledge and an inch below, cover with thick crust, and bake it about two hours. A tea-cupful of gravy or water may be put into the dish before the pie is baked, or some good gravy poured into it after it is taken from the oven.

A table-spoonful or two of mushroom catsup, or a flap mushroom, added to the steak, will greatly enrich this pie.

—Hale, *Ladies' New Book of Cookery* (1852), p. 268

With this recipe, Hale illustrates the point just made that many meat pies were baked without a bottom crust. Whether for emphasis, or, more likely, as an oversight, she gives this pie twice in *The Ladies' New Book of Cookery*. In its first appearance it is appended to a long discussion of raised paste. Oddly, Hale also gives another beef pie recipe, one for steak and oysters, twice in the same cookbook. Another of her meat pies, "Cold Beef Steak Pie," is little more than baked, crust-wrapped beef. She suggests that it be cut and served "sandwich fashion." Americans at midcentury were no strangers to mutton and veal pies, but as we can deduce from these offerings (and re-offerings) by Hale, their preference was for beef. One of the *OED*'s definitions for "flap" is "a large, broad mushroom."

20. TO MAKE A PIE OF A LEG OF PORK

Take a Leg of Pork well powdred and stuffed with all manner of good Herbs, and Pepper, and boil it very tender, then take off the Skin, and stick it with Cloves and Sage Leaves, then put it into your Pie with Butter top and bottom, close it and bake it, and eat it cold with Mustard and Sugar.

—Woolley, *Queen-like Closet* (1670), p. 137

A "well powdred" leg of pork has been preserved by dry salting, probably with a mixture of salt, saltpeter, and sugar. Enveloping the pork in butter makes of this a kind of cold potted ham pie. It is to be served with a mustard sauce, which, as we saw above (#17), was a traditional accompaniment for beef, pork, and mutton.

21. A CHESHIRE PORK-PYE

Take a Loin of Pork, skin it, cut it into Stakes, season it with Salt, Nutmeg, and Pepper; make a good Crust, lay a Layer of Pork, and then a large Layer of Pippins pared and cored, a little Sugar, enough to sweeten the Pye, then another Layer of Pork; put in half a Pint of White Wine, lay some Butter on the Top, and close your Pye: If your Pye be large, it will take a Pint of White Wine.

—Glasse, *Art of Cookery* (1747), p. 72

Glasse takes this recipe from *The Lady's Companion* (a later edition of *Whole Duty of a Woman*) but improves upon it by layering the meat and apples. Lehmann draws our attention to the sugar in this regional specialty, one of only a handful of savory meat pies in Glasse that contain the ancient flavoring. The Cheshire apple and pork pie tradition was carried forward, and to an American audience, by Leslie. However, for obvious reasons, she omitted the British name.

22. AN HAM PIE

Before you put your Ham to soak, cut it all round, so as to make it look handsome, and rather of a roundish Form. Put your Ham in water over Night to soak; and in the Morning boil it very tender, and skin and trim it; then season very well while hot with Mace, Pepper and a few Cloves pounded; then lay it in your Dish and lay whole Chickens, all around your Ham, seasoned in the same manner as your Ham putting into the Bellies of each a little piece of butter. Put in a quart of good Gravy just before it goes into the Oven, and cover all with a good Crust. An hour bakes it.

—Gardiner, *Family Receipts* (ca. 1770), pp. 53–54

Although Gardiner calls this a ham pie, the whole chickens move it toward the mixed category. Like Woolley's leg of pork, Gardiner's ham is boiled, skinned, and seasoned before being placed in the pie dish. It is not surprising that, as a member of the colonial mercantile elite, Gardiner includes directions for elegant presentation ("so as to make it look handsome").

23. RAISED HAM PIE

Choose a small ham, soak it, boil it an hour, cut off the knuckle, then remove the rind, trim the ham, and put it into a stew-pan with a quart of veal gravy to cover it: simmer till nearly done, when take it out and let it cool; then make a raised crust, spread on it some veal forcemeat, put in the ham, and fill round it with forcemeat; cover with crust, and bake slowly about an hour; when done, remove the cover, glaze the top of the ham, and pour round it the stock the ham was stewed in, having strained and thickened it, and seasoned it with Cayenne pepper. A ham thus dressed will be an excellent cold supper dish.

—Hale, *Ladies' New Book of Cookery* (1852), p. 270

This last of our pork and ham pie offerings shows Hale at work simplifying a richer British dish. Kitchiner's Madeira (or sherry), browning sauce, and explicit instructions to ornament the covering crust are excised by Hale. This is an instance of the general direction of her modifications—toward a pared down cuisine, which, by the end of the century, would be celebrated as historic, authentic, and typical of New England.

24. A LAMB PIE

Take a shoulder and cut it into small pieces, parboil it till tender, then place it in paste NO. 8, in a deep dish; add salt, pepper, butter and flour to each laying of lamb, till your dish be full; fill with water, and cover over with paste; put in a hot oven, bake one hour and a half.

—Simmons, *American Cookery* (Albany, 1796), pp. 23–24

The author of *The Cook Not Mad* copied this recipe, but the lamb pie did not otherwise catch on in America. Simmons's paste No. 8 (Chapter 9, #5), made with suet, butter, and cream, is "good for chicken or meat pie."

25. PIE, SQUAB, OR DEVONSHIRE

Take a few good baking-apples, pare, core, and slice them; chop some onions very small; line a deep dish with paste, put in a layer of the apples, strew a little sugar, and some of the chopped onions over them; season them, and lay lean mutton chops, also seasoned, more onions, then the apples, &c. as before, and so on till the dish is quite full; cover, and bake the pie.

—Lee, *Cook's Own Book* (1832), p. 143

Despite the name, there's not an unfledged pigeon in sight in this traditional pie. A secondary meaning of squab is fat, plump, or bulky, which adequately describes the dish. Probably, however, the appetizing name was given in hopes of dignifying—or disguising—the humble ingredients. But the trouble with mutton isn't its name. As Sir Pitt Crawley in Thackeray's *Vanity Fair* pronounces after being told that *mouton aux navets* is on offer for dinner, "Mutton's mutton."

Lee (lifting this time from Dolby) adapts the recipe from Glasse's "A Devonshire Squab-Pye" (which was itself copied from *Whole Duty of a Woman*) and Rundell's "Squab Pie." All four pies pretty much follow the *OED*: "A pie with a thick crust composed of mutton, pork, apples, and onions." The dictionary fails to mention the sugar which seems also to have been traditional—Glasse calls for "some" to be strewn over her pippins; Rundell adds "also some sugar"; and Lee/Dolby specifies "a little." Both Glasse and *Whole Duty* pour in water (*Whole Duty* calls for a half pint; Glasse doubles this), while neither nineteenth-century version includes any at all.

Devonshire had long been known as an apple-growing region. A writer later in the nineteenth century proclaimed that "Devonshire cider is simply the finest in the world. Devonshire pie, called also Squab pie, is made of Devonshire apples and of Devonshire (that is Dartmoor) mutton, or else of pork."

26. MUTTON PIE

Cut steaks from a loin of mutton, beat them and remove some of the fat; season it well, and put a little water at the bottom of the dish. Cover the whole with a pretty thick paste, and bake it.

—Howland, *New England Economical Housekeeper* (1845), p. 43

What can one say about mutton, water, and a "pretty thick" paste? Howland's mutton pie, shorn of apples and seasoning, is the mutton version of simplified forms of steak and ham pie (above, #19 and #23).

27. POT PIE, OF BEEF, VEAL, OR CHICKEN

The best way to make the crust is as follows. Peel, boil, and mash a dozen potatoes, add a teaspoonful of salt, two great spoonfuls of butter, and half a cup of milk, or cream. Then stiffen it with flour, till you can roll it. Be sure to get all the lumps out of the potatoes. Some persons leave out the butter.

Some roll butter into the dough of bread, others make a raised biscuit with but little shortening, others make a plain pie crust. But none are so good and healthful as the potato crust.

To prepare the meat, first fry half a dozen slices of salt pork, and then cut up the meat and pork; and boil them in just water enough to cover them, till the meat is nearly cooked. Then peel a dozen potatoes, and slice them thin. Then roll the crust half an inch thick, and cut it into oblong pieces. Then put alternate layers of crust, potatoes, and meat, till all is used. The meat must have salt and pepper sprinkled over each layer. The top and bottom layer must be crust. Lastly, pour on the liquor in which the meat was boiled, until it just covers the whole, and let it simmer till the top crust is well cooked, say half or three quarters of an hour. If you have occasion to add more liquor, or water, it must be *boiling hot,* or the crust will be spoilt. The excellence of this pie depends on having light crust, and therefore the meat must first be nearly cooked before putting it in the pie, and the crust must be in only just long enough to cook, or it will be clammy and hard. When nearly done, the crust can be browned, with hot coals on a bake-lid. Great care is needed not to burn the crust, which should not be put where the fire reached the pot on the bottom.

—Beecher, *Domestic Receipt-Book* (1846), pp. 38–39

Although, according to John Mariani, the term "pot pie" first appeared in print in the United States in 1792, we have found few instances of its use in our sources. What Beecher calls a pot pie is essentially a nineteenth-century chowder, with meat instead of fish, and with a potato-based pie crust playing the part of the crackers.

28. BEEF, OR MUTTON AND POTATO PIE

Take a deep dish, butter it, and put in it a layer of mashed potatoes, seasoned with butter, pepper, salt and minced onions. Take slices of beef, or mutton, and season them with pepper and salt, lay them with small bits of salt pork over the potatoes. Then fill the dish with alternate layers, as above described, having the upper one potatoes. Bake an hour, or an hour and a half.

—Beecher, *Domestic Receipt-Book* (1846), p. 42

Beecher, an advocate of potato crust for health reasons, offers slight variations on a theme. This recipe omits crust altogether and uses straight mashed potatoes, making it similar to a modern shepherd's pie.

Mince Pies

Mince (or shred) pies developed from small tarts and pasties, such as the "chewet" (see Chapter 11, #7), made with chicken or veal. For fast days, mince pies were made with fish, as in herring pie (see Chapter 11, #14). But the most popular mince pies were made with meat and by the Elizabethan period had become firmly associated with festive occasions such as Christmas. Basically, mince pies differed from the traditional medieval meat pie, in which fruits, sweetener, and spices were added to the meat, only in that the meat was always chopped very fine. Primarily in mince pie does the medieval fruit-and-meat combination survive into modern cookery. New Englanders carried the mince pie tradition forward, adding it to their Thanksgiving table and dousing it with their cider and molasses.

29. TO MAKE MINCE-PYES OF VEAL

From a Leg of Veal cut off four pounds of the fleshy part in thick pieces, and put them in scalding Water, and let it just boil; then cut the Meat in small thin pieces and skin it: it must be four pounds after 'tis scalded and skinned; to this quantity put nine pounds of Beef-suet well skinned, and shred them very well and fine with eight Pippins pared and cored, and four pounds of Raisins of the Sun stoned; when 'tis shred very fine, put it in a large Pan or on a Table to mix, and put to it one ounce of Nutmegs grated, half an ounce of Cloves, as much Mace, a large spoonful of Salt, above a pound of Sugar, the Peel of a Lemon shred exceeding fine; when you have seasoned it to your Palate, put in seven pounds of Currants, and two pounds of Raisins stoned and shred. When you fill your Pies, put into every one some shred Lemon with its Juice, some candied Lemon-peel and Citron in slices, and just as the Pies go into the Oven, put into every one a spoonful of Sack and a spoonful of Claret, so bake them.

—Smith, *Compleat Housewife* (1728), pp. 115–16

Some of the important features of modern mince pie, such as apples, raisins, nutmeg, cloves, mace, and wine or brandy, are present in Smith's recipe. As for the meat, veal (Smith's choice), mutton (as in a Markham recipe for "Minc't Pies"), and beef (as in a late-seventeenth-century manuscript recipe by "Mrs. Ann Blencowe") were equal contenders. Beef eventually won out. The presumably small, chewetlike size of Smith's pies—she instructs the cook to "put into every one a spoonful of Sack"—was another variation that remained popular in her day. Within the diverse realm of the English minced- or shredded-meat pie, Smith, along with Markham and Glasse, also offered a large pie called the "Florentine" or "Florendine," made with veal kidney. This "large, top-crust pie circular in shape" was made with puff paste, which was sometimes associated with Florence. Raisins of the sun are one of the varieties of Spanish or Malaga raisins.

30. TO MAKE MINCE-PIES THE BEST WAY

Take three Pounds of Suet shread very fine, and chopped as small as possible, two Pounds of Raisins stoned, and chopped as fine as possible, two Pounds of Currans, nicely picked, washed, rubbed, and dried at the Fire, half a hundred of fine Pippins, pared, cored, and chopped small, half a Pound of fine Sugar pounded fine, a quarter of an Ounce of Mace, a quarter of an Ounce of Cloves, two large Nutmegs, all beat fine; put all together into a great Pan, and mix it well together with half a Pint of Brandy, and half a Pint of Sack; put it down close in a Stone-pot, and it will keep good four Months. When you make your Pies, take a little Dish, something bigger than a Soop-plate, lay a very thin Crust all over it, lay a thin layer of Meat, and then a thin Layer of Citron cut very thin, then a Layer of Mince meat, and a thin Layer of Orange-peel cut thin, over that a little Meat; squeeze half the Juice of a fine Sevile Orange, or Lemon, and pour in three Spoonfuls of Red Wine; lay on your Crust, and bake it nicely. These Pies eat finely cold. If you make them in little Patties, mix your Meat and Sweet-meats accordingly: If you chuse Meat in your Pies, parboil a Neat's-Tongue, peel it, and chop the Meat as fine as possible, and mix with the rest; or two Pounds of the Inside of a Surloin of Beef boiled.

—Glasse, *Art of Cookery* (1747), p. 74

Glasse's boastful offering of mince pies "the best way" signals the final shape the pie was to take. The apples and brandy or sack remain, but the spirits have now become a means of preserving for later use all parts of the mincemeat except the shredded flesh meat. Indeed, the flesh meat may simply be omitted (as in #33), severing the link to medieval cooking altogether; if meat is to be retained, the preferred type is neat's (beef) tongue. Glasse also includes the unambiguously meatless "Lent Mince Pies," made with hard-boiled eggs.

31. A BRIDE'S PYE

Boil two Calf's-Feet, pick the Meat from the Bones and chop it very fine, shread small one Pound of Beef Suet and a Pound of Apples, wash and pick one Pound of Currants very small, dry them before the Fire, stone and chop a quarter of a Pound of Jar Raisins, a quarter of an Ounce of Cinnamon, the same of Mace and Nutmeg, two Ounces of candied Citron, two Ounces of candied Lemon cut thin, a Glass of Brandy and one of Champaign, put them in a China Dish with a rich puff Paste over it, roll another Lid and cut it in Leaves, Flowers, Figures, and put a Glass Ring in it.

—Raffald, *Experienced English House-keeper* (1769), p. 136

Although neat's tongue became the most common meat component in the mince pies of the eighteenth and nineteenth centuries, it never became the only one. Glasse mentions beef sirloin as an alternative, while Raffald gives us one mince pie with neat's tongue and this additional, more festive one with calf's feet.

Bride's Pie appears in various forms in English cookbooks from as early as the mid-seventeenth century to as late as the 1870s. For instance, along with the "Battalia Pye" included above (#3), Smith offers a second Battalia that she also names "Bride Pye." We can certainly understand why the idea of an elaborate pie (with the ring hidden inside) adorning the bridal banquet table held great appeal. Raffald's recipe was particularly popular.

According to Simon Charsley, "The earliest recipe recorded from Britain for a dish specifically for a wedding is in fact a pie." That pie was what Robert May, in *The Accomplish't Cook* (1660), called "an extraordinary Pie, or a Bride Pye." It was "only for a wedding to pass away time." Passing away time was accomplished by filling the pie with live animals, usually birds but sometimes more fearsome creatures such as snakes. Such "surprises" were culinary entertainments common at aristocratic weddings and other banquets. As Felipe Fernandez-Armesto points out, the surprise, part of "the theater of cookery," is as old as the "'blackbird' pies of the Middle Ages" and as "modern [as] bachelor night cakes which burst with dancing girls." Another strand of the tradition associates Bride's Pie more with a future rather than a present wedding—the girl who finds the ring in her piece will be the next bride.

Jar raisins were raisins of the sun, "so-called because they are imported in jars."

32. AN UMBLE PIE

Take the humbles of a buck, boil them, and chop them as small as meat for minced pies, and put to them as much beef suet, eight apples, half a pound of sugar, a pound and a half of currants, a little salt, some mace, cloves, nutmeg, and a little pepper; then mix them together, and put it into a paste; add half a pint of sack, the juice of one lemon and orange, close the pie, and when it is baked serve it up.

—Carter, *Frugal Housewife* (1772), pp. 111–12

Umble pie goes back to the Middle Ages and was essentially mince pie made with entrails (heart, kidney, liver, but also lung, spleen, intestines, and other organs), most often those of a deer. The examples in Woolley and the Martha Washington manuscript cookbook, both of them from the seventeenth century, lack the apples found here, which did not become standard in mince pie until the eighteenth century.

33. MINCE PIES, WITHOUT FLESH MEAT

One pound of Pippins, one pound of marrow and one pound of Raisins stewed, all minced very fine, two pounds of Currants, half a pound of candied or preserved Orange and the like quantity of candied or preserved Lemon (Orange Chips & Lemon Chips as they are called, are the best) and half a pound of Citron, one Ounce of Salt, a quarter of an Ounce of Cinnamon pounded and sifted, and the like quantity of Mace pounded & sifted. The Pippins, the marrow, the Orange the Lemon and the Citron, must be minced fine with half a pound of clayed, or whited brown, or powdered Sugar. Mix all well together, and put them down in a Crock, or Stone, or Earthen Pot. It will keep for 6 months. As you take it out for use, Add to it a little Brandy and Claret.

N.B. There is no mode of making Mince Pies, yet known, superiour, if equal, to this.

—Gardiner, *Family Receipts* (ca. 1770), p. 56

Despite Mrs. Gardiner's proclamation of the superiority of her mince pies without flesh meat (though not without an animal component—marrow), we shall see that mince pies with flesh meat remained abundantly on offer in nineteenth-century New England cookbooks. Sugar tinged with the brown residue of molasses was sometimes whitened ("whited") by covering the cone-shaped loaves with clay ("clayed") and dousing the whole with water to remove impurities. As we mentioned earlier, powdered sugar was the equivalent of our granulated rather than our confectioners' sugar. Gardiner adds brandy and claret not as a preservative but rather as a last-minute flavoring.

34. A FOOT PIE

Scald neets feet, and clean well, (grass fed are best) put them into a large vessel of cold water, which change daily during a week, then boil the feet till tender, and take away the bones, when cold, chop fine, to every four pound minced meat, add one pound of beef suet, and four pound apple raw, and a little salt, chop all together very fine, add one quart of wine, two pound of stoned raisins, one ounce of cinnamon, one ounce mace, and sweeten to your taste; make use of paste NO. 3—bake three quarters of an hour.

Weeks after, when you have occasion to use them, carefully raise the top crust, and with a round edg'd spoon, collect the meat into a bason, which warm with additional wine and spices to the taste of your circle, while the crust is also warm'd like a hoe cake, put carefully together and serve up, by this means you can have hot pies through the winter, and enrich'd singly to your company.

—Simmons, *American Cookery* (Hartford, 1796), pp. 23–24

This meaty mince pie, made with again fashionable grass-fed beef, calls for little suet compared to earlier recipes, where the amount of suet is usually equal to, and sometimes greater than, the amount of meat. Simmons also diverges from the established practice of excluding the meat from the filling when the filling is to be kept for later use. Like Glasse, she uses wine as a preservative, but like Gardiner, she also uses it as a flavoring added before serving. For the crust to be "warm'd like a hoe cake" was for it to be placed "before the fire," as Simmons puts it in her own recipe for "Johny Cake, or Hoe Cake" (see Chapter 14, #29). For "paste No. 3," see Chapter 9, #4. In adding a greater proportion of meat to suet and also in her reference to "hoe cake," Simmons has Americanized the English mince pie.

35. MINCED PIE OF BEEF

Four pound boild beef, chopped fine, and salted; six pound of raw apple chopped also, one pound beef suet, one quart of Wine or rich sweet cyder, one ounce mace, and cinnamon, a nutmeg, two pounds raisins, bake in paste NO. 3, three fourths of an hour.

—Simmons, *American Cookery* (Hartford, 1796), p. 24

Simmons Americanizes mince pie in yet another way—by offering "rich sweet cyder" as an alternative to wine. We will see subsequent New England cooks carrying on this tradition.

36. EGG MINCE PIES

Boil six eggs hard, shred them small; shred double the quantity of suet: then put currants washed and picked one pound, or more, if the eggs were large; the peel of one lemon shred very fine, and the juice, six spoon-fuls of sweet wine, mace, nutmeg, sugar, a very little salt: orange, lemon, and citron, candied. Make a light paste for them.

—Rundell, *New System of Domestic Cookery* (1807), p. 158

This recipe, which omits apples and substitutes eggs for meat, reappears in New England in both Lee and *The Roger Cookery*. As noted above (#30), egg mince pies are found in eighteenth-century cookbooks as a Lenten option. With suet, however, this recipe would not fill the Lenten bill.

Rundell gives another type of meatless mince pie made with lemons (and lots of sugar). These sweet-sour creations were apparently fashionable, as they turn up in Lee (from Dalgairns), *The Roger Cookery*, and Chadwick.

37. MINCE PIES

Boil a tender, nice piece of beef—any piece that is clear from sinews and gristle; boil it till it is perfectly tender. When it is cold, chop it very fine, and be very careful to get out every particle of bone and gristle. The suet is sweeter and better to boil half an hour or more in the liquor the beef has been boiled in; but few people do this. Pare, core, and chop the apples fine. If you use raisins, stone them. If you use currants, wash and dry them at the fire. Two pounds of beef, after it is chopped; three quarters of a pound of suet; one pound and a quarter of sugar; three pounds of apples; two pounds of currants, or raisins. Put in a gill of brandy; lemon-brandy is better, if you have any prepared. Make it quite moist with new cider. I should not think a quart would be too much; the more moist the better, if it does not spill out into the oven. A very little pepper. If you use corn meat, or tongue for pies, it should be well soaked, and boiled very tender. If you use fresh beef, salt is necessary in the seasoning. One ounce of cinnamon, one ounce of cloves. Two nutmegs add to the pleasantness of the flavor; and a bit of sweet butter put upon the top of each pie, makes them rich; but these are not necessary. Baked three quarters of an hour. If your apples are rather sweet, grate in a whole lemon.

—Child, *American Frugal Housewife* (1833), p. 66

Some nineteenth-century authors included several mince pies, ranked according to the richness and expense of the meat component. For example, in *The Good Housekeeper,* Hale (despite denouncing mince pie as "rich, expensive and exceedingly unhealthy") offers "Rich Mince Meat" (made with calf's tongue, copied from Dalgairns via Lee), along with "family" and "plain" recipes (made with lean beef, based on Leslie).

Child, of course, makes her mince pie with the most economical of these options—beef that may or may not be lean and free of bone and gristle. Another sign of Child's concern to accommodate the dish to people of limited means is that she makes her enhancements, such as nutmeg and crust-topping butter, optional.

38. TEMPERANCE MINCE-MEAT

Take three pounds of the lean of a round of fresh beef, that has been boiled the day before. It must be thoroughly boiled, and very tender. Mince it, as finely as possible, with a chopping-knife; and add to it two pounds of beef-suet, cleared from the skin and filaments, and minced very small. Mix the suet and the lean beef well together; and add a pound of brown sugar. Pick, wash, and dry before the fire, two pounds of Zante currants. Seed and chop two pounds of the best raisins. Sultana raisins have no seeds, and are therefore the most convenient for all cookery purposes. Grate the yellow rind of three large lemons or oranges into a saucer, and squeeze upon it their juice, through a strainer. Mix this with the currants and raisins. Prepare a heaped-up table-spoonful of powdered cinnamon; the same quantity of powdered ginger; a heaped tea-spoonful of powdered nutmeg; the same of powdered cloves; and the same of powdered mace. Mix all these spices into a quart of the best *West India* molasses. Then mix well together the meat and the fruit; and wet the whole with the spiced molasses; of which you must have enough to make the mixture very moist, but not too thin. If you want the mince-meat for immediate use, add to it four pounds of minced apple. The apples for this purpose should be pippins or bell-flowers, pared, cored, quartered, and chopped fine. Add, also, half a pound of citron, not minced, but cut into long slips.

If you intend the mince-meat for keeping, do not add the apple and citron until you are about to make the pies, as it will keep better without them. Mix all the other articles thoroughly, and pack down the mince-meat, hard, in small stone jars. Lay upon the top of it, a round of thin white paper, dipped in molasses, and cut exactly to fit the inside circumference of the jar. Secure the jars closely with flat, tight-fitting corks, and then with a lid; and paste paper down over the top on the outside.

West India molasses will be found a good substitute for the wine and brandy generally used to moisten mince-meat.

—Leslie, *Lady's Receipt-Book* (1847), pp. 138–39

Bliss also includes a recipe for mince pie in which molasses is the only moistening ingredient, but there are proclamations of temperance principles in neither title nor text. A mince pie recipe in Knight's *Tit-Bits* makes use of molasses but as supplement to, rather than substitute for, sherry and brandy. The Zante currant comes from Greece.

39. PLAIN MINCE PIE

Boil the meat with but little fat, thoroughly; prepare and chop fine with the meat, twice as much apple as meat; use for moistening some of the liquor the meat was boiled in; add chopped raisins: also currants and citron if liked; one half molasses and one half sugar; salt, cinnamon, a little clove and nutmeg to taste; the juice of a lemon; and if the use of sweet or boiled cider is objectionable, put in a little vinegar; if not moist enough use more of the meat-liquid or water. Stew all before filling the pies. This makes a simple but digestible and very good mince pie.

—*Aunt Mary's New England Cook Book* (1881), p. 31

Aunt Mary seeks to appeal to nontemperance and temperance cooks alike with her options of cider or vinegar. Molasses was becoming a standard ingredient in New England mince pies, for sweetening as well as moistening.

CHAPTER ELEVEN

Pies—Fowl, Fish

Fowl Pies

From the seventeenth to the nineteenth centuries in both England and New England, pies were built around domestic fowl and game birds, most notably chickens, geese, ducks, and pigeons but also turkeys, partridges, peacocks (although these were abandoned in the seventeenth century as too tough), and quail. More exotic fare such as swans and bustards were particularly fashionable in the 1690s but fell out of favor thereafter. Diners were as apt to encounter fowls baked into pies as they were to meet them roasted or fricasseed. The reasons for the fowl pie's immense popularity may be difficult for modern cooks to understand, as food preservation methods have changed dramatically since the pie's heyday. But before the advent of modern technology, pies served the flesh of birds particularly well. Enclosing tender fowl in a pie shell helped to retain moisture and promoted the blending of seasonings, wine, and butter in the gravy or caudle. Of course the shell itself, whether a rich short crust or an edible standing coffin designed for longer-term preservation, could be part of the attraction of the dish. Fowl pies were considered by many to be well worth the effort of constructing them. Their charms are still apparent in the following recipes.

1. A TURKEY PYE

Bone the Turkey, season it with savoury Spice, and lay it in the Pye with two Capons, or two Wild-Ducks cut in pieces to fill up the Corners; lay on Butter, and close the Pye.

—Smith, *Compleat Housewife* (1730), p. 13

Although Wilson says that turkeys were favored as bakemeats and ended up in Elizabethan pies, we found few examples of the turkey pie in later English or New England cookbooks. More's the pity. But like the goose that preceded it as the centerpiece of the festive English table, the turkey was large and juicy, thus favored for roasting. At the time the Plymouth Pilgrims were dining on wild turkey in 1621, domestic turkeys had long been sold in the markets of the old country. Smith's recipe, by the way, defies the 1541 order of Archbishop Cranmer, who counted turkeys among the "greater fowls" (crane and swan were the others) that ought not be combined with other birds in a single dish. Cranmer hoped his edict would check clergy gluttony.

2. A DUCK-PYE

Make a Puff paste Crust, take a Couple of Ducks, scald them, and make them very clean, cut off the Feet, the Pinions, the Neck and Head, all clean picked and scalded, with the Gizard, Liver and Hearts; pick out all the Fat of the Inside, lay a Crust all over the Dish, season the Ducks with Pepper and Salt, inside and out, lay them in your Dish, and the Gibblets at each End seasoned; put in as much Water as will almost fill the Pye, lay on the Crust, and bake it, but not too much.

—Glasse, *Art of Cookery* (1747), p. 72

In the 1830s, Richard Dolby adapted this pie, and Lee transmitted the adaptation to New England. Dolby/Lee reversed Glasse's caution about overbaking the pie, recommending instead to "let it be well baked." Pinions may mean either the whole wing or the segment of the wing farthest from the body.

3. A GIBLET PIE

Save the blood of the Geese, and have ready, before the Blood cools, two or three Spoonsfull of Groats pounded, or, for want thereof, of Oat-meal, boiled in a pint of sweet cream. Work the Blood and that well together. Season the Giblets, over Night with Pepper and Salt. In the morning get a Quart of sweet Cream, and add to it the Blood, one pound of good fresh Butter, a little Mutton Suet, a few Shallots shred, some grated Nutmeg, the Yolks of six Eggs and three of the Whites only, and a little Parsley cut small. Mix all together with the Blood and the Cream. Fill the Skins of the Necks with this Pudding. What is left pour into your Dish upon the Giblets. Then cover the Pie with a quarter of a pound of fresh Butter. Cover it with Paste and bake it. Before you serve it up, put in some warm or hot Gravy.

—Gardiner, *Family Receipts* (ca. 1770), pp. 52–53

Gardiner's giblet pie recipe is derived from Raffald's "A Yorkshire Giblet Pye." In Raffald's pie, however, the mixture of blood and thickening agent is not stuffed back into the goose neck skins to make a blood pudding (see Chapter 13) but put all together into the center of the pie. Raffald relies on beef suet to provide the fat in the pie; Gardiner uses instead a pound of butter mixed with a little mutton suet. The substitution of butter for beef fat continues: Gardiner seals her pie with a quarter-pound of butter; Raffald puts over her mixture a pound of beef fat. Both cooks call for groats (hulled grain) to thicken the mixture, while Raffald adds a grated penny loaf and Gardiner offers oatmeal as a possible substitute for the groats. Gardiner's pie seems a mere afterthought to her butter-and-egg-rich blood pudding.

Goose giblets are the heart, liver, gizzard (stomach), and intestines of the goose, or as the *OED* has it "odds and ends." Goose liver is of course now known exclusively as foie gras, and one can search high and low in modern cookbooks without finding a recipe for its use that includes the goose's other "giblets."

4. GIBLET PIE

Take two sets of goose giblets, clean them well and let them stew over a slow fire in a pint and a half of water, till they are half done; then divide the necks, wings, legs, and gizzards, into pieces, and let them lay in the liquor till the giblets get cold. When they are quite cold, season them well with a large tea-spoonful of pepper, a small one of salt, and half a salt-spoonful of Cayenne; then put them into a pie-dish, with a cupful of the liquor they were stewed in; cover it with paste for meat pies, and let the pie bake from one hour to an hour and a half.

Skim off the fat from the rest of the liquor in which the giblets were stewed, put it in a butter-sauce pan, thicken it with flour and butter, add pepper and salt to your taste; give it a boil up, and it is ready. Before the pie is served up, raise the crust on one side, and pour in the gravy.

—Hale, *Ladies' New Book of Cookery* (1852), p. 271

Hale presents a version of the bloodless goose giblet pie preferred in the nineteenth century—the giblets are stewed, mixed with other goose "odds and ends" (necks, wings, legs), seasoned, and baked with only a top crust. Preceding Hale in this tradition were Rundell (who supplements the giblets, which may be those of a duck instead of a goose, with beef, veal, or mutton steaks and potatoes) and Leslie (who also allows duck giblets to form the basis of the pie and includes potatoes and hard-boiled egg yolks).

5. A THATCHED HOUSE PYE

Take an Earthen Dish that is pretty deep, rub the inside with two Ounces of Butter, then spread over it two Ounces of Vermicelli, make a good puff Paste, and roll it pretty thick, and lay it on the Dish; take three or four Pigeons, season them very well with Pepper, and Salt, and put a good Lump of Butter in them, and lay them in the Dish with the Breast down, and put a thick Lid over them, and bake it in a moderate Oven; when enough, take the Dish you intend for it, and turn the Pye on to it, and the Vermicelli will appear like Thatch, which gives it the Name of Thatched House Pye.

It is a pretty Side or Corner Dish for a large Dinner, or a Bottom for Supper.

—Raffald, *Experienced English House-keeper* (1769), pp. 131–32

In her *Lady's Receipt-Book*, Leslie copied this novelty pie with a few minor alterations—stuffing each bird with a mushroom or chopped oyster, putting in some leftover veal gravy, adding nutmeg, leaving out butter, and seasoning "a very little" rather than "well" with salt and pepper.

Raffald's addendum about the placement of a vermicelli (or macaroni) pie on a formal table agrees with Margaret Bayard Smith's description of the elegant dinner party she was planning in Washington in 1835. To arrange this "small, genteel dinner" she consulted with the city's most fashionable waiter, who explained, "For side dishes you will have a very small ham, a small turkey, on each side of them partridges, mutton chops, or sweet breads [sic], a macaroni pie, and oyster pie." The foot of the table at this genteel dinner would be occupied with "a pyramid of anything, grapes, oranges, or anything handsome," though probably not the Thatched House Pie, which, as Raffald suggests, may be placed at the bottom of the table only for a less formal "supper." Impressive pyramids of meat to be displayed at the ends of banquet tables became popular in England in the early eighteenth century. This French-inspired fashion is reduced by Raffald to a quaint little dish of pigeons, puff paste, and vermicelli in the shape of an English cottage.

6. PARTRIDGE PIE IN THE ORDINARY WAY

Lay a veal cutlet in the bottom of the dish; line the inside of the birds with fat bacon, season them well and place them with the breast downwards; fill the dish with good gravy, and add forcemeat balls, with a few button mushrooms freshly gathered.

Pies of this sort may be made nearly in the same manner of every species of game; but the mixture of the brown and white meats is not desirable, as the former have a peculiar flavor which ought to be maintained, and is weakened by the admixture of the latter: also hare and venison, though each forming admirable pasties separately, yet spoil each other when put together.

—Hale, *Ladies' New Book of Cookery* (1852), p. 272

Hale provides a greatly attenuated reprise of the English savory pie tradition, the enhancements reduced to a few mushrooms and generic forcemeat balls. Her strictures against the mixture of brown and white meats (or of hare and venison) are idiosyncratic. Nevertheless, Hale's partridge pie, along with pigeon pies offered by Rundell (copied by Allen) and Leslie, indicate the persistence in New England cooking of pies made of smaller game birds.

7. A CHEWET PIE

Take the brawnes and the wings of *Capons* and *Chickens* after they haue been rosted, and pull away the skin; then shred them with fine Mutten suet very small;

then season it with *cloues, mace, cinamon, suger* and *salt;* then put to *raysins* of the Sunne and *currants,* and slic't *dates,* and *orange* pills, and being well mixt together, put it into small coffins made for the purpose, and strow on the top of them good store of *caraway* Comfets: then couer them, and bake them with a gentle heate, and these Chewets you may also make of rosted Veale, seasoned as before shewed, and of all parts the loyne is the best.

—Markham, *Countrey Contentments* (1623), p. 103

As noted in the Chapter 10 discussion of mince pies, a chewet is a small dish of minced and seasoned meat, poultry, or fish, made with or without pie crust. While brawn is most commonly boar's flesh, the word may also mean, as here, muscled, fleshy leg meat. Comfits, made of fruits, seeds, and the like preserved in a sugar syrup, were also known as sugarplums.

8. A SWEET CHICKEN PYE

Take five or six small Chickens, pick, draw and truss them for baking; season them with Cloves, Mace, Nutmeg, Cinnamon, and a little Salt; wrap up some of the Seasoning in Butter, and put it in their bellies; and your Coffin being made, put them in; put over and between them pieces of Marrow, *Spanish* Potatoes and Chesnuts, both boiled, peeled and cut, a handful of Barberies stript, a Lemon sliced, some Butter on the top; so close up the Pye and bake it, and have in readiness a Caudle made of White-wine, Sugar, Nutmeg, beat it up with yolks of Eggs and Butter; have a care it does not curdle; pour the Caudle in, shake it well together, and serve it up hot.

—Smith, *Compleat Housewife* (1728), p. 110

The distinction between savory and sweet pies emerged in cookbooks around 1720, shortly before the first edition of Smith's book. Nevertheless, Smith here preserves the medieval mixture of flavors, with her use of cloves, mace, nutmeg, cinnamon, wine, and sugar. The inclusion of marrow in pies also dates from the Middle Ages, yet with its lemon and barberries Smith's recipe also reflects more recent trends.

9. A CHICKEN PIE

Cut your Chicken in pieces, and season them with Salt and Pepper, a little beaten Mace; Lay in your Chickens, first laying at the bottom, if you chuse it, some slices of lean part of an Ham [or] Bacon. Season with Pepper and Salt, put in your Chickens and if you so chuse it, you may put in a fine beef Steak over the flour [sic] and under your Chickens — An Anchovy will do it no harm. Put in a full pint of water and cover the Pie; bake it well, and when it comes from the Oven, fill it with good Gravy.

—Gardiner, Family Receipts (ca. 1770), p. 56

In this as in most of the eighteenth-century chicken pie recipes we consulted, the chicken is not filleted, only cut up. The more notable feature of our first New England chicken pie recipe, however, is the contraction of ingredients from the expansive English chicken pies of the seventeenth and earlier eighteenth centuries. Gardiner offers a mixture of meats—chicken, ham or bacon, beefsteak—but dispenses with the variety meats and luxury additions of the earlier English versions. A brief inventory points the contrast: in seasoning, Markham specifies cloves, mace, cinnamon, sugar, salt; Smith adds nutmeg to the list; Glasse's "Chicken-Pye" is scaled back to pepper, mace, thyme, salt, and lemon peel; but Gardiner recommends only salt, pepper, and a little beaten mace. Likewise for embellishments, the truffles, morels, raisins, dates, currants, caraway comfits, sweet potatoes, chestnuts, marrow, barberries, sweetbreads, cockscombs, palates, and artichoke bottoms of Markham, Smith, and Glasse are less emphasized in Raffald (see Chapter 1, n. 35), and are reduced in Gardiner to "an Anchovy will do it no harm." The trend in tastes, in the Anglo-American gentry and upper middle classes to which the Gardiners belonged, is toward more lightly spiced, uncomplicated dishes. This reflects the influence, as refracted through Gardiner's two main sources, Glasse and Raffald, of the more spare French nouvelle cuisine of the 1730s and the tendency, also to be found in Glasse and Raffald, to affirm native English plainness over against French elaboration.

10. PIE, CHICKEN

Parboil, and then cut up neatly two young chickens; dry them; set them over a slow fire for a few minutes; have ready some veal stuffing or forcemeat, lay it at the bottom of the dish, and place in the chickens upon it, and with it some pieces of dressed ham; cover it with paste. Bake it from an hour and a half to two hours; when sent to table, add some good gravy, well seasoned, and not too thick. Duck pie is made in like manner, only substituting the duck stuffing instead of the veal. N. B.—The above may be put into a raised French crust and baked; when done, take off the top, and put a ragout of sweetbread to the chicken.

—Lee, Cook's Own Book (1832), p. 140

Lee takes this recipe from Kitchiner. Although ingredients are few and the sauce merely "some good gravy," added at the end in the English manner, the origin of this dish is nevertheless the *poupeton*, anglicized to pupton, one of the key dishes of the grand French court style, popular in England after the Restoration. The *poupeton* was, in Lehmann's words, "a kind of cake made with pigeons and a garnish, all these ingredients being placed inside a crust of veal forcemeat." According to Colin Spencer, pupton is from the French *pupe*, meaning chrysalis or case. The *poupeton* came in different sizes, serving either as one of the *hors d'oeuvres* (little dishes placed at the side of the dining table for use between courses at a banquet) or as an *entrée* (dishes which at a formal dinner were served during the first course along with larger dishes of roasted meat, poultry, or fish called *relevés*) within what has been aptly called "a landscape of dishes." In the Lee/Kitchiner version, chicken (or duck) substitutes for pigeon, and there is only a bottom crust of forcemeat. The final garnish, a "ragout of sweetbread," further indicates that the ultimate source is French court cuisine.

11. COLD CHICKEN PIE

A nice way of serving up cold chicken, or pieces of cold fresh meat, is to make them into a meat pie. The gizzards, livers, and necks of poultry, parboiled, are good for the same purpose. If you wish to bake your meat pie, line a deep earthen or tin pan with paste made of flour, cold water, and lard; use but little lard, for the fat of the meat will shorten the crust. Lay in your bits of meat, or chicken, with two or three slices of salt pork; place a few thin slices of your paste here and there; drop in an egg or two, if you have plenty. Fill the pan with flour and water, seasoned with a little pepper and salt. If the meat be very lean, put in a piece of butter, or such sweet gravies as you may happen to have. Cover the top with crust, and put it in the oven, or bake-kettle, to cook half an hour, or an hour, according to the size of the pie. Some people think this the nicest way of cooking fresh chickens. When thus cooked, they should be parboiled before they are put into the pan, and the water they are boiled in should be added. A chicken pie needs to be cooked an hour and a half, if parboiled; two hours, if not.

—Child, *American Frugal Housewife* (1833), pp. 56–57

Child's bake kettle reminds us that these pies might cook, like stews, over open hearths. Her claim to frugality is no mere gimmick, as her instruction to limit the amount of lard in the crust indicates (additional fat was to be supplied by the meat . . . supposedly).

12. CONNECTICUT THANKSGIVING CHICKEN PIE

In sufficient water to prevent burning, stew old not young fowls, jointed, all but tender enough for the table. Pour all into a dish, and season with salt and pepper to the taste. When about cold, place the parts in your pudding dish, lined with a thin common paste, adding about half a pound of butter to three pounds of fowl in alternate layers. Take more of the paste, roll it *nine times,* studding it each time with butter, (it must be made very rich;) be careful to roll out, each time, from you, and to roll up towards you, leaving it, at least, an inch thick. Add the upper crust; cut a lip in it; and ornament it with some of the reserved paste, having first lightly sprinkled the chickens with flour, after almost filling the dish with the liquor in which the chickens were stewed. Pin tight around the rim of the dish a cloth bandage, to prevent the escape of the juices; and bake from an hour to an hour and a half, in a quick oven. If the top burns, lay a paper over it.

—Webster, *Improved Housewife* (1844), p. 99

Webster identifies the chicken pie as a particular dish for a New England Thanksgiving table. In reminiscences of her youth in Salem, Massachusetts, in the early nineteenth century, Caroline Howard King describes Webster's pie exactly (although it's doubtful that her family feasted on old birds): "Frequently the feast began with a chicken pie, crowned with light and flaky puff paste, which was ornamented with small circles and diamonds cut out from the paste, and put on in patterns by my mother's own hands." Chicken pie supplemented roast turkey in the Thanksgiving dinners of nineteenth-century New England because, until the twentieth century, turkeys rarely weighed more than eight pounds and thus a single bird could not by itself meet the needs of this festive occasion.

13. CHICKEN PIE

Take young and tender chickens; cut up, wash and put into stew-kettle with water enough to cover. Add a little salt and stew till tender and well done. Then take a deep earthen dish and put in a layer of chicken; sprinkle with salt, pepper and bits of butter, also 1 cracker rolled fine. Proceed in this way until the dish is full. Place on top dices of salt pork and sprinkle with flour. Then fill with the chicken broth and cover with a nice rich crust of pastry with a hole in the center the size of a cup to let the steam and gasses escape. Place in a slow oven and let it remain until nicely browned.

—Whatsoever Circle, *King's Daughters Cook Book* (1903), p. 41

Our final chicken pie, from a community cookbook, is essentially a standard chowder from the previous century, made with chicken and sealed with crust.

Fish Pies

We might occasionally partake of the butter- and cream-drenched lobster and scallop "pies" that appear on the summertime menus of seaside restaurants, but we are unlikely to feature at a family dinner the herring, cod, pilchard, sole, oyster, or clam pies that were in times past both the joy and the bane of English and New England families. We hope the following selection of recipes will, on the one hand, engender respect for the creativity of cooks who had little to work with but pickled fish and a bit of pie crust and, on the other, revive enthusiasm for the classics of the Anglo-American fish pie tradition.

14. A HERRING PIE

Take white pickled *Herrings* of one nights watering, and boyl them a little: then pill of the skin, and take only the backs of them, and picke the fish cleane from the bones, then take good store off *raysins* of the Sunne, and stone them, and put them to the fish: then take a *warden* or two, and pare it, and slice it in small slices from the chore [core], and put it likewise to the fish: then with a very sharpe shredding knife shred all as small and fine as may be: then put to it good store of *currants, suger, cinamon,* slic't *dates,* and so put it into the coffin with good store of very sweete *butter,* and so couer it, and leaue only a round vent-hole on the top of the lid, and so bake like pies of that nature: When it is sufficiently bak't, draw it out, and take *Claret-wine* and a little *veriuice, suger, cinamon,* and sweete *butter,* and boyle them together; then put it in at the vent-hole, and shake the pie a little, and put it againe into the Ouen for a little space, and so serue it vp, the lid being candied ouer with *suger,* and the sides of the dish trimmed with *Suger.*

—Markham, *Countrey Contentments* (1623), p. 100

In medieval England, pickled herring ran second only to salt cod as "the most plentiful and least loved of Lenten delicacies," and the situation probably remained the same in Markham's time when "fysshe days" continued to be observed. Lenten fish pies made with butter, currants or raisins, spices, sugar, wine, and shredded fish are essentially mince pies (shredded fish substituting for shredded meat) and are to be baked in the manner of "pies of that nature." As with salt fish, pickled fish must be soaked or, as Markham puts it, watered before use to extract most of the preserving salt. Before the development of the seedless grape, the seeds of raisins had to be removed by the cook, thus Markham's instruction to "stone" them. The warden, short for warden-pear, may have been so named because it grew profusely near Warden Abbey, a twelfth-century Cistercian monastery.

15. A CARPE PYE

Take Carps scald them, take out the great bones, pound the Carps in a stone Morter pound some of the blood with the flesh which must be at the discretion of the Cook because it must not be too soft, then lard it with the belly of a very fat Eale, season it, and bake it like red Deere and eat it cold.

This is meat for a Pope.

—*Compleat Cook* (1658, 2nd ed.), p. 36

Not only is this pie baked like a venison pasty ("red Deere"), it is also pounded and larded like beef pies made to resemble venison pasties (see Chapter 10, #17). Of course, since the pie is intended for Lent, the larding must be carried out "with the belly of a very fat Eale" rather than with lard or suet. The carp is a large fish native to eastern Europe but now found in many parts of the world.

16. A FISH PYE

Take of Soles, or thick Flounders, gut and wash them, and just put them in scalding Water to get off the black Skin; then cut them in Scollops or Indentured, so that they will join and lye in the Pye, as if they were whole. Have your Pattipan in readiness, with Puff-paste at the bottom and a Layer of Butter on it; then season your Fish with a little Pepper and Salt, Cloves, Mace, and Nutmeg, and lay it in your Pattipan, joining the pieces together as if the Fish had not been cut; then put in Forc'd-balls made with Fish, slices of Lemon with the Rind on, whole Oisters, whole yolks of hard Eggs, and pickled Barberies; then lid your Pye and bake it; when 'tis drawn make a Caudle of Oyster Liquor and White-wine thickened up with yolks of Eggs and a bit of Butter; serve it hot.

—Smith, *Compleat Housewife* (1728), pp. 114–15

A northern European flatfish, sole has often been confused with other flatfish, especially flounder. In America, shortly after Smith's time, the term "sole" came to describe not a particular species of fish but "a method of preparing a white-fleshed fillet." Thus, for example, the American winter flounder was (and still is) called lemon sole. It is not a true sole although it is invariably served as a fillet. In 1887, Maria Parloa said of flounder, "Fashionable people always call it sole." This was undoubtedly because true sole could be had only in Europe, the cultural lodestar for Boston's Brahmins. Sole's European popularity is seen in the fact that it is the "most frequent choice" among the many fish dishes in the menu books of Charles Dickens's wife. But as we see in Smith's recipe for generic fish pie, sole and flounder (the fish) were as easily interchangeable on her side of the Atlantic in the eighteenth century as were sole and flounder (the terms) on this side of the Atlantic a hundred years later.

Smith's pie, with its lemon, barberries, butter, wine, forcemeat, and oysters for garnish, resembles any number of court ragouts and terrines but modified to suit English kitchens and tastes. It is also put into a pie crust, thus assimilating the continental tradition to the growing repertoire of English pies.

17. A SALMON PYE

Make a good Crust, cleanse a Piece of Salmon well, season it with Salt, Mace, and Nutmeg, lay a little Piece of Butter at the Bottom of the Dish, and lay your Salmon in. Melt Butter according to your Pye; take a Lobster, boil it, pick out all the Flesh, chop it small, bruise the Body, mix it well with the Butter, which must be very good; pour it over your Salmon, put on the Lid, and bake it well.

—Glasse, *Art of Cookery* (1747), p. 115

This pleasant spiced salmon, lobster, and butter pie, adapted from *Whole Duty of a Woman*, was copied by Gardiner. William Wood had long since commented that American salmon (East Coast, obviously) was "as good as it is in England and in great plenty."

18. A LOBSTER PIE

Take the Meat out of the Tail and claws of a boiled Lobster & cut them in Slices, & season them with grated Nutmeg, Pepper and Salt; then take the Meat out of the Body, and season it with the Yolk of an Egg, a little Flour, Nutmeg, Pepper and Salt. Make these Ingredients into Force Meat Balls and fry them brown with Butter; then put Paste in your Dish, and lay the pieces of Lobster in with some

Oysters, an Anchovy shred, & the Force-meat Balls over them, to which add half a pound of good fresh Butter, laying it uppermost. Close your Pie and bake it half an Hour, and then put in a Layer of good rich Gravy.

—Gardiner, *Family Receipts* (ca. 1770), p. 54

In this instance, Gardiner relies not on Glasse but rather on one of Glasse's main sources, *Whole Duty of a Woman.* Experience may have taught her to bake lobster pie only a short time, just as it probably taught Glasse and Raffald to cook lobsters quickly (see Chapter 6, #28). Harold McGee confirms this as best practice, citing Japanese studies which found that lobsters and several other fish and shellfish species have enzymes in their muscles that become mushy with slow cooking. This may be less important when the lobster is preboiled, though in many such cases, as here, short baking times are still preferred. Lobsters in eighteenth-century America were usually much larger than those for sale today, which weigh on average from one to three pounds.

19. COD PIE

Take a piece of the middle of a small cod, and salt it well one night: next day wash it; season with pepper, salt and a very little nutmeg, mixed; place in a dish, and put some butter on it, and a little good broth of any kind into the dish.

Cover it with a crust; and when done, add a sauce of a spoonful of broth, a quarter of a pint of cream, a little flour and butter, a grate of lemon and nutmeg, and give it one boil. Oysters may be added.

Mackarel will do well, but do not salt them till used.

Parsley picked and put in, may be used instead of oysters.

—Rundell, *New System of Domestic Cookery* (1807), p. 127

This English cod pie recipe fared well in New England. It was copied by Lee in the 1830s, adapted by Allen in the 1840s, and copied again in the early twentieth century by Helen S. Wright. But its popularity may serve more as testimony to cod's centrality to New England food traditions than to the dish's distinction.

20. OYSTER PATTIES

Make some rich puff-paste, and bake it in very small tin patty-pans. When cool, turn them out upon a large dish.

Stew some large fresh oysters with a few cloves, a little mace and nutmeg, some yolk of egg boiled hard and grated, a little butter, and as much of the oyster liquor as will cover them. When they have stewed a little while, take them out of the pan, and set them away to cool. When quite cold, lay two or three oysters in each shell of puff-paste.

—Leslie, *Seventy-five Receipts* (1830), p. 97

Wilson states that the English baked fish, first in "the traditional standing coffin of strong paste," then in a patty pan lined with puff paste, and finally in an open dish, sometimes with a protective topping of bread crumbs and butter. But the introduction of a new technique did not necessarily drive out an older one. This early-nineteenth-century light side dish might well be found on a luncheon table today, although we would be more likely to serve it warm. It was copied at least three times in the next twenty years, in Lee, *The Roger Cookery*, and Hale's *Ladies' New Book of Cookery*.

21. OYSTER PIE

Line a deep dish with pie-crust, fill with dry pieces of bread, and cover it with puff paste, bake, either in a bake pan or quick oven till it is a light brown; by this time have the oysters just stewed, take off the upper crust, take *out* the pieces of bread, put *in* the oysters, season with salt, pepper, and butter; walnut catsup: replace the upper crust.

—Webster, *Improved Housewife* (1844), p. 74

The technique of prebaking the crust with a temporary filling of dry bread before adding the oysters is adopted from Leslie, who explains that the bread will hold up the top crust during baking, "as the oysters will be too much done if they are cooked in the pie." But it is not only oyster pie that benefits from this treatment. Leslie also uses dry bread in her "Raised French Pie." Whatever filling is used (dried beans, pie weights, or a towel, as in Leslie's "French Oyster Pie," #25), this method is often called blind-baking.

Webster's recipe moves us a long way toward the plainer cookery of nineteenth-century New England, as compared to Dalgairns's English version, reproduced in Lee, which requires thin slices of "the kidney fat of a loin of veal," white pepper, mace, grated lemon peel, and a topping of marrow.

Walnut ketchup was one of the most common types. Webster calls for it in four additional recipes, although she does not explain how to make it. Here's a contemporary recipe.

22. WALNUT CATSUP

Bruise ten dozen young walnuts, add a quart of vinegar, and three-fourths of a pound of fine salt. Let them stand two weeks, stirring every day. Strain off the liquor, and add half an ounce of black pepper whole, thirty cloves, half an ounce of bruised nutmeg, half an ounce of ginger, and four sticks of mace. Boil the whole an hour, then strain and bottle tight.

—Beecher, *Domestic Receipt-Book* (1846), pp. 72–73

23. EEL PIE

Skin, and cut the eels in three inch lengths, season with salt and pepper, and place in the dish some small pieces of butter and a little water, and cover with a paste.

—Allen, *Housekeeper's Assistant* (1845), p. 129

The enduring eel, easy to catch, oily and rich like mackerel, and well-suited to pies, continued on the New England gastronomic scene for a very long time, sliding gracefully from the well-spiced dishes and pies of the seventeenth century (for example, Woolley's "Pie with Eels and Oisters") to the milder eighteenth-century preparations (Glasse's "Eel Pye"). At the time of Allen's exceedingly plain pie, eels were still part of the New England culinary repertoire, as we also saw in Chapter 6 (see #s 1–5). But before much longer, they would begin to suffer from the neglect that remains their lot today.

24. LOBSTER PIE

Boil two lobsters, or three small; take out the tails, cut them in two, take out the guts, cut each in four pieces, lay them in a dish. Put in the meat of the claws, and that you have picked out of the body; pick off the furry parts from the latter, and take out the lady; then take the spawn, beat it in a mortar, likewise all the shells. Set them to stew with some water, two or three spoonfuls of vinegar, pepper, salt, and some pounded mace. When the goodness of the shells is obtained, strain and roll a large piece of butter in flour, and put in; give a boil or two, strew some crumbs over, and put a paste over all. Bake slowly until the paste is done.

—Allen, *Housekeeper's Assistant* (1845), pp. 130–31

This recipe is based on Glasse's "Lobster Pye" and Leslie's version of the same. Allen simplifies Leslie's seasoning, omitting cayenne and mushroom ketchup. She adds a bread crumb topping that seems redundant here in a real pie with a top crust but that would become ubiquitous in New England shellfish "pies" of the twentieth century. In Glasse, bread crumbs are also used, but there they are mixed with lobster meat to make a kind of forcemeat. Like Glasse before her, Allen is not afraid to slow bake her preboiled lobsters. "The lady" is explained in Chapter 6, #31, "the goodness of the shells" in Chapter 6, #30.

25. FRENCH OYSTER PIE

Having buttered the inside of a deep dish, line it with puff-paste rolled out rather thick, and prepare another sheet of paste for the lid. Put a clean towel into the dish (folded so as to support the lid) and then put on the lid; set it into the oven, and bake the paste well. When done, remove the lid, and take out the folded towel. While the paste is baking, prepare the oysters. Having picked off carefully any bits of shell that may be found about them, lay them in a sieve and drain off the liquor into a pan. Put the oysters into a skillet or stew-pan, with barely enough of the liquor to keep them from burning. Season them with whole pepper; blades of mace; some grated nutmeg; and some grated lemon-peel, (the yellow rind only,) and a little finely minced celery. Then add a large portion of fresh butter, divided into bits, and very slightly dredged with flour. Let the oysters simmer over the fire, but do not allow them to come to a boil, as that will shrivel them. Next beat the yolks only, of three, four, or five eggs, (in proportion to the size of the pie,) and stir the beaten egg into the stew a few minutes before you take it from the fire. Keep it warm till the paste is baked. Then carefully remove the lid of the pie; and replace it, after you have filled the dish with the oysters and gravy.

The lid of the pie may be ornamented with a wreath of leaves cut out of paste, and put on before baking. In the centre, place a paste-knot or flower.

Oyster pies are generally eaten warm; but they are very good cold.

—Leslie, *Lady's Receipt-Book* (1847), pp. 30–31

Just as Leslie's temporary oyster pie filling of dry bread was copied by Webster (#21), so her temporary French oyster pie filling of a clean dish towel was copied by Hale. Given that the seasoning, the egg-and-butter gravy, and the ornamented puff paste are all well within the English pie tradition, it is unclear what, other than the desire to assert its elegance, makes this a French pie.

26. CLAM PIE

Take a sufficient number of clams to fill a large pie-dish when opened. Make a nice paste in the proportion of a pound of fresh butter to two quarts of flour. Paste for shell-fish, or meat, or chicken pies should be rolled out double the thickness of that intended for fruit pies. Line the sides and bottom of your pie-dish with paste. Then cover the bottom with a thin beef-steak, divested of bone and fat. Put in the clams, and season them with mace, nutmeg, and a few whole pepper-corns. No salt. Add a spoonful of butter rolled in flour, and some hard-boiled yolks of eggs crumbled fine. Then put in enough of the clam-liquor to make sufficient gravy. Put on the lid of the pie, (which like the bottom crust should be rolled out thick,) notch it handsomely, and bake it well. It should be eaten warm.

—Leslie, *Lady's Receipt-Book* (1847), pp. 31–32

At the time of this recipe, clams had to a considerable extent recovered from the image problems from which they had suffered since settlement. Doubtless the refined Leslie's deployment of them in this recipe furthered their upward mobility. Like the inclusion of veal and marrow in a contemporaneous oyster pie (see #21, commentary), the presence in this pie of both meat and fish signals the erosion of categories based on the observance of Lent.

27. CLAM PIE

Chop forty clams and two small onions, half green pepper. Boil four medium potatoes, cut fine and add to the above. Thicken with two tablespoons flour, one butter and cook all together. Make a biscuit crust, line a deep dish and fill. Spread over a top crust. When brown, pie is baked.

—Patten, *Our New England Family Recipes* (1910), pp. 82–83

This is essentially a clam pot pie. Such pies were often made with something other than a standard crust, such as the biscuit crust here or the "healthful" potato crust in Beecher's meat or fowl pot pie (Chapter 10, #27).

CHAPTER TWELVE

Pies—Vegetable, Fruit, Custard

AP-PLE-PYE,

Wb begin a sequence of three chapters filled primarily with sweet dishes by recalling that, as noted in Chapter 1, in early modern England such dishes constituted a separate department of food preparation, "confectionery," which was more prestigious than "cookery," the making of all other types of food. The ladies of the aristocracy and gentlewomen of the gentry participated directly in confectionery activities, while leaving cookery for the most part to their servants. This association of sweet dishes with upper-class female refinement, combined with the increasing availability of sugar, meant that when women came to the fore as cookbook authors in the eighteenth century, their "most important contribution to the continuing development of English cookery was in sweet dishes—puddings, tarts, pancakes, and cakes." And of course, pies (of all types, but especially of the sweet type). This emphasis was transferred intact to New England, where the farm wife, the merchant's wife, and the housekeeper also found personal expression and social elevation in making "decorative sweet dishes."

As regards vegetable and fruit pies specifically, in England, vegetables and fruits came into their own as primary ingredients in pie fillings—as opposed to serving as complements to meat, fowl, or fish—in the sixteenth century. By the seventeenth century, a significant portion of the orchard and garden yield of the typical yeoman farmstead was being dried or cold-stored for the specific purpose of making pies, and this practice was continued in New England. The place of vegetable and fruit pies in New England cooking was tied to the place of Thanksgiving in the New England agricultural calendar. Thanksgiving was a harvest festival, and in preparation for it much of the harvest was devoted straightaway to making "all manner of pies." The New England climate made it possible for many of these Thanksgiving pies to be stored away for later consumption, while throughout the winter and spring additional pies would be continually made from the cold-stored fruits and vegetables in the cellar and the dried fruits and vegetables hanging from the kitchen and attic rafters. Toward the end of the nineteenth century, Charles Dudley Warner reported that the rural districts of New England were "full of women" who would have been mortified "if visitors should catch them without a pie in the house." In an earlier day, most of New England had been rural, and this report would have been applicable almost everywhere in the region. Being able to have a pie always on hand meant that, for yet another year, the family and its farm were thriving.

Pumpkin Pie

We begin with pumpkin pie, and single it out from other vegetable pies, because of its prominent position in New England cuisine and culture. The New World gourd became the basis for the pie that came to occupy "the most distinguished niche" on the New England Thanksgiving table. Despite this starring role, pumpkin was often considered interchangeable with squash in pie-making, with some cooks, as seen in our selections, stating their preference for squash.

1. TO MAKE A PUMPION PYE

Take about halfe a pound of Pumpion and slice it, a handfull of Tyme, a little Rosemary, Parsley and sweet Marjoram slipped off the stalks, and chop them smal, then take Cinamon, Nutmeg, Pepper, and six Cloves, and beat them; take ten Eggs and beat them; then mix them, and beat them altogether, and put in as much Sugar as you think fit, then fry them like a froiz; after it is fryed, let it stand till it be cold, then fill your Pye, take sliced Apples thinne round wayes, and lay a row of the Froiz, and a layer of Apples with Currans betwixt the layer while your Pye is fitted, and put in a good deal of sweet butter before you close it; when the Pye is baked, take six yolks of Eggs, some white-wine or Verjuyce, & make a Caudle of this, but not too thick; cut up the Lid and put it in, stir them well together whilst the Eggs and Pumpions be not perceived, and so serve it up.

—*Compleat Cook* (1658, 2nd ed.), pp. 11–12

This is the standard English pumpkin pie of the sixteenth and seventeenth centuries. It is copied in one of Woolley's cookbooks; in another she offers two scaled-down versions. A century later in Boston, Gardiner gives an adaptation, with "some good fresh butter" instead of the caudle. While top crusts are sometimes broken up, here it seems that the cook is being instructed to cut open the top and pour in the caudle, mixing it only with the layer of apples. Clearly this is not the pumpkin pie that has become an American institution.

2. POMPKIN

NO. 1. One quart stewed and strained, 3 pints cream, 9 beaten eggs, sugar, mace, nutmeg and ginger, laid into paste NO. 7 or 3, and with a dough spur, cross and chequer it, and baked in dishes three quarters of an hour.

NO. 2. One quart of milk, 1 pint pompkin, 4 eggs, molasses, allspice and ginger in a crust, bake 1 hour.

—Simmons, *American Cookery* (Hartford, 1796), p. 28

Here are the first printed recipes for pumpkin pie in the form that Americans now know it—a pie crust filled with spiced pumpkin custard. The first of the two recipes, and possibly the second, is made with an ornamented top crust, a feature that the American pumpkin pie soon lost. Although this type of pumpkin pie represents a significant departure from the English pumpkin pie tradition, it nevertheless falls squarely within another English tradition of custardized vegetable and fruit (particularly apple) pies, of which we provide examples later in the chapter. We have not found any instances of custardized pumpkin in English cookbooks, despite pumpkin's suitability to this treatment. This is probably because in England pumpkin pie of any type fell into disfavor in the eighteenth century. We give Simmons's pastes in Chapter 9, #s 4 and 5. A dough spur, also called a jagging iron or jagger wheel, was "an instrument used for ornamenting pastry, in the form of a toothed wheel, set in a handle, frequently a product of the carving (scrimshaw) done on whaling vessels."

3. PUMPKIN AND SQUASH PIE

For common family pumpkin pies, three eggs do very well to a quart of milk. Stew your pumpkin, and strain it through a sieve, or colander. Take out the seeds, and pare the pumpkin, or squash, before you stew it; but do not scrape the inside; the part nearest the seed is the sweetest part of the squash. Stir in the stewed pumpkin, till it is as thick as you can stir it round rapidly and easily. If you want to make your pie richer, make it thinner, and add another egg. One egg to a quart of milk makes very decent pies. Sweeten it to your taste, with molasses or sugar; some pumpkins require more sweetening than others. Two tea-spoonfuls of salt; two great spoonfuls of sifted cinnamon; one great spoonful of ginger. Ginger will answer very well alone for spice, if you use enough of it. The outside of a lemon grated in is nice. The more eggs, the better the pie; some put an egg to a gill of milk. They should bake from forty to fifty minutes, and even ten minutes longer, if very deep.

—Child, *American Frugal Housewife* (1833), pp. 66–67

Here is a classic entry in Child's New England culinary scrapbook, both in terms of ingredients and writing style. Child's charmingly disjointed account of the best way to make pumpkin or squash pie reads so vividly that we can almost see the cook jotting down her observations and recommendations as they occur to her. While her near contemporary Catharine Beecher is concerned to streamline and rationalize the cooking process, Child's intimacy with her ingredients shows her concern for taste (as in her remark about the variable sweetness of pumpkins). But she also understands the common housewife's need to economize, as in her suggestion that "one egg to a quart of milk makes very decent pies."

We may wonder why Child recommends stewing rather than baking the pumpkin or squash that is to be used in this pie. Recall that for the open-hearth cook for whom she writes, kettles of water were often kept on the hearth for just such reasons. Bake ovens, on the other hand, required separate firing, along with considerable expertise to determine precisely when particular foods should be inserted into the falling heat. Oven-baking one's raw pumpkin in preparation for pie-making was simply impractical. Of course, Child assumes that her reader has access to an oven for the final pie-baking.

In an ensuing recipe for "Carrot Pie," Child adds that "squash [and pumpkin] pies should be baked without an upper crust, in deep plates." Henceforth, all New England pumpkin pie recipes would call for a bottom crust only.

A final note on pumpkin versus squash pies. Davidson highlights the "intractable problems of nomenclature" surrounding the genus *Cucurbita*. Within this "extensive family of plants with a vinelike habit of growth," pumpkins and squashes are not separate species. Rather, in at least two instances, *C. pepo* and *C. moschata,* both are found as varieties within the same species.

4. PIE, SQUASH

One pint of squash, stewed and strained; one pint of milk, and one of cream; ten eggs; half teacup of rosewater; quarter pound of sugar, and one grated nutmeg. Bake in plates lined with puff paste.

—Lee, *Cook's Own Book* (1832), p. 143

This is the lone recipe we have included from Lee the source of which, as mentioned in Chapter 2, we have been unable to identify. Her usual English sources do not include pumpkin or squash pies, since, as just noted, by the nineteenth century few such pies were being made in England. None of Lee's possible American sources, such as Child or Leslie's *Seventy-five Receipts,* contains this recipe.

Whoever created it, the recipe is squarely in the gourmandizing tradition of the entire Lee volume. Child speaks of one egg to a gill of milk as the ultimate in pumpkin pie richness. This would translate to eight eggs to a quart of milk. But the Lee recipe exceeds this standard by a considerable margin, not only in specifying ten eggs to a quart of dairy liquid but also in requiring that half of the liquid be cream rather than milk.

Rosewater, distilled from rose petals, perfumed and flavored Persian and Arabian dishes and was brought to Europe by the crusaders. It became a standard English flavoring and remained in use in New England into the nineteenth century.

5. PUMPKIN PIE

To one quart of stewed and strained pumpkin, add one quart of new milk, and sweeten it to your taste. For the crust, take wheat meal, wet with buttermilk to a sufficient stiffness to roll out. Bake it in deep dishes.

ANOTHER

Take a brown earthen pan, grease it, and sift Indian meal over it about the thickness of a quarter of an inch; prepare the pumpkin in good milk and sweetening, and add a little rice instead of eggs, with a little ginger. Ground rice, squashes, and sweet potatoes, may be made into pies in the same way, and are superior to pumpkins.

—Gilman, *Lady's Annual Register* (1840), p. 39

The first of these two austere pies is made without eggs, spices, and with the most minimal fat component in the crust. The term "meal" in the crust directions means that it is to be made with whole wheat flour, which was being promoted at this time by the nutritional reformer Sylvester Graham. The second recipe makes do with plain cornmeal for the bottom crust. Gilman's "little rice" has been boiled to a gelatinous mass before being mixed in with the pumpkin and milk. Ground rice has the consistency of coarse powder. Sweet potato pie is given below (#12).

6. PUMPKIN PIE (ENGLISH)

Take out the seeds, and grate the pumpkin till you come to the outside skin. Sweeten the pulp; add a little ground allspice, lemon peel and lemon juice; in short, flavor it to the taste. Bake without an upper crust.

—Hale, *Ladies' New Book of Cookery* (1852), p. 280

Hale includes this recipe immediately after giving what is close to a verbatim copy of the Child recipe, which she calls "Pumpkin Pie (American)." Although we have found no pies similar to this one in English cookbooks, the fact that the pumpkin is not custardized, or even stewed and strained, gives the recipe a rough family resemblance to early modern English pumpkin pies made with sliced pumpkin, such as #1 above.

7. SQUASH OR PUMPKIN PIE (*SQUASH IS THE NICEST.*)

Steam the squash, strain it carefully through a sieve, add two, four, or six eggs, according to convenience, to eight table-spoonfuls of squash, one quart of boiled new milk or cream, a glass of wine, a lemon, (the rind being grated,) and sugar, salt, and mace, to the taste. This pie needs only an under-crust and an edge.
—Mann, *Christianity in the Kitchen* (1857), p. 80

This is the thinnest pie in our selection, with only a quarter of a pint of pumpkin or squash to a quart of milk or cream—a one-to-eight ratio. Proportions of half as much pumpkin as dairy liquid constitute the distant second in thinness in the other recipes given here (Simmons No. 2 and Lee). Mann's inclusion of a glass of wine in her pumpkin pie marks her as one of those temperance advocates who, like Beecher, saw no need to "go beyond" a pledge to abstain from "intoxicating drinks as a beverage" and who therefore thought it "proper to use wine and brandy in cooking."

Other Vegetable Pies

Pies with vegetables—green and leafy or root—as the primary ingredients appeared with some frequency in English (and therefore colonial) cookbooks through the eighteenth century. In New England, they dwindled into insignificance by the middle of the nineteenth century.

8. TO MAKE AN ARTICHOKE PIE

Make your Paste as before named [i.e., as directed in the preceding recipe, "with fine Flower, Butter, cold Cream and the yolk and white of one Egg"], and roul it thin, and lay it into your baking-pan.

Then lay in Butter sliced thin, and then your bottoms of Artichokes tenderly boiled, season it with a little Salt, a little gross Pepper, and some sliced Nutmeg, with a blade or two of Mace and a little Sugar, then lay in some Marrow, Candied Orange and Citron Pill, with some Candied Eringo Roots; then cover it with butter, and close it with your Paste, and so bake it, then cut it up, and put in white Wine, Butter, and the yolks of Eggs and Sugar; cover it again, and serve it to the Table.
—Woolley, *Queen-like Closet* (1670), p. 95

This artichoke pie reflects both the lingering preferences of the Middle Ages, using spicy and sweet flavors to accent what we would consider savory dishes, and the newer trend toward making all manner of fruits and vegetables into pies.

9. TO MAKE A CARROT PUDDING

Take raw Carrots, and scrape them clean; then grate them with a grater, without a back. To half a pound of Carrot, take a pound of grated Bread, a Nutmeg, a little Cinamon, a very little Salt, half a pound of Sugar, half a pint of Sack, eight Eggs, a pound of Butter melted, and as much Cream as will mix it well together; stir it and beat it well up, and put it in a Dish to bake; put Puff-paste at the bottom of your Dish.

—Smith, *Compleat Housewife* (1728), p. 80

Here is our first instance of the English custardized vegetable or fruit pie that Amelia Simmons adapted for her originating recipes for American pumpkin pie. All the ancillary ingredients of the American pumpkin pie—milk or cream, eggs, sweetener, and spices—are found here. Glasse offered the Smith carrot pudding recipe with only minor alteration, and Carter copied Glasse's modified version. Simmons made more significant changes. Her carrot pudding is made with boiled and strained carrot pulp rather than grated raw carrot, just as her and subsequent American pumpkin pies are made with stewed and strained pumpkin pulp rather than sliced or grated raw pumpkin. Simmons also eliminates the bread crumbs. Although her carrot pudding is to be baked "without paste," essentially Simmons prepared the way for Child to state thirty years later that "carrot pies are made like squash [or pumpkin] pies." A hundred years before the open carrot and squash/pumpkin pie was made normative among American cooks, Smith omits the top crust in her contribution to the genre.

10. AN HERB PYE FOR LENT

Take Lettice, Leeks, Spinage, Beets, and Parsley, of each a Handful, give them a boil, then chop them small, and have ready boiled in a Cloth one Quart of Groats, with two or three Onions in them, put them in a Frying Pan with the Herbs, and a good deal of Salt, a Pound of Butter, and a few Apples cut thin, stew them a few Minutes over the Fire, fill your Dish or raised Crust with it: One Hour will bake it, then serve it up.

—Raffald, *Experienced English House-keeper* (1769), pp. 134–35

The presence of apples and the absence of sugar makes this a pie that is almost but not quite savory in the modern sense. Characteristically, Raffald simplifies the seasoning and general composition of her herb pie (for instance, no eggs or custard), as compared with those of Markham and Smith. As earlier noted, groats can mean hulled grain of any kind but most often means hulled oats. Boiling in a cloth is discussed in Chapter 13.

11. POTATOE PIE

Scald one quart milk, grate in four large potatoes while the milk is hot, when cold add four eggs well beaten, four ounces butter, spice and sweeten to your taste; lay in paste NO. 7—bake half an hour.

N.B. A bowl containing two quarts, filled with water, and set into the oven, will prevent any articles being scorched, such as cakes, pies, and the like.

—Simmons, *American Cookery* (Albany, 1796), p. 27

Simmons's custardized potato pie, similar to her pumpkin pies, appears in the second edition of her cookbook. Karen Hess points out that as early as 1597 John Gerard identified both sweet and white potatoes for his readers. The sweet potato was then being imported into England from Spain, hence its early name, Spanish Potato. Gerard called white potatoes "*Potatoes of Virginia.*" The extensive entry on potatoes in the marketing section of Simmons's first edition is almost entirely concerned with white potatoes. However, Simmons did not compose the marketing passages, indeed deleted them from the edition in which this recipe appears. So it is unclear which type of potato—sweet or white—is intended here. Simmons specifies the same crust as for the first of her pumpkin pies (#2). This recipe is copied in *The Cook Not Mad*.

12. SWEET POTATO PUDDING

Grate half a pound of parboiled sweet potatoes, and stir to a cream six ounces of sugar and six of butter, and then add the beaten yolks of eight eggs.

Mix the above, and add the grated peel and juice of a lemon, a glass of wine, and a grated nutmeg.

The last thing, put in the whites of the eggs beat to a stiff froth.

Common potatoes and carrots may be made as above, only they are to be boiled soft, and put through a colander, and more sugar used.

—Beecher, *Domestic Receipt-Book* (1846), p. 127

As the concluding comment indicates, Beecher's recipe is a sweet potato version of the potato and carrot pudding pies in Simmons (#11 and #9 commentary). The Simmons carrot pudding also omits milk or cream. Although Beecher mentions no crust, her section "Paste for Puddings and Pies" begins just down the page from this recipe (see Chapter 9, #s 12–14). What makes the recipe distinctive is Beecher's instruction to mix eight stiffly beaten egg whites into the pudding batter, making this a sweet potato (or white potato or carrot) soufflé.

13. TOMATO PIE

Pick green tomatoes, pour boiling water over them, and let them remain a few minutes; then strip off the skin, cut the tomatoes in slices, and put them in deep pie plates. Sprinkle a little ginger and some sugar over them in several layers. Lemon juice, and the grated peel, improve the pie. Cover the pies with a thick crust, and bake them slowly about an hour.

—Webster, *Improved Housewife* (1844), p. 92

Strictly speaking, this is a fruit pie, tomatoes being a fruit (called "apples of love" in the sixteenth and seventeenth centuries). In New England, tomatoes were only beginning to be accepted as a food item at the time Webster published this recipe. With its layering of the key vegetable ingredient, interspersed with sugar and spice, and with its omission of the bottom crust, the recipe is in the tradition of English pumpkin pie. Child included a "Tomatoes Pie" (custardized in the manner of her pumpkin/squash pie) in the appendix found in later editions of her cookbook.

Fruit Pies

In farm households in both Old and New England, a major, if not the principal, use of stored and preserved fruit was to make pies. An additional incentive to cooking fruit in pies was the opinion, prevalent until the nineteenth century, that fresh fruit was unhealthy. By the time conventional wisdom on this score had been overturned, sugar was becoming an ever more important part of the Anglo-American diet, even as the distinction between savory and sweet, in pies as in other dishes, was emerging. Fruit pies fell readily into this classification scheme, sugar having long been crucial to the preservation of fruit. The crisp, comforting apple was—and is—a perfect match with English and New England growing conditions and with Anglo-American tastes. The preponderance of apple pies and tarts in the following selections reflects this happy relationship.

14. A PIPIN TART

Take *Pippins* of the fairest, and pare them, and then diuide them iust in the halfes, and take out the chores [cores] cleane: then hauing rold out the coffin flat, and raysde vp a small verdge of an inch, or more high, lay in the *Pippins* with the hollow side downeward, as close one to another as may be: then lay here and there a *cloue,* and here and there a whole stick of *cinamon,* and a little bit of *butter;* then couer all cleane ouer with *suger,* and so couer the coffin, and bake it according to the manner of Tarts; and when it is bak't, then draw it out, and hauing boyld *butter* and *rose-water* together, anoynt all the lid ouer therewith, and then scrape or strow on it good store of *suger,* and so set it in the ouen againe, & after serue it vp.

—Markham, *Countrey Contentments* (1623), p. 105

Despite Markham's use of the term "coffin"—commonly understood to refer to a durable pastry able to hold its shape—and his inclusion of a top crust, the shallow-sided tart he describes would have been made with the richer pastry associated with open tarts. The "late-ripening, long-keeping" pippin was the most popular English cooking apple. According to *The Husbandman's Fruitful Orchard* (1609), in 1534 Richard Harris, fruiterer to Henry VIII, "fetched out of Fraunce great store of graftes especially pippins, before which time there were no pippins in England." Markham's instruction to "bake it according to the manner of tarts" refers to the fact that tarts, with their shorter crusts, required considerably less baking time than standing pies.

15. TO MAKE ORANGE OR LEMON TARTS

Take six large Lemons, and rub them very well with Salt, and put them in Water for two days, with a handful of Salt in it; then change them into fresh Water without Salt every other day for a fortnight; then boil them for two or three hours till they are tender, then cut them into half quarters, and then cut them thus ⤝| as thin as you can, then take six Pippins pared, cored, and quartered, and a pint of fair Water, let them boil till the Pippins break: Put the Liquor to your Orange or Lemon, and half the Pippin well broken, and a pound of Sugar, boil these together a quarter of an hour; then put it in a Gally-pot, and squeeze an Orange in it, if it be Lemon, or a Lemon if 'tis Orange, two spoonfuls is enough for a Tart: Your Pattipans must be small and shallow; put fine Puff-paste, and very thin; a little while will bake it. Just as your Tarts are going into the Oven, with a Feather or Brush do them over with melted Butter, and then sift double-refined Sugar on them, and this is a pretty Icing on them.

—Smith, *Compleat Housewife* (1728), p. 107

The filling for Smith's tarts amounts to an orange- or lemon-apple marmalade. In eighteenth-century Britain, sweet oranges, imported from Portugal, were preferred to bitter or Seville oranges in puddings and other confections. However, the designation of oranges as interchangeable with lemons in this recipe suggests that the bitter orange was meant. Smith's butter and sugar icing is similar to Markham's, except for the omission of rosewater. Double refined sugar, produced by a second cycle of boiling, crystallization, and refining, was off-white in color. In the eighteenth century, a gallipot was a small glazed earthenware pot, most often associated with apothecaries. This recipe was copied by Glasse, Carter, and Simmons (the latter probably taking it from Carter rather than Glasse or Smith).

16. AN APPLE PUDDING

Peel and quarter eight golden-runnets, or twelve golden-pippins; cast them into water, in which boil them as you do Apple-sauce; sweeten them with loaf sugar, squeeze in them two lemons, and grate in their peels; beat eight eggs, and beat them all well together; pour it into a dish cover'd, and with puff-paste, and bake it an hour in a slow oven.

—Smith, *Compleat Housewife* (1739), p. 104

Like Smith's carrot pudding, this is another instance of English custardized fruit or vegetable pie. Runnets were more often called rennets. The repetition of the instruction to beat the eggs was changed in the fourteenth edition to "break eight eggs, and beat them all well together." A recipe that differs from this one only in calling exclusively for pippins, in using butter, and in omitting the whites of the eggs appears in Glasse. As seen below, in New England some custardized apple pies would, in a small manifestation of the region's persisting culinary allegiance to the Mother Country, be given the English name "Marlborough."

17. TO MAKE DIFFERENT SORTS OF TARTS

If you bake in tin Patties, butter them, and you must put a little Crust all over, because of the taking them out: If in China, or Glass, no Crust but the top one. Lay fine Sugar at the Bottom, then your Plumbs, Cherries, or any other sort of Fruit, and Sugar at Top; then put on your Lid, and bake them in a slack Oven. Mince-pies must be baked in Tin-patties, because of taking them out, and Puff-paste is best for them. All Sweet Tarts the beaten Crust is best; but as you fancy. You have the Receipt for the Crusts in this Chapter. Apple, Pear, Apricock, &c. make thus: Apples and Pears, pare them, cut them in Quarters, and core them; cut the Quarters a-cross again, set them on in a Sauce-pan with just as much Water as will barely cover them, let them simmer on a slow Fire just till the Fruit is tender; put a good Piece of Lemon-peel in the Water with the Fruit, then have your Patties ready. Lay fine Sugar at Bottom, then your Fruit, and a little Sugar at Top; that you must put in at your Discretion. Pour over each Tart a Tea Spoonful of Lemon-juice, and three Tea Spoonfuls of the Liquor they were boiled in; put on your Lid, and bake them in a slack Oven. Apricocks do the same Way; only don't use Lemon.

As to Preserved Tarts, only lay in your preserved Fruit, and put a very thin Crust at Top, and let them be baked as little as possible; but if you would make them nice, have a large Patty, the Size you would have your Tart. Make your Sugar-Crust, roll it as thick as a Halfpenny; then butter your Patties, and cover it; shape your Upper-crust on a hollow Thing on purpose, the Size of your Patty, and mark it with a Marking-iron for that purpose, in what Shape you please, to be hollow and open to see the Fruit through; then bake your Crust in a very slack Oven, not to discolour it, but to have it crisp. When the Crust is cold, very carefully take it out, and fill it with what Fruit you please, lay on the Lid, and it is done; therefore if the Tart is not eat, your Sweet-meat is not the worse, and it looks genteel.

—Glasse, *Art of Cookery* (1747), p. 75

Glasse's fruit tarts are essentially variations on those offered by Markham in the previous century. Her "Preserved Tarts," constructed so that the fruit preserves will be visible, could appear on any twenty-first-century fancy dessert table, on which it remains desirable that the presentation be "genteel." The section on apple and pear tarts was copied by Carter.

18. AN APPLE PYE

Make a good Puff-paste Crust, lay some round the Sides of the Dish, pare and quarter your Apples, and take out the Cores, lay a Row of Apples thick, throw in half your Sugar you design for your Pye, mince a little Lemon-peel fine, throw over and squeeze a little Lemon over them, then a few Cloves, here and there one, then the rest of your Apples, and the rest of your Sugar. You must sweeten to your Palate, and squeeze a little more Lemon; boil the Peeling of the Apples, and the Cores in some fair Water, with a Blade of Mace, till it is very good; strain and boil the Syrup with a little Sugar, till there is but very little and good, pour it into your Pye, and put on your Upper-crust, and bake it. You may put in a little Quince and Marmalate, if you please.

Thus make a Pear-pye; but don't put in any Quince. You may butter them when they come out of the Oven; or beat up the Yolks of two Eggs, and half a Pint of Cream, with a little Nutmeg, sweetned with Sugar, and take off the Lid, and pour in the Cream. Cut the Crust in little three-corner Pieces, and stick about the Pye, and send it to Table.

—Glasse, *Art of Cookery* (1747), p. 114

The fruit pie, as opposed to the fruit tart, is now to be baked in a dish. This reflects the fact that by the beginning of the eighteenth century standing fruit pies were out of fashion. Note that there is no bottom crust. Glasse's apple pie would qualify as well as any to be prefixed by the phrase "As English as . . ." It was copied by both Carter and Gardiner.

19. ICEING FOR TARTS

Beat and sift a quarter of a pound of fine loaf sugar. Put it into a mortar with the white of one egg that has been well beat up. Add to these two spoonfuls of rose-water, and beat altogether till it be so thick as just to run, observing to stir it all one way. It is laid on the tart with a brush or small bunch of feathers dipped in the iceing. Set the tarts, when so done, into a cool oven to harden. But take care not to let them stand too long: for that will discolour them.

—Carter, *Frugal Housewife* (1772), p. 122

Tarts were frequently iced. In Markham's pippin tart (#14) and Smith's orange or lemon tarts (#15) an icing of butter and sugar (with or without rosewater) is recommended. Carter's variation, employing egg white in place of butter, produces a more striking hard white glaze.

20. A CODLING PYE

Gather small Codlings, put them in a clean Brass Pan with Spring Water, lay Vine Leaves on them, and cover them with a Cloth wrapped round the cover of the Pan to keep in the Steam, when they grow softish peel off the Skin, and put them in the same Water with the Vine Leaves, hang them a great height over the Fire to green, when you see them a fine green, take them out of the Water and put them in a deep Dish, with as much Powder or Loaf Sugar as will sweeten them, make the Lid of rich puff Paste and bake it, when it comes from the Oven take off the Lid, and cut it in little Pieces like Sippets, and stick them round the inside of the Pye with the Points upward, pour over your Codlings a good Custard made thus.—Boil a Pint of Cream, with a stick of Cinnamon, and Sugar enough to make it a little sweet, let it stand 'till cold, then put in the Yolks of four Eggs well beaten, set it on the Fire and keep stirring it 'till it grows thick, but do not let it boil, lest it Curdle, then pour it into your Pye, pare a little Lemon thin, cut the Peel like Straws, and lay it on your Codlings over the Top.

—Raffald, *Experienced English House-keeper* (1769), p. 134

Beware: Poison! Stewing apples along with vine leaves in a brass pan in order to make them turn green was a technique commonly used in the eighteenth century. Colquhoun explains that the process produced "highly toxic verdigris." Although Raffald condemns the practice as "Poison to a great degree," she nevertheless calls for it here and in another recipe.

A codlin or codling is an unripe apple ("codling" could also mean a young cod). The term was sometimes applied to a green, somewhat cone-shaped variety, but in all the recipes we have examined unripe apples are intended. In Markham's codling pie recipe, a cream or custard is, as here, to be poured over the filling after baking. Like Raffald's, Glasse's apple pie (#18) is decorated with pieces of the top crust. Raffald's recipe for "green codling Pudding" is a custardized apple pudding like Smith's (#16).

21. APPLE PIE

Stew and strain the apples, to every three pints, grate the peel of a fresh lemon, add cinnamon, mace, rose-water and sugar to your taste—and bake in paste NO.3.

Every species of fruit such as peas [peaches], plums, raspberries, black berries may be only sweetned, without spices—and bake in paste NO. 3.

—Simmons, *American Cookery* (Hartford, 1796), p. 24

22. DRIED APPLE PIE

Take two quarts dried apples, put them into an earthen pot that contains one gallon, fill it with water and set it in a hot oven, adding one handful of cramberries: after baking one hour fill up the pot again with water; when done and the apple cold, strain it, and add thereto the juice of three or four limes, raisins, sugar, orange peel and cinnamon to your taste; lay in paste NO. 3.

—Simmons, *American Cookery* (Albany, 1796), pp. 26–27

These two recipes use stewed and dried apples. Simmons includes another using tart raw apples. Together, these three apple pies from "the first American cookbook" are as English as English apple pie. The only mildly American touch is the cranberries in the dried apple pie. Simmons gives succinct directions for a forgotten art—reconstituting dried apples.

23. AN APPLE PUDDING DUMPLIN

Put into paste, quartered apples, lye in a cloth and boil two hours, serve with sweet sauce.

—Simmons, *American Cookery* (Hartford, 1796), p. 27

This is a boiled-down version, so to speak, of a recipe in Glasse for apple dumplings. Speaking of boiling, boiled pudding, sometimes a filling wrapped in cloth and boiled, sometimes a filling wrapped in a suet-rich dough and boiled, is closely connected to dumplings, which were sometimes made only of dough while at other times, as here, dough stuffed with fruit. Simmons swaddles her apple dumpling in both dough and cloth before boiling. Later, Beecher would leave out the "dumpling" designation, calling her version "Boiled Apple Pudding." Apples' sweet flavor and semi-soft texture when baked or boiled make them the perfect pudding or dumpling ingredient. For more on boiled puddings, see the first part of the next chapter.

24. MARLBOROUGH PUDDING

Take 12 spoons of stewed apples, 12 of wine, 12 of sugar, 12 of melted butter, and 12 of beaten eggs, a little cream, spice to your taste; lay in paste NO. 3, in a deep dish; bake one hour and a quarter.

—Simmons, *American Cookery* (Albany, 1796), p. 36

This custardized apple pudding pie resembles Smith's (#16), although Simmons adds cream. The recipes also differ somewhat in flavoring— Smith flavors hers with lemon, Simmons hers with wine. This is the first custardized apple pudding pie we have found that uses the name "Marlborough." The recipe is reproduced in *The Cook Not Mad*.

25. CHERRY PIE

Cherry pies should be baked in a deep plate. Take the cherries from the stalks, lay them in a plate, and sprinkle a little sugar and cinnamon, according to the sweetness of the cherries. Baked with a top and bottom crust, three quarters of an hour.

—Child, *American Frugal Housewife* (1833), p. 67

Child says nothing about pitting the cherries, but shortly before *The Frugal Housewife* was first published, Eliza Leslie states, in *Seventy-five Receipts*, that cherries going into pies "should be stoned."

26. APPLE PIE

When you make apple pies, stew your apples very little indeed; just strike them through, to make them tender. Some people do not stew them at all, but cut them up in very thin slices, and lay them in the crust. Pies made in this way may retain more of the spirit of the apple; but I do not think the seasoning mixes in as well. Put in sugar to your taste; it is impossible to make a precise rule, because apples vary so much in acidity. A very little salt, and a small piece of butter in each pie, makes them richer. Cloves and cinnamon are both suitable spice. Lemon-brandy and rose-water are both excellent. A wine-glass full of each is sufficient for three or four pies. If your apples lack spirit, grate in a whole lemon.

—Child, *American Frugal Housewife* (1833), pp. 67–68

This is another instance of Child's unique knack for turning a recipe into a conversation with the reader. She judiciously weighs the advantages and disadvantages of different options and offers reasons for the balance she ultimately chooses to strike. By her use of such phraseology as "the spirit of the apple," Child reminds us that cooking is the art of providing access to the energies and vitalities that are the earth's most important gift.

27. PIE, APPLE (2)

Pare, quarter, and core the apples; cut them into thin bits. Put into the bottom of a pie-dish a table-spoonful of brown sugar, with a tea-spoonful of grated ginger and lemon-peel, then a layer of apples, and so on alternately, till the dish is piled as full as it will hold. The next day wet the rim of the dish, line it with puff or tart paste, brush it with water, and cover it with paste; press the edge all round, notch it with a paste cutter, and make a small hole with the point of a knife in the middle. It may be seasoned with two table-spoonfuls of lemon or orange marmalade, pounded cinnamon, mace, and cloves, in addition to the ginger and lemon-peel.

—Lee, *Cook's Own Book* (1832), p. 139

Allowing thin slices of apple to marinate overnight in brown sugar, grated fresh ginger, and lemon peel is the key to this unique and delicious version of the most popular of all Anglo-American fruit pies. A dollop of marmalade along with cinnamon, mace, and cloves add to the richness and complexity of flavors. The recipe comes from Dalgairns.

28. RASPBERRY TART WITH CREAM

Roll out some thin paste, lay it in a pan of what size you choose; put in raspberries, strow over them fine sugar, cover with a thin lid and then bake. Cut it open, and have ready the following mixture, warm; half a pint of cream, the yolks of two or three eggs well beaten and a little sugar; and when this is added to the tart return it to the oven for five or six minutes.

—*Roger Cookery* (1838), p. 26

A few years before, Leslie recommended adding cream to raspberry or apple pies or tarts at the end of the baking process. This recipe elaborates the cream into a modified caudle (see Chapter 10, #1).

29. FRUIT PIES

When making pies from ripe summer fruits, such as raspberries, blueberries, cherries, damsons, &c. always take a deep plate, line it with paste, place a teacup inverted in the middle, and fill the pie with fruit, a good quantity of brown sugar, with very little spice or seasoning. The cup is placed to receive the juice, which will flow from the fruit as they bake, and which would otherwise ooze out at the edges. It will all settle under the cup, which must be removed when the pie is cut open.

—Hale, *Good Housekeeper* (1841), p. 83

Like the previous recipe, this one is heavily indebted to Leslie, who also recommends using an inverted teacup to trap the juice in a fruit pie. This recommendation and the subsequent instruction to remove the cup full of the trapped juices pose as many problems as they solve. First, why would the juices flow into the cup, and second, how does one remove an inverted cup full of juice without spilling the contents back into the pie? The answers to both questions are given in a midcentury British manual, *Cookery, Rational, Practical, and Economical* (1853): "The teacup will be found, when the pie is baked, to contain most of the juice, this having replaced the air expelled by the heat of the oven, but in slightly raising one side of it, the juice will flow down [into the cup] ready for use [elsewhere]." Of the nineteenth-century American cookbooks that recommend the teacup technique (first devised by the eighteenth-century scientist Stephen Hales), none includes as complete a description of the mechanics of the process. Webster copied Hale's exact wording of the technique.

30. PEACH PIE

Select mellow, juicy peaches; wash and place them in a deep pie plate lined with paste; strew a thick layer of sugar on each of the peaches, adding a spoonful of water, and a sprinkling of flour over the top of each layer; cover with a thick crust; and bake about an hour. The prussic acid of the stone imparts a most agreeable flavor to the pie. Stew peaches that are hard, before making them into pies. Also, stew dried peaches soft, and sweeten them; and give them no other spice than a few of the meats, blanched and pounded fine in a little rose-water.

—Webster, *Improved Housewife* (1844), p. 95

Webster offers three ways to cook peaches into pies, all unusual by modern standards. She recommends plunking several layers of either whole ripe peaches, whole, unripe stewed peaches, or dried, ripe stewed peaches into a pie paste, strewing with sugar, anointing with water, and sprinkling with flour before topping with a thick crust and baking. These are bold techniques. Her insistence on cooking the peach pits contradicts Leslie's instructions in *Seventy-five Receipts*. The "agreeable flavor" imparted by prussic acid released from the peach stone derives from cyanogen molecules, essentially cyanide. This phenomenon usually occurs in relation to the use of bitter almonds in cooking. William Augustus Guy, the eminent British forensic medical specialist, writing not long after the date of this recipe, reported that deaths both accidental and deliberate caused by ingestion of this poison were "on the increase." Guy noted that "the frequent use of essential oil of almonds in cookery . . . renders it a favorite instrument of suicide." But fear not. A great deal of peach-cum-pit pie would have to be consumed for death to ensue. Hale (from whom Webster plagiarized the tip about using an inverted teacup to trap pie juices) returned Webster's compliment by plagiarizing the first half of this recipe in *Ladies' New Book of Cookery*.

31. MARLBOROUGH TARTS

Quarter, and stew very tender, juicy tart apples. To a teacup of the pulp, rubbed through a sieve, put the same measure of sugar, the same of wine, half a teacup of melted butter, the juice and grated rind of a lemon, a tumbler of milk, four eggs, and half a nutmeg. Mix all the ingredients well together, and turn into deep pie plates that are lined with pastry, with a rim of puff paste round the edge. Bake the tarts about thirty minutes.

—Webster, *Improved Housewife* (1844), p. 96

This tempting recipe is similar to Simmons's Marlborough Pudding (#24), with more specific instructions regarding seasoning. Precedent for Webster's wine is found in Simmons, and for her lemon in Smith (#16). Webster also offers a Marlborough Pudding without a crust. Beecher copied it, adding a crust and insisting, in opposition to both Webster's pudding and tart, that "it is much better to grate than to stew the apples, for this and all pies."

32. PORK APPLE PIE

Make your crust in the usual manner, spread it over a large deep plate, cut some slices of fat pork very thin, also some slices of apple; place a layer of apples, and then of pork, with a very little allspice, and pepper, and sugar, between—three or four layers of each, with crust over the top. Bake one hour.

—Howland, *New England Economical Housekeeper* (1845), p. 41

Here is an apple pie whose filling is made in the manner of a chowder, interspersing layers of sliced apple (instead of cod fish) with layers of fat (that is, salt) pork. Howland even adds pepper, the conventional seasoning for chowder, to her sweet pie. The "Sea Dish" has come ashore but it's still a bit of a salty dog.

33. BLUEBERRY PIE

Wash the blueberries in a colander, with cold water, and let them drain a few minutes; then pour them into a deep dish (a soup plate) lined with Paste NO. 8, cover them with four table-spoonfuls of fine white sugar, dredge them with flour, cover them with the same paste, wet and pinch together the edges of the pastes, cut a slit in the centre of the top crust, through which the steam may escape, and bake in a quick oven forty-five minutes.

—Bliss, *Practical Cook Book* (1850), pp. 153–54

34. NO. 8. TART OR PUDDING PASTE

Rub one pound of butter into one and a half pounds of flour, with two tea-spoonfuls of salt; wet with cold water to a stiff paste, roll out to an eighth of an inch in thickness, brush beaten egg over it, sprinkle fine sugar upon it, and use it.

—Bliss, *Practical Cook Book* (1850), p. 151

Rather than collecting the berry juice in an upside-down teacup placed within the pie as Leslie and Hale recommend, Bliss thickens the juice by dredging the berries with flour. In her recipe for blackberry pie, virtu-ally identical to this one, Bliss notes that "ripe blackberries will not bear washing; pick them over nicely."

35. CRACKER APPLE PIE

Break in pieces one and half soda crackers, or one Boston cracker, and turn on a teacup of cold water. Let it stand while making the paste. Put it in a pie plate with a little nutmeg. Add a cup of sugar and the juice of one lemon—vinegar *may* do—and bake. *A real apple pie.*

—Webster, *Improved Housewife* (1855), p. 96

Not really. Crackers are used in various substitute capacities in nine-teenth-century New England cooking. For example, Howland suggests using "crackers, pounded fine," in place of eggs in a pumpkin pie recipe. We give additional specimens in the next chapter. The tradition contin-ues with the "Ritz Mock Apple Pie," now somewhat of a classic in its own odd way. A Boston cracker was simply a larger soda or common cracker.

36. POOR MAN'S PIE

Butter a pie plate; fill it with sliced apple, and put a crust over it. Bake it, and when done turn it over on to another plate. Sprinkle on the apple a little sugar and nutmeg, and serve hot.

—*Aunt Mary's New England Cook Book* (1881), p. 31

Bliss also includes a recipe for this very basic single-crust apple pie, which she says is sometimes called (for obvious reasons) "Turn-under Pie."

Cream and Custard Pies

In New England, cream and custard pies are perennial favorites of the holiday table, the church supper, and the scout-troop bake sale. Many of the pies in this chapter have included a cream or custard component mixed with a fruit or vegetable—for instance, pumpkin or Marlborough pie.

In the eighteenth century, creams and custards, with and without pie crust, often enriched with ground almonds, lemon peel, wine, and currants, came into their own in English cooking. They had a long pedigree. Sweetened curds with cream and cinnamon (called bonny-clabber by the Irish), "fresh cheese" (creamy curds with nutmeg, rosewater, and cinnamon—the name is perhaps a corruption of "French cheese"), spiced curd tarts, curds with eggs and currants—these were all seventeenth-century English favorites. By the middle of that century, "cheesecakes" were sometimes made without the traditional cheese curds. A mixture of eggs, butter, flour, and sweetened, unrenneted cream took their place. A few decades later, versions of these treats flavored with lemons or Seville oranges came into vogue. Behind all these variations was Anglo-Norman cooking. In medieval France, darioles (dariole molds are still sold), small pastry-lined custard tarts of egg, milk, sugar, cinnamon, and rosewater, were served at weddings. All these dishes descended ultimately from the egg dishes of ancient Rome.

But a more proximate and practical reality also underlay cooked creams and custards—the fear of unboiled milk. In the pre-pasteurization age, suspicions of fresh dairy products were rife, as Andrew Boorde attested: "Raw cream undecocted, eaten with strawberries or hurts [blueberries], is a rural man's banquet. I have known such banquets hath put men in jeopardy of their lives."

This was the route by which such desserts made their way to the New England table. The next time you eat a custard tart, a slice of coconut cream pie, or a cream puff, you might think back to the Elizabethans, or further back to the Romans, who enjoyed similar dishes.

37. ANOTHER WAY TO MAKE CHEESE-CAKES

Take a gallon of new Milk, set it as for a Cheese, and gently whey it; then break it in a Mortar, put to it the yolks of six Eggs, four of the whites, sweeten it to your

Taste; put in a grated Nutmeg, some Rose-water and Sack; mix these together, and set it over the Fire, a quart of Cream and make it into a Hasty-pudding, and mix that with it very well, and fill your Pattipans just as they are going into the Oven. Your Oven must be ready that you may not stay for that; when they rise well up, they are enough. Make your Paste thus:

    Take about a pound of Flour, and strew into it three spoonfuls of Loaf-Sugar beaten and sifted, and rub into it a pound of Butter, one Egg, and a spoonful of Rose-water, the rest cold fair Water; make it into a Paste, roll it very thin, and put it into your Pans, and fill them almost full.

            —Smith, *Compleat Housewife* (1728), pp. 105–6

A hundred years after Smith, Beecher emphasizes that once the curd is formed, it must be broken "gently . . . to make the whey separate. If this is not done gently, the milk runs off, the whey turns white, and the cheese is injured. The greener the whey, the better the cheese." This procedure is assumed in Smith's directions to "gently whey" the milk. Smith also offers a slightly richer cheesecake made with nine egg yolks. The six yolks and four whites in this recipe are inexplicably absent from a modern reprint based on the fifteenth edition.

38. TO MAKE ALMOND CHEESE-CAKES

Take four Ounces of Jordan Almonds, blanch them and put them into cold Water, beat them with Rose Water in a Marble Mortar, or Wood Bowl, with a Wood Pestle, put to it four Ounces of Sugar, and the Yolks of four Eggs beat fine, work it in the Mortar or Bowl, 'till it becomes White and Frothy, make a rich Puff Paste, which must be made thus: Take half a Pound of Flour, a quarter of a Pound of Butter, rub a little of the Butter into the Flour, mix it stiff with a little cold Water, then roll your Paste straight out, strew over a little Flour, and lay over in thin Bits, one Third of your Butter, throw a little more Flour over the Butter, do so for three Times, then put your Paste in your Tins, fill them and grate Sugar over them, and bake them in a gentle Oven.

        —Raffald, *Experienced English House-keeper* (1769), p. 236

Raffald explains how to make a rough approximation of almond milk, a venerable alternative to cow's or sheep's milk, used in the Middle Ages on fasting occasions. While Raffald simply pulverizes blanched almonds mixed with water and seasoned with rosewater, medieval cooks would have taken the extra step of straining the liquid to produce a rich almond milk. Smith also provides a recipe for almond cheesecakes in which the almonds are blanched, pounded, and softened with water but not strained. Raffald's Jordan almonds, not from Jordan but rather from Spain (a corruption of *jardín*, Spanish for "garden"), are the large variety and not, of course, candied as we find them today. These "cheesecakes" are an example of the kind made without cheese.

39. TO MAKE A BEEST CUSTARD

Take a Pint of Beest, set it over the Fire, with a little Cinamon, or three Bay Leaves, let it be boiling hot, then take it off, and have ready mixed one Spoonful of Flour and a Spoonful of thick Cream, pour your hot Beest upon it by Degrees, mix it exceeding well together, and sweeten it to your Taste; you may either put it in Crusts or Cups, or bake it.

—Raffald, *Experienced English House-keeper* (1769), p. 235

Like the famous syllabub recipes of the seventeenth and eighteenth centuries that "recommended milking the cow directly on to the liquor in the syllabub pot" in order to create a head of froth, this recipe provides a glimpse of a time when the routines of agriculture and the cook's productions were in touch with each other. Beest, or beestings, is milk from the "first milking of a freshly calved cow." Davidson informs us that it "contains much more of the lactalbumin proteins than usual, so that it is thick when raw and sets to a custard when cooked." It was often used in cooking for the sick.

40. CUSTARD PIE

Beat seven eggs, sweeten a quart of rich milk, that has been boiled and cooled—a stick of cinnamon or a bit of lemon-peel should be boiled in it—sprinkle in a salt-spoon of salt, add the eggs, and a grated nutmeg, stirring the whole together.

Line two deep plates with good paste, set them in the oven three minutes to harden the crust; then pour in the custard and bake twenty minutes.

—Hale, *Good Housekeeper* (1841), p. 84

Hale reprinted this recipe in *Ladies' New Book of Cookery*, adding the following: "For these pies roll the paste rather thicker than for fruit pies, as there is only one crust. If the pie is large and deep, it will require to bake an hour in a brisk oven."

41. MOCK CREAM

Beat three eggs well, and add three heaping teaspoonfuls of sifted flour. Stir it into a pint and a half of boiling milk, add a salt spoon of salt, and sugar to your taste. Flavor with rose water, or essence of lemon.

This can be used for cream cakes, or pastry.

—Beecher, *Domestic Receipt-Book* (1846), pp. 110–11

When poured into a pastry shell, this becomes a custard pie. When used as the filling for a sponge cake, it becomes the famously misnamed Boston Cream Pie (see Chapter 14, #46). The only difference between Beecher's recipe and modern pastry cream is the flavoring.

42. ALMOND CHEESE CAKE

Three well-beaten eggs.

A pint of new milk, boiling while the eggs are mixed in.

Half a glass of wine, poured in while boiling.

On adding the wine, take it from the fire, strain off the whey, and put to the curds sifted white sugar, to your taste, three eggs, well beaten, a teaspoonful of rose water, half a pound of sweet almonds, and a dozen of bitter ones, all blanched and pounded, and sixteen even spoonfuls of melted butter. Pour this into patties lined with thin pastry. Ornament the top with Zante currants, and almonds cut in thin slips. Bake as soon as done.

—Beecher, *Domestic Receipt-Book* (1846), p. 171

This is not an almond cheesecake in the same sense as the eighteenth-century recipe above (#38), for Beecher does not substitute pounded almonds for cheese but rather supplements or flavors it with them. Beecher intends the first three eggs to thicken the boiling milk, adding richness to the curds. McGee explains that egg protein bonds and stretches when heated. Here, it serves to coagulate the liquid. He also points out that, as Beecher implies in her mixing instructions, overmixing cheesecakes (or any custard for that matter) introduces air bubbles that will fill with steam during baking, only to deflate as the cake cools. Bitter almonds, which contain prussic acid and can be poisonous if eaten in large quantities (as discussed in the commentary to #30), are used here as flavoring. As with other custards, this one should be put in the oven as soon as it is mixed. Thus Beecher's somewhat cryptic direction to "bake as soon as done."

43. CREAM PIES

Put on a pint of milk to boil. Break two eggs into a bowl, and add a cup of white sugar, half a cup of flour, and after beating well, stir into the milk just as it commences to boil; keep on stirring one way till it thickens; take it off, and flavor with vanilla, or any other flavor you may prefer.

Previous to making the cream, make the paste for three pies, roll out and cover your plates, then roll out and cover a second time, and bake. When baked, and while warm, separate the edges gently with a knife, and lift the upper from the lower paste; fill in the cream, and put on the upper paste.

—Knight, *Tit-Bits* (1864), p. 63

The use of an upper crust for a custard pie is unusual, as is the instruction to prebake the two crusts together, one on top of the other. This is the first occurrence of vanilla in our selection. Soon it would replace the traditional flavors of rosewater, orange water, and wine.

CHAPTER THIRTEEN

Puddings

Over the river, and through the wood—
Now grandmother's cap I spy!
Hurra for the fun!
Is the pudding done?
Hurra for the pumpkin pie!

*M*any of us, we suspect, grew up as we did with the idea that when cake, pie, or ice cream was not to be had for dessert, pudding was the ho-hum fallback offering for that part of the menu. All those little dishes filled with chocolate-, vanilla-, or tapioca-flavored glop that were always lying in wait at the end of the school lunch line. The only thing worse—even more boring in taste and creepy in consistency—was Jell-O.

Like other items in our cuisine (succotash, for example), this insipid culmination conceals a more complex history. Along with sausage, pudding came into existence as a means of utilizing all the parts of a slaughtered animal. The Romans made sausage by stuffing tubes fashioned from hollowed-out intestines with mixtures consisting of ground-up offal or other less desirable meats, fat, cereal grain, herbs, and spices. A product of the slaughter that didn't go into sausage was the slain creature's blood. But that which had sustained one life must not be thrown away. Rather, it must be used to sustain other lives. Perhaps this semi-sacred dimension of blood—explicitly sacralized in most religious traditions—was part of what prompted the Romans to develop a separate and distinct blood-based food: *botellus*, in which a mixture of the blood, egg yolks (also suggestive of foundational vitality), pine kernels, onions, leeks, and pepper was placed in intestinal casings similar to those used for sausage.

In the course of the Middle Ages, *botellus* made its way into France as *boudin* and into Britain as pudding. Medieval British puddings weren't that much different from their Roman ancestors. As C. Anne Wilson writes, "The animal's blood was blended with minced onion and diced fat, spiced with ginger, cloves and a little pepper, and stuffed into lengths of intestine." Evidence for the notion that eating blood pudding always amounted to a kind of informal sacrament is provided by the fact that such pudding became part of the menu for "high days and holidays."

The term "blood pudding" in the previous sentence suggests that more than one kind of pudding was consumed in medieval Britain. Along with sausage, stuffed with shredded or ground meat, and *boudin*, stuffed with blood, the Norman Conquest brought *andouilles* to Britain, "large guts stuffed with . . . chopped entrails and well-seasoned." From *andouilles* developed white puddings, as opposed to blood or black puddings, made with liver or other organ meats, or with chicken or veal. According to Karen Hess, by the fifteenth century, a grain component—bread crumbs or oatmeal—was much more prominent in white puddings made in England than in those made in France, "where such practice is regarded as adulteration." By this time as well, English white puddings regularly included suet, cream, eggs, and dried fruits, along with the meat and grain or bread, and sugar along with other spices. As the ongoing requirement of meatlessness during much of the year led to the elimination of the meat in many recipes, the future of English pudding as a semi-solidified, sweetened blend of dairy products and cereals began to emerge.

Two developments of the sixteenth and seventeenth centuries completed the distancing of pudding from its origins in animal slaughter. Each allowed the dish to be cooked without an animal-gut container, and from each arose practices that remained prevalent in both England and New England into the twentieth century. One of these innovations was that puddings began to be baked in the bread oven that was now to be found in many households. The association between pies and baking was so strong that baked puddings were often called pudding pies, as seen in #17 below. Many dishes called puddings were also baked with a pie crust and are now considered pies, as in the type of pumpkin pie for which New England is famous. Those dishes are omitted here and included instead in Chapter 12.

The other early modern innovation in English pudding cookery was that puddings began to be boiled in a bag or cloth instead of a pouch consisting of the lining of an animal's entrails. An early recipe utilizing a pudding cloth, one from 1617 for "Cambridge Pudding," was essentially the mother of what became "one of England's national dishes," boiled suet pudding. The second recipe below is a virtually identical version of this dish from later in the seventeenth century. Plain or fancy, boiled-bag suet pudding was essentially a dumpling (consisting of suet, bread crumbs, and flour, with or without enhancements) that could be cooked in the same pot with some meat and then eaten as the course preceding the meat course. (In suet and other puddings consumed early on in the meal, the element of sweetness tended to be minimized.) In the midst of World War II, writing "in defence of English cooking," George Orwell mused that "south of, say, Brussels, I do not imagine that you would succeed in getting hold of a suet pudding. In French there is not even a word that exactly translates 'suet.'"

Many other kinds of boiled pudding were called forth by the convenience and flexibility of the pudding bag, and it remained an essential tool in the Anglo-American kitchen until the middle of the nineteenth century, when it was supplanted by the metal steamer. Already by the end of the seventeenth century, pudding had become so basic to English foodways that "come in pudding-time" had become one of the standard forms of invitation. Pudding came to be held in such high regard that "pudding-time" took on the broader meaning of "a time when one is in luck; a favourable time."

This English expression pudding time as a synonym for dinner or meal time became current in the American colonies and persisted well into the nineteenth century. Just as roast beef and pudding was a staple of the

English diet in the eighteenth century, so was pudding and meat likely to be found on the dinner table of the typical middle-class New England family around this same time. At a central Massachusetts wedding early in the nineteenth century, the fare consisted of the classic John Bull combination of roast beef and pudding.

It is not at all surprising, then, that New England pudding cookery was largely derivative of English pudding cookery. The varieties of pudding, especially the sweet varieties, developed in the seventeenth and eighteenth centuries in England were the varieties found in the cookbooks of nineteenth-century New England. New England's only distinctive contributions to the genre were Indian pudding and perhaps a somewhat greater utilization of apples and other fresh fruit. But since English pudding was, according the seventeenth-century French observer Henri Misson, "an excellent thing . . . a manna that hits the palates of all sorts of people," it reflects no discredit on New England cooks that they chose to fashion their puddings after such a pattern. We invite you to prepare, and then assay the proof of, the puddings that follow.

Boiled or Steamed Puddings

1. TO MAKE A QUAKING PUDDING

Take a pint and somewhat more of thick Creame, ten Egges, put the whites of three, beat them very well with two spoonfuls of Rose-water; mingle with your Creame three spoonfuls of fine flower, mingle it so well, that there be no lumps in it, put it altogether, and season it according to your Tast; Butter a Cloth very well, and let it be thick that it may not run out, and let it boyle for half an hour as fast as you can, then take it up and make Sauce with Butter, Rose-water and Sugar, and serve it up.

You may stick some blanched Almonds upon it if you please.

—*Compleat Cook* (1658, 2nd ed.), p. 17

This non-suet boiled pudding was popular in the seventeenth century. Woolley offers two minutely varied versions, one under this name and one under the common alternative designation shaking pudding. Its popularity persisted into the eighteenth century, with Smith, Glasse, Raffald, Carter, and Gardiner all including it. More often than not, in these later recipes, bread crumbs are used instead of flour, and in the one quaking pudding recipe in our nineteenth-century New England sample, that of Webster, the bread component takes the form of slices of white bread, turning the dish into a boiled bread pudding.

2. TO MAKE A CAMBRIDGE-PUDDING

Take grated bread searced through a Cullender, then mix it with fine Flower, minced Dates, Currans, beaten Spice, Suet shred small, a little salt, sugar and rosewater, warm Cream and Eggs, with half their Whites; mould all these together with a little Yest, and make it up into a Loaf, but when you have made it in two parts, ready to clap together, make a deep hole in the one, and put in butter, then clap on the other, and close it well together, then butter a Cloth and tie it up hard, and put it into water which boiles apace, then serve it in with Sack, Butter and Sugar.

—Woolley, *Queen-like Closet* (1670), p. 118

As noted above, this recipe for boiled suet pudding, enhanced with dried fruit, sugar, and other spices, is similar to the one from earlier in the seventeenth century that helped inaugurate the pudding-cloth era in English and New England kitchens. Where quaking pudding shifted from flour to bread crumbs as it made its way from the seventeenth to the eighteenth century, this dish went in the opposite direction—from sieved bread to flour. In eighteenth-century suet pudding recipes, dried fruit is included in some instances and omitted in others.

3. TO MAKE PUDDINGS WITH HOGS LIGHTS

Parboil them very well, and mince them small with Suet of a Hog, then mix it with bread grated, and some Cream and Eggs, Nutmeg, Rosewater, Sugar and a little Salt, with some Currans, mingle them well together, and fill the Guts and boil them.

—Woolley, *Queen-like Closet* (1670), p. 139

Here's a traditional white pudding recipe in which the organ meat is retained, as is the animal-skin container. Half a century later, Smith offers four versions of hog liver pudding, all to be boiled in skins, but thereafter the instances of organ meat white pudding are few and far between. The title of one of Raffald's recipes, "White Puddings in Skins," indicates that by her day the use of the animal gut container had become a deviation from the norm. Raffald's recipe includes "hog's lard" (Woolley's "Suet of a Hog") but not hog's liver.

4. TO MAKE BLACK HOGS PUDDINGS

Boil all the Hogs harslet in about four or five gallons of Water until 'tis very tender; then take out all the Meat, and in that Liquor steep near a peck of Groats; put in the Groats as it boils, and let them boil a quarter of an hour; then take the Pot off the Fire, and cover it up very close, and let it stand five or six hours; chop two or three handfuls of Thyme, a little Savory, some Parsley, and Penny-royal, some Cloves and Mace beaten, a handful of Salt; then mix all these with half the Groats, and two quarts of Blood; put in most part of the Leaf of the Hog; cut it in square bits, like Dice, and some in long bits; fill your Guts, and put in the Fat as you like it; fill the Guts three quarters full; put your Puddings into a Kettle of boiling-water; let them boil an hour, and prick them with a Pin to keep them from breaking. Lay them on clean Straw when you take them up.

The other half of the Groats you may make into white Puddings for the Family; chop all the Meat very small, and shred two handfuls of Sage very fine, an ounce of Cloves and Mace finely beaten, and some Salt; work all together very well with a little Flour, and put into the large Guts: Boil them about an hour, and keep them and the Black near the Fire till used.

—Smith, *Compleat Housewife* (1728), pp. 89–90

This is the latest black pudding recipe in our sample. Harslet is a pig's entrails, leaf the layer of fat around its kidneys, and pennyroyal a mint (*Mentha pulegium*). In white pudding recipes, groats (which we previously encountered in Chapter 11, #3 and Chapter 12, #10) were a common alternative to bread crumbs, as was rice. The white pudding portion of Smith's recipe is unusual in its omission of a liquid component, which leaves the mixture less a pudding than a forcemeat.

5. A BOILED PLUMB-PUDDING

Take a Pound of Suet cut in little Pieces, not too fine, a Pound of Currants, and a Pound of Raisins stoned, eight Eggs, half the Whites, the Crumb of a Penny-loaf grated fine, half a Nutmeg grated, and a Tea Spoonful of beaten Ginger, a little Salt, a Pound of Flour, a Pint of Milk; beat the Eggs first, then half the Milk, beat them together, and by degrees stir in the Flour and Bread together, then the Suet, Spice and Fruit, and as much Milk as will mix it all well together and very thick; boil it five Hours.

—Glasse, *Art of Cookery* (1747), p. 69

A quick comparison with #2 above reveals that this famous English Christmas treat is simply boiled suet pudding with a rather higher proportion of dried fruit, which constitutes the "plum" component. As with all other suet puddings, boiling in a pudding cloth is understood. Plum pudding seems to have had a dual lineage. Wilson states that, in a pattern similar to what we have seen with mince pie (see Chapter 10, #30 and #33), "meatless plum pudding" emerged during the eighteenth century from "the traditional meaty plum pottage of Christmas." Glasse's is indeed one of the earliest published recipes and reappears—sans the bread crumbs—in several cookbooks of the 1780s and '90s. Strikingly, there is no sugar in this plum pudding. The only other version among our eighteenth-century sources, that of Carter, includes "a large spoonful of sugar" and calls for the same amount of suet but omits the bread crumbs and reduces the quantities of eggs, flour, and "plums."

6. A PENNY LOAF PUDDING, COMMONLY SO CALLED

Take a stale Roll or a piece of white Bread, according to the Size of your intended Pudding, & Grate the Bread into a clean Pan; then put to it a little Cinnamon, Cloves, Mace, a small Nutmeg, grated, candied Orange Peel or Citron cut into little Bits, a large glass of Brandy. Mix these Ingredients well together with a good many Currants well washed and pickt, and some approve of Almonds chopped small. To the above Ingredients you must add Sugar melted with about half a pound of Butter, or as much as will wet all the above Ingredients well through; then add the Yolks of six Eggs well beat and strained thro' a coarse hair Sieve. Boil it in a Cloth as you would Dumplins. A small time will boil it. You may make it of what Size you please, proportioning your Ingredients accordingly.

. . . For Sauce—a Glass of Wine, Sugar, and butter to which you may add Rosewater.

—Gardiner, *Family Receipts* (ca. 1770), p. 60

The ellipsis dots in our transcription of this recipe mark the point at which one of Gardiner's descendants entered the comment that "Mrs. G. never weighed her Spices Sugar or Butter for the above Pudding, but guessed at the proper Quantities. It is very rich and universally liked." We should think so.

This is our first instance of a boiled pudding in which the bread crumbs are not cut with flour or mixed with something else, such as hog liver, but perform solo as the central ingredient. "Penny loaf" was one of the categories used in the English Assize of Bread, the system of price regulation for this staple food that was in effect from the thirteenth century until 1815. In #5 above, boiled plum pudding, Glasse (one of the authors upon whom Gardiner regularly relies) specifies the bread crumbs to be used as those from a penny loaf, and Glasse does so as well in her six other recipes explicitly designated as bread puddings. The same is true of Gardiner's other principal source, Raffald, in her two bread puddings. However, if there was a type of boiled bread pudding that was given the name penny loaf pudding, it is not to be found in any of our sources.

7. A NICE INDIAN PUDDING

NO. 3. Salt a pint meal, wet with one quart milk, sweeten and put into a strong cloth, brass or bell metal vessel, stone or earthen pot, secure from wet and boil 12 hours.

Errata: A nice Indian pudding, NO. 3; boil only 6 hours.

—Simmons, *American Cookery* (Hartford, 1796), pp. 26, Advertisement

Here is the first published recipe for the boiled form of this distinctively American type of pudding, made with cornmeal, just as "No. 1" and "No. 2," given below, are the first published recipes for the baked form of it. If these latter are any guide, the unspecified sweetening element could be either sugar or molasses. Simmons's basic formula was followed by many later writers. Despite Simmons's reduction of her cooking time, Beecher's comment, "the longer it is boiled the better," pretty much summed up the general view. The addition of suet was frequently mentioned, of eggs and spices (such as ginger) less frequently. Child notes that some people include slices of apple, and versions of both boiled and baked Indian pudding with various kinds of fruit were commonplace, as seen in #10 and #33 below.

Note the variety of alternatives to the pudding cloth or bag that were being utilized early on in American pudding cookery. The standard method of complying with Simmons's instruction to "secure from wet" was to tie a cloth over the top of the metal, stone, or earthen vessel. Only Child (and Lee and Hale, who copied her recipe) followed Simmons in allowing for the possibility of boiling in something other than a bag. By the time steamers had replaced pudding cloths as the default option in pudding boiling, Indian pudding was almost exclusively baked.

8. FLOUR OR BATTER PUDDING AND CRANBERRY PUDDING

Common flour pudding, or batter pudding, is easily made. Those who live in the country can beat up five or six eggs with a quart of milk, and a little salt, with flour enough to make it just thick enough to pour without difficulty. Those who live in the city, and are obliged to buy eggs, can do with three eggs to a quart, and more flour in proportion. Boil about three quarters of an hour. . . .

A pint of cranberries stirred into a quart of batter, made like a batter pudding, but very little stiffer, is very nice, eaten with sweet sauce.

—Child, *American Frugal Housewife* (1833), pp. 61, 64

Batter pudding was developed in England in the eighteenth century. Glasse's version is seasoned with ginger and optionally enhanced with currants or prunes, while Carter puts in sugar along with nutmeg. In Hale, the fruit is fresh rather than dried. Beecher reverts to Child's relatively plain style. Child's sweet sauce is made with sweetened flour and water, butter, rosewater, and, "if you want to make it very nice," wine and grated nutmeg.

9. BREAD PUDDING

A nice pudding may be made of bits of bread. They should be crumbled and soaked in milk over night. In the morning, beat up three eggs with it, add a little salt, tie it up in a bag, or in a pan that will exclude every drop of water, and boil it little more than an hour. No puddings should be put into the pot, till the water boils. Bread prepared in the same way makes good plum-puddings. Milk enough to make it quite soft; four eggs; a little cinnamon; a spoonful of rose-water, or lemon-brandy, if you have it; a tea-cupful of molasses, or sugar to your taste, if you prefer it; a few dry, clean raisins, sprinkled in, and stirred up thoroughly, is all that is necessary. It should bake or boil two hours.

—Child, *American Frugal Housewife* (1833), p. 62

Once again Child helps her readers make ends meet with a bread pudding, and even a plum pudding, made as simply as possible. The enriched, or plum, version lacks the fat of suet or butter that is a constituent of even the simplest eighteenth-century bread puddings. Further evidence (were any needed) that Child sits at the rather light end of the economy/luxury scale is the fact that subsequent writers, such as Allen, call their recipes resembling Child's "plum" pudding bread pudding. When it reappears in Beecher, Child's boiled bread pudding in its simplest form is fit only to be served to "Invalids, or Young Children." Here we must agree with

Beecher: a boiled pudding of stale bread soaked in milk, salted, and mixed up with a few beaten eggs is best suited to the nursery or sickroom.

10. WHORTLEBERRY PUDDING

Whortleberries are good both in flour and Indian puddings. A pint of milk, with a little salt and a little molasses, stirred quite stiff with Indian meal, and a quart of berries stirred in gradually with a spoon, makes a good-sized pudding. Leave room for it to swell; and let it boil three hours.

—Child, *American Frugal Housewife* (1833), p. 64

We omit the second section of the recipe, which is simply #8 with whortleberries. In this boiled Indian pudding with fruit, Child leaves out the ginger that is found in her boiled Indian pudding without fruit. Hale's "Indian Fruit Pudding," which is drawn from both of Child's Indian pudding recipes, recommends either chopped sweet apples or whortleberries. Lee and Webster simply copy Child's whortleberry version. Boiled or baked, Indian pudding with berries was nostalgically recalled in late-nineteenth-century New England memoirs.

11. ENGLISH PLUM PUDDING

Mix well, one and a half pound of flour, with one of well prepared currants, one of stoned and fine chopped raisins, one of fine chopped beef suet, and twelve ounces of sifted sugar; add two teacups of brandy, eight eggs, a nutmeg, and a little salt; stir all well together; add a teacup of milk, and mix the whole thoroughly.

Prepare the cloth; bag, and tie the pudding moderately close, and boil six hours; sauce; mix butter, sugar, wine, and rose-water.

—Webster, *Improved Housewife* (1844), p. 84

Almost all New England cookbooks of the nineteenth century included one or more recipes for plum pudding. Most are, like this one, strictly derivative of English practice. They could be made with flour or bread crumbs or both, most often with flour, as was also beginning to be the case in Britain in the previous century (see #5 and commentary). Hale prefaces her recipe by referring to plum pudding as a Christmas specialty, as of course it was in Britain. It was also featured on New England Thanksgiving menus.

12. SUET PUDDING, NO. 2

Sift your meal, chop your suet, and put it in the middle of the meal; strew over a little salt, then pour on boiling water, and mix it very stiff; then soften it by putting in half a cup or more of molasses. Wet your bag in boiling water; put the pudding in and tie it up tight; have the water boiling hot when you put it in; boil it an hour and a half.

—Howland, *New England Economical Housekeeper* (1845), p. 34

Although the term "meal," unmodified, was sometimes used in relation to rye or Graham (unbolted wheat), it was used far more often to mean cornmeal, which is doubtless what Howland has in mind here. As noted in the commentary to #7, suet was often included in boiled Indian pudding. Howland here simply gives it additional prominence, turning Indian pudding into an American version of the unenhanced forms of English boiled suet pudding.

13. CHERRY PUDDING

Into ten table-spoonfuls of flour, break six eggs, with a large tea-spoonful of salt; stir the egg and flour together until the whole is moistened with the egg, and no lumps remain; then add gradually one pint of rich milk. Have ready one quart of ripe cherries, stoned, and well dredged with flour, and when you have stirred the other ingredients quite smooth, put in the cherries, stirring them lightly; pour the whole into a pudding cloth, previously scalded and dredged with flour, tie it up firmly, and put it into a pot of boiling water, with a plate at the bottom of the pot; let it boil hard one hour; serve with sweet sauce.

—Bliss, *Practical Cook Book* (1850), p. 125

This is an instance (along with #8) of a batter pudding with fruit added. There was also the boiled fruit pudding/dumpling, in which the fruit served as the filling for a puff paste or suet crust (see Chapter 12, #23). Puddings of this latter type date from the seventeenth century in Britain. Of Bliss's two boiled berry puddings, one is of the eighteenth-century batter-pudding type and one is of the seventeenth-century pudding/dumpling type. In her general comments on pudding cookery, Bliss explains that the purpose of putting a plate at the bottom of the pot when boiling a pudding is "to prevent the pudding from adhering to the pot."

Of her various sauces for puddings, her "Plain Cream Sauce," consisting of whipped cream, sugar, and grated nutmeg, is, she states, "excellent for boiled puddings"; her "Hot Wine Sauce" is similar to the enhanced form of Child's basic pudding sauce, described in the commentary to #8.

If baked, this recipe would amount to the popular modern dessert cherry clafouti.

14. EVE'S PUDDING

Soak half a pound of stale bread in milk enough to moisten it, add half a pound of good beef suet chopped fine, half a pound of chopped dried apples, half a pound of currants, five eggs well beaten, and the rind of a lemon grated; beat all well together, add a little salt, tie it firmly in a cloth previously scalded and dredged with flour; boil three hours; serve with sweet sauce; if the apples are sweet, serve with lemon sauce.

—Bliss, *Practical Cook Book* (1850), pp. 131–32

This plum pudding with apples appears in Rundell under this name and was frequently found thereafter in New England cookbooks. Beecher offers a baked version, while Lincoln's can be either boiled or baked. Bliss's "Lemon Cream Sauce" is made with milk, flour, sugar, egg yolks, lemon rind, and lemon juice.

15. RICE AND APPLE PUDDING

Wash two tea-cups of rice, and spread it on your pudding cloth, with a tea-spoonful of salt; lay a dozen apples pared, cored, and quartered, upon the rice; tie the cloth up, and boil one hour; serve with sweet sauce, or lemon cream.

—Bliss, *Practical Cook Book* (1850), p. 143

Rice pudding has remained a standard Anglo-American pudding type from the seventeenth century to the present, with boiled and baked versions being offered with roughly equal frequency until the latter part of the nineteenth century. The type of "economical rice pudding" given here was developed in the eighteenth century, when, as in a recipe in the 1737 cookbook *The Whole Duty of a Woman* (copied by Glasse and Carter), the fruit would usually be raisins or currants and, as also in the same recipe, the dish would usually be eaten with a melted butter and sugar sauce. In this New England version, apples take the place of raisins or currants. Other New England recipes suggest gooseberries, apples, currants, or sometimes no fruit at all. By contrast, richer varieties mash the cooked rice with egg yolks, sugar, and butter, before adding fruit, flavoring with lemon and nutmeg, and boiling. The sauce for the richer versions is itself richer, usually wine sauce. Bliss's simple but delicious sauces are those described in numbers 13–14.

16. BROWN BREAD PUDDING

To half a pound of stale brown bread, finely and lightly grated, add an equal weight of suet, chopped small, and of currants cleaned and dried, with half a salt-spoonful of salt, three ounces of sugar, the third of a small nutmeg grated, two ounces of candied peel, five well-beaten eggs, and a glass of brandy. Mix these ingredients thoroughly, and boil the pudding in a cloth for three hours and a half. Send wine sauce to table with it. The grated rind of a large lemon may be added with good effect.

—Hale, *Ladies' New Book of Cookery* (1852), p. 294

In the nineteenth century, "brown bread" could mean either rye and Indian bread or whole wheat bread (also called Graham bread). Both in this book and in her earlier *Good Housekeeper*, Hale uses the term only in the latter sense. So this is bread or plum pudding made with whole wheat bread.

Baked Puddings

17. TO BAKE A PUDDING PIE

Take a quart of the best *creame*, and set on the fier, and slice a loafe of the lightest white bread into thin slices, and put into it, and let it stand on the fier till the *milke* begin to rise: then take it off, and put it into a bason, and let it stand till it be cold: then put in the yelkes of foure eggs, and two whites, good store of *currants, suger, cinamon, cloues, mace,* and plenty of *Sheepes* suet finely shred, and a good season of *salt;* then trim your pot very well round about with *butter,* and so put in your pudding, and bake it sufficiently, then when you serue it, strow *suger* upon it.

—Markham, *Countrey Contentments* (1623), p. 110

Markham provides an example of the early-seventeenth-century pudding pie mentioned at the beginning of this chapter. He does not call for lining the baking dish with a crust, which Wilson notes was only "an occasional practice in the seventeenth century," becoming "a more frequent one in the eighteenth." And indeed Glasse says at the end of her similar recipe for "A Bread and Butter Pudding" that "a Puff-paste under does best."

According to Lehmann, Glasse's bread and butter pudding is a Whitepot, a dish that was made with either bread crumbs or rice. The recipe in Markham's book that succeeds this one is called "A Whitepot" and is made with rice, but this pudding pie made (like the Glasse bread and butter pudding) with slices of bread would also seem to qualify for the title. Both of the other seventeenth-century cookbooks in our sample (*Compleat Cook* and Woolley) contain recipes called "Devonshire White-pot" (Devonshire being famous for its cream) that are made with slices of "penny Loaf." Glasse actually includes two recipes explicitly named "White-pot," one made with sliced bread, the other with rice. The one made with bread echoes Markham's call for half the number of egg whites to yolks. Simmons offers a bread-based "Whitpot" that is covered with puff paste.

18. THE IPSWICH ALMOND PUDDING

Steep somewhat above three ounces of the crum of white bread, sliced in a pint and half of cream, or grate the bread; then beat half a pound of blanched almonds very fine till they do not glister, with a small quantity of perfum'd water, beat up the yolks of eight eggs and the whites of four; mix all well together, put in a quarter of a pound of white sugar; then set it into the oven, but stir in a little melted butter before you set it in; let it bake but half an hour.

—Smith, *Compleat Housewife* (1739), p. 120

Ground or beaten almonds were a frequent enhancement of both baked and boiled puddings. Smith's recipe is similar to Markham's pudding pie, with the almonds and "perfum'd water" replacing Markham's currants and spices. Dolby's minimal alteration of this recipe, copied by Lee, specifies the aromatic water as "orange-flower water" and lines the baking dish with paper. Baked almond pudding occurs not infrequently in later New England cookbooks.

19. A YORKSHIRE PUDDING

Take a Quart of Milk, four Eggs, and a little Salt, make it up into a thick Batter with Flour, like a Pancake Batter. You must have a good Piece of Meat at the Fire, take a Stew-pan and put some Dripping in, set it on the Fire, when it boils, pour in your Pudding, let it bake on the Fire till you think it is nigh enough, then turn a Plate upside-down in the Dripping-pan, that the Dripping may not be blacked;

set your Stew-pan on it under your Meat, and let the Dripping drop on the Pudding, and the Heat of the Fire come to it, to make it of a fine brown. When your Meat is done and set to Table, drain all the Fat from your Pudding, and set it on the Fire again to dry a little; then slide it as dry as you can into a Dish, melt some Butter, and pour into a Cup, and set in the Middle of the Pudding. It is an exceeding good Pudding, the Gravy of the Meat eats well with it.

—Glasse, *Art of Cookery* (1747), p. 69

This famous English specialty is a type of baked batter pudding. Like boiled plum pudding, it first became popular in the eighteenth century. Glasse's laudatory comment at the end of her recipe suggests that the dish was in her day not yet fully established as a standard item. Lee includes a Yorkshire pudding similar to Glasse's, taken from Kitchiner. Yorkshire pudding occurs only occasionally in subsequent nineteenth-century New England cookbooks. A version of the 1840s is designed to accompany meat roasted over a hearth fire; by the 1860s, the meat, along with the pudding, are baked in the oven of a cast iron range. And of course by the early twentieth century oven baking is the only game in town.

20. A RICE PUDDING

NO. 2. Boil 6 ounces rice in a quart milk, on a slow fire 'till tender, stir in one pound butter, interim beet 14 eggs, add to the pudding when cold with sugar, salt, rose-water and spices to your taste, adding raisins or currants, bake [one and half hour].

Errata: Rice pudding, NO. 2; for one pound butter, read half pound—for 14 eggs read 8.

—Simmons, *American Cookery* (Hartford, 1796), pp. 25, Advertisement

This is one of six rice puddings Simmons includes, all baked; the baking time for this one is the same as that for her "No. 1." The ingredients and procedures Simmons recommends here, heavy on the butter and eggs (though less heavy after the author's errata page was printed), had been standard for baked rice pudding since the seventeenth century. Indeed, there is little to distinguish these puddings from the rice-based Whitepots mentioned in #17. What have become the other staple starches in our modern diet—potatoes and pasta—also served as the basis for puddings in the eighteenth and nineteenth centuries (for potato pudding, see #22 commentary).

21. A NICE INDIAN PUDDING

NO. 1. 3 pints scalded milk, 7 spoons fine Indian meal, stir well together while hot, let stand till cooled; add 7 eggs, half pound raisins, 4 ounces butter, spice and sugar, bake one and half hour.

NO. 2. 3 pints scalded milk to one pint meal salted; cool, add 2 eggs, 4 ounces butter, sugar or molasses and spice q. s. [as much as needed] it will require two and half hours baking.

—Simmons, *American Cookery* (Hartford, 1796), p. 26

Into the twentieth century, baked Indian pudding was made according to recipes similar to these, especially the second one. Molasses became the mandatory sweetening agent. The raisins in the first recipe were not called for that often. Child would be the first to suggest adding cold milk just before baking, in order to create a layer of whey on the top of the pudding. According to a later writer, after baking and cooling, this whey "makes a most delicious jelly." We agree.

22. A CROOKNECK, OR WINTER SQUASH PUDDING

Core, boil and skin a good squash, and bruize it well; take 6 large apples, pared, cored, and stewed tender, mix together; add 6 or 7 spoonsful of dry bread or biscuit, rendered fine as meal, half pint milk or cream, 2 spoons of rose-water, 2 do. [ditto] wine, 5 or 6 eggs beaten and strained, nutmeg, salt and sugar to your taste, one spoon flour, beat all smartly together, bake.

The above is a good receipt for Pompkins, Potatoes or Yams, adding more moistening or milk and rose water, and to the two latter a few black or Lisbon currants, or dry whortleberries scattered in, will make it better.

—Simmons, *American Cookery* (Hartford, 1796), pp. 27–28

Although Simmons recommends this mixture for pumpkins and potatoes as well as for squash, she also offers other recipes for potato and pumpkin pudding—that for pumpkin is to be baked with a crust and is the primordial version of the classic custardy American pumpkin pie, which we have included as Chapter 12, #2. Potato puddings were made with mashed potatoes, either sweet or white.

23. BIRD'S NEST PUDDING

If you wish to make what is called 'bird's nest pudding,' prepare your custard,— take eight or ten pleasant apples, pare them, and dig out the core, but leave them whole, set them in a pudding dish, pour your custard over them, and bake them about thirty minutes.

—Child, *American Frugal Housewife* (1833), p. 63

Child's introductory phrasing suggests that this pudding, which was to become a standard of the New England pudding repertoire, was relatively new in her day. Her custard "sufficiently good for common use" is made with "five eggs to a quart of milk, sweetened with brown sugar, and spiced with cinnamon, or nutmeg, and very little salt." The mixture is boiled, then cooled, before being poured over the apples. In later recipes, various fillings—sugar, a mixture of sugar, cinnamon and mace, or a flour-and-water paste enhanced with currants—were inserted into the hollows of the cored apples.

24. ARROW-ROOT PUDDING

From a quart of new milk take a small tea-cupful, and mix it with two large spoonfuls of arrow-root. Boil the remainder of the milk, and stir it amongst the arrow-root; add, when nearly cold, four well-beaten yolks of eggs, with two ounces of pounded loaf sugar, and the same of fresh butter broken into small bits; season with grated nutmeg. Mix it well together, and bake it in a buttered dish fifteen or twenty minutes.

—Lee, *Cook's Own Book* (1832), p. 157

Arrowroot is a starch made from the roots of *Maranta arundinacea*, a plant native to the West Indies and South America that is now grown elsewhere as well. It was exported to Britain beginning in the 1820s, where recipes soon began to appear for "American or West Indian blancmange" made with it. This was prepared in a manner similar to the operation outlined in the first part of this recipe. Lee, here plagiarizing from Dalgairns, was in turn plundered by Hale. Bliss offers a version without sugar (a deficiency supplied by serving with a sweet cream sauce) and seasoned with cinnamon rather than nutmeg. Beecher includes the egg whites, "cut to a stiff froth." Arrowroot starch is, as Davidson explains, "a delicate product, with remarkably fine grains, and is therefore a traditional invalid food" and a traditional children's food as well. Recipes abound in nineteenth-century cookbooks for arrowroot blancmanges, custards, jellies, and gruels for children and the sick. Arrowroot pudding itself is associated with sustenance for infants and the infirm, being one of the many types of milk puddings, made with one "bland starch" or another, that became popular in both Britain and the United States in the nineteenth century.

25. TAPIOCA PUDDING

Put four table-spoonfuls of tapioca into a quart of milk, and let it remain all night, then put a spoonful of brandy, some lemon-peel, and a little spice; let them boil gently, add four eggs, and the whites well beaten, and a quarter of a pound of sugar. Bake it.

—Lee, *Cook's Own Book* (1832), p. 166

Tapioca, made from cassava root, is the variety of milk pudding that has endured into our own day. Davidson remarks that baked tapioca pudding is "substantially improved" by adding the sorts of ingredients Lee, from Dolby, calls for here. We find the brandy a particularly felicitous enhancement, one that cannot of course be allowed into the tapioca puddings found on school lunch menus. The trend in subsequent nineteenth-century tapioca puddings was toward blandness, although Beecher and Webster did include wine in their versions, which are virtually identical. The last recipe in Beecher's book is actually one for a variety of tapioca pudding without eggs or milk that she grandiosely calls "the Queen of all Puddings." It turns out to be Bird's Nest Pudding with a solution of tapioca and water providing the custard. Later on in the nineteenth century, this came to be called Apple Tapioca Pudding.

26. BOSTON BEST

Mix with four quarts of milk, eight well beaten eggs; make this mixture quite thick, with stale bread, and four pounds of the best box raisins, adding sugar enough to make it *very* sweet, a little salt, and spices to the taste. Seed and flour the raisins. Bake about an hour and a half, or till done: it is excellent when cold.

—Webster, *Improved Housewife* (1844), p. 86

It had better be excellent when cold, since with her gallon of milk and four pounds of raisins, Webster has you make enough to feed an army. In the pudding domain, the honorific Boston was more often applied to various types of apple preparations, either of the boiled dumpling type or of the baked-with-a-crust type that we would now consider pie, than to bread puddings such as this one.

27. QUINCE PUDDING

Take six large ripe quinces; pare them, and cut out all the blemishes. Then scrape them to a pulp, and mix the pulp with half a pint of cream, and a half a pound of powdered sugar, stirring them together very hard. Beat the yolks of seven eggs, (omitting all the whites except two,) and stir them gradually into the mixture, adding two wine-glasses of rose-water. Stir the whole well together, and bake it in a buttered dish three quarters of an hour. Grate sugar over it when cold.

—Howland, *New England Economical Housekeeper* (1845), p. 38

Here we have another item that goes back to eighteenth-century Britain and that was kept alive in nineteenth-century New England. Glasse copied her recipe for this pudding from one of her sources. She was in turn plagiarized by Carter and, in nineteenth-century New England, by Allen. Beecher's and Hale's recipes each differ only in a few details from Howland's. Meanwhile, Lee (i.e., Dolby) offered a boiled bag version that was copied by Webster. Apparently, quince pudding recipes, like quince pudding itself, were too tempting to resist.

28. GREEN CORN PUDDING

Twelve ears of corn, grated. Sweet corn is best.
One pint and a half of milk.
Four well-beaten eggs.
One tea-cup and a half of sugar.
Mix the above, and bake it three hours in a buttered dish. More sugar is needed if common corn is used.

—Beecher, *Domestic Receipt-Book* (1846), p. 114

Despite Beecher's emphasis on sweetness, this custardy pudding was made without sugar as well as with it, although in such cases some sort of sweet sauce was usually recommended. For us, of course, corn custard or pudding has become a savory dish only.

29. COCOANUT PUDDING

Three quarters of a pound of grated cocoanut.
One quarter of a pound of butter.
One pound of sugar.
One half pint of cream.
Nine eggs.
One gill of rose water.

Stir the butter and sugar as for cake, add the eggs well beaten. Grate the co-coanuts, and stir it in with the butter and eggs. Put in the other ingredients, and bake with or without a crust.

It requires three quarters of an hour for baking. Some persons grate in stale rusk, or sponge cake.

—Beecher, *Domestic Receipt-Book* (1846), p. 124

Marco Polo alerted the European world to the existence of coconuts, which are probably native to the East Indies. They were widely culti-vated in the Western Hemisphere after their introduction by the Spanish and Portuguese. Baked with a bottom crust and topped with whipped cream, this is that favorite of our day, coconut cream pie. Recipes for this pudding, some with a crust and some without, are found in the majority of nineteenth-century New England cookbooks, from Lee onward. Leslie includes two recipes in *Directions for Cookery*, one with the grated rusk or sponge cake that Beecher gives as an optional addition. In a later edition of her work, Webster copied Beecher's recipe, one of the few instances in which the "borrowing" went in that direction. Personally, we can blame no one for wishing to promulgate coconut cream pudding. Samuel Johnson, in his 1755 *Dictionary*, is responsible for the spelling "cocoa-nut" (sometimes "cocoa-nut" or "cocoa nut") that was used in all these nineteenth-century sources. These forms, especially the hyphenated and two-word ones, suggest that the spelling may have arisen from some sort of confusion with "cocoa," itself a corruption of the Spanish *cacao*.

30. RASPBERRY PUDDING

Beat, until very light, six eggs with a quarter of a pound of fine sugar; mix a quar-ter of a pound of sugar with a quart of ripe raspberries, and add to the eggs and sugar, with a pint of cream and four spoonfuls of sifted flour, mix gently, grate nutmeg over the top, bake in a moderate oven half an hour, serve cold.

Similar puddings may be made with currants, adding a larger quantity of sugar.

—Bliss, *Practical Cook Book* (1850), p. 141

This cross between a custard and a baked batter pudding is exceedingly sweet and rich. Similar puddings may be made with currants, but believe us they won't be similar.

31. SAGO PUDDING

Wash a tea-cup of sago in cold water, soak it in one quart of milk; when the sago has absorbed half the milk, set the dish which contains the sago into a kettle of boiling water and let it scald; add a bit of butter, cover the sago closely, and let it cool; when cold, add three eggs well beaten, three table-spoonfuls of sugar, one table-spoonful of rose-water, a little salt, and a tea-cup of cold milk; stir all well together, and bake in a buttered dish forty-five minutes.

—Bliss, *Practical Cook Book* (1850), pp. 144–45

Like arrowroot and tapioca, sago is another light starch—made from the stems of palm trees—that was considered a useful ingredient in preparing food for invalids. Imported into Britain beginning in the late seventeenth century, it had turned up in New England by 1755, when, rather than being put to medicinal purposes, it figured in a murder plot. "Phillis" and "Phebe," the slave cooks of John Codman of Charlestown, Massachusetts, a saddler, sea captain, and merchant, were executed in that year for poisoning their master by adding arsenic to the "water-gruel," enhanced with "sagoe" and "plumbs," that they daily prepared for him.

Back in Britain, sago had become the basis for puddings by the 1740s, when Glasse included a recipe copied from another author, who had published it not long before. Sago's pudding career in New England begins with Lee, who provides both baked (from Dalgairns) and boiled (from Dolby) versions. Other authors besides Bliss who give recipes for sago pudding include Howland (four versions, one a Bird's Nest Pudding with a sago custard), Webster, Beecher (two versions, one differing from Webster in only a few details), Hale (closely based on the Lee/Dalgairns baked version), and Turner.

32. FLOUR AND INDIAN PUDDING

Four table-spoonfuls of flour, four of Indian meal, four eggs, one quart of boiling milk, one cup of molasses, one teaspoonful of salt; pour a cup of cream over it just before it goes into the oven. Bake three hours.

—Mann, *Christianity in the Kitchen* (1857), p. 66

Just as the "third bread" found in many cookbooks adds wheat flour to a recipe that traditionally relies on cornmeal and rye, so here Mann proposes adding wheat flour to cornmeal-based Indian pudding. As mentioned in the commentary to #21, the milk or cream poured over the top just before baking is designed to produce a coating of whey.

33. YANKEE PUDDING

One quart of milk boiled, one pint Indian meal, two cups of molasses, a dozen sweet apples cut in small pieces, and bake it with a steady fire three hours.

—Knight, *Tit-Bits* (1864), pp. 45–46

The Yankee-ness of this simple pudding consists presumably in the facts both that it is an Indian pudding and that it uses apples. As seen in the commentaries to #7 and #10, earlier writers such as Child and Hale had suggested putting apples in boiled Indian pudding, without making a fuss about promulgating a regional specialty. Parloa has a similar baked recipe, enhanced with butter or suet, ginger, and nutmeg, which she calls simply Indian and Apple Pudding.

34. THANKSGIVING PUDDING

Pound twenty crackers fine, add five cups of milk, and let it swell. Beat well fourteen eggs, a pint bowl of sugar, tea cup of molasses, two small nutmegs, two tea spoonfuls of ground clove, three of ground cinnamon, two of salt, and half a tea spoonful of soda, and add to the cracker lastly a pint bowl heaped of raisins, and citron if you like. This quantity will make two puddings.

—Knight, *Tit-Bits* (1864), p. 57

Knight neglects to mention how the two puddings are to be cooked, but almost certainly they are to be baked. Beginning with Child, many New England cookbooks include recipes for cracker plum pudding, most often baked for about two hours, which is probably a safe guess here. Knight follows Child in pulverizing the crackers, as do most subsequent recipes. In a few others, however, the crackers are split open, spread with butter, and layered with the raisins, all of which constituted a long-established procedure with the type of bread and butter pudding mentioned in #17. Whether the puddings served at New England Thanksgivings (see #11) were more often the traditional boiled bread plum pudding or this baked cracker plum pudding we do not know. New England cookbooks also found room for baked bread plum pudding.

35. DELICATE INDIAN PUDDING

One quart of milk, two heaping table-spoonfuls of Indian meal, four of sugar, one of butter, three eggs, one teaspoonful of salt. Boil the milk in the double boiler. Sprinkle the meal into it, stirring all the while. Cook twelve minutes, stirring often. Beat together the eggs, salt, sugar and half a teaspoonful of ginger. Stir the butter into the meal and milk. Pour this gradually on the egg mixture. Bake slowly one hour.

—Parloa, *Miss Parloa's New Cook Book* (1882), p. 267

The term "delicate" in a nineteenth-century New England cookbook usually indicates that egg whites are featured. That is not the case here. Parloa's pudding is perhaps delicate because it uses sugar (instead of molasses), eggs, and butter. In these ways it hearkens back to the first of Simmons's two recipes for baked Indian pudding (see #21).

In the heyday of the Indian pudding, this recipe had legs, as the journalists say, despite its misuse of the term "delicate." It reappeared in a souvenir collection from the 1893 Chicago Columbian Exposition signed by "Mrs. S. W. McLaughlin of North Dakota." With proper attribution to Parloa, it was also taken up by the suffragists in one of their charitable cookbooks. It even showed up in a cookbook associated with the White House.

36. CHOCOLATE PUDDING

Soak one-half cup dry or one cup of stale bread-crumbs in one pint of milk. To this add one level tablespoon of cocoa stirred in a quarter of a cup of sugar, and one beaten egg. Bake in a shallow pudding dish until firm throughout. Serve either hot or cold, with whipped cream, sweetened, and flavored with vanilla.

—Lincoln and Barrows, *Home Science Cook Book* (1911), p. 170

Although Leslie offered a recipe as early as 1847, chocolate pudding did not become a standard type until the last quarter of the nineteenth century. Leslie's version, like most today, is a custard. Yet into the twentieth century, as we see here, recipes with this name were about as likely to be made with bread as without it.

CHAPTER FOURTEEN

Breads and Cakes

Caroline Howard King, reminiscing about the foods of her Salem, Massachusetts, childhood in the 1820s and '30s, recounts that "pancakes also were great favorites, made of batter, sometimes raised with new-fallen snow, and eaten with sugar and wine or lemon. Then for tea, we had flapjacks, which were large griddle cakes often made with rice, which were cut in four quarters and eaten with powdered sugar and cinnamon. And pandowdy, a dark brown mixture of baked bread and apples, rich with spices, and sweetened with molasses. And brewis, which was little crusty bits of brownbread stewed in cream, and best of all every Sunday night a 'nimble cake,' light and flaky, which was baked on a board before an open fire . . . and in winter always buckwheat cakes every morning."

348

As King's account illustrates, milled cereals such as rice, wheat, and buckwheat (as well as corn, which we will discuss below) were regularly transformed into mouthwatering pancakes and bread puddings. King and her contemporaries happily consumed flapjacks, fire cakes, and brewis throughout the day, with fruit, spices, sweeteners, and sweet wine added to the batter. The appeal of these readily prepared treats is easy to understand.

Using bread crumbs and grains to thicken and flavor dishes was nothing new, as we've just seen with puddings. Frumenty, a wheat porridge made with meat broth or milk; wine possets made up with bread crumbs and egg whites; and crisp gingerbread of fine wheat crumbs, honey, and spices were among the glories of the English diet. The taste for porridge-like mixtures that included wheat, barley, or oats was brought by the first settlers to Plymouth and Massachusetts Bay. But in the harsh weather and harsher soil of their new home, the English found that their favorite grains did not grow well. So the old formulas for the best foods were quickly adapted for use with the one field crop that not only withstood the region's environmental challenges but flourished—Indian corn.

John Winthrop Jr. reports regarding "sampe," that simple dish of hulled and stewed corn that makes an appearance in these pages as Chapter 5, #9: "This was the most common diet of the planters, at the first beginning of planting in these parts and is still in use amongst them . . . [Samp] into which if Milke, or butter be put either with Sugar or without, it is a food very pleasant and wholesome . . . after it is Cold it groweth thicker, and it is Eaten commonly by mixing a good Quantity of Milke amongst it."

We might be excused for taking Winthrop's endorsement of this "very pleasant and wholesome" food (which grows even thicker when cold!) with a grain of salt—not to mention with milk, butter, and sugar. But a positive association was formed between this stick-to-your-ribs dish and New Englanders' stick-to-itiveness.

Thus Winthrop would have had no trouble in recognizing a twentieth-century New England recipe for "Hominy Cakes." These were composed of cold, leftover hominy (as discussed in Chapter 5, a de-germed and de-hulled gritlike corn dish), beaten eggs, and butter, the whole thing fried "like griddle cakes." These "cakes," like the frumenties, brewis, hearth breads, and samps they are related to, illustrate that the culinary distinctions we take for granted were not always so firm. For countless generations of New England cooks, cake, bread, and even puddings were categories as fluid as the batters of which they were made.

Despite their appeal, these slighter products of the hearth and stove always played second fiddle to the most desirable of grain-based foods— oven-baked yeast breads made with wheat. Unfortunately, the region's yearning for wheat bread to accompany the evening's salt pork or the morning's fried fish was not matched by a favorable climate and topography. Rye and barley grew fairly well, but even these grains failed to thrive as they had in Britain. The one grain that grew readily was native Indian corn, and so the New England tradition of making the most of it, both literally and figuratively, took hold.

Among the first products of these conditions was an item of diet that became one of the most cherished, and occasionally vilified, foods of the region, a cross between the Old World yeast breads and the New World samps and hominies. This was a bread constructed of the unlikely combination of granular cornmeal and heavy rye flour, leavened with yeast, and occasionally baked for added flavor on a bed of oak or cabbage leaves. For obvious reasons it was known as Rye and Indian; more often it was simply ryaninjun. With vast stores of cornmeal and supplies of rye flour sufficient to the task, New England cooks developed an everyday bread that was nourishing, dependable . . . and incredibly heavy.

It was a far cry from their cherished wheaten loaves, but Rye and Indian's solidity (some would say its indigestibility) was in time touted by the region's inhabitants, who took a kind of perverse pride in their ability to thrive on it. John Winthrop Jr. called it "very good Bread." Baking it on a bed of oak or cabbage leaves only made it more, well, distinctive.

As might be guessed, the opening of the Erie Canal in 1825, which brought ample supplies of cheap wheat into New England, did not obliterate the regional affection for the rigorous old bread. It, like virtually every material artifact and family lineage in New England, seemed destined for preservation. Henry James condemned this tendency to ancestral adulation as "the dreariness of the purely genealogical passion" and joked about New Englanders' concern with "perpetuation of race, especially in the backward direction." Indeed, reverence for history seems to have gotten an early and permanent grip on the New England sensibility. Yet in the case of rye and Indian bread, its last incarnation was not some desiccated scion better left in the family crypt but a surprisingly lively, fat, and sweet offspring—none other than the molasses-soaked, raisin-studded, soft, dark loaf known as Steamed Boston Brown Bread.

The bread of necessity had been transformed into a delectable steamed pudding. But the changes didn't stop there. From their humble origins, New England cakes evolved into some of the finest examples of the baker's art. By the late nineteenth century the descendants of the stony Puritans were regularly turning out multilayered Molly Starks (named for the wife of Revolutionary War hero John Stark), fruit-filled Scripture Cakes, baked by solving riddles of Bible references, exuberantly frosted Mont Blancs (named with French élan for New Hampshire's White Mountains), and wine-drenched Tipsy Cakes, to name a few. Even Old Tippecanoe got a Harrison Cake.

It seems unlikely that the source of fine baking can be traced back to a lump of bread dough. But unlikely or not, that is where the culinary detective must begin in searching for the genesis of cake. Given the exigencies of climate and terrain, yeast breads themselves were often a triumph of civilization, not only in New England where wheat was scarce but also in Europe, where centuries would pass before ordinary people were assured of a decent daily bread of wheat flour, rather than a sodden loaf of weeds, seeds, and heavy rye or barley. The recipes in this chapter outline the surprises, challenges, and accomplishments that ultimately let us eat cake.

Leavened Breads

Included here are examples of the most common leavened breads of England and New England from the seventeenth to the late nineteenth centuries. Because successful bread-baking depended as much on a cook's knowledge as on her ingredients, we also include some of the tips that appeared in early cookbooks for maintaining a bakehouse and preserving a good supply of yeast.

1. OF BAKING MANCHETS

Now for the baking of bread of your simple meales, your best and principall bread is manchet, which you shall bake in this manner; first your meale being ground vpon the black stones if it be possible, which makes the whitest flower, and boulted through the finest boulting cloth, you shall put it into a clean Kimnel, and opening the flower hollow in the midst, put into it of the best Ale barme the quantity of three pints to a bushel of meale, with som salt to season it with: then put in your liquor reasonable warme, and kneade it very well together, both with your hands, and through the brake, or for want thereof, fould it in a cloth, and with your feete tread it a good space together, then letting it lie an howre or thereabouts to swel take it foorth and mould it into manchets, round, and flat, scorcht about the wast to giue it leaue to rise, and prick it with your knife in the top, and so put into the Ouen, and bake it with a gentle heate.

—Markham, *English Hus-wife* (1615), p. 126

In 1542, physician and writer Andrew Boorde summed up the bread lust shared by many in his paean to this type of loaf: "I do love manchet breade, and great loves [loaves] the whiche be well mowlded and thorowe baken, the brande abstracted and abjected; and that is good for all ages."

For a rendition of the manchet approximating Markham's whitest flour in color and texture, the modern editors of an eighteenth-century manuscript cookbook suggest using "4 parts plain wheatmeal flour to 1 part strong white flour." Plain wheatmeal is 85 percent extraction, in other words mostly whole grain (including the bran and germ); strong white flour is flour high in protein, what we might call bread flour.

Markham offers two additional bread recipes in his chapter on brewing and baking—"cheate bread" and "bread for your hinde seruants which is the coursest bread for mans vse." With his three breads, he reproduces the cereal hierarchy of his day, which corresponded to the social hierarchy. Despite minor differences of nomenclature, a general outline can be traced: a light wheaten loaf for the upper classes; a less refined wheat loaf or a mixed loaf of wheat and rye or wheat and barley for average people or everyday use; and a loaf made of a compound of the lesser bread grains, along with peas, weeds, and other fillers, for "the inferior kind of people to feed upon."

The kimnel Markham mentions is a tub used in the preparation of bread, meat, ale, and cheese; a brake, or break, is a primitive machine used to knead large quantities of dough. The original dough brake was similar to the toothed instrument used to break flax fibers, or as a 1567 passage describes, "a braake to knede dowe withall, or to brake live hempe." Ale barm is yeast "drawn off fermenting malt," as Davidson explains. It is thought to have been put to use as a leaven first by the ancient Celts. The word survives in the name of an Irish fruit bread, barm brack.

2. GENERALL OBSERVATIONS IN THE . . . BAKEHOUSE

. . . then in your Bake-house you shall haue a faire boulting house with large Pipes to boult meale in, faire troughes to lay leauen in and sweet safes to receiue your branne, you shall haue boulters, searses, raunges and meale siues of all sorts both fine and course, you shal haue fair tables to mould on, large ouens to bake in the soales [soles, i.e., floors] thereof rather of one or two intire stones then of many brickes and the mouth made narrow, square and easie to be close couered: as for your peeles, cole-rakes, mankins [maukins] and such like, though they be necessary yet they are of such general vse they need no further relation.

—Markham, *English Hus-wife* (1615), p. 128

Markham's comments on the bakehouse point up the constant and careful labor required to make a household's everyday bread. Firing the oven, sweeping out the ashes, and determining when different items should be inserted was an art of considerable importance: without such knowledge, foods could burn or remain uncooked. Hours after the initial white-hot temperature inside the bake oven had been reached and the largest breads, cakes, puddings, and pots of beans had been baked, smaller items such as tarts, custards, small cakes, and biscuits (cookies) comprised the second or third "bakings."

The pipe was a large hollow cylinder of wood or metal used to transport and store wine, cider, and other liquors. Markham's use of the term in connection with dry storage is less common. A pipe of wine typically contained two hogsheads, or 477 liters, but the measure varied somewhat with the kind of wine stored.

The 1615 text's printer's error, "mankins," was changed in the second edition (1623) to "maukins," a variant spelling of "malkins" in the sense of "a mop; a bundle of rags fastened to the end of a stick, especially for cleaning out a baker's oven." The printer's error may have arisen from the fact that there is a suggestive similarity between another meaning of "malkin" ("an impotent or effeminate man; a weakling") and the meaning of "mankin" as "a diminutive or puny man; a manikin."

A malkin as a mop might perplex those who recall the opening scene of Macbeth, in which the first witch cries: "I come, Graymalkin!" Malkin also meant cat, graymalkin (sometimes grimalkin) being a common Elizabethan name for a gray cat. But the word's primary meaning is as a name for an untidy, lower-class (even sluttish) woman, an association that Shakespeare probably meant to suggest when he put that exclamation in the mouth of a witch. Chaucer also uses malkin in this sense in the fifth Canterbury tale, "The Man of Law's Tale": "It wol nat come agayn. Namoore than wol Malkyns maydenhede, Whan she hath lost it in hir wantownesse." To bring the etymological tale full circle, the use of the term to describe a bundle of sooty rags tied to the end of a stick and resembling a woman's form suggests the word's first meaning.

3. TO MAKE FRENCH BREAD

Take half a peck of fine Flour; put to it six Yolks of Eggs, and four Whites, a little Salt, a pint of good Ale-yeast, and as much new Milk made a little warm, as will make it a thin light paste; stir it about with your Hand, but by no means knead it: then have ready six wooden quart Dishes, and fill them with Dough; let them stand a quarter of an hour to heave, and then turn them out into the Oven; and when they are baked, rasp them. The Oven must be quick.

—Smith, *Compleat Housewife* (1728), pp. 128–29

"French Bread," a wheat loaf enriched with milk and eggs or an egg-butter combination (more like a modern brioche than a modern baguette), is also found in Woolley. In the eighteenth century, it became a standard item. Smith's instruction to rasp the crust after baking the bread also appears in Glasse's similar recipe. However, it seems that the French themselves actually liked their crusts hard and didn't scrape them off their bread as the English did.

To avoid increasing the number of tough gluten strands in this subtle dough, Smith warns against kneading. Cursory mixing is an aerating technique often used with dense cakes (spice cakes, for instance) that Harold McGee describes as "ingredients stirred together with minimal incorporation of air." Counterintuitive as it may seem, the technique as it is used here allows the yeast to leaven ("heave") without coarsening these small (quart-sized), rich loaves.

In her recipe, by deferring the addition of the flour until after the other ingredients have been mixed into a foam, Glasse approximates another of McGee's techniques for keeping delicate cake batters aloft: "Flour is often added only after the foam is formed and then by gently folding it in, not beating, to avoid popping a large fraction of the bubbles, and to avoid developing gluten." Glasse also walks the tightrope between mixing to achieve sufficient gluten (after all, she is making bread) and refraining from mixing to avoid popping air bubbles (after all, she is making cake-like bread). Thus her advice for mixing and baking French bread dough: "Mix it well, but the less you work it the better, make it into Roles, and have a very quick Oven, but not to burn." Smith offers the same kind of advice: "Stir it about with your Hand, but by no means knead it" and "The Oven must be quick." In both Smith's and Glasse's balancing acts we see opulent yeast doughs being treated like, but not yet completely evolved into, sensitive cake batters.

4. A METHOD TO PRESERVE A LARGE STOCK OF YEAST, WHICH WILL KEEP AND BE OF USE FOR SEVERAL MONTHS, EITHER TO MAKE BREAD OR CAKES

When you have Yeast in Plenty, take a Quantity of it, stir and work it well with a Whisk until it becomes liquid and thin, then get a large wooden Platter, Cooler or Tub, clean and dry, and with a soft Brush lay a thin Layer of the Yeast on the Tub, and turn the Mouth downwards that no Dust may fall upon it, but so that the Air may get under to dry it. When that Coat is very dry, then lay on another Coat, and let it dry, and so go on to put one Coat upon another, till you have a sufficient Quantity, even to two or three Inches thick, to serve for several Months, always taking Care the Yeast in the Tub be very dry before you lay more on; when you have occasion to make Use of this Yeast, cut a Piece off, and lay it in warm Water, stir it together, and it will be fit for Use.

—Glasse, *Art of Cookery* (1747), p. 151

Home bakers with experience of the vagaries of yeast often express curiosity about the leavens available in colonial days. Most often, yeast was obtained from the dregs of wine and ale casks. (As mentioned in Chapter 2 and as seen in the following recipe, in early America yeast of this type was called "emptins" or "emptings.") Glasse provides insight into the struggle of householders to preserve the temperamental live ingredient that was essential to successful baking. Addressing this problem from another direction, Glasse also offers a recipe for sourdough, which is made from a leftover piece of dough (or batch of batter) that has been allowed to ferment to the sour stage.

5. FLOUR BREAD

Flour Bread should have a sponge set the night before. The sponge should be soft enough to pour; mixed with water, warm or cold, according to the temperature of the weather. One gill of lively yeast is enough to put into sponge for two loaves. I should judge about three pints of sponge would be right for two loaves. The warmth of the place in which the sponge is set, should be determined by the coldness of the weather. If your sponge looks frothy in the morning, it is a sign your bread will be good; if it does not rise, stir in a little more emptings; if it rises too much, taste of it, to see if it has any acid taste; if so, put in a tea-spoonful of pearlash when you mould in your flour; be sure the pearlash is well dissolved in water; if there are little lumps, your bread will be full of bitter spots. About an hour before your oven is ready, stir in flour into your sponge till it is stiff enough to lay on a well floured board or table. Knead it up pretty stiff, and put it into well greased pans, and let it stand in a cool or warm place, according to the weather. If the oven is ready, put them in fifteen or twenty minutes after the dough begins to rise up and crack; if the oven is not ready, move the pans to a cooler spot, to prevent the dough from becoming sour by too much rising. Common sized loaves will bake in three quarters of an hour. If they slip easily in the pans, it is a sign they are done. Some people do not set a soft sponge for flour bread; they knead it up all ready to put in the pans the night before, and leave it to rise. White bread and pies should not be set in the oven until the brown bread and beans have been in half an hour. If the oven be too hot, it will bind the crust so suddenly that the bread cannot rise; if it be too cold, the bread will fall. Flour bread should not be too stiff.

—Child, *American Frugal Housewife* (1833), pp. 77–78

Child calls her recipe "Flour Bread" because, as we shall see in recipes that follow, the most common bread of New England was still the Rye and Indian discussed in the introduction to this chapter, which was made without wheat flour.

Child's suggestion to shake the bread pan is still a good test of doneness. As noted in Chapter 6 (#8), a gill is equivalent to four ounces. A modern packet of active dry yeast weighs one-quarter ounce, making the amount of liquid yeast in Child's recipe approximately sixteen times the amount of dry yeast called for in the average modern two-loaf bread recipe! Obviously, she was not using sixteen times the yeast we use today, so how to explain the discrepancy? (Baking the bread for only three-quarters of an hour also implies that these were small loaves.) Elizabeth David solves the mystery by pointing out that homegrown wet yeasts of the sort used by Child varied greatly in efficacy. In general they were far less potent than the modern dry product.

6. GOOD EYE AND INDIAN, OR WHEAT AND INDIAN BREAD

Two thirds Indian scalded and cooled, one third wheat or rye, good yeast, made pretty hard, put into pans to rise; baked one hour and a half in a hot oven.

—*Cook Not Mad* (1830), p. 34

This recipe is cook's shorthand for the now obsolete daily bread of New England, baked from settlement through the nineteenth century. Corn, and to a lesser extent rye, lacks the network of gluten strands that, when inflated by the carbon dioxide released from yeast, causes wheat bread to rise so dramatically. With its heavy, glutenless grains, Rye and Indian required mixing by a skilled hand and a long time in a hot oven to bake. As the opening of the Erie Canal made wheat more plentiful and cheaper, many cookbooks began including wheat in Rye and Indian, as is optional here, or offering "Third Bread," made with equal parts cornmeal, rye, and wheat.

The pleasures of this loaf may be debated, but as the regional bread it was included in all the important New England cookbooks of the nineteenth century. Some authors strained to find something good to say about it. Hale, for instance, called it "a sweet and nourishing diet, and generally acceptable to children." "It is economical," she added, "and when wheat is scarce, is a pretty good substitute for dyspepsia bread." The last is a strange comment, given the bread's reputation for causing dyspepsia (indigestion).

7. BOSTON BROWN BREAD

Good brown bread is as worthy to be apostrophized in poetry as the Scotch pudding, in praise of which Burns was so eloquent. To make it, take three pints of rye meal, and the same of Indian meal. (If this is sweet and fresh, do not scald it. When Indian meal is bitter, it must be scalded, but if good, almost every article in which it is used is much lighter without.) If you have a little boiled pumpkin, or a few spoonfuls of winter squash left of the last dinner, add it; also half a teacup of molasses, two teaspoonfuls of salt and one of saleratus, and half a teacup of yeast. Mix it with warm water. If you have saved that in which green corn or squash have been boiled, use it as far as it will go. Make it as stiff as can be conveniently stirred with the hand. Grease two earthen or iron pans very thickly, and put the bread in them. Have a bowl of water at hand, and smooth over the top, dipping your hand into the water. It will rise faster than other bread, therefore should not be made over night in summer, and in winter should stand in a cool place until after the fire is kindled in the oven. It requires a hot oven, and long baking. If you bake in the forenoon, such a loaf as one of these, will be done for tea, but if later, it must stand till morning.

—Cornelius, *Young Housekeeper's Friend* (1846), pp. 28–29

The lineage of this recipe, which appears to have been exceedingly popular based on the number of writers who copied it, begins with Child's "Brown Bread." Hale, who often copied Child, copied her in this matter as well but called her recipe "Rye and Indian Bread." Cornelius also copied Child. Or she may have taken elements of the recipe from both Child and Hale. Or she may have based her cribbed version on yet another cribbed version that appeared in Beecher the same year this recipe was published. In this tangled tale of authorship, one thing is clear: both Cornelius and Beecher include two relatively new additions to the old recipe. One of these is saleratus, an improvement on the pearl ash mentioned by Child (#5) and a precursor of baking soda. The year before, another writer claimed that saleratus prevented bread from turning sour. The other new addition is molasses, which would become increasingly important in New England breads made with cornmeal. Not everyone was happy about this trend. Bliss states that molasses makes brown bread "unwholesome and unpalatable. Good Indian meal, and sweet rye flour, are much better without molasses than with."

Bliss was fighting a rearguard action on the molasses question. Most of the midcentury recipes for this bread call for molasses. Recipes including this ingredient even made their way into government reports and documents. In 1863, the inmates of the Boston House of Correction were fed molasses-laced brown or rye and Indian bread three days a week.

Just as frequently as molasses was being added to the loaf, "Boston" was being added to the name, as seen in the title of this recipe. And just as the molasses was designed to enhance the culinary appeal of the bread, so the regional tag added to the name was designed to enhance its prestige. Other signs that such a movement was afoot included one brown bread recipe which began, "Good brown bread is . . . worthy to be apostrophized in poetry" and another in which it was stated that "a person once accustomed to this bread will never willingly live without it." The governing board of the Boston House of Correction boasted that the bread served to their prisoners was "such as is found on the bill of fare at the New York and Western hotels, under the name of '*Boston brown bread.*'" Moreover, "bread from the same batch is used at the tables of the Superintendents and officers, and is esteemed a luxury."

A final note about the boiled pumpkin Cornelius suggests as an enhancement. This had been added to cornmeal-based breads and cakes since colonial times and had been recommended more recently by Joel Barlow and Child. Beecher has a recipe for "Pumpkin Bread" made with nothing but cornmeal, stewed pumpkin, salt, and yeast.

8. CONNECTICUT BROWN BREAD

One quart of barley water; pour over one quart of corn meal; let it stand until milk-warm. Then put in one quart of rye meal, one cupful of molasses and a small teaspoonful of soda and one pressed yeast cake. Mix in one-half a cupful of water and a teaspoonful of salt; stir it with a spoon, and let it stand two hours. Then knead up with a little wheat flour in loaves. Let it rise. If it is desired sweeter, put in more molasses. Bake one hour.

—*Meriden Cook Book* (1898?), pp. 63–64

This late Rye and Indian shows that even at the end of the nineteenth century the old bread remained a part of the New England baking tradition. The recommendation of barley water to soften the cornmeal is idiosyncratic to this community cookbook, but otherwise this is the standard Rye and Indian. The place name is a simple case of regional boosterism.

New England's Saturday Night Bread

We've stressed that by midcentury "the *brown bread of New England*," described as what "all of our New England farmers have on their tables every day," had acquired a healthy dose of molasses, although the loaf was still baked. Further experiments aimed at improving the region's austere bread were under way in New England kitchens. Cookbooks began to reflect these innovations with the addition of a new recipe called Steamed Brown Bread (a little later, Boston Brown Bread), which was based on the old brown bread, with some important differences. The most significant was the manner in which the bread was to be cooked. In the new recipe, the former baked dough was made slightly looser with the addition of sweet or sour milk and more molasses, then placed in a pudding container to be steamed, sometimes atop the kitchen's newest appliance, the cast iron cookstove. A dough of cornmeal and rye flour, water, a little molasses, and yeast or soda had become a batter of cornmeal and rye flour (sometimes with the addition wheat flour), lots of molasses, milk, and soda or yeast, which was steamed like pudding and sometimes finished like bread in the oven. Quite rapidly, because of its relation to the venerable Rye and Indian, this new loaf took on an antique aura. Admonitions such as this one offered by Ella Shannon Bowles and Dorothy S. Towle in 1947 implied that the new "old" bread could be made and served properly only by following a seemingly immutable set of rules: "It is very important to remember that brown bread should never be cut with a knife, it should be sliced with the aid of a string."

9. STEAMED BROWN BREAD

For a very small family, take half a pint of rye meal, not sifted, and a pint of sifted Indian meal, a pint of sour milk, a half a gill of molasses, a teaspoonful of salt, and a large teaspoonful of saleratus. Mix all the ingredients except the saleratus, dissolve that (as it should always be) in a little boiling water, and add it, stirring the mixture well. Grease a tin pudding pan, or a pail having a close lid, and having put the bread in it, set it into a kettle of boiling water. The bread should not quite fill the pail, as it must have room to swell. See that the water does not boil up to the top of the pail, and also take care it does not boil entirely away. The bread should be cooked at least four hours. To serve it, remove the lid, and set it a few minutes into the stove oven, without the lid, to dry the top; then it will turn out in perfect shape.

If used as a pudding, those who have cream, can make an excellent sauce for it of thick *sour* cream, by stirring into it plenty of sugar, and adding nutmeg. This bread is improved by being made, and put into the pan or pail in which it is to be boiled, two or three hours before it is set into the kettle. It is good toasted the next day.

—Cornelius, *Young Housekeeper's Friend* (1862), p. 31

This is the first cookbook recipe we have found for brown bread in steamed form. By suggesting that steamed brown bread may also be used as a pudding, Cornelius allows that the dish may be placed on the dessert table. The recipe was copied in 1912 by Helen S. Wright.

Another recipe with the same name that appeared in the February 1862 issue of a New England farming periodical (and that called for "sweet skim" rather than sour milk) may have preceded this one. In 1864, around the same time that those residing at the Boston jail were eating baked Boston Brown Bread, "Steamed Brown Bread" was on the Tuesday supper menu for the students at the Massachusetts State Reform School in Westborough. In none of these 1860s appearances in print is the dish in this steamed form called Boston Brown Bread. This title does not appear to have been conferred upon it with any frequency until the 1870s.

10. BOSTON BROWN BREAD

One heaping cupful each of rye, corn and Graham meal. Sift carefully together and mix thoroughly with two cupfuls of New Orleans molasses, two cupfuls of sweet milk, one cupful of sour milk, one dessertspoonful of soda and one teaspoonful of salt. Pour into a tin mold, place in a kettle of cold water and boil four hours. Do not quite fill the mold, as the bread expands in cooking. When ready to serve, remove the lid and place for a few moments in a hot oven.

—*Meriden Cook Book* (1898?), p. 63

For centuries molasses, the liquid by-product of the sugar refining process, had been shipped directly to New England and used in the region's many distilleries to make rum. Perhaps the Meriden cook who contributed this recipe wished to minimize this connection by recommending the use of New Orleans molasses. According to the *OED*, a dessertspoon holds more than a teaspoon and less than a tablespoon.

The presence of no fewer than four recipes for steamed brown bread in this turn-of-the-century community cookbook points up the bread's importance as both food and symbol. As one of the present authors can testify, in the 1950s and early '60s, Steamed Boston Brown Bread—the name by which it was then invariably known—kept steady company with baked beans on the Saturday evening supper table, even in non-Yankee New England homes.

Sweet Breads, Small Cakes, and Biscuits

As we chart the Anglo-American baking tradition from the dense brown breads of the poor and the soft yellow manchets of the rich in the Middle Ages, to the plum-filled, egg-raised cakes of the eighteenth century, and on to the airy, egg-and-baking-powder sponges that could be speedily turned out a century later, a discussion of the smaller wonders of the baker's art—buns, sweet breads, small cakes, biscuits, and cookies—can seem little more than a bothersome distraction. But along the path from the wheaten loaf to the modern layer cake, some delectable culinary spandrels came into being. Warm little confections of various shapes and flavors—what one New Englander called the "special preparations [that] come naturally between bread and cake"—were happy by-products of fired-up freestanding bread ovens. And, as Wilson remarks, an additional oven, a kind of "cupboard fitted with an iron door in the kitchen wall," became another place to bake such small items when wall fireplaces and coal fires were introduced in the seventeenth century.

Elizabeth David reminds us of the complex origins even of such seemingly simple sweet breads as the bun:

> Bath buns, hot cross buns, spice buns, penny buns, Chelsea buns, currant buns—all these 'small, soft, plump, sweet, fermented' cakes are English institutions. . . . The simple spiced fruit bun, the original of our Good Friday hot cross bun without the cross . . . first became popular in Tudor days, at the same period as the larger spice loaves or cakes, and were no doubt usually made from the same batch of spiced and butter-enriched fruit dough. For a long time bakers were permitted to offer these breads and buns for sale only on special occasions.

David cites a decree issued by the London Clerk of the Markets during Elizabeth I's reign to the effect that spice cakes, buns, biscuits, and other spice bread, "being bread out of size and not by law allowed," could not be baked except for burials, on Good Friday, and at Christmas, "upon pain of forfeiture of all such spiced bread to the poor." But under James I, the laws were gradually liberalized and bakers began turning out these much-desired little treats at all times of year.

Later in the seventeenth century, as the gentry began to occupy town houses in the growing cities, these novel gustatory pleasures began to appear more frequently on urban breakfast tables alongside the still somewhat exotic hot drinks—coffee, tea, and chocolate—that were also coming into fashion. Heavy ales, thick slices of brown or white bread, pickled fish, cold joints, and hot porridge still sat ready to hand on the sideboards in most middle- and upper-class households, but the trendsetters were looking to break their fast with something lighter and sweeter.

A typical morning menu served to the lord and lady of a Northumberland estate around 1512 draws the contrast more pointedly: "First a loaf of bread in trenchers, 2 manchets, a quart of beer, a quart of wine, 2 pieces of salt fish, 6 baconned herring, 4 white herring, or a dish of sprats." The earl's oldest children had the same. Even the family's two youngest offspring ate "a manchet, a quart of beer, a dish of butter, a piece of salt fish, a dish of sprats or 3 white herring." The sprats and herring had been preserved in thick, salty brine. It being Lent, this was a relatively light breakfast.

Of course, poorer people ate less, and less well. Nevertheless, for those who performed manual labor breakfast was often the most substantial meal of the day. A warm cereal pottage, based on locally grown barley, oatmeal, or wheat, set up many an English peasant, small farmer, or housewife for the day's work. The fortunate might add milk, broth, a bit of salt fish, or some shredded meat to the mixture; ale and beer were drunk at every meal.

The shift that occurred at the end of the seventeenth century, away from such hearty morning fare and toward snacklike repasts, was nothing less than the beginning of the beginning of the day as we know it. It stands to reason that urban elites, whose work did not require the solid sustenance needed for manual labor, enthusiastically adopted the new style of morning collation. (The gentry also tended to break its fast at a later hour.) Modern physicians and health experts may rail, but the sweet roll and hot drink for breakfast that came into fashion in the late 1600s are still very much with us, although they are now enjoyed by all classes.

Spiced sweet breads were served not only at other times of year than Good Friday and Christmas but also, their breakfast popularity notwithstanding, at other times of day. Understandably, then, the early-twentieth-century New Englander cited above had some difficulty in deciding exactly where to place them in her cookbook: "For convenient classification, they are grouped under the title of Fancy Breads, though they might as well be classed as Plain Cakes." Yet she was unhesitating in her recommendation of them: "They serve a good purpose for variety, for luncheon, etc."

11. TO MAKE BISKET BREAD

To make Bisket bread, take a pound of fine flower, and a pound of suger finely beaten and searssed, and mix them together: Then take eight egges and put foure yelkes and beate them very well together: then strow in your flower and suger as you are beating of it, by a little at once, it will take very neere an houres beating; then take halfe an ounce of Anisseedes and let them be dried and rubbed very cleane, and put them in; then rub your Bisket panes with cold sweet butter as thinne as you can, and so put it in and bake it in an ouen: But if you would haue thinne Cakes, then take fruit dishes and rub them in like sort with butter, and so bake your Cakes on them, and when they are almost bak't, turne them and thrust them downe close with your hand. Some to this Bisket bread will adde a little Creame and a few Coriander seedes cleane rubed, and it is not amisse but excellent good also.

—Markham, *English Hus-wife* (1615), p. 72

Seventeenth- and eighteenth-century biscuits were "various small sugar cakes. Also sponge cakes." Markham's modern editor, Michael R. Best, believes "put four yolks" is probably an error for "but four yolks." This would make twice the number of whites to yolks (eight whites to four yolks), which is a possibility given the dry, crisp texture desirable for these biscuits. However, it is more likely that Markham did not intend to use more whites than yolks but rather the reverse. As seen in the next recipe, seventeenth-century cookbooks include types of small sweet breads or cakes in which egg whites alone are used. But when whites and yolks are to be separated and then both used, as they frequently are, more yolks than whites are called for in the great majority of cases. As Kate Colquhoun explains, this is due to the fact that in the humoral theory of health and cooking egg whites were considered cold and viscous and as such were often discarded.

Note that Markham uses the terms "bread" and "cake" interchangeably. John Ayto points out that early English cakes, of which this biscuit bread is a good example, were round, flat, and hardened on both sides by being turned during baking. Although now we mostly distinguish cakes by sweetness rather than shape, it was "this basic shape that lies behind the transference of the name to other, completely different foods." There is still nomenclatural confusion between the terms—for instance, pancakes and quickbreads, such as banana bread, are sweet, while rye bread, fish cakes, and uranium cakes, such as those sought by former Ambassador Joseph Wilson in Niger, are not. But, as Ayto also explains, "in England the shape and contents of cakes were gradually converging toward our present understanding of the term."

12. TO MAKE IUMBALS

To make the best Iumbals, take the whites of three egges and beate them well and take of the viell; then take a little milke and a pound of fine wheat flower and suger together finely sifted, and a few Aniseeds well rubd and dried; and then worke all together as stiffe as you can worke it, and so make them in what formes you please and bake them in a soft ouen vpon white Papers.

—Markham, *English Hus-wife* (1615), pp. 71–72

The phrase "take of the viell" was changed in the 1631 edition of *The English Hovse-wife* (the title was also changed) to "take off the froth." In a much later recipe, but one also involving beaten egg whites, Simmons instructs her readers to "take off the froth with a spoon."

While Markham's instructions are somewhat unclear—is it a pound each of flour and sugar, or a pound together?—we can see that his jumbles are anise-flavored small cakes.

The *OED* defines *jumble* as "a kind of fine sweet cake or biscuit, formerly often made up in the form of rings or rolls." Davidson mentions that the cakes were also known as knots, the thin rolls of dough being intertwined before baking. According to both Wilson and Hess, the word derives from the Latin *gemel* (twin) and is also associated with "gimbel," a peculiar double-finger ring of the sixteenth century. Both also think that the earliest jumbles were not simple circles but interlaced rings or knots. Woolley says to "tie them in Knots" and Hess cites a 1678 source that describes jumbles as "wreathed in knots." The jumble is related both linguistically and culinarily to the Italian *ciambelline* and the French *gimblettes*. Among English variant spellings are the *jombil* (Thomas Dawson, 1585), *jumbolds* (Woolley, 1670), *jemelloes*, and *jamballs* (Robert May, 1671). As Davidson also points out, in North America the term *jumble* or *jumbal*, meaning entwined rings, became confused with its homonym *jumble*, meaning a mixture. Simmons calls sugar cakes "Tumbles" (given below, #18), a variation that seems to confirm Davidson's point.

Simmons's tumbles are caraway-flavored, but the *OED* maintains that in the United States the jumble is a thin, crisp cake flavored with lemon peel or sweet almonds. Perhaps the notion derives from the fact that lemon peel is found in a recipe Beeton calls "California jumbles." Did Beeton's version of this old English treat originate in the United States?

In 1923, G. K. Chesterton simultaneously described and eulogized the jumble as "a brown flexible cake now almost gone from us." Flexible in-deed! They have been variously described as a soft butter cookie, a sugar cake, and a hard spiced biscuit, flavored with anise, lemon, or almonds. Only Chesterton colors them brown.

By a "soft" oven, Markham means one that has cooled down. Putting white paper underneath the jumbles prevents them from being scorched on the bottom during baking.

Markham also gives a "finer" jumble, made with more sugar, "halfe a dish of sweet butter," and blanched almonds. He says they taste more like macaroons.

13. TO MAKE SHREWSBURY CAKES

Take two pound of floure dryed in the Oven and weighed after it is dryed, then put to it one pound of Butter that must be layd an hour or two in Rose-water, so done poure the Water from the Butter, and put the Butter to the flowre with the yolks and whites of five Eggs, two races of Ginger, and three quarters of a pound of Sugar, a little salt, grate your spice, and it well [will] be the better, knead all these together till you may rowle the past, then roule it forth with the top of a bowle, then prick them with a pin made of wood, or if you have a comb that hath not been used, that will do them quickly, and is best to that purpose, so bake them upon Pye plates, but not too much in the Oven, for the heat of the Plates will dry them very much, after they come forth of the Oven, you may cut them without the bowles of what bignesse or what fashion you please.

—*Compleat Cook* (1658, 2nd ed.), p. 59

In view of the existence of this recipe, Davidson is obviously mistaken in his assertion that the "earliest recorded recipe" for Shrewsbury Cakes is that of Smith in the eighteenth century. A recipe of Woolley's represents at least one other seventeenth-century cookbook example. Davidson describes Shrewsbury Cakes as "a kind of biscuit (indeed occasionally known as Shrewsbury biscuits) of the shortbread type, made from flour, sugar, and butter, circular, fairly thin, and with scalloped edges. They are flavoured with spices, and sometimes rosewater." Here we have the rosewater and "two races of Ginger" (race means root, from the French *racine*). Cutting the cakes "without the bowles" means forming them into circular shapes by tracing them around the outside of ("without") in-verted bowls.

At first, this cake was associated exclusively with Shrewsbury. In 1602

Lord Herbert of Cherbury (a village south of Shrewsbury) sent his guardian "a kind of cake which our countrey people use and [is] made in no place in England but in Shrewsbury." Herbert was to become a philosopher of some note (his brother was the poet George Herbert), and he turned the properties of the cake into symbols with which to ingratiate himself with his guardian: "Measure not my love by the substance of it, which is brittle, but by the form of it which is circular." In time, Shrewsbury cakes were enjoyed more widely. William Congreve knew that the audience for *The Way of the World* (1700) would understand the expression "as short as a Shrewsbury cake."

Davidson mentions that in *The Ingoldsby Legends*, a trove of nineteenth-century poems and fables, Shrewsbury Cake plays an unlikely part. To set the scene: the heroine Mary-Anne is at the moment keeping a hungry cur at bay by feeding it pastry as she hides under the stairs. Her nemesis is the scoundrel Bloudie Jacke, whose name is a refrain throughout the poem:

> She has given him a bun and a roll,
> Bloudie Jacke!
> She has given him a roll and a bun,
> And a Shrewsbury cake,
> Of Pailin's own make,
> Which she happen'd to take ere her run
> She begun—
> She'd been used to a luncheon at One.

Pailin, "Prince of cake-compounders," was the namesake of the famous "Pailin's Original Shrewsbury Cakes," a flourishing enterprise in the late nineteenth century. ("The mouth liquefies at thy very name," says the poet.) Strange, though, that the lass from Shropshire didn't bake her own Shrewsbury Cakes. In any case, the poem concludes with an admonition to young ladies to take care when walking out at night with young men, because "some time or another, they'll make / A Mistake! / And lose—more than a Shrewsberrie Cake!!"

Shrewsbury Cakes were a standard item in eighteenth-century cookbooks. Smith, Glasse, and Raffald all include them, as does Simmons. There were minor variations. Glasse's rendering is sweeter than Smith's, and she uses cream, Smith butter. One of Raffald's versions is spiced with caraway seeds, the other with mace. Simmons is based on Raffald. In New England, Shrewsbury Cakes continued to appear into the nineteenth century, although in some cases their small size was forgotten. Beecher presents such a recipe. Otherwise, hers is the standard Shrewsbury Cake, flavored with rosewater and lemon peel.

14. TO MAKE BUNS

Take two pounds of fine Flour, a pint of Ale-yeast; put a little Sack in the Yeast, and three Eggs beaten; knead all these together with a little warm Milk, a little Nutmeg, and a little Salt; then lay it before the Fire, till it rise very light; then knead in a pound of fresh Butter, and a pound of rough Carraway-comfits; and bake them in a quick Oven on floured Papers, in what Shape you please.

—Smith, *Compleat Housewife* (1728), p. 128

As previously noted, comfits are nuts or seeds coated with a hard sugar paste. Popular from the seventeenth century to the nineteenth, they show up now only in the form of candied almonds. In the eighteenth century, comfits often took the place of currants and other dried fruits in sweet rolls, breads, and buns. Caraway comfits, called "kissing comfits" because they sweetened the breath, were said to have a "warm, sweet, biting taste." Glasse copied this recipe.

15. TO MAKE BATH CAKES

Rub half a Pound of Butter into a Pound of Flour, and one Spoonful of good Barm, warm some Cream, and make it into a light Paste, set it to the Fire to rise, when you make them up, take four Ounces of Carraway Comfits, work Part of them in, and strew the rest on the Top, make them into round Cakes the Size of a French Roll, bake them on Sheet Tins, and send them in hot for Breakfast.

—Raffald, *Experienced English House-keeper* (1769), p. 249

As mentioned above (#1 commentary), barm was the name given to yeast taken from fermenting malt. The spoonful measure for the barm implies that it has been "washed and purified," making it more potent than the "fairly weak and slow-working" liquid yeast of the type used above in #5. Elizabeth Davis says the modern equivalent would be two packets (a quarter ounce each) of dry yeast. Wilson associates Bath with both the Bath Cake or Bun and with "Lun's cake" (for more on Sally and her cake, see below, #24). The precise origins of the Bath and Lunn cakes (like the famous Sally Lunn herself) are unknown. Elizabeth David speculates that "somewhere along the line Bath cakes, which were very light, delicate tea cakes, developed into or became indistinguishable from Sally Lunns." However, the Bath Bun "was down-graded by the bakers into the amorphous, artificially coloured, synthetically flavoured and over-sugared confections we know today." David then distinguishes between the "London Bath bun" and the "Bath bun of Bath and the West Country." (We kid you not.) She cannot personally vouch for the superiority of the latter, but she relates that it is "said to be at least shapely and neatly rounded if not precisely light." There will always be an England.

While asserting that Raffald's "proportions and methods work perfectly," David updates the older recipe by replacing "over-lavish" cream with milk and substituting crystallized sugar for comfits and caraway seeds. She points out that Bath buns are closely related to French brioche.

16. GINGERBREAD CAKES, OR BUTTER AND SUGAR GINGERBREAD

NO. 1. Three pounds of flour, a grated nutmeg, two ounces ginger, one pound sugar, three small spoons pearl ash dissolved in cream, one pound butter, four eggs, knead it stiff, shape it to your fancy, bake 15 minutes.

—Simmons, *American Cookery* (Hartford, 1796), p. 36

Despite her proclamation of culinary independence, Simmons offers many conventional English recipes, and this one, based in part on Glasse's "Ginger-Bread Cakes," is among them. Simmons adds eggs, which make these cookies softer. Into the nineteenth century, cookies were often subsumed within the category of cakes.

The earliest gingerbreads were often colored red with sandalwood, yellow with saffron and ginger, or, as in a recipe in Markham, a deep violet with claret and turnsole (also known as heliotrope). At first sweetened exclusively with honey, in time sugar and molasses (treacle) took honey's place. Molasses not only sweetened the cakes but also turned them dark brown. King Charles II, we are told, favored treacle gingerbread. Early gingerbread was made of the grated crumbs of manchets (Markham's "three penny manchets finely grated") rather than raw flour. Slow baking dried them out until they were crisp. In 1670, Woolley gives two gingerbreads—one made with grated manchets, the other with flour—indicating the transition to the latter ingredient.

17. SOFT GINGERBREAD TO BE BAKED IN PANS

NO. 2. Rub three pounds of sugar, two pounds of butter, into four pounds of flour, add 20 eggs, 4 ounces ginger, 4 spoons rose water, bake as No. 1 [15 minutes].

—Simmons, *American Cookery* (Hartford, 1796), p. 36

As with her version of Shrewsbury Cake (see above, #13 commentary), Simmons offers a soft, cakelike gingerbread, although it is still denser than modern sponge cake gingerbread. This recipe is one that we have brought many times to our talks on New England cooking. With its light color, dense texture, and gingery bite, it's a crowd-pleaser.

18. TUMBLES

Three pound flour, two pound sugar, one pound butter and eight eggs, with a little carroway seed; bake on tins; add a little milk if the eggs are not sufficient.

—Simmons, *American Cookery* (Albany, 1796), p. 47

With the change of one letter, Simmons gives the already quaintly named British confection jumbles (#12) a jolt of American idiomatic energy.

19. TEA CAKES

Rub into a pound of flour, two ounces of butter, a beaten egg, and half a teaspoonful of salt; wet it with warmed milk; make the paste rather stiff, and let it remain before the fire, where it will be kept warm for an hour or two; then roll it thin, and cut it with the top of a tumbler, bake it quick.

—Hale, *Good Housekeeper* (1841), p. 102

"If I thought there was any hope of the advice being followed, I would say, do not eat any warm cakes at all," writes Hale. But acknowledging that many people choose warm cakes for breakfast and tea, she offers "directions for the sorts which seem likely to do the least injury." Although Hale is not explicit about the criteria she uses to determine which cakes minimize damage to health, this "warm cake" contains no sugar. It is essentially a cut biscuit with a beaten egg in place of baking soda. In calling this recipe "Tea Cakes," Hale illustrates that the cake category is still flexible.

20. VERY NICE EUSK

One pint of milk.
One coffee-cup of yeast. (Potato is best.)
Four eggs.
Flour enough to make it as thick as you can stir with a spoon.

Let it rise till *very* light, but be *sure* it is not sour; if it is, work in half a teaspoonful of saleratus, dissolved in a wine-glass of warm water.

When thus light, work together three quarters of a pound of sugar and nine ounces of butter; add more flour, if needed, to make it stiff enough to mould. Let it rise again, and when *very* light, mould it into small cakes. Bake fifteen minutes in a quick oven, and after taking it out, mix a little milk and sugar, and brush over the rusk, while hot, with a small swab of linen tied to a stick, and dry it in the oven. When you have weighed these proportions once, then *measure* the quantity, so as to save the trouble of weighing afterward. Write the measures in your receipt-book, lest you forget.

—Beecher, *Domestic Receipt-Book* (1846), p. 92

These rusks are shaped like round cakes and contain yeast, eggs, and even saleratus for leavening, making them a hybrid of modern bread and of egg- or baking powder–leavened cake. But dried in the oven as they are after baking, they are also the equivalent of the modern sweet biscuit or, as they are now universally known, biscotti. This Italian designation is apt in that the word "biscuit" comes from the language of the Romans—*panis biscoctus* means twice-cooked bread.

Since the Middle Ages, rusks, like their close kin ship's biscuits, have been favored for their keeping qualities and used to feed armies, navies, and other travelers. Their long shelf life made them a pantry staple in many homes.

21. GINGER SNAPS

One cup of molasses.
Half a cup of sugar.
Half a cup of butter.
Half a cup of warm water, the butter melted with it.
A small teaspoonful of pearlash, dissolved in the water.
Two tablespoonfuls of ginger.

The dough should be stiff; knead it well, and roll into sheets, cut into round cakes, and bake in a moderate oven.

—Beecher, *Domestic Receipt-Book* (1846), p. 134

Beecher neglects to mention that flour is added to make a stiff dough. Oliver maintains that pearl ash, which produced a softer crumb, gave rise "to the distinction in cookbooks between hard gingerbread and soft gingerbread." However, Simmons's soft gingerbread (above, #17) is made without pearl ash, while these hard gingersnaps are made with it. These discrepancies illustrate once again that early methods and recipes resist precise categorization.

22. NO. 1. GINGER NUTS

Dissolve six ounces of butter and four ounces of sugar in a pint of hot molasses; when cold, add one glass of rose-water, two table-spoonfuls of ginger, a tea-spoonful of salt, and sifted flour enough to make a soft dough; mix it well, roll it out thin, cut it into pieces an inch square, and bake on buttered tins fifteen minutes.
—Bliss, *Practical Cook Book* (1850), p. 178

We once made Beecher's version of ginger nuts for a book signing. With almost six times the amount of flour to the amount of butter, mixed with a quart of molasses and "kneaded hard for a long time," Beecher's cookies turned out to be so firm ("nuts" indeed) that we feared visitors to our table would break their teeth when they bit into them—and we would be sued for their dental expenses. We had nothing else to offer, however, so we issued a disclaimer of responsibility with each cookie we handed out. Despite our warnings, one gentleman returned to our table several times. Holding one cookie to his lips, he stuck others in his pockets. Eventually, perhaps embarrassed, he sent his wife to our table to request the recipe. She explained that her husband found Beecher's ginger nuts a perfect diet aid. Since he found them both delicious and virtually inedible he had to suck on them slowly rather than gobble them up. In our ongoing effort to avoid lawsuits, we give Bliss's softer version here. (In fairness to Beecher, we feel obliged to report that some say keeping her ginger nuts "for many months," as she boasts is possible, softens them.)

23. GINGERBREAD (MILK)

One cup molasses; two even teaspoons soda; one heaping teaspoon ginger; one and one half cups sweet milk; four cups flour; a little salt, and a piece of lard or butter (melted) size of two small hen's eggs. Butter is best.
—*Aunt Mary's New England Cook Book* (1881), p. 53

Aunt Mary's gives three gingerbreads differentiated by liquid—milk, water, and sour milk. She also gives a recipe for molasses cookies as part of her gingerbread section. Molasses had become the principal sweetener in New England gingerbreads, just as it was now invariably being added to brown bread and baked beans. Although Aunt Mary offers no advice on cooking time for her gingerbreads, she recommends baking her molasses cookies quickly.

24. SALLY LUNN

One quart of flour, a piece of butter the size of an egg, three tablespoonfuls of sugar, two eggs, two teacupfuls of milk, two teaspoonfuls of cream tartar, one of soda, and a little salt. Scatter the cream of tartar, the sugar, and the salt into the flour; add the eggs, the butter (melted), and one cup of milk; dissolve the soda in the remaining cup, and stir all together steadily a few moments. Bake in two round pans.

—Turner, *New England Cook Book* (1905), p. 132

The name Sally Lunn as applied to some form of tea cake dates from the late eighteenth century. Some maintain that it is a corruption of the name of a French cake "soleil et lune." In support of this thesis, "so-limemne" is the name of the French-style breakfast cake offered by Eliza Acton in 1845. Davidson quips that "the derivation of the name is a subject which has excited many pages of prose." The Sally Lunn is also associated with the Bath cake (above, #15).

All of the renowned English tea cakes of the eighteenth century continued to hold interest for New Englanders into the twentieth century.

Fried Cakes, Pancakes, and Hearth Cakes

These foods—quick to prepare, portable, and usually loaded or coated (or both) with sugar—seem particularly suited to the pace of life in a young country. And indeed, they have an illustrious history in New England and frontier America. The fried cakes known as doughnuts were packed up for picnics alongside the cheese and cold chicken, brought out to refresh churchgoers between morning and afternoon services, and, in colonial times, sold at the annual spring musters held throughout New England. Fried cakes and fritters were served to farmhands and servants at their mid-morning break. Pancakes and johnnycakes slid from griddles onto plates, to be dowsed with syrup or molasses before being gobbled up by family members about to embark on a day's work or coming in from an early morning in the barn or fields. In novels, memoirs, and cookbooks New Englanders spoke lovingly about the homemade doughnuts and johnny-cakes of their youth, although sometimes their memories inflated the significance and improved the taste of their everyday cakes. Nevertheless, by the end of the nineteenth century, many of these quickly cooked items were considered part of New Englanders' cultural heritage.

But small cakes cooked in a pan over an open fire, or on a piece of wood, stone, or iron near the hearth, or in a kettle of boiling lard had been known in Europe from time immemorial. In Britain, these foods had served much the same purpose and evoked much the same enthusiastic response as they would in New England. The particular versions consumed in North America were, like many of the people who consumed them, descended from English stock. Some of the recipes remained unchanged while others were modified to suit local conditions. In particular, cornmeal, the grain of the Indians (who also cooked hearth cakes) was used in place of oats, barley, or wheat. Later, as the cookstove replaced the open hearth, griddle cooking, oven baking, and pot boiling edged out hearthside baking. Just as fried cakes, pancakes, and hearth cakes made it easily across the Atlantic, they also made an easy transition to the new kitchen technologies.

25. TO MAKE FRITTERS

Take half a Pint of Sack and a Pint of Ale, a little Yest, the yolks of twelve Eggs, and six Whites, with some beaten Spice and a very little salt, make this into thick Batter with fine Flower, then boil your Lard, and dip round thin slices of Apples in this Batter, and fry them; serve them in with beaten spice and sugar.

—Woolley, *Queen-like Closet* (1670), p. 101

Woolley gives two apple fritter recipes, this one with slices of apple and another in which a "pomewater" (a type of large, juicy apple) is cut in small pieces. Fritter (and pancake) batter was used to coat raisins (Markham), herbs such as clary and tansy (Raffald), even the pulp of the tuberous skirret (Glasse). Fritters were also made without fruit, herb, or vegetable stuffings.

The distinction between fritter and pancake sometimes had to do with the composition of the batter, more often with the manner of cooking. In Woolley's day, fritters were usually deep-fat fried, while pancakes were cooked in a greased pan. Child reversed the terms. Fritters, she says, "are not to be boiled in fat, like pancakes." But others like Allen and Leslie stuck with crisping fritters in deep fat and frying pancakes in a greased skillet, which remain standard practices today.

26. TO MAKE PANCAKES SO CRISP AS YOU MAY SET THEM UPRIGHT

Make a dozen or a score of them in a little Frying-pan, no bigger than a Sawcer, then boil them in Lard, and they will look as yellow as Gold, and eat very well.

—Woolley, *Queen-like Closet* (1670), p. 117

Here Woolley anticipates Child's approach to pancakes. She also gives a more conventional pancake recipe. In a typical bill of fare for a gentleman's house for fish days—when wealthy diners often compensated for abstention from meat by partaking of all manner of rich breads and cakes—Woolley recommends pancakes or fritters as part of the second course. The irony of permitting such indulgences was apparently well understood, as conveyed in this passage from Shakespeare's *Pericles*: "Come, thou shalt go home, and we'll have flesh for holidays, fish for fasting-days, and moreo'er puddings and flapjacks."

27. TO MAKE PANCAKES

Take a pint of Cream, and eight Eggs, Whites and all, a whole Nutmeg grated, and a little Salt; then melt a pound of rare dish Butter, and a little Sack: Before you fry them, stir it in: it must be made as thick with three spoonfuls of Flour, as ordinary Batter, and fryed with Butter in the Pan, the first Pancake but no more: Strew Sugar, garnish with Orange, turn it on the backside of a Plate.

—Smith, *Compleat Housewife* (1728), p. 91

With a pound of butter already in the batter, it's no wonder that Smith only greases the frying pan once. According to Hess, the overuse of butter characterized Tudor cooking (in other words, through the early seventeenth century). But the tradition continued, as recipes such as this one a century later reflect the preceding age's elite dishes.

Among our sources, the phrase "rare dish butter" is found only in Smith, although butter measured by the dish appears in Markham (#12 commentary). In 1561, when Queen Elizabeth visited a country house, butter cost "7 pence the dish," and it seems that the best butter was sold by the dish. Smith follows Woolley in serving her pancakes with "the Juice of Orange and Sugar."

28. TO MAKE BATTER PANCAKES

Beat three Eggs, with a Pound of Flour, very well, put to it a Pint of Milk, and a little Salt, fry them in Lard or Butter, grate Sugar over them, cut them in Quarters, and serve them up.

—Raffald, *Experienced English House-keeper* (1769), p. 144

Raffald's batter pancakes, made of eggs, flour, and milk, fried in lard or butter, amount to what Andrew F. Smith calls "the basic American pancake." Milk became the standard liquid, in spite of Markham's warning against its use: "There be some which mixe Pancakes with new milke or creame, but that makes them tough, cloying, and not so crispe, pleasant and sauoury as running water." But few shared his preference, as we can see from this and the preceding recipe.

Oliver relates that pancakes were included among the nineteenth-century New England fisherman's everyday foods, which she calls the "three p's"—pot pies, pancakes, and pudding. From her we also learn that coastal New England slang for pancakes was joe-floggers. Nicknames for pancakes were nothing new. According to Elizabeth David, a recipe for yeast-leavened buckwheat pancakes was published in an 1817 cookbook under the curious name "Bockings" (from buck or buckwheat). Although buckwheat pancakes were associated primarily with American cooking, they appear to have been in vogue in the English Midlands around this time.

29. JOHNY CAKE, OR HOE CAKE

Scald 1 pint of milk and put to 3 pints of indian meal, and half pint of flower—bake before the fire. Or scald with milk two thirds of the indian meal, or wet two thirds with boiling water, add salt, molasses and shortening, work up with cold water pretty stiff, and bake as above.

—Simmons, *American Cookery* (Hartford, 1796), p. 34

The alternative name hoecake may have come from the fact that when the cakes were baked "before the fire" (later, they would be either baked in a brick oven or fried), they were sometimes placed on paddles shaped like hoes. As for the name johnnycake, we argue elsewhere that it and the cakes themselves are derived in part from Native American foodways. Hess and others link johnnycake primarily to Scottish oat cake.

30. INDIAN SLAPJACK

One quart of milk, 1 pint of indian meal, 4 eggs, 4 spoons of flour, little salt, beat together, baked on gridles, or fry in a dry pan, or baked in a pan which has been rub'd with suet, lard or butter.

—Simmons, *American Cookery* (Hartford, 1796), p. 34

Although the OED cites an 1805 recipe as the first instance of the term *slapjack* in print, Simmons's recipe obviously precedes that one. Her recommendations for baking pancakes are unusual. By frying in a "dry pan" Simmons may have meant frying not in an ungreased but rather in a well-seasoned skillet.

In nineteenth-century New England, the terms "flapjack" and "slapjack" were interchangeable. For instance, Hawthorne recorded that he had "a splendid breakfast of flapjacks, or slapjacks, and whortleberries." However, *flapjack* is the older word, with a first recorded use of 1600. (Child introduces yet another term, "flat-jacks," which she makes synonymous with fritters; Howland says flat-jacks when she means flapjacks.) The OED also gives flapjack as the name for an apple turnover, although we suspect that this is a case of similar terms—fritter, flapjack, slapjack, and pancake—being used interchangeably to describe fried quickbreads, some of which were stuffed with fruit. Nevertheless, the term flapjack was mostly used to mean pancake, which, in case you aren't yet sufficiently confused, was sometimes also called pan-pudding. In short, the nomenclature—and even the preparation—of these little cakes is as slippery as a pancake or flapjack or slapjack on a greased griddle.

31. DOUGH-NUTS

For dough-nuts, take one pint of flour, half a pint of sugar, three eggs, a piece of butter as big as an egg, and a tea-spoonful of dissolved pearlash. When you have no eggs, a gill of lively emptings will do; but in that case, they must be made over night. Cinnamon, rose-water, or lemon-brandy, if you have it. If you use part lard instead of butter, add a little salt. Not put in till the fat is very hot. The more fat they are fried in, the less they will soak fat.

—Child, *American Frugal Housewife* (1833), p. 73

Although it is often assumed that this particular fried cake was invented in America, doughnut recipes appear in virtually every medieval recipe collection. As Terence Scully puts it: "All that is needed is, on the one hand, hot grease in a pan or a pot, and, on the other, a dough or a batter to drop into it." Oliver says doughnuts came to America as "a Dutch sweet." So Hess is right to emphasize that "there is nothing specifically American" about doughnuts. On the other hand, this is true of many American foods, including hamburgers, French fries, and apple pie. The story of the doughnut embodies our prevailing national myth—a poor immigrant comes to this country and achieves fame and fortune.

We have seen Child calling for "emptings" (the lees or emptyings of beer or wine barrels) earlier in this chapter (#5). Here she employs this cheapest type of yeast as a substitute for eggs.

32. GRIDDLE CAKES

Rub three ounces of butter into a pound of flour with a little salt, moisten it with sweet buttermilk to make it into paste, roll it out, and cut the cakes with the cover of your dredging-box, and put them upon a griddle to bake.

—Howland, *New England Economical Housekeeper* (1845), p. 18

Griddle cakes were woven into the fabric of American life in the nineteenth century. In "A Mysterious Visit," an autobiographical short story by Mark Twain about his dealings with a man from the "U.S. Internal Revenue Department," the cakes put in an appearance. After unwittingly inflating his earnings to the tax collector, Twain calls out to his cook, "Hold me while I faint! Let Marie turn the griddle-cakes."

33. MUFFINS

Take a quart of wheat flour, mix it smoothly with a pint and a half of lukewarm milk, half a teacup of yeast, two eggs, a teaspoonful of salt, and two spoonfuls of lukewarm melted butter. Place the batter where warm to rise. When light, butter your muffin cups, pour in the mixture, and bake it till of a light brown.

—Webster, *Improved Housewife* (1844), p. 133

These muffins appear in a section of Webster's cookbook called "Hot Cakes," which includes recipes for corn cakes, johnnycakes, slapjacks, buckwheat cakes, and waffles. The phrase causes some categorical confusion—are hot cakes baked by the hearth like early johnnycakes, in the bake oven like corn cakes, on the griddle like slapjacks, or between hot irons like waffles? For muffins, the matter has been resolved in our day in favor of oven baking. But we place them here to point out that muffins originated in an overarching tradition whose emphasis was upon open fire rather than oven baking.

According to Wilson, in northern England the original muffins were made from a leavened batter and baked on a griddle. In much of the rest of England, the word "crumpet" was applied to this type of quickbread. Glasse does call such cakes muffins, or "muffings," but she says they were "like a Honey-Comb" when pulled open. That is, they were like an English crumpet rather than a soft American muffin. In New England, the term "crumpet" never took hold—we call it an English muffin!

In late-nineteenth-century New England, muffins or "gems," as they were also called, were sometimes baked in rectangular-shaped cast iron molds.

Cakes, Plain and Fancy

The larger cakes of the seventeenth century were massive productions that required yeast to rise. By the first quarter of the eighteenth century, cakes became smaller, and eggs began to replace yeast. These changes affected not only the final product but also the process of cake-making, as those accustomed to giving yeasted doughs plenty of time to rise had to learn the opposite lesson—that speed was needed to get egg-raised batters into the oven before they deflated. The transition from yeast to eggs in cakes took longer in New England, as illustrated by the popularity through the middle of the nineteenth century of the yeasted, plum-studded Election Cake.

The taste of yeast-raised cakes was generally considered superior, and such cakes were memorialized in sentimental accounts. Ultimately however, these slow foods could not compete with the newer types made quickly with eggs and chemical leavens. By the closing decades of the nineteenth century, even nostalgic New Englanders were exploring the range of styles, icings, and names that could be used to enhance the new cakes. A few complained that these products were tasteless compared with the old, yeasted spice cakes. But the quibbles of gastronomes were no match for the promises of convenience and the allure of lavish frostings.

34. TO MAKE A VERY GOOD GREAT OXFORD-SHIRE CAKE

Take a peck of flower by weight, and dry it a little, & a pound and a halfe of Sugar, one ounce of Cinamon, half an ounce of Nutmegs, a quarter of an ounce of Mace and Cloves, a good spoonfull of Salt, beat your Salt and Spice very fine, and searce it, and mix it with your flower and Sugar; then take three pound of butter and work it in the flower, it will take three hours working; then take a quart of Ale-yeast, two quarts of Cream, half a pint of Sack, six grains of Amber-greece dissolved in it, halfe a pint of Rosewater, sixteen Eggs, eight of the Whites, mix these with the flower, and knead them well together, then let it lie warm by your fire till your Oven be hot, which must be little hotter then for manchet; when you make it ready for your Oven, put to your Cake six pound of Currans, two pound of Raisins, of the Sun stoned and minced, so make up your Cake, and set it in your oven stopped close; it wil take three houres a baking; when baked, take it out and frost it over with the white of an Egge and Rosewater, well beat together, and strew fine Sugar upon it, and then set it again into the Oven, that it may Ice.

—*Compleat Cook* (1658, 2nd ed.), p. 11

Davidson points out that "no other language has a word which means exactly the same as the English 'cake' (although some echo it with strange-looking forms such as 'kek', when meaning to refer to English-type cakes)." On the continent, there are gateaux, tortes, babas, and the like, but they exist without a common generic name. The ancient world had its cakes. The Greek word for cake is *plakous,* meaning flat. From this comes the Latin word *placenta,* which we now associate with a fetus's food supply but which for Cato, in the second century BCE, was a kind of cheesecake. The Latin *pastillus* means a little cake or pie; it is possible that the word "cake," as it moved from Anglo-Saxon into English, also meant something small, as suggested by the various petite "cakes" we've seen in this chapter. (In the commentary on #11, we refer to the idea that a circular shape was also part of what made a cake a cake.) However, by the late fourteenth century, enormous cakes, dwarfing the one made with a peck (fourteen pounds) of flour described here, were common. Chaucer mentions a cake made with half a bushel (twenty-eight pounds) of flour.

By the end of the seventeenth century, five to seven pounds of flour were considered sufficient. We would still consider seven pounds of flour more than enough to make a big cake, but the trend was nevertheless downward. The invention of the tin hoop, at the end of the century, helped give a uniform shape and even rising to cakes that were increasingly made with the looser egg-raised batters. As we have noted, cakes continued to get smaller through the eighteenth century.

"Amber-greece," or ambergris, is the solid, waxy intestinal secretion (the bile) of the sperm whale, once used as a culinary aromatic. Even at the height of its popularity, one didn't need to hunt whales to obtain it—the substance (in pieces weighing a few ounces to two hundred pounds) could be found floating in the ocean or washed up on the sand. It appeared in recipes of the seventeenth century but mostly died out thereafter. Glasse uses it once, in "To Ice a great Cake another Way." There, it is pulverized with musk (the glandular secretion of the musk deer) and added to an icing of sugar, egg whites, and orange flower water. The six grains called for here would weigh less than a hundredth of an ounce—this was strong stuff.

35. A RICH SEED CAKE, CALLED, THE NUN'S CAKE

Take four pounds of your finest Flour, and three pounds of double-refined Sugar beaten and sifted; mix them together, and dry them by the Fire till you prepare your other Materials.

Take four pounds of Butter, beat it in your Hands till 'tis very soft like Cream; then beat thirty-five Eggs, leave out sixteen Whites, and strain out the Treddles of the rest, and beat them and the Butter together, till all appears like Butter, put in four or five spoonfuls of Rose or Orange-flower Water, and beat it again; then take your Flour and Sugar with six ounces of Carraway-seeds and strew it in by degrees, beating it up all the time for two hours together; you may put in as much Tincture of Cinnamon or Amber-grease as you please; butter your Hoop, and let it stand three hours in a moderate Oven.

—Smith, *Compleat Housewife* (1728), pp. 137–38

Smith gives seven recipes for seed cake. This one is copied by Glasse, who adds as a final line: "You must observe always in beating of Butter to do it with a cool Hand, and beat it always one Way in a deep Earthen Dish." Elsewhere, Smith also says to mix butter by "stirring it round with your Hand all one way." Smith and Glasse mean to beat the butter using your bare hands. This gives new meaning to the modern cooking direction to "beat by hand."

In Glasse, Smith's egg "treddles" become "treds" in the first edition and "threads" in the American 1805 edition. Davidson explains that "treds, or cock-treadings, are the coloured spots on the yolks of fertilized eggs. A treddle is not the same thing. It is the thread or string holding the yolk in position. In preparing a pale dish one would be especially concerned to remove the treds; in making a smooth-textured dish, the treddles." Here, where the dish is beaten for two hours to a silky smoothness, "treddles" is intended, and Glasse's substitution of "treds" indicates that she doesn't understand Smith's meaning. "Threads," in the later American edition of Glasse, though possibly a corruption of "treds," comes closer to Smith's intent.

At the height of their popularity in the eighteenth century, economical seed cakes were raised with yeast, richer ones with eggs. With thirty-five eggs (though "only" nineteen whites), Smith's cake certainly earns the designation "rich."

Although it seems obvious that the name of the cake derives from the caraway seeds (or comfits) it contained, English sources from the sixteenth to the nineteenth century also mention a seed cake made without seeds. This cake was so-named because it was served to agricultural workers during seed-time festivities. The connection to nuns in the alternate title presumably recalls the era in Britain when the rewards of monastic life included the baking and eating of rich cakes.

36. TO MAKE A BRIDE CAKE

Take four Pounds of fine Flour well dried, four Pounds of fresh Butter, two Pounds of Loaf Sugar, pound and sift fine a quarter of an Ounce of Mace, the same of Nutmegs, to every Pound of Flour put eight Eggs, wash four Pounds of Currants, pick them well and dry them before the Fire, blanch a Pound of Sweet Almonds (and cut them length-way very thin) a Pound of Citron, one Pound of candied Orange, the same of candied Lemon, half a Pint of Brandy; first work the Butter with your Hand to a Cream, then Beat in your Sugar a quarter of an Hour, beat the Whites of your Eggs to a very strong Froth, mix them with your Sugar and Butter, beat your Yolks half an Hour at least, and mix them with your Cake, then put in your Flour, Mace, and Nutmeg, keep beating it well 'till your Oven is ready, put in your Brandy, and beat your Currants and Almonds lightly in, tie three Sheets of Paper round the Bottom of your Hoop to keep it from running out, rub it well with Butter, put in your Cake, and lay your Sweetmeats in three Lays, with Cake betwixt every Lay, after it is risen and coloured, cover it with Paper before your Oven is stopped up; it will take three Hours baking.

—Raffald, *Experienced English House-keeper* (1769), pp. 242–43

37. TO MAKE ALMOND ICEING FOR THE BRIDE CAKE

Beat the Whites of three Eggs to a strong Froth, beat a Pound of Jordan Almonds very fine with Rose Water, mix your Almonds with the Eggs lightly together, a Pound of common Loaf Sugar beat fine, and put in by Degrees, when your Cake is enough, take it out and lay your Iceing on, and put it in to Brown.

—Raffald, *Experienced English House-keeper* (1769), p. 243

38. TO MAKE SUGAR ICEING FOR THE BRIDE CAKE

Beat two Pounds of double refined Sugar, with two Ounces of fine Starch, sift it through a Gawze Sieve, then beat the Whites of five Eggs with a Knife upon a Pewter Dish half an Hour, beat in your Sugar a little at a Time, or it will make the Eggs fall, and will not be so good a Colour, when you have put in all your Sugar, beat it half an Hour longer, then lay it on your Almond Iceing, and spread it even with a Knife; if it be put on as soon as the Cake comes out of the Oven, it will be hard by that Time the Cake is cold.

—Raffald, *Experienced English House-keeper* (1769), pp. 244

This is a large cake made according to the new yeastless method, with egg whites and yolks separated and beaten, and the entire batter whipped continually until it is put into the oven. Edible sculpture, the idea behind the wedding cake, was not new in Raffald's day. As discussed in Chapter 1, in the banquet courses of seventeenth-century feasts, molded sugar was shaped like birds or snails, sometimes even like the plates and cups on the table or the small structures (follies) that adorned gardens. But the edible edifice that the wedding cake would come to resemble was something new. The middle classes took enthusiastically to the idea of the architectural cake as a wedding symbol.

Raffald has been called "the most important single name in the history of the wedding cake." While her egg-raised cake has not yet assumed the shape of progressively smaller layers that would become the hallmark of the wedding cake, her use of a double icing begins the process of turning attention away from the cake itself and toward its decorative outer coatings. The double icing, by which the cake was in its earliest forms differentiated from the plum cake, was, as Simon R. Charsley notes, "her own idea, probably [developed] as a novelty for selling [the bride cake] in her shop in Manchester."

Lee, by copying a version in Dolby, brought Raffald's bride cake and almond icing to New England. Lee also includes a recipe for sugar icing for bride cake (taken from Kitchiner and loosely based on Raffald); however, Lee/Kitchiner say nothing about spreading the sugar icing upon a previously applied inner layer of almond icing.

39. PLUMB CAKE

Mix one pound currants, one drachm nutmeg, mace and cinnamon each, a little salt, one pound of citron, orange peal candied, and almonds bleach'd, 6 pound of flour, (well dry'd) beat 21 eggs, and add with 1 quart new ale yeast, half pint of wine, 3 half pints of cream and raisins, q: s:

—Simmons, *American Cookery* (Hartford, 1796), p. 33—

As this recipe illustrates, American cake-making at the end of the eighteenth century diverged from British practice in persisting in the use of yeast, although sometimes, as here, the yeast seems almost vestigial given the number of eggs. Simmons also offers recipes for two "Plain" cakes, which are made without raisins. One drachm, or dram, equals one-sixteenth of an ounce. Its weight is approximately equal to the Greek coin of the same name.

40. QUEENS CAKE

Whip half pound butter to a cream, add 1 pound sugar, ten eggs, one glass wine, half gill rose water, and spices to your taste, all worked into one and a quarter pound flour, put into pans, cover with paper, and bake in a quick well heat oven, 12 or 16 minutes.

—Simmons, *American Cookery* (Hartford, 1796), pp. 36–37

Queen's cakes have been served to the faculty and students of New College, Oxford, since at least the first quarter of the eighteenth century. Simmons bases this recipe on one in Carter. Patriotic fervor did not prevent fashionable British imports, even a cake with a royal name, from achieving popularity in New England after American independence. The primary difference between the Carter and Simmons versions is that

Simmons uses many more eggs than Carter. As we have seen with her soft gingerbread, Simmons favored cakey cakes. Simmons's instructions about using several pans implies dividing the batter into smaller cakes.

41. TIPSY CAKE

Cut a pan of sponge cake in halves, and place it in two glass dishes; stick it over full of blanched and quartered almonds. Wet the cake with wine. Drop raspberry jam about it, and then make a nice soft custard and pour over and around it.

—Chadwick, *Home Cookery* (1853), p. 61

This English triflelike cake was brought to New England by Lee (copying Dalgairns). It is interesting for several reasons: the sponge cake has become so common that no recipe for it need be given, and alcohol is treated with humor. Not everyone adopted this attitude. Temperance advocates countered with cakes of their own (see below, #45).

42. CIDER CAKE

Cider cake is very good, to be baked in small loaves. One pound and a half of flour, half a pound of sugar, quarter of a pound of butter, half a pint of cider, one teaspoonful of pearlash; spice to your taste. Bake till it turns easily in the pans. I should think about half an hour.

—Child, *American Frugal Housewife* (1833), p. 71

Typifying Child's frugality is this nice little eggless sponge cake raised with pearl ash and flavored with cider, made so obviously with what was to hand.

43. ELECTION CAKE

Old-fashioned election cake is made of four pounds of flour; three quarters of a pound of butter; four eggs; one pound of sugar; one pound of currants, or raisins if you choose; half a pint of good yeast; wet it with milk as soft as it can be and be moulded on a board. Set to rise over night in winter; in warm weather, three hours is usually enough for it to rise. A loaf, the size of common flour bread, should bake three quarters of an hour.

—Child, *American Frugal Housewife* (1833), p. 71

As noted, to many New Englanders Election Cake (also known as Dough Cake, March Meeting Cake, and Connecticut Loaf Cake) symbolized both the old way of baking and a tradition of sturdy democratic values, as it had long been served at the festivities surrounding colonial elections. The cake was often covered with a boiled sugar and egg white frosting. One nineteenth-century writer exclaimed: "The delicate frostings of white of egg and sugar, the rich, sweet, and spicy substance of the cake itself, and the raisins which were embedded in the toothsome compound were joys which no Connecticut boy could ever forgo or forget."

44. GRAHAM CAKE

Two tea-cups of buttermilk, two tea-cups of sugar, one nutmeg, one tea-spoonful of saleratus.

—Howland, *New England Economical Housekeeper* (1845), p. 31

Howland identifies a sugary buttermilk sponge cake with the dietary reformer Sylvester Graham. We can only assume that she means to thicken the batter with some of Graham's unbolted whole wheat flour.

45. TEMPERANCE CAKE, NO. 1

Three eggs, two cups of sugar, one cup of milk, one tea-spoonful of saleratus, nutmeg, flour enough to make it pour into the pan; bake it about twenty minutes. Allspice and raisins, instead of nutmeg, make a good plum cake.

—Howland, *New England Economical Housekeeper* (1845), p. 28

This "Temperance Cake" earns its name from the absence of the wine (or its equivalent) found in some "plum" cakes—for example, that of Simmons (#39).

46. BOSTON CREAM CAKE

One pint of butter rubbed into one quart of flour.
One quart of hot water, with the butter and flour stirred in.
When cool, break in from six to twelve eggs, as you can afford.
If needed, add flour till thick enough to drop on buttered tins in round cakes, the size of a tea-cup.
 When baked, open and fill with soft custard, or mock cream.

—Beecher, *Domestic Receipt-Book* (1846), p. 142

Another type of cream cake, made with cream in the batter (often clotted, thick, or sour), appears in many of our nineteenth-century sources, among them Lee/Dolby, Webster (one of hers is called "Boston Cream Cake"), Howland, Allen, Leslie, and even Beecher herself. Sometimes these cream cakes, sconelike in texture, are split open and spread with jam or butter. The cream- or custard-filled cake seen here, on the other hand, appears to be of French origin. In his *Royal Parisian Pastrycook and Confectioner,* published in London in 1834 (French original, 1815), Carême offers a "cream cake" (really a puff-paste shell) filled with mocha coffee cream or any of a variety of flavored creams or custards. In place of Carême's puff paste, Beecher deploys choux pastry (now used in eclairs and similar pastries, also discussed extensively by Carême).

Beecher's Boston Cream Cake is the first American recipe we have found in which a shell is filled with cream or custard. But a poem titled "Johnny Green and the Cream Cake" that appeared in a New York literary weekly in 1844 supplies evidence that the well-informed were familiar with the new French-derived filled cream cake, though its being a novelty to such rubes as Johnny *Green* is the basis of the poem's humor: "On the Fourth of July Johnny Green came to town; / 'Twas the very first time he had ever 'been down;' / . . . He eyed a plump cream cake, a nice one I'm sure— / (But Johnny had ne'er seen a cream cake before—)." Johnny proceeds to buy the cake from the "pie man" and takes a big bite, but spits it out when he finds the center soft. He concludes that his cake is uncooked: "'Here give me my money back, mister!' he cried; / 'Your cake is not *done*—see the *dough* that's inside!'"

The relationship between Beecher's Boston Cream Cake and the famous Boston cream pie is a bit on the paradoxical side, in that in Beecher's "cake," the cream or custard filling is placed within a pie-like shell, whereas in the earliest recipe we have found dubbed "Boston Cream Pie," from 1872, the filling is placed within a simple sponge cake. The two recipes—one for a "cream cake" (pie), the other for a "cream pie" (cake)—coexisted into the twentieth century, at which time Boston cream pie finally emerged in the form in which we now know it, topped with "satiny chocolate icing" (the earliest recipe we have found that calls for this crowning features dates from 1918).

Another aspect of "the murky evolution of the Boston cream pie" is the claim made by Boston's illustrious Parker House Hotel that the dessert was invented in the middle of the nineteenth century by one of its French chefs. Despite the tangled pedigree of this "much beloved half-cake, half-pie mutt," it has been designated the official dessert of Massachusetts, beating out Indian pudding and Toll House (chocolate chip) cookies to win the honor.

The second of Beecher's two fillings, her "mock cream," is given above (Chapter 12, #41).

47. WHITE MOUNTAIN CAKE

Four cups of flour, two of sugar, one of butter, one of milk, four eggs, one tea spoon cream of tartar, one of soda, flavor with lemon.

—Knight, *Tit-Bits* (1864), p. 109

48. WHITE MOUNTAIN CAKE

One cupful of butter,
Three cupfuls of sugar,
One pint of flour,
One and a half teaspoonfuls of Royal Baking Powder,
Whites of six eggs,
One cupful of milk,
Twenty drops Royal Extract Bitter Almonds,
Grated cocoanut.

Beat the butter and sugar together until they are a light white cream, add the whites of the six eggs that have been previously beaten to a dry froth, mix the flour and powder together and pass through a wire sieve; then add next the milk and extract, mix together thoroughly but carefully, and bake in jelly-cake tins in a quick oven fifteen minutes. Have ready a nice icing in the proportion of one tablespoonful of sugar to the white of one egg, beat very light, mix this with grated cocoanut in the proportion of two cupfuls of the icing to one of the cocoanut, arrange the cake when cool in layers, with this spread thick between each layer.

—*Godey's Lady's Book and Magazine* (May, 1883), p. 470

Our final two recipes trace the path of the White Mountain Cake from Knight's simple lemon cake (whose name seems arbitrarily to refer to the New Hampshire range) to a layer cake, complete with "snowy glaciers of frosting," also evocative of the New Hampshire range and possibly of the alpine Mont Blanc as well. The layer cake came into its own in the 1880s, as did brand names (e.g., Royal) and product promotion in recipes.

INTRODUCTION

1. "Pluck a Flamingo."

2. Sloat, *Old Sturbridge Village Cookbook*, 24 (quoting *Farmer's Monthly Visitor*).

3. Walsh, "Consumer Behavior," 235; Oliver, "Ruminations," 93. Such views are analogous to the broader denigration of "literary evidence" voices by the "new social historian" of a generation ago. For a brief summary and anlayhsis of the sociological perspective of the new social historians, see Stavely, *Puritan Legacies*, 8–9.

4. For a brief history of the sociology of wheat bread consumption, see Stavely and Fitzgerald, *America's Founding Food*, 10–11, 236–39.

5. Lehmann, *British Housewife*, 52–53.

6. Slater, *Appetite*, 9. Compare Charsley, *Wedding Cakes and Cultural History*, 34: "The history of the publication of recipes, while not the same thing as the history of dishes being consumed even amongst the book-buying classes, does . . . provide a basis for an account of trends and their approximate dating."

CHAPTER ONE. CULINARILY COLONIZED

1. Hess, *Martha Washington's Booke of Cookery*, 453; Simmons, *American Cookery* (introduction by Wilson), viii; Dexter, "Early Private Libraries," 143; Ford, *Boston Book Market*, 109–10, 133–34.

    Establishing that the works by Markham known to have been present in seventeenth-century New England included *The English Hus-wife* requires a brief account of the work's somewhat tangled bibliographic history. In the original 1615 edition, it appeared as book 2 of *Countrey Contentments*, book 1 of which was devoted to horsemanship. The title of the Markham work listed in the 1656 Miles Standish probate inventory is given as "Country Farmer," which may have been a garbled transcription of "Country Contentments" but is more likely to have been shorthand for Markham's 1616 edition and translation of *The Countrey Farme*, a sixteenth-century French husbandry manual by Charles Estienne. The relationship between this work and *The English Hus-wife* was quite close, in that Markham based the structure and much of the content of his own work on Estienne's book. A year after the publication of *The English Hus-wife*, in his capacity as editor and translator of *The Countrey Farme*, Markham added passages of his own composing to Estienne's text, "some of which were condensed versions of material [from] *The English Housewife*"; see Markham, *English Housewife* (1986), liv, xx; and Dexter, "Early Private Libraries," 143.

Most editions of *The English Hus-wife* after 1615 were issued as part of *A Way to Get Wealth*, a compendium of Markham's writings on husbandry, horsemanship, and housewifery. It was in this guise, as section 3 of "Markhams way to get wealth," that three copies of *The English Hus-wife* were sent to the Boston bookseller John Usher in 1684. The year before, Usher had received four copies of "Markhams Works." Worthington Chauncey Ford identifies this listing as "Markhams Master-piece revived," a work devoted exclusively to the care of livestock. But it might just as well have referred to *A Way to Get Wealth*, which, according to WorldCat, was reprinted that year, as well as in 1676; see Markham, *English Housewife* (1986), liv; and Ford, *Boston Book Market*, 133, 109.

2. Ford, *Boston Book Market*, 94, 103; Lehmann, *British Housewife*, 38–39, 67–68, 48; McKeon, *Secret History of Domesticity*, 487. Ford, 94, identifies the three copies of "queens Closet" appearing on a 1682 list of titles sent to John Usher as Woolley's *Queen-Like Closet*. However, the Woolley book appears as a separate entry on this same list, under its subtitle, "Rich Cabinet." There is no reason to suppose that the "queens Closet" entry referred to anything other than *The Queens Closet Opened*, of which there had been a reprint as recently as 1679. Ford's erroneous identification probably lies behind the mistaken assertion by Kevin J. Hayes that *The Queens Closet Opened* was a sequel to *The Queen-like Closet*; *Colonial Woman's Bookshelf*, 82. Leighton, *Early American Gardens*, 108–9, states that *The Queens Closet Opened* was to be found in Boston as early as the 1650s, but she offers no documentation for this assertion.

3. Lehmann, *British Housewife*, 96; Hayes, *Colonial Woman's Bookshelf*, 83. Evidence regarding the increased quantity and variety of books available in the colonies in the eighteenth century is summarized in Monaghan, *Learning to Read and Write*, 191–92, 391–92.

4. Lehmann, *British Housewife*, 108, 110; Hayes, *Colonial Woman's Bookshelf*, 85, 14; Gardiner, *Mrs. Gardiner's Family Receipts*, 64; Waters, "My Uncle, the Parson," 542. Milford, *Gardiners of Massachusetts*, though primarily concerned with the husband, son, and grandson of Anne Gibbons Gardiner, includes (36–37) a brief account of her manuscript cookbook.

5. Lehmann, *British Housewife*, 102, 105, 126; Hayes, *Colonial Woman's Bookshelf*, 86, 15.

6. DuSablon, *America's Collectible Cookbooks*, 3; Hayes, *Colonial Woman's Bookshelf*, 87; Lehmann, *British Housewife*, 402, 129, 131; Gardiner, Mrs. *Gardiner's Family Receipts*, 64.

7. Markham, *English Hus-wife* (1615), t.p.; Lehmann, *British Housewife*, 30, 38, 33. See also McKeon, *Secret History of Domesticity*, 487. Medicine was not yet principally the preserve of professional doctors, nor was "candying" or "confectionery" yet absorbed into "cookery."

8. Lehmann, *British Housewife*, 31. As Lehmann notes, the proportion of women able to read but not write was larger, although by how much is unclear.

9. Markham, *English Hus-wife* (1615), 46, 49–50, 47. Additional recipes appropriate for "every goodman's house" are listed by Markham's modern editor; see Markham, *English Housewife* (1986), xxxvii–xxxviii. For Markham's complete recipe for "ordinary wholsome boild-meats," see Chapter 5, #1.

10. Cahn, *Industry of Devotion*, 43–44; Korda, *Shakespeare's Domestic Economies*, 33–37; Markham, *English Hus-wife* (1615), 69; Lehmann, *British Housewife*, 35.

11. *Compleat Cook*, 34–36.

12. Woolley, *Queen-like Closet*, t.p.; Lehmann, *British Housewife*, 50–51.

13. Ibid., 49–50. The social position of Woolley's birth family is unclear from the available evidence.

14. Smith, *Compleat Housewife* (1728), sig. A4; Lehmann, *British Housewife*, 99.

15. Lehmann, *British Housewife*, 62. That the ideal of the lady of leisure was gaining widespread acceptance well before this, in the sixteenth and seventeenth centuries, is the central argument of Cahn, *Industry of Devotion*.

16. Glasse, *Art of Cookery* (1747), i, ii; Lehmann, *British Housewife*, 111–14.

17. Lehmann, *British Housewife*, 109–10.

18. Raffald, *Experienced English Housekeeper* (1769), sig. A2, ii; Glasse, *Art of Cookery*, i; Lehmann, *British Housewife*, 131.

19. Lehmann, *British Housewife*, 130; Raffald, *Experienced English Housekeeper* (1997), xii–xiv; Raffald, *Experienced English House-keeper* (1769), t.p. Minimal reliance on other cookbooks certainly distinguishes the book from Glasse's *Art of Cookery*, the dependence of which on other cookbooks has been demonstrated in great detail; see Glasse, *Art of Cookery* (1747), xv–xxxvii.

20. Lehmann, *British Housewife*, 130; Raffald, *Experienced English House-keeper* (1769), ii; Hill, *Women, Work, and Sexual Politics*, 144.

21. Anderson, "Solid Sufficiency," 153–56.

22. *Compleat Cook*, 22, 28, 42, 56, 6, 24, 49, 54.

23. Ibid., 12; Markham, *Countrey Contentments* (1623), 93; Anderson, "Solid Sufficiency," 155–56; Mennell, *All Manners of Food*, 88.

24. *Compleat Cook*, 7, 13, 25, 36, 53, 31, 33, 46, 30, 40; Lehmann, *British Housewife*, 40–41. "Humoral physiology is based on the idea that four major fluids dominate the human body: blood, phlegm, choler, and black bile (melancholy) . . . [and] that each food also had its own complexion or dominant humor and would thus interact with the humoral balance of the individual who consumed it" (*Cambridge*

World History of Food, 2:1205–6). In this perspective, "the process of digesting foods was actually a form of cooking." But by the middle of the seventeenth century, physicians began to argue that "digestion involved fermentation rather than cooking. . . . Eventually Europe's middle classes emulated the aristocracy" in following the new theory, which "seemed to offer a certain refinement, not just in the sense of good taste but also in a chemical sense." The most advanced cuisine came to mean, "as the authors of the gastronmic treatise, *The Gifts of Comus*, published in Paris in 1739, put it . . . 'analyzing, digesting, and extracting the quintessence of foods, drawing out the light and nourishing juices, mingling and blending them together'"; Laudan, "Birth of the Modern Diet," 76–81. Montanari (*Culture of Food*, 119) provocatively suggests that the principle that "elite demand is driven by the rarity, expense and exclusive character of the goods consumed" was a major factor in the emergence of *nouvelle cuisine*. "Spices, which for a millennium had distinguished the cuisine of the rich" became commonly available with the "globe-encircling voyages of exploration and conquest" of the sixteenth century, and very soon thereafter European elites turned to "more delicate flavours."

25. Lehmann, *British Housewife*, 45–46, 51–53.

26. Davidson, *Woman's Work Is Never Done*, 47–48 (quoting Bradley trans. of Chomel, *Dictionnaire Oeconomique* [1725]); Glasse, *Art of Cookery* (1747), 77. For the "Eel Soop" recipe in full, see Chapter 5, #31.

27. Lehmann, *British Housewife*, 235, 176 (quoting *The Court and Country Cook* [1702]); Glasse, *Art of Cookery* (1747), 45, xxxii.

28. Smith, *Compleat Housewife* (1728), 9, 11, 11–12, 27, 36–37, 72; Smith, *Compleat Housewife* (1730), 4, 34; Raffald, *Experienced English House-keeper* (1769), 71. Many of the savory pies in both Smith and Glasse are filled with the "truffles, morels, cockscombs, . . . artichoke bottoms," and other enhancements that were thought to add a French dimension to a dish of any sort.

29. Lehmann, *British Housewife*, 355–56 (quoting *Tatler*, March 1709).

30. Stereotyping along these lines was not confined to the English defining themselves over against the French. French writers had not been above placing their own nation at the unpretentious and aboveboard pole of such antitheses. In 1654, in *Les Delices de la campagne*, Nicolas de Bonnefons advocated simplicity in cookery, urging that "the depraved ragouts" and indeed all made dishes (his French term for which is "*deguisemens*") be left "to foreigners"; see Wheaton, *Savoring the Past*, 125 (quoting Bonnefons, *Delices*). Earlier, during the long interval in the sixteenth century when the Florentine Catherine de' Medici held court in Paris, first as queen, then as queen mother to her three sons in succession, there had been a vogue for all things Italian among the French aristocracy, followed by a virulent anti-Italian backlash. The "attenuated elegance" of Catherine's court festivities came in for much criticism, particularly her gluttonous fondness for "artichoke hearts, coxcombs, and kidneys." After Catherine's line died out, propagandists for the first of the Bourbon monarchs, Henri IV, portrayed his predecessor's courtiers as "curled, crimped, waxed, and unnaturally powdered hermaphrodites, who awkwardly [ate] artichokes, asparagus and peas with little pronged forks." The image of the new ruler that was disseminated, on

the other hand, was that of "a rugged, garlic-smelling king on horseback who . . . stood for 'a chicken in every pot, every Sunday'"; see Young, "Catherine de' Medici's Fork," 447–48.

31. Smith, *Compleat Housewife* (1728), sig. A4 (typography reversed).

32. Glasse, *Art of Cookery* (1747), ii. See Lehmann, *British Housewife*, for analysis of the contradiction between this outburst and the heavily French content of the book itself (113–14) and for similar expressions of hostility to French cooking in other eighteenth-century English cookbooks (118, 119). According to Kate Colquhoun (*Taste*, 363), this set of stereotypes persisted into the second half of the twentieth century. A popular 1973 cookbook was based on the premise that "a distinctive British national cuisine" must be one that is "unencumbered by French chicanery."

33. Lehmann, *British Housewife*, 103 (quoting Harrison, *Housekeeper's Pocket-book* [1733]), 355 (quoting de Saussure, *Lettres et Voyages* [1725–29]).

34. Raffald, *Experienced English House-keeper* (1769), iii; Lehmann, *British Housewife*, 163.

35. Raffald, *Experienced English House-keeper* (1769), 133.

36. Monaghan, *Learning to Read and Write*, 374. These figures indicate more distinct improvement in female literacy during the eighteenth century than the research in Lockridge, *Literacy in Colonial New England*, 38–42, had indicated.

37. Monaghan, *Learning to Read and Write*, 31–32, 43–44; Hall, *Cultures of Print*, 58; Hall, *Worlds of Wonder*, 34, 32.

38. Hall, *Worlds of Wonder*, 248 (citing Main, "Standard of Living in Southern New England").

39. Carson, "Consumer Revolution in Colonial British America," 499; Sweeney, "High-Style Vernacular," 4.

40. McMahon, "Comfortable Subsistence," 44–45.

41. Monaghan, *Learning to Read and Write*, 392; Hayes, *Colonial Woman's Bookshelf*, 11–16; Crain, "Print and Everyday Life," 71.

42. Sweeney, "High-Style Vernacular," 5; Carson, "Consumer Revolution in Colonial British America," 620. For a succinct summary of the eighteenth-century consumer revolution, see Conforti, *Saints and Strangers*, 174–78.

43. Carson, "Consumer Revolution in Colonial British America," 624, 587–96, 597–605. The first house plan in America with a designated dining room dates from 1681, for a house in Boston. A quarter century or so later, the fashion began to catch on in more provincial areas, for sometime after 1701 the Providence merchant Nicholas Power built a house that was the first one in town "to feature its own dining room"; see Smith, *Oxford Encyclopedia of Food and Drink in America*, 1:393; Austin, "One Line of the Power Family," 18–19; and Rappleye, *Sons of Providence*, 10.

44. Carson, "Consumer Revolution in Colonial British America," 596–97 (quotation from *True Gentlewoman's Delight* [1653]).

45. Sweeney, "High-Style Vernacular," 9; Hooker, *Food and Drink in America*, 90–91; Breen, *Marketplace of Revolution*, 53; Carson, "Consumer Revolution in Colonial British America," 652–53.

46. Breen, *Marketplace of Revolution*, 43 (quoting Eliot, *Continuation of the Essay on Field-Husbandry*); McMahon, "Comfortable Subsistence," 33, 36–41, 45, 52–59; McMahon, "'All Things in Their Proper Season,'" 132–36.

47. Gardiner, *Mrs. Gardiner's Family Receipts*, 52–53, 8; Raffald, *Experienced English House-keeper* (1769), 137; Glasse, *Art of Cookery* (1747), 65. For Gardiner's giblet pie, see below, Chapter 11, #3; and for Glasse's Scotch barley broth, see Chapter 5, #2.

48. Carson, "Consumer Revolution in Colonial British America," 653.

49. Mennell, *All Manners of Food*, 103–108; Fischer, *Albion's Seed*, 135–36.

50. "John Winthrop's Experiencia, 1616–18," in *Winthrop Papers*, 1:193–94.

51. Morgan, *Puritan Family*, 16 (quoting Cotton, *Practical Commentary upon John*).

52. Crowley, *This Sheba, Self*, 3, 17–18, 50; Hall, *Worlds of Wonder*, 51–52; Williams, *Correspondence*, 2:615 (To Major John Mason and Governor Thomas Prence, 22 June 1670).

53. Ibid.; Foster, *Their Solitary Way*, 121 (quoting Cotton, *Christ the Fountaine of Life*). These doctrines were viewed by those hostile to Puritanism as nothing but threadbare rationalizations of hypocrisy. Thus in Ben Jonson's play *Bartholomew Fair*, the representative Puritan character, Zeal-of-the-Land-Busy, argues that one may satisfy "a longing to eat pig . . . so it be eaten with a reformed mouth"; Jonson, *Bartholomew Fair*, 58, 59 (I, vi, 39, 68–69; quoted in Poole, *Radical Religion*, 58).

54. Johnson, *Johnson's Wonder-Working Providence*, 210. Puritan divines sometimes used the language of gastronomic pleasure to describe the state of grace. Being reborn spiritually was analogous to being healthy physically, said John Cotton, and "its a signe of health to rellish a sweetnesse in our meat [food]"; Knight, *Orthodoxies in Massachusetts*, 118 (quoting Cotton, *Christ the Fountaine of Life*). Max Weber's arguments regarding the relations between "the Protestant ethic and the spirit of capitalism" have been endlessly debated. The view of the issue taken here is based on that in Stavely, *Puritan Legacies*, 63–68.

55. Milton, "Sonnet XVII," in *Poems of John Milton*, 410 (ll. 1, 9–12).

56. Jonson, "Inviting a Friend to Supper," in *Anchor Anthology*, 68–69 (ll. 9–29).

57. For an instance of Jonson's ridicule of Puritanism, see above, n. 53.

58. Carter, *Frugal Housewife*, 105–10, 63–64, 65, 69, 55. Some of Carter's savory pies show a similar ancestry; see 112, 115–16.

59. Breen, *Marketplace of Revolution*, xvi (quoting *New-London Gazette*, 27 November 1767); Breen, "Baubles of Britain," 468 (quoting sources cited in Larned, *History of Windham County, Connecticut*).

60. Gardiner, *Mrs. Gardiner's Family Receipts*, 2, 9, 17, 56–57, 9–10.

61. Neustadt, *Clambake*, 32 (quoting Ezra Stiles). For the disapprobation of Indian

corn and most types of shellfish in early New England, see Stavely and Fitzgerald, *America's Founding Food*, 8–12, 76–77, 88–89.

62. Neustadt, *Clambake*, 32 (quoting Old Colony Club Records cited in Albert Matthews, "Term Pilgrim Fathers and Early Celebrations of Forefathers' Day" [1915], and *Boston Gazette*, 28 December 1772).

63. Sweeney, "High-Style Vernacular," 31, 46, 51, 57.

64. Parkman, Diary, 30 May 1760, American Antiquarian Society.

65. Franklin, *Autobiography*, 81 (quoted in Breen, *Marketplace of Revolution*, 154).

66. Hess and Hess, *Taste of America*, 28 (quoting Franklin).

CHAPTER TWO. THE YOUNG REPUBLIC

1. The political significance to Americans of no longer taking their "cultural cues" from Great Britain during the decade preceding the American Revolution is discussed in Breen, "Baubles of Britain," 444–82. Despite the success of the Revolution, the work of dissociating from "the bonds of empire," as Breen describes the psychological ties to British goods and culture, continued in the first decades after independence and are evident in Simmons.

2. Simmons, *American Cookery* (introduction by Wilson), ix–x; Simmons, *American Cookery* (introduction by Hess), ix.

3. Simmons, *American Cookery* (Wilson), "Advertisement."

4. Ibid., xi, xvii–xviii, and "Advertisement." Simmons, *American Cookery* (Hess), 5. Ironically, Hannah Woolley, among English cookbook writers "the first woman writer to proclaim herself as such on the title-page of her books," ran into similar trouble. Her *Gentlewoman's Companion* (1673) carried Woolley's name but was, in its published form, "apparently the result of a fraudulent transformation of her manuscript," in this case by her publisher. Woolley too complained that "her reputation as an author . . . [would be] ruined by the changed text." Strangely, in spite of her complaints, the text of the second edition of Woolley's book, brought out by a different publisher, "was identical to that of the first" (Lehmann, *British Housewife*, 48, 49). Simmons, at least, bothered to correct what she perceived as errors.

5. Simmons, *American Cookery* (Wilson), ix–x; Simmons, *American Cookery* (Hess), xii, xv.

6. Matthews, *"Just a Housewife,"* 7; Theophano, *"Eat My Words,"* 233. The most significant discussions of the "Republican Mother" are Kerber, *Women of the Republic*, 228–31, and Norton, *Liberty's Daughters*, 242–50. Norton (251–55) and Cathy Davidson (*Revolution and the Word*, 131–34) note that while the writings of Mary Wollstonecraft contributed distinctly to the propagation in the early republic of a feminism that went well beyond republican motherhood, the alleged promiscuity of Wollstonecraft's life contributed even more distinctly to the discrediting of such an outlook. Davidson in particular argues that the demise of Wollstonecraft-style feminism cleared the ground for republican motherhood to evolve into the nineteenth-century cult of domesticity.

7. Theophano, *"Eat My Words,"* 233, 235; Simmons, *American Cookery* (Wilson),

x. Jessamyn Neuhaus (*Manly Meals,* 10) notes that "anti-British propaganda had long co-opted English characterizations of America as an unruly child." Simmons's Americanizing of cuisine was one of a number of such nationalistic initiatives undertaken around this time, ranging (to mention only a couple of examples) from the American epic poems of Timothy Dwight and Joel Barlow in the 1780s to Bernard McMahon's *American Gardener's Calendar* in the first decade of the nineteenth century. Like that of Simmons, many of these other declarations of cultural independence were based—ironically—upon models provided by the former mother country, such as Milton's *Paradise Lost* or English month-by-month gardening manuals; see Stavely, "World All before Them," 148–49, and Hatch, "Bernard McMahon."

8. Dudden, *Serving Women,* 10, 20; Shammas, *History of Household Government in America,* 61–62.

9. Towner, "Good Master Well Served," 108, 110–12.

10. Simmons, *American Cookery* (Wilson), 3–4.

11. Ibid., 3.

12. Cathy Davidson has analyzed the development of the early American novel during the decade in which *American Cookery* was published, from *The Power of Sympathy* (1789) by William Hill Brown (grandiosely advertised as the "FIRST AMERICAN NOVEL," with the publicity timed "to coincide with the preparations for the inauguration of the first American president") to *The Coquette* (1797) by Hannah Webster Foster. She concludes that in these novels the victims of the incomplete realization of republican ideals in early national society are not only orphans and widows, as Simmons would primarily have it, but rather all women: "Sentimental novels in the new Republic are ultimately about silence, subservience, stasis (the accepted attributes of women as traditionally defined) in contradistinction to conflicting impulses toward independence, action, and self-expression (the ideals of the new American nation)"; *Revolution and the Word,* 83–150, quotations at 90, 84, 147.

13. Dudden, *Serving Women,* 10.

14. Simmons, *American Cookery* (Wilson), 3; Lehmann, *British Housewife,* 138–39. Among the indications that Simmons was keenly aware of class are her reference to "All Grades of Life" on her title page and, in her second edition preface, to "all classes of citizens," a phrase that combines the hopefulness of republican ideology ("citizens") with a sense of the permanence of social hierarchy ("all classes"). See Simmons, *American Cookery* (Hess), 6.

15. Simmons, *American Cookery* (Hess), 5. Throughout the prefaces to the two editions, Simmons expresses deference to the upper classes, at the same time indicating that her book will also be helpful to all Americans. In this she adapts the British conventions we have seen in Glasse and Raffald (gratitude for the patronage of ladies, instruction of servants) to American republican ideals.

16. Ibid., 5–6.

17. Simmons, *American Cookery* (Wilson), xviii–xix, xxiv.

18. Glasse, *Art of Cookery* (1747), 160–64; Smith, *Compleat Housewife* (1750), 1–12 (copied in part from Glasse); Lehmann, "Birth of a New Profession," 14, 19, 22, 23, 24; Dudden, *Serving Women*, 136; Rundell, *New System of Domestic Cookery*, 1–3, 23–25, 79–81; Child, *American Frugal Housewife*, 43–46, 53, 57–58; Lee, *Cook's Own Book*, xxxiii–xxxv; Beecher, *Domestic Receipt-Book*, 26–30.

19. Compare, for example, Simmons, *American Cookery* (Wilson), 5, 8–9 (choosing beef, capons, hares, leveret, rabbits), with the corresponding advice in Glasse, *Art of Cookery* (1747), 161, 162, 163.

20. Simmons, *American Cookery* (Hess), x, 7.

21. Ibid., 5; Simmons, *American Cookery* (Wilson), Errata.

22. Indeed, plagiarism had long been widespread among English cookbook authors. For Glasse's considerable engagement in it, see above, Chapter 1, n. 19.

23. Theophano, *Eat My Words*, 235; Simmons, *American Cookery* (Hess), xv; Simmons, *American Cookery* (Wilson), t.p.

24. Ibid., xi–xvii; Simmons, *American Cookery* (Hess), 43–44.

25. Simmons, *American Cookery* (Hess), xii–xv; Glasse, *Art of Cookery* (Hess), ix–x; above, Chapter 1, nn. 61–66. Hess catalogs the use of many of these same American products in earlier British and even French cookbooks and gives examples of recipes in which Simmons substitutes an American foodstuff in making traditional English dishes, as in her replacement of oatmeal with cornmeal in her "Indian Pudding" recipes; see xiii. Other historians argue that pearl ash was also not an American innovation but rather "one of the professional secrets of European bakers"; see Smith, *Oxford Encyclopedia of Food and Drink in America*, 1:217. For critiques of Hess's denials of the Americanness of johnnycake and pumpkin pie specifically, see Stavely and Fitzgerald, *America's Founding Food*, 292–93, n. 92, 67, 301, n. 62.

26. Simmons, *American Cookery* (Hess), xii, xiv, x.

27. Lehmann, *British Housewife*, 260, 194, 231, 267; above, Chapter 1, nn. 29–35.

28. Fernandez-Armesto, *Near a Thousand Tables*, 114, 122.

29. Simmons, *American Cookery* (Hess), 31, 13, 34–35, 41–42, xiii–xv.

30. Simmons, *American Cookery* (Wilson), xviii–xix. On the consumer revolution, see above, Chapter 1, nn. 41–48.

31. Simmons, *American Cookery* (Wilson), 29, 46, 32, 24; see also ibid., 30, 47.

32. Ibid., xix. In some instances, foods thought to originate in the New World had long, if forgotten, histories in the Old. See, for instance, the discussion of the origins of doughnuts in Stavely and Fitzgerald, *America's Founding Food*, 354, n. 90.

33. Karcher, *First Woman in the Republic*, 2.

34. Ibid., chap. 1, esp. 33–37. See chaps. 1–6 for Child's early years and writing career from the publication of *Hobomok* to *The Frugal Housewife*; and for her conversion to abolitionism and its adverse effect on her career, see chaps. 7–8. Some of the scholarship on "the theme of the disappearing Indian" in early-nineteenth-

century New England culture, as well as on the continuing Indian presence in the region, is cited in Stavely and Fitzgerald, *America's Founding Food*, 296–97, n. 136.

35. Karcher, *First Woman in the Republic*, xix–xxv, 47–49.

36. Ibid., 1–4, 38.

37. Ibid., 14.

38. Ibid., 69. Whatever her emotional commitments, in nineteenth-century legal terms Child's husband's financial difficulties were her own. As Karcher (102) explains, because of coverture law, "she found herself at the mercy of David's spiraling debts."

39. Child, *American Frugal Housewife*, t.p. verso; Karcher, *First Woman in the Republic*, 129, 646, n. 10.

40. On the eighteenth-century preference for the English imprint over the American, see Breen, "Baubles of Britain," 459. See also above, Chapter 1, n. 41 (colonial imprints v. book imports).

41. *Feeding America*, "Mary Randolph Biography"; Nylander, *Our Own Snug Fireside*, 212–13.

42. Nylander, *Our Own Snug Fireside*, 213 (no source given).

43. Karcher, *First Woman in the Republic*, 131, 128; Matthews, *"Just a Housewife,"* 12–14.

44. Karcher, *First Woman in the Republic*, 128–29; Leslie, *Seventy-five Receipts*, 37–38, 54–55.

45. Child, *American Frugal Housewife*, t.p.; Karcher, *First Woman in the Republic*, 130–31. Other advocates of domestic self-reliance also rose to prominence in the 1830s, but their messages tended to emphasize dietary reform rather than economy. Primary among them was Sylvester Graham, whose recommendation that housewives return to making their own bread offered women a sense of control over their families' health and thus an important social role. The housewife following Graham's advice may also have saved money, but that was not his primary purpose. On Graham and other nutritional reformers, see Nissenbaum, *Sex, Diet, and Debility*.

46. Karcher, *First Woman in the Republic*, 133–35, discusses some specific ways in which Child violates "the genteel code" in the language she uses in the first edition; a painfully diligent student of refinement when it came to literary style, Child removed in the second edition many of these "vulgarisms," for example, changing "emptings" to "yeast" and "nice" to "good." On genteel consumerism, see, among many others, Bushman, *Refinement of America*; on nineteenth-century New England cookbooks as responses to such consumerism, see Stavely and Fitzgerald, *America's Founding Food*, 133–47 (134–37, 138–40 devoted specifically to Child); and on the forms that consumerism took in the eighteenth century, see above, Chapter 1, nn. 41–48. The cultural developments that historians call the ideal of woman's sphere and the cult of domesticity were closely linked to genteel consumerism. Karcher, *First Woman in the Republic*, 129–30, states that

"the ideology governing *The Frugal Housewife* is not the cult of domesticity," although she notes one passage, added after the book became *The American Frugal Housewife*, in which Child speaks of "domestic life as the gathering place of the deepest and purest affections; as the sphere of woman's *enjoyments* as well as of her *duties*; as, indeed, the whole world to her" (*AFH*, 95). At the time Child was writing, it was not yet firmly established that a household in which the woman's supportive role would be primarily emotional was also expected to be a household that was expensively refined in its furnishings, decor, and way of life. Thus, Child could simultaneously affirm the "affections," oppose extravagance, and advocate for frugality and housewifely expertise on thoroughly hardheaded grounds as the key to the family's economic survival and security.

47. Karcher, *First Woman in the Republic*, 647, n. 11 (quoting Alcott, *Young Wife*), 126–28; Nylander, *Our Own Snug Fireside*, 213. For additional discussion of the many alarms that were sounded about the loss of housewifely skills among the young women of the nineteenth century, see below, Chapter 3, nn. 44, 47–48, and Stavely and Fitzgerald, *America's Founding Food*, 139, 142.

48. Child, *American Frugal Housewife*, 7.

49. Karcher describes Child's ideological intent, or lack thereof, when she began *The Frugal Housewife*: "At bottom, however, the impetus that generated *The Frugal Housewife* was practical rather than ideological. Only as an afterthought had Child incorporated into the book the 'Hints to People of Moderate Fortune' she had begun publishing in the *Massachusetts Journal* six months earlier. In its original form she had geared *The Frugal Housewife* simply toward offering pointers on how to cope with the day-to-day tasks a low-income housewife must perform." Nevertheless, the book as it appeared in print, with the addition of those "Hints," and the "Introductory Chapter," was highly ideological, as Karcher outlines. The larger political implications of Child's domestic advice were also clear, at least to her more astute readers: "It would be through these articles, many of which were reprinted in other newspapers, that she would attract the attention of William Lloyd Garrison. As a cultural critic, Child staked out an ambiguous position. Her 'Hints' on domestic economy, though squarely within woman's sphere, articulated political values that applied to larger public issues, as Garrison recognized." See Karcher, *First Woman in the Republic*, 130, 129–30, 118.

50. Child, *American Frugal Housewife*, 99–103.

51. Ibid., 102–3; above, Chapter 1, n. 63.

52. Few careers are more interesting than that of Benjamin Thompson, aka Count Rumford (1753–1814), a loyalist American who was a physicist, inventor, reformer, and who had been made a count of the Holy Roman Empire for his services to Bavaria. Mennell, *All Manners of Food*, 147–48, points out that the famous nineteenth-century French chef Antonin Carême could not have popularized soufflés had Rumford not invented a stove that allowed better control of heat. Nylander, *Our Own Snug Fireside*, 217–18, provides a succinct explanation, with illustrations, of the construction and workings of the Rumford range, as well as a discussion of its drawbacks. As discussed in Chapter. 1, n. 26, the stew hole or stew stove was a charcoal-fueled hearth set slightly below waist height

that allowed the cook better control of heat than did the open hearth. Imported into England from France in the early eighteenth century as part of the keen interest among the English upper classes in all things relating to French cookery, the stoves arrived in the colonies around the same time. See Ferry, "French Connection," www.chowdc.org/Papers/Ferry%202001.html. For descriptions of stew stove cooking as practiced by the American elite, see Fowler, ed., *Dining at Monticello*, 25, 99. For the development of the cookstove, see Strasser, *Never Done*, 36–38, 40, and Brewer, *From Fireplace to Cookstove*.

53. Brewer, *From Fireplace to Cookstove*, 79. On cooking in the traditional hearth setting, see the sources cited in Stavely and Fitzgerald, *America's Founding Food*, 284, n. 32. Significant investments in kitchen equipment had been made by this time in some households. Dudden, *Serving Women*, 132, points out that "in the 1830s food supply patterns, and therefore cooking, began to change, thanks to refrigeration and railroads. By 1838 the New York *Mirror* could remark that although it was only a few years since the refrigerator had come into common use, it was now considered an 'article of necessity' as much as a carpet or a dining table." But for the many for whom a carpet or a dining table proved too expensive, the improvements brought by technology and transportation were equally inaccessible.

54. Brewer, *From Fireplace to Cookstove*, 80 (quoting Goodrich, *Recollections of a Lifetime*, and Hazen and Hazen, *Keepers of the Flame*). We use the stove to exemplify the profound domestic changes taking place as part of the Industrial Revolution. However, even small technological advances had the capacity to effect large change, as seen in this example from Dudden, *Serving Women*, 128: "The introduction of friction matches in the 1830s probably saved as much work as coal stoves, for 'locofocos,' or lucifer matches, eliminated the need for constant vigilance to keep a fire of some sort going."

55. Brewer, *From Fireplace to Cookstove*, 92, 18–24, 31, 41. As fireplaces were replaced by stoves, the desire to rekindle the old spark only grew among sentimental writers; see ibid., 99–104, and Stavely and Fitzgerald, *America's Founding Food*, 53–55. In Britain as in the United States, the preference for fireplaces over stoves persisted well into the nineteenth century; see Davidoff and Hall, *Family Fortunes*, 380–81. New Englanders' and other Anglo-Americans' appreciation of their open fireplaces also amounted to disapproval of stoves because of their association with German-Americans. Brewer (*From Fireplace to Cookstove*, 33) informs us that manufacturers were responsive to this ethnic antipathy: "Before 1750, most American stoves were decorated with traditional German images. . . . Thereafter, English words began to replace their German equivalents in inscriptions, and . . . stove plates sprouted flower pots, sheaves of wheat, and eight-pointed stars . . . floral patterns . . . and other naturalistic motifs [that] harmonized well with fashionable Anglo-American interiors." Hearths were sometimes maintained alongside cookstoves for culinary reasons as well: "roasting and brick oven baking gave superior results at the hearth, whereas griddle foods were easier to prepare on the stove"; Smith, *Oxford Encyclopedia of Food and Drink in America*, 2:214.

56. This predilection for outdated open-hearth cooking continued among subse-

quent Anglo-American cookbook writers such as Esther Allen Howland and Sarah Josepha Hale; see Brewer, *From Fireplace to Cookstove*, 113–17, and below, Chapter 3, nn. 19, 28.

57. Ibid., 65.

58. Roberts, *House Servant's Directory*, 161–62, 160 (quoted in Brewer, *From Fireplace to Cookstove*). This work offers an intriguing counterpoint to *The Frugal Housewife*, which it preceded into print by two years. In its emphasis on instructing servants on such matters as "general rules for setting out tables and sideboards in first order" and "cleaning plate, brass, steel, glass, mahogany," *The House Servant's Directory* seems at first glance virtually a handbook of the new luxuriating gentility that Child found so pernicious. However, the relationship between the two works is complicated by the fact that the author, Robert Roberts, was a free African American long employed by various elite families in the Boston area, for whom the possession of tables, sideboards, and plate and the establishment of stable "client relationships" with black male servants signified gentility not as ruinous extravagance but rather as settled manner of living. There is no evidence that Child objected to such traditional gentility. Christopher Gore, Roberts's employer at the time he composed *The House Servant's Directory*, may have encouraged and assisted Roberts with his book project, thus being "useful and generous" in the manner that Child claimed the practice of economy would enable her lower-middle-class readers to achieve as well; see Roberts, *House Servant's Directory*, t.p.; *Feeding America*, "Robert Roberts Biography"; Dudden, *Serving Women*, 34; and O'Leary, *At Beck and Call*, 56, 59, 175–76.

59. Cowan, *More Work for Mother*, 47–48; Strasser, *Never Done*, 24.

60. Dudden, *Serving Women*, 35 (quoting Tillson, *Woman's Story of Pioneer Illinois*).

61. Ibid., 39 (quoting Briggs, *Reminiscences and Letters*). "Help" was a form of extrafamilial household labor rooted in the colonial tradition of neighborhood exchanges of goods and services; see ibid., chap. 1; and Lasser, "Mistress, Maid and Market," chaps. 1–2.

62. Conforti, *Imagining New England*, 150–66 (164–66 on Child; quotation on 166); Hall, *Cultures of Print*, 36–78. For an instance from later in the century of nativistic deployment of Yankee virtues, one for which Harriet Beecher Stowe and her sister Catharine Beecher were responsible, see below, Chapter 3, n. 54.

63. Dudden, *Serving Women*, 124–25.

64. Child, *American Frugal Housewife*, 98; Dudden, *Serving Women*, 124; Child, *Appeal*, 23. For instances of the Northern view of Southern slaveholders as lolling in the lap of luxury, see Essig, *Bonds of Wickedness*, 99 (1789 quotation from Morse, *American Universal Geography*); Mason, *Slavery and Politics in the Early American Republic*, 53 (quoting *Connecticut Courant*, 20 December 1814); and Hale, *Northwood* (1827), 1:212, 215–16; and for a discussion of "the servant problem" in Catharine Beecher's works, see below, Chapter 3, nn. 50–54.

65. Child, *Appeal*, 195–96.

66. Child, *American Frugal Housewife*, 99.

67. Ibid., 97; Karcher, *First Woman in the Republic*, 70–71, 634, n. 50; Stavely and Fitzgerald, *America's Founding Food*, 136–40. For a calculation of the dollar value of Child's domestic recommendations, see Boydston, *Home and Work*, 133–35.

68. Mills, *Cultural Reformations*, 6, 2.

69. Karcher, *First Woman in the Republic*, 131–33; Child, *American Frugal Housewife*, 8–22. Among the first to criticize the book for incoherence was Sarah Josepha Hale: "There is not sufficient system in the arrangement of items" (quoted in Karcher, *First Woman in the Republic*, 133). On Catharine Beecher's systematizing tendencies, see below, Chapter 3, n. 63.

70. Brewer, *From Fireplace to Cookstove*, 105 (quoting Stowe, *Uncle Tom's Cabin*).

71. Nylander, *Our Own Snug Fireside*, 212 (quoting Randolph, *Virginia Housewife*).

72. Lowenstein, *Bibliography of American Cookery Books*, 32.

73. *The Cook's Own Book* and Leslie's *Seventy-five Receipts* were both published by Munroe and Francis of Boston, which reissued the Lee book bound together with *Seventy-five Receipts* several times. See *Feeding America*, "Introduction: *The Cook's Own Book*," and Lowenstein, *Bibliography*, 112. In at least one of these joint editions, and quite probably in all of them, the two recipes that we know Lee lifted from Leslie appear in both the Lee and Leslie sections of the volume.

74. Story, *Forging of an Aristocracy*, 124–29; Story, "Class and Culture in Boston," 184–88.

CHAPTER THREE. CUISINE AND CULTURE AT MIDCENTURY

1. Hale, *Good Housekeeper*, v. The available biographies of Hale, neither of them entirely satisfactory, are Finley, *Lady of Godey's*, and Rogers, *Sarah Josepha Hale*. For a brief summary of Hale's life and development, particularly her shift from an adherence to republicanism's approach to an egalitarian view of women to the Victorian notion of separate spheres, see Okker, *Our Sister Editors*, 38–46, 54–55. The next several paragraphs are based on these sources.

2. Hale, *Northwood* (1827), 4; Hale, *Northwood* (1852), iii (Hale's emphasis).

3. Hale, *Good Housekeeper*, vi. Okker, *Our Sister Editors*, 44, 229–30, n. 16, maintains that Hale was offered her first editorial position "not because of [*Northwood's*] success but because friends of her husband came to her aid." She also speculates, 230, n. 17, that financial difficulties at *The Ladies' Magazine* motivated the merger with *Godey's*. Nineteenth-century periodicals were often issued under variant titles; we shall refer to both *Ladies' Magazine* and *Godey's* only by their best-known names.

4. Hale, *Good Housekeeper*, vi–vii. Hale was also instrumental in the establishment of Thanksgiving as a national holiday; see Rogers, *Sarah Josepha Hale*, 96–102, and Smith, "First Thanksgiving," 81–84.

5. The claim is that John Roulstone wrote the first twelve lines. Hale denied the theft. See Finley, *Lady of Godey's*, 279–305. Okker notes that "more has been written about Hale's authorship of 'Mary's Lamb' than any other facet of her career"; *Our Sister Editors*, 2, 221, n. 2.

6. Karcher, *First Woman in the Republic*, 133 (quoting Hale's review in *Ladies' Magazine*).

7. *Feeding America*, "Eliza Leslie Biography."

8. Stavely and Fitzgerald, *America's Founding Food*, 251. According to Joyce Appleby (*Inheriting the Revolution*, 266), by the 1820s regional differences had become sufficiently marked that there had developed in the North a view of "America's revolutionary heritage as a call to innovation, enterprise, and reform," while the South "clung to values that pushed them apart" from the rest of the nation.

9. *Feeding America*, "Eliza Leslie Biography." Leslie wrote fiction as well as cookbooks, but most of her income came from the cookbooks; Smith, *Oxford Encyclopedia of Food and Drink in America*, 2:31.

10. Fernandez-Armesto, *Near a Thousand Tables*, 196–97.

11. Finley, *Lady of Godey's*, 68; Tonkovich, *Domesticity with a Difference*, 129.

12. Finley, *Lady of Godey's*, 160. Hale used the term elsewhere, for instance, in relation to women's formerly "inferior position." But there too the word was carefully chosen for its powerful religious overtones; see Okker, *Our Sister Editors*, 35.

13. Finley, *Lady of Godey's*, 161.

14. Ibid., 162; Tonkovich, *Domesticity with a Difference*, esp., 128–47.

15. Strasser, *Never Done*, 14–15.

16. Ibid., 16–17; above, Chapter 1, n. 46; Brewer, *From Fireplace to Cookstove*, 112.

17. Rogers, *Sarah Josepha Hale*, 120.

18. Above, Chapter 2, nn. 55–56; Brewer, *From Fireplace to Cookstove*, 114 (quoting Hale, *Mrs. Hale's New Cook Book*).

19. Tonkovich, *Domesticity with a Difference*, 105–6.

20. Ibid., 106 (quoting Hale, *Manners; or, Happy Homes and Good Society All the Year Round*).

21. Strasser, *Never Done*, 38.

22. Davidoff and Hall, *Family Fortunes*, 375.

23. Carson, "Consumer Revolution in Colonial British America," 664, 607.

24. Ibid., 612, 614.

25. Above, Chapter 1, nn. 42–43; Carson, "Consumer Revolution in Colonial British America," 630, 635.

26. Carson, "Consumer Revolution in Colonial British America," 675.

27. Ibid., 615.

28. Bushman, *Refinement of America*, xviii. Carson, "Consumer Revolution in Colonial British America," 659, points out that "the man who boasted in 1744 that 'his little woman att [sic] home drank tea twice a day,' might have found sympathy from pioneer housekeepers in Kentucky fifty years later, almost every one of whom, it was said, 'had some bowl or dish she brought from the old states . . . as proof of her primitive gentility.'" But fifty years after that, the Kentucky

housekeeper's bowl or dish would have been a dime a dozen, thus no indication of gentility. Okker, *Our Sister Editors*, 67, speculates that Hale might have realized that her promotion of the sewing machine "represented a potential challenge to the ideology of separate spheres, in collapsing the distinction between the industrial and domestic worlds." It seems to us more likely that concern with social boundary maintenance, not concern with ideological consistency, dictated Hale's approach to the latest developments.

29. Finley, *Lady of Godey's*, 268 (quoting Hale, source not identified); Hale, *Good Housekeeper*, 103–4.

30. Tonkovich, *Domesticity with a Difference*, 74, 79 (quoting Hale in *Godey's*, 1853), 81.

31. Hall, *Cultures of Print*, 44.

32. Hale, *Good Housekeeper*, vi, 11, Preface to 2nd ed.

33. Ibid., 19, 12–15, 22.

34. Ibid., 24–30.

35. Ibid., 31.

36. Ibid., 127–28; below, n. 44; Child, *American Frugal Housewife*, 91–97, esp. 92–93.

37. Hale, *Good Housekeeper*, 122, 126. Most of the material on mistresses and servants is reprinted in *Ladies' New Book of Cookery*, 437–44.

38. *Feeding America*, "Introduction: The Ladies' New Book of Cookery"; Hale, *Ladies' New Book of Cookery*, 134–36, 116.

39. Hale, *Ladies' New Book of Cookery*, iv. Of course, as we have seen with her poem about Mary's lamb, Hale was among those responsible for the development of children's literature as a distinct genre.

40. Ibid., iii–iv; Finley, *Lady of Godey's*, 217. On Hale's involvement with the curriculum at Vassar College, see ibid., 217–18.

41. Boydston, ed., *Limits of Sisterhood*, 15–17; Hedrick, *Harriet Beecher Stowe*, 4–5, 12.

42. Boydston, ed., *Limits of Sisterhood*, 17–19. Sklar, *Catharine Beecher*, 29–42, provides a detailed account of Beecher's twin crises of her failed conversion and her fiancé's death. For discussions of the Hartford Female Seminary, see ibid., 64–104; and Hedrick, *Harriet Beecher Stowe*, 31–43. And for discussions of the education of women in the late eighteenth and early nineteenth centuries, see Kerber, *Women of the Republic*, 189–231; Norton, *Liberty's Daughters*, 256–94; and Kelly, *In the New England Fashion*, 70–76.

43. Beecher, *Miss Beecher's Domestic Receipt-Book*, xi; Glasse, *Art of Cookery* (1747), i.

44. Ibid., ii; above, Chapter 1, nn. 15–16; Beecher, *Treatise on Domestic Economy*, t.p., 27.

45. Lehmann, *British Housewife*, 70 (quoting Haywood, *Female Spectator*). See also Lehmann, "Birth of a New Profession," 15–17.

46. Gardiner, *Mrs. Gardiner's Family Receipts*, 12–13, 42, 56, 60.

47. *New Letters of Abigail Adams*, xxxiii (quoting *Diary of William Bentley*); *Letters of Mrs. Adams*, 265 (AA to Elizabeth Smith Shaw Peabody, 5 June 1809). See also, for example, *Adams Family Correspondence*, 1:61–62 (AA to Mary Smith Cranch, 31 January 1767), 377 (AA to Mercy Otis Warren, 13 April 1776), 2:212–13 (AA to John Adams, 17 April 1777), 5:364 (AA to Mary Smith Cranch, 10 July 1784), 395 (AA to Elizabeth Smith Shaw, 11 July 1784); *New Letters of Abigail Adams* (all letters, AA to Mary Smith Cranch), 74 (30 October 1791), 114 (28 November 1797); *Letters of Mrs. Adams*, 245 (AA to Colonel W. S. Smith, 3 May 1801). The examples of Gardiner and Adams may suggest a need to qualify Mary Beth Norton's argument (*Liberty's Daughters*, 3–33) that the model of the "notable housewife," an expert all around the house, was not by and large willingly followed but was rather the joint product of necessity and male imposition.

48. Boydston, ed., *Limits of Sisterhood*, 15, 24, 27; Stowe, *House and Home Papers*, 125–47; Tonkovich, *Domesticity with a Difference*, 4, 7.

49. *Adams Family Correspondence*, 6:241 (AA to Mary Smith Cranch, 8 July 1785). For the servant question in nineteenth-century America, see among others, Dudden, *Serving Women*; Diner, *Erin's Daughters in America*, 80–94; Hotten-Somers, "Relinquishing and Reclaiming Independence"; Katzman, *Seven Days a Week*; Lasser, "Mistress, Maid and Market"; Lynch-Brennan, "Ubiquitous Biddy"; Sutherland, *Americans and Their Servants*; Ryan, *Love, Wages, Slavery*; and O'Leary, *At Beck and Call*.

50. Beecher, *Miss Beecher's Domestic Receipt-Book*, 269–70; Beecher, *Treatise on Domestic Economy*, 199.

51. Ibid., 197; Beecher, *Miss Beecher's Domestic Receipt-Book*, 280–82. Of course, the servants of an earlier day were not always obedient and cooperative either. In 1721, a Massachusetts clergyman complained of servants who "must have liberty for their tongues to speak almost what and when they please; liberty to give and receive visits of their own accord; liberty . . . to go & come almost when they will without telling why or wherefore. . . . may be the work they are set about, they reckon 'tis beneath or below them, they wont stoop to do it"; Gildrie, *The Profane, the Civil, & the Godly*, 93 (quoting Wadsworth, *Well-Ordered Family*).

52. Beecher, *Treatise on Domestic Economy*, 198, 202.

53. Beecher, *Miss Beecher's Domestic Receipt-Book*, 270, 247.

54. Beecher and her sister were not above indulgence in the standard nativist denigrations of Irish servant girls as constitutionally incompetent. In *The American Woman's Home*, 230–31, they contrast "a raw Irish maid-of-all-work, a creature of immense bone and muscle, but of heavy, unawakened brain" who "establish[es] . . . a reign of Chaos and old Night in the kitchen and through the house," with a "daughter of a neighboring farmer . . . a tall, well-dressed young person, grave, unobtrusive, self-respecting, yet not in the least presuming," who in short order gives this same kitchen and home "that neat, orderly appearance that so often strikes one in New-England farm-houses." This passage was drafted by Harriet Beecher Stowe (compare Stowe, *House and Home Papers*, 140–41), but by her

coauthorship with Stowe of *The American Woman's Home*, Beecher assumed responsibility for it.

55. Beecher, *Miss Beecher's Domestic Receipt-Book*, xi, 121–30, 146–53, 165–82.

56. Ibid., 11, 13, 50–56.

57. Ibid., xi, 127. For a similar contradiction in the work of Hale, as regards styles in female dress, see above, n. 30. Hale, by the way, also expressed disapproval of pie crust; *Good Housekeeper*, 81.

58. Hess, ed., *Martha Washington's Booke of Cookery*, 451; *Compleat Cook*, 54; Beecher, *Miss Beecher's Domestic Receipt-Book*, 147, 138, 60.

59. Tonkovich, *Domesticity with a Difference*, 58 (quoting *Reunion Hartford Female Seminary, June 9, 1892*); Sklar, *Catharine Beecher*, 64–77, 88, 93. A few of Beecher's recipes are identical, or nearly so, to recipes in Webster, *Improved Housewife*, which was first published in Hartford in 1841. We note some instances of this in Part 2. Given that Beecher is otherwise less prone to cookbook plagiarism than most of her contemporaries, it may be that these recipes are among those that made their way into her book via the Hartford area alumnae of her school.

60. Tonkovich, *Domesticity with a Difference*, 8, 11; Hedrick, *Harriet Beecher Stowe*, 12.

61. Sklar, *Catharine Beecher*, 88. On the matters summarized in this paragraph, see among others Smith, *Revivalism and Social Reform*; Bushman, *Refinement of America*; and Kasson, *Rudeness and Civility*.

62. Tonkovich, *Domesticity with a Difference*, 5; Boydston, ed., *Limits of Sisterhood*, 15–16; Beecher, *Miss Beecher's Domestic Receipt-Book*, 14, 11, 46, 59.

63. Beecher, *Treatise on Domestic Economy*, 144, 369–71; Beecher, *Miss Beecher's Domestic Receipt-Book*, 247, 252–68; Tonkovich, *Domesticity with a Difference*, 9; Mathews, "Second Great Awakening as an Organizing Process," 23–43; Beecher and Stowe, *American Woman's Home*, 27–94, 116–21, 296–307.

64. Beecher, *Miss Beecher's Domestic Receipt-Book*, 234–46 (quotations on 234, 239).

65. Ibid., xi. Harriet Beecher Stowe never produced a cookbook. Nevertheless, as already implied by our use of a character from *Uncle Tom's Cabin* to illuminate the advantages of Child's unsystematic procedures, Stowe wrote about cooking in a lighter, more engaging manner than did her older sister. In addition to the numerous descriptions of cooking in her novels, Stowe drafted much of the chapter on "Good Cooking" in *The American Woman's Home*, 129–45 (compare with *House and Home Papers*, 225–65).

CHAPTER FOUR. THE CIVIL WAR AND AFTER

1. Cummings, *American and His Food*, 75, 53–59. Of course, for most people the aim was to consume larger quantities of fresh produce and whole grains, rather than to subsist on them as an exclusive diet.

2. Ibid., 12 (quoting Volney, *View of the Soil and Climate of the United States of America*).

3. "Amos Bronson Alcott." For an illuminating discussion of this issue as manifested

in Europe since the middle decades of the nineteenth century, see Montanari, *Culture of Food*, 152–71.

4. Romines, "Growing Up with the Methodist Cookbooks," 76.

5. McPherson, *Battle Cry of Freedom*, 481; Longone, "'Tried Receipts,'" 20–21.

6. Ibid., 21–22.

7. Kirshenblatt-Gimblett, "Moral Sublime," 147.

8. Ross, "Ella Smith's Unfinished Community Cookbook," 163–65.

9. Cummings, *American and His Food*, 67; Longone, "'Tried Receipts,'" 18; Neuhaus, *Manly Meals*, 17; Romines, "Growing Up with the Methodist Cookbooks," 84. Borden's condensed milk got its start, like so much of the modern food industry, during the Civil War, when Gail Borden made his fortune selling it, along with cider and blackberry juice, to the Union Army. Borden had patented a vacuum process to extract water from the milk and fruit juices. The final product was highly sweetened with sugar, then canned. It had the singular advantage of an indefinite shelf life. From returning soldiers, the civilian population soon learned to enjoy its morning coffee and tea sweetened with Borden's condensed milk; see "Gail Borden."

10. Betsky, "Inside the Past," 251; Butler, "Another City upon a Hill," 19–20.

11. Betsky, "Inside the Past," 251 (quoting Wharton).

12. On New England building styles such as those found in Litchfield, Connecticut, being viewed as the most representative American architecture, see Butler, "Another City upon a Hill," 15–51.

13. Hedrick, *Harriet Beecher Stowe*, 346 (quoting Harte).

14. Ibid., 345 (quoting the *Nation*).

15. Ibid., 320–21.

16. Ibid., 320 (quoting McLoughlin, *Meaning of Henry Ward Beecher*).

17. Conforti, *Imagining New England*, 205–6. Stowe's domestic verisimilitude is what led us to draw frequently upon her four New England novels in our earlier study of the history of New England cooking; see Stavely and Fitzgerald, *America's Founding Food*, passim.

18. Conforti, *Imagining New England*, 225–27 (quoting Earle, *Margaret Winthrop*).

19. Ibid., 227; above, Chapter 1, n. 63.

20. Shapiro, *Perfection Salad*, 37.

21. For the idea that the supervision of servants constituted the equivalent in the household of the emerging managerial approach in business and industry, see Dudden, *Serving Women*, 155–92.

22. Shapiro, *Perfection Salad*, 48.

23. Ibid., 47–70. For an account of the slightly later New England Kitchen project, also aiming to alter the foodways of the urban working class, also Boston-based, and also purporting to be "scientific," see Levenstein, *Revolution at the Table*, 44–59.

24. Shapiro, *Perfection Salad*, 53, 55, 60, 56. Parloa's role in late-nineteenth-century American cuisine was similar to that of Woolley, Smith, and Glasse in seventeenth- and eighteenth-century England. She adapted for the middle class the sophistications of French cuisine that were becoming fashionable in the upper class; see Levenstein, *Revolution at the Table,* 19–20.

25. Shapiro, *Perfection Salad*, 60–61, 52, 59. Similarly, such success as the New England Kitchen achieved was with middle-class people, not workers; see Levenstein, *Revolution at the Table,* 52–53, 55, 58–59.

26. Neuhaus, *Manly Meals*, 19; Shapiro, *Perfection Salad,* 55.

27. Dudden, *Serving Women,* 65–66.

28. Shapiro, *Perfection Salad,* 57–58.

29. Ibid., 62–63; Neuhaus, *Manly Meals*, 21. For the trend toward increased or modified sweetening of various long-established New England dishes, see Stavely and Fitzgerald, *America's Founding Food,* 28–29, 57–59, 250–52. The fare offered by the New England Kitchen likewise consisted of "fish, clam, and corn chowders, 'Pilgrim Succotash,' . . . baked beans, and Indian pudding"; Levenstein, *Revolution at the Table,* 56–57.

30. Shapiro, *Perfection Salad,* 65. For the involvement of the New England Kitchen in the provision of school lunches in Boston, see Levenstein, *Revolution at the Table,* 51.

31. Shapiro, *Perfection Salad,* 68.

32. Ibid., 70.

33. Ibid., 114–17; Smith, *Oxford Encyclopedia of Food and Drink in America,* 1:451; Davidson, *Oxford Companion to Food,* 288–89; Carlin, "Weights and Measures," 67–77 (quotations at 76, 77).

34. Shapiro, *Perfection Salad,* 112, 118–19, 121, 125–26. Like some other colonial revivalists, such as Thomas Robinson Hazard, Farmer could be refreshingly skeptical when it came to some of the more blatantly "ye olde" aspects of the movement. Thus, she questioned the notion that "the fine reputation which Boston Baked Beans have gained" was due to "the earthen bean-pot with small top and bulging sides in which they are supposed to be cooked," maintaining that "equally good beans have often been eaten where a five-pound lard pail was substituted for the broken bean-pot"; Farmer, *Boston Cooking-School Cook Book,* 212 (partially quoted in Davidson, *Oxford Companion to Food,* 289). For Hazard's ridicule of Boston Brown Bread, see Stavely and Fitzgerald, *America's Founding Food,* 29.

35. Farmer's work is so widely available that we have included very little from it in our recipe selections.

36. Ames, "Introduction," 12; Roth, "New England, or 'Olde Tyme,' Kitchen Exhibit," 162.

37. Ibid., 164, 172.

Sources for Part 2
Recipes and Commentaries

CHAPTER FIVE. POTTAGES, CHOWDERS, SOUPS, AND STEWS

Introduction: Wilson, *Food and Drink in Britain*, p. 199 (quoting Boorde); Stavely and Fitzgerald, *America's Founding Food*, pp. 214, 338, n. 62; Wood, *New Englands Prospect*, p. 72; Karr, *Indian New England*, p. 80 (quoting Gookin); Montanari, *Culture of Food*, pp. 102–3; Mood, "John Winthrop, Jr., on Indian Corn," p. 123 (quoting Gerard, *Herball* [1636 ed.]).

English Grain Pottages Introduction: Colquhoun, *Taste*, pp. 58–59; Wilson, *Food and Drink in Britain*, p. 207.

#1: Lehmann, *British Housewife*, pp. 46, 44, 276; Wilson, *Food and Drink in Britain*, pp. 199 (quoting Boorde), 204, 205, 351–52, 355, 361; Davidson, *Oxford Companion to Food*, pp. 167, 88; Hess, *Martha Washington's Booke of Cookery*, p. 40.

#2: Gardiner, *Mrs. Gardiner's Family Receipts*, p. 8; Hess, *Martha Washington's Booke of Cookery*, pp. 44, 67, 15; Acworth, *Margaretta Acworth's Georgian Cookery Book*, p. 21; Wilson, *Food and Drink in Britain*, pp. 215–16, 195; Markham, *English Hus-wife* (1615), pp. 37, 39; McGee, *On Food and Cooking*, p. 248.

#4: Fernandez-Armesto, *Near a Thousand Tables*, pp. 125, 124 (quoting Camporesi, *Magic Harvest*); Wilson, *Food and Drink in Britain*, pp. 199–200.

New England Succotash Introduction: Whitehill, *Food, Drink, and Recipes of Early New England*, p. 9; Barlow, "Hasty Pudding," p. 91; Stavely and Fitzgerald, *America's Founding Food*, p. 42; Deetz, *In Small Things Forgotten*, p. 170.

#7: Hale, *Good Housekeeper*, p. 105.

Hominy Introduction: Williams, *Key into the Language of America*, pp. 11–12; Hardeman, *Shucks, Shocks, and Hominy Blocks*, pp. 142–43.

#9: Mood, "John Winthrop, Jr., on Indian Corn," pp. 130, 131.

Baked Beans Introduction: Drummond and Wilbraham, *Englishman's Food*, p. 25; Anderson, "Solid Sufficiency," pp. 221–22.

#13: Henisch, *Fast and Feast*, p. 112.

#14: McMahon, "Comfortable Subsistence," p. 45; Stavely and Fitzgerald, *America's Founding Food*, pp. 56, 59–60.

#15: Beecher, *Miss Beecher's Domestic Receipt-Book*, p. 78; Howland, *New England Economical Housekeeper*, p. 69.

Chowder Introduction: Oliver, *Saltwater Foodways*, p. 294; G. H. Bent Co., "Bent's Cookie Factory," www.bentscookiefactory.com/history.html; Lehmann, *British Housewife*, p. 53.

#18: Glasse, *Art of Cookery* (1747), p. 182; *OED*, "lute," "morel," "pepper"; Booth, *Hung, Strung, and Potted*, p. 16; Fernandez-Armesto, *Near a Thousand Tables*, p. 122.

#19: Hooker, *Book of Chowder*, p. 4; Wolcott, *Yankee Cook Book*, p. 6; Simmons, *American Cookery* (introduction by Wilson), p. 18; Lee, *Cook's Own Book*, p. 49; Dolby, *Cook's Dictionary*, p. 151.

#21: Ibid., p. 167; Davidson, *Oxford Companion to Food*, p. 12; Glasse, *Art of Cookery* (1747), p. 194; *OED*, "pepper"; Lee, *Cook's Own Book*, p. 51; Kitchiner, *Cook's Oracle* (1822), p. 365.

#22: *Roger Cookery*, p. 18; Lee, *Cook's Own Book*, p. 51; Kitchiner, *Cook's Oracle* (1822), p. 365.

#23: Stowe, *Pearl of Orr's Island*, p. 142 (chap. 14).

#25: Chadwick, *Home Cookery*, pp. 89–90, 93.

#26: Turner, *New England Cook Book*, pp. 51–52.

Soups Introduction: Wilson, *Food and Drink in Britain*, p. 223; Hess, *Martha Washington's Booke of Cookery*, pp. 65, 40; Smith, *Compleat Housewife* (1728), pp. 4–5.

#29: Wilson, *Food and Drink in Britain*, p. 256; Markham, *English Hus-wife* (1615), pp. 126–27; Lehmann, *British Housewife*, pp. 42–43; *OED*, "leer."

#30: Carter, *Frugal Housewife*, p. 81; Lehmann, *British Housewife*, pp. 207, 210–11.

#31: Wilson, *Food and Drink in Britain*, p. 225; Carter, *Frugal Housewife*, pp. 89–90; Fowler, *Dining at Monticello*, pp. 21, 23, 24–25.

#32: Wilson, *Food and Drink in Britain*, pp. 223–24; Smith, *Compleat Housewife*, (1728), pp. 4–5; Simmons, *American Cookery* (introduction by Hess), pp. 19, 20.

#33: Rombauer and Becker, *Joy of Cooking*, p. 590; Gardiner, *Mrs. Gardiner's Family Receipts*, p. 7; Glasse, *Art of Cookery* (1747), pp. 76–77; Beecher, *Miss Beecher's Domestic Receipt-Book*, pp. 60–61.

#34: Stavely and Fitzgerald, *America's Founding Food*, p. 156.

Stews Introduction: Raffald, *Experienced English House-keeper* (1769), p. 8; Beecher, *Miss Beecher's Domestic Receipt-Book*, pp. 40–41.

#35: McCance and Widdowson, *Breads White and Brown*, pp. 20, 1; Davidson, *Oxford Companion to Food*, pp. 235, 650–51; Wilson, *Food and Drink in Britain*, p. 287; Hess, *Martha Washington's Booke of Cookery*, p. 385 (quoting Gerard, *Herball* [1636 ed.]).

#36: Ibid., pp. 183–84, 174; Lehmann, *British Housewife*, pp. 42, 247–49, 101–3.

#38: Ibid., pp. 175–77, 179, 211, 123–26, 52–53, 41; Spencer, *British Food*, pp. 152–53; Willan, *Great Cooks*, p. 56.

#39: Lehmann, *British Housewife*, pp. 249, 47.

SIX. FISH AND SHELLFISH

Introduction: Davidson, *Oxford Companion to Food*, pp. 301 (quoting Bernard Read), 302 (quoting Graham, *Modern Domestic Medicine*); Stavely and Fitzgerald, *America's Founding Food*, pp. 76–77, 89; Oliver, *Saltwater Foodways*, p. 332; Hale, *Good Housekeeper*, p. 64; U.S. Census Bureau, 2008 Statistical Abstract, www.census.gov/compendia/statab/cats/health_nutrition/food_consumption_ and_nutrition.html, Table 205; Anderson, "Solid Sufficiency," p. 80 (quoting Hartley, *Food in England*); Drummond and Wilbraham, *Englishman's Food*, p. 38 (quoting Boorde); *Journal of the Pilgrims at Plymouth*, p. 48; Hawthorne, *Old Seaport Towns of New England*, pp. 117–18.

Eels Introduction: Schweid, *Consider the Eel*, p. 17; Davidson, *Oxford Companion to Food*, pp. 268–69; Wilson, *Food and Drink in Britain*, p. 37; Redon, *Medieval Kitchen*, pp. 7, 8; Spencer, *British Food*, p. 95; *Journal of the Pilgrims at Plymouth*, p. 97; Markham, *Countrey Contentments* (1623), p. 94.

#1: Josselyn, *John Josselyn, Colonial Traveler*, pp. 79–80; *OED*, "posnet"; Woolley, *Queen-like Closet*, pp. 68, 71, 79, 80, 81, 82; Howard, *England's Newest Way*, p. 137; Fearnley-Whittingstall, *River Cottage Cookbook*, p. 318; Colquhoun, *Taste*, pp. 263–64.

#2: Glasse, *Art of Cookery* (1747), pp. 194, xxxiii; *OED*, "spitchcock," "spatchcock"; *Whole Duty of a Woman*, p. 240; Carter, *Frugal Housewife*, p. 52; Raffald, *Experienced English House-keeper* (1769), p. 30; Lee, *Cook's Own Book*, p. 69; Allen, *Housekeeper's Assistant*, p. 129.

#3: Dalgairns, *Practice of Cookery*, p. 65; Lehmann, *British Housewife*, pp. 51–52, 183; Smith, *Compleat Housewife* (1728), p. 14; Carter, *Frugal Housewife*, p. 15.

#4: Davidson, *Oxford Companion to Food*, p. 676.

#5: Farmer, *Boston Cooking-School Cook Book*, p. 155.

Fish Miscellany Introduction: Stavely and Fitzgerald, *America's Founding Food*, pp. 109–10, 112–13; Davidson, *Oxford Companion to Food*, pp. 685, 758, 467, 806, 715; Oliver, *Saltwater Foodways*, pp. 389, 393, 378–79, 376, 384, 395, 391 (quoting Whymper, *Fisheries of the World*); Simmons, *American Cookery* (introduction by Wilson), p. 7; Trumbull, *Memorial History of Hartford*, 1:380–81.

#6: Oliver, *Saltwater Foodways*, p. 366.

#7: Davidson, *Oxford Companion to Food*, pp. 282, 154, 357, 432, 60–61, 758, 596; Hess, *Martha Washington's Booke of Cookery*, p. 177; Smith, *Compleat Housewife* (1739), p. 71; Glasse, *Art of Cookery* (1747), pp. 130–31; Florida Fish and Wildlife Conservation Commission, Fish and Wildlife Research Institute, Gallery: Saltwater Fish/Saltwater Fish Catalog/Southern Kingfish, research.myfwc.com /gallery/image_details.asp?id=13493; Encyclopedia Britannica Online, "Hind," http://library.eb.com/eb/article-9040508; Gardiner, *Mrs. Gardiner's Family Receipts*, p. 74.

#8: *OED*, "gill."

#9: Carter, *Frugal Housewife*, p. 76; Davidson, *Oxford Companion to Food*, p. 760.

#10: Smith, *Oxford Encyclopedia of Food and Drink in America*, 1:334; Glasse, *Art of Cookery* (1747), p. 186; Davidson, *Oxford Companion to Food*, p. 728.

#11: Webster, *Improved Housewife* (1844), p. 68; Oliver, *Saltwater Foodways*, p. 392; Davidson, *Oxford Companion to Food*, p. 612; Farmer, *Boston Cooking-School Cook Book*, p. 152.

#15: Stavely and Fitzgerald, *America's Founding Food*, pp. 10–11, 217, 236–39, 339–40; Oliver, *Saltwater Foodways*, p. 379.

#16: Cummings, *American and His Food*, p. 44.

Oysters Introduction: Swift, *Polite Conversation*, p. 130; Smith, *Oxford Encyclopedia of Food and Drink in America*, 2:224, 225; Clark, *Oysters of Locmariaquer*, pp. 39–40 (quoting Swift and Pliny), 6; Wilson, *Food and Drink in Britain*, pp. 21, 35, 43, 55; Spencer, *British Food*, p. 55; Davidson, *Oxford Companion to Food*, p. 563; Earle, *Home Life in Colonial Days*, pp. 118–19; Stavely and Fitzgerald, *America's Founding Food*, pp. 105–7; Pillsbury, *No Foreign Food*, p. 24; Hooker, *Food and Drink in America*, pp. 145–46; Oliver, *Saltwater Foodways*, pp. 386, 385; Hess, *Martha Washington's Booke of Cookery*, p. 74; Fisher, *Consider the Oyster, passim*, p. 45; Jacobsen, *Geography of Oysters*, p. 112.

#18: Raffald, *Experienced English Housekeeper* (1997), p. 203; Kitchiner, *Cook's Oracle* (1822), p. 199; Lee, *Cook's Own Book*, p. 131.

#19: Hess, *Martha Washington's Booke of Cookery*, p. 46; Davidson, *Oxford Companion to Food*, p. 204; Wilson, *Food and Drink in Britain*, p. 88; *OED*, "scallop, scollop"; Smith, *Compleat Housewife* (1728), menu section, November; Smith, *Compleat Housewife* (1968), menu section, September, October, November; Glasse, *Art of Cookery* (1747), p. 95; Gardiner, *Mrs. Gardiner's Family Receipts*, p. 30; Raffald *Experienced English House-keeper* (1769), p. 31; Thorne, *Simple Cooking*, p. 169.

#20: Beecher, *Miss Beecher's Domestic Receipt-Book*, p. 64.

#21: Ibid.; Wilson, *Food and Drink in Britain*, pp. 17, 54–55; Jacobsen, *Geography of Oysters*, pp. 8, 245–46.

Clams Introduction: Davidson, *Oxford Companion to Food*, pp. 524, 188; Spencer, *British Food*, p. 54; Stavely and Fitzgerald, *America's Founding Food*, pp. 76–77 (quoting Wood), 89, 306, n. 68; Wilson, *Food and Drink in Britain*, p. 43;

Woolley, *Queen-like Closet*, p. 124; Smith, *Compleat Housewife* (1728), p. 76; Glasse, *Art of Cookery* (1747), pp. 77, 95–96, 116, 135; Gardiner, Mrs. *Gardiner's Family Receipts*, pp. 19, 27, 30–31, 32; Simmons, *American Cookery* (introduction by Wilson), p. xix; Oliver, *Saltwater Foodways*, pp. 370, 372–73 (quoting Edward Knapp); Smith, *Oxford Encyclopedia of Food and Drink in America*, 1:258–59.

#22: Webster, *Improved Housewife* (1844), p. 73; Beecher, *Miss Beecher's Domestic Receipt-Book*, p. 66; Bliss, *Practical Cook Book*, p. 41; Chadwick, *Home Cookery*, pp. 93–94; Dean, *Cooking American*, pp. 33–34.

#23: Beecher, *Miss Beecher's Domestic Receipt-Book*, p. 66; Bliss, *Practical Cook Book*, p. 41.

#24: Hale, *Ladies' New Book of Cookery*, p. 64; Beecher, *Miss Beecher's Domestic Receipt-Book*, p. 66; Leslie, *Lady's Receipt Book*, p. 32.

#25: Lincoln and Barrows, *Home Science Cook Book*, p. 123; Dean, *Cooking American*, p. 33.

#s 26–27: Turner, *New England Cook Book*, p. 115; Wolcott, *New England Yankee Cook Book*, p. 61; Wolcott, *Yankee Cook Book*, p. 58; Dean, *Cooking American*, pp. 34–35.

Lobsters Introduction: Wilson, *Food and Drink in Britain*, pp. 21, 43–44, 49, 55, 57; Stavely and Fitzgerald, *America's Founding Food*, p. 102; Oliver, *Saltwater Foodways*, pp. 381 (quoting Higginson), 381–82 (quoting Capt. Thomas Fairfax, in *New York Times*), 344; Bradford, *Of Plymouth Plantation*, p. 130; Glasse, *Art of Cookery* (1747), pp. 95, 115; Gardiner, Mrs. *Gardiner's Family Receipts*, pp. 19, 23–24, 54; Raffald, *Experienced English House-keeper* (1769), p. 40; Webster, *Improved Housewife* (1844), p. 65; Lee, *Cook's Own Book*, p. 111; Davidson, *Oxford Companion to Food*, p. 457 (quoting Lord, *Crab, Shrimp and Lobster Lore*).

#28: Woolley, *Queen-like Closet*, p. 108; Glasse, *Art of Cookery* (1747), p. 95; Raffald, *Experienced English House-keeper* (1769), p. 33; McGee, *On Food and Cooking*, pp. 220–21.

#30: Dalgairns, *Practice of Cookery*, p. 67; McGee, *On Food and Cooking*, pp. 220, 223; Bliss, *Practical Cook Book*, p. 41; Chadwick, *Home Cookery*, p. 94; Mendall, *New Bedford Practical Receipt Book*, p. 12; Rombauer and Becker, *Joy of Cooking*, p. 385.

#31: Wilson, *Food and Drink in Britain*, pp. 44, 55; Raffald, *Experienced English House-keeper* (1769), p. 32; Beecher, *Miss Beecher's Domestic Receipt-Book*, pp. 64–65; Fussell, *Masters of American Cookery*, p. 190.

#32: Raffald, *Experienced English House-keeper* (1769), p. 32; Poole, *Radical Religion*, p. 64 (quoting Taylor, *Brownists Conventicle*).

Cod Introduction: Davidson, *Oxford Companion to Food*, pp. 198, 688; Oliver, *Saltwater Foodways*, pp. 373, 374, 375; Kurlansky, *Cod*, pp. 33, 19–21, 44, 24, 26, 27–29, 79; Day, *Fishes of Great Britain and Ireland*, 1:279 (partially quoted in Davidson, *Oxford Companion to Food*); Wilson, *Food and Drink in Britain*, pp. 34, 48; Innis, *Cod Fisheries*, p. 71 (quoting Martin Pring); Vickers, *Farmers and Fishermen*, p. 90; McManis, *Colonial New England*, p. 10; Stavely and Fitzgerald,

America's Founding Food, pp. 117–19, 77, 60; Spencer, *British Food*, pp. 55–56, 83–84, 94–95; Glasse, *Art of Cookery* (1747), Contents, Index, "cod," "salt fish," "salt fish pie"; Hamilton, *Gentleman's Progress*, p. 108; Bowles and Towle, *Secrets of New England Cooking*, p. 16; Drake, *Nooks and Corners of the New England Coast*, p. 314.

#34: Davidson, *Oxford Companion to Food*, pp. 454, 365; Alaska Fish and Game, Wildlife Notebook, "Lingcod," www.adfg.state.ak.us/pubs/notebook/fish/lingcod.php; Oliver, *Saltwater Foodways*, pp. 373, 377; Hamilton, *Gentleman's Progress*, p. 108; Mariani, *Dictionary of American Food and Drink*, p. 117.

#35: King, *When I Lived in Salem*, p. 98; Oliver, *Saltwater Foodways*, p. 373; Bowles and Towle, *Secrets of New England Cooking*, p. 15; Early, *New England Cookbook*, p. 19; Bliss, *Practical Cook Book*, p. 33; Beecher, *Miss Beecher's Domestic Receipt-Book*, p. 64; Brown, *Recipes from Old Hundred*, p. 40.

#36: Dolby, *Cook's Dictionary*, p. 175.

#37: Kurlansky, *Cod*, p. 34; Glasse, *Art of Cookery* (1747), pp. 57, 90; Carter, *Frugal Housewife*, p. 51; Dalgairns, *Practice of Cookery*, p. 48; Oliver, *Saltwater Foodways*, p. 368.

#38: Dalgairns, *Practice of Cookery*, p. 45; Davidson, *Oxford Companion to Food*, p. 201; Woolley, *Queen-like Closet*, p. 106; Smith, *Compleat Housewife* (1728), p. 8; Glasse, *Art of Cookery* (1747), p. 87; Raffald, *Experienced English House-keeper* (1769), pp. 15–16; Carter, *Frugal Housewife*, pp. 23–24; OED, "milt"; Rossi-Wilcox, *Dinner for Dickens*, p. 238; Hale, *Good Housekeeper*, pp. 64–65; Webster, *Improved Housewife* (1844), p. 69; Bliss, *Practical Cook Book*, p. 32.

#39: Wilson, *Food and Drink in Britain*, p. 44 (quoting *Goodman of Paris*); Bliss, *Practical Cook Book*, p. 34.

#40: Brown, *Recipes from Old Hundred*, p. 40.

#s 41–42: Putnam, *Mrs. Putnam's Receipt Book*, p. 18; Gould, *Two Half Dollars*, p. 106; Mariani, *Dictionary of American Food and Drink*, p. 358; *Dictionary of Americanisms* (1951), 2:1479; Bartlett, *Dictionary of Americanisms*, p. 561; Hale, *Good Housekeeper*, p. 66; Bowles and Towle, *Secrets of New England Cooking*, p. 20; American Classics, "Boston Baked Scrod," www.foodreference.com/html/boston-scrod.html.

CHAPTER SEVEN. FOWL, WILD AND TAME

Introduction: *Frontline*, "Modern Meat," www.pbs.org/wgbh/pages/frontline/shows/meat/safe/howmuch.html; OED, "fowl"; Wilson, *Food and Drink in Britain*, pp. 120–21; Spencer, *British Food*, pp. 120, 118–19, 117; Redon, *Medieval Kitchen*, pp. 18, 83–92; Stavely and Fitzgerald, *America's Founding Food*, pp. 162–63 (quoting Brillat-Savarin).

Wildfowl, Ducks, Geese Introduction: Wilson, *Food and Drink in Britain*, pp. 121 (quoting *Proper Newe Booke of Cokerye*), 130; Willan, *Great Cooks*, p. 50 (quoting Bartolomeo Scappi).

#1: Wheaton, *Savoring the Past*, p. 117; Wilson, *Food and Drink in Britain*, pp. 134,

101, 223; Glasse, *Art of Cookery* (1747), p. 41; Lehmann, *British Housewife*, pp. 282, 40, 38, 42, 44, 276, 34; Davidson, *Oxford Companion to Food*, p. 773; *OED*, "sippet," "sop."

#2: Examination of Smith editions 2 –7, 9–11, 13–14, in *Eighteenth-Century Collections Online*; Glasse, *Art of Cookery* (1747), pp. xxxii–xxxiii, 5, 6, 42; Lehmann, *British Housewife*, pp. 96, 162–63; Wilson, *Food and Drink in Britain*, p. 121; Oliver, *Saltwater Foodways*, p. 273.

#3: Lehmann, *British Housewife*, pp. 253–54.

#4: Glasse, *Art of Cookery* (1747), p. 10; Stavely and Fitzgerald, *America's Founding Food*, pp. 152–56; Lehmann, *British Housewife*, pp. 40–41, 214–18; *OED*, "ruff," "reif."

#5: Wilson, *Food and Drink in Britain*, pp. 113, 121.

#6: Dolby, *Cook's Dictionary*, pp. 218–19; Lehmann, *British Housewife*, pp. 249–51; Stavely and Fitzgerald, *America's Founding Food*, p. 322, n. 21.

#7: Wilson, *Food and Drink in Britain*, pp. 117, 133; Hale, *Good Housekeeper*, pp. 53–54.

#8: Stavely and Fitzgerald, *America's Founding Food*, pp. 154–56; Wilson, *Food and Drink in Britain*, pp. 56–57.

#9: Davidson, *Oxford Companion to Food*, p. 851.

#10: Ibid., p. 731; Wheaton, *Savoring the Past*, p. 117.

Chicken Introduction: Davidson, *Oxford Companion to Food*, pp. 378, 166; McGee, *On Food and Cooking*, p. 139, Stavely and Fitzgerald, *America's Founding Food*, pp. 156–57; Plymouth Archaeological Rediscovery Project, "European Chicken," plymoutharch.tripod.com/id8.html.

#11: Lehmann, *British Housewife*, pp. 48, 49, 51; Davidson, *Oxford Companion to Food*, p. 133; Wilson, *Food and Drink in Britain*, p. 135.

#12: Wheaton, *Savoring the Past*, p. 117; Davidson, *Oxford Companion to Food*, p. 683; Smith, *Oxford Encyclopedia of Food and Drink in America*, 2:13.

#13: *OED*, "fowl"; Simmons, *American Cookery* (introduction by Wilson), pp. 7–8, 12–13, 45; Hess, *Martha Washington's Booke of Cookery*, pp. 50, 46; Redon, *Medieval Kitchen*, p. 169; Markham, *English Hus-wife* (1615), p. 61; McGee, *On Food and Cooking*, p. 364; Wilson, *Food and Drink in Britain*, pp. 328–29, 332–33.

#s 14–15: Hess, *Martha Washington's Booke of Cookery*, pp. 41–43; Lehmann, *British Housewife*, pp. 40–41, 178–79, 44, 248.

#16: Dalgairns, *Practice of Cookery*, p. 163.

#18: Beecher, *Miss Beecher's Domestic Receipt-Book*, p. 42.

#s 19–20: Glasse, *Art of Cookery* (1747), p. 52; Lehmann, *British Housewife*, pp. 255–57.

#21: Bliss, *Practical Cook Book*, p. 79.

#22: Smith, *Oxford Encyclopedia of Food and Drink in America*, 1:151–52; Oliver, *Food in Colonial and Federal America*, pp. 43, 176; Oliver, *Saltwater Foodways*, p. 107.

#23: Early, *New England Cookbook*, pp. 107–8.

#25: Wilson, *Food and Drink in Britain*, p. 290.

Turkey Introduction: Spencer, *British Food*, pp. 107–10, 112, 150–51; Davidson, *Oxford Companion to Food*, pp. 809–10; Schorger, *Wild Turkey*, pp. 9–11; Wheaton, *Savoring the Past*, pp. 13, 81–82; Stavely and Fitzgerald, *America's Founding Food*, p. 161; Hazard, *Jonny-Cake Papers*, p. 73; Wilson, *Food and Drink in Britain*, p. 136.

#26: *Eighteenth-Century Collections Online*, Smith eds.; OED, "crop"; Wilson, *Food and Drink in Britain*, p. 131; Spencer, *British Food*, p. 163.

#27: Smith, *Compleat Housewife* (1728), p. 40; Glasse, *Art of Cookery* (1747), pp. 18, 35, 36, xxxii; Raffald, *Experienced English House-keeper* (1769), pp. 49–50, 108–9.

#28: Gardiner, *Mrs. Gardiner's Family Receipts*, pp. 9–14; Glasse, *Art of Cookery* (1747), pp. 186, 54.

#29: Simmons, *American Cookery* (introduction by Wilson), p. 18; Stavely and Fitzgerald, *America's Founding Food*, p. 325, n. 71.

#31: Kitchiner, *Cook's Oracle* (1822), p. 177; Fagan, *Little Ice Age*, p. 50; McGee, *On Food and Cooking*, pp. 143–44.

#32: Lee, *Cook's Own Book*, p. 227; *Roger Cookery*, p. 15; Bliss, *Practical Cook Book*, p. 80; Knight, *Tit-Bits*, p. 20; Turner, *New England Cook Book*, pp. 61–62; OED, "drawn," "butter"; Glasse, *Art of Cookery* (1747), p. 25.

#33: Schorger, *Wild Turkey*, pp. 141–43, 365–67.

CHAPTER EIGHT. GAME AND MEAT

Introduction: Wilson, *Food and Drink in Britain*, p. 97; Anderson, *Creatures of Empire*, p. 58; Como, *Blown by the Spirit*, p. 329, n. 8 (quoting High Commission charge); Stavely and Fitzgerald, *America's Founding Food*, pp. 177–78; Stowe, *Pearl of Orr's Island*, p. 61 (chap. 8); Dwight, *Travels in New England and New York*, 4:249; Martin, *Standard of Living in 1860*, p. 46; Hale, *Good Housekeeper*, pp. 21–22.

Game Introduction: Stavely and Fitzgerald, *America's Founding Food*, pp. 148–50, 170–71.

#1: Anderson, "Solid Sufficiency," pp. 187–88; Markham, *English Hus-wife* (1615), pp. 54–55; Markham, *English Housewife* (1986), pp. 304, 310; Davidson, *Oxford Companion to Food*, pp. 444, 825; Hess, *Martha Washington's Booke of Cookery*, pp. 48, 90; Smith, *Oxford Encyclopedia of Food and Drink in America*, 1:335. Until the third edition (1631), Markham's passage regarding when meat is "rosted enough" contained the printer's errors, "stroke" for "smoake" and "offendeth" for "ascendeth"; Markham, *English Housewife* (1986), p. 221.

#2: Anderson, "Solid Sufficiency," pp. 78–79; Smith, *Compleat Housewife*, (1728), p. 52; Smith, *Compleat Housewife* (1968), glossary.

#3: Anderson, "Solid Sufficiency," pp. 58, 74–75; Mariani, *Dictionary of American Food and Drink*, p. 327; Lee, *Cook's Own Book*, p. 170; Kitchiner, *Cook's Oracle* (1822), p. 152; OED, "warren."

#4: Stavely and Fitzgerald, *America's Founding Food*, p. 185.

Veal Introduction: Oliver, *Food in Colonial and Federal America*, p. 46; Derven, "Wholesome, Toothsome, and Diverse," pp. 56–57; Oliver, *Saltwater Foodways*, p. 14; Nylander, *Our Own Snug Fireside*, p. 204.

#5: Davidson, *Oxford Companion to Food*, p. 797.

#6: Stavely and Fitzgerald, *America's Founding Food*, pp. 185–86; Raffald, *Experienced English House-keeper* (1769), p. 89.

#7: Pope, *Poems*, pp. 475–76; Glasse, *Art of Cookery* (1747), p. 19 (first knuckle recipe); Smith, *Compleat Housewife* (1739), p. 43.

#8: Beecher, *Miss Beecher's Domestic Receipt-Book*, pp. 116–17; Stavely and Fitzgerald, *America's Founding Food*, pp. 193–96.

Lamb Introduction: Oliver, *Food in Colonial and Federal America*, pp. 46–47; Hale, *Good Housekeeper*, p. 47; Derven, "Wholesome, Toothsome, and Diverse," pp. 56–57; Hooker, *Food and Drink in America*, p. 113.

#10: Lehmann, *British Housewife*, pp. 177, 51–53.

#11: Markham, *English Hus-wife* (1615), pp. 39–42; Davidson, *Oxford Companion to Food*, p. 682 (quoting Evelyn, *Acetaria* [1699]).

#14: Allen, *Housekeeper's Assistant*, p. 116; Patten, *Our New England Family Recipes*, p. 5.

Mutton Introduction: Wilson, *Food and Drink in Britain*, pp. 80, 78, 88; Johnson, *Johnson's Wonder-Working Providence*, p. 210; Vickers, *Farmers and Fishermen*, p. 169; Nylander, *Our Own Snug Fireside*, pp. 204, 267; Karcher, *First Woman in the Republic*, p. 86; Stowe, *Pearl of Orr's Island*, pp. 122–23 (chap. 13); Lehmann, *British Housewife*, p. 374; Stavely and Fitzgerald, *America's Founding Food*, p. 326, n. 82.

#15: Woolley, *Queen-like Closet*, p. 113; *Meriden Cook Book*, p. 26.

#16: Davidson, *Oxford Companion to Food*, p. 690.

#18: Hess, *Martha Washington's Booke of Cookery*, pp. 48–49; *Compleat Cook*, p. 44; Woolley, *Queen-like Closet*, pp. 125, 104; Smith, *Compleat Housewife* (1728), p. 28; Raffald, *Experienced English House-keeper* (1769), pp. 62–63, 66; Glasse, *Art of Cookery* (1747), pp. 25, 59.

#19: Simmons, *American Cookery* (introduction by Wilson), p. 19.

#20: Lee, *Cook's Own Book*, p. 99; Davidson, *Oxford Companion to Food*, p. 407.

Pork Introduction: Anderson, "Solid Sufficiency," pp. 68–69; Wilson, *Food and Drink in Britain*, pp. 88, 89–90, 103–4; Stavely and Fitzgerald, *America's Founding Food*, pp. 181, 193–96; Walsh, "Consumer Behavior," p. 242; Davidson, *Oxford Companion to Food*, p. 624; King, *When I Lived in Salem*, p. 99.

#21: Raffald, *Experienced English House-keeper* (1769), p. 43; Allen, *Housekeeper's Assistant*, p. 101; Markham, *English Housewife* (1986), p. 260; OED, "scorch," "scotch"; Glasse, *Art of Cookery* (1747), p. 4; Lee, *Cook's Own Book*, p. 144; Kitchiner, *Cook's Oracle* (1822), p. 176; *Roger Cookery*, p. 16; Markham, *English Hus-wife* (1615), p. 55. Best does not include the change from "scorch" to "scotch" in his list of textual variants. See Markham, *English Housewife* (1986), p. 221; Markham, *English Hus-wife* (1615), p. 58; and Markham, *Countrey Contentments* (1623), p. 83.

#23: Simmons, *American Cookery* (introduction by Wilson), pp. 5–6.

#24: Smith, *Compleat Housewife* (1750), pp. 18–19; Raffald, *Experienced English House-keeper* (1769), pp. 43–44; Carter, *Frugal Housewife*, pp. 6–7; Glasse, *Art of Cookery* (1747), p. 5; Simmons, *American Cookery* (introduction by Hess), p. 12; Lee, *Cook's Own Book*, pp. 143–44; Kitchiner, *Cook's Oracle* (1822), p. 177.

#25: Lee, *Cook's Own Book*, p. 148; Kitchiner, *Cook's Oracle* (1827), p. 135; Stavely and Fitzgerald, *America's Founding Food*, pp. 193–96; Child, *American Frugal Housewife*, pp. 40–41; Anderson, "Solid Sufficiency," p. 107.

#26: Hale, *Good Housekeeper*, p. 42; Beecher, *Miss Beecher's Domestic Receipt-Book*, p. 27; Acton, *Modern Cookery*, p. 203; Davidson, *Oxford Companion to Food*, pp. 623, 12; *High Beam Encyclopedia*, "Hand of Pork," www.encyclopedia.com/doc/1O39-handofpork.html.

#27: *Practically Edible*, "Pork Chine," www.practicallyedible.com; Spencer, *British Food*, p. 115; Carter, *Frugal Housewife*, p. 16; Emerson, *New-England Cookery*, p. 24; Willan, *Great Cooks*, p. 87; Bliss, *Practical Cook Book*, p. 74.

#29: Webster, *Improved Housewife* (1844), p. 44; Stavely and Fitzgerald, *America's Founding Food*, p. 175.

#30: Davidson, *Oxford Companion to Food*, p. 623; Stavely and Fitzgerald, *America's Founding Food*, pp. 193–96; Bliss, *Practical Cook Book*, pp. 74–75; Child, *American Frugal Housewife*, p. 60.

#31: Hale, *Good Housekeeper*, p. 42; Beecher, *Miss Beecher's Domestic Receipt-Book*, p. 27.

#32: Farmer, *Boston Cooking-School Cook Book*, p. 210; Lincoln and Barrows, *Home Science Cook Book*, pp. 138–39; Stavely and Fitzgerald, *America's Founding Food*, pp. 28–29, 57–58.

Beef Introduction: Lehmann, *British Housewife*, pp. 24, 36, 373–74; Fielding, *Complete Works*, p. 259 (*Grub Street Opera*, 3, 3, air 45); Tate Online, "William Hogarth, 1697–1764: O the Roast Beef of Old England ("The Gate of Calais"), 1748," www.tate.org.uk/servlet/ViewWork?workid=6617; Mennell, *All Manners of Food*, pp. 102–3; Nylander, *Our Own Snug Fireside*, p. 267 (quoting *Hampshire Gazette*, 23 December 1801); Brewer, *From Fireplace to Cookstove*, p. 93 (quoting Whitney, *Homespun Yarns*); Beecher and Stowe, *American Woman's Home*, p. 63 (quoted in Strasser, *Never Done*); Davidson, *Woman's Work Is Never Done*, pp. 184–85.

#33: Lehmann, *British Housewife*, p. 48; Willan, *Great Cooks*, pp. 101, 103; Ockerman, *Animal By-Product Processing*, p. 75.

#34: OED, "alamode," "fillet"; Davidson, *Oxford Companion to Food*, pp. 8–9; Proust, *Remembrance of Things Past*, 2:1114.

#35: Carter, *Frugal Housewife*, p. 1; Lehmann, *British Housewife*, p. 24.

#37: Karcher, *First Woman in the Republic*, p. 134 (quoting Willis); Thorne, *Mouth Wide Open*, pp. 79–98.

#38: Farmer, *Boston Cooking-School Cook Book*, pp. 181–82; Lee, *Cook's Own Book*, p. 11; Dalgairns, *Practice of Cookery*, pp. 86–87; Davidson, *Oxford Companion to Food*, pp. 479–80; Webster, *Improved Housewife* (1844), p. 34; Beecher, *Miss Beecher's Domestic Receipt-Book*, pp. 37–38; Sanborn, *Bronson Alcott*, pp. 9–12.

#39: Dolby, *Cook's Dictionary*, p. 59; McGee, *On Food and Cooking*, pp. 166–67; Davidson, *Oxford Companion to Food*, p. 320; Allen, *Housekeeper's Assistant*, p. 96; Leslie, *Directions for Cookery*, p. 86.

#41: McGee, *On Food and Cooking*, p. 355.

#42: Beecher, *Miss Beecher's Domestic Receipt-Book*, pp. 223, 221–22.

#43: Ibid., p. 26; Mariani, *Dictionary of American Food and Drink*, p. 367; *OED*, "steak."

#44: Stavely and Fitzgerald, *America's Founding Food*, pp. 42–43; Beecher, *Miss Beecher's Domestic Receipt-Book*, p. 26; Hale, *Good Housekeeper*, p. 36.

#45: McGee, *On Food and Cooking*, p. 131; Rombauer and Becker, *Joy of Cooking*, pp. 450–52, 454.

#47: Knight, *Tit-Bits*, pp. 7–10.

#48: Smith, *Oxford Encyclopedia of Food and Drink in America*, 1:332; McGee, *On Food and Cooking*, p. 164; Parloa, *Miss Parloa's New Cook Book*, pp. 165–66.

CHAPTER NINE. PIE CRUSTS

Introduction: Wilson, *Food and Drink in Britain*, p. 271; Colquhoun, *Taste*, pp. 81, 391; Lehmann, *British Housewife*, pp. 41 (quoting Marnette), 42, 48, 183, 197; Hess, *Martha Washington's Booke of Cookery*, p. 11.

#2: Wilson, *Food and Drink in Britain*, pp. 56, 254; Markham, *English Housewife* (1986), p. 309; *OED*, "seam."

#3: Hess, *Martha Washington's Booke of Cookery*, pp. 157, 156, 96; Wilson, *Food and Drink in Britain*, pp. 142, 351; Lehmann, *British Housewife*, p. 199.

#4: Simmons, *American Cookery* (introduction by Hess), p. 37; Glasse, *Art of Cookery* (1747), p. 75.

#5: *OED*, "sweetmeat"; Simmons, *American Cookery* (introduction by Wilson), p. xxx.

#6: Carter, *Frugal Housewife*, p. 111; Simmons, *American Cookery* (introduction by Hess), p. 38; Hess, *Martha Washington's Booke of Cookery*, p. 159.

#8: Leslie, *Directions for Cookery*, p. 276; Webster, *Improved Housewife* (1844), pp. 37–38.

#14: Stavely and Fitzgerald, *America's Founding Food*, pp. 242–43; Hess and Hess, *Taste of America*, pp. 56–69; Beecher, *Miss Beecher's Domestic Receipt-Book*, pp. 128–29.

#15: Leslie, *Lady's Receipt Book*, pp. 100–2.

CHAPTER TEN. PIES—MIXED, MEAT, MINCE

Introduction: Hale, *Good Housekeeper,* p. 83; Hale, *Ladies' New Book of Cookery,* p. 451; Fernandez-Armesto, *Near a Thousand Tables,* pp. 108, 112.

Mixed Pies Introduction: Wilson, *Food and Drink and Britain,* p. 253.

#2: Hess, *Martha Washington's Booke of Cookery,* pp. 127–28, 87; Glasse, *Art of Cookery* (1747), pp. 119–20; Beecher, *Miss Beecher's Domestic Receipt-Book,* p. 195; *Cook Not Mad,* pp. 93–94; Allen, *Housekeeper's Assistant,* p. 137 (flour caudle copied from *Cook Not Mad*); OED, "sack."

#3: OED, "battalia," "shiver"; Mennell, *All Manners of Food,* p. 147; Lehmann, *British Housewife,* pp. 212, 193–94, 275; Carter, *Frugal Housewife,* p. 115; Glasse, *Art of Cookery* (1747), p. 192.

#4: Ibid., p. 73; Rundell, *New System of Domestic Cookery,* p. 133; Lee, *Cook's Own Book,* p. 141; Leslie, *Lady's Receipt Book,* pp. 100–2; OED, "tun-dish"; Wilson, *Food and Drink in Britain,* pp. 56, 57, 105; Lehmann, *British Housewife,* p. 34.

#5: Oliver, *Saltwater Foodways,* pp. 110–11; Simmons, *American Cookery* (introduction by Hess), p. 24; Lee, *Cook's Own Book,* p. 143; Hale, *Ladies' New Book of Cookery,* p. 270; Glasse, *Art of Cookery* (1747), p. 125.

#6: Dalgairns, *Practice of Cookery,* p. 247; Redon, *Medieval Kitchen,* p. 133.

#7: Davidson, *Oxford Companion to Food,* p. 584; Stavely and Fitzgerald, *America's Founding Food,* pp. 211–13; Smith, *Turkey,* p. 36.

#8: Hale, *Ladies' New Book of Cookery,* p. 345; Stavely and Fitzgerald, *America's Founding Food,* p. 246; McGee, *On Food and Cooking,* p. 601.

#10: *Encyclopedia Britannica Online,* "British Imperial System," library.eb.com/eb/article-9016522; Rombauer and Becker, *Joy of Cooking,* p. 595; Cressy, *Coming Over,* p. 8; Hess, *Martha Washington's Booke of Cookery,* pp. 83–84; Lehmann, *British Housewife,* pp. 44, 53; Woolley, *Queen-like Closet,* pp. 155, 159–60.

#11: Allen, *Housekeeper's Assistant,* p. 54.

#13: Wilson, *Food and Drink in Britain,* p. 85; Smith, *Compleat Housewife* (1728), pp. 111, 118–19; Rundell, *New System of Domestic Cookery,* p. 130.

#14: OED, "lumber"; Smith, *Compleat Housewife* (1968), glossary; Simmons, *American Cookery* (introduction by Wilson), p. 44; Fernandez-Armesto, *Near a Thousand Tables,* p. 125; Wilson, *Food and Drink in Britain,* p. 90.

#16: McGee, *On Food and Cooking,* pp. 533, 534.

#17: Markham, *English Hus-wife* (1615), pp. 66–67; *Compleat Cook,* pp. 59, 7; Hess, *Martha Washington's Booke of Cookery,* pp. 80–83, 83–84; Woolley, *Queen-like Closet,* pp. 136–37; Wilson, *Food and Drink in Britain,* pp. 95, 85.

#18: Glasse, *Art of Cookery* (1747), p. 71; Raffald, *Experienced English House-keeper* (1769), p. 131; Simmons, *American Cookery* (introduction by Hess), p. 23; Dalgairns, *Practice of Cookery,* p. 240; Lee, *Cook's Own Book,* p. 140.

#19: Hale, *Ladies' New Book of Cookery,* pp. 91–92, 268–69, 273; OED, "flap."

#20: Anderson, "Solid Sufficiency," p. 103.

#21: Glasse, *Art of Cookery* (1747), p. xxxvii; *Lady's Companion*, 2:113; Lehmann, *British Housewife*, p. 231; Leslie, *Directions for Cookery*, p. 122.

#23: Kitchiner, *Cook's Oracle* (1822), p. 476.

#24: *Cook Not Mad*, p. 21.

#25: Thackeray, *Vanity Fair*, p. 92 (chap. 8); Dolby, *Cook's Dictionary*, pp. 397–98; Glasse, *Art of Cookery* (1747), pp. 72, xxxiii; *Whole Duty of a Woman*, p. 504; Rundell, *New System of Domestic Cookery*, p. 132; OED, "squab-pie"; *Black's Guide to Devonshire*, pp. xvi–xvii; Dallas, *Kettner's Book of the Table*, pp. 156–57.

#27: Mariani, *Dictionary of American Food and Drink*, p. 315; Smith, *Oxford Encyclopedia of Food and Drink in America*, 2:242.

Mince Pies Introduction: Wilson, *Food and Drink in Britain*, p. 254.

#29: Markham, *Countrey Contentments* (1623), pp. 103–4, 107–8; Blencowe, *Receipt Book*, p. 28; Smith, *Compleat Housewife* (1728), pp. 111–12; Smith, *Compleat Housewife* (1730), p. 13; Glasse, *Art of Cookery* (1747), pp. 59, 184; Hess, *Martha Washington's Booke of Cookery*, p. 125; *Henriette's Herbal Homepage*, "Uvae.—Raisins," www.henriettesherbal.com/eclectic/kings/vitis-vini_uva.html.

#30: Wilson, *Food and Drink in Britain*, p. 273; Glasse, *Art of Cookery* (1747), p. 116.

#31: Charsley, *Wedding Cakes and Cultural History*, pp. 47–49; Smith, *Compleat Housewife* (1728), p. 102; Fernandez-Armesto, *Near a Thousand Tables*, p. 115; Butler, *Arithmetical Questions*, p. 59.

#32: Wilson, *Food and Drink in Britain*, pp. 94, 86; Woolley, *Queen-like Closet*, p. 115; Hess, *Martha Washington's Booke of Cookery*, p. 93.

#33: Glasse, *Art of Cookery* (1747), p. 201.

#36: Lee, *Cook's Own Book*, pp. 140, 142; *Roger Cookery*, pp. 25–26; Rundell, *New System of Domestic Cookery*, p. 158; Chadwick, *Home Cookery*, p. 53.

#37: Dalgairns, *Practice of Cookery*, pp. 254–55; Lee, *Cook's Own Book*, p. 141; Hale, *Good Housekeeper*, pp. 85–86; Leslie, *Directions for Cookery*, pp. 283–84.

#38: Bliss, *Practical Cook Book*, p. 158; Knight, *Tit-Bits*, pp. 64–65; *Henriette's Herbal Homepage*, "Uvae.—Raisins," www.henriettesherbal.com/eclectic/kings/vitis-vini_uva.html.

CHAPTER ELEVEN. PIES—FOWL, FISH

Fowl Pies Introduction: Wilson, *Food and Drink in Britain*, pp. 126–29.

#1: Ibid., pp. 136, 125, 129; Davidson, *Oxford Companion to Food*, p. 344.

#2: Lee, *Cook's Own Book*, p. 140; Dolby, *Cook's Dictionary*, p. 220; OED, "pinion."

#3: Raffald, *Experienced English House-keeper* (1769), p. 137; Glasse, *Art of Cookery* (1747), p. 186; OED, "giblet."

#4: Rundell, *New System of Domestic Cookery*, p. 133; Leslie, *Ladies' New Book of Cookery*, p. 103.

#5: Ibid., pp. 99–100; Cummings, *American and His Food*, p. 41 (quoting Smith, *First Forty Years of Washington Society*); Lehmann, *British Housewife*, p. 188.

#6: Rundell, *New System of Domestic Cookery*, p. 134; Allen, *Housekeeper's Assistant*, p. 121; Leslie, *Directions for Cookery*, p. 157.

#7: *OED*, "chewet," "brawn," "comfit"; Wilson, *Food and Drink in Britain*, p. 254.

#8: Lehmann, *British Housewife*, pp. 195, 44; Wilson, *Food and Drink in Britain*, p. 91.

#9: Markham, *Countrey Contentments* (1623), p. 103; Glasse, *Art of Cookery* (1747), pp. 72, xxvi.

#10: Kitchiner, *Cook's Oracle* (1822), pp. 474–75; Lehmann, *British Housewife*, pp. 178, 179, 99, 131–32; Spencer, *British Food*, pp. 163–64; Hertzmann, "Service à la Française," www.hertzmann.com/articles/2004/service; Colquhoun, *Taste*, p. 158 (quoting Strong, *Feast*).

#12: King, *When I Lived in Salem*, p. 25; Sloat, *Old Sturbridge Village Cookbook*, pp. 22–23.

#14: Henisch, *Fast and Feast*, p. 35; Drummond and Wilbraham, *Englishman's Food*, p. 63; Oliver, *Food in Colonial and Federal America*, p. 69; Brewer, *Dictionary of Phrase and Fable* www.bartleby.com/81/17275.html.

#15: Davidson, *Oxford Companion to Food*, p. 139.

#16: Oliver, *Saltwater Foodways*, p. 376; Rossi-Wilcox, *Dinner for Dickens*, p. 230; Lehmann, *British Housewife*, pp. 34–35, 193–94.

#17: Glasse, *Art of Cookery* (1747), p. xxxiii; *Whole Duty of a Woman*, pp. 519–20; Gardiner, *Mrs. Gardiner's Family Receipts*, pp. 54–55; Wood, *New Englands Prospect*, p. 35.

#18: *Whole Duty of a Woman*, p. 520; McGee, *On Food and Cooking*, pp. 212, 222; Davidson, *Oxford Companion to Food*, p. 457; Oliver, *Saltwater Foodways*, pp. 380–81.

#19: Lee, *Cook's Own Book*, p. 140; Allen, *Housekeeper's Assistant*, p. 122; Wright, *New England Cook Book*, p. 22.

#20: Wilson, *Food and Drink in Britain*, p. 56; Lee, *Cook's Own Book*, p. 130; *Roger Cookery*, p. 17; Hale, *Ladies' New Book of Cookery*, p. 63.

#21: Leslie, *Directions for Cookery*, p. 60; Leslie, *Lady's Receipt Book*, pp. 100–102; Dalgairns, *Practice of Cookery*, p. 251; Lee, *Cook's Own Book*, p. 130; Webster, *Improved Housewife* (1844), pp. 53, 55, 63, 74.

#23: Oliver, *Saltwater Foodways*, pp. 376, 382; Woolley, *Queen-like Closet*, p. 88; Glasse, *Art of Cookery* (1747), p. 115.

#24: Ibid., p. 115; Leslie, *Directions for Cookery*, p. 64.

#25: Hale, *Ladies' New Book of Cookery*, pp. 62–63.

#26: Stavely and Fitzgerald, *America's Founding Food*, pp. 88–95.

Introduction: Above, chap 1, n. 7, chap. 2, n. 27; Stavely and Fitzgerald, *America's Founding Food*, pp. 215–18; Lehmann, *British Housewife*, pp. 197–98, 278; Wilson, *Food and Drink in Britain*, p. 349; Anderson, "Solid Sufficiency," p. 224; McMahon, "All Things in Their Proper Season," p. 141; McMahon, "Laying Foods By," p. 185; Oliver, *Saltwater Foodways*, p. 244; Warner, *Backlog Studies*, p. 36.

Pumpkin Pie Introduction: Hale, *Northwood* (1827), 1:110.

#1: Wilson, *Food and Drink in Britain*, p. 349; Woolley, *Gentlewoman's Companion*, pp. 145–46; Woolley, *Queen-like Closet*, pp. 100, 109; Gardiner, *Mrs. Gardiner's Family Receipts*, p. 55.

#2: Wilson, *Food and Drink in Britain*, p. 349; Simmons, *American Cookery* (introduction by Wilson), p. xxix; Early, *New England Cookbook*, p. 113.

#3: Stavely and Fitzgerald, *America's Founding Food*, pp. 13–14, 55–56; Child, *American Frugal Housewife*, p. 67; Davidson, *Oxford Companion to Food*, p. 231.

#4: Ibid., p. 673.

#6: Hale, *Ladies' New Book of Cookery*, p. 280.

#7: Beecher, *Miss Beecher's Domestic Receipt-Book*, p. 183.

#9: Glasse, *Art of Cookery* (1747), p. 107; Carter, *Frugal Housewife*, pp. 140–41; Simmons, *American Cookery* (introduction by Wilson), p. 27; Child, *American Frugal Housewife*, p. 67.

#10: Markham, *Countrey Contentments* (1623), p. 110; Smith, *Compleat Housewife*, (1728), p. 114; Glasse, *Art of Cookery* (1747), p. 186.

#11: Hess, *Martha Washington's Booke of Cookery*, p. 86; Simmons, *American Cookery* (introduction by Wilson), pp. 10–11; *Cook Not Mad*, p. 25.

#12: Simmons, *American Cookery* (introduction by Wilson), p. 27.

#13: Markham, *English Hus-wife* (1615), p. 37; Wilson, *Food and Drink in Britain*, p. 346; Smith, *Oxford Encyclopedia of Food and Drink in America*, 2:545–46; Child, *American Frugal Housewife*, pp. 114–15.

Fruit Pies Introduction: Anderson, "Solid Sufficiency," p. 224; McMahon, "All Things in Their Proper Season," p. 141; McMahon, "Laying Foods By," p. 185; Stavely and Fitzgerald, *America's Founding Food*, pp. 207–8; Wilson, *Food and Drink in Britain*, p. 302.

#14: Amherst, *History of Gardening in England*, pp. 101–2 (quoting *Husbandman's Fruitful Orchard* [quotation also appears, unattributed, in Watson, *Cider Hard and Sweet*, 20]); Davidson, *Oxford Companion to Food*, p. 30; Glasse, *Art of Cookery* (1747), p. 174.

#15: Wilson, *Food and Drink in Britain*, pp. 358–59; Glasse, *Art of Cookery* (1747), pp. 201, 185, 74–75; *OED*, "gallipot"; Carter, *Frugal Housewife*, pp. 121–22; Simmons, *American Cookery* (introduction by Wilson), p. 31.

#16: Smith, *Compleat Housewife* (1968), glossary; *Eighteenth-Century Collections Online*, Smith eds., 10–11, 13; Smith, *Compleat Housewife* (1750), p. 129; Glasse, *Art of Cookery* (1747), pp. 174, 107.

#17: Carter, *Frugal Housewife*, pp. 120–21.

#18: Wilson, *Food and Drink in Britain*, p. 350; Carter, *Frugal Housewife*, p. 119; Gardiner, Mrs. *Gardiner's Family Receipts*, p. 58.

#20: Wilson, *Food and Drink in Britain*, p. 349; Colquhoun, *Taste*, p. 207; Raffald, *Experienced English House-keeper* (1769), pp. 321, 325, 153; Glasse, *Art of Cookery* (1747), p. 174; Markham, *Countrey Contentments* (1623), p. 106.

#s 21–22: Simmons, *American Cookery* (introduction by Wilson), p. 25.

#23: Glasse, *Art of Cookery* (1747), p. 113; Beecher, *Miss Beecher's Domestic Receipt-Book*, p. 112.

#24: *Cook Not Mad*, p. 30.

#25: Leslie, *Seventy-five Receipts*, pp. 23–24.

#27: Dalgairns, *Practice of Cookery*, p. 256.

#28: Leslie, *Seventy-five Receipts*, p. 25.

#29: Ibid., p. 24; Reid, *Cookery, Rational, Practical, and Economical*, pp. 133–34; Mangione, *Physical Diagnosis Secrets*, p. 23; Webster, *Improved Housewife* (1844), p. 98.

#30: Leslie, *Seventy-five Receipts*, p. 23; McGee, *On Food and Cooking*, pp. 258–59; Guy, *Principles of Forensic Medicine*, p. 450; Hale, *Ladies' New Book of Cookery*, p. 281.

#31: Webster, *Improved Housewife* (1844), p. 84; Beecher, *Miss Beecher's Domestic Receipt-Book*, p. 126.

#s 33–34: Bliss, *Practical Cook Book*, p. 153.

#35: Howland, *New England Economical Housekeeper*, p. 42; Smith, *Oxford Encyclopedia of Food and Drink in America*, 1:43–44; Mariani, *Dictionary of American Food and Drink*, p. 49.

#36: Bliss, *Practical Cook Book*, p. 152.

Cream and Custard Pies Introduction: Lehmann, *British Housewife*, p. 279; Wilson, *Food and Drink in Britain*, pp. 267, 172–73, 141, 157 (quoting Boorde, *Dyetary*); Redon, *Medieval Kitchen*, p. 160.

#37: Beecher, *Miss Beecher's Domestic Receipt-Book*, p. 205; Smith, *Compleat Housewife* (1728), p. 105; Smith, *Compleat Housewife* (1968), p. 152.

#38: Redon, *Medieval Kitchen*, pp. 222–23; Smith, *Compleat Housewife* (1728), p. 119; Davidson, *Oxford Companion to Food*, p. 12.

#39: Wilson, *Food and Drink in Britain*, p. 170; Glasse, *Art of Cookery* (1747), p. 146; Raffald, *Experienced English Housekeeper* (1997), p. 201; Davidson, *Oxford Companion to Food*, p. 69.

#40: Hale, *Ladies' New Book of Cookery*, p. 280.

#42: McGee, *On Food and Cooking*, p. 84, 98.

#43: Smith, *Oxford Encyclopedia of Food and Drink in America*, 2:569.

Introduction: Wilson, *Food and Drink in Britain*, pp. 308–11, 318, 316, 321 (quoting Misson); Hess, *Martha Washington's Booke of Cookery*, p. 102; Spencer, *British Food*, p. 96; Davidson, *Oxford Companion to Food*, pp. 638, 762; Lehmann, *British Housewife*, pp. 198, 355; Orwell, *Collected Essays*, p. 40; *OED*, "pudding time"; *Dictionary of American Regional English*, 4:363; Bowles and Towle, *Secrets of New England Cooking*, p. 175; Bushman, *Refinement of America*, p. 74; Nylander, *Our Own Snug Fireside*, p. 258.

#1: Wilson, *Food and Drink in Britain*, p. 316; Woolley, *Queen-like Closet*, pp. 70, 138; Smith, *Compleat Housewife* (1728), p. 84; Glasse, *Art of Cookery* (1747), p. 112; Raffald, *Experienced English House-keeper* (1769), p. 156; Carter, *Frugal Housewife*, p. 134; Gardiner, *Mrs. Gardiner's Family Receipts*, p. 61; Webster, *Improved Housewife* (1844), p. 80.

#2: Wilson, *Food and Drink in Britain*, p. 316; Smith, *Compleat Housewife* (1728), p. 84; Glasse, *Art of Cookery* (1747), pp. 69, 124; Carter, *Frugal Housewife*, p. 136 (copy of Glasse, p. 69).

#3: Smith, *Compleat Housewife* (1728), pp. 88–89; Smith, *Compleat Housewife* (1732), p. 97; Raffald, *Experienced English House-keeper* (1769), p. 155.

#4: *OED*, "harslet"; Smith, *Compleat Housewife* (1968), glossary; Wilson, *Food and Drink in Britain*, p. 311.

#5: Ibid., pp. 316–17, 273, 106, 228; Lehmann, *British Housewife*, p. 262; Carter, *Frugal Housewife*, p. 135.

#6: Stavely and Fitzgerald, *America's Founding Food*, p. 347, n. 15; Glasse, *Art of Cookery* (1747), pp. 109, 111; Raffald, *Experienced English House-keeper* (1769), pp. 148–49.

#7: Child, *American Frugal Housewife*, p. 61; Webster, *Improved Housewife* (1844), p. 77; Beecher, *Miss Beecher's Domestic Receipt-Book*, pp. 112–13; Lee, *Cook's Own Book*, p. 161; Hale, *Ladies' New Book of Cookery*, p. 296.

#8: Glasse, *Art of Cookery* (1747), p. 108; Carter, *Frugal Housewife*, pp. 133–34; Hale, *Good Housekeeper*, p. 79; Beecher, *Miss Beecher's Domestic Receipt-Book*, p. 110; Child, *American Frugal Housewife*, p. 65.

#9: Glasse, *Art of Cookery* (1747), p. 109; Raffald, *Experienced English House-keeper* (1769), pp. 148–49; Allen, *Housekeeper's Assistant*, p. 53; Beecher, *Miss Beecher's Domestic Receipt-Book*, p. 114.

#10: Child, *American Frugal Housewife*, p. 61; Hale, *Good Housekeeper*, pp. 104–5; Lee, *Cook's Own Book*, p. 167; Webster, *Improved Housewife* (1844), p. 83; Hazard, *Jonny-Cake Papers*, p. 53.

#11: Simmons, *American Cookery* (introduction by Hess), pp. 36–37; Hale, *Good Housekeeper*, p. 80; Beecher, *Miss Beecher's Domestic Receipt-Book*, p. 123; Bliss, *Practical Cook Book*, pp. 138–39; Nylander, *Our Own Snug Fireside*, p. 275.

#12: Stavely and Fitzgerald, *America's Founding Food*, p. 28.

#13: Wilson, *Food and Drink in Britain*, p. 320; Bliss, *Practical Cook Book*, pp. 123, 120, 209.

#14: Rundell, *New System of Domestic Cookery*, p. 142; *Cook Not Mad*, p. 31; Leslie, *Directions for Cookery*, pp. 296–97; Webster, *Improved Housewife* (1847), p. 216; Parloa, *Miss Parloa's New Cook Book*, p. 266; Beecher, *Miss Beecher's Domestic Receipt-Book*, pp. 122–23; Lincoln, *Mrs. Lincoln's Boston Cook Book*, pp. 332–33; Bliss, *Practical Cook Book*, p. 208.

#15: Wilson, *Food and Drink in Britain*, p. 321; Glasse, *Art of Cookery* (1747), pp. xxxiii, 111; Carter, *Frugal Housewife*, p. 137; Child, *American Frugal Housewife*, p. 63; Howland, *New England Economical Housekeeper*, pp. 33–34; Raffald, *Experienced English House-keeper* (1769), pp. 148, 146; Dalgairns, *Practice of Cookery*, p. 286; Lee, *Cook's Own Book*, p. 165.

#16: Stavely and Fitzgerald, *America's Founding Food*, p. 28; Hale, *Good Housekeeper*, pp. 27–28; Hale, *Ladies' New Book of Cookery*, pp. 379–80.

#17: Wilson, *Food and Drink in Britain*, p. 318; Glasse, *Art of Cookery* (1747), pp. 111, 79; Lehmann, *British Housewife*, p. 232; Markham, *Countrey Contentments* (1623), p. 111; *Compleat Cook*, p. 10; Woolley, *Queen-like Closet*, p. 15; Simmons, *American Cookery* (introduction by Wilson), p. 26.

#18: Wilson, *Food and Drink in Britain*, pp. 319, 316; Dolby, *Cook's Dictionary*, p. 8; Lee, *Cook's Own Book*, p. 156; Allen, *Housekeeper's Assistant*, pp. 47, 48; Leslie, *Directions for Cookery*, pp. 286–87; Hale, *Ladies' New Book of Cookery*, pp. 290–91 (two versions, one a copy of Leslie, the other a copy of Smith); Parloa, *Miss Parloa's New Cook Book*, pp. 269–70.

#19: Wilson, *Food and Drink in Britain*, p. 321; Kitchiner, *Cook's Oracle* (1822), pp. 346–47; Lee, *Cook's Own Book*, p. 167; Allen, *Housekeeper's Assistant*, pp. 81, 82; Mendall, *New Bedford Practical Receipt Book*, p. 21; Lincoln and Barrows, *Home Science Cook Book*, p. 40.

#20: Woolley, *Queen-like Closet*, pp. 68–69; Smith, *Compleat Housewife* (1728), p. 86; Glasse, *Art of Cookery* (1747), pp. 108, 79; Carter, *Frugal Housewife*, p. 139; Markham, *Countrey Contentments* (1623), p. 111; Smith, *Compleat Housewife* (1739), p. 122; Allen, *Housekeeper's Assistant*, p. 52.

#21: Child, *American Frugal Housewife*, p. 61; Lee, *Cook's Own Book*, p. 161; Hale, *Good Housekeeper*, p. 105; Webster, *Improved Housewife* (1844), p. 78; Mann, *Christianity in the Kitchen*, p. 65; Mendall, *New Bedford Practical Receipt Book*, p. 46; Knight, *Tit-Bits*, pp. 49–50; *Godey's*, June 1880, p. 561; Turner, *New England Cook Book*, p. 161.

#22: Simmons, *American Cookery* (introduction by Wilson), pp. 27, 28; Bliss, *Practical Cook Book*, p. 140.

#23: Child, *American Frugal Housewife*, p. 62; Beecher, *Miss Beecher's Domestic Receipt-Book*, pp. 108–9; Bliss, *Practical Cook Book*, p. 124; Webster, *Improved Housewife* (1844), p. 81.

#24: Davidson, *Oxford Companion to Food*, pp. 36, 502; Wilson, *Food and Drink in Britain*, p. 226; Dalgairns, *Practice of Cookery*, p. 277; Hale, *Good Housekeeper*, p. 77; Bliss, *Practical Cook Book*, p. 122; Beecher, *Miss Beecher's Domestic Receipt-Book*, pp. 124, 194, 197; Webster, *Improved Housewife* (1844), pp. 185–86; Child, *American Frugal Housewife*, p. 31; Farmer, *Boston Cooking-School Cook Book*, p. 499.

#25: Davidson, *Oxford Companion to Food*, p. 782; Dolby, *Cook's Dictionary*, p. 464; Hale, *Good Housekeeper*, pp. 77–78; Allen, *Housekeeper's Assistant*, p. 46; Howland, *New England Economical Housekeeper*, p. 37; Bliss, *Practical Cook Book*, p. 145; Beecher, *Miss Beecher's Domestic Receipt-Book*, pp. 109, 293; Webster, *Improved Housewife* (1844), p. 80; Parloa, *Miss Parloa's New Cook Book*, pp. 264–65; Lincoln, *Mrs. Lincoln's Boston Cook Book*, p. 333.

#26: Lee, *Cook's Own Book*, p. 158; Allen, *Housekeeper's Assistant*, p. 51; Howland, *New England Economical Housekeeper*, p. 32.

#27: Glasse, *Art of Cookery* (1747), pp. xxxvii, 107; Carter, *Frugal Housewife*, p. 141; Allen, *Housekeeper's Assistant*, p. 46; Beecher, *Miss Beecher's Domestic Receipt-Book*, p. 127; Hale, *Ladies' New Book of Cookery*, p. 301; Dolby, *Cook's Dictionary*, p. 428; Lee, *Cook's Own Book*, p. 164; Webster, *Improved Housewife* (1844), pp. 82–83.

#28: Howland, *New England Economical Housekeeper*, p. 35; Leslie, *Directions for Cookery*, p. 290; Webster, *Improved Housewife* (1844), p. 77; Bliss, *Practical Cook Book*, p. 126; Knight, *Tit-Bits*, pp. 46, 58; Turner, *New England Cook Book*, pp. 155–56.

#29: Davidson, *Oxford Companion to Food*, p. 199; Lee, *Cook's Own Book*, pp. 159–60; Leslie, *Directions for Cookery*, pp. 287–88; Allen, *Housekeeper's Assistant*, pp. 52–53; Hale, *Ladies' New Book of Cookery*, p. 302; Bliss, *Practical Cook Book*, pp. 125–26; Knight, *Tit-Bits*, p. 46; Turner, *New England Cook Book*, p. 157; Webster, *Improved Housewife* (1847), p. 227; *OED*, "coco," "cocoa."

#31: Wilson, *Food and Drink in Britain*, p. 214; Davidson, *Oxford Companion to Food*, p. 681; Smith, *Compleat Housewife* (1750), p. 377; Beecher, *Miss Beecher's Domestic Receipt-Book*, pp. 197, 109, 115; *Proceedings of the Massachusetts Historical Society*, pp. 122–23, 130; Glasse, *Art of Cookery* (1747), pp. xxxiii, 106; Raffald, *Experienced English House-keeper* (1769), pp. 150, 152; Dalgairns, *Practice of Cookery*, pp. 266–67; Dolby, *Cook's Dictionary*, p. 441; Lee, *Cook's Own Book*, p. 165; Howland, *New England Economical Housekeeper*, p. 35; Webster, *Improved Housewife* (1844), p. 84; Hale, *Ladies' New Book of Cookery*, pp. 297–98; Turner, *New England Cook Book*, p. 157.

#32: Stavely and Fitzgerald, *America's Founding Food*, p. 26.

#33: Parloa, *Miss Parloa's New Cook Book*, p. 268.

#34: Child, *American Frugal Housewife*, pp. 64–65; Howland, *New England Economical Housekeeper*, pp. 32, 36; Beecher, *Miss Beecher's Domestic Receipt-Book*, pp. 125, 123; Whatsoever Circle, *King's Daughters Cook Book*, p. 61; Glasse, *Art of Cookery* (1747), p. 111; Lincoln and Barrows, *Home Science Cook Book*, p. 171; Farmer, *Boston Cooking-School Cook Book*, p. 337; Bliss, *Practical Cook Book*, p. 139.

#35: Beecher, *Miss Beecher's Domestic Receipt-Book*, p. 96; Webster, *Improved Housewife* (1844), p. 115; Lincoln, *Mrs. Lincoln's Boston Cook Book*, pp. 344–45; Bliss, *Practical Cook Book*, p. 129; Shuman, *Favorite Dishes*, p. 141; Burr, *Woman Suffrage Cook Book*, p. 68; Gillette, *White House Cook Book*, pp. 351–52.

#36: Leslie, *Lady's Receipt-Book*, pp. 127–28; Wilcox, *Buckeye Cookery*, p. 199; Parloa, *Miss Parloa's New Cook Book*, p. 261; Burr, *Woman Suffrage Cook Book*, p. 58;

"*Aunt Babette's*" *Cook Book*, pp. 232–33; Shuman, *Favorite Dishes*, pp. 143–44; Curtis, *Good Housekeeping Woman's Home Cook Book*, pp. 78–80.

CHAPTER FOURTEEN. BREADS AND CAKES

Introduction: King, *When I Lived in Salem*, p. 99; Anderson, "Solid Sufficiency," p. 175; Smith, *Compleat Housewife* (1728), p. 152; Mood, "John Winthrop, Jr., on Indian Corn," pp. 130–31; Lincoln and Barrows, *Home Science Cook Book*, pp. 19–20; Stavely and Fitzgerald, *America's Founding Food*, pp. 8–12, 234–44; Earle, *Home Life in Colonial Days*, p. 67; James, "Miss Woolson," p. 8.

#1: McCance and Widdowson, *Breads White and Brown*, p. 10 (quoting Boorde); Acworth, *Margaretta Acworth's Georgian Cookery Book*, p. 94; Markham, *English Housewife* (1986), pp. 289, n. 25 (quoting Harrison, *Description of England*), 304; Markham, *English Hus-wife* (1615), pp. 126–27; Stavely and Fitzgerald, *America's Founding Food*, pp. 234–44; OED, "brake" (quoting Thomas, *Principal Rules of the Italian Grammer*); Davidson, *Oxford Companion to Food*, p. 60; Wilson, *Food and Drink in Britain*, p. 231.

#2: Acworth, *Margaretta Acworth's Georgian Cookery Book*, p. 90; OED, "pipes," "malkin," "mankin," "grimalkin." Best does not include the change from "mankin" to "maukin" in his list of textual variants. See Markham, *English Housewife* (1986), p. 224; Markham, *English Hus-wife* (1615), p. 128; and Markham, *Countrey Contentments* (1623), p. 233.

#3: Woolley, *Queen-like Closet*, p. 23; Glasse, *Art of Cookery* (1747), p. 150; Raffald, *Experienced English House-keeper* (1769), p. 255; Acworth, *Margaretta Acworth's Georgian Cookery Book*, p. 94; McGee, *On Food and Cooking*, pp. 557–58.

#4: Glasse, *Art of Cookery* (1747), p. 151; Stavely and Fitzgerald, *America's Founding Food*, p. 239.

#5: David, *English Bread and Yeast Cookery*, p. 98.

#6: McGee, *On Food and Cooking*, pp. 521–26; Child, *American Frugal Housewife*, p. 78; Bliss, *Practical Cook Book*, p. 110; Hale, *Good Housekeeper*, pp. 27–28.

#7: Child, *American Frugal Housewife*, pp. 76–77; Hale, *Good Housekeeper*, p. 28; Beecher, *Miss Beecher's Domestic Receipt-Book*, p. 89; Prescott, *Valuable Receipts*, p. 16; Bliss, *Practical Cook Book*, p. 110; Blake, *Farmer's Every-day Book*, p. 555; Hall, *Practical American Cookery*, p. 295; United States Patent Office, *Report*, p. 163; Boston, *Seventh Annual Report*, pp. 13–14; Stavely and Fitzgerald, *America's Founding Food*, p. 67.

New England's Saturday Night Bread Introduction: Boston, *Seventh Annual Report*, p. 13; Stavely and Fitzgerald, *America's Founding Food*, pp. 28–29; Bowles and Towle, *Secrets of New England Cooking*, p. 144.

#9: Wright, *New England Cook Book*, pp. 184–85; *New England Farmer*, p. 104; Massachusetts, *Eighteenth Annual Report*, p. 33; Chase, *Dr. Chase's Family Physician*, p. 152; *Tried and True Recipes*, p. 182; *Home Cook Book*, p. 280.

#10: Stavely and Fitzgerald, *America's Founding Food*, pp. 262–66; Hooker, *Food and Drink in America*, p. 86; OED, "dessert."

Sweet Breads, Small Cakes, and Biscuits Introduction: Turner, *New England Cook Book*, p. 132; Wilson, *Food and Drink in Britain*, pp. 269, 210–11, 265–66, 45; David, *English Bread and Yeast Cookery*, pp. 473–74.

#11: Prospect Books, *Glossary of Cookery*, "Bisket," dspace.dial.pipex.com/town/lane/ kal69/shop/pages/glossb.htm; Markham, *English Housewife* (1986), p. 265, n. 180; Markham, *English Hus-wife* (1615), pp. 75–76; Hess, *Martha Washington's Booke of Cookery*, pp. 314–15, 334–35, 337, 348; *Compleat Cook*, pp. 9, 11, 13–14, 22–23, 43–44, 54, 56; Woolley, *Queen-like Closet*, pp. 14, 16, 18, 30, 40, 49, 51, 54, 57, 62; Colquhoun, *Taste*, p. 53 (citing *Tacuinum sanitatis*); Davidson, *Oxford Companion to Food*, p. 123 (quoting Ayto, *Diner's Dictionary*); Olver, "Cake," www.foodtimeline.org/foodcakes.html (quoting Ayto, *A to Z of Food and Drink*).

#12: Markham, *English Housewife* (1986), p. 265, n. 178; Simmons, *American Cookery* (introduction by Wilson), pp. 32–33; *OED*, "jumble"; Davidson, *Oxford Companion to Food*, p. 423; Wilson, *Food and Drink in Britain*, p. 269; Hess, *Martha Washington's Booke of Cookery*, p. 349, Smith, *Oxford Encyclopedia of Food and Drink in America*, 1:318; Woolley, *Queen-like Closet*, p. 49; Simmons, *American Cookery* (introduction by Hess), p. 47; Markham, *English Hus-wife* (1615), p. 72; Acworth, *Margaretta Acworth's Georgian Cookery Book*, p. 90.

#13: Davidson, *Oxford Companion to Food*, p. 722; Hess, *Martha Washington's Booke of Cookery*, p. 284; Ingoldsby, *Ingoldsby Legends*, pp. 399, 405; Smith, *Compleat Housewife* (1728), pp. 129–30; Glasse, *Art of Cookery* (1747), p. 141; Raffald, *Experienced English House-keeper* (1769), pp. 248–49; Simmons, *American Cookery* (introduction by Wilson), p. 37; Beecher, *Miss Beecher's Domestic Receipt-Book*, p. 150.

#14: Davidson, *Oxford Companion to Food*, p. 208; Glasse, *Art of Cookery* (1747), pp. xxxiii, 141.

#15: David, *English Bread and Yeast Cookery*, pp. 98, 479–80; Wilson, *Food and Drink in Britain*, pp. 265–66; Davidson, *Oxford Companion to Food*, p. 684.

#16: Glasse, *Art of Cookery* (1747), p. 139; Beecher, *Miss Beecher's Domestic Receipt-Book*, pp. 134, 137; Stavely and Fitzgerald, *America's Founding Food*, pp. 244–46; Markham, *English Hus-wife* (1615), p. 71; *OED*, "turnsole (heliotrope)"; Woolley, *Queen-like Closet*, pp. 60–61.

#19: Hale, *Good Housekeeper*, p. 101.

#20: Davidson, *Oxford Companion to Food*, pp. 676, 75–76.

#21: Oliver, *Food in Colonial and Federal America*, p. 154.

#22: Beecher, *Miss Beecher's Domestic Receipt-Book*, pp. 141–42.

#23: *Aunt Mary's New England Cook Book*, p. 54; Stavely and Fitzgerald, *America's Founding Food*, pp. 249–52.

#24: Davidson, *Oxford Companion to Food*, p. 684.

Fried Cakes, Pancakes, and Hearth Cakes Introduction: Stavely and Fitzgerald, *America's Founding Food*, pp. 256–59, 30–31.

#25: Woolley, *Queen-like Closet*, pp. 116–17; *OED*, "pomewater," "clary," "tansy," "skirret"; Raffald, *Experienced English House-keeper* (1769), pp. 141, 159–61, 144; Glasse, *Art of Cookery* (1747), pp. 81, 202, 82; Markham, *Countrey Contentments* (1623), p. 68; Colquhoun, *Taste*, p. 71; Child, *American Frugal Housewife*, p. 74; Allen, *Housekeeper's Assistant*, p. 26; Leslie, *Directions for Cookery*, p. 312.

#26: Woolley, *Queen-like Closet*, pp. 133, 160–61; Shakespeare, *Pericles* (II, i, 84–87), in Harrison, *Shakespeare*, p. 1359.

#27: Hess, *Martha Washington's Booke of Cookery*, p. 9; Woolley, *Queen-like Closet*, p. 133.

#28: Smith, *Oxford Encyclopedia of Food and Drink in America*, 2:234–35; Markham, *English Hus-wife* (1615), p. 45; Oliver, *Saltwater Foodways*, p. 132; David, *English Bread and Yeast Cookery*, p. 416 (quoting Hammond, *Modern Domestic Cookery and Useful Receipt Book*).

#29: Stavely and Fitzgerald, *America's Founding Food*, pp. 29–39, 292–93, n. 92.

#30: OED, "flapjack," "slapjack"; Child, *American Frugal Housewife*, p. 74; Howland, *New England Economical Housekeeper*, p. 25.

#31: Scully, *Art of Cookery in the Middle Ages*, p. 217; Oliver, *Food in Colonial and Federal America*, p. 154; Stavely and Fitzgerald, *America's Founding Food*, p. 25; Willan, *Great Cooks*, p. 132.

#32: Twain, "Mysterious Visit," pp. 384, 387.

#33: Wilson, *Food and Drink in Britain*, p. 266, Glasse, *Art of Cookery* (1747), p. 151; Oliver, *Saltwater Foodways*, p. 57.

Cakes, Plain and Fancy Introduction: Stavely and Fitzgerald, *America's Founding Food*, pp. 239–44, 253–56; Lehmann, *British Housewife*, p. 200.

#34: Davidson, *Oxford Companion to Food*, pp. 122–24, 14, 523; Wilson, *Food and Drink in Britain*, pp. 269–70, 297; Glasse, *Art of Cookery* (1747), p. 138; OED, "grain."

#35: Glasse *Art of Cookery* (1747), pp. 139, 202; Glasse, *Art of Cookery* (1805), pp. 164–65; Smith, *Compleat Housewife* (1728), p. 134; Wilson, *Food and Drink in Britain*, p. 270; Davidson, *Oxford Companion to Food*, p. 712.

#s 36–38: Lehmann, *British Housewife*, p. 35; Barham, *Science of Cooking*, pp. 151–52; Charsley, *Wedding Cakes and Cultural History*, pp. 56, 70–71; Dolby, *Cook's Dictionary*, pp. 93, 7; Kitchiner, *Cook's Oracle* (1822), p. 500; Lee, *Cook's Own Book*, pp. 33–34, 2, 98.

#39: Simmons, *American Cookery* (introduction by Wilson), p. 33; OED, "drachm."

#40: Ayres, *Ralph Ayres' Cookery Book*, pp. 10, 75; Carter, *Frugal Housewife*, pp. 126–27.

#41: Dalgairns, *Practice of Cookery*, p. 339; Lee, *Cook's Own Book*, p. 222.

#43: Smith, *Oxford Encyclopedia of Food and Drink in America*, 1:157; Oliver, *Saltwater Foodways*, p. 22 (quoting Redfield, *Life in the Connecticut River Valley, 1800–1840*).

#46: Lee, *Cook's Own Book*, p. 35; Dolby, *Cook's Dictionary*, p. 189; Howland, *New England Economical Housekeeper*, p. 22; Allen, *Housekeeper's Assistant*, p. 19;

Leslie, *Directions for Cookery*, pp. 372–73; Beecher, *Miss Beecher's Domestic Receipt-Book*, pp. 100–101, 136; Carême, *Royal Parisian Pastrycook*, pp. 102–5, 71–74; Morrell, "Johnny Green," p. 79; *Methodist Almanac*, p. 57; Wilcox, *Buckeye Cookery*, p. 63; "Wheatless Recipes," p. 63; Smith, *Oxford Encyclopedia of Food and Drink in America*, 2:273; St. George, "Parker House"; Massachusetts, "State Symbols," www.sec.state.ma.us/cis/cismaf/mf1a.htm.

#s 47–48: Stowe, *Minister's Wooing*, p. 256 (chap. 30); Bowles and Towle, *Secrets of New England Cooking*, p. 221; Hooker, *Food and Drink in America*, p. 249.

Bibliography

Acton, Eliza. *Modern Cookery, in All Its Branches: Reduced to a System of Easy Practice.* Philadelphia: Blanchard and Lea, 1858.

Acworth, Margaretta. *Margaretta Acworth's Georgian Cookery Book.* Edited by Alice Prochaska and Frank Prochaska. London: Pavilion, 1987.

Adams, Abigail. *Letters of Mrs. Adams, the Wife of John Adams.* Introduction by Charles Francis Adams. 2 vols. Boston: Little, Brown, 1840.

——. *New Letters of Abigail Adams, 1788–1801.* Edited by Stewart Mitchell. Boston: Houghton Mifflin, 1947.

Adams Family Correspondence. Edited by Lyman Henry Butterfield et al. 9 vols. to date. Cambridge, Mass.: Belknap Press, 1963–.

Alaska Department of Fish and Game, *Wildlife Notebook Series,* "Lingcod." www.adfg .state.ak.us/pubs/notebook/fish/lingcod.php.

Alcott, William A. *The Young House-Keeper.* Boston: George W. Light, 1838.

Allen, Ann. *The Housekeeper's Assistant.* Boston: James Munroe, 1845.

American Classics by the Editors of Cook's Illustrated Magazine. "Boston Baked Scrod." www.foodreference.com/html/boston-scrod.html.

Ames, Kenneth L. "Introduction." In *The Colonial Revival in America,* edited by Alan Axelrod, 1–14. New York: Norton, 1985.

Amherst, Alicia. *A History of Gardening in England.* 2nd ed. London: Bernard Quaritch, 1896.

"Amos Bronson Alcott." *Dictionary of American Biography,* base set. American

Council of Learned Societies, 1928–1936. Reproduced in History Resource Center. Farmington Hills, Mich.: Gale.

Anchor Anthology of Seventeenth-Century Verse, The. Vol. 2. Edited by Richard S. Sylvester. Garden City, N.Y.: Doubleday, 1969.

Anderson, Jay Allan. "'A Solid Sufficiency': An Ethnography of Yeoman Foodways in Stuart England." Ph.D. diss., University of Pennsylvania, 1971.

Anderson, Virginia DeJohn. *Creatures of Empire: How Domestic Animals Transformed Early America.* Oxford: Oxford University Press, 2004.

Appleby, Joyce. *Inheriting the Revolution: The First Generation of Americans.* Cambridge, Mass.: Harvard University Press, 2000.

"Aunt Babette's" Cook Book. Cincinnati: Bloch, 1889.

Aunt Mary's New England Cook Book. Boston: Lockwood, Brooks, 1881.

Austin, John O. "One Line of the Power Family." *Narragansett Historical Register* 7 (1889): 17–24.

Ayres, Ralph. *Ralph Ayres' Cookery Book.* Introduction and glossary by Jane Jakeman. Oxford: Bodleian Library, 2006.

Barham, Peter. *The Science of Cooking.* New York: Springer-Verlag, 2001.

Barlow, Joel. "The Hasty Pudding" (1793). In vol. 2 of *The Works of Joel Barlow*, edited by William K. Bottorff and Arthur L. Lord, 85–99. Gainesville, Fla.: Scholars' Facsimiles and Reprints, 1970.

Bartlett, John Russell. *Dictionary of Americanisms: A Glossary of Words and Phrases Usually Regarded as Peculiar to the United States.* 4th ed. Boston: Little, Brown, 1877.

Beecher, Catharine E. *Miss Beecher's Domestic Receipt-Book: Designed as a Supplement to Her Treatise on Domestic Economy* (1858, 1846). Introduction by Janice (Jan) Bluestein Longone. Mineola, N.Y.: Dover, 2001.

———. *A Treatise on Domestic Economy* (1841). Edited by Kathryn Kish Sklar. New York: Schocken, 1977.

Beecher, Catharine E., and Harriet Beecher Stowe. *The American Woman's Home: Or, Principles of Domestic Science* (1869). Reprint, edited by Nicole Tonkovich. Hartford, Conn.: Harriet Beecher Stowe Center; New Brunswick, N.J.: Rutgers University Press, 2004, 2002.

Beeton, Isabella. *The Book of Household Management.* London: Ward, Lock, 1888.

Betsky, Celia. "Inside the Past: The Interior and the Colonial Revival in American Art and Literature, 1860–1914." In *The Colonial Revival in America*, edited by Alan Axelrod, 241–77. New York: Norton, 1985.

Black's Guide to Devonshire. Edited by A. R. Hope Moncrieff. 17th ed. London: Adam and Charles Black, 1902.

Blake, John Lauris. *The Farmer's Every-day Book.* Auburn, N.Y.: Derby, Miller, 1850.

Blencowe, Ann. *The Receipt Book of Mrs. Ann Blencowe, A. D. 1694.* Introduction by George Saintsbury. London: The Adelphi, Guy Chapman, 1925.

Bliss, Mrs. [of Boston]. *The Practical Cook Book.* Philadelphia: Lippincott, Grambo, 1850.

Booth, Sally Smith. *Hung, Strung, and Potted: A History of Eating in Colonial America.* New York: Clarkson N. Potter, 1971.

Boston, City of. *Seventh Annual Report of the Board of Directors of Public Institutions for the Year 1863* (City Document No. 10).

Bowles, Ella Shannon, and Dorothy S. Towle. *Secrets of New England Cooking.* 1947. Reprint, Mineola, N.Y.: Dover, 2000.

Boydston, Jeanne. *Home and Work: Housework, Wages, and the Ideology of Labor in the Early Republic.* New York: Oxford University Press, 1990.

Boydston, Jeanne, Mary Kelley, and Anne Margolis, eds. *The Limits of Sisterhood: The Beecher Sisters on Women's Rights and Woman's Sphere.* Chapel Hill: University of North Carolina Press, 1988.

Bradford, William. *Of Plymouth Plantation, 1620–1647.* Edited by Samuel Eliot Morison. New York: Random House, 1952.

Breen, T. H. "'Baubles of Britain': The American and Consumer Revolutions of the Eighteenth Century." In *Of Consuming Interests: The Style of Life in the Eighteenth Century,* edited by Cary Carson, Ronald Hoffman, and Peter J. Albert, 444–82. Charlottesville: University of Virginia Press, 1994.

———. *The Marketplace of Revolution: How Consumer Politics Shaped American Independence.* New York: Oxford University Press, 2004.

Brewer, E. Cobham. *Dictionary of Phrase and Fable.* 1898. New York: Bartleby.com, 2000. www.bartleby.com/81/.

Brewer, Priscilla J. *From Fireplace to Cookstove: Technology and the Domestic Ideal in America.* Syracuse, N.Y.: Syracuse University Press, 2000.

Brown, Nellie I. *Recipes from Old Hundred: 200 Years of New England Cooking.* New York: M. Barrows, 1939.

Burr, Hattie A., comp. *The Woman Suffrage Cook Book.* Boston: The Author, [1890?].

Bushman, Richard L. *The Refinement of America: Persons, Houses, Cities.* New York: Knopf, 1992.

Butler, William. "Another City upon a Hill: Litchfield, Connecticut, and the Colonial Revival." In *The Colonial Revival in America,* edited by Alan Axelrod, 15–51. New York: Norton, 1985.

Butler, William. *Arithmetical Questions, on a New Plan.* 2nd ed. London, 1795.

Cahn, Susan. *Industry of Devotion: The Transformation of Women's Work in England, 1500–1660.* New York: Columbia University Press, 1987.

Cambridge World History of Food, The. Edited by Kenneth F. Kiple and Kriemhild Corneè Ornelas. 2 vols. Cambridge: Cambridge University Press, 2000.

Carême, Marie Antonin. *The Royal Parisian Pastrycook and Confectioner.* Edited by John Porter. London: F. J. Mason, 1834.

Carlin, Joseph M. "Weights and Measures in Nineteenth-Century America." *Journal of Gastronomy* 3, no. 3 (Autumn 1987): 67–77.

Carson, Cary. "The Consumer Revolution in Colonial British America: Why Demand?" In *Of Consuming Interests: The Style of Life in the Eighteenth Century,* edited by Cary Carson, Ronald Hoffman, and Peter J. Albert, 483–697. Charlottesville: University of Virginia Press, 1994.

Carter, Susannah. *The Frugal Housewife; or Complete Woman Cook* (1765). Boston, 1772.

Chadwick, Mrs. J. *Home Cookery: A Collection of Tried Receipts both Foreign and Domestic.* Boston: Crosby, Nichols, 1853.

Charsley, Simon R. *Wedding Cakes and Cultural History.* London: Routledge, 1992.

Chase, A. W. *Dr. Chase's Family Physician, Farrier, Bee-keeper, and Second Receipt Book.* Toledo, Ohio: Chase Publishing, 1874.

Child, Lydia Maria. *The American Frugal Housewife*. 12th ed. Boston: Carter & Hendee, 1833. Reprint, Bedford, Mass.: Applewood Books, 1989.

———. *An Appeal in Favor of That Class of Americans Called Africans*. New York: John S. Taylor, 1836. First published 1833 by Allen and Ticknor, Boston.

Clark, Eleanor. *The Oysters of Locmariaquer*. New York: Pantheon, 1964.

Colquhoun, Kate. *Taste: The Story of Britain through Its Cooking*. New York: Bloomsbury, 2007.

Como, David R. *Blown by the Spirit: Puritanism and the Emergence of an Antinomian Underground in Pre-Civil-War England*. Stanford: Stanford University Press, 2004.

Compleat Cook, The. 2nd ed. London, 1658. Reprint, Whitefish, Mont.: Kessinger, n.d. [= cookery section of *The Queens Closet Opened*].

Conforti, Joseph A. *Imagining New England: Explorations of Regional Identity from the Pilgrims to the Mid-Twentieth Century*. Chapel Hill: University of North Carolina Press, 2001.

———. *Saints and Strangers: New England in British North America*. Baltimore: Johns Hopkins University Press, 2006.

Cook Not Mad, The. Watertown, N.Y.: Knowlton and Rice, 1830.

[Cornelius, Mrs. Mary Hooker]. *The Young Housekeeper's Friend*. Boston: Charles Tappan; New York: Saxton & Huntington, 1846.

———. *The Young Housekeeper's Friend*. Rev. and enl. ed. Boston: Frederick A. Brown, 1862.

Cowan, Ruth Schwartz. *More Work for Mother: The Ironies of Household Technology from the Open Hearth to the Microwave*. New York: Basic Books, 1983.

Crain, Patricia. "Print and Everyday Life in the Eighteenth Century." In *Perspectives on American Book History: Artifacts and Commentary*, edited by Scott E. Casper, Joanne D. Chaison, and Jeffrey D. Groves, 47–78. Amherst: University of Massachusetts Press, 2002.

Cressy, David. *Coming Over: Migration and Communication between England and New England in the Seventeenth Century*. Cambridge: Cambridge University Press, 1987.

Crowley, J. E. *This Sheba, Self: The Conceptualization of Economic Life in Eighteenth-Century America*. Baltimore: Johns Hopkins University Press, 1974.

Cummings, Richard Osborn. *The American and His Food: A History of Food Habits in the United States*. Chicago: University of Chicago Press, 1941.

Curtis, Isabel Gordon, comp. *The Good Housekeeping Woman's Home Cook Book*. Chicago: Reilly & Britton, 1909.

Dalgairns, Mrs. *The Practice of Cookery, Adapted to the Business of Every Day Life*. 3rd ed. Edinburgh: Robert Cadell, 1830.

Dallas, Eneas Sweetland. *Kettner's Book of the Table: A Manual of Cookery, Practical, Theoretical, Historical*. London: Dulau, 1877.

David, Elizabeth. *English Bread and Yeast Cookery*. American ed. Notes by Karen Hess. New York: Penguin, 1982; © 1980.

Davidoff, Leonore, and Catherine Hall. *Family Fortunes: Men and Women of the English Middle Class, 1780–1850*. Chicago: University of Chicago Press, 1987.

Davidson, Alan. *The Oxford Companion to Food*. Oxford: Oxford University Press, 1999.

Davidson, Caroline. *A Woman's Work Is Never Done: A History of Housework in the British Isles, 1650–1950*. London: Chatto & Windus, 1986; © 1982.

Davidson, Cathy N. *Revolution and the Word: The Rise of the Novel in America*. New York: Oxford University Press, 1986.

Day, Francis. *The Fishes of Great Britain and Ireland*. 2 vols. London: Williams and Norgate, 1880–84.

Dean, Sidney W. *Cooking American*. New York: Bramhall House, 1957.

Deetz, James. *In Small Things Forgotten: An Archaeology of Early American Life*. Rev. ed. New York: Anchor, 1996.

Derven, Daphne L. "Wholesome, Toothsome, and Diverse: Eighteenth-Century Foodways in Deerfield, Massachusetts." In *Foodways in the Northeast*, edited by Peter Benes, 47–63. Boston: Boston University, 1984.

Dexter, Franklin B. "Early Private Libraries in New England." *American Antiquarian Society, Proceedings*, new ser., 18 (1907): 135–47.

Dictionary of American Regional English. Edited by Frederick Gomes Cassidy. 4 vols. Cambridge, Mass.: Harvard University Press, 1985.

Dictionary of Americanisms on Historical Principles. 2 vols. Chicago: University of Chicago Press, 1951.

Diner, Hasia L. *Erin's Daughters in America: Irish Immigrant Women in the Nineteenth Century*. Baltimore: Johns Hopkins University Press, 1983.

Dolby, Richard. *The Cook's Dictionary, and House-keeper's Directory*. London: Henry Colburn and Richard Bentley, 1830.

Drake, Samuel Adams. *Nooks and Corners of the New England Coast*. 1875. Reprint, Detroit: Singing Tree Press, 1969.

Drummond, J. C. and Anne Wilbraham. *The Englishman's Food: A History of Five Centuries of English Diet*. Rev. ed. London: Jonathan Cape, 1957.

Dudden, Faye E. *Serving Women: Household Service in Nineteenth-Century America*. Middletown, Conn.: Wesleyan University Press, 1985; © 1983.

Durham Women's Club. *The Durham Cook Book: A Collection of Tested and Approved Recipes*. Concord, N.H.: Rumford Press, 1898.

DuSablon, Mary Anna. *America's Collectible Cookbooks: The History, the Politics, the Recipes*. Athens: Ohio University Press, 1994.

Dwight, Timothy. *Travels in New England and New York*. Edited by Barbara Miller Solomon. 4 vols. Cambridge, Mass.: Harvard University Press, 1969.

Earle, Alice Morse. *Home Life in Colonial Days*. 1898. Reprint, Williamstown, Mass.: Corner House, 1975.

Early, Eleanor. *New England Cookbook*. New York: Random House, 1954.

Echoes from South County Kitchens. Wickford, R.I.: The Farm Home and Garden Center, n.d. [ca. 1940s].

Eighteenth Century Collections Online.

Emerson, Lucy. *The New-England Cookery*. Montpelier, Vt.: Josiah Parks, 1808.

Encyclopedia Britannica Online. Public Library ed.

Essig, James D. *The Bonds of Wickedness: American Evangelicals against Slavery, 1770–1808*. Philadelphia: Temple University Press, 1982.

Fagan, Brian. *The Little Ice Age: How Climate Made History, 1300–1850.* Basic Books, 2002; © 2000.

Farmer, Fannie Merritt. *The Boston Cooking-School Cook Book.* 1896. Reprint, New York: Weathervane Books, n.d.

Fearnley-Whittingstall, Hugh. *The River Cottage Cookbook.* Berkeley: Ten Speed Press, 2008.

Feeding America: The Historic American Cookbook Project. Online digital archive, digital.lib.msu.edu/projects/cookbooks/index.html.

———. "Eliza Leslie Biography." digital.lib.msu.edu/projects/cookbooks/html/authors/author_leslie.html#bio.

———. "Introduction: *Seventy-five Receipts for Pastry, Cakes, and Sweetmeats.* By Miss Leslie." digital.lib.msu.edu/projects/cookbooks/html/books/book_09.cfm.

———. "Introduction: *The Cook's Own Book.*" digital.lib.msu.edu/projects/cookbooks/html/books/book_08.cfm.

———. "Introduction: *The Ladies' New Book of Cookery.*" digital.lib.msu.edu/projects/cookbooks/html/books/book_19.cfm.

———. "Mary Randolph Biography." digital.lib.msu.edu/projects/cookbooks/html/authors/author_randolph.html.

———. "Robert Roberts Biography." digital.lib.msu.edu/projects/cookbooks/html/authors/author_roberts.html.

Fernandez-Armesto, Felipe. *Near a Thousand Tables: A History of Food.* New York: Free Press, 2002.

Ferry, John. "The French Connection: Stew Stoves in America." Talk presented to The Culinary Historians of Washington, D.C., 11 February 2001. www.chowdc.org/Papers/Ferry%202001.html.

Fielding, Henry. *The Complete Works of Henry Fielding, Esq.* Vol. 9. London: William Heinemann, 1903.

Finley, Ruth E. *The Lady of Godey's: Sarah Josepha Hale.* Philadelphia: Lippincott, 1931.

Fischer, David Hackett. *Albion's Seed: Four British Folkways in America.* New York: Oxford University Press, 1989.

Fisher, M. F. K. *Consider the Oyster.* 1941. Reprint, San Francisco: North Point Press, 1988.

Florida Fish and Wildlife Conservation Commission Fish and Wildlife Research Institute. "Gallery: Saltwater Fish." research.myfwc.com/gallery.

Ford, Worthington Chauncey. *The Boston Book Market, 1679–1700.* 1917. Reprint, New York: Burt Franklin, 1972.

Foster, Stephen. *Their Solitary Way: The Puritan Social Ethic in the First Century of Settlement in New England.* New Haven: Yale University Press, 1971.

Fowler, Damon Lee, ed. *Dining at Monticello: In Good Taste and Abundance.* Chapel Hill: University of North Carolina Press, 2005.

Franklin, Benjamin. *Benjamin Franklin's Autobiography and Selected Writings.* Edited by Dixon Wecter and Larzer Ziff. 1948, 1959. New York: Holt, Rinehart and Winston, 1964.

Frontline. "Modern Meat: How Much Meat We Eat." www.pbs.org/wgbh/pages/frontline/shows/meat/safe/howmuch.html.

Fussell, Betty. *Masters of American Cookery: M. F. K. Fisher, James Andrew Beard, Raymond Craig Claiborne, Julia McWilliams Child. 1983.* Lincoln: University of Nebraska Press, 2005.

G. H. Bent Co. "Company History." www.bentscookiefactory.com/history.html.

"Gail Borden." *Dictionary of American Biography*, base set. American Council of Learned Societies, 1928–1936. Reproduced in History Resource Center. Farmington Hills, Mich.: Gale.

Gardiner, Anne Gibbons. *Mrs. Gardiner's Family Receipts from 1763, Boston.* Edited by Gail Weesner. Boston: Rowan Tree Press, 1988.

Gildrie, Richard P. *The Profane, the Civil, & the Godly: The Reformation of Manners in Orthodox New England, 1679–1749.* University Park: Pennsylvania State University Press, 1994.

Gillette, Fanny Lemira, comp. *White House Cook Book.* Chicago: R. S. Peale, 1887.

Gilman, Caroline. *The Lady's Annual Register and Housewife's Almanac for 1840.* Boston: Otis, Broaders, 1840.

Glasse, Hannah. *The Art of Cookery Made Plain and Easy.* London, 1747. Reprint, with introductory essays by Jennifer Stead and Priscilla Bain, glossary by Alan Davidson, *"First Catch Your Hare . . .": The Art of Cookery Made Plain and Easy,* Totnes, Eng.: Prospect, 1995.

———. *The Art of Cookery Made Plain and Easy.* 6th ed. London, 1758.

———. *The Art of Cookery Made Plain and Easy.* Alexandria, Va.: Cottom and Stewart, 1805. Reprint, with historical notes by Karen Hess, Bedford, Mass.: Applewood Books, 1997.

Godey's Lady's Book and Magazine. February 1880–April 1891.

Gould, Adeline Eunice. *The Two Half Dollars and Other Tales: A Gift for Children.* Boston: Tappan and Dennet, 1844.

Guy, William A. *Principles of Forensic Medicine.* 2nd ed. London: Henry Renshaw, 1861.

Hale, Sarah Josepha. *The Good Housekeeper.* Boston, 1841, 1839. Reprint, *Early American Cookery: "The Good Housekeeper," 1841.* Introduction by Janice (Jan) Bluestein Longone. Mineola, N.Y.: Dover, 1996.

———. *The Ladies' New Book of Cookery.* New York: H. Long & Brother, 1852.

———. *Northwood: A Tale of New England.* 2 vols. Boston: Bowles and Dearborn, 1827.

———. *Northwood: Or, Life North and South: Showing the True Character of Both.* 2nd ed. New York: H. Long & Brother, 1852.

Hall, David D. *Cultures of Print: Essays in the History of the Book.* Amherst: University of Massachusetts Press, 1996.

———. *Worlds of Wonder, Days of Judgment: Popular Religious Belief in Early New England.* New York: Knopf, 1989.

Hall, Elizabeth M., comp. *Practical American Cookery and Domestic Economy.* New York: C. M. Saxton, Barker, 1860.

Hamilton, Alexander. *Gentleman's Progress: The Itinerarium of Dr. Alexander Hamilton, 1744.* Edited by Carl Bridenbaugh. Chapel Hill: University of North Carolina Press, 1948.

Hardeman, Nicholas P. *Shucks, Shocks, and Hominy Blocks: Corn as a Way of Life in Pioneer America.* Baton Rouge: Louisiana State University Press, 1981.

Harrison, G. B., ed. *Shakespeare: The Complete Works.* New York: Harcourt, 1948.

Hatch, Peter J. "Bernard McMahon, Pioneer American Gardener." www.twinleaf.org/articles/mcmahon.html.

Hawthorne, Hildegarde. *Old Seaport Towns of New England.* New York: Dodd, Mead, 1916.

Hayes, Kevin J. *A Colonial Woman's Bookshelf.* Knoxville: University of Tennessee Press, 1996.

Hazard, Thomas Robinson. *The Jonny-Cake Papers of "Shepherd Tom"* (1888). Introduction by Rowland Gibson Hazard. Boston: Merrymount Press, 1915.

Hedrick, Joan D. *Harriet Beecher Stowe: A Life.* New York: Oxford University Press, 1994.

Henisch, Bridget Ann. *Fast and Feast: Food in Medieval Society.* University Park: Pennsylvania State University Press, 1976.

Henriette's Herbal Homepage. "Uvae.—Raisins." www.henriettesherbal.com/eclectic/kings/vitis-vini_uva.html. Data drawn from Harvey Wickes Felter and John Uri Lloyd, *King's American Dispensatory.* Cincinnati: Ohio Valley, 1898).

Hertzmann, Peter. "Service à la Française." www.hertzmann.com/articles/2004/service.

Hess, John L., and Karen Hess. *The Taste of America.* 1972. Urbana: University of Illinois Press, 2000.

Hess, Karen, ed. *Martha Washington's Booke of Cookery; and Booke of Sweetmeats.* New York: Columbia University Press, 1995

High Beam Encyclopedia. "Hand of Pork." www.encyclopedia.com/doc/1O39-handofpork.html. Data drawn from David Bender, *A Dictionary of Food and Nutrition.* New York: Oxford University Press, 2005.

Hill, Bridget. *Women, Work, and Sexual Politics in Eighteenth-Century England.* Oxford: Basil Blackwell, 1989.

The Home Cook Book, Compiled from Recipes Contributed by Ladies of Chicago. Chicago: J. Fred. Waggoner, 1876.

Hooker, Richard J. *The Book of Chowder.* Harvard, Mass.: Harvard Common Press, 1978.

———. *Food and Drink in America: A History.* Indianapolis: Bobbs-Merrill, 1981.

Hotten-Somers, Diane M. "Relinquishing and Reclaiming Independence: Irish Domestic Servants, American Middle-Class Mistresses, and Assimilation, 1850–1920." *Eire-Ireland* 36, 1–2 (2001): 185–201.

Howard, Henry. *England's Newest Way in All Sorts of Cookery.* 3rd ed. London, 1710.

Howland, E[sther] A[llen]. *The New England Economical Housekeeper, and Family Receipt Book.* 2nd ed. Worcester, Mass.: S. A. Howland, 1845.

Hunt, William. *Good Bread: How to Make It Light without Yeast or Powders.* 2nd ed. Boston, 1858.

Ingoldsby, Thomas. *The Ingoldsby Legends, Or Mirth and Marvels.* London: John Lane, 1903.

Inman, LeValley A. *A Rhode Island Rule Book.* Edited by Leah Inman Lapham. Providence, R.I., 1939.

Innis, Harold A. *The Cod Fisheries: The History of an International Economy.* Rev. ed. Toronto: University of Toronto Press, 1978.

Jacobsen, Rowan. *A Geography of Oysters: A Connoisseur's Guide to Oyster Eating in America*. New York: Bloomsbury USA, 2007.

James, Henry. "Miss Woolson." In *Constance Fenimore Woolson*, edited by Clare Benedict, 1–14. London: Ellis, [1932].

Johnson, Edward. *Johnson's Wonder-Working Providence, 1628–1651* (1654). Edited by J. Franklin Jameson. New York: Scribner's, 1910. Reprint, New York: Barnes and Noble, 1959.

Jonson, Ben. *Bartholomew Fair*. Edited by Eugene M. Waith. New Haven: Yale University Press, 1963.

Josselyn, John. *John Josselyn, Colonial Traveler: A Critical Edition of "Two Voyages to New-England"* (1674). Edited by Paul J. Lindholdt. Hanover, N.H.: University Press of New England, 1988.

Journal of the Pilgrims at Plymouth [Mourt's Relation], The. Edited by George B. Cheever. New York: Wiley, 1848.

Karcher, Carolyn L. *The First Woman in the Republic: A Cultural Biography of Lydia Maria Child*. Durham, N.C.: Duke University Press, 1994.

Karr, Ronald Dale, ed. *Indian New England, 1524–1674: A Compendium of Eyewitness Accounts of Native American Life*. Pepperell, Mass.: Branch Line Press, 1999.

Kasson, John F. *Rudeness and Civility: Manners in Nineteenth-Century Urban America*. New York: Hill and Wang, 1990.

Katzman, David M. *Seven Days a Week: Women and Domestic Service in Industrializing America*. New York: Oxford University Press, 1978.

Kelly, Catherine E. *In the New England Fashion: Reshaping Women's Lives in the Nineteenth Century*. Ithaca: Cornell University Press, 2002, 1999.

Kerber, Linda K. *Women of the Republic: Intellect and Ideology in Revolutionary America*. Chapel Hill: University of North Carolina Press, 1980.

King, Caroline Howard. *When I Lived in Salem, 1822–1866*. Edited by Louisa L. Dresel. Brattleboro, Vt.: Stephen Daye Press, 1937.

Kirshenblatt-Gimblett, Barbara. "The Moral Sublime: The Temple Emanuel Fair and Its Cookbook, Denver, 1888." In *Recipes for Reading: Community Cookbooks, Stories, Histories*, edited by Anne L. Bower, 136–53. Amherst: University of Massachusetts Press, 1997.

Kitchiner, William. *The Cook's Oracle, Containing Receipts for Plain Cookery*. 4th ed. London and Edinburgh: Hurst, Robinson; A. Constable, 1822.

———. *The Cook's Oracle; Containing Receipts for Plain Cookery*. New ed. London, Edinburgh, and Dublin: Simpkin and Marshall; G. B. Whittaker; Cadell; John Cumming, 1827.

Knight, Janice. *Orthodoxies in Massachusetts: Rereading American Puritanism*. Cambridge, Mass. Harvard University Press, 1994.

Knight, Mrs. S. G. *Tit-Bits: Or, How to Prepare a Nice Dish at Moderate Expense*. Boston: Crosby and Nichols, 1864.

Korda, Natasha. *Shakespeare's Domestic Economies: Gender and Property in Early Modern England*. Philadelphia: University of Pennsylvania Press, 2002.

Kurlansky, Mark. *Cod: A Biography of the Fish That Changed the World*. New York: Penguin, 1998. First published 1997 by Walker, New York.

Lady's Companion, The. 4th ed. Vol. 2. London, 1743.

Lasser, Carol S. "Mistress, Maid and Market: The Transformation of Domestic Service in New England, 1790–1870." Ph.D. diss., Harvard University, 1981.

Laudan, Rachel. "Birth of the Modern Diet." *Scientific American,* August 2000, 76–81.

[Lee, Mrs. N. K. M.]. *The Cook's Own Book: Being a Complete Culinary Encyclopedia.* Boston: Munroe and Francis, 1832.

Lehmann, Gilly. "The Birth of a New Profession: The Housekeeper and Her Status in the Seventeenth and Eighteenth Centuries." In *The Invisible Woman: Aspects of Women's Work in Eighteenth-Century Britain,* edited by Isabelle Baudino, Jacques Carée, and Cécile Révauger, 9–25. Aldershot, Eng.: Ashgate, 2005.

———. *The British Housewife: Cookery Books, Cooking, and Society in Eighteenth-Century Britain.* Totnes, Eng.: Prospect, 2003.

Leighton, Ann. *Early American Gardens: "For Meate or Medicine."* Boston: Houghton Mifflin, 1970. Reprint, Amherst: University of Massachusetts Press, 1986.

Leslie, Eliza. *Directions for Cookery in Its Various Branches.* 10th ed. Philadelphia: E. L. Carey & A. Hart, 1840.

———. *The Lady's Receipt-Book.* Philadelphia: Carey and Hart, 1847.

———. *Seventy-five Receipts for Pastry, Cake, and Sweetmeats.* 3rd ed. Boston: Munroe and Francis, 1830.

Levenstein, Harvey A. *Revolution at the Table: The Transformation of the American Diet.* New York: Oxford University Press, 1988.

Lincoln, Mary J. *Mrs. Lincoln's Boston Cook Book.* Boston: Roberts Brothers, 1884.

Lincoln, Mary J., and Anna Barrows. *The Home Science Cook Book.* 1902. Boston: Whitcomb and Barrows, 1911.

Lockridge, Kenneth A. *Literacy in Colonial New England: An Enquiry into the Social Context of Literacy in the Early Modern West.* New York: Norton, 1974.

Longone, Janice Bluestein. "'Tried Receipts': An Overview of America's Charitable Cookbooks." In *Recipes for Reading: Community Cookbooks, Stories, Histories,* edited by Anne L. Bower, 17–28. Amherst: University of Massachusetts Press, 1997.

Lowenstein, Eleanor. *Bibliography of American Cookery Books, 1742–1860.* 3rd ed. Worcester, Mass.: American Antiquarian Society, 1972.

Lynch-Brennan, Margaret. "Ubiquitous Biddy: Irish Immigrant Women in Domestic Service in America, 1840–1930." Ph.D. diss., State University of New York, Albany, 2002.

McCance, R. A., and E. M. Widdowson. *Breads White and Brown: Their Place in Thought and Social History.* Philadelphia: Lippincott, 1956.

McGee, Harold. *On Food and Cooking: The Science and Lore of the Kitchen.* Rev. ed. New York: Scribner, 2004.

McKeon, Michael. *The Secret History of Domesticity: Public, Private, and the Division of Knowledge.* Baltimore: Johns Hopkins University Press, 2005.

McMahon, Sarah F. "'All Things in Their Proper Season': Seasonal Rhythms of Diet in Nineteenth Century New England." *Agricultural History* 63 (Spring 1989): 130–51.

———. "A Comfortable Subsistence: The Changing Composition of Diet in Rural New England, 1620–1840." *William and Mary Quarterly,* 3d ser., 42 (January 1985): 26–65.

————. "Laying Foods By: Gender, Dietary Decisions, and the Technology of Food Preservation in New England Households, 1750–1850." In *Early American Technology: Making and Doing Things from the Colonial Era to 1850*, edited by Judith A. McGaw, 164–96. Chapel Hill: University of North Carolina Press, 1994.

McManis, Douglas R. *Colonial New England: A Historical Geography*. New York: Oxford University Press, 1975.

McPherson, James M. *The Illustrated Battle Cry of Freedom: The Civil War Era*. Oxford: Oxford University Press, 2003.

Mangione, Salvatore, ed. *Physical Diagnosis Secrets*. Philadelphia: Hanley & Belfus, 2000.

Mariani, John F. *The Dictionary of American Food and Drink*. New York: Ticknor and Fields, 1983.

Mann, Mrs., Horace. *Christianity in the Kitchen: A Physiological Cook Book*. Boston: Ticknor and Fields, 1857.

Markham, Gervase. *Countrey Contentments, or The English Huswife*. London, 1623.

————. *The English Housewife*. Edited by Michael R. Best. Montreal & Kingston, Ont.: McGill-Queen's University Press, 1994, 1986.

————. *The English Hus-wife*. London, 1615.

Martin, Edgar W. *The Standard of Living in 1860*. Chicago: University of Chicago Press, 1942.

Mason, Matthew. *Slavery and Politics in the Early American Republic*. Chapel Hill: University of North Carolina Press, 2006.

Massachusetts, Commonwealth of. *Eighteenth Annual Report of the Trustees of the State Reform School, at Westborough*. Public Document No. 20. Boston: Wright & Potter, 1864.

————. Office of the Secretary. Citizens Information Service. "State Symbols." www .sec.state.ma.us/cis/cismaf/mf1a.htm.

Mathews, Donald G. "The Second Great Awakening as an Organizing Process, 1780–1830." *American Quarterly* 21 (Spring 1969): 23–43.

Matthews, Glenna. *"Just a Housewife": The Rise and Fall of Domesticity in America*. New York: Oxford University Press, 1987.

Mendall, P. H. *The New Bedford Practical Receipt Book*. New Bedford, Mass.: Charles Taber, 1862.

Mennell, Stephen. *All Manners of Food: Eating and Taste in England and France from the Middle Ages to the Present*. 2nd ed. Urbana: University of Illinois Press, 1996.

Meriden Hospital Women's Executive Committee. *Meriden Cook Book*. Meriden, Conn., [1898?].

Methodist Almanac, The. New York: Carlton & Lanahan, 1872.

Milford, T. A. *The Gardiners of Massachusetts: Provincial Ambition and the British-American Career*. Hanover, N.H.: University Press of New England, 2005.

Mills, Bruce. *Cultural Reformations: Lydia Maria Child and the Literature of Reform*. Athens: University of Georgia Press, 1994.

Milton, John. *The Poems of John Milton*. Edited by John Carey and Alistair Fowler. London: Longmans, 1968.

Monaghan, E. Jennifer. *Learning to Read and Write in Colonial America*. Amherst: University of Massachusetts Press, 2005.

Montanari, Massimo. *The Culture of Food*. Translated by Carl Ipsen. Oxford: Basil Blackwell, 1994.

Mood, Fulmer. "John Winthrop, Jr., on Indian Corn." *New England Quarterly* 10 (March 1937): 121–33.

Morgan, Edmund S. *The Puritan Family: Religion and Domestic Relations in Seventeenth Century New England*. Rev. ed. New York: Harper Torchbooks, 1966.

Morrell, Arthur. "Johnny Green and the Cream Cake." *The Rover: A Weekly Magazine of Tales, Poetry, and Engravings* 3 (1844): 79.

Neuhaus, Jessamyn. *Manly Meals and Mom's Home Cooking: Cookbooks and Gender in Modern America*. Baltimore: Johns Hopkins University Press, 2003.

Neustadt, Kathy. *Clambake: A History and Celebration of an American Tradition*. Amherst: University of Massachusetts Press, 1992.

New England Farmer, The, 14 (February 1862).

Nissenbaum, Stephen. *Sex, Diet, and Debility in Jacksonian America: Sylvester Graham and Health Reform*. Westport, Conn.: Greenwood Press, 1980.

Norton, Mary Beth. *Liberty's Daughters: The Revolutionary Experience of American Women, 1750–1800*. Boston: Little, Brown, 1980.

Nylander, Jane C., *Our Own Snug Fireside: Images of the New England Home, 1760–1860*. New York: Knopf, 1993.

Ockerman, Herbert W., and Conly L. Hansen. *Animal By-product Processing and Utilization*. Boca Raton, Fla.: CRC Press, 1999.

Okker, Patricia. *Our Sister Editors: Sarah J. Hale and the Tradition of Nineteenth-Century American Women Editors*. Athens: University of Georgia Press, 1995.

O'Leary, Elizabeth L. *At Beck and Call: The Representation of Domestic Servants in Nineteenth-Century American Painting*. Washington, D.C.: Smithsonian Institution Press, 1996.

Oliver, Sandra L. *Food in Colonial and Federal America*. Westport, Conn.: Greenwood Press, 2005.

———. "Ruminations on the State of American Food History." *Gastronomica* 6 (Fall 2006): 91–98.

———. *Saltwater Foodways: New Englanders and Their Food, at Sea and Ashore, in the Nineteenth Century*. Mystic, Conn.: Mystic Seaport Museum, 1995.

Olver, Lynne, ed. "Cake." In *Food Timeline*. www.foodtimeline.org/foodcakes.html.

Orwell, George. *The Collected Essays, Journalism and Letters of George Orwell*. Vol. 3. Edited by Sonia Orwell and Ian Angus. New York: Harcourt, Brace & World, 1968.

Oxford English Dictionary. Online edition.

Parkman, Ebenezer. Diary, 1723–78. In Parkman Family Papers, American Antiquarian Society, Worcester, Mass.

Parloa, Maria. *Miss Parloa's New Cook Book*. Boston: Estes and Lauriat; New York: Charles T. Dillingham, 1882.

Patten, Mrs. Francis Jarvis. *Our New England Family Recipes*. New York: Tobias A. Wright, 1910.

Pillsbury, Richard. *No Foreign Food: The American Diet in Time and Place*. Boulder, Colo.: Westview Press, 1998.

"Pluck a Flamingo." *Economist*. 18 December 2008. www.economist.com.

Plymouth Archaeological Rediscovery Project. "European Chicken (Gallus gallus) and Native American Culture." plymoutharch.tripod.com/id8.html.

Poole, Kristen. *Radical Religion from Shakespeare to Milton: Figures of Nonconformity in Early Modern England.* Cambridge: Cambridge University Press, 2000.

Pope, Alexander. *The Poems of Alexander Pope.* Edited by John Butt. New Haven: Yale University Press, 1963.

Practically Edible. "Pork Chine." www.practicallyedible.com.

Prescott, J. H. *Valuable Receipts.* Boston: Mead and Beal, 1845.

Proceedings of the Massachusetts Historical Society, 1st ser., 20 (1882–83): 122–57.

Prospect Books. *A Glossary of Cookery and Other Terms.* dspace.dial.pipex.com/town/lane/kal69/shop/pages/gloss.htm.

Proust, Marcel. *Remembrance of Things Past.* 2 vols. Translated by C. K. Scott Moncrieff and Frederick A. Blossom; introduction by Joseph Wood Krutch. New York: Random House, 1932–34.

Putnam, Elizabeth. *Mrs. Putnam's Receipt Book and Young Housekeeper's Assistant.* Boston: Ticknor, Reed, and Fields, 1849.

Raffald, Elizabeth. *The Experienced English House-keeper.* 1st ed. Manchester, 1769.

———. *The Experienced English Housekeeper* (1769). Edited by Roy Shipperbottom. Lewes, Eng.: Southover Press, 1997.

Rappleye, Charles. *Sons of Providence: The Brown Brothers, the Slave Trade, and the American Revolution.* New York: Simon & Schuster, 2006.

Redon, Odile, Françoise Sabban, and Silvano Serventi. *The Medieval Kitchen: Recipes from France and Italy.* Chicago: University of Chicago Press, 1998.

Reid, Hartelaw. *Cookery, Rational, Practical, and Economical: Treated in Connexion with the Chemistry of Food.* Edinburgh: John Menzies; London: W. S. Orr, 1853.

Roberts, Robert. *The House Servant's Directory, or A Monitor for Private Families.* Boston: Munroe and Francis; New York: Charles S. Francis, 1827.

Roger Cookery, The: Being a Collection of Receipts, Designed for the Use of Private Families. Boston: Joseph Dowe, 1838.

Rogers, Sherbrooke. *Sarah Josepha Hale: A New England Pioneer, 1788–1879.* Grantham, N.H.: Tompson & Rutter, 1985.

Rombauer, Irma S., and Marion Rombauer Becker. *The Joy of Cooking.* Indianapolis: Bobbs-Merrill, 1975.

Romines, Ann. "Growing Up with the Methodist Cookbooks." In *Recipes for Reading: Community Cookbooks, Stories, Histories,* edited by Anne L. Bower, 75–88. Amherst: University of Massachusetts Press, 1997.

Ross, Alice. "Ella Smith's Unfinished Community Cookbook: A Social History of Women and Work in Smithtown, New York, 1884–1922." In *Recipes for Reading: Community Cookbooks, Stories, Histories,* edited by Anne L. Bower, 154–72. Amherst: University of Massachusetts Press, 1997.

Rossi-Wilcox, Susan M. *Dinner for Dickens: The Culinary History of Mrs Charles Dickens's Menu Books.* Totnes, Eng.: Prospect, 2005.

Roth, Rodris. "The New England, or 'Old Tyme,' Kitchen Exhibit at Nineteenth-Century Fairs." In *The Colonial Revival in America,* edited by Alan Axelrod, 159–83. New York: Norton, 1985.

Rundell, Maria Eliza Ketelby. *A New System of Domestic Cookery*. New ed. London, 1807.

Ryan, Barbara. *Love, Wages, Slavery: The Literature of Servitude in the United States*. Urbana: University of Illinois Press, 2006.

St. George, Donna. "The Parker House: Grant Ate Pie Here." *New York Times*. 22 January 1997.

Sanborn, Franklin Benjamin. *Bronson Alcott: At Alcott House, England, and Fruitlands, New England (1842–1844)*. Cedar Rapids, Iowa: Torch Press, 1908.

Schorger, A. W. *The Wild Turkey: Its History and Domestication*. Norman: University of Oklahoma Press, 1966.

Schweid, Richard. *Consider the Eel: A Natural and Gastronomic History*. Chapel Hill: University of North Carolina Press, 2002.

Scully, Terence. *The Art of Cookery in the Middle Ages*. Woodbridge, Eng.: Boydell Press, 1995.

Shammas, Carole. *A History of Household Government in America*. Charlottesville: University of Virginia Press, 2002.

Shapiro, Laura. *Perfection Salad: Women and Cooking at the Turn of the Century*. New York: Farrar, Straus and Giroux, 1986.

Shuman, Carrie V., comp. *Favorite Dishes. A Columbian Autograph Souvenir Cookery Book*. Chicago: R. R. Donnelley, 1893.

Simmons, Amelia. *American Cookery*. 1st ed. Hartford, Conn., 1796. Reprint, with an introduction by Mary Tolford Wilson, New York: Dover, 1984.

———. *American Cookery*. 2nd ed. Albany, N.Y. [1796]. Reprint, with an introduction by Karen Hess, Bedford, Mass.: Applewood Books, 1996.

Sklar, Kathryn Kish. *Catharine Beecher: A Study in American Domesticity*. New Haven: Yale University Press, 1973.

Slater, Nigel. *Appetite: So What Do You Want to Eat Today?* New York: Clarkson N. Potter, 2002. First published 2000 by Fourth Estate, London.

Sloat, Caroline, ed. *Old Sturbridge Village Cookbook*. Chester, Conn.: Globe Pequot Press, 1984.

Smith, Andrew F. "The First Thanksgiving." *Gastronomica* 3 (Fall 2003): 79–85.

———. *The Turkey: An American Story*. Chicago: University of Illinois Press, 2006.

Smith, Andrew F., ed. *The Oxford Encyclopedia of Food and Drink in America*. 2 vols. New York: Oxford University Press, 2004.

Smith, E. *The Compleat Housewife: Or, Accomplish'd Gentlewoman's Companion*. 2nd ed. London, 1728.

———. *The Compleat Housewife: Or, Accomplish'd Gentlewoman's Companion*. 4th ed. London, 1730.

———. *The Compleat Housewife: Or, Accomplish'd Gentlewoman's Companion*. 5th ed. London, 1732.

———. *The Compleat Housewife: Or, Accomplish'd Gentlewoman's Companion*. 9th ed. London, 1739.

———. *The Compleat Housewife: Or, Accomplish'd Gentlewoman's Companion*. 14th ed. London, 1750.

———. *The Compleat Housewife: Or, Accomplish'd Gentlewoman's Companion*. Reprint, compiled from the 15th (1753) and 18th (1773) eds., London: Literary Services and Production, 1968.

Smith, Timothy L. *Revivalism and Social Reform: American Protestantism on the Eve of the Civil War.* New York: Harper, 1965. First published 1957 by Abingdon Press, New York.

Spencer, Colin. *British Food: An Extraordinary Thousand Years of History.* New York: Columbia University Press, 2002.

Stavely, Keith W. F. *Puritan Legacies: Paradise Lost and the New England Tradition.* Ithaca: Cornell University Press, 1987.

———. "The World All before Them: Milton and the Rising Glory of America." *Studies in Eighteenth-Century Culture* 20 (1990): 147–64.

Stavely, Keith, and Kathleen Fitzgerald. *America's Founding Food: The Story of New England Cooking.* Chapel Hill: University of North Carolina Press, 2004.

Story, Ronald. "Class and Culture in Boston: The Athenaeum, 1807–1860." *American Quarterly* 27 (1975): 178–99.

———. *The Forging of an Aristocracy: Harvard and the Boston Upper Class, 1800–1870.* Middletown, Conn.: Wesleyan University Press, 1980.

Stowe, Harriet Beecher. *House and Home Papers.* 1864. 8th ed. Boston: Houghton Mifflin, 1890.

———. *The Minister's Wooing.* 1859. Edited by Susan K. Harris. New York: Penguin, 1999.

———. *The Pearl of Orr's Island: A Story of the Coast of Maine.* 1862. Edited by Joan D. Hedrick. Boston: Houghton Mifflin, 2001.

Strasser, Susan. *Never Done: A History of American Housework.* New York: Pantheon, 1982.

Sutherland, Daniel E. *Americans and Their Servants: Domestic Service in the United States from 1800 to 1920.* Baton Rouge: Louisiana State University Press, 1981.

Sweeney, Kevin M. "High-Style Vernacular: Lifestyles of the Colonial Elite." In *Of Consuming Interests: The Style of Life in the Eighteenth Century,* edited by Cary Carson, Ronald Hoffman, and Peter J. Albert, 1–58. Charlottesville: University Press of Virginia, 1994.

Swift, Jonathan. *Polite Conversation in Three Dialogues* (1738). Edited by George Saintsbury. London: Charles Whittingham, 1892.

Tate Online. "William Hogarth: O the Roast Beef of Old England ('The Gate of Calais')." www.tate.org.uk/servlet/ViewWork?workid=6617.

Thackeray, William Makepeace. *Vanity Fair: A Novel without a Hero.* Afterword by V. S. Pritchett. New York: New American Library, 1962.

Theophano, Janet. *Eat My Words: Reading Women's Lives through the Cookbooks They Wrote.* New York: Palgrave, 2002.

Thorne, John. *Mouth Wide Open: A Cook and His Appetite.* New York: North Point Press, 2007.

———. *Simple Cooking.* New York: North Point Press, 1996.

Tonkovich, Nicole. *Domesticity with a Difference: The Nonfiction of Catharine Beecher, Sarah J. Hale, Fanny Fern, and Margaret Fuller.* Jackson: University Press of Mississippi, 1997.

Towner, Lawrence William. "A Good Master Well Served: A Social History of Servitude in Massachusetts, 1620–1750." Ph.D. diss., Northwestern University, 1955.

Tried And True Recipes: The Home Cook Book, Compiled from Recipes Contributed by Ladies of Toledo. Toledo, Ohio: T. J. Brown, Eager, 1876.

Trumbull, James Hammond, ed. *The Memorial History of Hartford, Connecticut, 1633–1884.* 2 vols. Boston: Edward L. Osgood, 1886.

Turner, Alice M., comp. *The New England Cook Book: The Latest and Best Methods for Economy and Luxury at Home.* Boston: Chas. E. Browne, 1905.

Twain, Mark. "A Mysterious Visit." In *Sketches New and Old,* 384–89. New York: Harper, 1922.

United States Census Bureau. *The 2008 Statistical Abstract: The National Data Book.* www.census.gov/compendia/statab.

United States Patent Office. *Report of the Commissioner of Patents for the Year 1855.* Washington: A. O. P. Nicholson, 1856.

Vickers, Daniel. *Farmers and Fishermen: Two Centuries of Work in Essex County, Massachusetts, 1630–1850.* Chapel Hill: University of North Carolina Press, 1994.

Walsh, Lorena S. "Consumer Behavior, Diet, and the Standard of Living in Late Colonial and Early Antebellum America, 1770–1840." In *American Economic Growth and Standards of Living before the Civil War,* edited by Robert E. Gallman and John Joseph Wallis, 217–64. Chicago: University of Chicago Press, 1992.

Warner, Charles Dudley. *Backlog Studies.* 18th ed. Boston: Houghton Mifflin, 1886.

Waters, John. "My Uncle, the Parson." *The Knickerbocker, or New-York Monthly Magazine* 24 (December 1844): 541–44.

Watson, Ben. *Cider Hard and Sweet: History, Traditions, and Making Your Own.* 2nd ed. Woodstock, Vt.: Countryman Press, 2009.

[Webster, Mrs. A. L.]. *The Improved Housewife.* 2nd ed. Hartford, Conn.: Richard H. Hobbs, 1844.

———. *The Improved Housewife.* 9th ed. Hartford, Conn.: Richard H. Hobbs, 1847.

———. *The Improved Housewife.* 20th ed. Boston: Phillips, Sampson; New York: James C. Derby, 1855.

Whatsoever Circle. *King's Daughters Cook Book.* Newport, N.H.: Barton and Wheeler, 1903.

"Wheatless Recipes from Washington Headquarters." *Hotel Monthly* 26 (May 1918): 60–65.

Wheaton, Barbara. *Savoring the Past: The French Kitchen and Table from 1300 to 1789.* Philadelphia: University of Pennsylvania Press, 1983.

Whitehill, Jane. *Food, Drink, and Recipes of Early New England.* Sturbridge, Mass.: Old Sturbridge Village, 1963.

Whole Duty of a Woman, The. London, 1737.

Wilcox, Estelle Woods, comp. *Buckeye Cookery, and Practical Housekeeping.* Minneapolis: Buckeye Publishing Co., 1877.

Willan, Anne. *Great Cooks and Their Recipes: From Taillevent to Escoffier.* London: Pavilion, 2000.

Williams, Roger. *The Correspondence of Roger Williams.* Edited by Glenn W. LaFantasie. 2 vols. Hanover, N.H.: University Press of New England, 1988.

———. *A Key into the Language of America.* 1643. New York: Russell and Russell, 1973.

Wilson, C. Anne. *Food and Drink in Britain: From the Stone Age to the Nineteenth Century*. Chicago: Academy Chicago, 1991.

Winthrop Papers. 5 vols. Boston: Massachusetts Historical Society, 1929–47.

Wolcott, Imogene. *The New England Yankee Cook Book*. Preface by Wilbur L. Cross. New York: Coward-McCann, 1939.

———. *The Yankee Cook Book*. New York: Ives Washburn, 1971.

Wood, William. *New Englands Prospect*. London, 1634. Boston [?]: Reprinted for E. M. Boynton, 1898 [?].

Woolley, Hannah. *The Gentlewomans Companion*. London, 1673.

———. *The Queen-like Closet*. London, 1670. Reprint, Boston: IndyPublish.com, n.d. [author on t.p.: "Hannah Wolley"]

Wright, Helen S. *The New England Cook Book*. New York: Duffield, 1912.

Young, Carolin. "Catherine de' Medici's Fork." In *Authenticity in the Kitchen: Proceedings of the Oxford Symposium on Food and Cookery, 2005*, edited by Richard Hosking, 441–53. Totnes, Eng.: Prospect, 2006.

Art Credits for Part 2

PAGE 13. Frontispiece to Elizabeth Raffald, *The Experienced English Housekeeper*, 10th ed., 1786. Raffald offers her cookbook to her readers. (Courtesy the Schlesinger Library, Radcliffe Institute, Harvard University)

PAGE 24. Porcelain teapot, ca. 1740–1760. Tea drinking was the most widely adopted custom associated with the emergence at this time of consumerism. (Courtesy Newport Historical Society; photograph by Michael Osean)

PAGE 44. Amelia Simmons, *American Cookery*, Hartford edition, 1796. These two recipes, an Americanized pumpkin pie and a verbatim copy of an English recipe for orange pudding, exemplify the dual nature of Simmons's work. (Courtesy American Antiquarian Society)

PAGE 47. Engraving from a portrait of Lydia Maria Francis (Child) by Francis Alexander, 1826. Original held by Medford Historical Society. (Courtesy Library of Congress)

PAGE 53. Study for Lilly Martin Spencer, *The Young Wife: First Stew*, 1856. The work portrays the emotional toll taken by the loss of culinary skill among nineteenth-century young women, a loss Child's *American Frugal Housewife* addresses. (Courtesy Ohio Historical Society)

PAGE 67. Engraving from a portrait of Sarah Josepha Hale by W. B. Chambers, *Godey's Lady's Book*, December 1850. (Courtesy the Schlesinger Library, Radcliffe Institute, Harvard University)

PAGE 81. Daguerreotype portrait of Catharine Beecher, 1848. (Courtesy the Schlesinger Library, Radcliffe Institute, Harvard University)

PAGE 87. Engraving for Kate Sutherland, "Cooks," *Godey's Lady's Book*, May 1852. Conflict between householders and servants was a constant theme in nineteenth-century domestic manuals and cookbooks. As here, servants were often depicted as coarse and disobedient. (Courtesy the Schlesinger Library, Radcliffe Institute, Harvard University)

PAGE 97. Back matter page, *Meriden Cook Book*, 1898[?]. Product promotion was regularly featured in community cookbooks. (Courtesy the Schlesinger Library, Radcliffe Institute, Harvard University)

PAGE 103. Engraving, *Frank Leslie's Illustrated Newspaper*, 3 April 1880. (Courtesy Harvard College Library, Widener Library, XPS 527PF, vol. 48)

PAGE 108. Cover, *Harper's Weekly*, 21 January 1911. The dialogue between cookbook writer and cook, depicted earlier in the frontispiece to Elizabeth Raffald's *Experienced English Housekeeper*, continues into the twentieth century. (Courtesy Harvard College Library, Widener Library, P207.6F, vol. 55)

PAGE 113. Engraving for T. S. Arthur, "The Chowder Party," *Godey's Lady's Book*, August 1849. (Courtesy the Schlesinger Library, Radcliffe Institute, Harvard University)

PAGE 141. Engraving for William H. Bishop, "The Lobster at Home," *Scribner's Monthly*, June 1881. (Courtesy Harvard College Library, Widener Library, P137.4A, vol. 22)

PAGE 175. Engraving from *Dame Trot and Her Comical Cat*, 1817. (Courtesy Library of Congress)

PAGE 195. Engraving, *Harper's Weekly*, 22 November 1890. (Courtesy Harvard College Library, Widener Library, P207.6F, vol. 34)

PAGE 206. *Miss Beecher's Domestic Receipt-Book*, 1846. (Courtesy the Schlesinger Library, Radcliffe Institute, Harvard University)

PAGE 244. Engraving, "Dame Punch was delighted to hear of a feast, / And said she'd make haste & the dainties prepare," *Pug's Visit to Mr. Punch*, 1810. (Courtesy the Historical Society of Pennsylvania)

PAGE 255. Engraving, *A Little Pretty Pocket Book*, 1787. Following English tradition, New England Christmas pies were often mince pies. (Courtesy American Antiquarian Society)

PAGE 282. Engraving, *Harper's Weekly*, 26 December 1885. (Courtesy Harvard College Library, Widener Library, P207.6F, vol. 29)

PAGE 299. Engraving, *The History of Little King Pippin*, 1814. (Courtesy American Antiquarian Society)

PAGE 325. Engraving, Lydia Maria Child, "The New-England Boy's Song about Thanksgiving Day," *Flowers for Children*, vol. 2, 1845. (Courtesy Houghton Library, Harvard University)

PAGE 348. Woodcut from "The History of Mrs. Williams and Her Plumb-Cake," in *Nurse Truelove's New-Year's Gift*, 1786. Mrs. Williams has "drawn the Cake from the Oven, all befrosted over with Egg and white Sugar." (Courtesy American Antiquarian Society)

Index

evangelicalism, 90; Hartford Female Seminary, 81; Litchfield Female Academy, 90–91; and Puritanism, 88, 91; and refinement, 90; and servants, 82, 84–88, 405n. 54; and systematizing, 91, 220, 302; and women's education, 81. See also *Miss Beecher's Domestic Receipt-Book*

beef
—about, 230–32, 243
—cuts: brisket, 239; cheek, 232; round, 238; shoulder clod, 238; sirloin, 239; tenderloin, 240
—recipes: alamode, 232, 234–35; boiled dinner, 237, 240–41; braised, 242; brisket, stewed, 239; bullock's cheek, baked, 232; calf's head, 234; corned, 238; fillet, roast, 239–40; pot roast, 243; roast, 233; sauces for, 240; steak, 238; stew, 242; stewed with apples, 237; tripe, 236
—steak, 239
—variety meat, 235–36.
—*See also* pies (meat); pies (mince); pottage; soups; stews

beest, 322
Beeton, Isabella, 365
Bell Seasoning, 201
Benham, R., 205
Bentley, William, 84
Berry, Edward, 8
Biddle, Arthur, 74
biscuit, 371. *See also* cakes (small)
bisques. *See* potage
blanc dessore, 114
blancmange, 114, 341
Blencowe, Ann, 274
blind baking, 295
Bliss, Mrs. (of Boston). See *Practical Cook Book*
bockings, 376
bonny-clabber, 320
books and publishing: colonial, 7–8, 21–22; nineteenth-century, 59, 77
Boone, Daniel, 205
Boorde, Andrew, 115, 209, 320, 352
Borden, Gail, 407n. 9

Borden murders, 218
Boston, Massachusetts, 63, 102; anglophilia, 64; architecture, 31; booksellers, 7–8; and refinement, 22, 75
Boston Cooking School. *See* domestic science
Boston Cooking-School Cook Book: style, 107; measurement in, 107; popularity, 107; revisions, 108
Boston Cream Pie, 323, 387–88
Boston House of Correction, 358–59
Bradford, William, 162, 263
Bradley, Martha, 8
brake, 352
brawn, 287
breads
—about, 337, 345, 350–52, 354–57, 359–60
—Indian corn in, 350, 357
—recipes: rich white, 354; Rye and Indian, 357–59; steamed brown, 360–61; white, 355–56; whole wheat (manchet), 351–52
—yeast, 352, 355–56, 368; recipe, 355
breads and cakes, 348–51, 361–64, 368–69, 371; Indian corn in, 349–50
breakfast, 362–63
Brewer, Stephen, 23
brewis, 114, 348
brick ovens, 56, 72–73, 303, 327, 353, 362, 366
bride's pie, 276
Brillat-Savarin, Anthelme, 176
British Housewife, 8
browning sauce, 190
Brown, William Hill, 396n. 12
Bulfinch, Charles, 31
butter: beating, 381–82; dish, 375–76; sauce, 203; and Tudor cooking, 375

Cabot, John, 167
cakes
—about, 351, 354–55, 379–84, 386–88
—recipes: cider, 385; cream (cream puff), 386; Election, 385; Graham, 386; layer (White Mountain), 388;

and, 100–101; and consumerism,
100–101; and cooking, 106, 109,
146, 241; Farmer and, 108–9, 146;
Harriet Beecher Stowe and, 99–100;
and industrialization, 98–99; Lincoln
and, 106; and nativism, 110; New
England Kitchen exhibit, 109–10
comfits, 287, 368, 382
Compleat Cook
—plagiarized from, 301
—recipes: cake, 380; cakes, small,
366; duck, 177; mutton, 218; pie,
carp, 292; pie, pumpkin, 301; quaking pudding, 328; soup, 132–33
Compleat Housewife
—anti-French attitudes, 18
—audience, 11–12
—editions, 8, 22, 178
—French influence, 17
—in New England, 8
—plagiarism, 178
—plagiarized from, 28–29, 41, 133,
248, 258, 306, 310, 368, 381
—popularity, 2, 8
—recipes: bread, 354; buns, 368;
cake, 381; caudle, 257; cod,
168–69; goose, 178; lear, 257;
lobster, 163; mutton, 218–19;
pancakes, 375; pie, apple, 310; pie,
battalia, 258; pie, carrot, 306; pie,
cheesecake, 320–21; pie, chicken,
287; pie, mince, 274; pie, orange
or lemon, 309–10; pie, sole or
flounder, 292; pie, turkey, 283; pie,
veal, 266; pie, venison, 263; pie
crust, 247; pudding, almond, 338;
pudding, black, 330; soup, 133;
turkey, 199
Complete House-keeper, 179
Complete System of Cookery, 180
confectionery, 9, 11, 299–300, 391n. 7
Congreve, William, 367
conspicuous consumption, 10, 31, 55,
100–101
consumerism: and American
Revolution, 29, 32; eighteenth-

century, 21–25, 28, 31–32, 74–75,
403–4n. 28; and mobility, 74–75;
nineteenth-century, 53, 74–76, 90,
100, 398–99n. 46
cookbooks: audience, 2–3, 9, 21–23;
brand names in, 97–98, 388; charitable, 96; chefs as authors, 232; community, 95–98; housekeepers as
authors, 11–12, 14, 63; influence,
3–4, 389n. 6; manuscript, 3, 16;
marketing advice, 39–40; popularity,
1–2, 4; promotional pamphlet, 98;
sources, 3, 89; women as authors, 11,
71, 232, 299–300
*Cookery, Rational, Practical, and
Economical,* 316–17
cookies. *See* cakes (small)
Cook Not Mad: plagiarism, 271, 307,
314; Rye and Indian (bread) recipe,
357
Cook's Dictionary: plagiarized from, 63,
128, 171, 181, 236, 272, 342, 384
Cook's Oracle: plagiarized from, 63,
202, 271, 289; and Plymouth,
Massachusetts, 129; and shellfish,
129
Cook's Own Book
—anglophilia, 63–64
—authorship, 63
—plagiarism, 63–64, 128, 145, 164,
171–72, 181, 190, 202, 236, 260–
61, 272, 279, 289, 294–95, 315,
341–42, 334, 384
—plagiarized from, 172, 181, 226,
341
—recipes: chicken, 190; chowder,
128; cod, 171–72; duck, 181; eels,
145; lobster, 164; pie, apple, 315;
pie, chicken, 288; pie, mixed,
260–61; pie, mutton, 271; pie,
squash, 303; pudding, arrowroot,
341; pudding, tapioca, 342; tripe,
236; turkey, 202
—and *Seventy-five Receipts,* 402n. 73
cookstoves. *See* industrialization
coral, 165

Cornelius, Mrs. Mary Hooker. See *Young Housekeeper's Friend*

Cotton, John, 26–27, 394n. 54

coulis. *See* French cooking

Countrey Contentments. See *English Hus-wife*

Cox, Edward, 8

crackers, 319, 346; Boston, 319; Medford, 46; pilot, 125, 131

cradle spit, 226

Cranmer, Thomas (archbishop of Canterbury), 283

craw, 199

cream cake, 386–87

crimping, 126

crop, 199

crumpets, 379

Cunningham, Marion, 107

curds, 320

currants, 137, 281

curry, 191

cusk, 146; creamed recipe, 152

custard recipe, 341

Dalgairns, Mrs. See *Practice of Cookery*

darioles, 320

Dawson, Thomas, 365

Defoe, Daniel, 197

delicate, 347

de Medici, Catherine, 198, 392n. 30

dessertspoon, 361

Dickens, Mrs. Charles, 293

Dickinson, Emily, 98

diet: colonial, 21, 23–24, 27–28; nine-teenth-century, 71–72, 94–95

dining, formal: courses, 10, 264, 289, 375, 383; dishes, 289; pyramids, 286; surprises, 276; table arrangement, 200, 285–86, 289

dining room, 22–23, 393n. 43

Directions for Cookery: popularity, 69; rabbit recipe, 210

Dolby, William. See *Cook's Dictionary*

Domestic Receipt-Book. See *Miss Beecher's Domestic Receipt-Book*

domestic science: Beecher and, 91, 101; Boston Cooking School, 102–7; and

colonial revival, 106, 108–9; Hale and, 79; and periodicals, 106; and public schools, 106; and woman's sphere, 101

domestic skills: attitudes toward, 12, 78–79, 82–84; and education, 54, 104, 241–42

doughnuts, 378. *See* hotcakes

dough spur, 302

drachm, 384

drawing (meat or fowl), 203, 223

drawn (sauce), 203

duck, 177, 181; boiled recipe, 177; roast recipe, 180; stewed recipe, 179, 181. *See also* pies (fowl)

dumpling, 314, 327, 335

dunfish, 173

Durham Cook Book: halibut recipe, 152–53

Dwight, Timothy, 207, 395–96n. 7

Earle, Alice Morse, 100–101

Echoes from South County Kitchens: chicken recipe, 194

eels
— about, 142–44, 292, 296
— recipes: baked, 145; broiled, 144; fried, 146; stewed, 143, 145.
— *See also* pies (fish); soups

egerdouce, 114

Election Cake, 379, 385–86. *See also* cakes

Emerson, Lucy, 227

emptins, 42, 355, 378

English cooking, 14–19, 25, 137, 203, 375; anti-French attitudes, 17–19, 288, 393n. 32; characteristics, 18–19; creams and custards, 43–44, 320; French influence, 15–17, 133, 138–39, 145, 178–81, 189–90, 215, 289, 293, 320, 392n. 28; and lemon, 263–64; pastry, 245; pies, 43–44, 245, 262, 288, 293, 299–300; pot-tage, 113, 133; puddings, 245, 299; roasting, 199, 209, 245

English Hus-wife
— baking equipment, 353

fruit: and health, 308; preservation, 300, 308

frumenty, 118, 349

gallipot, 310

game and meat, 203, 206–8. *See also* beef; hare; lamb; mutton; pies (meat); pies (mince); pork; pottage; rabbit; soups; stews; veal; venison

Gardiner, Anne Gibbons, 30, 83. See also *Mrs. Gardiner's Family Receipts*

Gay, John, 213

gems, 379

Gerard, John, 114, 307

gill, 149, 356

Gilman, Caroline. See *Lady's Annual Register*

gingerbread, 369–70, 373; and ginger-snaps, 372. *See also* cakes (small)

Glasse, Hannah: biography, 12; *Compleat Confectioner*, 8. See also *Art of Cookery Made Plain and Easy*

Godey's Lady's Book: cake recipe, 388

Good Bread: baked beans recipe, 124–25

Good Housekeeper
—and diet, 78
—and domestic skills, 78–79
—and economy, 76
—and health, 77–78
—plagiarism, 120, 172, 226, 316, 341
—plagiarized from, 317
—popularity, 77
—recipes: cakes, small, 370; par-tridge, 182; pie, custard, 322; pie, summer fruit, 316; pork, pickled, 225–26; stew, 138; veal, 213
—and servants, 79
—sources, 77

Gookin, Daniel: succotash recipe, 117

goose, 177, 181; giblets, 284; and pot-ting, 260; roast recipe, 178, 180–81. *See also* pies (fowl)

Gore, Christopher, 401n. 58

Gosnold, Bartholomew, 167

Graham, Sylvester, 77–78, 94, 255–56, 304, 386, 398n. 45

gridiron, 150

groats, 284, 307, 330

grouper, 148

Guy, William Augustus, 317

haddock, 170, 174. *See also* chowder

hair bag, 200

hair sieve, 200

Hale, Sarah Josepha (Buell): biography, 65–68, 402n. 3; and brick ovens, 72–73, 75; and Child, 68, 76–77; and children's literature, 404n. 39; and clothing, 77; as cultural arbiter, 75–77; and domestic science, 79; *Godey's Lady's Book*, 66–67, 76–77, 402n. 3; and industrialization, 70, 72–73; *Ladies' Magazine*, 66, 77, 402n. 3; *Mary Had a Little Lamb*, 68, 402n. 5; and meat consump-tion, 207–8; and meat pies, 258; and New England, 66, 73, 80; and Thanksgiving, 402n. 4; and tourism, 71; and woman's sphere, 80, 402n. 1, 403–4n. 28; and women's education, 79–80. See also *Good Housekeeper*; *Ladies' New Book of Cookery*

Hales, Stephen, 317

halibut, 146; baked recipe, 152–53

hare: jugged recipe, 209

Harris, Richard, 309

Harrison, Sarah, 8

Harrison, William Henry, 351

harslet, 330

Harte, Bret, 99

Hartford, Connecticut, 147

hash, 220, 238

hasty pudding: about, 119–20; and po-lenta, 119; recipes, 120

Haywood, Eliza, 83

Hazard, Thomas Robinson, 199

health and cookbooks, 9, 77–78, 107, 142, 257, 333, 341–42, 391n. 7

hearth cooking, 56, 192, 289, 303, 374; attitudes toward, 57, 62, 231, 400n. 55, 400–401n. 56. *See also* brick ovens

heliotrope, 137, 369

Henri IV (king of France), 392–93n. 30

Henrietta Maria, 7

Henry VIII (king of England), 309
Herbert, Edward (first baron of Cherbury), 366–67
Herbert, George, 367
herbs, 115–16, 213
herring, 291; pie recipe, 291
Higginson, Francis, 146, 161–62
hind, 149
hoecake, 377
Hogarth, William, 230
Home Cookery: cake recipe, 385; chowder recipe, 130–31
Home Science Cook Book: clams recipe, 160–61; pot roast recipe, 243; pudding recipe, 347
hominy: about, 120–21, 349; and health, 121; recipes, 121–22
hotcakes
—about, 373–79
—Indian corn in, 374
—recipes: doughnuts, 377–78; fritters, 374; griddle cakes, 378; johnnycake, 376; muffins, 378; pancakes, 375–77
Housekeeper's Assistant
—plagiarism, 296–97
—recipes: beef, 239; ketchup, 139–40; mackerel, 151; pie, lobster, 296; pie, venison, 264
House-Keeper's Pocket-Book, 8
Howard, Henry, 144
Howland, E. A. See *New England Economical Housekeeper*
humoral theory, 15, 364, 391–92n. 24
Hunt, William. See *Good Bread*
Huntley, Joseph, 69
Husbandman's Fruitful Orchard, 309

Improved Housewife
—plagiarism, 172, 317, 334, 344
—plagiarized from, 317
—recipes: clams, 159; eels, 145; lobster, 165; muffins, 378; oysters, 157; pie, apple, 318; pie, chicken, 290; pie, cracker apple, 319; pie, oyster, 295; pie, peach, 317; pie, tomato, 308; pie crust, 251; pig's head

cheese, 228; pudding, bread, 342; pudding, plum, 334; shad, 150
India pepper, 126
industrialization: appliances, 72; attitudes toward, 56–58, 62, 70, 72–74, 93–95, 98–99; and community cookbooks, 95–98; cookstoves, 56–57, 72, 192, 231, 374; and diet, 71–72, 94–95; and fairs, 109; and food production, 58, 69, 72, 94–95, 407n. 9; fuel, 57–58; matches, 400n. 54; refrigerators, 400n. 53; transport, 58, 94–95, 350, 357; and women, 70
Ingoldsby Legends, 367
Inman, LeValley A. See *Rhode Island Rule Book*
Irish as servants, 104, 405n. 54
Irish stew, 221

jagger wheel, 302
Jamaica pepper, 128
James II (king of England), 197
James, Henry, 350
Jefferson, Thomas, 134
jelly, 262. See also calf's foot jelly
joe-floggers, 376
johnnycake, 377. See also hotcakes
Johnson, Edward, 27, 217
Johnson, Samuel, 344
Jonson, Ben, 28, 394n. 53
Josselyn, John, 143–44, 146
jumbles, 365, 370. See also cakes (small)

ketchup: 137–38, 190; mushroom recipe, 139; tomato recipe, 216; and tomatoes, 127–28, 137, 190; walnut, 295; walnut recipe, 296
kimnel, 352
King, Caroline Howard, 170–71, 290, 348
kingfish, 148–49
King's Daughters Cook Book: chicken pie recipe, 290; chicken recipe, 194; sparerib recipe, 229
Kitchiner, William. See *Cook's Oracle*
Knight, Mrs. S. G. See *Tit-Bits*
knots, 365

La Chapelle, Vincent, 133, 139

Ladies' New Book of Cookery
—and Catholics, 79
—and children, 79
—and consumerism, 79
—plagiarism, 271, 295, 304, 317, 343
—recipes: beef and sauces, 239–40;
clams, 160; eels, 146; pie, beef,
269; pie, giblet, 285; pie, ham, 271;
pie, partridge, 286; pie, pumpkin,
304; pie, venison, 264–65; pork,
226–27; pudding, bread, 337

"lady in the lobster," 165

Lady's Annual Register: pumpkin pie
recipes, 304

Lady's Companion: plagiarized from, 270

Lady's Receipt-Book: clam pie recipe,
298; mince pie recipe, 280; oyster
pie recipe, 297

lamb: about, 214, 216; casserole recipe,
216; knuckle, 215; ragout recipe,
215; roast recipe, 215; shank, 215;
shoulder roast recipe, 216. *See also*
pies (meat)

Lamb, Patrick, 200

langdebeef, 115

larding, 209, 218, 240, 268, 292; and
stuffing, 234, 236

larding pork, 132

La Varenne, François Pierre de, 15, 126,
139, 178, 184, 187, 189

leaf, 330

lear, 257–58

leavens, chemical, 124, 252, 267, 358,
379

Lee, Mrs. N. K. M. (pseud.), 63. *See*
also *Cook's Own Book*

leer bacon, 133

lemon, 190, 263–64; and mince pie, 279

Lent, 125, 141, 168, 275, 279, 291–92,
298, 306, 363

Leslie, Eliza: biography, 68, 403n. 9;
and industrialization, 70; as north-
erner, 68–69; popularity, 69; and
tourism, 70–71. See also *Directions
for Cookery; Lady's Receipt-Book;
Seventy-five Receipts*

libraries, 8, 21–22

lights (variety meat), 224

Lincoln, Mary J.: biography, 105; and
colonial revival, 106; and refinement, 105. See also *Home Science
Cook Book; Mrs. Lincoln's Boston
Cook Book*

ling, 169

lingcod, 169

literacy: American women, 20–21;
English women, 9, 391n. 8; and
Simmons, 41. *See also* servants

lobsters
—about, 161–65, 294
—recipes: boiled, 165–66; fricassee,
164; roasted, 163; salad, 164.
—*See also* pies (fish)

lumber pie, 266

lute, 126

luxury. *See* refinement

mackerel, 146–47; recipe, 151; and caveach, 148

Madam Johnson's Present, 8

made dishes, 15–17, 29, 139, 191

malkin, 353–54

manchets, 137, 352

Mann, Mrs. Horace. See *Christianity in
the Kitchen*

Marco Polo, 344

marjoram, 236

Markham, Gervase: *Cheape and Good
Husbandry,* 185. See also *English
Hus-wife*

Marlborough pudding, 310, 314. *See also*
pies (fruit)

marrow, 266, 287

Martha Washington's Booke of Cookery,
137, 148, 220, 249, 257, 263, 268,
277

Martin, Joseph, 205

Martin, Samuel, 205

Massachusetts State Reform School,
360–61

Massasoit, 185

Massialot, François, 16, 133, 139, 189

mawmenees, 114

Practical Cook Book
  —recipes: baked beans, 124; calf's
    foot jelly, 261–62; chicken, 192;
    cod, 173; fowl, boning, 262; ginger-
    snaps, 372; oysters, 157; pie, blue-
    berry, 318; pie, New Year's, 261; pie
    crust, 319; pork chops, 229; pud-
    ding, cherry, 335; pudding, plum,
    336; pudding, raspberry, 344; pud-
    ding, rice, 336; pudding, sago, 345;
    salmon, 151; scrod, 173; succotash,
    119; turkey 204–5; woodcock, 183
Practice of Cookery: plagiarized from,
    63, 145, 164, 171–72, 190, 260–61,
    315, 341
Prescott, J. H. See *Valuable Receipts*
Proust, Marcel, 233
prussic acid, 317
puddings
  —about, 284, 314, 325–28, 335,
    337–39, 341–42, 347, 360
  —boiling: cloth, 203, 314, 327, 332;
    steamer, 327, 332, 359–60
  —and pies, 327
  —recipes: almond, 338; arrowroot,
    341; batter (baked), 344; bat-
    ter (boiled), 333, 335; bird's nest,
    340–41; black (blood), 300; bread
    (baked), 337, 342; bread (boiled),
    331, 333, 337; cherry, 335; choco-
    late, 347; coconut, 343–44; corn,
    343; cranberry, 333; Indian (baked),
    340, 345–47; Indian (boiled), 332,
    334–35; plum (baked), 346; plum
    (boiled), 330, 334, 336–37; quaking,
    328; quince, 343; raspberry, 344;
    rice (baked), 339; rice (boiled), 336;
    sago, 345; suet, 329, 335; squash,
    340; tapioca, 342; white, 329; whor-
    tleberrry, 334; Yorkshire, 338–39
pudding-time, 327
pumpkin, 303. *See also* pies (pumpkin)
Puritanism: and cooking, 25–28; and
    gluttony, 26; and Protestant ethic,
    26–27, 83; and temperance in diet,
    26–28, 256, 394nn. 53–54

Queen-like Closet
  —French influence, 16
  —in New England, 7–8, 390n. 2
  —recipes: beef, 232; chicken, 186;
    eels, 143; fritters, 374; pancakes,
    375; pie, artichoke, 305; pie, beef,
    267; pie, pork, 269; pudding, suet,
    329; pudding, white, 329
  —sociology, 11
Queen's cake, 384
Queens Closet Opened: in New England,
    7, 390n. 2; "secrets" book, 9; sociol-
    ogy, 10, 15; sources, 15, 89. See also
    Compleat Cook

rabbit, 210; boiled and baked recipe,
    194; fricassee recipe, 210
race (root), 366
Raffald, Elizabeth: biography, 14; and
    weddings, 276, 383–84. See also
    Experienced English House-keeper
ragout, 139, 181, 215
raisins, 292; jar, 276; of the sun, 275–76
Randolph, Mary. See *Virginia Housewife*
recipe format, 239
red sanders (sandalwood), 137
refinement: and cookbooks, 23–25;
    eighteenth-century, 22–25, 31–33,
    75, 403–4n. 28; nineteenth-century,
    52–53, 55, 60–61, 75–76, 90, 152,
    214, 216–17, 221, 223, 398–99n. 46;
    and tea drinking, 23, 31–32
rennet, 310
republican mother, 36, 395n. 6
restaurants, 154
Revere, Paul, 29
Rhode Island Rule Book: chowder recipe,
    132; ham recipe, 229–30
rice, 193; ground, 304
roasting, 209, 223; and baking, 218,
    225, 231; basting, 211, 215, 233–34,
    240; brown, 199; dredging, 211, 215,
    216; papering, 199–200, 211, 233–
    34; and pie crust, 211; white, 199
Roberts, Robert, 401n. 58; *House
    Servant's Directory*, 401n. 58
Rockwell, Norman, 195

venison: roast recipes, 208, 210–11; variety meat, 277. *See also* pies (meat); pies (mince)

verdigris, 313

verjuice, 188–89

Verral, William, 180

Virginia Housewife: audience, 51–52; and Child, 50–51, 62; and New England, 51; popularity, 51; southern style, 68–69

warden, 292

Warner, Charles Dudley, 300

warren, 210

water-cod, 170

Webster, Daniel: chowder recipe, 129–30

Webster, Mrs. A. L. See *Improved Housewife*

wedding: cake, 383–84; pie, 276

Wharton, Edith, 98–99

Whitepot, 338–39

Whitney, Adeline D. T., 231

Whole Duty of a Woman, 16, 270, 336; plagiarized from, 144, 293–94

whole spice, 144

widgeon recipe, 180

wildfowl, 177; garnishes, 180. *See also* pies (fowl); *and under individual species*

Williams, Roger, 26–27, 120–21

Willis, Nathaniel P., 235

Wilson, Joseph, 364

Windham, William, 203

Winslow, Edward, 142–43, 161, 185

Winthrop, John, 25–26

Winthrop, John, Jr.: hominy, 349; hominy recipe, 121; Rye and Indian, 350; succotash recipe, 117

Wollstonecraft, Mary, 395n. 6

Woman's Education Association, 102, 104

woman's sphere: domestic science and, 101; Hale and, 80, 402n. 1, 403–4n. 28; and refinement, 398–99n. 46; republican mother and, 395n. 6

Wood, William, 146, 158, 293

woodcock, 183; and potting, 260; roast recipe, 183

Woolley, Hannah: biography, 11, 391n. 13; *Gentlewoman's Companion,* 43, 395n. 4. See also *Queen-like Closet*

Wright, Helen S. See *New England Cook Book* (Wright)

Young House-Keeper: hominy recipes, 121–22

Young Housekeeper's Friend: plagiarism, 358; plagiarized from, 360; Rye and Indian (bread) recipe, 357–58; steamed brown bread recipe, 360

About the Authors

Keith Stavely is a writer, scholar, and former library director whose interest in the Puritan influence on American and English culture has resulted in a number of critically-esteemed books and articles. He has been a Guggenheim and American Council of Learned Societies fellow and a winner of the Modern Language Association Prize for Independent Scholars. The place of food in Anglo-American culture is a more recent passion.

Kathleen Fitzgerald holds a Master of Divinity degree and a Master of Library Studies. She has worked as a college chaplain, a soup kitchen coordinator, and for many years as a public librarian in urban settings. A native New Englander of Irish descent and an avid cook, she has a deep interest in the region's complex social and culinary history.

Independent scholars Stavely and Fitzgerald are also husband and wife. Their previous book, *America's Founding Food: The Story of New England Cooking* (2004), was widely acclaimed. They make their home in Jamestown, Rhode Island.